SOCIAL PSYCHOLOGY
Explorations in Understanding

ADVISERS & CONTRIBUTORS

Chief Academic Adviser

Kenneth Gergen

Academic Advisers

Genevieve Clapp

Richard Nisbett

David Rosenhan

Contributors

William Barton

Lola Bogyo

Genevieve Clapp

Alice Eagly

Sheldon Feldman

Kenneth Gergen

Mary Gergen

James Jones

Louise Kidder

Robert Liebert

Harvey London

Bert Moore

Stanley Morse

Stanton Peele

Rita Poulos

Robert Siegler

Siegfried Streufert

Susan Streufert

Dalmas Taylor

Bill Underwood

SOCIAL PSYCHOLOGY
Explorations in Understanding

CRM BOOKS
Del Mar, California

Library of Congress Catalog Card Number:
73-88658

Standard Book Number:
87665-174-0
Text

87665-720-X
Trade

Manufactured in the
United States of America

9
8
7
6
5
4
3
2
1

PREFACE

As human society grows increasingly complex, many of our social needs become more difficult to satisfy in fulfilling and constructive ways. We still desire relationships that are mutually supportive and enduring. But the prospects for such relationships lessen with our accelerating mobility and transience. We still need work that is creative and self-expressive. But these satisfactions are beyond the grasp of many people because of intense specialization. And we still crave a sense of community, of cooperative effort and common purpose. This theme supplies the rhetoric for politicians and ideologists of all persuasions. But despite our essential interdependence, we often live lives of insulation from our neighbors and colleagues. Furthermore, we frequently live by codes of competition at the expense of others. Yet when we all compete for the same rewards, we all tend to lose. The victor reaches his goal, only to find it unsatisfying. The loser leaves the field in frustration.

Scientists from every discipline are gathering information that can contribute to an understanding of our experiences and, hopefully, to an improvement of the human condition. This book is an attempt to add to that understanding.

Social-psychological research has been fruitful in yielding insights into the dilemmas faced by each of us. It suggests means of resolving these dilemmas. This volume focuses on the fruits of this research. The authors have also drawn liberally from research findings in other disciplines—from psychology, sociology, and anthropology, in particular—when these findings have shed light on the pursuits of social psychologists.

The text is organized into five relatively distinct and independent units. In Unit I, the methodological underpinnings of the discipline of social psychology are outlined. Unit II focuses on the ways in which propensities for all social behavior are transmitted and expressed. Unit III explores the ways in which people encounter one another—perceptually, emotionally, evaluatively, and behaviorally. After examining the ways by which we influence one another, Unit IV presents some fundamental human alternatives: conformity and deviance, violence and altruism, competition and cooperation. Many social scientists feel that their research in these areas is running a race with time. If attempts to reduce propensities toward aggression, violence, and competition do not soon succeed, the opportunity may be lost forever. Because each prosocial or antisocial act may well cause other people to behave similarly, the decision as to what sort of world we will live in may be influenced by each of us. The focus of Unit V is on groups, on the interfaces between the individual and the group and between the group and the larger society. The spectrum of groups discussed ranges from the informal and formal groups with which we spend much of our individual lives to the governmental bodies and mass movements that shape our national and cultural lives.

The many persons who contributed to this undertaking profoundly influenced one another and the final product. Involvement took many forms. The volume began to take shape at an initial seminar. The manuscripts were then written by the authors and advisers and underwent several cycles of editing, reviewing, and further revision. (Authors, reviewers, and other contributors are named on pages 598-601.) To all the professionals who contributed to this volume, our sincere thanks.

Social psychology is an expanding field, and much of its subject matter is continually changing. The textual material in this volume refers to many recent aspects of our common cultural and political histories. Two devices have been particularly useful in keeping the book current and lively. *Topical inserts* appear throughout and serve to amplify or illustrate major ideas, lines of research, and applications. Some topical inserts are independent of the textual material; others elaborate on issues that are only briefly summarized in the text. The *graphic illustrations* portray both current and historical events in the form of literary passages, still photographs from old films, cartoons, legends and fables, and both documentary and interpretive photographs and prints. In addition, graphs, charts, tables, and diagrams are included where they can help the reader understand concepts. The graphic illustrations are intended to clarify concepts and to relate material to readers' experiences. Our special thanks to Corita Kent, the highly respected poster artist and serigrapher, for her calligraphic rendering of the *haiku* at the beginning of each unit. Like the Japanese poet who captures his feelings in concise, evocative images and the calligrapher whose fluid brush strokes preserve the moment, the social psychologist tries to characterize the flow of human interaction so that we can better understand human social experience in all its complexity. The Japanese poet Sion seems to have captured the essence of the task . . .

Life? butterfly
   on a swaying grass
      that's all . . .
but exquisite!

CONTENTS

ENCOUNTERING
OTHERS:
PERCEPTIONS,
FEELINGS &
THOUGHTS

III

INTERACTING WITH OTHERS: LIFE & DEATH TOGETHER

IV

BEHAVIOR IN
GROUPS:
PLANNED &
UNPLANNED

V

If you wish to KNOW the ROAd up the MOUNTAIN you MUST ASK the MAN WHO goes bACK ANd foRtH ON it. ZeNRiNKushu

I

INTRODUCTION

The photographic sequence at the opening of each chapter represents the substance of that chapter, as interpreted by a troupe of actors and actresses in the commedia dell'arte tradition—a stylization, exaggeration, or parody of life. This form of "folk theater" has been used in the past as a vehicle for social comment. Here, it is adapted to the concepts of social psychology. In this first sequence, members of the troupe give an impressionistic interpretation of some of the problems that confront researchers in their quest to understand human interaction. The experimenter (in black coat and cap) is doing his best to "measure" three subjects, or, more precisely, to weigh them on a produce scale. This particular researcher appears confident that his "scale" is assessing some characteristic of his subjects. In contrast, many researchers have voiced concern that the loves, hates, and interactions of human beings cannot be measured as precisely as can meat and vegetables. As suggested by the expressions of the subjects in these photographs, even the measurement process itself can affect the attitudes and responses of human subjects.

1

A Science of
Social Behavior

BEFORE DEFINING WHAT SOCIAL PSYCHOLOGY IS, or what it *can* be, a few events that have occurred in the recent past will be instructive. The names are changed, some specifics are modified, and some details are omitted. Nonetheless, all of the events are segments of reality.

EVENT 1:   The time is ten P.M. on a Thursday night. Tom Wilson—good looking, afro hairstyle, well dressed—is pacing back and forth along the wall of a small meeting room, telephone in hand. He obviously is upset, annoyed. The other voice on the phone is not audible, but whatever it is saying seems to make Tom even angrier. He finally interrupts the lengthy verbiage from the other side: "Shit, you can't tell me that the president of this goddam university won't talk to me. You bastards don't care, do you?" As though his words need further amplification, Tom bangs the telephone set onto the table. "If the president won't see us by midnight, and if he doesn't meet our demands, this school is going up in smoke, you hear?" Suddenly a smile develops on Tom's face, and he turns around to the small group of friends who are sitting, waiting, and listening. Tom makes a sign with his hand and continues into the receiver: "You listen to me. Have the great Mr. President call me. You got the number. Just make sure he calls before it's midnight. Tell him that if he doesn't, there's trouble." With a triumphant turn of his wrist, Tom throws the receiver down. Very slowly he laughs: "Now we'll see what happens."

EVENT 2:   It is Wednesday afternoon. Mrs. Jane Philips has been shopping most of the day and is in a hurry to get home to cook dinner for her family. Luckily, she gets a taxi quickly, climbs into it, and tells the driver where she wants to go—not too far away in a residential area. The driver nods and drives off. When he has gone approximately two-thirds of the way, he suddenly pulls over to the side of the road, parks his cab, and says, "Excuse me a minute." He gets out of the taxi and leaves. He disappears behind a house and is gone. Mrs. Philips waits and notices that the taxi meter is still running. She feels a little disturbed about the situation. After some time, the taxi driver reappears and sits down in his seat. "Oh," he says, "Let me

3

show you this letter I just got today." Mrs. Philips takes the letter and reads it. It is written on cab company stationery and addressed to the driver. It tells him that he had been found negligent in his duties and that the company disapproves of his behavior. As a consequence he is in danger of losing his job. Mrs. Philips is hardly surprised at the content of the letter. After all, she herself has just had an experience that suggested that this cab driver is not exactly reliable. She gives the letter back to the driver as they arrive at their destination. Reaching for her purse, she wonders how much she should pay him and how much she should tip him. After all, he has overcharged her: The meter was running the entire time he was gone.

EVENT 3: Bob is on his way to visit his girl friend, taking the subway as usual. He enters one of the cars of the express train, sits down, and casually looks around. The car is half full of men and women, but none of them seems particularly interesting. Several newcomers enter the car at the next stop. Among them is a young black man, probably college age, carrying a cane. He walks a few steps forward, toward the end of the car where Bob is sitting, and suddenly collapses. Bob thinks, "What should I do?" He has doubts about whether or not he should help. He feels the impulse to get up and walk away from the stricken man. "But I should go and help him," he believes. But while Bob is trying to make up his mind, a black man and two white men come to the aid of the fallen man.

EVENT 4: One Sunday afternoon, John K. Paulton is sitting in his living room, watching television. He is waiting to be contacted for an experiment in which he has agreed to participate, an experiment that is to last two weeks. He does not hear the police car pull up outside. He does not see the curious faces of neighbors as they watch a policeman walk up to his door. But he does hear the forceful knock on the door. The policeman sternly informs Paulton that he is charged with suspicion of armed robbery, informs him of his legal rights, and handcuffs him. As the neighbors watch, Paulton is led to the back of the police car and driven to the station. There he is fingerprinted and placed in a detention cell. Later he is blindfolded and taken to a prison where he has to strip, is sprayed with what seems to be a delousing spray, and is photographed. After some time he is given a loosely fitting muslin smock with a number printed on front and back. He is also told to wear a nylon cap and rubber sandals. After being placed alone in a small cell, he is instructed to be quiet.

All this time John K. Paulton wonders if any of this is real. To his knowledge, he has not committed any kind of criminal act, and certainly not robbery, an armed one at that. Could this be part of the experiment in which he had agreed to participate? The experiment, after all, was to be concerned with the behavior of prison inmates. But why then was he arrested by a *real* police officer? It just does not

Figure 1.1 Social psychology is the study of interpersonal behavior, which can occur in a wide variety of situations, including intimate relationships, decision-making groups, panics, and one person merely thinking about another or being observed. Shown here (*left to right*) are examples of social behavior that are dealt with in this text: a confrontation between students and police (what causes a demonstration to become violent?); teenagers at a party (what effect does being a "wallflower" have on a young person, and why does this occur?); life on a Chinese commune (what are the effects of customs and life style on socialization of the young?); a racial demonstration in South Africa (why does it erupt, and why have such demonstrations not led to revolution or social changes in South Africa?). This volume posits answers to these and many other questions of contemporary interest.

make sense. He had asked the arresting policeman whether or not this arrest was related to the experiment. But the policeman had not given him any helpful information. What is going on? Does someone actually think that he might be a criminal?

All four of these situations involved social psychologists and represent some of the types of research that will be explored throughout this volume. The first event occurred in an experimental simulation of campus unrest. In this research, Siegfried Streufert, Susan Kliger, Carl Castore, and Michael Driver (1967) wanted to know what factors influence moderate students to support either campus radicals or their campus administrations. (Ways in which people influence one another are explained in Chapters 9 and 10).

The events in the taxi cab were also part of an experiment. Howard Fromkin, Robert Baron, and Timothy Brock (1973) wanted to determine how a frustrated person (the passenger) would react to another person (the cab driver) who was either derogated (as in this example) or praised by his superiors. (The origins and effects of negative prejudices are discussed in Chapter 7, and those of neutral and positive predispositions are the major topics of Chapters 5 and 6.)

The man collapsing on the subway train was a confederate of three experimenters, and he feigned his disability. Irving Piliavin, Judith Rodin, and Jane Piliavin (1969) were interested in whether or not the race of a victim would affect helping behavior. Helping behavior has only recently captured a great deal of interest among social psychologists; Chapter 12 is devoted to the phenomenon that researchers call "prosocial behavior" or "altruism." As it turned out, Piliavin, Rodin, and Piliavin found that race was not important in helping a crippled victim, but when the victim's mishap appeared to be due to drunkenness instead of illness, only members of his own race were likely to help.

Finally, arrest and imprisonment were part of a simulation designed by Philip Zimbardo, Craig Haney, and Curtis Banks (1973) to study the behavior of prisoners and guards. As explained in Chapter 11, Zimbardo found that the situational demands of his mock prison were so compelling that seemingly well-adjusted persons whom the investigators assigned to par-

ticipate as prisoners or as guards quickly assumed aggressive or passive roles accordingly. Guards became aggressive and often sadistic. Prisoners became passive, dependent, helpless, and self-deprecating. The simulation had to be terminated before half the time originally planned had elapsed because the actions of many participants became pathological.

SOCIAL PSYCHOLOGY DEFINED

These and other studies conducted by social psychologists have an underlying focus in common. Whereas psychology in general can be defined as the scientific study of individual behavior, social psychology focuses on the scientific study of *interpersonal* behavior. This focus is not limiting, however. Most human behavior is either specifically interpersonal (as is a conversation) or occurs in interpersonal contexts (as does eating in a restaurant), and it is consequently molded by social events.

From a strictly human viewpoint, social psychology can be viewed as the hub of a wheel. Each spoke touches another science or applied profession. For example, sociology is the study of interaction among groups. For political science these groups are political ones. But the groups studied by both sociologists and political scientists all consist of individuals who interact with other individuals in their own and other groups; social psychology can make relevant contributions to these fields, and vice versa. Economics is the study of the economic behavior of people who compete or cooperate with one another; competition and cooperation among individuals and groups of individuals is an area of great interest to social psychologists, as becomes apparent at several points throughout this book, and the principles of exchange that pervade many social interactions are discussed in Chapters 6 and 13. Biologists are concerned with the physiological composition of individuals; social psychologists are concerned with the effects of different physiologies on interpersonal behavior. (For example, they study prejudice that some people direct toward other persons whose skin color, a physiological trait, is different.) Advertising is aimed at persuading the consumer; social influence, persuasion, and attitude change are central areas of social psychology (see Chapters 9 and 10). There are many more examples, but it is sufficient to note that social psychology is or could be concerned with any human interaction.

Any time that two or more people interact, something of interest to the social psychologist is likely to occur. But the discipline encompasses even more than specifically human behavior. Social psychologists do comparative work; for example, Bibb Latané, Emily Schneider, Peter Waring, and Richard Zweigenhaft (1971) have studied the social behavior of laboratory rats. They are interested in such questions as: What happens when one rat looks different from others in the group, as when the hair on its tail has been shaved? Do other rats respond to it differently? Latané and his colleagues' purpose was to find out whether rejection of the idiosyncratic individual is a strictly human characteristic or a phenomenon that occurs in various species. Another topic that might interest social psychologists is dreaming, which often features imaginary social encounters. Social psychologists might also study psychosomatic illness—illness that is produced by social stresses under which individuals function. Some researchers have become interested in the problem of obesity from the viewpoint of social psychology (Nisbett, 1968; Schachter, 1968). Although earlier investigators may have viewed the problem of obesity as rooted in physiological malfunctioning, intrapsychic difficulties, thyroid imbalance, and the like, these social psychologists have shown that obesity is often acquired through learning; children whose parents feed them every time they cry—whether their discomfort is due to lack of attention or actual hunger or a skinned knee—may as adults eat in response to a wide range of emotional states. Thus, these researchers have been able to demonstrate that the appetites of obese people are governed by situational cues and emotional responses, whereas trimmer persons tend to eat in response to caloric needs. This view of obesity as a learning problem places it squarely in a context that is ultimately social rather than in a context in which its origins are attributed to the internal physiological or psychological workings of the individual. All of these areas of interest can be, and in many cases already are, subject matter for research conducted by social psychologists.

THE WORLD THROUGH SOCIAL-PSYCHOLOGICAL GLASSES

Do social psychologists have a different world view than do other people? If so, is it different even from that of other social scientists? Although they differ from others in some ways, social psychologists inevitably have much in common with other members of their culture; in fact, their theories and research typically reflect the concerns of the cultures of which they are a part. Nevertheless, in certain respects their approach to social behavior is different. To appreciate the ways in which a social-psychological approach differs from others, consider an incident that is not uncommon in daily life:

You are eating lunch with two friends and the subject of religion is raised. One of your friends, Ron, argues that the Catholic Church is contributing to the misery of millions of people in its position on birth control. Ron feels that the birth rates in many underdeveloped countries are increasing because their largely Catholic populations are encouraged by the Church to have large families. As the birth rates increase there is less food per capita, less space, and greater pollution; the economies of these countries are thereby further stagnated. Your other friend, Sue, is mildly interested in the conversation, but as Ron continues his argument she begins to raise minor objections. She mentions that there are also many non-Catholic countries in which there are increasing birth rates, so that it may not be fair to blame the Church. Ron discounts Sue's argument, and she raises other points: many Catholics do practice forms of birth control, the Pope has strong religious traditions to maintain, and so on. The intensity of Ron's arguments increases. Sue begins to become angry. Finally Sue accuses Ron of prejudice, and Ron attacks Sue for her blindness. They both leave the table in fits of anger.

There are many common reactions to incidents of this nature. In similar situations, the concern may be with the feelings of our friends toward one another, and we may try to patch things up. We may evaluate the correctness of their arguments and try to come to balanced conclusions of our own. Or we might join with one side or another and form stronger friendships that will exclude those we side against. The social psychologist might have any or all of these reactions as well. However, if he or she could behave only as a professional, the social psychologist's approach would be quite different. First the social psychologist would try to discern whether or not there was some *general principle* that would account for this chain of events. This general principle would take a specific form: When certain conditions (a, b, and c, perhaps) exist, certain behaviors (x, y, and z) are likely to result. The present incident might suggest, among other possible principles: "When two persons hold opposing opinions and voice these opinions in the presence of a third person, their disagreements will not lessen but will become more intense." As you can see, this is a statement of *cause and effect.* It implies that certain conditions cause, or determine, certain behaviors. The social psychologist also considers it a *hypothetical* statement. There are no absolute or essential truths for the social psychologist, only hypothetical approximations to the truth. Some approximations, nevertheless, are better than others.

The social psychologist is not particularly concerned with his or her own reaction to the argument or interested in the argument in and of itself. Rather, the social psychologist is interested in how this incident can contribute to a system of general laws or principles that can be used to understand not only this incident but thousands of others like it. Such a deterministic system leaves little room in this explanation of the world for notions such as "free choice" and "will." There is also a hesitancy in the approach, a form of conservatism. The social psychologist rarely says, "Obviously this happened because. . . . " A dim view is taken in the field toward overbearing confidence in one's knowledge of "why." This posture protects the social psychologist's openness to new insights and new phenomena and also reduces biases from his or her personal opinions that find their way into both theory and data. (For an example, see the history of research on authoritarianism in Chapter 7.)

There are still further differences in the social psychologist's approach. In formulating general principles, it is necessary for the psychologist to break an incident into smaller pieces. Reality cannot be accepted in its totality. Rather, *smaller units must be isolated for analysis.* For example, to formulate the foregoing principle, the analyst needed to identify three separate persons and to note that the opinions of two of them differed. Then, from the myriad events that occurred, the analyst centered on the change in opinion intensity of the two persons arguing.

Critics of this approach feel that it does injustice to reality. It seems akin to reducing the totality of Beethoven's Ninth Symphony to the interaction between the first and second oboists. However, there is considerable advantage in isolating segments of social reality in this way. As already noted, the social psychologist is interested in formulating principles that can successfully predict behavior. By stating the principle in a way that segments reality, one can know when and where the principle can be applied. The principle under discussion does not say that all arguments will end up in intense disagreements but rather that those arguments that take place in the presence of a third person will tend to escalate in intensity.

This segmentation also allows the social psychologist to test the validity of a theory. It also suggests conditions that match the theoretical statement and facilitates a comparison of the effects of these conditions with the effects of contrasting conditions. For example, it may be that the presence of a third person is unnecessary to produce the accelerating disagreement. Using experimental means, one could allow pairs of people to argue, half in the presence of a third person and the other half by themselves. If the principle is correct, the experimental group with an audience should show greater differences of opinion at the conclusion of the experiment than should the group of solitary debaters. Without isolating segments of reality, it would be impossible to carry out tests such as this.

This segmentation of reality permits the social psychologist to refine a theory. The researcher does not emerge from one well-designed study with the evidence needed to construct or validate a theory. On the contrary, the important findings that social psychologists have contributed have typically emerged from series of individual studies in which researchers have isolated one variable after another. The findings of a researcher's previous studies often supply indications of variables that can be isolated in future studies, and the composite data from many such studies can provide a view of the ways in which many variables interact in complex relationships. An example of how the experimenter tracks down his or her quarry in a series of controlled studies is provided by Stanley Milgram, whose work on obedience is described in Chapters 10 and 11. Milgram (1963) originally found that a startling number of people (65 percent of his subjects) would obey an experimenter's orders to administer painful electric shock to a fellow subject. Milgram thereafter conducted a series of variations on his original experiment, pinning down the specific conditions that increased or decreased subjects' inclinations to inflict pain on others for the sake of obedience. He found that obedience at the expense of others is likely to increase as physical, visual, or auditory contact between subject and victim decrease. In still other variations of his experiment, Milgram found that willingness to disobey increased with decreasing contact between subjects and the experimenter who was giving the orders and that disobedience also increased when other subjects provided social support for disobedience. These variations provide a fuller understanding of the specific conditions that foster obedience than did Milgram's prototype experiment and suggest, as well, some measures that can be taken in real-life situations to deter harmful obedience.

Still another distinguishing feature of most social-psychological thought is the feeling that it is difficult to understand or predict social behavior without reference to the *internal state* of the individual. Whereas sociologists usually place a strong emphasis on the social structure or on large arrangements of people and biologists are primarily interested in the physical or organic composition of people, the social psychologist is concerned with a person's feelings, values, motives, personal definitions of the world, and so on. The principle of opinion disagreement that was tentatively formulated above makes no reference to internal states. However, if pushed further to explain why the principle should work, the social psychologist might well speak in terms of the "embarrassment" one feels upon appearing to change his or her opinion, "the desire" to appear firm, the "loss in feelings of esteem" when shown to be wrong, and so on.

The view of the social psychologist is different from that of other scientists. However, it is adopted in order to solve pressing problems. Whether or not it is the most successful approach to these problems is a matter you may wish to decide for yourself as you read this volume.

DOES THE INDIVIDUAL COUNT IN SOCIAL PSYCHOLOGY?

Aldous Huxley has pointed out that when we study *motion,* we do not study the moving *objects.* A similar problem occurs in social psychology: If we study behavior, we do not study the individual who engages in that behavior. Most social psychologists favor this *nomothetic approach;* that is, they suggest that it is sufficient to know how the "average" person will respond in a social situation. In other words, social psychologists as scientists can aspire to predict the behavior of most persons in particular situations but cannot predict the behavior of any specific person. The late Gordon Allport (1937) strongly argued against this "statistical" approach to the study of social behavior. Rather, Allport favored an *ideographic approach*—one that focuses on the individual and on that individual's response to his or her social environment.

The sometimes competitive ideographic and nomothetic trends in social psychology have existed for some time. Although few social psychologists value studying the unique individual, many see merit in taking account of *individual differences* among people (see Chapter 4). The individual-difference approach to social psychology had an especially strong impact directly after the conclusion of World War II. At that time social scientists from several disciplines were attempting to make sense of the fascistic movements that had swept and devastated Europe. They wanted to know whether or not there was something peculiar to Italians, Austrians, Germans, and Spanish people that led them to embrace fascistic philosophies. Or was a similar proclivity present in nonfascistic nations as well? For

Figure 1.2 The ideographic approach in social psychology involves studying individuals and their unique responses to various situations. Although such an approach would permit more accurate evaluation of, for example, the old woman in the center of this photograph, to study in depth the reactions of each individual in this gathering would be an overwhelming task. For this reason, social psychologists prefer to study the reactions of the average individual and risk being wrong part of the time when making predictions about individual behavior.

I Introduction

example, could an "authoritarian personality" be found among Americans? A wave of research, using the *F* scale (a measure of authoritarianism), demonstrated that many Americans do fit the "fascistic" personality. The ubiquitous fascistic presence called for extensive scientific analysis. Volumes of research documented the social behavior of authoritarians and nonauthoritarians. Other personality tests followed: Social psychologists became interested in the characteristics of those scoring high or low on rigidity, on dogmatism, on Machiavellianism, and on many other measures. For these researchers, it was important to ask: "How do the specific personality characteristics of an individual produce (or contribute to) his or her social behavior?"

The ideographic ideal of studying individuals has seldom been realized, however. It is cumbersome to study each individual carefully and to predict his or her personal behavior. No social psychologist has the time, the personnel, or even the methods to reliably predict what person X who has personality characteristic Y will do. It is much easier to predict what several persons will do "on the average." Predictions about groups of people that are based on probability permit social psychologists to be wrong part of the time, as long as they are not wrong most of the time. Researchers who use individual-difference measures tend to make predictions for smaller groups of people than do researchers who are more nomothetic in their orientations. For example, they might predict and demonstrate that persons scoring high on the *F* scale are on the average more aggressive toward a subordinate than are persons scoring low on that scale. The prediction may or may not hold for any specific individual subject. As a consequence, personality approaches typically diverge from the ideographic ideal and become somewhat nomothetic.

Researchers choosing a completely nomothetic route to social psychology have tended to ignore individual-disposition variables altogether. Instead, they often consider environmental factors the major determinants of social behavior. Their work has recently been given more impetus by the prison-simulation findings of Zimbardo and his colleagues, described earlier, and by the findings of Stanley Milgram (1963), described in Chapters 10 and 11, that normal, well-adjusted adults will shock others with dangerous levels of electric current (450 volts) if they are told to do so by someone who represents authority. Why did Zimbardo's subjects become sadistic when assigned to play the role of prison guard? Why did they humiliate their prisoners? And did Milgram's subjects willingly endanger the lives of other subjects? The answer seems to lie in situational influences. And these situational factors were strong enough, at least in most cases, to override any individual predilections not to harm their fellow human beings. The setting of the experiment—the reality of the simulated prison for Zimbardo's subjects and the presence of an insistent "scientist" who ordered Milgram's subjects to hurt a fellow subject—produced behavior that the subjects themselves were often unable to explain after the experiment was over. As it turns out, harmdoing and altruism (see Chapters 11 and 12) are both closely linked to situational factors that are capable of evoking both types of behavior in the same individual at different times.

The nomothetic and individual-differences approaches can be united into yet another approach. It is quite conceivable (and has been demonstrated) that, at least in some situations, personality (the characteristics of an individual) and environment combine to influence interactions among individuals and among groups. For social psychologists who favor this *interactive approach,* the primary question is, "How do the effects of an individual's personality and the effects of his or her environment combine to determine social behavior?"

STRATEGIES OF INQUIRY

The purpose of any science lies in the investigation of the phenomena in its purview. It attempts to define its area, to describe the phenomena within that area, to determine which phenomena relate to which others, and finally to establish whether or not any causal relationships are present. Knowledge of relationships among events, particularly if they are causal, permits one to predict events in the future. Understanding and prediction are the goals of science.

Every science must adapt its methods of research and analysis, its ways of stating and testing models and theories, to the phenomena with which it is dealing. For social psychology, four methods have been found most appropriate: the *case study,* the *survey,* the *simulation,* and the *standard laboratory experiment.* All of them will be discussed at some length here. However, the field is not necessarily limited to these strategies of inquiry; others may well come into use as they are developed or become appropriate. The discussion of research methods in this chapter, then, should not be viewed as exhaustive. The focus of the present discussion will begin with the most broadly based of the methods—the one that is most sensitive to the complexities of a real-world situation—and move to the method that is least broad in scope. At the same time, the focus will move from the method permitting least inference of causality to that permitting most. Thus, the discussion begins with the case study, then turns to the survey, considers simulations, and looks last at the standard laboratory experiment.

The Case Study

A physicist who is interested in the free fall of an object can climb the leaning tower of Pisa (or any similar structure, for that matter) and drop the object from the top of it. Or, if more controlled laboratory conditions are desired, the physicist can pump air out of a long glass tube and measure free fall in a vacuum. If, however, he wants to study the effects of radiation from a nuclear explosion on the environment, his exploding a bomb may be called immoral. Social psychologists must face a similar problem rather frequently. Many experiments have been attacked as unethical, and research must often be carefully designed to avoid ethical problems. Certain situations for which the need for information is great present insurmountable problems. For example, it would be of great value to know more about how people react to disasters—earthquakes, flash-floods, and so forth. Knowledge about human behavior in crisis situations might suggest emergency programs that, if developed, might save many lives. However, an investigator whose enthusiasm is fueled by a desire to contribute this knowledge cannot open up the flood gates of a dam in order to study the reactions of people to the ensuing crisis. The investigator must wait until a crisis occurs naturally and then collect as much information as possible during and after the crisis. But because the progress of naturally occurring crises cannot be controlled, investigators cannot infer causality from any of the data they obtain. Yet they can learn to make increasingly "educated guesses" about events during a crisis, and their predictions regarding reactions to future crises may be somewhat improved as a result.

Similar problems arise when investigators want to study any event that cannot be faithfully created in the laboratory. Consider, for example, the dilemma of researchers who want to study the ways in which votes (and potentially attitudes) are changed during Democratic and Republican conventions to select presidential candidates. The number of people involved, their various commitments, the emotionally charged atmosphere, and so forth cannot be re-created in a laboratory. Certainly investigators can study parts of the process in the laboratory, but they cannot study the ways in which the parts fit together unless they observe them in the real-world context of the convention itself. As with crisis situations, then, the investigators must resort to the case-study approach when studying political conventions. And again, they will not be able to draw conclusions about which events caused which other events; simultaneously occurring events may be unrelated—that is, they may occur at the same time by accident—or may both be produced by some third phenomenon. But at the very least, case studies can yield knowledge that assists investigators in designing more appropriate and representative laboratory experiments.

The best way to describe any research strategy is to give an illustrative example. To better understand the advantages and limitations of the case-study method, consider a disaster that yielded a great deal of knowledge to researchers about possible reactions to this type of situation.

Case Study—When Disaster Strikes. On June 16, 1965, a catastrophic flood hit the city of Denver, Colorado. City officials learned of this disaster in advance. Policemen drove down the streets of low-lying areas of the city and announced through loudspeakers that a twenty-foot-high wall of water was approaching. They told residents in these areas that they would have five to fifteen minutes to leave for higher ground. Residents who turned on radios and televisions found that some stations were continuing regular broadcasting while others sporadically covered the approaching flood, at times presenting contradictory information. The contradictions produced disbelief; many persons simply would not believe that the oncoming flood

Figure 1.3 The case study is employed to study human behavior in rare situations that cannot be re-created for research purposes, such as natural disasters and national events. Here, Mississippi young people sandbag the river banks in an attempt to prevent threatened flood damage to their town.

represented a severe threat. Those who had friends, families, or business establishments in the endangered area, as well as sightseers, started to converge on threatened ground. Fortunately the time available for evacuation was much longer than initially announced. The police began evacuating people at about 4 P.M., but the flood waters did not arrive until about 8:15 P.M. The water reached its crest about 11 P.M., carrying tons of debris. Bridges were ripped out, houses were destroyed. The flood damage was estimated at $325 million. The police department and other agencies that were involved in the evacuation efforts had been effective; no lives were lost. The success of the effort to save the lives of people living in the area threatened by the flood was facilitated by the fact that more than four hours elapsed between the time information about the impending disaster became available and the actual arrival of the flood waters. The time available for preparing for many other disasters has been much shorter.

What can be learned from the Denver disaster for potential future use? Thomas Drabeck and John S. Stephenson (1971) interviewed a random sample of 278 out of approximately 3,700 families that lived in the stricken area. Drabeck arrived in Denver three days after the disaster and initially interviewed local officials who were involved in the attempt to avert greater disaster. The purpose of these interviews was to establish a descriptive account of what had been done and why it had been done. Official records, including police-department radio logs, were obtained. Based on the information these interviews yielded, a forty-five page interview schedule was developed. The questions led each respondent to reconstruct the sequence of events as the disaster affected his or her family. These reports were given in yes-no answers and verbal descriptions that were recorded verbatim. The investigators also obtained background data on the ages, occupations, and so on of all family members. After pretesting this interview schedule, a final questionnaire was developed. Every tenth family within the boundaries of the stricken area was then interviewed, and the average interview took about one and one-half hours; again, verbatim responses were recorded, in addition to yes-no answers.

Drabeck and Stephenson obtained a number of response patterns that are of potential value for planning actions in future disasters. Here are some of them: Families acted and thought as groups, not as individuals. For separated families, the primary concern was locating the other family members. Officials had more difficulty evacuating family members who were cut off from one another than families that were together. Although the mass media were effective in getting danger warnings to the families, they were relatively ineffective in producing action. Telephone communications among relatives and friends apparently produced much more action toward evacuation than did television or radio messages; they appear to be of vital importance in mobilizing people during a disaster. Therefore, a policy of not tying up telephone lines appears to be a bad one. Telephone communications also served to make transportation available. As many as 17 percent of the families relied on evacuation transportation arranged in telephone conversations. Officials had expected a panic, but it did not occur. This finding is not unusual. Had officials known that a panic was not to be expected, they could have used a different evacuation strategy. To begin with, they could have been more honest about the length of time people had before the disaster would strike. This time could have been used to save valuable possessions. Families did not have any plans about what to do in case of disaster. They had no idea about where to meet if separated. Their important papers were not stored in safe places. Many families did not know how to shut off gas, water, electricity, and so on in order to avoid possible additional damage. Warning messages could have been more effective if, for example, they had been more consistent.

Obviously, results such as these are of considerable importance to any administrator who must cope with an impending disaster. These results are also useful in defining areas in which more small-scale laboratory studies can be designed. For example, although the investigators cannot be certain that the inconsistency of information released by the media produced public inaction, the results are suggestive and deserving of further investigation.

The Survey

Case studies usually concern events that take place rarely or perhaps only once. Disasters are usually infrequent. Conventions for the selection of presidential candidates occur only once every four years, and their characteristics differ from one time to another. But some other events and phenomena occur almost continuously—for example, the spread of venereal disease in the United States, the use of drugs by a large part of the population, and political attitudes.

These continuing phenomena can be studied with survey methods as they are occurring, and not just in retrospect as in the case of disasters. Surveys are techniques for obtaining beliefs, opinions, attitudes, intentions, and so on of selected members of a population. The purpose of surveys often is to describe or to attempt to make predictions for:

1. the frequency with which a particular response occurs (for example, in predicting the percentage of the voter turnout that a particular candidate or issue will capture);
2. the relationships between people's feelings about or responses to certain objects (for example, the relationship between conservatism and preference for a political candidate);
3. the relationships between beliefs and past or intended actions (for example, the views held about the rightness of a political action and the intent to vote for or against the person who engaged in that action); or
4. the relationships between certain actions and other actions (for example, the degree to which grades in college are related to the use of drugs).

All these aims, as well as the specific examples cited, are represented throughout this book. Typically, survey researchers carefully select a *sample* from the relevant population, because they cannot usually survey every individual in the population. For example, if they are interested in studying college students, they will select students from representative colleges, perhaps matching urban with rural respondents, government with private representatives, or East Coast students with Midwestern students with students from West Coast schools. The researchers will interview representatives of each group in proportion to that group's incidence in the population. (Thus, for example, the ratio of male to female college students being interviewed should reflect the female-to-male ratio in the United States college population.) Several research organizations have samples of this sort permanently available.

All members in a sample are asked to respond to carefully pretested questions or statements. The answers are then scored, and statistical techniques are used to establish the incidence of the obtained responses (for example, the incidence of votes for one presidential candidate as opposed to another) and the relationship of that incidence to other responses (for example, the incidence of persons who claim to be liberal rather than conservative and intend to vote for the candidate). The methods and means of evaluating data, as well as some of the problems involved, are described in Chapter 8.

Survey research is limited in its capacity to yield inferences of causality, although not as severely limited as is the case-study method. If it is found that conservatives are planning to vote for candidate Simon Short, then the temptation is to say that these people will vote for him because they are conservative. This conclusion may or may not be accurate. Some third phenomenon might have intervened and produced this result. Nonetheless, the information obtained about voting preferences might prove quite useful. For example, if Simon Short intends to win more votes, it might be advantageous for him to spend his time persuading liberal voters rather than conservatives, who already back him. Candidate Short may not care why the conservatives favor him; he may simply want to know where he currently lacks support so that he can plan his strategy accordingly.

A survey can sometimes help to combat certain causal assumptions that are made on the basis of little or no knowledge. For example, it is sometimes asserted that use of marijuana leads to use of hard drugs. Survey research could test part of that proposition; by questioning two groups of equal size, one composed of marijuana users and the other of persons who have not used marijuana, a researcher could ascertain the frequencies with which members of the two groups have used harder drugs. If the researcher found that the two groups did not differ in this respect, then the assumption that marijuana use leads to hard drugs would likely be erroneous. And if the investigator were to find that marijuana users had tried hard drugs more often than nonusers had, the contention would be neither supported nor refuted. This point will be discussed later in the chapter, but first consider the findings of three researchers who used the method to study characteristics of marijuana users. Kenneth Gergen, Mary Gergen, and Stanley Morse (1972) were interested in the incidence of marijuana smoking among college students and in the relationship of marijuana usage to other factors.

Survey—Marijuana and College Students. Gergen, Gergen, and Morse compared college students who had smoked marijuana with others who had not. They selected a sample of thirty-eight colleges and universities from the *Education Directory.* Students at each college or university were selected at random, yielding 5,050 respondents to a questionnaire. The questionnaire was four pages long, and the responses were anonymous and self-administered. Students took about twenty-five minutes to complete the forms. Questions dealt with political opinions, characteristics of the institution attended, demographic background, and drug experiences.

The researchers found that 36.7 percent of the students had used marijuana at least once; 11.7 percent reported experience with hallucinogens such as LSD and mescaline; 8.2 percent had used stimulants or depressants like amphetamines and barbiturates; and 1.9 percent reported the use of heroin and/or cocaine. Relating the incidence of marijuana use to the characteristics of the institutions, the investigators found that marijuana use is greatest at the most academically competitive institutions. Marijuana users included 55.6 percent of the students at institutions that demand scholastic excellence. The percentage of students who used marijuana drop-

Figure 1.4 Survey methods are often used in social-psychological research to ascertain attitudes and intentions. Predictions based on surveys are sometimes unreliable, however, because of last-minute opinion swings, dishonest or inadequate responding, or poor sampling procedures. Although pollsters have generally fared well in their predictions, there have been notable errors of large significance, such as *(below)* their predictions of a Dewey landslide in 1948. For the most part, however, surveys yield useful information about their respondents. Sample items *(opposite)* used by sociologists Charles Glock and Rodney Stark in surveying the attitudes of Americans toward Jews and the relationship between those attitudes and such variables as religious beliefs, socioeconomic status, and level of education. In this case, some of the statements about Jews *do* tend to be accurate. Thus, agreement (Column A) that, for example, Jews tend to drink less than non-Jews should not be interpreted as prejudice against Jews unless the accompanying response in Column B indicates an unfriendly attitude toward Jews who do not drink.

I Introduction

ped consistently with decreasing difficulty of the school. Only 27 percent of junior-college students reported experience with the drug. Grade-point average was also related to marijuana usage. The best students reported greater use of marijuana: 37.2 percent of those with an A average used marijuana, 36.3 percent of those with a B average, 32.6 percent with a C average, and 23.3 percent of those with a D average had smoked marijuana. The academic degree that the student viewed as the highest he or she hoped to earn was also important: Those students wanting to earn doctorates reported the highest incidence of marijuana use (51.5 and 46.9 percent respectively for Ph.D. and M.D. hopefuls); those aspiring to master's degrees reported 34.5 percent usage; only one quarter of the students hoping to obtain a bachelor's degree used marijuana (26.9 percent); and 27.7 percent of the students intending to obtain an associate's degree reported usage. Those who reported using marijuana were also opposed to the war in Vietnam.

The results of this survey clearly suggest that the incidence of marijuana use is considerably greater than is the use of other drugs. In other words, a simplistic supposition that those who smoke marijuana are also using harder drugs is apparently unjustified. And those who assume that "bums" and "dropouts" are the marijuana users should be somewhat surprised by the finding that marijuana use increases with schools' academic difficulty and with quality of academic performance. However, the reasons for these findings are not clear. The investigators do not know, for

---

We turn now to relations between Christians and Jews. There is a great deal of disagreement about what Jews are like. Here are some things people have said at one time or another about Jews. For each statement, we would ask you to do two things:

First read the statement and decide whether you tend to think Jews are like this or not, and put your answer in Column A.

Then, whether or not you think Jews are like this or not, we would ask you to suppose that the statement actually were true. If the statement were true, how would it tend to make you feel toward Jews? Would you tend to feel friendly or unfriendly toward them because of this? Put your answer in Column B.

COLUMN A Do you feel Jews tend to be like this?

COLUMN B If Jews were like this would it tend to make you feel:

Yes	Somewhat	No		Friendly	Unfriendly	Neither Way
☐	☐	☐	Jews are particularly generous and give a great deal of money to charity	☐	☐	☐
☐	☐	☐	On the average, Jews are wealthier than Christians	☐	☐	☐
☐	☐	☐	Jews are more likely than Christians to cheat in business	☐	☐	☐
☐	☐	☐	Jewish children tend to get better grades in school than Christian children do	☐	☐	☐
☐	☐	☐	Jews are less likely than Christians to oppose Communism	☐	☐	☐
☐	☐	☐	The movie and television industries are pretty much run by Jews	☐	☐	☐
☐	☐	☐	On the average, Jews tend to drink less than non-Jews	☐	☐	☐

example, whether or not brighter people tend to explore more, whether or not the stress they experience provokes them to seek escape routes, whether or not marijuana is most easily available to students who are bright and to those who are at demanding institutions, and so on. The findings seem to indicate with some certainty that marijuana use does not adversely affect academic performance, but they cannot indicate whether or not it has helped academic performance. Again, the results are suggestive and deserve to be followed up with more research, preferably long-term research that would follow individuals' development over several years. Some of the data from this study may also provide the basis for laboratory-research designs in future studies of marijuana use.

The Simulation

The term "simulation" is now a familiar one. We have perhaps all seen the word on television screens as the capsule of an Apollo moonshot separated from its booster rocket or as the lunar-landing module took off from the surface of the moon.

A simulation is a representation of reality in simplified form, attempting to maintain the essential (for immediate purposes) components of the reality it represents. Engineers have been using simulations for a much longer time than have social scientists. For example, engineers have built precise miniature replicas of future aircraft to test their aerodynamic properties in wind tunnels. Social scientists have only in the past decade designed simulations for their own purposes. Simulations are useful to social psychologists when they want to learn about the characteristics of some more-or-less complex event or sequence of events that occurs in the real world. If the relevant components of an event can be re-created in a laboratory or on a computer, a simulation is possible.

Social psychologists have used three different kinds of simulation techniques: man-machine simulations, all-man simulations, and computer simulations. The all-man simulation puts the participants in a laboratory environment that is as similar as possible to the real-world environment it

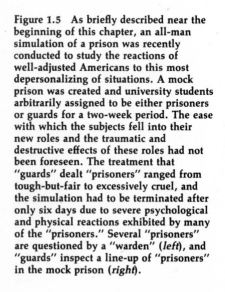

Figure 1.5 As briefly described near the beginning of this chapter, an all-man simulation of a prison was recently conducted to study the reactions of well-adjusted Americans to this most depersonalizing of situations. A mock prison was created and university students arbitrarily assigned to be either prisoners or guards for a two-week period. The ease with which the subjects fell into their new roles and the traumatic and destructive effects of these roles had not been foreseen. The treatment that "guards" dealt "prisoners" ranged from tough-but-fair to excessively cruel, and the simulation had to be terminated after only six days due to severe psychological and physical reactions exhibited by many of the "prisoners." Several "prisoners" are questioned by a "warden" (*left*), and "guards" inspect a line-up of "prisoners" in the mock prison (*right*).

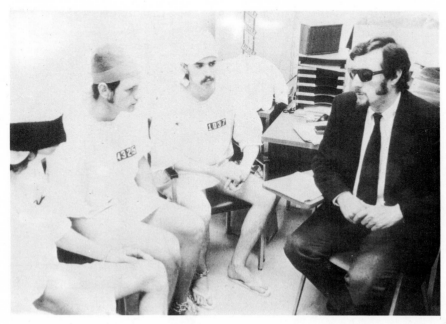

represents. For example, when Drabeck and Stephenson (1971) were interested in measuring certain aspects of police decision making, the police dispatcher and his equipment were moved into the laboratory. There he did his work as usual, except that some additional calls were received to which he had to respond. Because he did not know which calls were "real" and which were "experimental," he had to respond meaningfully to all of them. Consequently, his responses could be measured. Similarly, the campus-unrest study and the research by Zimbardo, Haney, and Banks with prisoners and prison guards, both mentioned at the beginning of this chapter, are simulations and have been designed to collect systematic data about human behavior in specific situations.

These examples point toward an advantage of simulation over the two techniques that were considered earlier: The researcher has *control* over what happens in the laboratory. That is, the researcher determines the information flow to the participant and/or determines the specific conditions under which the participant must work. For example, Harold Guetzkow (1970) and his associates have used the Inter Nation Simulation (INS)—a method of *free simulation*—to place subjects in the positions of national leaders who make decisions about economic, military, and other components of domestic and international politics. These leaders of various nations can interact freely. Each participant must begin with the resources, political system, and so on assigned by the researcher. Nevertheless, each nation's circumstances may change drastically because its fortune is necessarily linked to the actions of the other players. Consequently, the experimenter can try to measure the "typical" sequence of events, given certain predetermined antecedent conditions. The outcome of a number of "runs" of the simulation can then be used to build a theoretical model of behavior among nations.

Howard Fromkin and Siegfried Streufert (1973) have suggested that Guetzkow's simulation technique has value as a theory of behavior but that it lacks usefulness as an experimental method. Because the experimenter in a free simulation has little or no control over subsequent events beyond the

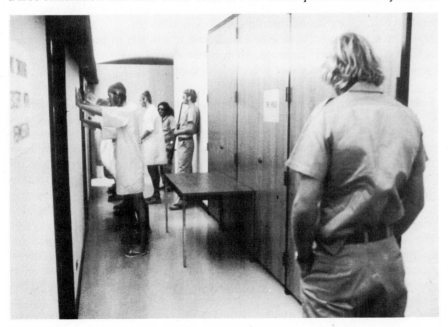

initial starting point of the simulation, he cannot know precisely what conditions led to what outcomes. To alleviate this problem, Siegfried Streufert, Carl H. Castore, Susan C. Kliger, and Michael Driver (1967) developed the *experimental-simulation* technique, which involves man-machine simulations.

The participant in the experimental simulation is pitted against a computer program that responds to each action with a predetermined countermove. A simple form of a man-machine simulation would be a chess game between a person and a computer. In a more complicated example, the computer may represent decision makers of one nation while the participants in the simulation represent decision makers of another nation. The computer might be programed to respond to each move made by the participants in a predetermined way, or it may only appear to respond meaningfully, because its responses are preprogramed and independent of the participants' moves. To develop a computer program that would meaningfully respond to the actions of participants, the "typical" responses of a nation of the kind represented by the computer would have to be known. In other words, advance knowledge about the parameters—the relationships between fixed input and output—are needed. These parameters must be known before a researcher can design a computer program. The type and number of these parameters determine the characteristics and complexity of the program and also determine the extent of the investigator's control over the simulation.

Whether among corporations, other organizations or groups, or between individuals, human participants can be eliminated from a simulation of interaction to the extent that all the parameters are known. This procedure is called a computer (all-machine) simulation. Although this technique can produce the greatest quantity of data in the smallest amount of time, it is accurate only to the degree that the parameters are accurate. A computer is never better than the program that is used in operating it.

One final comment on simulations as a technique is that they should be distinguished from role playing. Some psychologists have argued that there is no need to experiment, that it would be enough merely to ask people to imagine what they would do in a specific situation (Brown, 1965). Research has shown, however, that individuals find it difficult to predict their own behavior, and others' behavior is not necessarily any simpler to predict. Role playing produces more than its share of errors in prediction.

Simulation—War and Peace in Shamba. The Tactical and Negotiations Game (TNG), developed by Siegfried Streufert, Carl Castore, Susan Kliger, and Michael Driver (1967), is an experimental simulation that permits participants to make decisions about the economic, negotiation, military, and intelligence operations of a nation involved in a limited war. When the participants arrive for the simulation, they are placed in groups of two or four in a room that resembles a strategic-command meeting room. It is equipped with a three-dimensional map of Shamba (a fictional peninsula), a telephone, video communication equipment, flags, and many other props. The participants read a manual on the historical background of Shamba and on the current conditions there, and are informed about their resources, capacities, and so on. After a two-hour reading period and a strategy consultation with one another, they are ready to play the game. They believe that they are playing against another team representing an opposing nation. For example, if the team members represent a large powerful

Figure 1.6 Man-machine simulation can pit an individual against a computer, as in this chess game. Each of the individual's moves elicits a countermove that is determined by a computer program. As with any computer simulation, its success depends on how complete the program is that it is based on.

nation assisting the local government in Shamba against a rebel movement, they believe that the other team represents the rebels. If they play the role of rebels, they assume that the opposing team represents the foreign power. The team members can divide up their work or operate as a unit. The way in which they handle the simulated problem is up to them.

These events in the simulation are carefully preprogramed so that the illusion of reality is maintained. However, the teams are receiving information (via written messages, telephone calls, or video-news broadcasts) that has been predetermined by the experimenters. In this fashion, the experimenters control the conditions at the beginning of the simulation, and they also know exactly what information is being received by the participants at any point in time. In other words, all teams in any experiment can receive information in exactly the same way (the same information in the same or random order).

Implications of the results of this and similar studies for decision making in "high places," particularly in international relations, are a topic discussed in Chapter 15.

Experimental-simulation techniques lend themselves to a variety of experimental purposes. The University Game, described at the beginning of this chapter, was an experimental simulation. It was devised to study decision making and to measure the attitudes of college students. Attitudes can be measured with the TNG, too. For example, Siegfried Streufert and Sandy Sandler (1971) were interested in testing Urie Bronfenbrenner's mirror-image hypothesis. After visiting the Soviet Union, Bronfenbrenner (1961) concluded that the Russians view the United States exactly as many North Americans view the Russians: as aggressors. Is it true that mirror-image perceptions occur easily? Do nations often view one another incorrectly as "bad" and as "aggressive" even when neither view is accurate? Streufert and Sandler found that only two hours of indoctrination (reading the TNG manual) resulted in mirror-image perceptions. Even though the TNG manual for the large foreign power contained the same factual information for both sides as did the manual for the rebel movement, the information was "colored" by a means similar to the subtle propaganda techniques used by national governments. The two versions of the manual varied in some of the adjectives used in such a way that a participant's own position was always favored; the players thereby tended to become persuaded that their side was right and the other wrong. Regardless of what their own actions had been, players tended to view the other side as aggressive and themselves as much less so. Even participants who displayed pacifist symbols engaged in violently aggressive acts against their opponents when the other side did not respond to initial peace overtures. Later they often asked themselves why they had acted in a manner so inconsistent with their own values. This simulation suggests that people are highly susceptible to propaganda, even when it is presented subtly, particularly when they feel involved in the ongoing events.

Involvement is the key characteristic of a good simulation. Participants in simulations often refuse to quit even after hours. They can get completely carried away with ongoing situations, perhaps confusing reality with simulated events. The advantages of the simulation are that it measures behavior similar to naturally occurring human behavior, that it usually elicits feelings of involvement from subjects that heighten their sense of realism, and that the experimenter has control over events as they proceed. There are some disadvantages as well: The simulation is a compromise between such real-world techniques as the survey and the standard laboratory experiment, which permits more precise control over variables by experimenters. As a compromise, the simulation necessarily has advantages and disadvantages and is probably most effectively used in combination with other approaches, particularly with the standard laboratory experiment, which can usually yield more precise information about relationships among clearly defined conditions.

The Standard Laboratory Experiment

Most published research in social psychology, most theory testing, and even a good deal of applied research has employed the standard laboratory experiment as its method of research. The laboratory in which it probably takes place may vary from a sophisticated, electronically equipped suite of rooms to a regular classroom. The researcher typically exposes subjects to a limited number of stimuli and then measures their responses to the stimuli with some predetermined research instrument. The stimuli that represent independent variables in laboratory experiments—stimuli that are under the control of the experimenter—vary widely. For example, these stimuli can take forms as diverse as a momentary tachistoscopic projection of a picture with an interpersonal theme, information about the attitudes of another person, or a description of an event. The measure on which the subject responds can vary equally widely. The experimenter may measure the physiological response to a picture (perhaps noting increases in heart rate or galvanic skin response as the subject is shown a sexually explicit photograph), ask the subject to respond by placing a checkmark on an attitude scale, observe and record subjects' responses to other subjects who are present during the experiment, and so on.

There are good reasons for the predominance of the laboratory-research method in social-psychological research. This method more than any other allows the researcher to control the environment in which the experiment takes place. The laboratory can be arranged and the manipulation of the independent variable designed so that only the *independent variable*—the variable that is manipulated by the experimenter—gains the major portion of a subject's attention. Potentially irrelevant confounding effects can be eliminated or at least held constant at some level at which they are not likely to interfere with measuring the relationship between independent and *dependent variables* (those experimental variables that change in response to changes in the independent variable). Because of the clarity of the data obtained with a good laboratory-research design, and because of the clear inference of causality for relationships among variables that this type of research permits, supporters of the laboratory experiment have often argued that it is the only meaningful research method.

There are other advantages as well. Assuming that the required research space is available, most laboratory experiments are relatively inexpensive and can be conducted in reasonably short time periods. The relative speed with which data can be obtained either allows the researcher to try several approaches to a research problem without much loss of time or permits the investigator to perfect techniques for obtaining information about relationships among the variables being studied. After the laboratory researcher has obtained the results, he or she can feel relatively sure that the obtained relationships among variables are *reliable*—that is, that these same relationships would be obtained again if someone repeated the experiment under essentially the same conditions. In other words, the experimenter can place a relatively large degree of trust in data obtained in a laboratory experiment.

An ingenious researcher can sometimes turn the "real world" into a laboratory. Examples are the taxi-cab experiment and the subway study described at the beginning of this chapter. Experiments carried out in this fashion are usually called *field experiments.* This form of experimentation suffers from some lack of experimental control over extraneous variables that might intervene in the measurement of independent and dependent variables; for example, the results of the experiment could in part be due to the particular subway route along which the experiment was carried out. Nevertheless, the data obtained in a field experiment are often more representative of the real behavior of real people in the real world than are data from studies conducted under antiseptic laboratory conditions. The subject who arrives at the laboratory to participate in an experiment may be painfully alert for signs that he or she is being evaluated, may not want to participate, may be eager to help the experimenter obtain results that the experimenter wants, or may respond in an uncharacteristic way as a result of feeling uncomfortable in the laboratory environment. In contrast, subjects in a field experiment typically are not aware that they are participating in research. Consequently, subjects behave as they normally would. Unfortunately, however, many research problems are not amenable to field-research designs.

How useful is the frequently employed laboratory experiment? This method has often been described as artificial by real-world standards, and it often deals with so few variables at one time that it is not clear whether or not the results would stand up in a more complicated real-world setting. For example, as explained in detail in Chapter 6, Donn Byrne (1971) has repeatedly demonstrated that "similarity attracts." The finding is not surprising if one considers that a proverb has stated this phenomenon rather clearly, unless one becomes aware that the opposite view is also represented by a proverb—the old saying that "opposites attract." Byrne's research is based on paper-and-pencil responses: The subject fills out an attitude scale, finds that another person has filled out the scale either similarly or quite differently, and is then asked on a paper-and-pencil measure how attracted he or she is to that other person. Typically, Byrne

Figure 1.7 The standard laboratory experiment is the research strategy most commonly used by social psychologists. The control it allows the experimenter, the clarity and reliability of the data it yields, and the ease with which it can be carried out account for its popularity. Because of its artificiality, however, relationships identified in the laboratory should only be generalized to "real-world" situations with a great deal of caution. (*Left*) from behind a one-way window, an experimenter observes an interaction between an adult and a child. (*Right*) four subjects participate in a study of social perception without being able to directly observe one another's actions.

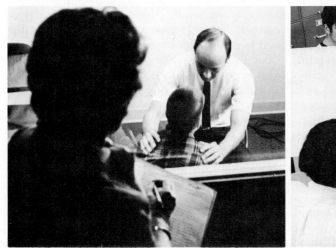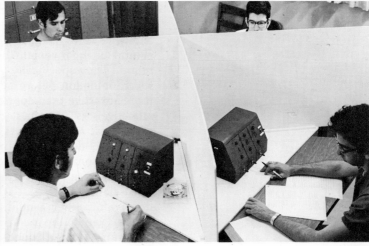

finds that the similar other is perceived by a respondent as more attractive than the dissimilar other, even though the information subjects have about these two individuals differs only in their responses to an attitude scale. The Byrne theory of attraction and the proverb that similarity attracts are thereby supported.

However, this result may be artificial because it might not hold on a measure other than a paper-and-pencil test. Does it generalize to more natural situations? Donn Byrne, Glenn Baskett, and Louis Hodges (1971) decided to find out. They arranged a situation in which subjects learned that another person was similar or dissimilar to themselves and were then placed in a situation in which they were free to sit close to or far away from the other person. As it turned out, their behavior reflected the paper-and-pencil results; subjects preferred to sit near a similar person rather than near a dissimilar person.

But even these results were obtained in a laboratory setting. The subjects knew little about the person they were to sit with, except that the person was similar or dissimilar in certain attitudes. In addition, many other phenomena influence our interactions in the real world: task requirements, strategic considerations, external constraints, and more. Byrne's data merely show that under some conditions similarity attracts. Other researchers (see Chapter 6) have used different variables and have obtained divergent results. Which combination of factors will facilitate or discourage attraction in any particular real-world setting cannot be predicted with absolute certainty.

The laboratory experiment, then, can yield precise *causal* information about the relationship of one variable to another. However, it provides information about only one stone in the overall mosaic that is human social behavior in real-world settings. An inability to generalize to other situations is apparently the price of precision and vice versa.

Some laboratory experiments are more applicable to complex situations than others are. Grounds for generalizing from the results of an experiment are strengthened when the phenomenon is a rather important and overriding one, when the real-world behavior is determined by a limited number of variables, or when the same experimental results have been obtained by others. An experiment by Elliot Aronson and Judson Mills might qualify as having greater generality than most.

Laboratory Experiment—Severity of Initiation. In a hypothesis derived from work in cognitive-dissonance theory (a topic of Chapter 8), Aronson and Mills (1959) suggest that it is inconsistent for individuals to engage in painful or inconvenient behavior without gaining something valuable in return. They specifically proposed that an individual who must undergo a severe initiation before being admitted to a group should find that group more attractive than does one who need not undergo severe treatment. The attractiveness of some groups to members—fraternity brothers, early Christians, and members of lodges and country clubs—who must make painful sacrifices for their memberships are real-world manifestations of the phenomenon Aronson and Mills studied in a laboratory.

The researchers recruited college women to participate in a series of discussions about sex. Each subject entered the laboratory individually and underwent either a mild, a moderate, or a severe initiation; the experimenter varied the severity of the initiation as follows: he entered the laboratory and explained that some persons had difficulty discussing sex and asked whether or not subjects felt free to discuss the topic. All subjects stated that they would have no problems. Subjects who had randomly been placed in the mild initiation group were then told that they could now join the group discussion. Those in the moderate- and severe-initiation conditions were then told that the experimenter had developed a screening device that separates those who do not feel free to discuss sex from those who do. In the severe-initiation condition, the experimenter asked the subjects to read to him two vivid descriptions of sexual activity and twelve erotic words. (Remember, the subjects were women and the experimenter was a male.) In the moderate condition, subjects were asked to read a number of words that were related to sex but could not be considered erotic.

Subjects from all groups were then individually told that they would join a group that had met for some weeks already. Moreover, subjects learned that on their first day they would merely be allowed to listen to the group, to get the hang of what was going on. The experimenter also explained that the group members found it easier to talk to one another if they did not see one another. Each subject was thus placed in a cubicle and given an earphone. All subjects heard the same tape-recorded discussion, which was notably dull. At the end of the discussion the experimenter returned and gave the subjects rating scales that asked how worthwhile the discussions had been. As expected, the girls in the severe-initiation condition rated the discussion group as much more attractive than did the subjects in either of the other two conditions. Apparently, the subjects who had undergone the most severe initiation to be admitted to the group were most in need of justifying their sacrifices. (See Chapters 8 and 9 for more detailed discussions of dissonance studies.)

PROBLEMS WITH RESEARCH: ARTIFACTS

Different research methods have different advantages and disadvantages. As the discussion has moved from the case study to the survey technique to the simulation to the standard laboratory experiment, the precision of the research tool consistently grew but the price of diminishing applicability to real-world problems also became steeper and steeper. Nonetheless, all the problems that plague research have not yet been covered. Another problem, which became a major focus of attention during the 1960s, has been *experimental artifacts*—phenomena that produce erroneous results because of some problem inherent in the research methodology (Orne, 1959). Only a few of the more important artifacts that a good experimenter must avoid will be mentioned here.

Researchers have known about some artifacts for a long time—for example, as explained in Chapter 4, *social desirability.* Given the opportunity, some subjects will try to respond in ways that make them "look good" to the experimenter, particularly on survey questions or personality tests. These "right" or "correct" responses are given in conformity to the standards of the culture to which the subjects belong. Socially desirable responses in one country may be quite different from those in other parts of the world. There are ways to avoid getting responses that are given because they are socially desirable. For example, the experimenter may pit equally desirable alternatives against one another in a forced-choice test: Respondents cannot decide on the basis of which choice is more desirable, so they presumably must decide on the basis of factors that are more intrinsic to the issues mentioned in the test. Or the experimenter may weave *lie scales* into the test or survey that detect patterns of responding that stretch the truth for the sake of social desirability. Another problem is *experimenter-demand characteristics* (Orne, 1962). The experimenter may communicate to the subject that a particular response is expected or desirable in that situation. The experimenter may relay this information by his or her manner of dress, by instructions during the experiment, or by some other means. In any case, many subjects respond in ways that they feel will make the experimenter happy. Other subjects will do exactly the opposite. In either case, the data will be *biased*.

Still another source of bias may result if the experimenter is aware of the particular experimental condition into which subjects have been placed.

THE KOOL-AID ACID TEST

AN IMPORTANT PROBLEM faced by researchers in social psychology is that they may unwittingly bias the reactions of subjects under study. Thus, subjects may not respond so much to the appropriate stimulus but rather to cues given off by the experimenter as to how they should respond if they are to validate a hypothesis. Social psychologists call these cues "demand characteristics."

Martin Orne and Frederick Evans demonstrated demand characteristics in the context of hypnosis. They believed that many persons supposedly under hypnotic spells might actually be responding to demand characteristics—that is, responding to the demands on them that are implicit in the situation and the hypnotist's behavior. To put this belief to the test, Orne and Evans challenged the power of hypnotic trances by asking hypnotized subjects to do dangerous things, such as handling poisonous snakes, putting their fingers in bubbly acid, and then throwing the acid in the experimenter's face. What Orne and Evans wanted to do was to see if people who had not undergone hypnosis would do similar things. Subjects were therefore either hypnotized or instructed to simulate hypnosis—to act as though they had been hypnotized.

Subjects in each group had three opportunities to engage in dangerous acts. How would the groups differ from one another? Orne and Evans found that there were no significant differences between the hypnotized and the simulation groups. The subjects who were pretending to be hypnotized willingly handled a "dangerous" snake, gingerly dipped their fingers in "acid," and perhaps even gleefully splashed the experimenter with it.

Orne and Evans reasoned that the feigning experimental subjects were not acting as they would have normally but rather saw themselves as under the aegis of the experimenter. Everyone "knew" in spite of warnings to the contrary that the scientists in the white coats would not risk serious injury to their subjects or to themselves. Thus, as in a play-acting situation, the subjects tried to satisfy the demands of the situation. The experimenter desired them to throw acid. As good subjects they would throw the acid, leaving it up to the experimenter to worry about the consequences.

Taken seriously, the implications of this study cast doubt on many otherwise clear-cut interpretations of experimental data. At many points throughout this volume, it may be helpful for the reader to ask whether subjects behaved as free agents or conformed to subtle cues, which acted as demand characteristics in particular situations. If conformity is involved, then knowledge about the situation itself lends a fuller understanding of subjects' feelings and attitudes and enhances one's ability to predict the behavior of others in comparable situations.

Source: Adapted from M. T. Orne and F. J. Evans, "Social Control in the Psychological Experiment," *Journal of Personality and Social Psychology,* 1 (1965), pp. 189–200.

The experimenter may give out subtle cues, perhaps influencing the results of the study. This type of influence often yields results that confirm the experimenter's expectations. For example, as described more fully in Chapter 7, Robert Rosenthal (1966) assigned graduate students to be experimenters in the same experiment but told each one that he expected a different outcome. Interestingly enough, most of the student experimenters obtained exactly the results that they had been told were expected. To avoid this problem, the experimenter ideally should be "blind" to the purpose of the experiment, or at least to the condition into which a particular subject has been placed. There are other artifacts as well (Aronson and Carlsmith, 1969; Fromkin and Streufert, 1973); however, the preceding list is probably sufficient to point out the necessity for extreme care in designing social-psychological research.

Avoiding artifacts is but one of the problems that is encountered when designing experiments. Another question that should be asked is how far the experimenter should go in causing subjects physical or psychic pain.

ETHICAL ISSUES IN RESEARCH

In recent years social psychologists have become increasingly concerned with the ethical implications of their research. Most especially, American military involvement in Southeast Asia has sensitized psychologists to the possibility that their research might be used to dehumanize, oppress, and bring undue pain to the subjects of their studies in the same way that the nation seemed to be doing abroad. Still other psychologists came to feel that too much research was being conducted for selfish or parochial reasons and that not enough was dedicated to the significant problems facing contemporary society. Greater social conscience was needed in the way research was conducted as well as in its goals.

Much of the research discussed in the present volume has been touched by these concerns; much has not. However, there are two ethical issues that occur with particular frequency, and these deserve attention at the outset. The first has to do with the creation of false impressions. In numerous studies the experimenter creates a reality for the experimental subjects that has no basis in fact. For example, subjects may be informed that another person likes them, that others' decisions are better than theirs, that they are inflicting intense pain on others, that the building they are in is burning down, and so on. To put it bluntly, these are all lies. Although most researchers probably do not enjoy duplicity for its own sake and are fully willing to admit its ethical shortcomings, many researchers maintain that duplicity is an occupational hazard. The earlier discussion of experimentation provides a rationale: Scientific knowledge depends importantly on our capacity to test the effects of isolated factors. The natural environment seldom offers an opportunity to observe the effects of a single factor and to hold all others constant. Thus, the experimenter often resorts to creating situations in which the factor is present and comparing the effects with those of situations in which the factor is absent or of lesser intensity.

The subject cannot be informed of the experimenter's manipulation until after the effects on the subject have been observed, because this information might well bias the subject's reactions. Perhaps it would encourage even more than the usual attention to responses that are socially desirable. Alternatives to this approach are continuously being sought, and most experimenters attempt to minimize the "unreal" aspects of the situation. However, developing knowledge of sufficient validity that it can be used to reduce social conflict and increase cooperation may require a certain amount of deception on the part of experimenters.

A second important problem stems from the pain that is often inflicted on experimental subjects. Psychologists who are interested in contributing findings that can be used to alleviate conflict, reduce aggression, or understand stress often create situations in which people experience undue emotional stress. The experiment may place subjects in a state of conflict, inflict physical pain, or induce stress. In many instances subjects for such research are informed beforehand of the noxious aspects of the research. However, because of problems of biased results, subjects are not always so candidly apprised of the situation. In almost all cases the experimenter introduces as little pain or stress as he can; ethical considerations prevent laboratory study of some issues, such as the psychology of extreme pain. In addition, investigators almost invariably talk with participants after unpleasant experiences to inform them about why the pain was inflicted and to assure them of the value of their contribution to knowledge. In almost all cases in which subjects have been deceived or have experienced discomfort, a debriefing session has followed. The attempt is made to ensure that no one leaves with a false picture of what has happened or with a feeling of having been uselessly abused.

(Specific ethical problems are described throughout this book when they affect the studies being discussed.)

The ethics of social-scientific study is one type of research problem. A different sort of problem is that of making clear conclusions about relationships between independent and dependent variables. Statistics, a branch of mathematics, is useful to social psychologists in "describing" the degree to which a finding is *significant,* or unlikely to have occurred by chance alone.

---

*Social Science &
the Image of Man:*

THROUGH A GLASS DARKLY

THIS CHAPTER IS ABOUT the "rules of the game" in social psychology. Not all social scientists agree with this system. Some argue for a radical departure from present practices. One critic, Charles Hampden-Turner, says:

When we search the literature of socio-psychological experiments what do we find? We find an astonishing number of experiments on pain inflicting, prejudice, obedience, conformity, cheating, aggression, inauthenticity, and scapegoating. . . . In nearly every case *it is the anti-social subjects who confirm the experimental hypothesis and confirm the experimenter as a scientist.* The dissenters who resisted these pressures are shown to be creative, impulsive, affectionate, intelligent, interpersonally skillful, tolerant, imaginative, philosophical, self-aware, humorous, etc.

. . . It is not that the investigators themselves have a savage eye, but rather that their predicting and controlling tools demand the predictable and controllable man in order to consummate the Good Experiment! And what a misery the man turns out to be! The highly respected Dr. Jekyll discovers Mr. Hyde, the beast in man uncovered by inhuman instruments. (1970, page 4)

What is the image of human beings put forth by social psychology? Do its methods corrupt their users as well as their subjects, as Hampden-Turner suggests? You may want to keep this critique in mind as you read the rest of the book.

Source: Adapted from C. Hampden-Turner, *Radical Man* (Cambridge, Mass.: Schenkman, 1970).

A good research design must be amenable to statistical treatment. Haphazardly collected data simply cannot be analyzed, because no relevant statistical methods are available. How does the social psychologist use statistics?

THE PLACE OF STATISTICS IN RESEARCH

What is statistics? The word is certainly familiar enough. So are the television commercials that attempt to persuade viewers that a particular product is better than Brand X by overwhelming them with statistics. The fact is that the manufacturers of any product, or the promoters of any cause or candidate, can "prove" the superiority of even the shoddiest commodity by using statistics selectively. It seems that many people in this age of advertising have a reverence for numbers that is often undeserved. Advertisers, political propagandists, and others frequently capitalize on this reverence. A closer look at what statistics actually can and cannot reveal is in order.

Statistics is often used to compare two classes of persons, objects, or events. These classes will be easy to compare if all members of the first group are similar to one another, if all members of the second group are also similar to one another, and if all members of the first group are different from all members of the second group. For example, if one group contains only children and the other group contains only adults, then it can be stated that the members of the first group are younger than those of the second, and clear-cut comparisons can be made.

Unfortunately, it is not often that easy to compare two groups. The membership of groups often overlaps, characteristics are often similar, and differences may be very small. One is justified in saying that two groups are different from each other if one (1) knows the characteristics of all their members and (2) knows that one member who differs from all the others is present in only one group. Say, for example, that the racial characteristics of two groups are being compared. If one group contains only lower-class whites from the South and the second group contains one middle-class black person from the North among several lower-class Southern whites, then the two groups are indeed different. To be aware of a difference such as this, it is necessary to research the appropriate characteristics of the total *populations* of both groups. A "population" refers to the total membership of a group, class of objects, or class of events. Studying entire populations is often unwieldy if the populations are large. Consequently, social scientists usually must be content with a *sample* of the relevant population—that is, with a representative group of population members. For example, if a researcher wanted to know whether or not the French are better lovers than Americans, it would be impossible to test and interview every French person and every American. On the other hand, if only one French person and one American were studied, the investigator might find that the American is a better lover or that the French person is better or that they are equally good lovers. In the first instance, the researcher's prejudice may be unconfirmed, in the second it may be confirmed, and the finding that the two persons did not differ in their love-making abilities would probably confuse the investigator. But what would any of these results imply about the abilities of French people and Americans as lovers? Nothing.

Rather than focus on an individual who may be the exception rather than the rule, the investigator usually selects a sample of persons from the populations being studied, taking care to select a sample that is as representative of the general population as possible. Only then can results be relatively reliable, so that other researchers following the same research design will probably obtain the same results.

If you were a researcher studying the relative love-making abilities of French and American people and were concerned about basing your data on a sample large enough to permit comfortable generalizations to the populations at large, you might select 500 Americans and 500 French persons and *match* subjects from rural areas with subjects from urban areas, laborers with professionals, males with females, and so on. In other words, the French sample will include the same proportion of, for example, female subjects as is included in the American sample. You might have developed a paper-and-pencil "lover's test" that distinguishes between "good" and "bad" lovers. There is no question that some Americans will score high. So will some French subjects. Other American and French subjects will score low. Still others will score in the middle range. You will have two distributions of scores: one for the French, one for the Americans. You can address two central questions with statistics on the basis of these distributions: (1) Are the French and American distributions different from each other? And (2) how sure can one be that the differences obtained (if any) between the sample distributions of your French and American subjects accurately reflect actual differences between the populations of French and American people? The answer to this latter question is typically given as a probability statement. For example, if you had found that the French indeed make better lovers and that the probability of French superiority in this respect was beyond the .05 *level of significance,* or 5 percent *level of confidence,* you could state with reasonable confidence that the probability that your sample differences reflect population differences is better than 95 percent. Or you could express this finding from the opposite direction and say that your conclusion about French love-making abilities has only a 5 percent chance of being wrong. These are both ways of saying that you are confident that the differences you found between your samples reflect differences in the population; in both cases, the odds would be twenty to one that your results reflected real population differences. Had the odds been one hundred to one, you could be even more confident in your conclusions, stating that your hypothesis can be accepted at the .01 level of significance, or 1 percent level of confidence. Had your results fallen below the .05 level of significance, then you would not be warranted in concluding that your hypothesis is accurate, because the odds are too great that the results could be due to chance variation. Clearly, then, the term "significance" does not mean that data are "important"; it refers, rather, to the confidence with which one can believe that the results reflect a characteristic of some larger population.

Uses and Abuses of Statistics

Statistics are not of value to the scientist in their own right. They may be fun, unpleasant, or whatever, depending on the individual's point of view, but they are not "science." Rather, they are a tool for the scientist just like the hammer is a useful tool for the carpenter. The better the hammer and the more appropriate the hammer for the kind of nail being used, the more successful the carpentry job will be. The same is true of statistics. There are many statistical methods. All of them have limited usefulness, all of them can be abused, and most of them can be used either to confuse or to elucidate issues.

Consider two simple examples. If you are told by an authoritative

Figure 1.8 Social-psychological phenomena such as attraction, love, attitudes, social influence, and aggression are not as easily measured as is a side of beef or a crate of tomatoes. For any research endeavor to be meaningful, the social psychologist must precisely define what it is she or he wants to study, must determine how the concept can be measured by one and preferably several tools, must select a representative population for study, and must take other precautions, as well. By analyzing how data have been obtained, you can guard against a common fallacy—jumping to unwarranted conclusions by assuming that a set of figures means more than it actually does mean.

I INTRODUCTION

television personality that nine out of ten lawyers prefer chocolate bars over hard candy, then you have been given insufficient information (the claim has been altered somewhat here in order not to embarrass the manufacturer). The implication is that many lawyers were sampled. In fact, the sample might have consisted of only ten lawyers, nine of whom worked for the chocolate-bar company that produced the advertisement. This is an example of a probability statement that is not accompanied by information about how the probability was obtained. Or you may be told that you should eat fruit sugar because it gets into the bloodstream twice as fast as cane sugar does. If fruit sugar takes fifteen minutes and cane sugar takes thirty, that would be quite a difference. But if one takes two milliseconds and the other takes four, then the real difference is not significant enough to warrant a change in your shopping habits; it only sounds impressive. This is a descriptive statement that lacks sufficient information. Both of these examples represent abuses of statistics.

Erroneous or misleading use of statistical methods can occur in social-psychological research. For example, recall the hypothetical study of French and American love making. Among the assumptions on which the study was based was that there would be a paper-and-pencil test measuring the ability to be a good lover. But just as the statistical underpinnings of the TV commercials just described were questionable, the love-making test is also questionable. Is the test *valid?* That is, does it actually measure love-making excellence, or does it measure something else? For example, it may not be surprising that French subjects appeared to excel if the test had been developed by a French researcher, who was particularly sensitive to what the French consider good loving. Americans may have different beliefs, may enjoy different activities, and consequently the test may be valid in France but less valid in the United States. Or the test may tend to elicit socially desirable responses from both French and American subjects, so that differences are more revealing of what are considered socially acceptable sexual activities than they are of differences in what the subjects actually do. In either case, the results obtained in this hypothetical experiment may not mean what they are interpreted to mean.

One should be aware of another characteristic of statistics. Often data are reported that suggest that a significant relationship between two variables has been found. For example, if the reported significance level is .05 or better, the probability that this finding would be obtained erroneously is less than 5 percent. What does this "significance" imply? As discussed earlier, if all the relevant characteristics of two populations are known to an investigator, then only one observation is a sufficient basis for drawing conclusions about that population. By implication, the larger the sample (the more closely it approaches the size of the population), the smaller the difference required to be significant. For example, if data are obtained from six or seven subjects in each of two samples, then there can be practically no overlap between their distributions if a difference is to be statistically significant. If, on the other hand, the samples contain hundreds of subjects, then very small differences will be significant. From a statistical, or mathematical, standpoint this makes sense. However, from a practical standpoint, the implications of sample size should be understood: When a researcher reports a significant difference between two groups, two subjects, or two conditions, the size (and thus the importance) of this difference should be noted. The difference may well support a theory, it may well be interesting, but it may or may not be a large difference, and it

Figure 1.9 The mean, median, and mode each give an estimate of a distribution's central tendency, but each is used in different circumstances. (*Top*) the mean, or average, is generally the most reliable. (*Center*) in a distribution with a few extreme scores falling on one end (for example, 90, 70, 67, 65, 61), the mean would yield a distorted picture and the median, or middle, score would be preferable. (*Bottom*) at times the mode, or most frequent score, indicates the most useful information about a distribution; for example, if you wished to join a social club you might be interested in the modal age of its membership.

thus may or may not have practical application. This point will be explored further after some of the statistical terminology has been discussed.

Statistical Terminology

The following discussion is not intended to provide a complete catalog of statistical methods but merely to give the flavor of the means by which most of the data in this volume has been interpreted. The reader may wish to return to these brief explanations to understand findings presented later in the book. First, consider the distribution of a sample—the various scores obtained by members of a group.

Central Tendency, Variance, and Scales. Most distributions tend to be (and are assumed to be) normal; that is, most people's responses fall near the middle of the range of scores, and fewer and fewer scores occur toward the two extremes of the distribution. Distribution can be described using any of three measures of central tendency: (1) the *mean,* or average score of the distribution; (2) the *median,* or middle score (for example, the fourth highest, or lowest, score in a group of seven scores); and (3) the *mode,* or most frequently occurring score.

The degree to which scores spread, or distribute, across a potential number of points on any measure can also be described. For example, if subjects could score anywhere between 1 and 80 on a test and if each of eighty subjects had obtained a different score, so that each scoring possibility would be occupied by one person, then the *variance* of the distribution would be very high; in other words, scores would vary considerably. On the other hand, if on the same test all persons scored either at 39, 40, or 41 points on the scale, then the variance would be very low. As the square root of variance, the *standard deviation* of a distribution reflects these characteristics.

When investigators intend to compare the statistical properties of two distributions, they must first know whether the scales on which the subjects responded were nominal, ordinal, equal-interval, or ratio scales. Had they, for example, merely asked subjects to tell them whether they favored the Republican or the Democratic party, then they would have obtained a *nominal scale;* only a name would distinguish one kind of response from the other. Had they asked them, however, to report (1) whom they would most prefer as the next president, (2) whom they considered the next best person (if the first were not available), (3) the next-best choice, and so forth, the result would be an *ordinal scale.* If the subjects had placed all the candidates on a scale consisting of several points from "good" to "bad," then an *equal-interval scale* would have been obtained. For example, one subject might have placed candidates A, B, C, and D as follows:

good__ : A : B : __ : C : D : __ bad

This rating yields ordinal information: The subject prefers A to B, B to C, C to D, and A to C and D, and so on. In addition one could infer that this subject's preference for A over B is just about as great as the preference for C over D. In other words, the intervals in the scale are assumed to be of equal size. Numbers can now be assigned to the preferences; on an evaluative scale, which a good-to-bad scale represents, the respondent's attitude can be scored as 2 for candidate A, 3 for candidate B, 5 for C, and 6 for D. Values of 1 through 7 have simply been assigned to the seven points of the scale. This assignment is arbitrary; the good end of the scale could just as well be represented as 7 and the bad end as 1. The possibility of inversion suggests that one cannot infer that, for example, a subject likes candidate B twice as much as candidate D. Division and multiplication, which terms such as "twice as much" imply, are possible only when a scale has a meaningful zero point. Such is the case with age: Someone who is eight years old is twice the age of someone who is four, because there is such a thing as zero age—the point of birth. Few psychological scales have such a meaningful zero point. Thus, few *ratio scales* exist in psychology.

Why is it important to know about characteristics of scales? Different statistical techniques involve specific assumptions about the data to which they are applied. *Nonparametric statistics* are specifically designed for use with nominal and ordinal data. *Parametric statistics,* on the other hand, are designed for equal-interval and ratio data. And statistical techniques often involve additional assumptions: The number of subjects in each of the samples often must be the same as in the other samples; the data in each sample should be normally distributed; and so on. The well-informed researcher knows which assumptions can or cannot be violated to still obtain meaningful results. In other words, just as the size of a hammer is an important consideration when a particular size of nail is to be pounded into a wall, only specific statistics fit specific data. For this reason, it is important for the researcher to plan appropriate statistical procedures before even attempting to run an experiment. There are simply no statistical techniques available for analyzing certain kinds of data.

Correlations and Their Kin. After collecting data, the researcher is faced with the task of analyzing them to find out whether or not the responses of subjects in the samples have any meaningful implications for the populations from which those samples were drawn.

Assume that the researcher has asked subjects to rate presidential candidate A on the good-bad scale described above. Then the subjects rated themselves on another seven-point scale that represented the range from liberal to conservative. As it turns out, this researcher is employed by the campaign committee for candidate A, and her job is to contribute information about candidate A's potential constituency that will help in mapping a strategy for the campaign. The managers of candidate A's campaign want to plan speeches and schedule speaking time so as to capitalize on candidate A's areas of greatest potential strength in the constituency. They need to know, for example, just how liberal or conservative candidate A's present strength is. Thus their researcher has decided to find out how respondents' evaluative attitudes toward candidate A correlate with their liberalism-conservatism scores. The strength of the *correlation* tells the investigator about the degree of association between the scores on the two scales. A correlation of zero would indicate that there was no relationship between them—that candidate A's strength is almost equally divided between conservatives and liberals. Or all the respondents may have rated him in the middle of the scale.

The more the *correlation coefficient* (the statistic used to describe relatedness, symbolized by *r*) departed from zero and approached the value of either −1.0 or +1.0, the greater the relationship between the two measures. For example, if all conservatives had rated candidate A as very good and all liberals had rated him as very bad, then the obtained correlation would have been very high. Correlation coefficients can be either positive or negative, indicating the direction of relationship between scores on the two scales. A negative correlation indicates that persons scoring high on one scale tend to score low on the second, and vice versa.

Whether or not a correlation is significant depends on the sample size. For example, correlations as low as $r = .19$ are significant at the .05 level if sample size exceeds 100 subjects. If sample size were limited to ten subjects for each observation, however, the correlation coefficient would have to reach a value of about $r = .50$ to be significant at the same level. Clearly, it is important to look for more information than a simple statement that "significance" was obtained.

Still another problem with correlations must be considered. Correlations merely imply that two variables are associated with each other—not whether they are causally related. The fact that persons scoring high on one measure also score high on another does not imply that a characteristic of either measure produces the response on the other. A third factor might produce both tendencies. Consider an old and frequently used example: There is a significant correlation between soft viscosity of asphalt and incidence of poliomyelitis. Does this mean that polio causes asphalt to soften? Or does it mean that soft asphalt is a great breeding ground for polio? Neither. Both effects are produced by a third phenomenon—heat. In other words, a correlational statement is not a statement of causality. Consider another example: It has often been suggested that marijuana use causes use of harder drugs. The rationale for the argument is based on a correlation: Most of the persons who are addicted to hard drugs previously used marijuana. However this correlation does not demonstrate whether or not marijuana use leads to the use of other drugs. Instead, a third variable may cause both marijuana use and hard-drug use, such as the greater openness of some individuals to novel experiences or the relatively high availability of both types of drugs in the same neighborhoods.

Even more sophisticated statistical techniques that are based on correlations—factor analysis and regression analysis, for example, both of which describe intercorrelations among several responses from the same subjects—suffer from the same limitation: Inferences of causality cannot safely be made on the basis of these techniques. Correlation-based statistics and the research methods on which they depend are consequently rather limited. What means are available to an experimenter who wants to infer causality, who wants to know whether or not one event is actually *caused* by another?

Experimental Research. Investigators can obtain information about causal relationships by manipulating independent variables and measuring their effects on dependent variables as described earlier. Typically, the researcher creates two or more different conditions (either in the laboratory or in the field) by varying one aspect of the situation and then measuring the effects. Leonard Berkowitz (1971), for example, was interested in the degree to which the presence of a weapon would result in aggression. After placing his subjects in a frustrating situation, he measured their aggression toward others under two conditions: (1) when a gun was placed visibly in the room and (2) when it was not present. He found that subjects who were in a room that contained a gun were more aggressive than were those who were in a room that did not contain a gun. Berkowitz drew a causal conclusion on the basis of this finding—the conclusion that the presence of the gun did indeed

Figure 1.10 Correlation coefficients merely indicate that two variables are associated with one another, not that one causes the other. Often a third, unidentified, factor is responsible for the occurrence of both variables. Correlations between two variables, however, have been sources of countless old-wives' tales, quack medical treatments, and religious and social fears. Unfortunately, correlations are frequently misinterpreted and abused even by fairly sophisticated individuals. Refusing to legalize marijuana because it leads to more serious drug use is a case in point. Such fears are based solely on correlations, with no factual basis for inferring a causal relationship.

"As surely as smoke leads to fire, the devil's weed will lead one to the needle!"

I INTRODUCTION

result in greater aggression—and used statistical techniques to demonstrate how this causal relationship operated.

Clearly, then, statistics has many uses. But the use of a scientific tool does not in itself make social psychologists scientists. In fact, whether or not social psychology is a science is a question, like ethics, that social psychologists must ask themselves.

IS SOCIAL PSYCHOLOGY TRULY A SCIENCE?

Social psychology has been defined here as the scientific study of interpersonal behavior. But is social psychology really a science? Science is usually defined in a rather circular way. Any field that uses the "scientific method" to establish laws may be called a science. It is rather easy for the physicist to demonstrate that physics is a science. If you have taken an introductory physics course, you may have noticed that it took the physics professor very little time to demonstrate this fact, perhaps less than five minutes. The chemist takes a little longer; the biologist, much longer. But the psychologist, to explain why the term "science" is justifiably used for the field of psychology, may take half a lecture or longer. The sociologist takes longer yet; the economist may need several days; and, if home economics or physical education is to be viewed as a science, the instructor may need all semester to get the point across.

This discrepancy does not reflect any higher level of intellect among the teachers of "hard" sciences as compared to the social, or "soft," sciences. The statement that one's field is indeed a science simply becomes more and more difficult to defend as one moves from "hard" to "soft" sciences. Laws in physics are long-established and easy to demonstrate. The free fall is $1/2gt^2$; furthermore, the formula holds in Europe as well as in Australia. It even holds on the moon, if one allows for the differences between earth gravity and moon gravity. Laws in economics, on the other hand, are much less reliable. In many cases, for example, cost is controlled by supply and demand; in other cases, however, this hypothesis fails. In other words, the hypothesis that supply and demand determine costs cannot be elevated to the status of law. Similar problems occur in social psychology, even though they may not be as trying as are the problems faced by economists who want to attain scientific status for their principles. Some social-psychological theories approach the status of law. An example might be Theodore Newcomb's (1953) A-B-X principle, discussed in Chapter 8. Newcomb suggests that if persons A and B like each other but disagree about object X, which is of importance to them both, then some change either in their relationship or in the opinion of one of them with regard to X will occur. In most cases this theory indeed holds. However, there are persons for whom it does not hold, as well as situations in which the theory is typically refuted. The results are not universally true; consequently they cannot be described as law.

How, then, can laws in social psychology be established? A solution that is often proposed is equivalent to *infinite regress,* which involves focusing on smaller and smaller segments of the interpersonal process. Proponents of this solution suggest that the reasons for exceptions to laws lie in the confounding of several variables in theoretical predictions; in other words, two or more variables are likely to affect data, although the researcher may assume that there is only one variable. The consequences are erroneous conclusions. The solution, according to the advocates of infinite regress, is to develop finer and more specific measures of variables and to adapt theories to finer discriminations among situations. The problem with solutions of infinite regress is that increasingly finer distinctions among situations also result in greater and greater differences between the science of interpersonal behavior and interpersonal behavior in the real world. In effect, the ability to make applicable predictions may be lost, although closer approximations to scientific laws may be obtained.

Most social-psychological research has not followed the principle of infinite regress. Rather, it has remained at some intermediate level between mundane realism—the broadest scope of events—and regress. Theories are still tested in more-or-less realistic (and consequently more-or-less confounded) situations. How close does standard social-psychological theory come to the desired status of "science"?

Kenneth Gergen (1973) has offered a view that may be disturbing to many theorists and researchers who have sought to establish for themselves reputations as scientists in the purest sense. He suggests that social psychology may not be a science at all. The problem, he points out, has little to do with the use of scientific method. Rather, the difficulty lies in the fact that the social scientists are attempting to predict characteristics of subject matter that is not itself constant. A physicist who describes the free fall of an object as $^1/_2gt^2$ can rely on the fact that twenty years, two hundred years, or thousands of years later, an object dropped under the same

A BOX FOR DR. SKINNER

WHAT KIND OF MAN would deny that human beings are capable of self-determination and free will? Who would dare say that attitudes, beliefs, perceptions, values, and culture are not useful concepts in studying human behavior? What man would call a defense of human dignity a deterrent to the welfare of man? None other than the noted psychologist B. F. Skinner. Skinner, the dreamer of a utopia where social controls would eliminate the need for human beings to be "good" and the likelihood that man would be "bad," stresses the predominance of environmental control over behavior.

Skinner points to a contrast between the traditional "prescientific" view of human beings and the view he espouses:

In what we may call the prescientific view . . . a person's behavior is at least to some extent his own achievement. He is free to deliberate, decide, and act, possibly in original ways, and he is to be given credit for his successes and blamed for his failures. In the scientific view . . . a person's behavior is determined by a genetic endowment traceable to the evolutionary history of the species and by the environmental circumstances to which as an individual he has been exposed. (1972, page 101)

For comparison, Skinner describes first in "prescientific" and then in "scientific" terms the experience of a young man who has just undergone a major change in his life, such as having graduated, been fired, or entered the military:

he lacks assurance or feels insecure or is unsure of himself
(*his behavior is weak and inappropriate*);

he is dissatisfied or discouraged
(*he is seldom reinforced, and as a result his behavior undergoes extinction*); . . .

he feels guilty or ashamed
(*he has previously been punished for idleness or failure, which now evokes emotional responses*); . . .

he becomes hypochondriacal
(*he concludes that he is ill*)

or neurotic
(*he engages in a variety of ineffective modes of escape*); . . .

he experiences an identity crisis
(*he does not recognize the person he once called "I"*). (pages 146–147)

Skinner would rate parts of this book "prescientific." Yet there are strong arguments against the behavioral approach. There is still time for you to decide (*or for your reinforcement history to shape your behavior*).

Source: Adapted from B. F. Skinner, *Beyond Freedom and Dignity* (New York: Knopf, 1972).

conditions is likely to fall at exactly the same speed. In contrast, societies change, and attitudes change, and so is everything else likely to change that is at least in part culturally determined. In other words, attitudes may not be the same today as they will be two thousand years from now, or even two years from now, and the way that attitudes change may also change.

Sociologists and cultural anthropologists have often said that the rate of cultural change is much greater today than it was one hundred years ago and greater still now than a thousand years ago. In part, as explained further in Chapter 3, this increasing rate of cultural change is due to the rapid advancement of communication facilities and of other technological abilities as well. In part, however, the increasing rate of social change is due to social science itself. When research results are published, social scientists directly or indirectly communicate to the other individuals in their society what they are expected to do. When people learn how they are likely to behave, they often match their behavior to these prescriptions or else rebel against them. In effect, then, the statements made by social scientists can directly produce or discourage the kind of behavior that these scientists are trying to describe. Consequently, the descriptions are not laws; they can merely be temporary historical statements about the state of society at a particular time.

There are social scientists who disagree with Gergen's point of view. Some say that many of the underlying tendencies of human behavior in groups are really rather constant. They believe, for example, that attitudes may be affected by changes in society but that attitude-change *processes* will not be affected. They believe, also, that social needs for power, achievement, uniqueness, and so on can be demonstrated throughout and across cultures and over time. In fact, much of the research presented in

Figure 1.11 The universe as conceptualized by a medieval artist, before presently accepted laws of physics and astronomy were established. Can social-psychological principles become established in the future to the extent that the principles of the "hard" sciences have been established since the Middle Ages? Or does the nature of social-psychological subject matter preclude such a possibility?

this volume is based on the assumption that there are certain basic laws that govern the behavior of human beings and other animals. For example, the line of investigation pioneered by B. F. Skinner, which is discussed in detail in Chapter 2, is based on the idea that certain learning processes pervade otherwise diverse aspects of behavior. In sum, although they would acknowledge that some changes occur and that some findings of social scientists may become outdated, these social scientists believe that most findings describe underlying processes that are constant over time.

Which of these points of view will be widely accepted (and perhaps substantiated) in the future remains to be seen. But in either case, some researchers suggest that social psychology has many contributions to make to the human condition, even if it is not as pure a science as the physical sciences and even if it is not going to provide an abundance of laws that are as hard and fast as the laws of physical scientists. Many of these contributions are suggested throughout this volume.

SUMMARY

Social psychology is the scientific study of *interpersonal* behavior. As scientists, social psychologists look for the general principles underlying events that interest them. Social psychologists then attempt to challenge their own *hypotheses* about the underlying principles of these events. Because human interaction is complex, a social psychologist must often isolate small units of behavior for study, formulating principles that can be tested and that can be used to predict behavior.

There are two main, sometimes competitive, approaches to the study of social behavior. The *nomothetic approach,* favored by most contemporary social psychologists, predicts what people "on the average" are likely to do; the *ideographic approach* focuses on a person's response to his or her social environment. Another approach, the *individual-differences approach,* is both ideographic (it tests the personality traits of individuals), and nomothetic (on the basis of many tests, it predicts what groups of people will do). One other approach, which unites the nomothetic and individual-difference approaches, is the *interactive approach;* it looks at the ways in which individuals' personalities and their environments, in combination, affect social behavior.

The methods most often used by social psychologists are the case study, survey, simulation, and standard laboratory experiment. The *case study,* which examines interpersonal behavior in an actual event, is the research method most sensitive to real-world complexities but permits the most limited inferences about causality. *Survey* research obtains data from selected members of a population about their beliefs, opinions, attitudes, intentions, and the like. Statistical analyses of these data are limited in the inferences of causality they yield, but less so than are analyses of data from case studies. In contrast to the case study, the survey can be used to study continuing phenomena. *Simulation,* as the name suggests, re-creates an event or situation in a partially controlled setting. Sometimes computers are used in simulations. Simulations elicit human behavior that is much like that in the real world, and they do permit the researcher some control over the situational variables. Inferences of causality permitted by simulation are more reliable than those permitted by the case study or the survey. In *standard laboratory experiments,* the researcher exposes subjects to a limited number of stimuli (independent variables) and measures their responses (dependent variables). Data obtained through these controlled means offer the most reliable and precise basis for causal inferences about behavior under similar conditions, but many psychologists feel that this type of study is too narrow in scope to allow generalizations about real-life situations.

Besides the limitations of each research method just described, general methodological problems—called *experimental artifacts*—plague experimenters. Some phenomena that produce erroneous results are a subject's desire to appear socially desirable and his or her response to what seems to be the experimenter's aim in running the experiment. In fact, sometimes the experimenter unintentionally sends out subtle cues revealing his or her expectations—another experimental artifact.

One recent research problem has centered around the *ethics* of deceiving subjects about an experiment or subjecting them to stress or pain. Social psychologists are aware of these problems; many experimenters are searching for alternative methods; and almost all researchers do their best to minimize the unethical aspects of their manipulations of human subjects.

Experiments should also be designed in a way that makes the resulting data amenable to *statistical analysis.* Social psychologists use statistical techniques as tools to check the *validity* of their data (do they in fact measure what the investigators set out to measure?); the *reliability* of their results (will other researchers who follow the same research designs be able to obtain the same results?); and the *significance* of their results (how confident can they be that their results reflect reality?).

A basic problem in social psychology centers on the definition of social psychology as *science.* There is a controversy between psychologists who believe that social-psychological methods should try to approach those of sciences like physics as closely as possible (by focusing on segments of the interpersonal process small enough to allow specific measures) and those who feel that researchers are mistaken in trying to formulate universal laws for constantly changing phenomena. Other social psychologists stand midway in this controversy, saying that many processes of human behavior in groups are constant, although their manifestations may change with time. All these approaches are represented in this volume.

SUGGESTED READINGS

Back, Kurt W. "The Proper Scope of Social Psychology," *Social Forces,* 41 (1963), 368–376.

Di Renzo, Gordon J. (ed.). *Concepts, Theory and Explanation in the Behavioral Sciences.* New York: Random House, 1966.

Festinger, Leon, and Daniel Katz (eds.). *Research Methods in the Behavioral Sciences.* New York: Dryden, 1953.

Gergen, Kenneth J. "Social Psychology as History," *Journal of Personality and Social Psychology,* 26 (1973), 309–320.

Homans, George C. *The Nature of Social Science.* New York: Harcourt, Brace and World, 1967.

Lana, Robert E. *Assumptions of Social Psychology.* New York: Appleton-Century-Crofts, 1969.

As to icicles
  i often wonder
  why they grow
some long... some short
      ONitsuRA

II

SOCIALIZATION: BEING HUMAN

2

Socialization: The Humanizing Processes

WHAT ESSENTIAL QUALITIES are involved in "being human"? Are these qualities present in each of us at birth, forming an inherent pattern that adds up to "human nature"? By the time you are old enough to read a book such as this one, you probably feel that humanness is instinctive. Your behavior, which has long been that of a human being, is distinctly different from that of other animals. (So different, in fact, that you may flinch inwardly at being classified as an animal.)

But what sort of human would you be today had your parents chosen to chain you in a dark corner of the basement, provide you with a blanket, throw you some food three times a day, keep your water container filled—and otherwise ignore your existence? Treated in this inhuman manner, you would probably have become an unhuman being. Children are occasionally found who have not been treated humanly, and their behavior shows few of the characteristics that are considered essential to being human. They may not interrelate at all with other people, they may defecate and urinate at any time and place, and they cannot communicate verbally. Scientists call these children *feral*. Although a few feral children have shown considerable learning ability, none has ever become socially "normal" (Davis, 1940, 1947, 1949).

Being human, then, is not just a matter of having upright carriage, prehensile hands, a well-developed brain, and organs that allow speech. Physiological and biological characteristics provide the capacity to be human and also set limits on the human condition; they provide the "what" that makes up the human animal. But turning this "what" into a "who" requires *socialization,* the process by which we learn how to be human.

43

During this process—which goes on throughout our lives—we acquire the complex sets of behaviors, emotions, standards, attitudes, and personal characteristics that define us, both as individuals and as members of groups.

Socialization is a broad concept that is studied by anthropologists, sociologists, and psychologists, who apply varying emphases of varying theoretical frameworks. But particular aspects of socialization are recognized by all three disciplines. For example, every society provides its members with training in such specific areas of socialization as aggression, altruism, cooperation, dependence, eating, elimination, moral values, and sex. The content of the teaching varies considerably, as does the degree of emphasis that different societies place on each area.

Every society has *norms,* or rules that define the behavior it considers acceptable. These norms are passed along by *agents* of socialization, including parents, peers, the mass media, and teachers of academic and religious topics.

Parents are potent agents of socialization. Mothers are particularly influential, because in most societies they spend more time with the child during the formative years than do any other agents. In societies that are relatively unchanging, parental influence may be particularly long-lasting, so that one carries on the traditions of one's mother and father, grandmother and grandfather. Peers become increasingly important as the child advances to adolescence and adulthood; they serve as models of what individuals feel they ought to be, and they provide standards against which individuals can measure their own performance.

The roles of agents, particularly those concerned with education and religion, vary widely from culture to culture. The prime educational agents in the socialization of adolescents whose parents are wealthy upper-class Bostonians may be teachers at elite schools, who give formal instruction in Latin, deportment, rhetoric, and riding horseback. For a young Bedouin nomad, however, equivalent socialization may be provided in informal learning situations by elders who know how to predict the weather, heal sick camels, make cheese, and ride horses. In each situation, the young person receives instruction in the kinds of knowledge that are considered important in a specific environment. Although the ability to ride well may be valued in both Boston and Jidda, in each place this skill is valued for different reasons, and the standards by which individuals are recognized as good horseback riders also differ.

Several specific learning mechanisms are basic to socialization. Social psychologists are interested in analyzing these mechanisms, because an understanding of them could lead to more effective socialization—which, in turn, could perhaps provide a means of lessening conflict among individuals as well as among nations. Some of the most important theories of socializa-

tion are based on these learning mechanisms. Learning theorists focus on classical conditioning, instrumental (or operant) conditioning, and observational learning. Other theorists present socialization as a process that occurs in consecutive stages of maturation.

The role of learning mechanisms and developmental processes in socialization are the first topics of discusssion in this chapter, and then the focus shifts to some particular areas of socialization: dependence, sex roles, and morality. Finally, some of the issues that are currently of particular importance to social psychologists are considered: the impact of early social experiences, socialization in adulthood, and political socialization. (Communication and personality, both of which involve important aspects of socialization, are discussed in detail in Chapters 3 and 4.)

LEARNING PROCESSES: SHAPING UP TO BE SOCIAL

Socialization begins at birth. The newborn infant has no values, no attitudes, no beliefs. The infant does have certain physiological needs, however, among which food is the most obvious. The ways in which this particular need is met may vary considerably, even within a single society; some infants receive food from mothers who nurse them, others from bottles propped up on pillows in their cribs. Although the influences of agents may vary, the processes by which humans and many other animals learn are apparently universal. The basic learning mechanisms that apparently underlie all socialization are classical conditioning, instrumental conditioning, and observational learning.

Classical Conditioning: From Salivation to Social Attitudes

The classic studies in learning processes that were carried out by Russian physiologist Ivan Pavlov began during his investigations of the digestive processes of dogs (which won him a Nobel Prize in 1904). In a laboratory situation, dogs salivated when food was placed on their tongues—to no one's great surprise. But Pavlov noted that after a time, the dogs salivated at the mere sight of the food. He reasoned that salivating at the taste of food was an instinctive or unlearned response but that salivation at the sight of it was a response that had been learned, or acquired, as a result of environmental conditions.

Pavlov pursued this initial observation scientifically by substituting several other stimuli for the sight of food—a bell, a ticking sound, a light, a rotating disk. He presented these stimuli to dogs shortly before they received the unconditioned stimulus of food. Eventually, salivation occurred when these stimuli were presented—even when food did not follow.

In formulating his startling discovery, Pavlov (1927) established ingested food as an *unconditioned stimulus* (UCS) and salivation at the inges-

tion of food as an *unconditioned response* (UCR). He considered the sight of food, the light, the sound of the bell, and so on to be *conditioned stimuli* (CS) and salivation at the hearing or sight of them to be a *conditioned response* (CR).

(Therapists have been able to use classical-conditioning procedures in treating some real-life problems. For example, the norms of our society decree that, beyond a certain age, the wetting of one's bed is unacceptable behavior, and classical conditioning has proved to be an effective method of treatment (Baker, 1969). In the conditioning, a liquid-sensitive pad is connected to an alarm placed under the bedsheet. When the pad is wetted, an alarm sounds (UCS) and the subject awakens (UCR). The desired CS is the physical awareness of a full bladder, and the desired CR is awakening in time to go to the bathroom. Eventually, the CS is usually strengthened to the point where the desired CR becomes habitual.)

Pavlov also observed that a CR, once learned, could be *extinguished*. When a CS was repeatedly presented without being followed by the UCS of food, its power to bring about a CR gradually diminished and eventually disappeared. (The permanence of the conditioning treatment for bedwetting, therefore, depends greatly on how much the subject wishes to be socialized in this direction. If a child considers the wetting of a bed to be an effective and "accidental" means of punishing mother, the CR that mother desires may tend to be rather quickly extinguished.)

In perhaps even more important experiments, Pavlov discovered that after initial conditioning to a CS—a ticking sound, for instance—dogs salivated in response to a similar but different ticking sound. The greater the similarity between the two stimuli, the greater the degree to which they elicited similar responses. This phenomenon, in which the response learned in reaction to one stimulus is elicited by different but similar stimuli, is called *generalization*. Because generalization of learned responses may occur in situations that are not identical to those of the past, it is of considerable importance in explaining behavior. For example, an adult whose life is made difficult by an unreasonable fear of all animals may have been frightened in infancy by a teddy bear that an older brother or sister used to scare the infant.

Pavlov also observed a corollary of generalization—*discrimination*. In one experiment, an animal was always presented with food (UCS) after the

Figure 2.1 A wide variety of involuntary responses can be classically conditioned. Consider the experience of this young woman, who finds that she blushes at the sight of a trench coat. Originally, trench coats had been neutral stimuli for her, although she blushed (UCR) at the sight of male nudity (UCS). One day a man in a trench coat exposed himself to her, causing her to blush. After this experience, the sight of a trench coat alone (CS) was sufficient to cause her to blush (CR).

presentation of a circle (CS) but was never given the UCS after being presented with an ellipse. This dog learned to salivate whenever it saw a circle, but it did not salivate when shown the ellipse. Pavlov changed the ellipse to shapes that by gradations became less ovoid and more nearly circular. When the dog finally became unable to discriminate between near-circles and perfect circles, its behavior changed dramatically:

The hitherto quiet dog began to squeal in its stand, kept wriggling about, tore off with its teeth the apparatus for mechanical stimulation of the skin, and bit through the tubes connecting the animal's room with the observer, a behaviour which had never happened before. On being taken into the experimental room the dog now barked violently, which was also contrary to its usual custom; in short it presented all the symptoms of a condition of acute neurosis. On testing the cruder differentiations they also were found to be destroyed . . . . (1960, page 291)

It is not difficult to understand the desperation shown by this animal. Human beings have broken down under less frustrating conditions than those faced by Pavlov's dog, and the effects of the inability to discriminate are relevant to socialization. Overeager parents who push children beyond their capabilities by expecting complete control of elimination at an early age or, later, expecting difficult athletic achievements may produce emotional problems, thus destroying the effects of earlier successful training.

John Broadus Watson, the father of modern behaviorism, was the first to demonstrate the direct implications that classical conditioning has for human behavior. Watson rejected the popular views of his time, in which behavior was attributed to mental processes such as consciousness, will, and imagery. Instead, he believed that behavior should be studied in terms of the stimulation available in the environment. He voiced this belief in words that have since become both famous and infamous:

Give me a dozen healthy infants, well-formed, and my own specified world to bring them up in and I'll guarantee to take any one at random and train him to become any type of specialist I might select—doctor, lawyer, merchant, chief and yes, even beggar-man and thief, regardless of his talents, peculiarities, tendencies, abilities, vocations, and race of his ancestors. (Watson, 1962, page 104)

Watson was not able to pursue his conviction this far, but he carried out a classic experiment in conditioning with a child called "Little Albert" (Watson and Rayner, 1920). Little Albert, who was eleven months old, was not afraid of a white rabbit, but when a very loud noise was made behind

Figure 2.2 Ivan Pavlov *(center, with white beard)* and his original apparatus for controlling dogs' salivation by means of the phenomenon later termed classical conditioning. Pavlov had initially been studying the physiology of digestion; he happened upon the conditioning phenomenon by chance when he observed that the mere sight of food, or even the sound of his footsteps in the laboratory, activated the dogs' salivary responses. He then shifted his attention to this phenomenon and studied it systematically for many years. The apparatus consisted of a harness that restricted the subject's extraneous movement; a container for food; and a tube through which saliva ran from the dog's mouth into a container, where a device recorded the amount of salivation.

him, he cried and tried to crawl away. Watson and Rayner systematically presented Little Albert with a white rabbit and then made the loud noise. After seven such pairings, the baby cried and tried to crawl away when he saw the rabbit, even when the noise was not presented. Later, this fear proved to have become generalized; Little Albert was also afraid of furry things in general, including Santa Claus' beard, although he had not previously been afraid of such things.

Since Watson's time, researchers have classically conditioned a wide range of behaviors in people of all ages, using a variety of stimuli. There is evidence that classical conditioning can account for learning that is considered complex. For example, attitudes regarding topics as complex as politics and religion are sometimes learned by means of classical conditioning; an example is provided by the life-long, "dyed-in-the-wool" Democrat or Republican who automatically votes for the entire party ticket without knowing the attributes of the individual candidates.

A series of experiments by Jum Nunnally, Albert Duchnowski, and Ronald Parker (1965) demonstrate that previously neutral words can be classically conditioned to have evaluative meanings. In one set of experiments, elementary-school children were asked to spin a wheel on which one of three nonsense syllables—*ZOJ, MYV,* and *GYQ*—had been placed at each of eighteen possible stopping points. Each child spun the wheel thirty times. According to which nonsense syllable the wheel stopped on, the child received two pennies, received nothing, or lost a penny. This served as a conditioning process to specifically associate one stimulus (a nonsense word) with another stimulus (pennies).

Other tests were given to the children after this conditioning process. One was a verbal-evaluation task. The experimenter showed each child three stick figures. Each stick had a different label—*ZOJ, MYV,* or *GYQ*—and an experimenter told the child that each stick represented a different boy. The investigator then read five positive, five neutral, and five negative questions from a list; the subject was asked to select a stick to match each question. For example, the children had to answer: "Who would you like to play with?" and "Who walked down the street?" and "Who is mean to animals?" The children's answers indicated that they had been conditioned through their experience with the wheel-spinning game to associate nonsense syllables with evaluative meanings; "good" meanings were associated with syllables that had been connected with reward and "bad" meanings were associated with the syllables that had been related to losses in the wheel-spinning game. Consequently, the children's conceptual worlds changed somewhat from what they had been before the conditioning.

In a somewhat similar study, Arthur and Carolyn Staats (1958) demonstrated that complex attitudes can be conditioned in adults. College students were asked to participate in an experiment, which they were told was an investigation of simultaneous visual and auditory learning. Subjects were asked to look at a specific proper or national name—such as Tom, Bill; Swedish, Dutch—which served as a CS. At the same time, they were to pronounce aloud a specific word with either a positive or negative connotation—such as gift, sacred, happy, bitter, and ugly—that served as a UCS. A relatively short period of this conditioning produced dramatic differences in subjects' attitudes toward the names. Typical results for "Bill" and "Swedish" appear in Figure 2.3.

Other experiments suggest that the conditioning of attitudes may occur early in life and that white children as young as preschoolers associate

Figure 2.3 Previously neutral words can take on positive connotations when people learn to associate them with positive stimuli, and negative stimuli can lend unfavorable connotations to neutral words with which they are paired. Shown here are the mean evaluations for the previously neutral words "Bill" and "Swedish" after brief conditioning sessions, as reported by Staats and Staats in 1958. Classical conditioning may play a similar role in forming the emotional connotations that the words "red," "pig," "flag," and "blacks" have for many people.

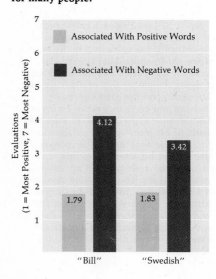

II SOCIALIZATION: BEING HUMAN

"white" with positive adjectives and "black" with adjectives that are negative. In a typical experiment, investigators presented subjects with drawings that included both white and black figures, but they did not indicate how the activities of the figures could be evaluated in terms of "good" and "bad." The children were then asked questions such as, "Everyone likes one of these little boys, because he is always doing good things for people. Which do you guess is the good little boy?" White children regularly selected white figures over black; so, usually, did black children. As explained in Chapter 7, however, evaluations by black children seem to be shifting dramatically. Although in previous years most black children shared white preferences—or said that they did—there are recent indications that they are now tending to prefer black to white on tests such as the one just described (Hraba and Grant, 1970; Rosenberg and Simmons, 1971; Ward and Braun, 1972).

From this evidence, it is clear that during the course of socialization children often acquire deep-seated attitudes toward school, toward minority groups, and even toward themselves. Adults, too, may acquire values and attitudes through classical conditioning; the origins of many stereotypes can be traced to its effects. However, classical conditioning is only one means by which socialization takes place. Other processes, just as important and somewhat more complex, are described in the following sections.

Instrumental Conditioning: From Bar Pressing to Utopian Society

Research with classical conditioning suggests that we can be strongly influenced without being aware of it. A state of passivity, therefore, does not make one immune to influences from the environment. Research in instrumental conditioning suggests, in addition, that we are also influenced while being actively engaged in the social world. Whether we are active or passive, then, our behavior, feelings, and thoughts are molded by our experiences.

The notion of instrumental learning was first introduced by Edward Thorndike, who studied the behavior of animals in problem-solving situations (1907). In a typical experiment, Thorndike placed a cat in a cage and food outside the cage; to escape and obtain the food, the cat had to press a lever. By trial and error, the cat eventually pressed the lever "accidentally" and succeeded in escaping. Subsequently, the frequency of the previously accidental behavior increased. Observing this, Thorndike formulated the *law of effect,* which states that an act that is followed by satisfaction is more likely to recur than is an act that is followed by discomfort. Thorndike, like Watson, attributed tremendous power to the effects of basic learning mechanisms in influencing human behavior. He wrote of his law of effect:

[It] is the fundamental law of learning and teaching. . . . By it animals are taught their tricks; by it babies learn to smile at the sight of the bottle or the kind attendant, and to manipulate spoon and fork; by it the player at billiards or golf improves his game; by it the man of science preserves those ideas that satisfy him by their promise, and discards futile fancies. It is the great weapon of all who wish—in industry, trade, government, religion or education—to change men's responses, either by reinforcing old and adding new ones, or by getting rid of those that are undesirable. (cited in Joncich, 1962, pages 79–80)

Although extensive investigations have been based on Thorndike's formulations, one behavioral scientist—B. F. Skinner—stands out as having made profound contributions not only to the basic knowledge of instrumental learning but also to its application. Skinner was the first to apply the term "instrumental" to actions that operate on the environment and thereby result in outcomes that either weaken or strengthen those actions. (Others have called this process *operant conditioning*.) Working with pigeons and rats in controlled experimental situations, Skinner has discovered a great deal about the process of instrumental learning.

Reinforcement. All organisms have biological needs—food, water, and sexual satisfaction are the most frequently cited examples. Any behavior that temporarily reduces these needs without also bringing punishment is *positively reinforced* and will gradually increase. It might be expected, then, that if a hungry infant's crying results in someone's providing her with food, she will soon learn to cry when she is hungry. On the other hand, behavior that results in the removal of punishing stimulation is *negatively reinforced.* ("Negative reinforcement" is often confused with "punishment." However, a reinforcer is *any* stimulus that increases behavior. Punishment results in a decrease of the behavior it follows. Negative reinforcement produces an increase in the behavior that stops or diminishes the aversive stimulation.) For example, the frequency with which you clean your room may increase if in the past this action has eliminated parental wrath.

New behaviors are also strengthened by *secondary reinforcement,* which occurs when one of the relatively few biological reinforcers becomes associated with other stimuli that then become reinforcing in themselves. Thus, the mother who provides food for a crying infant becomes associated with satisfaction in the infant's thoughts; gradually, her presence alone becomes a secondary reinforcer, even when food is absent. The infant then may cry just for the presence of the mother or may learn other actions, such as babbling or saying "Mama," that result in the mother's return. In an individual's later years, secondary reinforcement may be supplied by the attention or pleasure of parents, peers, or spouses; such reinforcement may influence a person to excel in long-distance running or mathematics, to

Figure 2.4 Alcoholism is an example of a complex behavior that can develop through instrumental learning. Drinking behavior can be reinforced and therefore strengthened by the pleasant effects of the alcohol itself, reduction of anxiety, and freedom to behave in ways considered unacceptable under other circumstances. Conditioning techniques have also been used successfully in the treatment of alcoholism, as is done at Patton State Hospital in California. As shown here, the Patton staff sets up an actual bar (*left*). Under these familiar conditions, alcoholic patients are permitted to drink until they collapse. The sequence of events is videotaped and later played back to the patients (*right*). The purpose is to lead patients to associate their drinking behavior with the physical sensations of nausea and collapse as well as with auditory and visual feedback of themselves as sick and intoxicated—both of which they usually find quite aversive.

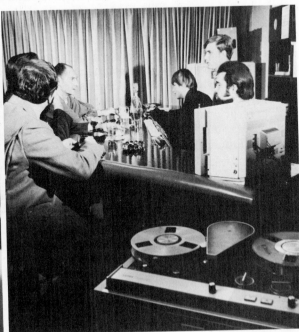

steal from the Internal Revenue Service but not from friends, to become a doctor, or to engage in any number of enterprises. In fact, secondary reinforcement can account for much of human behavior: Work that earns money, politeness that brings a smile from parents, and studying that results in an A derive their strength from the fact that money, parental approval, and social recognition of certain achievements have become reinforcing events for the individual.

Like classically conditioned behavior, instrumentally learned behavior can be extinguished by withdrawing reinforcers. How readily extinction occurs depends somewhat on the conditions under which the behavior was learned—that is, on the patterning, or *scheduling,* of the reinforcement. In *continuous reinforcement,* every correct or desired response brings a reward; in *partial reinforcement,* on the other hand, a response is only occasionally reinforced. Some schedules of reinforcement, though not continuous, offer rewards on a regular basis.

Studies have shown that the behavior learned under continuous reinforcement or under regular schedules of reinforcement becomes extinguished more easily than behavior that was rewarded sporadically. For example, parents who reward a child *every time* he earns an A on his schoolwork or *every time* he cleans his room should expect that when the child leaves home, his room-cleaning behavior or study habits are likely to disappear faster than if the child had been rewarded only sometimes for those actions. The child who does not always receive a reward for every desired act will not later be subject to the same frustrations as the child who comes to expect a reward each and every time he performs the act; he will be used to waiting for rewards. In more subtle ways, too, parents can better pass on their moral values to their children if they do not reinforce every desired act or statement the child makes. Like other types of learning, moral learning will endure longer if it is not invariably reinforced. Robert Lundin suggested in 1961 that the success of partial over continuous reinforcement may explain why, as adults, some people break down easily, whereas others are "like the Rock of Gibraltar." His examples illustrate one way in which early socialization practices may dramatically affect later behavior:

> The application of the principle in training for adult maturity is clear. "Spoiled" or overindulged children are poor risks for later life. In looking into their past histories of reinforcement, we find that those who break down easily or are readily set to aggression were as children too often *regularly* reinforced. Every demand was granted by their acquiescent parents. In youth they may have been so sheltered that failure was unknown to them. (page 32)

The message to parents seems to be that if they want their children to develop a sense of internal control over their lives, they will do best not to try to reward every desired response their children make. Their children will consequently come to feel that there is a chance of greater rewards if they persist. (Individual differences in feelings of internal versus external control are discussed in more detail in Chapter 4.)

Discrimination and Generalization. Classical and instrumental conditioning set the stage for much social interaction, and two additional processes that vitally increase the impact of learning should be considered. These are the processes of discrimination and generalization.

In the case of discrimination, a person learns to progressively make finer and finer distinctions regarding the environment, so that his or her behavior becomes more and more efficiently tuned to getting the most out of social life. The ability to discriminate is present in the human fetus and is surprisingly well developed by the end of the first year of life. The infant's ability to discriminate, for example, may not be suspected by those who observe the baby only in a home environment. In an experiment conducted by Lewis Lipsitt (1967), however, an infant learned that the sound of a buzzer meant there was a bottle on his left and that the sound of a bell meant the bottle was on his right. What does this simple experiment indicate? It has shown that the infant could distinguish a buzzer from a bell, that he could tell his right side from his left, and that he could figure out the system that the researcher had added to his environment.

This kind of discrimination is essential to socialization. Consider the ways in which you talk to different people. Say, for example, that the following five people were to ask you what you did last night: a five-year-old girl, your roommate, your father, the president of your school, and somebody you sit next to on a bus. The content of your account would probably be different in each conversation; so would your choice of words and accompanying facial and bodily expressions. The story you would tell your father might also vary greatly from the story you would tell your mother. Such discrimination may seem instinctive, but it is actually learned behavior.

Whereas discrimination involves responding differently to two stimuli, stimulus generalization involves equivalent responses to different stimuli. Stimulus generalization is much more likely to occur within a particular stimulus dimension (such as the spectrum of visible light) than between dimensions (such as those of light and sound). Generalization does not necessarily imply lack of discrimination; for example, a child who has learned to respond to the brightness of white light will respond to other lights on the basis of brightness rather than color, although the child can also distinguish between different colors.

Fortunately, there are limits on the extent to which discrimination and generalization affect normal behavior. A person who carried discrimination to it logical extreme would see every event as different from all other events; if this were normal, a child who had been burned by fire would not hesitate to touch it again, because the second time it would look different from the first. On the other hand, an individual whose behavior was completely generalized would react in exactly the same way to all situations.

Shaping Behavior. Interpreted narrowly, shaping refers to a procedure in which a large class of responses that are relevant to a desired behavior are initially reinforced. Then the shaper requires closer and closer approximations to the desired behavior before dispensing reinforcements. For example, a parent can successfully shape children to pick up their toys, by first giving positive regard for *any* behavior in that direction, perhaps only for being in their own rooms, then for picking up one toy at a time. Eventually, the parent could withhold reinforcement until the child had put away all stray toys. In a more general sense, shaping also encompasses the efforts that human beings make in attempting to direct, through reinforcement, the course of entire societies. Many proponents of instrumental learning believe, as Watson did, that people can shape one another to engage in virtually any behavior.

In his controversial novel *Walden Two,* B. F. Skinner (1948) proposed that people can attain a utopian state by systematically shaping and controlling each individual's behavior from the moment that he or she is born. Skinner, unlike many people, does not view social control as an unmitigated evil. In fact, he suggests that individuals can learn to deal even with frustrating experiences and remain optimistic, fulfilled, and happy. Inevitably, the world is sometimes a frustrating place. Skinner believes that people could learn to lead basically happy and fulfilling lives if, as children, they were exposed to a series of increasingly frustrating situations. Thus, in *Walden Two*, adults give three- and four-year-olds lollipops that are coated with powdered sugar, which comes off with the slightest touch of a child's tongue. The children are told that they will be allowed to eat the lollipops later in the day only if there are no signs that the candy has been licked. Skinner explains the conditioning process:

. . . children are urged to examine their own behavior while looking at the lollipops. This helps them to recognize the need for self-control. Then the lollipops are concealed, and the children are asked to notice any gain in happiness or any reduction in tension. Then a strong distraction is arranged—say, an interesting game. Later the children are reminded of the candy and encouraged to examine their reaction. The value of the distraction is generally obvious. (pages 107–108)

The children learn to put out of their minds frustrating situations about which they can do nothing. They are given concrete examples of how to accomplish this end, such as putting the physical reminders of their frustration out of sight and allowing something else to distract their attention. What the children actually learn is to delay small gratifications in order to obtain larger rewards—a behavior that is highly valued in our society. There is little doubt that people do indeed learn to delay gratification in our present culture, although not as systematically as Skinner would have it and not in the manner he proposes (Mischel and Liebert, 1966).

Skinner's prescriptions are basically conservative, as many critics have pointed out. The specific applications of learning theory that he has set forth are essentially coping strategies—ways in which people can adapt to the culture Skinner knows best. In this culture, traits such as ambition, productivity, and ability to delay gratification have the status of virtues. This culture is changing, however, and alternative goals are emerging; some of them place less than the traditional emphasis on competition and delayed gratification and more emphasis on cooperation and more immediate gratification. But the basic socializing processes that Skinner has proposed can be used toward any behavioral end. Potentially, they can make human beings competitive or cooperative, aggressive or peace-loving, devoid of imagination or highly creative. The question of who is to decide which ends should be pursued is basic in applying Skinner's proposals, and no satisfactory answer has yet been provided. For this and other reasons, his utopian proposals have been criticized by many other psychologists (notably by Carl Rogers in 1969).

The Effects of Punishment. Skinner believes that behavior is shaped almost exclusively through reward and not punishment, which is any aversive event that follows a response. He bases this opinion on laboratory research, which indicates that in animals punishment may suppress certain responses only temporarily and may also have undesirable side effects, such as fear. Outside the laboratory, however, punishment plays a prominent role in the child-rearing practices of many parents. In one survey, 98 percent of the parents questioned said they punish their children at least occasionally (Sears, Maccoby, and Levin, 1957). Punishment seems to be a potent socializing tool under some circumstances, but its effects vary, and misuse is common.

Recent research reveals aspects of punishment that influence its effectiveness in inhibiting unacceptable behavior. Timing of punishment is an important factor in punishment. Justin Aronfreed and Arthur Reber (1965), in investigating the effects of delayed punishment, presented fourth- and fifth-grade boys with pairs of toys, one attractive and the other considerably less so, and told them that they could select one to tell about. When the boys chose the more attractive toy, however, the experimenter said firmly, "*No!* That's for the older boys." (This reprimand was the punishment.) The children were divided into three groups. Those in one group were reprimanded just as they began to touch the forbidden toy. Those in a second group were allowed to pick up the forbidden toy and hold it for several seconds before they were reprimanded and had the toy taken forcibly from them. Boys in the control group were warned not to pick up the forbidden toy and were then told to point to the one they wanted; thus, they had neither an opportunity to actually pick up either toy nor an occasion to receive an explicit rebuke. During this training phase of the experiment, all the children quickly learned to avoid the more attractive but forbidden toy.

An investigator then placed two toys, including a forbidden toy, in front of the children and left the room, ostensibly to fetch some forgotten papers. Actually, the children were observed during the experimenter's absence. A hidden observer noted the influence of the previous punishment on children's later resistance to touching attractive but forbidden toys when the young subjects thought that they were not being observed—a real test of socialization.

What were the effects of punishment in this situation? The frequency of transgression is shown in Figure 2.5. Even mild punishment was effective in inducing resistance to temptation (as measured against the frequency of transgression among control-group children). But timing proved to be critical: Reprimands that had been made as a child picked up the toy proved to be more effective than reprimands uttered after the child had held the toy for a time.

As a general rule, delay weakens the effectiveness of mild punishment. A transgression usually produces some positive outcome; thus, in Aronfreed and Reber's study, the longer the toy was held, or savored, the more likely that this satisfaction would balance the negative experience of punishment. Then, too, the purpose of late punishment may be confusing. A youngster who breaks an important rule at home may subsequently try to be "good" during the rest of the day (perhaps to restore a positive balance). If punishment is delayed until the child's father arrives at home and delivers a spanking, however, negative consequences do not follow the transgression; they may follow some very desirable behaviors.

The intensity of punishment is also a factor that determines its effectiveness. Research with animals has consistently shown that very mild levels of punishment usually do not permanently eliminate undesirable responses and that moderate punishment often tends only to suppress the behavior that it follows. Very intense punishments, however, are apparently effective in completely eliminating certain kinds of habitual responses (Solomon, 1964).

Ethical considerations obviously preclude using intense punishments with human subjects, but a few carefully designed studies have been used in

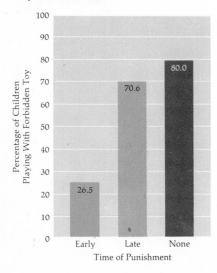

Figure 2.5 Mild punishment is most effective in reducing specific behaviors when applied immediately after a transgression begins rather than after the transgression has been allowed to continue for some time or if it has not been allowed to happen at all. This was the finding of Aronfreed and Reber, who reported in 1965 that fourth- and fifth-grade boys who were reprimanded immediately after reaching for a toy (early-punishment group) were subsequently least likely to play with the forbidden toy when they thought they were unobserved.

II SOCIALIZATION: BEING HUMAN

investigating the effects on children of varying intensities of punishing noise (Parke, 1969, 1970). These studies substantiate the findings, just mentioned, of researchers who have studied the effects of varying degrees of punishment on animals. Moreover, a particularly striking finding is the manner in which the intensity and the timing of punishment interact. Ross Parke in 1970 reported evidence that late punishment is less effective than early punishment *only* when the punishment is relatively mild. When late punishment is intense, children are quite responsive.

Other factors, too, influence the effectiveness of punishment. Punishment delivered by a rewarding and nurturant adult is apparently more effective than that given by one who is cold and distant (Aronfreed, 1968; Parke, 1967; Whiting, 1954). In addition, punishment is likely to be more effective when an experimenter offers a reason for the prohibition (Parke, 1969). Finally, certain types of consistency in the use of punishment are important; for example, the reprimands of parents who "practice what they preach" are usually more effective than are the punishments of those who do not practice what they preach (Mischel and Liebert, 1966). When parents

---

A Preschooler Probe:
CIVIL DISOBEDIENCE

ASK THE PARENTS of any small child and they will probably confess that the child is on occasion a recalcitrant monster who delights in doing the opposite of what they say. This same child might also be praised by a neighbor for her sweet, agreeable nature. Which is the real child? Is the child capable of being both angel and devil? Perhaps the difference is in the adults who are evaluating the child. Parents may demand more obedience from their children than neighbors do. Why, then, call a child disobedient if the fault lies with the adult?

Tom Landauer, J. Merrill Carlsmith, and Mark Lepper studied mothers and children at the Stanford University nursery school in an effort to pinpoint the source of obedience. They asked each mother to request three children, including her own, to do something she wanted. Each child received requests from three different mothers, including his or her own. Here are some of their findings:

1. There were no great differences in the obedience levels of different children. In other words, there were no "good" or "bad" children.

2. There were no great differences in the mothers' abilities to elicit obedient responses. There were no "strong" or "weak" mothers.

3. Children were more likely to obey someone else's mother than their own. Of fifty-two children, forty-four were less obedient to their own mothers than to other women.

It is interesting to speculate about why children are inclined to obey other people before their own mothers. Contributing factors may include fear of unknown punishments for disobeying a stranger, the familiar patterns of their own mothers, a desire for social approval, or the possible attractiveness or niceness of a stranger.

Although this study revealed no tendency for some children to be more obedient than others or for some mothers to be more controlling than others, this may be the result of some weakness in the manipulation, in the research design, or in the type of sample that was tested. A different study might discern differences among children or mothers or both.

Source: Adapted from T. K. Landauer, J. M. Carlsmith, and M. Lepper, "Experimental Analysis of the Factors Determining Obedience of Four-Year-Old Children to Adult Females," *Child Development*, 41 (1970), pp. 601–611.

practice what they preach, they can enlist the assistance of a potent mechanism of socialization in transmitting values and standards of behavior—that of observational learning.

Observational Learning: From Aristotle to Bobo

Aristotle, writing some 2,300 years ago, suggested that human beings are the most imitative of living creatures and that through imitation they learn many of their earliest lessons and some of their later ones as well. Despite general agreement with this view, it is only rather recently that investigators have studied observational learning in sufficient detail to reveal important implications for socialization. Perhaps one of the reasons for this lack of interest has been the assumption that imitation is the mere copying of a particular response and that, as such, it can account only in a limited way for human behavior.

Careful analyses show that this reasoning is misleading; observational learning is far from a simple process. For example, observing another's behavior can sometimes *reduce* the probability of copying; the child who sees someone bitten by a dog will become less likely to approach dogs. Generalization also broadens the applicability of observational learning. Thus, a youngster who observes a movie that features shooting and brawling may become more likely to yell at or push a younger sibling. In this case, viewing the film has reduced the child's inhibitions regarding aggressive behavior in general—not just the specific acts of aggression (shooting and brawling) portrayed in the film. Similarly, a youngster who sees that his father respects his mother and considers her intelligent may grow up to have a positive view of women generally.

Because everyone observes the behavior of others from day to day—directly as well as indirectly through books, movies, and other media—a more detailed analysis of the relevant processes of observational learning is worthwhile.

Acquisition Versus Performance. The effects of observational learning are not always immediately apparent, because observation made at one point may affect behavior in another setting that is far removed from the influential situation in space and time. To demonstrate that children can learn observationally without immediately performing what they have learned, Albert Bandura has conducted many experiments. Many of these involved systematic manipulations of vicarious consequences, or outcomes that accrue to a model for his or her behavior. When the consequences are positive or desirable, they carry vicarious rewards for an observer; negative or undesirable consequences carry vicarious punishments.

In one study, Albert Bandura (1965) showed nursery-school children a five-minute film in which an adult model punched, kicked, and threw balls at a plastic Bobo doll. The movie had three different endings. Some of the children saw a final scene in which the model was rewarded generously. Other children watched the model receive punishment for his aggression. The children who served as a control group saw a version of the film that had no scene in which the model's aggression brought consequences. Bandura subsequently left each child alone for ten minutes with an assortment of toys that included a Bobo doll, a mallet, and a doll house; the child's behavior was periodically recorded by judges from behind a one-way screen. Children who had seen the model receive punishment for his actions exhibited far fewer imitative aggressive responses than did those who had seen the model's behavior bring either rewards or no consequences at all.

But a question remained: Did these young witnesses to punished aggression actually learn fewer aggressive responses? In order to obtain a measure of aggressive skills that might have been acquired, the experimenter reentered the room supplied with incentives, such as colored pictures, and told the children individually that they would earn a reward for every act of aggression they could reproduce. Their success in reproducing the aggressive behavior they had witnessed showed that children in all three groups had learned the aggressive behavior—although they did not imitate the punished model when they were alone in the playroom.

The results of this study, which have been replicated many times, have particularly important implications. Consider, for example, that sponsors often justify popular entertainment featuring larceny or homicide on the grounds that in the end the villains are punished. However, although spontaneous imitation by viewers who witness punished crimes is unlikely, the punishment does not impede learning. After they have been learned, violent acts may be reproduced in real life when environmental conditions make those tactics expedient or rewarding for the viewer.

Characteristics of the Model. The characteristics of the model can also influence how much an observer imitates his or her behavior. For example, Bandura demonstrated in 1969 that high-status and nurturant models are more likely to elicit imitation than are models who are low in status and nurturance. Perhaps the observer responds to the power that these models appear to have; the observer may want to reap rewards and avoid punishment as the high-status model has done or may want to be like an important individual. (The effects of different characteristics of models on the likelihood that a person will imitate aggressive or altruistic behavior are fully discussed in Chapters 11 and 12.)

Thus far, several basic mechanisms of learning have been discussed. It should not be concluded, however, that this discussion completely accounts for the socialization of the person. Some theorists even consider learning processes of secondary importance, of less importance than maturational factors. These investigators have emphasized the importance of biologically determined developmental stages and thus are more sensitive than are social-learning theorists to stable, predictable changes in the individual's receptivity to socialization—a process that seems to occur regardless of learning context.

Developmental Learning: The Stage Is Set

Sigmund Freud was the first psychologist to theorize that individuals invariably pass through qualitatively different stages during the process of maturation. Freud was vitally interested in socialization, parent-child relationships, and a variety of cultural phenomena, all of which he felt were products of the biological nature of human beings.

Freud's Theory of Emotional Development. Freud (1938) argued that individuals progress through a series of stages from infancy to adulthood. In particular, he stressed the importance of infancy and early childhood experiences in determining an individual's later personality. He described the developmental process as a series of *psychosexual stages* in which central roles were played by sexual impulses, and he associated each stage with a particular conflict that must be resolved before the individual can proceed to the next stage. Thus, in infancy sexual energy is invested in the oral region. In about a year, the source of sexual energy becomes the anal area.

The genital region becomes the focus of instinctual pleasure in humans at about the age of four, according to Freud, and at this stage the child experiences conflict between a desire to possess the parent of the opposite sex and fear of retaliation from the parent of the same sex. Freud called the conflict in the male child the "Oedipal complex." He suggested that the boy resolves this conflict through *defensive identification,* in which he identifies with his father by adopting the father's behavior, attitudes, and values (Mussen, 1969). Defensive identification allows him to reduce his fear of his father and to experience vicarious possession of his mother.

Freud postulated a female corollary of the Oedipal complex—the "Electra conflict." This theory is not as elegant or as tidy as is his explanation of male development because the mother is the first object of love for the girl as well as the boy. Freud hypothesized that the girl transfers her love from her mother to her father when she notices that she has no penis, concludes that she had a penis but lost it, and blames her mother for this loss. Her affection for her mother consequently diminishes. And as her affection for her father simultaneously increases, believed Freud, her mother may disapprove of the child's incestuous desire for her father—which produces further deterioration of the mother-daughter relationship. The girl resolves this conflict through *anaclitic identification,* in which she identifies with her mother by adopting the mother's behavior, attitudes, and values. Anaclitic identification, says Freud, lets the little girl possess her father vicariously.

There is little factual basis to support Freud's theory of identification,

SOCIALIZATION & PROSTITUTION

NOT ALL RESEARCH on socialization comes from the laboratory. Some social scientists attempt to construct theories about humankind based on case studies. By going beyond statistics into the intimate details of someone's life, these investigators hope to capture the essential dynamics of a person that they feel cannot otherwise be adequately understood. One of these investigators is Thomas Cottle. The following are the words of a Boston prostitute who told Cottle her feelings about her father and what he meant to her as she was growing up:

I try to imagine what my father looked like. Was he big or small. How much he weighed. How come it was I never met him. . . . But there *is* something extremely special about him—this man I don't even know. I always think that I was destined to become a prostitute. . . . I always think that I had to; that maybe it would be the only way that I would find my father. Like one night I would be making it with some guy and then I'd know. All of a sudden in some way I would just know that the guy was my

real father. Pretty queer, huh? . . . [I]f somehow I could just meet him my life . . . would fit together better. . . . [I]f you don't know one of your parents at all, like your father in my case, then you don't really have a whole life. It's not only the past that seems all screwed up, it's the future too. Like when I'm dreaming I think all the time that my future can't get going until my father comes, or until something way back then has been settled. (pages 527–528)

To keep it a vital human science, psychology must reflect the "stuff" of human existence, which is in some cases more likely to be found in a prostitute's apartment than in a controlled laboratory. There are, however, limits to research based on case studies, because they are vulnerable to personal biases that we bring to our perceptions and that determine how and to whom we become attracted.

Source: Adapted from T. J. Cottle, "Matilda Rutherford, She's What You Would Call a Whore," *The Antioch Review,* 31 (Winter 1971–1972), pp. 519–543.

and its validity is now doubted. Social-learning theorists have suggested an alternative: that male as well as female children come to imitate their parents because of the satisfaction, warmth, comfort, and love that the parents may provide. In addition, becoming like the parents in attitudes and behavior may be strongly reinforced by the parents. Identification may also be instigated by children's desire to reap rewards similar to those that they have been given by their parents rather than by envy or fear of the parents. This kind of positive and constructive identification is a powerful factor in the acquisition of sex roles and other social roles, of moral values, and of dependence.

Piaget's Theory of Cognitive Development. More demanding of current psychological interest is Jean Piaget's view of normal development. Piaget (1956) based his theory initially on intensive observation of his own children, and he focuses on cognitive processes rather than emotional ones. Unlike most learning theorists, who view learning as a cumulative process by which new bits of information are constantly being acquired, Piaget believes that there are successive, well-defined stages of cognitive development and that the kind of learning that can occur at each level is qualitatively different from the types of learning that were possible during preceding stages. When a child matures to a new level, he or she reaches a more sophisticated level of conceptualization. As a result, the child will perceive the world from a qualitatively different framework than before. The kind of socialization to which one is responsive is limited by one's level of maturation, and so is the speed with which socialization can be achieved. Piaget's view of cognitive development is discussed later as it applies to moral development and in Chapter 3 as it applies to the acquisition of language.

The basic learning mechanisms and developmental processes are apparently much the same in all individuals, and in all societies they underlie socialization. Perhaps because these mechanisms and processes have such universal applicability, they have been presented here in somewhat abstract form. The discussion now moves to three specific applications of these phenomena; in doing so, the focus will turn to some of the vital issues that confront any society—what makes people dependent or independent, why the sexes differ, and how people come to acquire concepts of morality.

AREAS OF SOCIALIZATION

People who live together in a society must develop ways of getting along with one another. Some of the problems they face continue from generation to generation, and some problems are apparently universal in all cultures. For example, human young in all societies are unable to care for themselves for an extended length of time and are dependent on others during this period. However, at some point individuals must learn to take care of themselves, and this issue is not always easily resolved. For some of us, it is never satisfactorily resolved. In fact, it probably is never completely resolved by most of us, which may testify to our essential interdependence and not necessarily to inadequacies. The handling of dependence, then, is a problem that all societies must face.

Dependence

A socialized individual, one psychologist has said, "attaches importance and pays attention to people and the rules that have been developed to mold them into and keep them functioning as a society" (McCandless, 1967). He noted further that the child's early dependence on others appears to be the foundation of socialization. It is the basis for the power and influence that parents and other socializing agents have over the young. There are several views of how dependence is acquired.

The Psychoanalytic View. According to Freudian theory, the emotional bond between infant and adult—especially the mother—is central in the development of dependence. At first, the infant is aware only of biological needs that create tensions, and later the child becomes attached to the experience of satisfaction itself. Toward the end of the first year, the infant is able to perceive the mother or other principal caretaker as a source of gratification, and she becomes the child's first love object. Although this attachment becomes directed toward secondary satisfactions such as affection and approval, it is rooted in the satisfaction of primary needs, such as those for food, water, and warmth.

The Learning View. A learning approach to dependence also emphasizes early childhood experiences, although the processes are viewed quite differently by learning and Freudian theorists (Hartup, 1963). Learning theorists believe that dependence develops through reinforcement of help-seeking responses, such as crying. Gradually, the agents of satisfaction bestow secondary reinforcements, such as attention and approval.

Edward Zigler and Irvin Child (1969) reviewed the results of many investigations of the effects of reinforcement and punishment on dependence, which they have summarized as follows:

1. Dependent acts increase as a function of positive consequences.
2. Punishment appears to result in anxiety about being dependent, thereby inhibiting it.
3. Unavailability of social reinforcement appears to increase dependence.

The Developmental View. In a provocative series of experiments, Harry Harlow and his associates (Harlow and Harlow, 1970; Harlow and Zim-

Figure 2.6 The nurturant features of a mother are more important than her biological link with the infant. Even when surrogate mothers were neither alive, nor warm, nor a source of food, infant monkeys studied by Harlow and his associates showed a definite preference for a cloth surrogate over a wire apparatus (*left*). Women have functioned as surrogate mothers for human infants in many parts of the world. An example are the surrogate mothers in an Israeli kibbutz (*right*). An infant's attachments are determined by his or her environment and can be distributed among several individuals. Although children raised in communal settings may not have as much individual contact with specific adults as those raised in family situations, their emotional, social, and intellectual development is normal.

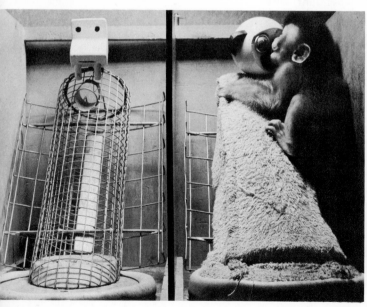
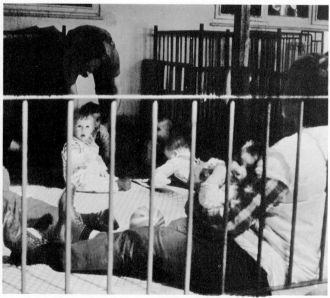

merman, 1959) substituted surrogate mothers for the natural mothers of young rhesus monkeys. In one experiment, half the young monkeys were fed from bottles held by wire surrogate mothers and the other half from bottles held by soft terry-cloth surrogates. All the monkeys spent more time with the cloth mother-substitutes, regardless of which was the source of food (see Figure 2.7). Contact with cloth surrogates also appeared to be more effective in reducing the fear of young monkeys who were exposed to fear stimuli, such as a moving toy bear or a bug-like creature. Pleasurable physical contact, then, apparently contributes to dependence at an early age—at least among monkeys.

Another extensive investigation reported by Rudolph Schaffer and Peggy Emerson in 1964 explored three aspects of early social attachment in sixty infants: the age at which it occurred, its intensity, and the objects to which the infants became attached during the first sixteen months or so of their lives. These investigators devised a series of situations paralleling everyday life. They obtained descriptions of the youngsters' reactions, such as crying when left alone in a room, during extensive interviews with the mothers of their young subjects. The onset of attachment to specific individuals occurred for most infants between the ages of six and nine months, and in many cases attachment was not to the person who fed and cared for them. What seemed more important in determining whom an infant became attached to was the responsiveness of the individual to the child. Schaffer and Emerson noted:

Whom an infant chooses as his attachment object and how many objects he selects depend, we believe, primarily on the nature of the social setting in which he is reared and not on some intrinsic characteristic of the attachment function itself. This view receives strong support from anthropological data: Margaret Mead . . . , on the basis of her observations of different types of family structure, has seriously questioned the view that exclusiveness of attachment to one mother-figure is biological in origin and that attachments cannot be safely distributed amongst several figures. (page 71)

An additional finding was that the intensity of attachment for specific individuals peaked between forty-one and forty-four weeks. The investi-

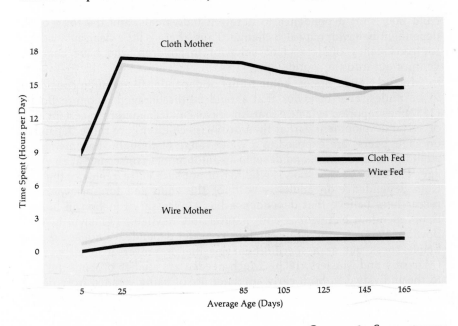

Figure 2.7 Whether the infant monkeys studied by Harlow and Zimmerman (1959) were fed by a wire or a cloth mother, the cloth surrogate was the preferred source of comfort and the object of affection. This preference, reflected by the amount of time the infants chose to spend with each surrogate, suggests that contact and comfort are important factors in the early development of dependence.

gators concluded from observing the children that new motor skills—such as crawling, sliding, and walking, which often developed between forty-four and seventy-eight weeks—may have been responsible for the subsiding of dependence at about the same age. The children apparently became absorbed in their new feats and consequently were more willing to leave their mothers. Even when dependence is strong—or perhaps particularly because there is someone to depend on—the young child begins to explore the world.

The Widening World.   Exploratory behavior facilitates survival, because the infant moves away from the caretaker and begins to learn about his or her surroundings. Figure 2.8 illustrates that the distance an infant travels from the mother increases with age in a variety of species. The mother's presence stimulates exploration and suppresses attachment in the older infant, apparently providing a secure base from which the surroundings can be explored (Ainsworth and Wittig, 1969). In contrast, the absence of the mother reverses the process, severely inhibiting exploration and intensifying attachment behavior.

Environmental changes may induce children to leave their mothers and venture forth to explore. After observing the responses of human infants to novel toys, Harriet Rheingold and Carol Eckerman (1970) concluded that the speed at which their subjects entered a new environment, how far they ventured from their mothers, and how long they stayed away varied according to the number, location, and novelty of the toys. They also noted that when children returned to their mothers they often sounded happy and made signs of relief.

Thus, although reduction of fear is one motive underlying the attachments that individuals form toward one another, pleasure in the company of others also plays a role. Moreover, the motivation for dependence changes as the child becomes older. If at first infants must be brought food, later they are able to fetch their own; still later, they become capable of tying their shoelaces or traveling next-door to seek a playmate. But at the same time, as they mature they begin to become more dependent on others to fill abstract needs, such as those for attention and approval. Thus, the child may shift dependence to different individuals, and the form of the dependent behavior may also change. Thus, there is little clear-cut evidence for consistency of dependent behavior in children who have begun to venture out into the world.

In the United States, some forms of dependence are often considered to be undesirable behavior that should be discouraged. Leonore Boehm (1957) has reported evidence that American children mature in certain areas of social development earlier than do Swiss children, are more dependent on their peers, are exposed to a wider range of thought, become free of adult influence sooner, and develop an autonomous conscience at an earlier age. The essential question is whether or not such early freeing of the child from dependence on adults is best for the child and for society. Some researchers believe that dependence has a necessary function in life and that dependent behavior is both natural and inevitable (Ainsworth, 1961; Bowlby, 1961). And most researchers consider dependence not as a state of helplessness but as a specific behavior that is universal in all societies (Maccoby and Masters, 1970). Much needed are studies probing the costs to the individual in both early and later life of being weaned from dependence at an early age.

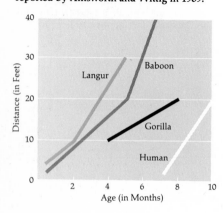

Figure 2.8   Exploratory behavior increases with an infant's age in a variety of species. Here, the average distances that various types of primates wander from their mothers at various ages are shown. The worlds of these primate infants continue to widen beyond the distances shown here. For example, the normal ten-month-old baboon ventures about ninety feet from its mother, as reported by Ainsworth and Wittig in 1969.

II Socialization: Being Human

In American society, independent behavior is encouraged in males to a much greater extent than in females. This and other aspects of socialization supply the content of sex roles.

The Development of Sex Roles

Our society decrees a double standard for females and males almost from the moment of birth. Pink and blue name-tag bracelets in maternity wards mark the beginning of this pervasive shaping, sometimes blatant and sometimes subtle, of sex-role behavior and attitudes. A result of this shaping process is that gender is one of the most significant factors in an individual's life, determining to a very great extent his or her life-long behavior, attitudes, and opportunities. Failure to fulfill these expectations or to adopt appropriate sex-role behaviors frequently results in negative sanctions ranging from mild criticism to near ostracism.

Constitutional Factors. Physiology sets the stage for the development of sex roles. In general, men have more muscular strength than women. Women mature faster and have a lower incidence of several genetically determined and sometimes deleterious traits, such as hemophilia, color blindness, and baldness. Women have lower rates of mortality at all ages because they have more resistance to most diseases. In parts of the world where childbirth is no longer likely to be the cause of mothers' deaths, women live longer than men do.

Biological differences are soon overshadowed by effects of social and cultural factors in a child's development. Sex roles are products of socialization. The arduous work carried out by women in developing nations offers adequate evidence that strength and stamina are not exclusively male attributes. Some researchers—the anthropologist M. F. Ashley Montagu

Figure 2.9 Indoctrination in "appropriate" sex-role behavior begins almost at birth. The ways others respond to children; the expectations held of them; the toys they are given; the models they pattern their behavior after; and the instructions, rewards, and punishments they receive for "appropriate" sex-role behavior all contribute to this learning process. In contrast to these Chinese boys and girls (*left*), who from an early age help both their mothers and fathers in heavy labor, this American child (*below*) is being taught that little girls are supposed to look pretty and be "feminine."

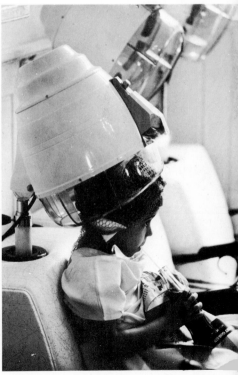

(1968), for example—have in fact suggested that woman is the stronger sex, although in most cultures tasks involving danger or aggressiveness are assigned to males (D'Andrade, 1966).

But all males do not automatically adopt, or even prefer, vigorous and aggressive behavior. Indeed, individuals of either sex may acquire a predominance of opposite-sex styles. Furthermore, a person's sex-typed behavior may be quite specific to the situation. A little boy who is dependent on his mother for praise may react passively to being pushed by another child if she encourages passive behavior, even though he may also enjoy football and may be boisterous on the playground. Evidently, then, much sex-role development is the result of the child's unique experiences. As Eleanor Maccoby (1966) has noted:

> . . . the sex-typed attributes of personality and temperament . . . are the product of the interweaving of differential social demands with certain biological determinants that help to produce or augment differential cultural demands upon the two sexes. The biological underpinnings . . . set limits to the range of variation of these demands from one cultural setting to another. Still, within these limits considerable variation does occur . . . . (page 50)

How, then, are these variations in sex-role behavior brought about? Primarily by socialization, which begins at home.

Shaping Within the Family.　Sex roles are learned within the family at an early age in most societies. By about two-and-one-half years of age, the child is aware of his or her own sexual identity, and after this identity has been established it is almost impossible to reverse.

Parents are the primary agents in establishing sex roles. But which kind of parent do children identify with more readily—the warm provider or the stern taskmaster? Paul Mussen and Ann Parker (1965) asked mothers whom they had previously classified as either nurturant or nonnurturant to teach their daughters to solve maze problems. At the experimenters' request, the mothers also engaged in irrelevant behavior, such as drawing loops and curves in the lines or hesitating unnecessarily. The children of nurturant mothers proved more likely to be imitative.

However, the sex-role behavior of a given individual may also vary strikingly from situation to situation. The girl who likes to play with dolls may also be a better sandlot first-baseman than her older brother is. A teen-aged male athlete, on the other hand, may also like to cook (although he might prefer to get grease on his clothes than wear a symbol of the female role, his mother's apron). And because sex-role behavior is so variable, different measures that researchers use to detect it yield differences in indications of this type of behavior. A good summary of the various findings regarding the relationships between different measures of sex-role behavior was provided by Walter and Harriet Mischel in 1971:

> The low intercorrelation obtained among components of sex-typed behavior gives little support to the belief that sex typing is the result of a unitary identification process that exerts highly generalized effects . . . . The findings, instead, indicate that an individual's sex-typed behaviors may be quite specific rather than highly generalized. (page 365)

Most parents have rather clear-cut ideas about the behavior that is appropriate for males and females. To varying degrees, parents pass along their own concepts of appropriate behavior to their offspring. In the early 1950s, for example, middle-class fathers stated that they would be concerned if their sons were too passive, too conforming, or cried too much

(Aberle and Naegele, 1952). Although today's fathers would probably voice similar concerns, parental views of the haircuts and clothing that are appropriate for males have probably changed considerably since the early 1950s.

Behavior that is considered appropriate may be encouraged during the child's early years by punishment of inappropriate behavior and reinforcement of the behavior that is desired. A study of the child-rearing practices of some 380 parents of boys and girls of about five years of age, who represented all socioeconomic levels, indicates that they used punishment and reinforcement as a means of encouraging behavior that they considered appropriate (Sears, Maccoby, and Levin, 1957). The investigators found, for example, that the socialization of aggression was carried out quite differently for boys than for girls:

Aggression was the area of child behavior in which the greatest sex distinctions were made by parents. Boys were allowed more aggression in their dealings with other children in the neighborhood, and were more frequently encouraged to fight back. (page 403)

Girls, in contrast, were punished for aggression and disobedience and praised for conformity, obedience, and sweetness.

Children do not seem to be equally responsive to all socializing agents. At certain ages, in fact, they seem to become progressively more responsive to people of their same sex. In a series of experiments, Joan Grusec and Dale Brinker (1971) have shown that when five- and seven-year-old boys and girls are shown movies of male and female adults performing simple actions, they are better able to remember the behavior of the adult of their own sex. The investigators point to the following intriguing implications of their findings:

While boys at an early age may even be equally familiar with the behaviors displayed by both their mothers and fathers, as they grow older and are exposed to more and more direct training for masculine behavior, they may come to be less familiar with the behaviors that females in our culture display. When they grow up they may be unskilled at sweeping, dusting, and making beds not just because they have not had practice in doing these things, but because they have never really concentrated too closely on how they are done. (page 155)

This process of sexual identification affects many more traits than awareness of and competence at household chores. It may well be a major factor, for example, in the mystiques of masculinity and femininity that fill our movies, advertisements, legends, offices, bedrooms, and divorce courts— that provide some of the magic in male-female relationships and that also fuel many of the misunderstandings and double standards that come between the sexes.

Not surprisingly, differences in the amount of importance placed on sex-appropriate behavior at home shape many aspects of personality. Patricia Minuchin (1965), for example, found that girls from home environments that emphasized individuality were less likely to display and adhere to conventional sex-role standards than were girls who came from relatively traditional backgrounds. It should not be concluded from this research that sex-role learning is determined exclusively by the behavior of the same-sex parent, however. Benjamin Rosenberg and Brian Sutton-Smith concluded in 1968 that sex-role preferences vary in complex interaction with family structure; sibling affects sibling, parents affect their children, and children affect their parents. Fathers, for example, are less feminine in families that have only girls than in families that include both girls and boys. And a boy with two sisters tends to express more masculinity than does a boy with only one sister (Rosenberg and Sutton-Smith, 1964). Orville Brim (1958) showed that children having a sibling of the opposite sex had more cross-sex traits than did those whose siblings were of the same sex.

Rejection of Sex Roles. One of the more important changes taking place in our society today is being made through the efforts of women who want to obtain rights equal to those of men and also to expand the range of behavior considered appropriate for both sexes.

Women's liberation is not a new idea—nor is women's dissatisfaction with being born female. In three different studies spanning almost twenty years (Gallup, 1955; Roper, 1946; Terman, 1938), investigators have asked women questions such as, "If you could be born over again, would you rather be a man or a woman?" The answers have been consistent. Between 20 and 30 percent of the females interviewed would have preferred to be male. Fewer than 4 percent of the men, on the other hand, would rather have been women.

Daniel Brown (1957) evaluated sex-typed preferences of children in kindergarten through the fifth grade by showing them pictures of objects or people that are socially defined as masculine or feminine. For example, he asked subjects to choose eight of sixteen pictures of toys, half of which were masculine (including a tractor and a rifle) and half of which were feminine (a doll and dishes). Boys of all ages preferred masculine stimuli. Girls demonstrated no sex-typed preference at kindergarten age, but then they turned sharply in the direction of masculine interests; in the fifth grade, they again made an abrupt change, this time choosing female over male stimuli. Brown found a parallel pattern of role preferences: more than twice as many kindergarten girls as boys expressed a preference for the parental role of the opposite sex. Between the first and the fifth grades, the disparity became even greater; from three to twelve times as many girls as boys expressed a cross-sex preference. It can be expected, however, that the rising social and economic status of women in our society will ultimately

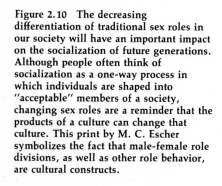

Figure 2.10 The decreasing differentiation of traditional sex roles in our society will have an important impact on the socialization of future generations. Although people often think of socialization as a one-way process in which individuals are shaped into "acceptable" members of a society, changing sex roles are a reminder that the products of a culture can change that culture. This print by M. C. Escher symbolizes the fact that male-female role divisions, as well as other role behavior, are cultural constructs.

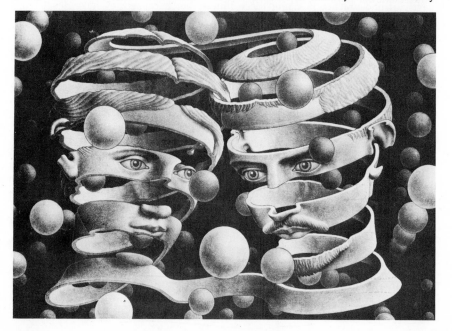

improve the subjective ratings of their sex group. As shown in Chapter 7, the racial concepts of black people in the United States have undergone such a transformation.

If females in our culture are rewarded for passivity and sweetness and do indeed adopt the habits of behavior traditionally assigned to them, it may be informative to ask how rejection of their traditional role is coming about. First, it appears that as children, females enjoy a wider latitude of behavior than they do as adults. Tomboys are considerably more acceptable than sissies are. Thus, in early life young girls learn and engage in many activities that they are later expected to give up. In addition, extensive education now provides many females with rewarding learning and job

Growing Up in the U.S.:

LOSING YOUR MARBLES

IMAGINE THAT YOU are a child of five sitting across the table from another five-year-old. An experimenter has put a marble board between the two of you. You can choose between two sides of the board, A or B. The other player takes the marbles that are left after you choose. In Case 1 you may (A) choose three marbles and let your partner take three or (B) take three marbles and let your partner have only one. In Case 2 you have a board with these alternatives: Will you choose three and give the other child four? Or would you go for two and leave him with one?

In a series of trials using these and other marble boards, Spencer Kagan and Millard Madsen have assessed the propensity for rivalry in children that leads them to try to win more than other children, even at the cost of their own resources. In Case 2, for example, a choice that would reduce the other child's resources (B) would also reduce the chooser's amount by one marble. This is the rivalry choice.

The experimenters investigated differences in rivalry and in the development of rivalry with age between Anglo-American and Mexican children. This study involved children five to six years old and eight to ten years old from both Mexico and the United States. Each child was paired with another child of the same age and gender. The marbles were of some value to the young subjects because they could exchange the marbles for desirable prizes.

The table, developed from the two cases shown above, exemplifies Kagan and Madsen's findings. It shows that rivalry tended to increase with age in both groups. Apparently, this form of competitiveness is a characteristic that is learned during the process of socialization, because older children seem to place greater value than younger children on making more than their partners.

The table also shows a relatively stronger tendency for the Northern children to behave in a rivalrous manner than for the Mexican children to do so. These are strong indications of different cultural values regarding competition with one's peers. There were also sex-role differences between the groups. In the Mexican sample, the differences between the sexes were insignificant, whereas in the Anglo-American group the boys became increasingly more rivalrous than the girls did. Closer analyses of the data show that Anglo-American boys chose to relinquish material rewards in order to vanquish their co-players.

This study, and others of a similar nature, support the idea that socialization has a marked impact on the values placed on resources and on their proper distribution. And apparently, the golden rule practiced by America's young men is "Do Unto Others . . . Before They Do Unto You."

Average Percentage of Rivalrous Responses, Cases 1 and 2

AGES OF CHILDREN	ANGLO-AMERICAN		MEXICAN	
	Boys	Girls	Boys	Girls
5–6	57.0%	42.0%	27.0%	15.5%
8–10	86.5	59.5	46.0	50.0

Source: Adapted from S. Kagan and M. Madsen, "Rivalry in Anglo-American and Mexican Children of Two Ages," *Journal of Personality and Social Psychology,* 24 (1972), pp. 214–220.

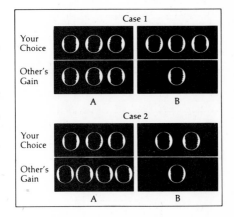

experiences that are unrelated to the skills necessary for housekeeping. Then, too, individuals of both sexes learn that society bestows greater rewards on the masculine role and values it more highly than the feminine role. In view of these factors as well as other prevailing social circumstances, such as women's increasing economic independence, the demands by women for sex-role change are understandable and timely.

In sum, the impact of socialization greatly outweighs the behavioral constraints imposed by biology in determining sex-role behavior. As women seek new roles for themselves, researchers are trying to pinpoint the specific ways in which sex roles have traditionally been conferred. Their findings promise to be of immense importance to all who are constrained by sex roles.

The Development of Moral Values

A child comes into the world ignorant of moral values; honesty, loyalty, responsibility for others, and any other qualities beyond mere selfishness must be taught.

Some social scientists have lamented that the learning of moral values is not more effective. In our society, people seem to hesitate so little in exploiting one another. However, other critics suggest that morals that are extremely strong produce social antagonism. Strong moral commitments tend rapidly to split the world into camps of "good" and "bad."

The teachings of many religions and other ethical systems suggest that morality is dichotomous; they present good and evil as polar opposites and assume that a person who is moral tends to act uniformly in accord with higher principles in all dealings with other people. However, an early investigation that was inspired by just such a view revealed that there was surprisingly little uniformity in children's moral conduct. The investigators (Hartshorne and May, 1928; Hartshorne, May, and Shuttleworth, 1930) placed thousands of children in a wide variety of situations in which they could transgress without being detected, as far as they knew. For example, they had opportunities to lie, steal, and cheat. The principle findings:

1. Children cannot be classed as invariably honest or dishonest. Almost every child cheats some of the time. But if a youngster cheats in one situation, it does not necessarily mean that he or she cheats in another. One child may cheat in school but rarely lie at home, whereas another may never cheat at school but quite willingly lie to the parents. Clearly, then, there is no single character trait for "honesty."
2. Children's verbal statements about honesty and other moral issues have little to do with the ways in which they actually behave. Those who cheat, for example, express as much (and sometimes even more) moral disapproval of cheating than do those who do not cheat.
3. It appears that the decision to cheat is largely determined by expedience, depending on the degree of risk involved and the amount of effort required to break a particular rule.
4. Moral behavior appears to be determined largely by immediate situational factors, such as approval and example.
5. The cultural values that influence honesty appear to be specific to the individual's social class or immediate group rather than being universal ideals.

These findings have many implications for understanding the socialization of morality. First, they seem to cast serious doubt on the assumption that individuals harbor any general tendencies to be either dishonest or honest. Moral character appears to be a matter not of fixed and general virtues such as honesty but rather of behavior that can be understood only in terms of an individual's needs, the values of his or her immediate group, and the demands of the situation the person faces.

But children do show marked changes in moral behavior as they mature, both in their behavior and in their stated moral values and judgments. One of the more helpful approaches that has been developed by psychologists to understand these changing values is the cognitive-developmental approach.

Maturation and Morality. The work of Swiss psychologist Jean Piaget (1956) has inspired investigations of the development of moral concepts in children. Piaget has not been interested in moral behavior per se but in the types of judgments that the child formulates as she or he matures. Piaget believes that moral development proceeds through a sequence of three stages: (1) blind obedience, involving *objective morality,* in which the child's moral concepts are simply based on what the parents permit and forbid; (2) an *interpretation-of-the-rules* stage in which a child, in *shifting from moral "realism" to moral "relativism,"* learns that the spirit is more important than the letter of a rule and thus makes subjective moral judgments; and (3) an *interpretation-of-act* stage in which people develop a sense of ethical and moral responsibility for their behavior.

According to this model, children younger than seven usually judge deviant acts in terms of the severity of the consequences; they evaluate a transgression simply in terms of the amount of damage it does. Later, however, youngsters judge transgressions according to intent rather than damage, thus shifting from the notion of objective responsibility to that of subjective responsibility. To illustrate this transition, Piaget presented pairs of stories to youngsters of various ages and then carefully questioned them regarding their reactions.

The paired stories usually differ from each other on two dimensions—the objective amount of damage done and the intentions of the transgressor. Consider these examples:

1. John was in his room when his mother called him to dinner. John goes down and opens the door to the dining room. But behind the door was a chair, and on the chair was a tray with fifteen cups on it. John did not know the cups were behind the door. He opens the door, the door hits the tray, bang go the fifteen cups, and they all get broken.

2. One day when Henry's mother was out, Henry tried to get some cookies out of the cupboard. He climbed up on a chair, but the cookie jar was still too high, and he couldn't reach it. But while he was trying to get the cookie jar, he knocked over a cup. The cup fell down and broke.

Piaget's research has revealed evidence of a shift from objective to subjective moral judgments. For example, younger children usually respond to the above example by saying that John (the boy in the first story) is naughtier than Henry because he broke fifteen cups, whereas Henry broke only one. Older children, in contrast, are more critical of Henry, pointing out that he did his damage while purposely committing a forbidden act.

Later, at about age eleven, children enter the final stage of development as they recognize the applicability of abstract principles to moral behavior. Jean Piaget and Bärbel Inhelder (1969) have put it this way:

[The child acquires] the concept of social justice and of rational, aesthetic, or social ideals. As a result . . . decisions, whether in opposition to or in agreement with the adult, have an altogether different significance than they do in the small social groups of younger children. . . . The possibilities opened up by these new values are obvious in the adolescent, who differs from the child in that he is not only capable of forming theories but is also concerned with choosing a career that will permit him to satisfy his need for social reform and for new ideas. (page 151)

Kohlberg's Approach. Building on Piaget's pioneering analyses, Lawrence Kohlberg (1969) has advanced a somewhat more complex and comprehensive description of the course of moral development. The child, says Kohl-

---

BOYS WILL BE BOYS
(With Class Distinctions)

FROM THE SOCIAL-LEARNING point of view, crime should breed criminality; that is, after a person begins a life of crime, his or her values are likely to change accordingly. Earlier values will be replaced with criminal values. The social-learning theorist might expect, for example, that juvenile delinquents would come to resemble one another in their attitudes concerning morality, regardless of class background or other indications of earlier learning experiences. "Serving time" should augment these characteristics learned by delinquents.

A study by Leon Fannin and Marshall Clinard is interesting in this regard. Fannin and Clinard interviewed and tested fifty white adolescent lawbreakers who were serving time in delinquency "training schools" in the Midwest. The boys were equally divided as to whether their family backgrounds were lower-class or middle-class. Each boy was given two types of adjective lists. He was first asked to rank the adjectives in describing himself and then asked to sort them according to his ideal of how he would really like to be.

The table shows some of the personality qualities with which the boys evaluated themselves. Overall, the lower-class boys believed themselves more dangerous, tough, and violent than did the middle-class boys, and they also admired those qualities more. Middle-class boys saw themselves as more loyal, friendly, kind, sympathetic, and loved than did lower-class boys, although in general both middle- and lower-class boys

Average Ratings of Personal Characteristics for Lower-Class and Middle-Class Juvenile Delinquents*

TRAIT LISTS	ACTUAL SELF		IDEAL SELF	
	Lower Class	Middle Class	Lower Class	Middle Class
List A				
Bad	1.14†	1.57†	0.84	1.05
Dangerous	1.11†	0.57†	0.95	0.67
Loyal	3.05†	3.71†	2.63†	3.71†
Tough	1.88†	1.45†	1.63†	0.91†
Violent	0.95	0.76	0.95†	0.29†
List B				
Friendly	2.84†	3.52†	3.05	3.10
Kind	2.89†	3.33†	3.21	3.29
Loved	2.58†	3.33†	3.74	3.66
Respectable	2.63	2.43	3.00†	3.62†
Sympathetic	1.53†	2.57†	1.32	1.81

*On a scale from 0 (lowest) to 4 (highest)
†Significant difference between lower-class and middle-class groups

desired these traits in their ideal selves.

Middle-class boys rated themselves as more "bad" than did lower-class boys, in spite of the fact that they had committed fewer and less serious crimes.

These findings suggest that social-class differences can persist in our self-images as well as our ideals even in the face of strong learning experiences to the contrary. New experiences can change us, but this does not mean that earlier lessons are totally lost. For example, within Fannin and Clinard's data one can find evidence suggesting the conclusions that middle-class homes are more love-oriented, devalue violence more, and engender greater susceptibility to guilty consciences than do lower-class homes.

Source: Adapted from L. Fannin and M. Clinard, "Differences in the Self-Conception of Self as a Male Among Lower- and Middle-class Delinquents," in E. Vaz (ed.), *Middle-class Juvenile Delinquency* (New York: Harper & Row, 1967), pp. 101–114.

berg, is a moral philosopher in his or her own right. To illustrate, Kohlberg shows the child a series of hypothetical moral dilemmas such as this one:

In Europe, a woman was near death from cancer. One drug might save her, a form of radium that a druggist in the same town had recently discovered. The druggist was charging $2,000, ten times what the drug cost him to make. The sick woman's husband, Heinz, went to everyone he knew to borrow the money, but he could only get together about half of what it cost. He told the druggist that his wife was dying and asked him to sell it cheaper or let him pay later. But the druggist said, "No." The husband got desperate and broke into the man's store to steal the drug for his wife. Should the husband have done that? Why? (page 379)

On the basis of children's responses to this and similar dilemmas, Kohlberg has identified three levels in the maturation of moral thinking: *preconventional, conventional, and postconventional.* The preconventional child interprets the ideas of good and bad simply in terms of their physical consequences—for example, punishment, reward, exchange of favors—or in terms of the power of those who enunciate the rules. The conventional level of moral development goes further, emphasizing the social value of conformity to rules. Finally, at the postconventional level, the individual conceptualizes universally applicable social contracts and moral principles that should be followed apart from the power of those who hold them or those who break them. Kohlberg's basic stages are clearly similar to those that Piaget proposed.

Kohlberg goes on to suggest, however, that there are two stages within each of his three major levels. Thus, he proposes a total of six stages of moral development. Some concrete examples of the type of moral judgments associated with each are provided in Figure 2.12 by typical responses to Heinz's dilemma, described above. Note that the stages are not differentiated by the *actions* an individual proposes but rather by the *reasons* the person gives for either supporting or denouncing Heinz's decision.

Social Learning. Some psychologists have proposed that maturation alone cannot fully account for a child's moral values and behavior. This view, representing the social-learning approach to socialization, suggests that much moral behavior is acquired and modified through learning experiences. Researchers who support this approach have sought detailed information about the ways in which learning of moral values and behavior can occur; one such investigator is Albert Bandura, whose research on observational learning was discussed earlier.

It is clear that children have ample opportunity to observe the moral behavior of others. Almost daily they see their parents lie or tell the truth, keep their promises or break them, and set relatively high or low personal standards for themselves. Children also watch their friends, teachers, and other adults. Research suggests that such observation is a potent means of learning moral values.

In an early study, Albert Bandura and Frederick McDonald (1963) demonstrated that the moral judgments a child makes are less age-specific than Piaget had suggested and that these values can be developed and modified by exposure to social models. Adopting part of Piaget's basic method, Bandura and McDonald presented youngsters with pairs of stories, such as the two stories presented on page 69, which they took directly from Piaget's work. They noted the frequency with which each child made objective and subjective judgments. As illustrated in Figure 2.11, Bandura and McDonald found support for the general age pattern described by

Figure 2.11 As they grow older, both girls and boys tend increasingly to make subjective moral judgments—that is, to take transgressors' intentions into account when making moral judgments. Evidence of this is the rising mean percentages of subjective moral judgments given by young subjects in response to Piagetian stories, as reported by Bandura and McDonald in 1963. However, these two researchers also found that the quality of moral judgment is variable within each age group, which suggests that morality may be less age-specific than hypothesized by Piaget.

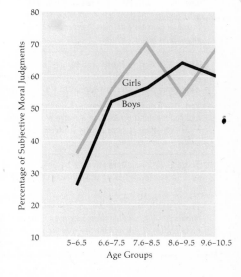

Figure 2.12 Kohlberg (1969) proposes
that there are six stages of moral
development. In response to Heinz's
dilemma, presented on the preceding
page, these types of moral judgments are
typical of the thinking at each stage of
moral development. Note that an
individual's stage of moral development
is not identified so much by the pro or
con direction of the moral decision
as by the reasoning used in reaching
that decision.

Piaget: Older children tended to make more subjective judgments than did younger children. This study also underscored the variability in morality at all age levels. For example, the younger children often based at least some of their judgments on the intentions of the transgressor, and older children sometimes weighed intent less heavily than resultant damage.

Then Bandura and McDonald used three different procedures to demonstrate that these moral orientations could change as a result of social learning. In the first, youngsters were reinforced with praise whenever they changed their original judgments to opposing judgments. In the second and third procedures, adult models consistently expressed moral judgments that were in opposition to each child's initial moral orientation; that is, the adult always made objective judgments in the presence of "subjective" children,

Stage 6 Concern about self-condemnation for violating one's own principles. (Differentiates between community respect and self-respect, and differentiates between self-respect for achieving rationality and self-respect for maintaining moral principles.)

Pro *If you don't steal the drug and let your wife die, you'd always condemn yourself for it afterward. You wouldn't be blamed and you would have lived up to the outside rule of the law but you wouldn't have lived up to your own standards of conscience.*

Con *If you stole the drug, you wouldn't be blamed by other people but you'd condemn yourself because you wouldn't have lived up to your own conscience and standards of honesty.*

Stage 5 Concern about maintaining respect of equals and of the community (assuming that their respect is based on reason rather than emotions). Concern about own self-respect to avoid judging oneself as irrational, inconsistent, nonpurposive.

Pro *You'd lose other people's respect, not gain it, if you don't steal. If you let your wife die, it would be out of fear, not out of reasoning it out. So you'd just lose self-respect and probably the respect of others too.*

Con *You would lose your standing and respect in the community and violate the law. You'd lose respect for yourself if you're carried away by emotion and forget the long-range point of view.*

Stage 4 Action motivated by anticipation of dishonor, that is, for institutionalized blame for failure of duty, and by guilt over concrete harm done to others. (Differentiates formal dishonor from informal disapproval. Differentiates guilt for bad consequences from disapproval.)

Pro *If you have any sense of honor, you won't let your wife die because you're afraid to do the only thing that will save her. You'll always feel guilty that you caused her death if you don't do your duty to her.*

Con *You're desperate and you may not know you're doing wrong when you steal the drug. But you'll know you did wrong after you're punished and sent to jail. You'll always feel guilty for your dishonesty and lawbreaking.*

Stage 3 Action motivated by anticipation of disapproval from others — actual, imagined, or hypothetical (for example, guilt). (Differentiation of disapproval from punishment, fear, and pain.)

Pro *No one will think you're bad if you steal the drug but your family will think you're an inhuman husband if you don't. If you let your wife die, you'll never be able to look anybody in the face again.*

Con *It isn't just the druggist who will think you're a criminal, everyone else will too. After you steal it, you'll feel bad thinking how you've brought dishonor on your family and yourself; you won't be able to face anyone again.*

Stage 2 Action motivated by desire for reward or benefit. Possible guilt reactions are ignored and punishment viewed in a pragmatic manner. (Differentiates own fear, pleasure, or pain from punishment.)

Pro *If you do happen to get caught you could give the drug back and you wouldn't get much of a sentence. It wouldn't bother you much to serve a little jail term, if you have your wife when you get out.*

Con *He may not get much of a jail term if he steals the drug, but his wife will probably die before he gets out so it won't do him much good. If his wife dies, he shouldn't blame himself, it wasn't his fault she has cancer.*

Stage 1 Action is motivated by avoidance of punishment, and "conscience" is irrational fear of punishment.

Pro *If you let your wife die, you will get in trouble. You'll be blamed for not spending the money to save her and there'll be an investigation of you and the druggist for your wife's death.*

Con *You shouldn't steal the drug because you'll be caught and sent to jail if you do. If you do get away, your conscience would bother you thinking how the police would catch up with you at any minute.*

and vice versa. Some of the children who observed the models were praised for changing to the models' judgments, and others were not.

After this training, an experimenter asked each child to evaluate twelve additional pairs of stories. During this test the agent of training was absent, and the children received neither praise nor criticism for their judgments. The results, presented in Figure 2.13, suggest that the models exerted a powerful influence in modifying children's moral orientations, although praise alone was relatively ineffective. Thus, observational learning was effective in changing children's moral dispositions. This does not necessarily mean that maturation has no effects on moral choice, but whatever dispositions do emerge with increasing age are highly susceptible to modification through social learning.

Most children—indeed, most of us—live in a sea of mixed observations. We see that adults act honestly some of the time and dishonestly at other times. The same is true of friends and of models observed on television. Adults can convey moral and personal values to children in two ways: by verbalizing or by demonstrating. Their preaching may or may not be consistent with their practices. Most adults who tell their children not to steal may usually be honest themselves. However, all children are exposed at times to dilemmas when their parents and teachers say one thing and do another. What happens to the child in this sort of situation?

This question has been investigated in a number of studies conducted during the past ten years (Hill and Liebert, 1968; McMains and Liebert, 1968; Mischel and Liebert, 1966; Rosenhan, Frederick, and Burrowes, 1968). The results of the various investigations are remarkably clear: When an adult imposes a standard on a child, the likelihood that the child will adopt it is substantially strengthened if the child sees adults adhering to that standard and substantially weakened when other adults violate the standard. Jae Hill and Robert Liebert (1968), for example, asked children to play a bowling game in which four scores were possible—5, 10, 15, and 20. An adult instructed each child to take a token reward only when he or she obtained a score of 20 and never for other scores. The tokens were valuable to the children, because they could be exchanged for prizes at the end of the game. Some children—those in the control group—played the game alone while a hidden observer determined how often they broke the rule. Other children watched one, two, or three adult models play before they played

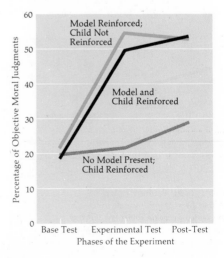

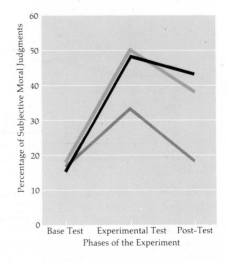

Fig. 2.13 The relative effects of three social-learning strategies (modeling, reinforcement, and the two combined) in altering children's moral orientations. *(Left)* the percentages of responses reflecting objective morality given by children with a subjective moral orientation in each of the three social-learning conditions. *(Right)* the percentages of responses reflecting subjective morality given by "objective" children. Bandura and McDonald's (1963) data show that observational learning, in addition to maturation, plays an important role in moral development.

themselves. Half the children observed models who behaved dishonorably, taking rewards for scores of 15 as well as for scores of 20. The remaining children saw models abide strictly by the 20-only rule. When the children then played alone, the results, shown in Figure 2.14, were truly striking. The likelihood of children adhering to the imposed rule when alone increased or decreased dramatically, depending on whether they had watched models obey or disobey.

In sum, then, there is truth in both the cognitive-maturational view of the development of moral judgments and in a social-learning view. Learning theorists focus on the potential malleability of children's morality but allow that the cumulative effects of learning can give the adult a different moral structure than the child's. Likewise, cognitive-developmentalists focus on the stages that people's moral concepts progress through while recognizing the variability in moral decisions that specific situations evoke.

THE LONG-TERM IMPACT OF EARLY SOCIALIZATION

Thus far it has been shown that various learning processes have an immense impact in shaping the social behavior of the individual. The bulk of the research that has revealed these processes has been conducted with very young subjects. The effects of early learning experiences can be persistent as well as immediately observable, but opinions vary as to the *degree* to which early experiences influence adult behavior. How irreversible are the habits of dependence, sex role, and morality acquired during these "formative" years? Are habits, good or bad, locked in for life?

Early Social Deprivation: The Creation of Terror

A good deal of research suggests that the early years are indeed significant. One line of research, for example, has investigated the effects of early contact with others on later social behavior. The most important conclusions have been based on extensive experimental work with nonhumans;

Figure 2.14 Results of Hill and Liebert's experiment (1968), which strongly suggest that parents should practice the values that they preach if they expect their children to adhere to those values. All subjects, who were children, were instructed to reward themselves only for scores of 20 and not for scores of 15 or lower. But whether or not they obeyed this rule when they believed that they were alone and unobserved was greatly influenced by whether the model that they previously observed had obeyed or disobeyed.

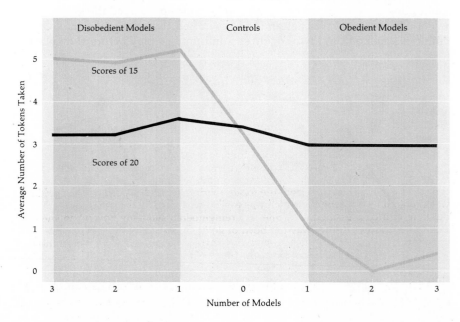

II SOCIALIZATION: BEING HUMAN

Harry Harlow has played the central role in this inquiry. As noted earlier, he has used young rhesus monkeys in experiments involving their own mothers, surrogate mothers made of terry cloth, and surrogate mothers made of wire that merely provide food. In 1970 Harlow reported the results of a study in which he and his wife Margaret isolated newborn monkeys in steel chambers with diffused light, controlled temperature, regulated air flow, and no sounds whatsoever. Adequate food and water were provided and the cage was regularly cleaned by remote control. All of the monkeys' physical needs were met, but no contact with other living creatures was available during the course of development.

After living in this manner for three, six, or twelve months, each young monkey was then exposed to a peer—another monkey who also had been reared in isolation—and to two other monkeys of the same age who had been reared in open cages with other members of their species. The experimenters placed all four animals in a special playroom, usually for half an hour every day, for five days a week, for six months. The results, closely paralleling those of earlier studies by the Harlows and other investigators, are clear: Deprivation has dramatic and almost irreversible effects on social behavior. In the Harlows' own words:

> Fear is the overwhelming response in all monkeys raised in isolation. Although the animals are physically healthy, they crouch and appear terror-stricken by their new environment. Young that have been isolated for only three months soon recover. . . . But the young monkeys that had been isolated for six months adapt poorly to each other and to [those reared in normal, open cages]. They cringe when approached and fail at first to join in any of the play. . . . When the other animals become aggressive, the isolates accept their abuse without making any effort to defend themselves. . . . Fear prevents them from engaging in social interaction and consequently from developing ties of affection.
>
> Monkeys that have been isolated for twelve months are very seriously affected. . . . Even primitive and simple play activity is almost nonexistent. . . . Their behavior is a pitiful combination of apathy and terror as they crouch at the sides of the room, meekly accepting the attacks of the more healthy control monkeys. We have been unable to test them in the playroom beyond a ten-week period because they are in danger of being seriously injured or even killed by the others. (page 95)

Effects of Early Learning: From Asthma to Autonomy

The impact of early learning experiences is also evident from studies involving human beings. For example, a number of asthma cases were traced in adults to accidental forms of classical conditioning that apparently occurred during early childhood (Dekker and Groen, 1956). It was found that asthmatic attacks in some patients appear to have resulted from exposure to stimuli as varied as the sight of dust, knitting, sunshine, and someone else swallowing an aspirin. Consider, for example, the case of Patient L:

> Patient L had told us that she got an asthmatic attack from looking at a goldfish . . . a goldfish in a bowl was brought into the room. . . . Under our eyes she developed a severe asthmatic attack with loud wheezing, followed by a gradual remission after the goldfish had been taken from the room. During the next experiment the goldfish was replaced by a plastic toy which was easily recognized by the patient as such . . . but a fierce attack resulted. . . . She . . . remembered suddenly how when she was a child her mother threw away her bowl of goldfish, which she loved so much. The patient had saved her pocket-money to buy them. Mother threw the fishes into the water closet and flushed them through. (page 62)

The therapists associated the childhood incident, which had apparently produced severe gasping reactions, with the patient's adult problem of suffering an asthmatic attack whenever she saw a goldfish or any stimulus suggestive of them.

Being rewarded for certain types of behavior during childhood or adolescence can also have a powerful impact on later thoughts and action, even when the original contingencies no longer apply. The late Gordon Allport, a pioneer in the study of personality development, believed that stable motives that are maintained in the face of changing contingencies have become *functionally autonomous* from their original bases in learning. As an example, Allport (1961) shows that functional autonomy of motives can be decisive in choosing a vocation:

Now the original reason for learning a skill may not be interest at all. For example, a student who first undertakes a field of study in college because it is required, because it pleases his parents, or because it comes at a convenient hour may end by finding himself absorbed in the topic, perhaps for life. The original motives may be entirely lost. What was a means to an end becomes an end in itself. (pages 235–236)

Or consider the following example:

Joe, let us say, is the son of a famous politician. As a young lad he imitates everything his father does, even perhaps giving "speeches." Years pass and the father dies. Joe is now middle-aged and is deeply absorbed in politics. He runs for office, perhaps the self-same job his father held. What, then, motivates Joe today? Is it his earlier father fixation? . . . The chances, however, are that his interest in politics has outgrown its roots in "father identification." There is historical continuity but no longer any functional continuity. Politics is now his dominant passion; it is his style of life; it is a large part of Joe's personality. The original seed has been discarded. (pages 228–229)

IS THAT ALL THERE IS?—THE SOCIALIZATION OF THE ADULT

Socializing processes do not cease when maturity is reached. In all societies—from the most industrialized to the least—the acquisition of beliefs, customs, habits, information, and technology is a lifelong process.

One reason that the acquisition of such knowledge is continuous is that, as people age, their roles change. In some cases, the individual is prepared for future roles long before attaining them: The child learns how to be a parent (or perhaps how not to be) long before he is either emotionally or physically able to assume this particular role. Even sexual activity, which might seem to involve instinctive knowledge, must be learned; monkeys that have been raised in isolation have failed to learn how to engage in intercourse, even after being placed in the company of monkeys of the opposite sex (Harlow and Harlow, 1970). The acquisition of an education and an occupation also requires years of preparation. The college graduate faced with his first job may require years of socialization before he is thoroughly acclimated to the work environment. If he is promoted, he may be further socialized to fill a higher-status social and occupational role. Every time he changes jobs, he will need to undergo some degree of job socialization. And if he switches occupations, he will probably face an even more thoroughgoing process of socialization.

Another reason why socialization is continuous is that societies change. In our time, rapid social change often becomes a problem. The carriage maker has been supplanted by the automobile manufacturer, whose industry in turn is being threatened by increasing concern for the effects of automobiles on the environment. To the individual who is past maturity, change may seem equally threatening: A man may long for the days when computers did not involve his business in complex procedures

"What's wrong with that damned kid?"

II Socialization: Being Human

and systems analyses; a woman may resent the army of electric gadgets that have elevated the standards of "good housekeeping" and in many ways added to her burden instead of lightening it.

Idealism and Realism: The Case of Political Socialization

The concepts with which people are provided during childhood socialization often do not sufficiently equip them with strategies for successful coping as adults. Furthermore, the strategies acquired during one generation inevitably fall short during subsequent generations when the individual is faced with a rapidly changing social environment. In studying the development of political attitudes in childhood and adolescence, Robert Hess and Judith Torney (1960) found evidence that, as they mature, children replace some of their earlier attitudes with more realistic ones. One aspect of the child's emerging political attitudes that Hess and Torney investigated involved conceptualizations of the president:

The child's initial relationship with governmental authority is with the President, whom he sees in highly positive terms, indicating his basic trust in the benevolence of government. Indeed, interviews of first- and second-grade children indicated that the President is the major figure in the child's emerging political world. The small child believes the President is available to the individual citizen, either by visits to the White House or by telephone. The President's concern is personal and nurturant. He is the tie to the governmental system through which other objects—institutions, processes—become familiar and understood. The Vice President, for example, is described in interviews as the President's helper, and the Congress frequently is seen as working for the President. The President is the critical point of contact for the child in the political socialization process.

The early image of the President centers around personal qualities. With increasing age of a child, the President's qualities directly related to his office become more prominent than his personal attractiveness, and the child develops a concept of the *Presidency* as separate from the President. (page 214)

Hess and Torney concluded that the school was the most important agent of political socialization and that it "stresses ideal norms and ignores the tougher, less pleasant facts of political life in the United States." These researchers believe that political socialization in the United States, to be effective, should present a more realistic view of legal, social, political, economic, and environmental conditions.

Although adult and childhood socialization share many of the features already described in this chapter, a central difference is that the agents of socialization for adults are typically no longer family and friends; for adults, the most important agents appear to be "people-processing" organizations: schools, colleges, corporations and factories, mental hospitals, jails. (Chapter 16 reveals the immense power that organizations, such as schools and business enterprises, have over most people's attitudes, behavior, and life alternatives.) The media are also powerful agents of socialization that monitor and evaluate reality, providing a continuous source of indirect experience for people of all ages. Also, much adult socialization takes place through direct experience, so that what is learned is tempered by the reality of the surroundings. Perhaps, as Hess and Torney suggest, the socialization of children should include more "facts of life," even if they are unpleasant, so that young people do not make demands that are impossible to fulfill in light of the actual, concrete realities of a situation and so that they are better prepared to work with the concrete. However, the primary agents of children's socialization—the parents—generally seek to instill ideals in their children that they know are unattainable. They believe that some ideals are

Figure 2.15 Socialization is not always a one-way process. The younger generation often influences the older generation.

appropriate to the needs of the young, even if those ideals will have to be modified later. Furthermore, most parents mourn the loss of their own innocence, whether that innocence be conceptualized as political, sexual, economic, ethical, or religious innocence. They still hope for a better world and know that to seek it, idealism is needed. Thus, in spite of a lack of grounding in fact, ideals may be necessary for social change. As such, ideals contain the seeds of tomorrow's reality.

Adults sometimes turn to groups of peers for *resocialization.* For example, consciousness-raising groups have been formed by blacks, women, Chicanos, and other individuals who share similar problems of social adjustment. Parallel functions are served by organizations such as Synanon and Alcoholics Anonymous. In the supportive atmosphere of such a group,

BEING SOCIALIZED FOR OBSOLESCENCE

THERE IS ONE disadvantaged minority group to which most of us will eventually belong—that of old people. If we stay around long enough, we may face diminishing opportunities and loss of status: We may be forced by arbitrary rules to stop working while we still want to work and are physically capable of doing so. Many of our social ties may dissolve through death and geographical separation. We may experience prolonged declines in physical capabilities that further limit our social contacts. Financial problems may severely circumscribe how and where we can live. Our closest relatives may remove us from our homes and place us in nursing facilities, despite our objections. People may withhold information from us and lie to us "for our own good." We may find that we are deprived of the power to make medical, legal, and other personal decisions for ourselves. And all the while, we may be plagued by a growing fear of what the future holds. In short, we may sustain losses of the lifetime social, psychological, and physical freedoms that we have become accustomed to. This erosion of personal freedoms is a common experience for the elderly; in fact, it may be inevitable for those who live long enough.

What is responsible for the frequent prematurity of the downward spiral of social, psychological, and physical deterioration? It is certainly enhanced by the expectations of old people themselves—a prognosis perhaps shared by all but the youngest age groups. Young and middle-aged persons are likely to perceive old people as helpless and incompetent. These views cause people as they become old to feel and act helpless and incompetent. After all, the oldsters are probably perpetuating the concepts they themselves had when they were younger. Conceptions of old age that affect the attitudes of all age groups toward elderly individuals are transmitted by means of the same socialization processes to most members of the culture.

Sociologists Aaron Lipman and Richard Sterne have contributed significantly to an understanding of these expectations; they characterize dependent behavior by old persons as constituting a sick role from which, unlike many other sick roles, no one expects the patient to recover. This social role may not be one that the old person chooses; it is frequently ascribed by society to elderly persons while they are still physically, psychologically, and socially capable of functioning independently. In contrast to achieved roles that are assigned on the basis of individual characteristics, ascribed social roles are occupied by persons for arbitrary reasons. For example, Lipman and Sterne suggest that, considering the range of capacities commanded by individual sixty-five-year-olds, compulsory

members can examine their own maladaptive social roles, can search for more adaptive strategies, and can experiment with new roles. This process of shedding old self-concepts and behavioral styles and adopting more fulfilling ones is discussed in greater detail in Chapter 7. It is a process by which the individual can replace the unusable products of past socialization with more adaptive concepts and strategies.

The Adult Learns From The Child

Most research on socialization, and much of that described thus far in this chapter, concentrates on the effects of adults on children, no doubt because the research is conducted by adults. It may appear to most adults that socialization is a one-way street down which the child travels toward

retirement is an arbitrary designation of old age.

Lipman and Sterne believe that society "rescues" the elderly from economic helplessness through the sick role that renders them dependent on Medicare, Old Age Assistance, Social Security, subsidized housing, and other institutionalized "cures" for the economic sick role. However, old persons are likely to harbor feelings of resentment because of this enforced dependence and of guilt at not being able to repay these "debts." A dependent role among adults is typically scorned in the United States.

Independence has assumed the status of a cardinal virtue throughout much of Western society. According to major social theorist Talcott Parsons, the essential economic independence of the individual serves an achievement ethic. The inability to be economically self-sufficient is inevitably associated with failure, especially for males. Self-sufficiency may be doomed at an unusually early age because the knowledge required for many occupations is made obsolete with ever-increasing frequency by rapid social and technological change. The conflict between the ideal of independence and the reality of enforced dependence may leave the retired person with a degraded view of his or her own worth.

The psychological price of the sick role thus involves many frustrations for the elderly: They have fewer opportunities to influence their world than they had during their earlier

years, but they still have the human capacity and desire to control their environment. They may have lost those they loved, but they still need to love and be loved. They may have no friends left, but they still have the capacity for friendship. A rapidly changing environment may make some of their knowledge and skills obsolete, and they may be deprived of opportunities for social as well as occupational fulfillments, but they still have the desire to be useful to others.

Solutions to the plight of the elderly have been offered. For example, sociologist Irving Rosow suggests that the stigma of old age can be alleviated by more comprehensive assistance programs, such as those in Scandinavia, the Low Countries, England, France, Germany, and Israel. If programs such as these were well established, there might be an accompanying cultural shift from viewing benefits for the aged as charity to thinking of them as well-deserved *rights*. But a real change in attitudes toward the elderly may require nothing short of a reorganization of our cultural attitudes regarding human resources and a realization of the essential interdependence of all people.

Source: Adapted from A. Lipman and R. Sterne, "Aging in the United States: Ascription of a Terminal Sick Role," *Sociology and Social Research,* 53 (1969), pp. 194–203.
I. Rosow, "And Then We Were Old," *Trans-Action,* 2 (1965), pp. 20–26.

civilized adulthood. However, there is also evidence that the child, too, is an agent of socialization for the parent. As B. F. Skinner (1971) has proposed:

The behavior with which a parent controls his child, either aversively or through positive reinforcement is shaped and maintained by the child's responses. A psychotherapist changes the behavior of his patient in ways which have been shaped and maintained by his success in changing that behavior. A government or religion prescribes and imposes censures selected by their effectiveness in controlling citizen or communicant. An employer induces his employees to work industriously and carefully with wage systems determined by their effects on behavior. The classroom practices of the teacher are shaped and maintained by the effects on his students. In a very real sense, then, the slave controls the slave driver, the child the parent, the patient the therapist, the citizen the government, the communicant the priest, the employee the employer, and the student the teacher. (page 161)

In this way, each of us influences others and is in turn influenced. Chapter 3 discusses the acquisition of language and of other means of communication—a process that is essential in humanizing beings and that is remarkably similar from culture to culture. Socialization is responsible as well for individual differences within a given culture, and Chapter 4 focuses on these differences in personalities.

SUMMARY

Every society has the task of rearing its young so that they function adequately in the culture. This process of socialization involves the learning of expected behaviors, emotions, values, and attitudes. Two major approaches to studying socialization have developed—that of theorists who emphasize the effects of cumulative learning and that of psychologists who believe that development proceeds in stages.

One of three mechanisms of socialization identified by learning theorists is *classical conditioning,* first described by Ivan Pavlov. This type of learning may be responsible for a wide variety of complex social behaviors, including emotional reactions and attitudes. Another mechanism, *instrumental conditioning,* refers to the shaping of behavior by its consequences. Behaviors can be strengthened by positive reinforcement—satisfaction of a need—or by negative reinforcement—the removal of an aversive stimulus. Previously neutral activities and stimuli—for example, money—sometimes become secondary reinforcers by association with such primary satisfactions as food, water, or sexual activity. Although B. F. Skinner and others have noted that punishment often only temporarily suppresses an act and may have undesirable side effects, recent research indicates that punishment can be a potent socializer, depending on its intensity, its timing, and on other factors. A third socialization mechanism that is pervasive and very effective is *observational learning.* Exposure to a model's behavior can lead to imitation of that behavior or of similar behavior. But it can also result in decreased copying if the model's behavior yields unpleasant results.

One of two major developmental theories was originally hypothesized by Sigmund Freud, who believed that *identification* accounts for an individual's acceptance of the behaviors, emotions, and attitudes of parents or caretakers. A developmental approach to socialization that enjoys more current popularity originated with Jean Piaget. According to him, learning depends on the child's stage of cognitive development—in effect, on the child's intellectual readiness to grasp concepts of varying complexity.

One important area of socialization is *dependence* on others, which underlies the influence of parents and other socializing agents on the growing child. Freudian theorists view dependence as a function of the emotional bond between mother and child, and learning theorists see dependence as arising from reinforcement of the young child's attempts to get help. Studies of human infants have shown that the function of dependence changes gradually with age from a means of satisfying physical needs to a means of satisfying social needs and that the object of their dependence shifts from parents to others.

Gender is one of the most significant determinants of the individual's behavior throughout life. Although biological and physiological differences between males and females do exist, the effect of these on sex-role behavior is greatly overshadowed by cultural expectations that the child learns to abide by. Important in this learning process are identification with adults and the influence of socializing agents like parents, who shape the child and are models for imitation. Not surprisingly, in view of the traditionally inferior status of women in American society, women more often than men reject the sex roles expected of them.

The development of moral values is at the heart of the individual's ability to exist as a social being. Morality is apparently not a virtue that is consistently displayed by people; it is influenced to a very large extent by situational contexts. Cognitive developmentalists propose that moral development proceeds through a series of stages. Social-learning theorists contend that learning experiences are more formative than maturity is.

Regardless of theoretical orientations, social psychologists agree that early social experience has important effects on later behavior. Support for this position comes from both animal studies, particularly Harry Harlow's work with infant primates and surrogate mothers, and from studies with human beings. Although childhood experiences can influence adult life, a person can continue to develop and to assimilate novel experiences long after physical growth ceases. For example, political attitudes have been shown to change greatly from childhood to adulthood; ideals tend to give way to more realistic views. Also, socialization is not a one-way street; as in other forms of social interaction, the target of socialization in turn shapes the behavior of the socializer. Thus, the processes of socialization pervade all human interaction.

SUGGESTED READINGS

Bandura, Albert, and Richard Walters. *Social Learning and Personality Development.* New York: Holt, Rinehart and Winston, 1963.

Bronfenbrenner, Urie. "Freudian Theories of Identification and Their Derivatives," *Child Development,* 31 (1960), 15–40.

Hartup, Willard. "Dependence and Independence," in H. W. Stevenson (ed.), *Child Psychology: The Sixty-Second Yearbook of the National Society for the Study of Education.* Chicago: University of Chicago Press, 1963, pp. 333–363.

Kohlberg, Lawrence. "Stage and Sequence: The Cognitive-Developmental Approach to Socialization," in D. A. Goslin (ed.), *Handbook of Socialization Theory & Research.* Chicago: Rand McNally, 1969, pp. 347–479.

McCandless, Boyd. *Children: Behavior and Development,* 2nd ed. New York: Holt, Rinehart and Winston, 1967.

Mussen, Paul. "Early Sex-Role Development," in D. A. Goslin (ed.), *Handbook of Socialization Theory & Research.* Chicago: Rand McNally, 1969, pp. 707–731.

Mussen, Paul (ed.). *Carmichael's Manual of Child Psychology,* Vols. 1 and 2, 3rd ed. New York: Wiley, 1970.

Zigler, Edward, and Irvin Child. "Socialization," in G. Lindzey and E. Aronson (eds.), *The Handbook of Social Psychology,* Vol. 3. Reading, Mass.: Addison-Wesley, 1969, pp. 450–489.

3

Language &
Communication

An ESSENTIAL FEATURE OF SOCIAL relationships is communication. Without communication there would be no relationships. What we communicate, and how, influences the ways in which others perceive us, feel about us, and act toward us. Much of this communication is verbal in nature, but it need not be; Charlie Chaplin could keep his audience in tears and in stitches before movies had sound tracks. To understand social relationships, all the phenomena of communication must be considered. What does it mean to communicate? Do nonverbal signals communicate basically the same content and emotions as words do, only in a less precise fashion? How are communicative skills acquired, and how are they related to thought? This chapter is devoted to these issues.

PRIMATE COMMUNICATION: DID TARZAN HAVE AN ADVANTAGE?

Young Sarah recently turned the tables on her teacher and started asking multiple-choice questions. Another preschooler named Washoe, while preparing for a bath, was struck by the insight that the word "open" applied not only to a brief case or to the door of a room or refrigerator but also to a faucet. These instances of intellectual precocity are remarkable only because Sarah and Washoe are not human children. They are chimpanzees. Sarah was taught to "speak" in a laboratory training program directed by David Premack (1970). The program used many of the principles, such as those of operant conditioning, investigated in Chapter 2. Washoe was trained more informally by Allan and Beatrice Gardner (1969) in a situation more comparable to those that most human infants encounter: Washoe simply lived with some interested (and accepting) communicative adults, who spent time playing with her, caring for her, and talking to her. Sarah "spoke" by manipulating colored disks of various shapes on a magnetic board; Washoe used American Sign Language (the standard dialect of hand motions used by deaf people). Both chimpanzees showed the capacity to "speak" in sentences and to make requests. Can it be concluded, then, that chimpanzees are language users?

One of the more persistent vanities expressed by human philosophers has been the belief that only people are capable of language composed of a system of symbols. This ability has even been referred to as the defining characteristic of humanness. Humans have been referred to as *the* symbol-using animals, as the only animals capable of negation, and as the only animals that can predicate. What becomes of these notions of human uniqueness if Sarah and Washoe—and by implication, all chimpanzees— are granted the capacity for language? Might other animals also be able to use language, if they were provided with well-designed training programs and language mediums that they could use? (The choice of medium is important: Two earlier experiments on chimpanzees' language-learning abilities failed because trainers tried to teach chimpanzees to *speak* English; it is now known that the chimpanzee pharynx lacks the fine musculature needed to speak human languages.)

The accomplishments of Sarah and Washoe highlight some difficult conceptual questions that researchers often prefer to ignore. Are human beings uniquely capable of language? Before this question can be answered, "capable of language" must be defined, and a means of evaluating an organism's capabilities according to that definition must then be found.

Suppose, for example, that chimpanzees can learn particular linguistic structures. How many and what kinds must they learn before they can, in principle, be considered language users? Must they know a particular set of structures or a particular number of them? Or must the structures be organized in a particular manner?

Jacob Bronowski and Ursula Bellugi (1970), for example, have hypothesized a set of criteria for ascertaining whether or not an animal possesses language. They note that Washoe did not *seem* to differentiate between appropriate and inappropriate word orders. Her inattentiveness to linguistic ordering, or *structure,* suggests that her knowledge of the signs she learned was itself unstructured. However, the Gardners and a new wave of psycholinguists counter that rigid word order does not now seem as important in defining language ability as it once did, even in outlining the linguistic development of human children. Washoe, like deaf or very young children, reversed the structure that is used by adult models and placed the modifier after the noun in two-word combinations, as in "clothes white" and "baby mine." The linguistic development of chimpanzees may be seen, therefore, as remarkably similar to the development of young children.

Human flexibility depends a great deal on the ability to extract information from the environment by analysis and to structure and restructure it as the context demands. Children become capable of just such analysis and structuring in the course of their development, and it is this capacity, Bronowski and Bellugi suggest, that may be unique to human thought. Although most two-year-old children can put together blocks of different sizes and different colors, they usually cannot sort them by color or by shape, and they certainly cannot sort blocks using both criteria simultaneously. As they mature, however, they come to use each of these criteria, first independently and then in combination.

Premack has proposed that Sarah was attentive to some syntactic constraints, such as word order. Sarah differentiated, for example, between "blue on green" and "green on blue." Similarly, after being trained to respond appropriately to "Sarah insert banana cup" and to "Sarah insert apple dish," Sarah was easily trained to respond first to the combination "Sarah insert banana cup (and) Sarah insert apple dish" and then to the combination with deletions, "Sarah insert banana cup apple dish." This last sort of success, Premack believes, indicates that Sarah was able to comprehend principles of ordering.

How can it be determined whether or not the Gardners' or Premack's data satisfy the criteria set forth by Bronowski and Bellugi? Are these criteria valid? The "X on Y" structure that Sarah learned is a single relationship that other species can also learn. In fact it is very similar, in principle, to "light before food" in classical conditioning paradigms. And Washoe was capable of such complex combinations as "You me go out there hurry" early in her training. It may be argued that even if Sarah and Washoe could learn elementary ordering from their training programs, their behavior was rote and human behavior is creative. However, even the criterion of creativity seems to be satisfied by one of the Gardners'

Figure 3.1 Many attempts have been made to teach animals the use of human language. (*Top*) Washoe, a chimpanzee, uses American Sign Language at about five years of age to name the object "fruit"; the object "hat"; and the quality "sweet." (*Bottom*) a dolphin named Peter takes part with his trainer in an experiment in which he is learning to approximate human speech. There is a striking resemblance between the sound-wave patterns of the trainer saying "ball" and Peter's subsequent vocalization of the word. However, the dolphin's pitch is somewhat higher than the trainer's, and he tends to raise the pitch at the end of the word rather than lower it.

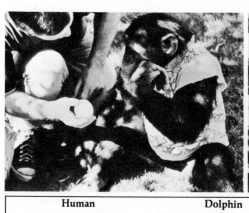

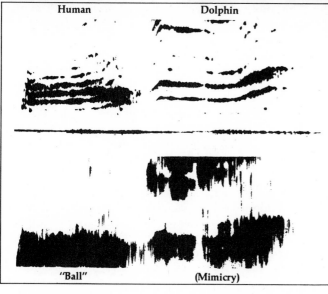

Human   Dolphin

"Ball"   (Mimicry)

Figure 3.2 Hockett's (1960) thirteen design features. (1) The communication leaves the remainder of the body free for other activities. (2) Anyone within hearing range can hear a vocal signal and can usually locate its source. (3) Human language signals do not linger as do writing and animal tracks. (4) Any message that is understood can be reproduced by any speaker. (5) Each speaker hears all linguistically relevant aspects of her or his own communication. (6) Speech has only one function—that of signaling. (7) There is an association between each language signal and the environment. (8) These associations are arbitrary. (9) Human words are discrete entities rather than elements in a continuum of sound. (10) People can talk of objects that are not present. (11) People can say totally new things and be understood by others. (12) Language is learned. (13) The vast number of words in a language are formed with different arrangements of a relatively small number of distinguishable sounds.

experiences with Washoe: what they signed as "cold box" (refrigerator), Washoe spontaneously dubbed "open food eat."

No conclusions can yet be drawn concerning the specific language capacities of chimpanzees. To fully understand the meaning that human language has (or *can* have), whether for a chimpanzee or for a human being, it is necessary to define what language is: What criteria must a communication meet to be called linguistic? What functions must it perform, and what degree of structure must it have? Studies such as the Gardners' and Premack's force us to reexamine assumptions, to isolate critical phenomena in behavior and training, and to specify more clearly just what is known about language. This chapter will first deal with the design and the functions of language, considerations that lead to a second major focus: the development of language in the child. Then the emphasis will shift to the adult and the problems of cross-cultural communication.

THE DESIGN OF LANGUAGE

One approach to defining language is to find out how language differs from other communication systems. The major features of human spoken languages, like those of many other systems of communication, can be analyzed using a *design-features approach*. These features can also be compared

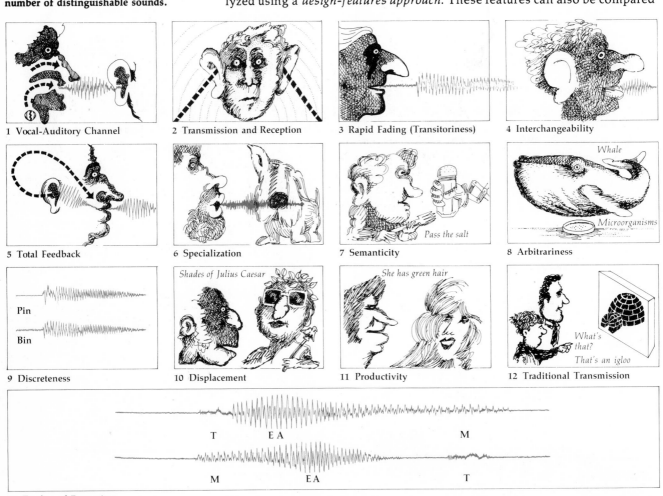

1 Vocal-Auditory Channel

2 Transmission and Reception

3 Rapid Fading (Transitoriness)

4 Interchangeability

5 Total Feedback

6 Specialization

7 Semanticity   *Pass the salt*

8 Arbitrariness   *Whale*   *Microorganisms*

9 Discreteness   Pin   Bin

10 Displacement   *Shades of Julius Caesar*

11 Productivity   *She has green hair*

12 Traditional Transmission   *What's that? That's an igloo*

13 Duality of Patterning   T E A M   M E A T

with design features observed in communication systems used by other species. Comparisons drawn from observation of other species would also help to identify design features that are unique to human language.

For example, the spoken word does not normally leave a physical trace of its occurrence. But neither do the calls of, say, gibbons. Hence, the *rapid fading* of an instance of communication is not a critical design feature of human language. And the number of sentences that might be uttered in human communication is infinite. There is no longest sentence, for it is always possible to add adjectives and clauses. This feature—the *openness* of the system—seems to be lacking in messages sent by other animals; hence, it may be a central design feature of human language. The criteria suggested by Bronowski and Bellugi form one example of a set of central design features. Another example, an early set of design features suggested by Charles Hockett in 1960, is given in Figure 3.2.

THE FUNCTIONS OF LANGUAGE

The design-features approach focuses on structures of the communication system and on comparisons among different species. Another approach, the *functional approach*, focuses on the *sorts of messages* that are transmitted in a communication system and on the ways in which they are *related to behavior* outside that system. An analogy can be made to studies of sexual behavior: The pure design-features approach might yield information about the anatomy of the sexual systems of various species and might suggest certain conclusions about similarities between species, the uniqueness of particular features, and perhaps the evolutionary development of such features. In contrast, the functional approach might yield information about the ways in which the sex organs are used, not only in reproductive behavior but also in grooming behavior, play, and other everyday activities of the animals studied.

Psychologists using the functional approach have concentrated on describing relationships between the frequencies of particular behaviors

Figure 3.3 In the midst of controversy about the possibility that television may increase aggressiveness in its viewers, Marshall McLuhan suggests that it may have positive consequences as well; in fact, he speculates that television may lead to increased humanitarianism. He bases this hypothesis on the inability of television to provide its viewers with complete enough information to allow total understanding. To fill in the missing gaps, viewers must become more involved than is necessary to assimilate messages from other media, and they develop increased empathy and understanding for their fellow human beings as a result.

and the effects of those behaviors on the social and physical environment. For example, some psychologists have been interested in the effects of particular reinforcement schedules on different sorts of verbal behavior. Along these lines, Joel Greenspoon reported in 1955 that he could condition subjects to use many more plural nouns than usual simply by supplying minimal signs of approval for doing so. This finding may prove useful, for example, in helping children overcome emotional and speech difficulties (Lovaas, Berberich, Perloff, and Schaeffer, 1966) and in teaching adults foreign languages. Psychologists have also been interested in the effects of particular sorts of messages and in determining just what information various messages actually carry.

Nonverbal Communication

Currently there is great interest among functionally oriented psychologists in *nonverbal* communication. The functional approach calls attention to *messages*, which may not be "linguistic" or even verbal. In studying the ways in which warnings are given, for example, one has to include outcries and contorted facial expressions as well as utterances such as "I think there's a man-eating tiger in our tent."

Messages that are transmitted by words and sentences are called *linguistic*, and those transmitted by behavior that is involved in the production of linguistic communication are called *paralinguistic*. Paralinguistic messages may take the form of accompanying sounds, such as "um" and "uh," changes in pitch and inflection, and so forth. The term *extralinguistic* refers to messages that are transmitted by other means, such as hand gestures, facial expressions, and so on.

The means, or modality, by which a message is communicated is the *channel*. Messages sent by the nonverbal channels—that is, paralinguistic

---

SPEAKING WITHOUT TONGUES

A WELL-KNOWN ARCHITECT, famous for his witty, erudite, and sometimes outrageous behavior, was often the center of attention at office parties. His wife, more taciturn and serious, never seemed to bat an eye at his antics or involve herself in the frenetic whirl of conversation that surrounded her husband. Nevertheless, at some point in the party, the two of them would separately but simultaneously say their good-byes to those around them. Within five minutes, without an apparent exchange of views, they had disappeared Cinderella-like into the night. The other guests were left to ponder the nature of their communication system. Was it ESP or some type of secret language?

Although some people may be more successful in transmitting their silent thoughts than others are, most people have at some time experienced a relationship in which a private language is possible. With hardly a word spoken, each can read the other's thoughts. What type of couple is most able to do this? Who should be least likely to? Psychologists have been able to test out some ideas concerning this matter. One major factor expected to affect language comprehension is the similarity between speakers. For example, it has been found that people who belong to the same social class understand one another better than do those from different levels. Harry Triandis, a psychologist from the University of Illinois, was interested in looking at the effect of similarities in conceptualization on communication. Triandis believed that people who use the same concepts when they think about something can understand one another better than those who use dissimilar concepts. Triandis evaluated his subjects' cognitive similarity by looking at their judgments of twelve triads of pictures that portrayed

and extralinguistic messages—may convey different types of information than do linguistic messages. Jurgen Ruesch and Weldon Kees suggested in 1956 that nonverbal channels are especially useful for sending messages about *degrees* of response. For example, the intensity of a scowl or a shove can communicate the degree of anger a person feels. The verbal channel, on the other hand, is thought to be better suited to sending messages about *categories* of response, such as the reasons for anger. It may be that messages in different channels call up different responses in receivers.

Marshall McLuhan and his followers have given us many interesting speculations regarding the different effects of messages transmitted in the *mass media*—the various public channels of human communication, including films and television. For example, according to McLuhan (1964), television requires greater involvement on the part of the human receiver because the material it provides is incomplete and needs further structuring by the audience. McLuhan believes that frequent exposure to television produces a habit of mind that leads people to much greater empathetic understanding of one another. This empathy evolves as people strive to fill in the gaps in their knowledge and, McLuhan believes, will ultimately lead people to a more humanitarian way of living together on this planet. This movement, McLuhan has suggested, runs counter to Western society's previous trend toward fractionalization of knowledge, development of specialities and restricted expertise, and lack of concern for global issues. According to McLuhan (1962), this earlier trend was based on the invention and spread of printing, in which the receiver and the sender of messages are separated from one another, and bits of knowledge are presented as if knowledge were amenable to division and encapsulation. Although McLuhan's thesis has many weaknesses, it does point out the potential value of studying the processes by which people send messages. In order to appreciate the full

expressions of human emotions. Each subject looked at the three pictures in each group, picked one as being different from the other two, and described that difference.

During the second stage of the experiment, pairs of subjects played a guessing game six times. Each partner was given two of the pictures that they had previously judged. One picture was the same for each partner; the other was different. The question for the subjects was, "Which one is the same?" They could not see one another, and they were only able to communicate with written, rating-type notes. For twelve minutes they were free to pass these special messages back and forth, and at the end of the game they each had to guess which picture was identical to the partner's. Each pair was judged on three factors: (1) cognitive similarity, which depended on the pregame picture ratings; (2) communicative similarity,

which was a measure of similarity between the subjects' messages during the games; and (3) communication efficacy, which was the subjects' success in guessing which picture they had in common. The findings support the similarity hypothesis. People were better able to guess the correct picture (1) the greater the similarity between concepts they had used in describing the first sets of pictures, and (2) the greater the communication similarity when they sent messages during the games.

This research lends support to the belief that individuals and groups can better understand one another when they use the same conceptual constructs.

Source: Adapted from H. Triandis, "Cognitive Similarity and Communication in a Dyad," *Human Relations,* 13 (1960), pp. 175–183.

impact of nonverbal communication, it is useful to consider message content and what happens when the content of different messages conflict.

Nonverbal Content: The Sounds of Silence

The most obvious reason for studying nonverbal communication is to determine the sorts of messages communicated by nonverbal means and to isolate their effects. Novelists, psychiatrists, and lovers, among others, have often noted that people convey information through eye contact, choice of clothing, gestures such as hand-wringing, and so forth. Furthermore, these nonverbal signs are often interpreted as indications of character, anxiety, or sexual interest. Paul Ekman and Wallace Friesen (1969b) have provided a useful analysis of the various functional types of nonverbal messages, identifying five in particular. These are (1) *illustrative* (such as hand gestures indicating the size of an object); (2) *affective*, or emphasizing (such as table thumping indicating finality); (3) *regulatory* (such as glancing at one's audience, encouraging a reply); (4) *adaptive* (such as recoiling in

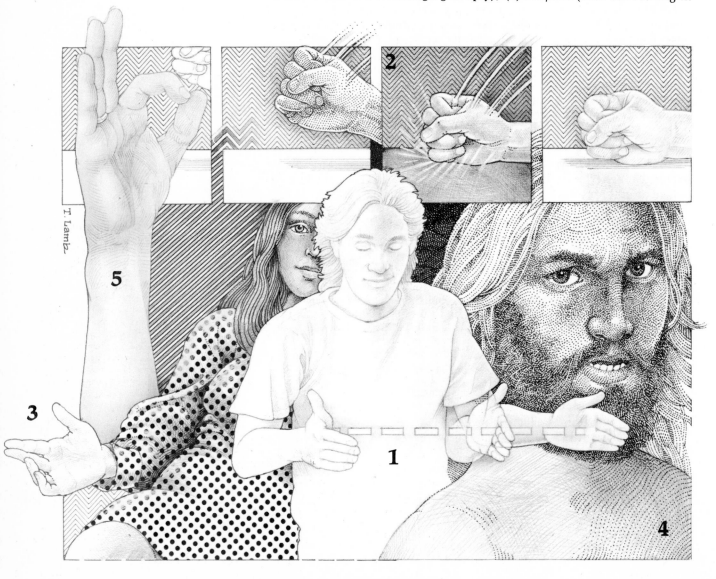

describing a bad experience, thus repeating a movement that originally accompanied it); and (5) *emblematic,* or symbolic (such as signaling "okay" by making a circle with the thumb and forefinger). Different parts of the body, including the face, the hands, and the legs and feet, are used in sending messages. These are frequently referred to as *display systems.* Particular display systems are often related to particular types of messages.

For example, eye contact can be used to communicate several different types of messages. In the realm of affective messages, Zick Rubin (1970) has documented what lovers have always known: People in love spend much more time gazing into each other's eyes than do people who are not in love. In contrast, however, eye contact can also be used to communicate threat and unwillingness to yield territory. In a demonstration of this point, Ralph Exline and Absalom Yellin (1969) challenged rhesus monkeys with bold stares. The head-on stares first evoked fang-baring, attacking postures, and lunges from the monkeys (who were safely caged, of course). As the stares continued and the monkeys were unable to reach their tormentors, they backed away and assumed submissive postures. In control conditions, Exline and Yellin made brief eye contact with caged monkeys and then looked down. This behavior did not evoke attack.

Eye contact also has regulatory functions, as Adam Kendon (1967) has shown. A speaker tends to look at his listener toward the end of each phrase and to look away just before, or as, he begins a new phrase. If he looks away but does not speak further, the listener tends to allow him to "keep the floor," as if he were being given a respite to gather his thoughts. If he looks away and then back to the listener, however, it is as if he had given the listener license to respond, and this behavior tends to evoke reply. In much the same way, facial expressions, gestures, postures, and other nonverbal behaviors have great communicative value, and many span the range of functions discussed by Ekman and Friesen.

The fact that many different functions may be served by messages that are sent through the same channels poses a problem, however. If eye contact serves both to communicate love and to communicate threat, for example, how is the receiver to know which message the sender is trying to convey? Perhaps because messages sent nonverbally are open to ambiguity, people use verbal channels more often than nonverbal channels for sending complex information. Investigators need to find out whether or not nonverbal messages can be interpreted reliably. They also need to know whether nonverbal communication can be said to be structured, as verbal communication is said to be.

The Identification of Emotions

Complete answers to the problems just raised cannot be given at the present time, but studies of facial expressions offer important insights. For many years social psychologists have tried to determine how successful people are in identifying others' emotions from their facial expressions. A thorough review of this research by Paul Ekman, Wallace Friesen, and Phoebe Ellsworth in 1972 showed that observers can correctly identify emotions if they see photographs of people they know have experienced those particular emotions during the photographic sessions. (In other experiments, drawings failed to elicit correct judgments.) Researchers have also been able to predict how subjects will interpret photographs showing certain facial expressions; for example, it seems to make a difference whether the lips of the photographed persons are open or closed, whether

Figure 3.4 Ekman and Friesen's (1969b) five functions of nonverbal messages (*opposite page*). (1) Illustrative messages depict or accent verbal message content; they are shared within cultural, ethnic, or social-class groups and are socially learned through imitation. (2) Affective expression augments, emphasizes, or conflicts with verbal content and varies according to the norms governing the consequences of that expression in a cultural group, social class, or family. (3) Regulatory devices are learned habits almost involuntarily employed to maintain and otherwise regulate the flow of a conversation; they do not represent the specific topics discussed. Regulatory messages vary with roles, demography, and cultures and can be sources of intergroup misunderstandings. (4) Adaptive messages are triggered by feelings and are generally restrained by a communicator who is aware of them and politely ignored by the audience; they are based in learned habits that can be either shared or idiosyncratic to the individual. (5) Emblematic messages are informative substitutes for explicit verbal messages, often signaled physically with symbols that are culturally specific and often learned at the same time as a language.

their upper eyelids are raised or lowered, whether or not their lower lids are wrinkled, and so forth. It would appear, then, that facial displays of emotion are, at least under some conditions, readily understood and easily described by an observer who is familiar—either consciously or unconsciously—with the norms of the observed person's culture. Thus, this research indicates that at least some nonverbal behavior, like verbal behavior, has a complex structural organization.

A remarkable feature of verbal communication is its flexibility. In contrast, the basics of facial communication may be heavily influenced by heredity. *Affective* facial expressions may be programed in humans, as is the bristling of a porcupine that is confronted by danger. Many facial expressions seem to be similar in all cultures (Ekman, 1970). Differences apparently stem mainly from the situations eliciting particular facial expressions and from the emphasis placed on particular affects, or meanings. Thus, for example, the Japanese show disgust in the same ways as do Americans but tend to inhibit displays of disgust and to make them much more brief than Americans do. The fact that a nonverbal communication system is the same from culture to culture suggests the presence of a strong biological component that is fixed in structure but subject to cultural conditioning. Although the expression of different messages may be biologically programed and universal for some communication systems, the case with spoken and written systems is different. As shown in a following section, particular message forms not only vary from culture to culture, but they also vary from situation to situation within any culture.

Conflicting Messages

Because messages can be transmitted by several means, simultaneous messages may sometimes refute one another. The understanding of situations in which messages conflict has been enriched by Gregory Bateson, Don Jackson, Jay Haley, and John Weakland (1956) who have studied *double-bind messages.* As an example, they point out that a parent may fuss over his child verbally while simultaneously resisting the child's attempts to get physically close. The simultaneous conflicting verbal and tactile messages set up a conflict for the child: He receives verbal messages that he is loved and nonverbal indications that he is not. Bateson and his co-workers theorize that continually having to deal with conflicting messages in early life may be a factor in psychiatric disorders, especially schizophrenia, that later develop in some individuals.

Paul Ekman and Wallace Friesen (1969a) have observed that simultaneous but conflicting messages sent through different channels may indicate a speaker's confidence (or lack of it) or his sincerity. They note, for example, that the facial muscles are capable of sending highly differentiated messages but that the feet and legs, in contrast, are relatively incapable of sending most affective or adaptive messages. One's face, they also note, is closely monitored both by oneself and by others, whereas one's legs and feet are not. Hence, if a person is feeling guilty or nervous he will usually be able to keep his feelings from showing in his face but may not be able to keep them from being conveyed through leg movements and leg positions.

In their investigations, Ekman and Friesen studied films of hospitalized psychiatric patients made at the time of admission, during the hospital stay, and shortly before discharge. Noting that patients often attempt to project an image of well-being that they do not actually feel, Ekman and Friesen hypothesized that they would be able to identify these discrepancies by watching nonverbal behavior. For example, a woman might try to act flirtatious and in control of a situation, although she might actually be quite frightened and upset. She might smile coquettishly while constantly shifting her feet in agitation. Ekman and Friesen asked observers to review edited versions of some of their films. In some of these, head and face cues were shown; in others, body and leg cues. The results clearly supported their prediction that undesirable, conflicting messages could unintentionally be communicated by feet and legs. The analysis of simultaneous messages sent through different channels may be useful, then, in gauging the sincerity of the impression a person is trying to convey.

THE ACQUISITION OF LANGUAGE

Without understanding how human beings acquire the ability to communicate, knowledge about the nature and function of language and the ways in which people differ from other mammals remains incomplete. Learning processes and their importance in infancy and early childhood are detailed in Chapter 2. It would be quite convenient to simply suggest that language is acquired by the child in the same way that any other complex habit is acquired. For many years psychologists wrote accounts of language learning in much that way. Those accounts of language acquisition made good theoretical sense to psychologists, whether they adhered to a Skinnerian position or to one emphasizing inner processes. However, as the pioneering linguistic work of Noam Chomsky (1957, 1965) has shown, learning theories fail to present an adequate account of the speed with which human beings acquire language and knowledge of language structure, although a learning approach may still provide some insights.

Learning-Theory Approaches

Generally speaking, a learning-theory account of language development might run as follows: The infant's babbling is only one of a series of relatively random activities in which the infant engages in an attempt to fulfill its needs. However, babbling is an activity that is rapidly reinforced by parents and older children, who shape the infant's vocalizations by praise and other feedback mechanisms until the vocalizations match those of the culture. After infants have learned the proper sounds, they are encouraged to combine them, and those combinations that resemble culturally recognized words are in turn praised or otherwise reinforced, as by giving the baby milk when his babbling comes close to the sound cluster signifying "milk" in that culture. Finally, through a combination of praise, direct reinforcement, and perhaps the secondary reinforcement that arises from meeting internalized standards for having pleased his parents, the infant learns to string words together. First, two-word sentences are formed (such as "daddy go"); then longer sentences (such as "daddy go car"); and finally sentences that are well formed by adult standards.

Although it is highly plausible, and no doubt valid in many respects, there is much about the foregoing theoretical account that is open to doubt. For example, until the age of about six months, deaf babies babble as much as normal infants and in the same way (Lenneberg, 1967). Nevertheless, the clearest, most acceptable part of the learning-theory account is the notion that children are sensitive to the models of language behavior that they encounter. Children learn the language used in their environment, regardless of their ethnic backgrounds. For example, the child of Bulgarian immigrants in America will learn English, if that is what her parents speak or what they allow her exposure to. For the first few months of life, the babble of most infants sounds alike. In fact, infants everywhere seem to make sounds from all languages—including French vowels and Spanish rolled Rs—sounds that they later find difficult to form (Atkinson, Mac-Whinney, and Stoel, 1969). But soon the sounds of the language that an infant hears begin to predominate in his babbling. Furthermore, there is evidence that children who have no language model (children with no human contact, or so-called feral children like those whose linguistic deficits were described by Roger Brown in 1958) fail to learn language, as is discussed further on in this chapter. Nonetheless, the exact contribution of learning to language capability is still an issue.

In general, children must be sensitive to utterances that are addressed to them if they are to learn a language. However, they must also discriminate between the normal speech of their language models and utterances that contain ungrammatical or complex content or that are marked by hesitations and errors. Even though adults modify their speech when they speak to children, as Catherine Snow (1972) has shown, children can

A CHILD'S GUIDE TO ENGLISH

HAVE YOU EVER KNOWN a child who always seemed to give you trouble no matter what you said? He answered back, disobeyed you and sometimes told lies about how you had treated him? If so, perhaps some of your troubles were resulting from a communication breakdown.

A recent review of the available data regarding the development of language in children after the age of four reports the following findings, which might clarify some aspects of the generation gap between you and that child.

1. Children under eight do not fully understand the words "promise," "ask," and "tell." If you say, "Mom promised Laura to give her a spanking if she was bad," the child may assume that Mother is going to get the spanking.

2. Children under seven have difficulty with loose pronouns such as in the sentence, "Billy knew he had to take out the trash." Who has the garbage detail is unclear to young children.

3. When a first-grader says, "He hit me *because* I fell down on the floor," she may mean that he struck her and *then* she fell on the floor.

4. If you tell a child under ten, "Don't go out unless I say so," it may mean, "Don't go out if I tell you," to her.

5. First-graders have a confused sense of largeness. Not only do they judge the largeness of something by its height, regardless of width; they also believe that a "slightly large" piece of cake would be larger than a "rather large," "large," or "quite large" piece of cake.

6. Young children also do not discriminate among adjectives very well. For the average six-year-old, "good," "pretty," and "happy" all mean the same, and she will enjoy hearing any of them. But if you call her "sweet," she may lick her skin and call you a liar.

It is clear that the understanding of words continues to develop long after the basic gains of early childhood, even after words have become part of a child's vocabulary. David Palermo and Dennis Molfese, the compilers of the review from which these findings were taken, believe that the available data support Jean Piaget's view of cognitive development as proceeding in a stage-like sequence. Between ages five and seven, when a child shifts from preoperational to concrete operations (in which the child adds to intuition the ability to coordinate and classify different types of information), and between twelve and fourteen, when a child develops the power to think abstractly, changes in language processing occur. As children switch from one mode to another, they are likely to go through stages of linguistic confusion and may even suffer temporary setbacks in their abilities to process language in its "proper" forms.

Source: Adapted from D. Palermo and D. Molfese, "Language Acquisition From Age Five Onwards," *Psychological Bulletin,* 78 (1972), pp. 409–427.

evidently still separate out and disregard nonstandard adult utterances as they develop their own speech patterns.

Furthermore, children are apparently not as sensitive to selective reinforcement as was initially thought. David McNeill (1966) recounts a typical dialogue between a mother and her child:

CHILD: Nobody don't like me.

MOTHER: Nobody likes me.

CHILD: Nobody don't like me.

(eight repetitions of this dialogue)

MOTHER: No, now listen carefully; say "*Nobody likes me.*"

CHILD: Oh! Nobody don't likes me.

Children's resistance to corrections of their language becomes even clearer when one adds to this example common observations about the difficulty of getting a three-year-old to say "went" instead of "goed." Again, consider the task of getting a child to say "please" or "thank you," even with selective reinforcement of either a material or nonmaterial sort. It is difficult to shape a child's linguistic behavior, although the response may be decipherable, the reinforcements may be carefully administered, and the feedback may be immediate and pertinent to the specific behavior at issue. Thus, it seems unwise to attribute to selective reinforcement the importance in language acquisition that it occupies in the traditional learning-theory model of language.

A basic assumption of most learning-theory models is that each word is learned in the context of other words. We learn not single words but words in a context. As a result, the presentation of any one word increases the probability that a particular type of word will follow. Thus, for example, we can view the sentence as composed of a sequence of words in which the choice of each word is partly governed by its prior linguistic context. In formal terms, one can estimate each word's *transitional probability.*

A number of interesting examples of the dependence of verbal behavior on transitional probabilities have been described. For example, Davis

Mother's Utterance	Child's Imitation	Child's Utterance and Mother's Reply
Tank car.	*Tank car.*	
Wait a minute.	*Wait a minute.*	CHILD: *See truck, Mommy.*
Daddy's brief case.	*Daddy brief case.*	*See truck.*
Fraser will be unhappy.	*Fraser unhappy.*	MOTHER: *Did you see the truck?*
		CHILD: *No I see truck.*
He's going out.	*He go out.*	MOTHER: *No, you didn't see it?*
That's an old time train.	*Old time train.*	CHILD: *There go one.*
		MOTHER: *Yes, there goes one.*
It's not the same dog as Pepper.	*Dog Pepper.*	CHILD: *See a truck.*
		See truck, Mommy.
No, you can't write on Mr. Cromer's shoe.	*Write Cromer shoe.*	*See truck.*
		Truck.
		Put truck, Mommy.
		MOTHER: *Put the truck where?*
		CHILD: *Put truck window.*
		MOTHER: *I think that one's too large to go in the window.*

Figure 3.5 **Children's early sentences are not strict imitations of adult speech but are approximations. A child's imitations of the mother's utterances and a dialogue between child and mother appear here. Words that primarily serve relational functions, such as prepositions, articles, and auxiliary verbs, are generally omitted, resulting in sentences that are short and simple.**

Howes and Charles Osgood (1954) asked people to free associate (make quick verbal responses to verbal stimuli) to sets of four words. People were three times more likely to respond with "hell" to the set "devil, fearful, sinister, dark," than to "devil, eat, basic, dark." In the former context, each word tends to be related to the meaning or associations of "hell." Context does influence the words that are emitted, then, whether in sentences or in a free-association exercise.

A classic study by George Miller and Jennifer Selfridge (1950) provides another example of the importance of transitional probabilities in language performance. Miller and Selfridge devised samples of language whose approximation to the statistical structure of English varied. For example, the zero-order passages contained words randomly chosen from the dictionary. Seventh-order passages were created by asking a subject to add a word to a six-word phrase such as "The boy saw an old man _____," asking another subject to respond to "boy saw an old man walking _____," another to "saw an old man walking down _____," and so forth. A new group of subjects was then asked to learn ten-, twenty-, thirty-, or fifty-word passages from these materials. As shown in Figure 3.6, recall improved markedly as the order of approximation to English went from zero-order to fourth- or fifth-order, and was then fairly stable, regardless of the lengths of the passages assigned. Thus, materials that exhibit familiar sequential probabilities do aid learning.

Sequential probabilities, then, do figure in language performance, but there are limitations to their effects. Noam Chomsky (1957) has shown, for example, that the transitional-probability model is not applicable to sentences having certain dependent parallel structures, such as "If . . . then . . . ," and "Not only . . . but also . . . ." It also fails to account for sentences containing *embedded* elements, such as "John called him up," where "him" has intruded between elements of the unit "called up." The learning of transitional probabilities also fails to take into account the human capacity to form new combinations with relative ease. Seldom do we ever speak the same sentence twice, a fact that is difficult to comprehend in terms of reinforcement histories.

Another focus of the learning theorist is on the phenomenon of *generalization* of grammatical rules. As noted earlier, young children tend to use words such as "goed," which is a construction that they form on the basis of a generalization from many other verbs in which the past-tense ending is "ed." This generalization is actually more strictly consistent—it adheres more closely to the rules of English grammar—than the irregular form "went" that adults use. Children also use regular (though incorrect) plural nouns, such as "sheeps." The implication is that children do not learn language word by word but rather learn general rules that they unconsciously apply to language.

Roger Brown (1957) presented nonsense words to preschool children, each in a context that defined the word as being (1) a verb, (2) a mass noun, or (3) a count noun. For example, a child was shown a picture of a pair of hands performing a kneading activity with a mass of red confetti-like material piled into (and overflowing) a blue-and-white round container. Brown told some children that the picture showed (1) *sibbing,* others that it showed (2) *some sib,* and still others that it depicted (3) *a sib.* Each child was then shown three other pictures, one reproducing the motion with other materials, one showing another action performed on a similar mass of material, and one showing a similar container. To determine whether the

Figure 3.6 Miller and Selfridge's (1950) experimental results suggest the importance of linguistic context to language performance. Passages that varied in their approximations to the statistical structure of English were better remembered by two groups of ten subjects the closer they were to at least the fourth or fifth order of approximation, regardless of their length. These results indicate that it is easier for subjects to learn materials that are characterized by familiar sequential probabilities than to learn those that reflect less typical word orders.

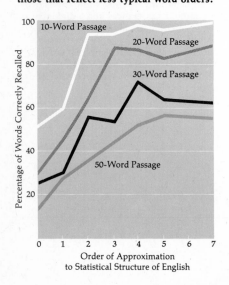

II Socialization: Being Human

child had attended to the verbal labels, the investigators asked the child to point out the picture that was like the original. Thus, for example, if the child had been told that the original picture showed *sibbing*, the young subject could be expected to choose the picture showing a similar motion performed on other materials. Children did quite well at this task, and the strong implication is that they were able to distinguish between verbs and types of nouns and to generalize, as well, from previous knowledge of which word form was relevant to an unfamiliar situation.

The capacities for generalization shown by Brown's young subjects are not likely to be present in very young children. As the child grows older the capacity seems to improve. This dependence on maturation suggests that a child's native capacities for language must be seriously considered if language acquisition is to be understood.

Nativism: The Natural Birth of Language

Thus far, this chapter has shown that learning-theory approaches seem to explain some facets of language acquisition but leave others unexplained. These inadequacies can be pursued further. If language were learned in a straightforward fashion, how much could be learned?

George Miller and Noam Chomsky (1963) studied this question and concluded that if a person were to develop a vocabulary of a mere 1,000 words, was restricted to sentences of fifteen or fewer words, had choices between words restricted to one of four word-form categories at each point in the sentence, and had to learn a new sentence every second, waking or sleeping, that person would require more than thirty years to learn all the sentences possible under these seemingly narrow constraints!

The complexity, open-endedness, and novelty of language behavior clearly require an investigation beyond the simple principles of learning. People seem to have a *generative* mechanism, or ability for creating endless combinations and novel configurations from a finite number of structures and rules. In other words, people seem to be able to extract or develop, unconsciously, rules for structuring language that let them invent forms and sentences that they have never heard and thus could not have simply learned by memory. As yet, there is no convincing account of how such structures and rules are learned. The obvious question is thus whether or not these rules and structures are innate.

Some strong evidence in support of the nativist hypothesis that linguistic competence is innate is derived from data on *linguistic universals*. Although the world's languages differ in their surface characteristics, important structural similarities among them are revealed at a more basic level. These similarities are outlined in Figure 3.8. It is certainly unlikely

Figure 3.7 Children can apparently grasp the structure of their language and effectively use it in conveying their thoughts, even though their vocabulary is quite limited.

If I were a mile
I would have a big smile
And whenever you smiled
I'd be 55 miles.

—LAURA NOTMAN,
FOURTH GRADE

Gush, mush, yum,
 rich, red fruit,
dribble down your
 bathing suit,
then you go back to the pond.

—ALANNA HEIN, FIFTH GRADE

I saw a man riding a
motorcycle.
He feels fast.

—STUART WAX, FOURTH GRADE

that these similarities are a matter of chance; their existence is a good argument for innate language tendencies. If language competence is innate, it might be possible to find that language development among children follows roughly similar patterns. There have been a number of provocative studies of language acquisition, particularly in English—such as those by Roger Brown and Colin Fraser (1963) and by Wick Miller and Susan Ervin (1964)—that have uncovered several sequences through which children's speech passes. Dan Slobin (1972) is currently carrying out a direct test of the sequence through which children acquire linguistic structures to see how general the sequence is. In this test, investigators are using standardized methods to collect information on language acquisition from different cultures and are periodically comparing the results. They have uncovered signs that some general patterns of acquisition do indeed exist.

One useful approach to the universals of language development rests on the foundation laid by Jean Piaget and his followers. Although not a nativist, Piaget proposes that the child goes through a standard sequence of intellectual development. This maturation in intellectual style has implications for language and communication.

In some of Piaget's earliest work (1926, 1928), he noted that young children often fail to evaluate how knowledgeable or ignorant their listeners are. For example, in retelling a story with several female characters, the child will continuously say "she" without specifying *which* female—a lapse that clearly would confuse any listener not familiar with the story. In another example from that study, children again omitted critical factors in a situation requiring an explanation. While explaining how a water tap works, one child pointed to diagrams of an open tap and a closed tap and said: "That and that is that and that because there it is for the water to run through, and that you see them inside because the water can't run out. The water is there and cannot run." This young speaker was astonished to learn that the listener (another child) had no idea what he was saying. He began again, saying: "This is a thing [pointing to the handle] like this; this way it's that the water can't run." Although the second time the child at least identified the handle of the tap for his listener, he still failed to communicate the relationship between the handle, the pipe, and the act of turning the handle. In more recent experiments, John Flavell (1966) has shown that children describing a game do not take into account whether or not the listener can even see the game board.

Perhaps the best data on this phenomenon come from a series of experiments by Robert Krauss and his colleagues (Glucksberg, Krauss, and Weisberg, 1966; Krauss and Glucksberg, 1969). These researchers developed a set of six unusual shapes for which no particular names existed. Each shape was stenciled on four sides of a cube, which had a hole through the center so that it might be mounted on a dowel. Six cubes (one with each design) were laid in front of a young child (the communication receiver), who was separated by an opaque screen from a second child (the sender). The children were invited to play a game in which the sender was to tell the receiver the proper order for stacking the cubes on the dowel, by naming or describing the shapes of the stencils. (The order the sender was to use was determined by the order in which he removed a companion set of blocks from a dispenser on his side of the screen, as seen in Figure 3.9.)

When older children or adults were senders in this experiment, they tended to refer to the shapes in terms having some social currency, such as "motorboat" or "hammer." If adult senders were told that the message was

Figure 3.8 The identification of structural features, termed linguistic universals, that characterize all languages provides support for the contention that certain language tendencies are innate to human beings. Several categories of universals have been identified, including a category, as outlined here, that pertains to the ordering of words and sounds. (One example of a rule in that category is that the subject always precedes the object in a declarative sentence.)

Basic Linguistic Universals

Syntactic rules (about the order of words in sentences)

Hungry five squirrels gray nuts gathered fallen.

Five hungry gray squirrels gathered fallen nuts.

Phonological rules (about the placement of sounds and their symbols in words)

stchl
satchel

Discrete lexical items (words) that are sequences of sound segments.

Ther ainin Spa infal lsma inlyo nth epla in.

The rain in Spain falls mainly on the plain.

unclear, they tended to elaborate the description or to try out another one. In contrast, children were far more likely to pick idiosyncratic descriptions initially, such as "my mommy's hat," and were likely to repeat that description without elaboration when asked to clarify. Apparently, mental maturity carries with it an ability to mold language in order to communicate effectively with others.

Cognitive Development and Social Interaction

Both the learning and the nativist orientations to language acquisition, considered thus far, indicate that the question is not simply whether language is a purely genetic endowment or whether it is taught. Normal human beings can clearly acquire language, although it is not as clear that animals can. But whatever people inherit, the endowment is obviously not so specific that it produces a French speaker or a Swahili speaker without environmental influences. Human beings simply cannot acquire language without *some* environmental tutoring. Reports of children who have been isolated from human contact indicate that they do not have *any* language when they are discovered (Brown, 1958). However, biological factors are also implicated in studies of children who have been deprived of human contact. Eric Lenneberg proposed in 1967 that isolated children who are brought into human society beyond a certain age seem to have passed a *critical period* and to be incapable of acquiring language. At this point, social learning seems totally ineffective. Even well-educated individuals often have great difficulty learning new languages as adults. How, then, does the environment interact with genetic endowments, and what are some of the limits on the effects of the environment?

The transaction between the child and his or her verbal environment is important in understanding the interrelationship between genetic development and learning. Consider but one example.

It is likely that children must pay attention to adult models at *selected* times. In order for pertinent information about language to be communicated in one form or another, children must have adult models at some point; otherwise, they could not even begin to learn the words appropriate to the culture. Conversely, if they were to pay attention to *all* adult speech within hearing, they would be flooded with complex information that probably would do more to confuse them than to enable them to progress

Figure 3.9   Krauss and Glucksberg (1969) studied the development of communication abilities as a function of age by placing their child subjects on opposite sides of an opaque screen (*left*). One child was required to describe to the other the order in which each of six blocks should be placed on a dowel; each block could be identified only by the novel shape stenciled on it. Young children's descriptions of the shapes were idiosyncratic and without elaboration, but older children used socially relevant descriptions and elaborated on them when necessary. The six novel shapes used by Krauss and Glucksberg (*below*).

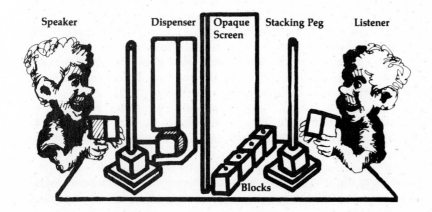

linguistically. The information that is communicated must be of sufficient novelty and complexity to be engaging but not so ambiguous or complex as to be overwhelming. Both novelty and complexity can be, and probably are, controlled by adults in their interactions with children. Furthermore, children exercise some degree of control over the novelty and complexity of their communications with one another. Control over these variables may be necessary in enabling the child to acquire language.

Several examples of the ways in which adults influence the selection of what the child learns can be cited. *Baby talk,* for example, involves the adult adding certain endings to words, such as "doggie" and "milkie-poo," or repeating words, like "no-no." A peculiarly saccharine voice quality is often used when talking to children. Also common is altering the baby's name ("Does Rumpelstiltskin want more milk?") or using the name rather than the pronoun "you" in questions or descriptions ("Oh, Martha is playing pat-a-cake!"). Another common way of engaging the child is to simplify sentences. Finally, parents often rely on nonverbal signals, such as exaggerated use of illustrators (such as pointing) or of emphasizers (such as tone or stress). Charles Ferguson reported in 1964 that similar phenomena are found in a wide variety of languages. But does baby talk actually help the child to develop language abilities?

A recent study by Elizabeth Shipley, Carlota Smith, and Lila Gleitman (1969) shows that children attend to adult speech differently depending on these special signals. The results of this study also highlight the importance of presenting the child with materials of optimum complexity. In this experiment, mothers delivered various commands to their young children. The commands ranged from well-formed ones, such as "Throw me the ball," to telegraphic commands, such as "Throw ball," to isolated noun commands, "Ball," to nonsense forms, "Throw ronta ball," "Gor ronta ball," and "Gor ball." These command forms differ both in their surface syntax and in the use of known and unknown words. ("Gor" and "ronta" are nonsense to adults; but to the child they are, like "sibbing" in our earlier example, simply members of the enormous class of words that he or she has not yet learned.)

The investigators recorded several classes of responses to each command: any action on the part of the child; an action related to the stimulus object named (including touching or looking at it); answering (including "Mommy get it" and "Where?"); and simply repeating the command. Considering only the appropriate action responses, the children who spoke primarily in one-word sentences (holophrastically) responded to the one-word and two-word commands far more than to the well-formed commands. On the other hand, the children who were able to speak telegraphically ("Throw ball"; "Doggie bark"; "Daddy go office") responded to the well-formed commands far more than to the more childlike commands. These results suggest that children attend selectively to language and respond best to language that is somewhat—but not greatly—more complex than that which they themselves can produce.

Given the present level of understanding, it cannot be predicted whether some particular speech element will fit the child's developing competence at a given moment or will be just relevant enough or just complex enough to stimulate progress. (Recall the lack of success of the mother who responded to her child's "Nobody don't like me" with "Nobody likes me.") But it is possible to be sensitive to the interaction process and to provide the child with models of the appropriate linguistic complexity that will allow the fastest possible progress in learning the language. What may be required of the adult, then, is to engage the child in the communication process with a degree of novelty and complexity adapted to the developing level of ability.

These various research studies suggest that the problems of language development and their solutions may be universal for humans. In other words, human cognitive development is likely to pass through stages that are determined by our biological heritage rather than through those that are culturally unique. However, the particular strategies of teaching employed at any given stage and the resulting language form may be culturally determined. Furthermore, the rapidity of development of children's learning processes may be influenced by patterns of communication and feedback that are peculiar to given cultures.

COMMUNICATING ACROSS CULTURAL BOUNDARIES

In August of 1945 the United States dropped an atomic bomb on Hiroshima, Japan. Two days later another was dropped on Nagasaki. More than 400,000 people were killed—either instantly or more slowly from the effects of radiation poisoning. Many people feel that the bombing was inexcusable, a brutal and inhumane act. Others argue that the bombing was necessary to bring World War II to a rapid halt; many more lives would have been taken, so they say, if fighting had continued. These latter arguments are based in part on the analysis made at the time of the Japanese Emperor's messages to his people. From the American standpoint, the messages indicated that each person should fight the invaders to the death. It was later learned that, to the Japanese, the messages had a much different meaning—a certain but honorable surrender was implicit. Had Americans been able to understand what the Emperor's messages meant to the Japanese, the bombs might never have been dropped. This unfortunate situation underscores the importance of cross-cultural communication.

Can cultural differences in language be overcome, so that appropriate translations are attainable, regardless of the complexity of the ideas and regardless of apparent differences between languages? Or is the member of any given group unable to see beyond his group's *Weltanschauung*, or vision of the world, as Benjamin Lee Whorf (1956) and others have argued?

The answers to these questions involve further questions: Are language and thought separable? Can we think without language? If we *can* think independently of language, it might be possible to design better vehicles for transmitting thought and hence for communicating with one another. If our ability to think and the form of our thoughts rely primarily on language, and languages differ markedly from one another, it may be that speakers of different languages will never be able to communicate fully with one another.

The notion that language patterns influence thought processes has affected the daily lives of some people. For example, students used to be urged to study Latin for the practice it would give them in learning to think logically, although studies of transfer of training indicate that no such transfer exists. There are those today who recommend instruction in computer languages for the same purpose. Similarly, some literary critics have held that the rhetorical structures favored by eighteenth-century writers, such as a use of parallel clauses, showing a frame of mind given to rational contemplation of similarities and differences, are much to be admired and much to be imitated, especially in contrast to such modern devices as stream-of-consciousness writing.

A far more important outcropping of this same point of view on the relationship of language to thought may be seen in discussions of the status of minority dialects, such as Black English. Some observers feel that the upbringing of black Americans is deficient. They argue that the cognitive abilities of blacks tend to compare poorly with those of others as demonstrated with standard IQ tests or certain associative-reasoning tests (Jensen, 1968). They go on to suggest that this deficiency is reflected in black culture generally and in black people's speech in particular. According to this view, black dialect is insufficient for dealing with the complex technological world of the mid-twentieth-century West. Proponents of this explanation point to supposed deficits in black people's speech patterns to explain their problems in public schools. Black language, they say, is not differentiated enough to allow for the intellectual work required by the educational system. The effects of this view are too important to pass by, and they will receive more detailed attention after a consideration of the general relationship between language and thought.

On the assumption that thought precedes language, attempts have been made to develop international communication systems. However, invented languages such as Basic English and Esperanto have failed to catch on, partly because of the impoverished vocabularies and structures to which their use has been restricted. Attempts have also been made to develop formal languages modeled after mathematical languages or computer-programed languages. These seem to have been successful only within very narrow ranges; they certainly do not possess the richness of natural languages. A third set of attempts has centered on developing rules for sentence usage, such as those of general semantics (Hayakawa, 1941; Korzybski, 1933). An example of such a rule would be one requiring the speaker of "Jones is a good man" to clarify whether he intended the listener to understand that Jones is the "good" that means "moral"; the "good" that means "capable of burnishing widgets in his daily job"; "a good man," implying male chauvinism; or whatever. These attempts seem to have had only limited success, because they run counter to the uses of ambiguity and redundancy in natural language.

The attempt to find a common second language for all people is doomed to failure if language really constrains thought. If people think differently because they speak different languages, then how can they agree on a single language? If children beginning to develop their thought processes are exposed to different languages with different structures that influence their thought patterns in relatively permanent ways, then each child will be unable to verify his or her version of reality, because each will have a different reality. If we cannot fully communicate our ways of viewing the world, then we can neither verify nor disconfirm our perceptions of reality to others.

Several different kinds of research bear on this issue. The following discussion describes the results of some interesting studies on the behavioral effects of linguistic differences and the results of studies on cross-cultural comparisons of different languages.

Linguistic Relativity

The possibility that differences in language might indicate differences in thought was scrutinized by anthropologists in the late nineteenth century.

Figure 3.10 Examples of Esperanto. Although several attempts have been made to establish an international communication system, none has been successful. Esperanto, which has a strong Latin base, is one such attempt.

LA HOMO ESTAS MORTEMA,
Man is mortal.

ESTAS BILDO SUR LA MURO,
There is a picture on the wall.

These scholars were exposed to the astounding variety of human behavioral and cultural differences and to the enormously popular Darwinian theory of evolution. Not surprisingly, they hypothesized that language and culture have also shown evolutionary development from the simple and concrete to the complex and abstract. They and their twentieth-century followers, such as Benjamin Lee Whorf (1956) and Edward Sapir (1949), accepted the corollary that if languages differ in terms of an evolutionary continuum, as might the cultures using them, then the thought processes of members of those cultures must also vary on a continuum. It later became clear that the languages of relatively "primitive" cultures were, in fact, in many cases more differentiated in grammar than those of "advanced" cultures, but the idea that language constrains thought has remained. Advocates of this view suggest that the child is born into a community that uses a relatively fixed language. The language of his community structures the view of reality to which the developing child is exposed, and as he becomes competent in that language, he adopts its inherent view of the world. Thus, the linguistic relativists conclude, the individual's view of reality—the concepts or mental

WOULD SOME OF THE PROBLEMS of the world be solved by having the same language used everywhere? Would brotherhood evolve from a common tongue? Perhaps this could be so. But even if a world language were created, could it be maintained?

Language is an organic entity in that it changes constantly. Words and expressions that are common during one age fall into disuse in the next. How could a unified international language persist in a single form? We would encounter difficulties in trying to understand the common expressions of even our own language of one hundred years ago. The following, for example, are found in the book of *Slang and Its Analogues, Past and Present,* Volume 3, which was published during that period and begins with "Flabbergast" and ends with "Hyps" (the blue devils). The dates are those when the terms were most recently in common usage. How many do you understand without referring to the equivalents that follow each term? For that matter, how many of the equivalents do you recognize? —These equivalents date from 1909.

Flash-tail: a prostitute (1868)
Flat fish: a dullard (1868)
Flimping: stealing (1857)
Frost: a complete failure (1885)
Gob stick: a silver tablespoon (1859)

Greens, to have, get, give one's: to enjoy, procure or confer the sexual favour (1835)
Grog blossom: a pimple caused by drinking to excess (1835)
Guy: an ill-dressed person, from Guy Fawkes (1858)
Hairy: difficult or splendid (1861)
Halfling: betwixt and between (1818) (Usually said of a boy or a girl just leaving childhood)
Handle: the nose (1887)
Hankin: trick of putting off bad work for good (1887)
Hansel: first money taken in the morning, hence lucky money (1821)
Hard-head: a man of good parts—physical, intellectual, or moral (1824)

Many of the words found in this dictionary of slang are still in use. Some have even passed into the most respectable speech. Others are so obscure that they seem nonsensical. Changes occur so rapidly that even within the past ten years a few words have become passé. What will our grandchildren think of our present language? Probably that it is funny, old-fashioned, or downright obscure.

Source: Adapted from J. Farmer and W. Henley, *Dictionary of Slang and Its Analogues, Past and Present.* (London: Harrison and Sons, 1893).

FROM HARD-HEADS TO HARD-HATS

categories that he or she uses in structuring it—can only be that view present in the person's native language.

One of the foremost proponents of this view was Benjamin Lee Whorf. Whorf (1956) compared the languages of different cultural groups and reported that there were vital differences in the conceptions of reality that each implied. He noted, for example, that Eskimos use several words for "snow," depending on whether it is falling or has fallen, what its moisture content is, and so forth; English speakers do not make such distinctions. The Navaho language does not differentiate time and motion in the same way that the English language does. It may be impossible to state many basic laws of physics in the language of the Navahos.

Two tentative conclusions emerged from Whorf's observations, the first more dramatic than the second. Essentially, it is possible that language is a mold into which the individual's thoughts are poured. Thus, speakers of English may be unable to see the many snows the Eskimos know and the Navahos may not be able to conceive of "the white man's" laws of physics. Secondly, it is possible that language does not determine as much as it gently nudges. Rather than locking the individual's thoughts in place, his or her experiences with language simply suggest certain paths of perception and thought—paths that can be altered in light of learning, or experience.

In one of the more systematic explorations of the Whorfian hypothesis, Roger Brown and Arnold Horowitz (1958) showed that Navahos and Harvard students made different groupings of colored chips given

Figure 3.11 Language has taken many forms, as illustrated on these two pages. Early examples are *(left)* Egyptian hieroglyphics; *(upper center)* Chinese writings; and *(upper right)* music notations. Specialized languages also exist, such as *(opposite, from left to right)* sign language used by the deaf; mime, demonstrated here by contemporary master Marcel Marceau; and computer language, represented here by a portion of the coded message "Now is the time for all good men to come to the aid of their party" punched into paper tape. Mass media—including *(far right)* television and publications made possible by the invention of movable type such as *(this page, lower right)* the Gutenberg Bible—have had profound social and political effects: More ideas and events now reach more people in shorter periods of time than ever before, and the speed of change as well as the content of public opinion are thereby affected.

different nonsense names. They did so in accordance with *phonemic* (sound) distinctions in their respective languages. Because vowel length is very important in the Navaho language, the Navaho subjects tended to distinguish between chips labeled "ma" (with a short *a*) and "ma" (with a long *a*). Since vowel length is not particularly significant in English, the Harvard students did not use this distinction in sorting the chips. It is possible, therefore, that a difference in language does affect behavior.

The difference between Navahos and Harvard students in the Brown and Horowitz experiment was not necessarily the result of some deep, unconscious process stamped in by linguistic experience and resistant to change in response to new contingencies. Brown and Horowitz interviewed their subjects after the experiment and asked the Harvard students whether or not they had heard the difference between the two pronunciations of "ma." The typical answer was, "Yes, of course. But I didn't think it made a difference." Although self-reports must always be treated with caution, there is reason to trust these reactions. People are often able to distinguish many aspects of an event that they tend to ignore until they have some reason for attending to those features. In other words, the sort of behavioral differences isolated by Brown and Horowitz may reflect habitual responses to certain linguistic features. If so, the basis of the differences lies in convenience and simplicity rather than in permanent cognitive structures imposed by linguistic differences.

Research suggests that behavioral differences may indeed stem from habitual rather than conceptual differences. For example, Eric Lenneberg

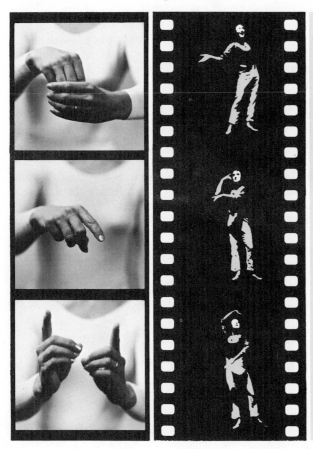

and J. M. Roberts (1958) showed that members of different cultural groups divide the color spectrum differently, as indexed by varying ranges of color-denoting words. Roger Brown and Eric Lenneberg (1954) went on to show that individuals within a culture are able to recall colors better and faster when those colors are associated with shorter and more widely used color names in that culture. Thus, semantic differences are associated with behavioral differences. However, these behavioral effects are far from unchangeable. Thus, skiers who spend much time around snow come to differentiate various sorts of snow, and those who must refer to unusual colors tend to shorten the labels in order to be able to recall and describe them more readily.

Approaching the problem in a slightly different way, John Carroll and Joseph Casagrande (1958) predicted that Navaho speakers would be more likely than English speakers to pay attention to the shape of objects they handle, because in Navaho one must alter the verb denoting the handling according to the shape of the object. Carroll and Casagrande reasoned, therefore, that if a Navaho speaker were given a blue stick and asked to pair it with either a yellow stick or a blue block, he would choose the yellow stick. In a test of this hypothesis they found that Navahos who spoke primarily in the Navaho language tended to sort on the basis of shape far more than did Navahos who relied primarily on English for communication. These results seemed to show influences of language habits on behavior, but a control group of English-speaking Boston children were found to attend to the shapes of things just as the Navaho-speaking Navahos had. In explanation, Carroll and Casagrande suggest that the American children may have been affected by practice with toys that emphasized form. Another possibility is that many non-Navahos "lose touch" with some sensations, or at least become less aware of them, as they become older. It follows from this explanation, however, that linguistic habits are *not sufficient* to create permanent differences in thinking or behavior between language groups. Thus, Whorf's more dramatic hypothesis seems untenable.

A third example may help to clarify this point. Roger Brown and Albert Gilman (1960) point out that many languages force the speaker to designate his relationship to the listener in an explicit way. In French and Spanish, for example, the speaker learns to address a listener in the second-person familiar form (*tu* in both languages) when speaking to family, friends, and those of lower status and to use the second-person formal form (*vous, usted*) in other relationships; furthermore, the speaker of French or Span-

Figure 3.12 Eskimos make finer discriminations between different types of snow than other groups do, and they have words to identify each of these types. This does not necessarily reflect underlying perceptual or cognitive differences shaped by language. A more plausible hypothesis is that the Eskimos' environment necessitates attention to these differences, which are of little consequence in most other parts of the world. The finer discriminations in identifying types of snow of which the Eskimos are capable may thus be habitual.

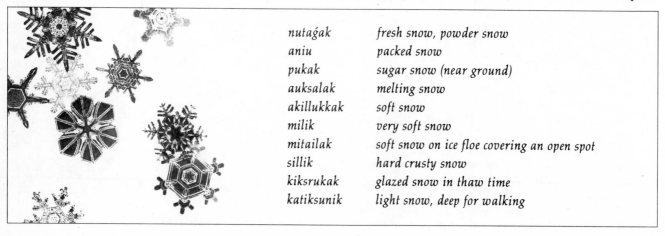

nutaġak	fresh snow, powder snow
aniu	packed snow
pukak	sugar snow (near ground)
auksalak	melting snow
akillukkak	soft snow
milik	very soft snow
mitailak	soft snow on ice floe covering an open spot
sillik	hard crusty snow
kiksrukak	glazed snow in thaw time
katiksunik	light snow, deep for walking

ish must make a similar choice in conjugating and uttering every verb referring to the actions of the listener. English-speakers need not make these explicit commitments. Are English-speakers therefore less likely to be sensitive to the formality of the relationships or to the relative status of those to whom they speak? One view of Whorf's hypothesis (buttressed by our democratic ideology or longings) might lead most of us to say that English-speakers, at least in the United States, are relatively less respectful of status and formality. However, speakers of English are probably just as sensitive to these factors but simply communicate the information in less obvious (and perhaps less frequent) ways. For example, our posture, physical distance, facial expression, and eye contact in a relationship often convey similar messages as do the distinctions between the singular and plural forms of French and Spanish pronouns and verbs. And speakers of English often find themselves forced to decide whether to use first names or last names when addressing people or whether to use their listeners' titles (Brown and Ford, 1961)—and recently, whether to address a particular woman as Mrs., Miss, or Ms.

In sum, evidence does suggest that a weaker form of the Whorfian hypothesis has some validity. Language does encourage certain ways of looking at and understanding the world. However, the effects of language do not seem permanent or unchangeable; on the contrary, at least some of its effects seem easily modified. In this light, cross-cultural understanding seems well within the realm of possibility.

Connotative Meanings Across Cultures

One other approach to the study of psychological differences related to language and culture differences is worth discussion. Starting in the early 1950s, Charles Osgood, Percy Tannenbaum, and George Suci (1957) developed an extremely useful research tool, the *semantic differential,* based on individual responses to words and other concepts along various descriptive scales. For example, subjects would be asked to rate the concept "freedom" or "democracy" on such dimensions as "pleasant-unpleasant" and "soft-hard." The researchers then analyzed whether various dimensions were used in a manner similar to one another (as, perhaps, "pleasant-unpleasant" and "beautiful-ugly"—most things judged pleasant are also judged more beautiful than ugly) or in an essentially unrelated manner (as, perhaps, "pleasant-unpleasant" and "soft-hard"—some pleasant things are soft, and some are hard). Osgood and his colleagues thus determined underlying dimensions along which concepts were judged. These dimensions, they felt, were used to express the connotative meaning of concepts.

One interesting result of the initial research of Osgood and his colleagues was the finding that speakers of English tend to judge heterogeneous sets of concepts along a very small number of dimensions: Ratings of a concept's "goodness," "strength," and "activity" seem to account for most of the variations in ratings of different concepts. These dimensions seem little related to anything specific about English and the ways in which concepts are labeled in English. But are these dimensions culturally universal? Or is there some subtle aspect of language that predisposes its users to respond to concepts in culturally specific ways? Might members of another language group respond along different underlying dimensions?

In order to test the cross-cultural generality of the dimensions of connotative meaning found in English, Osgood and his colleagues undertook a broad-scale investigation of connotative meaning in nearly two dozen other cultures. They chose groups speaking languages as different from one another in origin and development as possible. They included groups living in virtually the same culture but speaking different languages as well as groups living in different cultural settings but speaking the same language. In order to ensure the cultural fairness of the set of concepts being studied (surely an Afghan cannot have the sort of response to "astronaut" or "traffic jam" as does a resident of the United States), they began with a list of words judged to be of standard importance in known cultures. They developed rating scales by securing word associations to each of the standard concepts *within* each culture and choosing those adjectives that seemed most common within the given group, thus further avoiding the pitfalls of judging whether or not translations of measuring instruments are accurate and culturally fair. This research was the most extensive and carefully designed cross-cultural survey undertaken up to that date. Osgood and his colleagues also took great pains to secure data that would refute their hypothesis of cross-cultural uniformity, if indeed it was unfounded.

These semantic-differential studies, then, were aimed at determining whether language differences are reflected in people's use of judgmental dimensions. If Whorf's hypothesis were correct in asserting that language differences determine or reflect differences in underlying views of the world, then this should be reflected in differences in the underlying dimensions along which concepts are judged by users of different languages. In other words, the strong-weak dimension might be central in judging a particular concept in one language, whereas the hot-cold dimension might be more relevant in evaluating the same concept in another language.

Charles Osgood, Yasumasa Tamaka, and Tadasu Oyama (1963) found great differences across human groups in the ways in which *particular concepts* are judged; for example, Americans might judge "progress" very good, and another group might judge it very bad. However, they found that the basic *underlying dimensions* of judgment are universal. There is no evidence in their research with heterogeneous concepts, or in their continuing research with verb structure (Osgood, 1970), or in studies by other researchers of communication via facial expressions (Cuceloglu, 1967) that language differences make an important psychological difference in judgmental behavior.

In the light of these findings, the chances for effective cross-cultural communication seem high. If all people share certain ways of evaluating reality, then major obstacles to understanding need not be overcome. The United States might not have dropped the atomic bomb had greater efforts been made by Americans to comprehend another people's communication.

Black Dialect

So far, this chapter has focused on the possibility that linguistic differences are associated with differences in other psychological processes. The major question is whether or not linguistic differences lead to those other psychological differences. No compelling evidence of this possibility has yet been found, as already discussed. An alternative possibility is that linguistic performance is a direct indication of innate cognitive skills. That is, it may not be that language locks in our thought processes, but our thoughts may have a direct impact on our language performance. This hypothesis has been looked at most closely in societies with subcultures that show differences in their use of language. Those differences in language performance may or may not have practical importance; may or may not be related to cognitive differences; and may or may not arise as a result of environmental or of genetic factors.

The practical importance of differences in linguistic performance is readily evident in the problems of primary education for black children. As noted earlier, some people explain away the school system's failings with many black pupils from deprived environments as failings of the children themselves or of black culture generally. They consider the alleged deficiencies of Black English as prima facie evidence of the cognitive inferiority of black people, and they ask how blacks could possibly be expected to succeed in intellectual endeavors with such limited ways of expressing themselves. There are several difficulties with an argument of this sort.

First, note the erroneous logic of this argument: Because (1) black children do not do as well in school and (2) their language is different, therefore (3) their language must be inferior. The proposition that "different" is "inferior" is clearly ethnocentric, and it is without basis in fact. There is simply no reason to believe that Black English (or *any* language or dialect) is inherently inferior or superior to any other for logical or social communication. In extensive and penetrating critiques of this issue, William Labov (1970) presents detailed analyses of the linguistic and logical processes of speakers of nonstandard dialects of English. In one of these studies of adolescent black males, the interviewer talked with the subjects and recorded these conversations in the streets of Harlem, rather than in the perhaps forbidding and demeaning office of a white man. Labov asked each subject to repeat after him the sentence: "I asked Alvin if he knows how to play basketball." One subject replied, "I ax Alvin do he know how to play basketball." A second said, "I ax Alvin if—do he know how to play basketball." The argument for inferiority of black children rests on such

Figure 3.13 The language spoken by contemporary blacks, far from being an inferior medium of communication, has been found to have complex and consistent grammatical and syntactic rules and to differ from Standard English only in particular surface details. The main pronunciation differences between Black English and Standard English are given here (*left*), as are those features of Black English grammar that are the most distinguishable from Standard English (*below*).

The spelled "r" in the middle and at the end of words is not pronounced.

guard = god	four = foe
sore = saw	Paris = Pass
Carol = Caal	

The "l" is usually not pronounced, especially after vowels.

toll = toe	all = awe
help = hep	fault = fought

Consonant clusters at the end of words are simplified. The clusters most commonly involved in this simplification are those that end in "t" or "d," and "s" or "z."

past = pass	hold = hole
test = tess	meant = mend = men

Final consonants are dropped.

boot = boo	seat = seed = see
road = row	

The copula (linking words, such as "to be") is not required.
   He gone.
   She over there.
   He a bad boy.

Possession does not require the use of the possessive marker.
   The lady hat.
   Sam cousin.
   The man car.

Number agreement of subject and verb is not required.
   Mr. Gibson have a dog.
   He do?
   I goes away.

Plurals are indicated differently.
   I got five marble.
   The mens.
   The childrens.

The "double negative" is acceptable.
   I don't got no bread.
   Didn't he want nothing?

The verb "be" may be used as a time-extension indicator.
   He busy. (standard English: He is busy right now.)
   He be busy. (standard English: He is always busy.)

data as their use of the nonstandard "he know" in place of "he knows" and their nonstandard pronunciation of "ask." As Labov points out, however, these are all surface differences. The basic content and structure of the utterances clearly have been processed and communicated in a manner apparently identical to the equivalent features of the standard dialect.

A second weakness in the argument that black failings in the classroom reflect racial inferiorities is that the data on black achievement in the school system and in standard test situations are not clear-cut. Tests of intelligence and achievement are often culture-bound, and the social milieu in which blacks are tested—indeed, the social milieu of schools generally—often seems to interfere with the capabilities of black test takers. Consider one example, reported by James Ledvinka in 1971. He studied job interviews of blacks applying to the state employment service in a large Midwestern city. Each applicant was randomly assigned to either a white or a black registration interviewer and then to a counselor of the other race. With either order of interviewers (white-black or black-white), the applicants showed more richness in their language, more creative use of words, and longer sentences when interviewed by another black than by a white.

As you may recognize from your own experience, your speech patterns are likely to be imaginative and rich when you are in a comfortable situation. It is reasonable to assume that when a person's language or dialect is different from the one that authorities use, that person's use of language is even more sensitive to social contexts than if the individual feels linguistically "at home." This sensitivity to social contexts is bound to be even more evident when strain exists between members of a person's own group and the group in social control.

For numerous reasons having to do with social history and with the history of dialects, black people in the United States share dialects that differ somewhat from the dialects used by most whites, called Standard English. It contains forms, for example, that seem to stem from the African

Figure 3.14 Although black jive talk may be a handicap in a predominantly white, middle-class school system, it is neither necessarily simplified nor restricted. In fact, it is a mark of distinction in many black subcultures.

"Now I'm goin tell you how the jive really started. I'm going to tell you how the club got this big. 'Bout 1956 there used to be a time when the Jackson Park show was open and the Stony show was open. Sixty-six street, Jeff, Gene, all of 'em, little bitty dudes, little bitty... Gene wasn't with 'em then. Gene was cribbin (living) over here.

Sixty-six (the gang on sixty-sixth street), they wouldn't allow us in the Jackson Park show. That was when the parky was headin it. Everybody say, If we want to go to the show, we go! One day, who was it? Carl Robinson. He went up to the show... and Jeff fired on him. He came back and all this was swelled up 'bout yay big, you know. He come back over to the hood (neighborhood). He told and them dudes went up there....

They went on up there, John, Roy and Skeeter went in there. And they start humbuggin (fighting) in there. That's how it all started. Sixty-six found out they couldn't beat us, at that time. They couldn't whup seven-o. Am I right Leroy? You was cribbin over here then. Am I right? We were dynamite! Used to be a time, you ain't have a passport, Man, you couldn't walk through here. And if didn't nobody know you it was worse than that...."

languages spoken by their ancestors. Superficial variations in the use of language have to do with group identity, language models, and so on, and they accord well with the idea that the poor school performances of black children do not reflect underlying differences in intellectual abilities or competence. Social reality, in other words, complicates the study of differences in dialects. There is a strong possibility that none of the performance differences in language that have been isolated by students of ethnic and social-class differences actually reflect differences in intellectual abilities or competence.

In a British version of the attempt to account for social-group differences in school performance on the basis of language-related intellectual differences, Basil Bernstein suggested in 1970 that the development of verbal behavior is greatly affected by social-class membership. (In Britain the most marked social division is not racial, as it is in the United States, but social-class.) He found that working-class parents, in contrast to middle-class parents—in Britain, at least—tend to socialize their children to attend to social role and position rather than to personal differences and feelings and tend to emphasize commands and universalistic rules. Bernstein goes on to say that working-class children develop a *restricted* language suitable for the communication of egocentric, directive, and affective information in close relations, but middle-class children develop an *elaborated* language that is suited for expressing alternate realities in nonegocentric, informative, and differentiated communication. Bernstein also says that middle-class children are able to use either the elaborated or the restricted code, whereas working-class children cannot.

As yet there is little support for Bernstein's hypothesis. The problem is that it founders on the same shoals as do those hypotheses discussed with respect to Black English. There *are* class differences in the ways in which mothers talk to their children and answer their questions, as Robert Hess and Virginia Shipman (1965) and W. P. Robinson and Susan Rackstraw (1967) have shown. As was noted in the earlier discussion of language acquisition, these environmental differences in social interaction may affect the speed of development from stage to stage (from an egocentric to a more mature view of the world, for example), and they may well affect moral development, as Lawrence Kohlberg (1971) proposes. At least one study has shown, however, that working-class children can use what Bernstein called the elaborated code when called upon to do so (Robinson, 1965), much as the elaboration of Black English is context-sensitive.

All human languages seem to share certain basic features and to be acquired everywhere through the same basic processes. Apparently, some conceptual and linguistic features are universal enough that real communication between members of even the most diverse human cultures is possible. The studies of Black English and of the dialects used by working-class Britons show that language performance relies on more than training and innate capabilities; an individual's abilities at self-expression can rise and fall from situation to situation, depending largely on how comfortable that speaker feels with his or her audience. However, history, everyday experience, and mythology all offer numerous examples of misunderstandings among members of various groups. The focus of this volume will return in Unit III to some of the situational factors that can influence an individual's success in communicating. First, however, the discussion will turn to personality differences that may well account for many misunderstandings. As suggested earlier, human thought processes are probably shaped to some

Figure 3.15 This plaque, affixed to the side of a Pioneer spacecraft bound for outer space, locates the creators of the plaque in time and space for the benefit of unknown beings who may someday find the craft. The row of circles (*bottom*) represents the sun and planets in our solar system, with the Pioneer trajectory starting from the circle that represents earth; the radial design (*center left*) indicates in binary language the relative position of the solar system within the galaxy at the time the spacecraft was launched; and the other symbols can be used to calculate the height in centimeters of the female figure (*right*). If the plaque is ever found, it could take many thousands of earth-years for a reply to reach earth, unless beings find the plaque who are capable of compressing space, which would eliminate the need to travel through space. The chances are slim that another being capable of deciphering this message will be at the right place at the right time to receive it and that beings capable of deciphering a reply will reside on earth when a response arrives. But the fact that people made this effort testifies to the strength of their motivation to communicate.

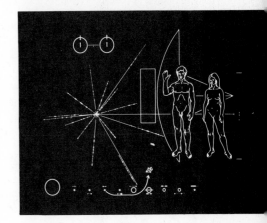

extent by language. But people in turn shape language to suit their individual purposes. Thus, even individuals who share similar cultural and linguistic experiences may differ dramatically in their perceptions, values, intentions, and expressive styles.

SUMMARY

All living animals have methods of communicating. It has long been thought, however, that only we human beings can use abstract language to communicate. Two chimpanzees, Sarah and Washoe, have inadvertently fueled challenges to this theory by learning to use symbols to communicate with human beings; it also appears that they are able to manipulate word order, another skill previously considered the exclusive province of human beings. One of our most cherished assumptions—human supremacy in the capacity to creatively restructure information in a linguistic form—may yet be shattered by the accomplishments of chimpanzees.

Some researchers who have tried to define language in systematic ways follow the *design-features approach,* which concentrates on the basic design features of a language system. A central feature of human language seems to be openness, or the number and variety of possible elements that can elaborate a basic communication.

The *functional approach* analyzes the usefulness of various kinds of communication—both verbal and nonverbal—in a variety of situations. Users of this approach note that messages can be transmitted through a variety of *channels,* and the medium through which a message is sent often affects the meaning of the message. But a nonverbal message can have a variety of meanings; for example, eye contact can display either love or threat. Facial expressions are often important in the expression of emotions. The fact that people in so many cultures use many of the same facial expressions in conveying the same meanings implies that nonverbal expressions of basic emotions may in part result from biological factors.

Often messages conflict; in these *double-bind* messages, verbal content does not match nonverbal or other verbal content.

The acquisition of language is an important area of investigation, because language is central to human communication. Learning theory explains language acquisition as a selective-reinforcement process that encourages the child to gradually approximate adult language. Learning theorists also believe that words are learned in the context of other words, through *generalizations* of grammatical rules, which makes future uses of language dependent on what has been learned before.

However, these principles cannot explain the ability of humans to *generate* new language combinations and innovations. Biological capacities and normal maturation also play a role. The structural similarities of languages throughout the world indicate a genetic basis. Jean Piaget has found that the sequence of intellectual development sets the stage for the acquisition of language.

But the development of language is not entirely an automatic unfolding of innate capabilities; environmental factors and social interaction also play important roles. For example, although children seem to learn better from communications that are only somewhat more complex than their own, adults can influence the language development of the child by controlling the complexity and novelty of their communications.

Some theorists feel that thought processes are influenced by cultural language patterns. To promote the sharing of perceptions between cultures, several attempts have been made to develop a common language for the world's people. In explaining the development of various cultural outlooks, Benjamin Whorf hypothesized that each language structures differently the view of reality developed by the children who learn that particular language. Research indicates, however, that although language encourages certain viewpoints in a cultural group, these viewpoints are neither permanent nor unchangeable.

A variety of cultural groups seem to have evolved similar basic modes of evaluating diverse experiences. For example, dimensions of goodness, activity, and strength seem to be universal, but particular concepts are apparently judged differently in different cultures.

Black dialect, like many other dialects, is often belittled by those who speak the standard dialect. Black English is actually structured like Standard English; therefore, those who belittle the conceptual abilities of blacks on the basis of language differences have little evidence to back them up. The language "disabilities" that blacks sometimes exhibit are likely to reflect the psychological discomfort blacks feel in situations biased against them. Although our thought processes may be influenced by the languages we speak, they also influence the ways that we use language.

SUGGESTED READINGS

Brown, Roger. *Psycholinguistics.* New York: Free Press, 1970.

Chomsky, Noam. *Language and Mind.* New York: Harcourt Brace Jovanovich, 1968.

Ekman, Paul, Wallace V. Friesen, and Phoebe Ellsworth. *Emotion in the Human Face: Guidelines for Research and an Integration of Findings.* New York: Pergamon Press, 1972.

Furth, Hans. *Thinking Without Language.* New York: Free Press, 1966.

Lenneberg, Eric. *The Biological Foundations of Language.* New York: Wiley, 1967.

Premack, David. "A Functional Analysis of Language," *Journal of the Experimental Analysis of Behavior,* 14 (1970), 107–125.

Vygotsky, Lev. *Thought and Language.* Cambridge, Mass.: MIT Press, 1962.

Whorf, Benjamin. *Language, Thought, and Reality.* New York: Wiley, 1956.

4

Personalities:
Pegs, Round &
Square

IMAGINE THAT YOU ARE ATTENDING a political rally, and the major speech is being given by a woman who speaks with clarity and authority. According to many principles developed by social psychologists, the audience should be much swayed. But the word "people," when considered a little more carefully, implies no limits—all of us are included—and it takes no account of differences among us. Three people attending the rally might have the following reactions:

> ROBIN: "What a fantastic speech! She sure tells it like it is. They can count on my vote, and if there's a mass demonstration, I'll be there."

> TERRY: "This really stinks. They just knew she'd be a crowd-pleaser. People aren't really listening to what she's saying; they're just looking at how beautiful she is. She's being used, and I bet she doesn't even know it. I can't wait to get out of this place."

> MARTY: "I really wish I could be like that. She's really beautiful—so cool, standing up there in front of this mob. I've got to try to have more self-confidence, let people know what I think. I bet I could really . . . ."

As you can see, at the level of individuals, statements about "people" seem very misleading. In this case, Robin is reacting as "people" in general may be predicted to react. Terry, however, is reacting in just the opposite way, and Marty's mind is not really on politics at all. Many of the important processes shaping these reactions are discussed in Chapter 2. However, in developing general principles of social behavior it is important to realize that many people will not fit those general principles. Individuals differ, and the present chapter is concerned with these differences.

The psychological study of personality differences involves taking *systematic* account of the ways that people differ in their responses to events.

For example, if a researcher's goal was to understand how children respond to one another in a nursery-school environment, it would be important to discover in exactly which respects the children differ. What are the important dimensions on which their behavior varies? Thus, the researcher seeks efficient ways of summarizing and describing the varied forms of behavior that occur. In the nursery-school situation, for example, it might be useful to describe children as differing in the traits of "aggressiveness" and "friendliness." A major goal is to evolve a description of behavioral differences in terms of differences along a relatively small set of trait dimensions that can be measured in some way. When pursued in depth, a study of this nature also explores the background behind these differences. Someone trying to understand cooperation among nursery-school children should first find out the ways in which the children differ in cooperation and then study factors that may cause them to be cooperative or uncooperative. Differences in self-esteem, for example, might be relevant. Perhaps those who view themselves most positively are the most cooperative. If the investigator could measure differences in self-esteem, and if these differences proved to be good predictors of tendencies to cooperate, the investigator would have taken a significant step toward understanding cooperative behavior in nursery-school children. The researcher might then explore further the types of home environment or neighborhoods or peer groups that contributed to the different levels of self-esteem.

The present chapter first explores the problem of assessing individual dispositions. (For example, how can it be established that someone is high in a trait such as self-esteem? What measures should be used?) Then the chapter considers three different trait measures and how they developed; this discussion focuses on the measuring of differences in feelings of personal control, differences in the need for approval from others, and differences in self-esteem. Then the chapter considers some of the shortcomings and failings of contemporary work on individual differences. A critique of this sort suggests possible improvements in the orientation of the work on individual differences, which is the topic of the chapter's final discussion.

THE STUDY OF INDIVIDUAL DIFFERENCES

A psychologist studying individual differences in a particular area of behavior often starts out with a hunch about some kind of fairly stable dimension of behavior on which people differ. Psychologists usually refer to a fairly stable tendency along a behavioral dimension as a *trait* or as a disposition. Psychologists posit traits in the hope that they will be good predictors of behavior—convenient tools for relating stimuli to the responses that typically follow.

A trait or a disposition can be defined as a tendency to respond to a given class of stimuli in a particular way. Psychologists often make a distinction between traits and motives, usually reserving the term motivation for goal-directed behavior. However, because goal-directed behavior may involve certain specified reactions to a class of stimuli, motives can be considered as a specialized class of traits. For this reason, in this chapter the terms motive, motivation, trait, and trait dimension will be used rather interchangeably.

Suppose that a psychologist suspects that college students differ in their academic success partly because they vary in the strength of their motivation to achieve. By assuming differences along this *trait dimension*—

the motivation to achieve—the psychologist implies that people with similar motivational strengths in this respect are similar in their achievement behavior and that people of different motivational strengths are different in their achievement behavior. Thus, the investigator would expect people possessing a high level of the trait to behave consistently in particular ways (such as always reading assigned material), whereas people possessing a low level would behave in ways that are consistently different from those who are highly motivated to achieve (such as never doing any of the assigned reading).

What supplies the psychologist with the initial hunch about the trait dimensions that are important in a social situation? Psychological theories frequently provide clues. For example, one of the traits discussed in this chapter—feelings of personal control—was derived from a social-learning theory formulated by Julian Rotter (1954). But more often, the assistance provided by another theory or past research is less formal. Sometimes intuitions about important traits flow from informal observation.

Many ideas about the ways in which particular traits operate just do not succeed. Before a trait gains scientific importance, researchers must demonstrate that people do, in fact, differ along the dimension and that knowing people's positions on the dimension aids in predicting their behavior. It would be helpful, then, to understand some of the methods that researchers use in trying to establish these facts.

Personality Assessment

After a researcher has formulated a trait, the next step is to attempt to measure the trait by singling out one or more *behavioral indicators* of the trait that are stable over time and across situations. Suppose you are interested in differences in people's tendencies to affiliate—to form personal relationships. You want to know who may be predicted to become

Figure 4.1 Unlike the twins shown here, from whom the name "Siamese twins" is derived, most individuals have unique genetic and environmental histories, which produce the wide variety of reactions and behavioral patterns that we observe in those around us. These Siamese twins not only shared identical sets of genes but, because they were joined from birth, had identical environments. They both married and had nineteen normal children between them. It would be interesting to know to what extent they differed on the various personality dimensions that are discussed in this chapter.

highly social and who may be predicted to become isolated. You would first specify a particular behavior (or a group of them) that you believe may indicate a desire to affiliate. Perhaps you would conclude that the frequency with which people smile in social situations is a good indicator of how strongly they want to affiliate with others. Next, you must demonstrate that a person's smiling frequency is fairly stable when measured at different points in time and in different situations. If frequency of smiling *is* stable, then smiling has high *reliability.* But if a person's tendency to smile changes from moment to moment—so that sometimes he or she is a smiler and sometimes a frowner—smiling behavior would not be reliable—that is, it is not a stable, predictable characteristic.

Even if frequency of smiling turned out to be a reliable characteristic, you would still have to show that it is a good indicator of the tendency to affiliate. After all, you could be wrong in your intuition that smiling has a positive relationship to affiliation—that, in other words, this tendency really is an *index* of the trait you are interested in. How well an index measures the trait it is supposed to measure is called the *validity* of the index. How would you establish the validity of smiling as an index of the tendency to affiliate? You might link differences in the frequency of smiling to differences in other behaviors, or indices, that psychologists also think are affected by the tendency to affiliate. Thus, the smiling index might be compared with the number of friendships a person has, the number of people he talks to during a day, the frequency with which he says "hello," the number of people he approaches at a party, and so on. Positive correlations between the smiling index and these other affiliative behaviors would give you confidence that the smiling index is, in fact, a valid indicator of the affiliative tendency.

One problem that investigators encounter is that most behavior is influenced by many factors. Smiling frequency, for example, is probably a function of more than just the affiliative tendency. One's mood, the nature of the social situation (a party versus a classroom, for example), social roles (in most cultures, women may tend to smile more than men), or something else (such as whether the person thinks he has ugly teeth) may also influence smiling. If the tendency to affiliate accounts for only a small part of the tendency to smile, smiling would not be a useful index of the trait. Yet multiply determined behaviors are the rule rather than the exception. Thus, how can you be sure that your measure is tapping, in this case, primarily affiliative tendencies and that the other factors are minor?

One way that psychologists deal with this problem is to use not a single response, such as smiling, but rather a *set* of relevant behaviors as indices of

Figure 4.2 We cannot directly observe a trait; we can only infer its existence from behavior. But can we validly make such an inference on the basis of any one type of behavior? Smiling may be related to affiliative needs, but like any behavior, smiling is multiply determined. The expressions of each of these individuals may have been influenced by different circumstances. To minimize potential errors, psychologists do not make inferences about traits unless a variety of an individual's behaviors point to the existence of that trait.

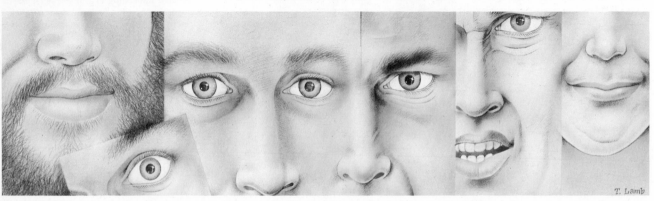

a trait. They assume that each of these behaviors is at least somewhat influenced by the trait in question, although each is also influenced by a variety of other factors that are irrelevant to the trait being studied. The fact that these other factors generally differ across the set of behaviors makes it useful to study the whole set of traits because they then tend to cancel one another out. By becoming a set of behaviors rather than a single behavior, the index has become a better indicator of the trait. For example, if you not only assessed a woman's tendency to smile but also charted the number of clubs to which she belonged and the amount of time she spent alone each day, you would probably have a better indicator of her affiliative tendencies than if you considered smiling alone. Many of the additional factors influencing smiling—sex role, attractiveness of teeth, and so on—would not have much influence on these other behaviors. Additional factors that influenced them would not interfere with smiling. Looking at a combination of the three behaviors thus provides a much better index of affiliation than looking at any one alone.

Most commonly, the set of behaviors that psychologists use to gauge a personality trait consists of a set of answers to a questionnaire made up of statements with which the person is asked to agree or disagree. The subject's response to each statement is taken to reflect the degree to which he or she possesses the trait under investigation. Responses are summed across the various statements.

For example, Irving Janis and Peter Field (1959) developed a scale to measure aggressiveness. The scale was composed of ten items, including the following:

How often do you lose your temper?

Do you ever feel mean and full of hatred toward other people?

Do you find that you often have to tell people to mind their own business?(page 304)

The respondent answered each question on a five-point scale, ranging from "not at all" (scored 1) to "very often" (scored 5). The aggressiveness score was obtained by summing the numerical ratings for all ten items.

It is not legitimate, however, just to write a set of statements and to assume that they all measure the same thing. The set of statements must also be *internally consistent:* responses to one must be correlated with responses to the others. There are statistical procedures, referred to by the general name of *item analysis,* that allow the researcher to examine the internal consistency of the set of statements and thereby to determine whether or not it is appropriate to sum across the statements. One way of establishing the internal consistency of a test by using item analysis is to correlate subjects' responses to each statement with their cumulated responses to all statements in the set (that is, with their "total score"). For example, in the case of the aggressiveness scale, the individual's score on the item "How often do you lose your temper" should be correlated with the summed scores for the entire set of items. The person who frequently loses his or her temper should generally show high scores on the other items, if the scale is internally consistent. Statements eliciting responses that are inconsistent with the total score must be eliminated. This same technique is also used in developing attitude scales (see Chapter 8).

Not all trait measures are assessed by agree-or-disagree answers to verbal statements. For example, in a technique that goes under the general title of Thematic Apperception Test (TAT), the subject is presented with a number of pictures, usually of people involved in somewhat ambiguous situations, and is asked to write a story about each. These descriptions are then scored (by "content analysis") to determine the extent to which they include certain themes or reflect needs or desires thought to represent the personality trait in question. Other investigators have used sentence-completion tests in which subjects are given beginning phrases and asked to invent endings for the sentences. The themes that appear in their "spontaneously" created endings are used to assess personality traits.

The Underside of Personality Assessment. A major problem with studying personality through personality-assessment tests is that any number of variables other than the personality trait in question can be systematically related to a person's responses. For example, people whose responses to a self-esteem scale indicate high self-esteem may be those who are rather concerned with responding in a socially acceptable way. If a person's score on the self-esteem scale is used as a predictor of a certain response tendency, such as the tendency to be persuaded, the relationship might have occurred because the items on the self-esteem scale call into play the person's desire to respond in a socially desirable way, rather than feelings of self-esteem. Or, if intelligence turns out to be correlated with self-esteem, intelligence could account for some of the response tendencies mistakenly attributed to self-esteem. Because a response to *any* personality test is probably correlated with other personality variables—such as a desire

Figure 4.3 An ambiguous picture similar to one used in the Thematic Apperception Test and stories written in response to it by two men. The author of the first story seems bound by conventional standards and tends to ignore or deny his unacceptable desires by projecting them onto others. He seems unable to admit his own weakness and seems to rigidly defend himself against revealing any feelings of inadequacy. Such reactions are characteristic of an individual disposition labeled by psychologists as an authoritarian personality. In contrast, the second story does not reflect authoritarian tendencies. The author appears to try to understand his own behavior and to be sensitive to others' thoughts and feelings.

Oh, oh! This is apt to be rather sordid. It doesn't represent a family scene to me! It may be a prostitute, and I see the old bottle there. This may be a young American down in the tropics; he is dressed in white because of the temperature. As for the woman, it's difficult to say because of the shadows, but she appears of darker skin. The place has crude furnishings. (What preceded?) The natural assumption is that they had sexual intercourse. The fellow is about half drunk and is about to consume more. The fellow looks kind of "hang-dog"; perhaps he regrets his recent act or perhaps his station in life. He is down and out and liquor isn't much of a boon to him. He has sufficient depth of character to take himself out of a place like that and to genuinely regret what he did to the woman. She doesn't enter into the story, except to be the object of his lust. He is a better type than she. He can take care of himself. He finally drags himself out of such surroundings and gradually amounts to something. Do I take too long? I get quite involved in these stories.

This is a young fellow who drinks a lot. His clothes are all messed up. In a dingy hotel room, he feels he has lost all of his friends. He thinks all of the troubles of the world are on his shoulders. He contemplates suicide. The trouble is with a woman he had an affair with. He doesn't know whether to injure her or destroy himself. To kill her or commit suicide. She isn't much good herself, and he isn't too much better. He is in a mixed up mental state. He is pausing there to make some decision. He will try to get revenge on the woman. (Revenge for what?) He has been going with her and giving her money and thinks of marrying her. She fools him and is unfaithful, going around with other men. He kills her.

to get a course credit, a job, or a scholarship or a wish to appear socially desirable—one can never be entirely sure that a particular trait, rather than some other variable, is causing the behavior in question.

Experimental Manipulation of Traits

There is another important way to study the effects of individual differences—one that permits a clear causal inference in a particular situation. This approach consists not of studying the differences that already exist between people but of trying to use experimental means to alter a particular disposition on a temporary basis. Psychologists create situations designed to elicit behavior typical of persons having varying levels of a particular trait. The logic of this procedure is that the proper situation will temporarily bring on a psychological state typical of one who is generally high (or low) in the trait in question. A researcher studying self-esteem, for example, could present some of the subjects with information that gives them a feeling of high self-esteem: they might be told that tests show them to be mature, creative, and highly intelligent. Subjects receiving treatment to induce low self-esteem, on the other hand, would receive unfavorable information characterizing them as immature, not very creative, and not particularly intelligent. (Experimenters tell subjects that the information was false after such experiments.) By loading the information subjects receive, then, the experimenter can determine the effects of these artificially established levels of self-esteem. Thus, if the researcher is interested in the effect of self-esteem on the ease with which people are persuaded, the self-esteem manipulation would be followed by an attempt at persuasion.

This situational approach to personality study has attractive features. In particular, investigators can make inferences about "what-causes-what" with some confidence. The differences in behavior that occur in the two experimental conditions (high self-esteem and low self-esteem) are very likely caused by the differences that the experimenter created in the two situations, not by some other factor. Thus, a difference in persuasibility between the two groups is caused by the prior difference in information by which the researcher established either high or low self-esteem. This conclusion follows if this inequality of information was, in fact, the only respect in which the two groups of subjects received systematically different treatment. The advantage in making clear causal inferences, therefore, makes the experimental-manipulation approach strong in precisely the respect that the personality-assessment approach is weak.

Skeletons in the Experimental Closet. Experimental manipulation, even though it has the advantage of tracing cause and effect, also has a major disadvantage. This disadvantage stems from the fact that psychologists studying personality are primarily concerned with stable dispositions, and the nature of these dispositions may not be reflected in the character and dynamics of temporary states.

Although the differences that exist between people can be simulated in experimental manipulations, a manipulation nevertheless produces a simulation—an attempt to set up a state that is like the "real thing." There always remains the question: How adequate is this particular simulation? The experimental manipulation may create temporary states that are not fully comparable to the "chronic" levels of the trait. For example, does the favorable information designed to give subjects high self-esteem really make them respond just like someone with chronically high self-esteem?

This question is not easily answered. However, the investigator's position is much improved if he or she can conduct subsequent research with subjects who have been classified as having high or low self-esteem on the basis of their prior responses to a personality test. Very similar findings in the two types of studies would lend confidence to the assumption that the experimental manipulation had established a state close to that typical of people with chronically high self-esteem. Investigators thereafter could be reasonably confident that a temporary state of self-esteem, even one established through experimental manipulations, is comparable to a more chronic state of self-esteem. Findings that differed for chronic and temporary states would be more ambiguous and might reflect essential differences in these two types of states, defects in the experimental manipulation, or defects in the personality test.

THE EFFECTS OF PERSONALITY

The major methods of personality research have been generally described, and three important trait dimensions will now be considered. These dimensions, which are especially challenging for psychologists who are interested in understanding social relations, are internal versus external control, the need for social approval, and self-esteem.

Internal Versus External Control

Picture yourself getting into an argument with one of your best friends. It is a very hot day, you are in the school cafeteria among friends, and the food is as lousy as usual. The argument mounts in intensity, and you begin to make angry statements. Finally you refuse to speak with your friend any further. Later you meet and begin to talk it over. Whose fault was it that the argument became so heated and abusive? You might feel that it was your fault. You generally know what you are doing; your friend was acting unfairly, and to teach him a lesson you decided to let him have it. The events were largely under your control. Or perhaps you do not see the situation that way at all. Perhaps you feel like a victim of circumstances. After all, it was a hot day, the food was terrible, and there were all those people looking on. How could you help it? The circumstances were beyond your personal control.

Psychologists have been particularly interested in these two different ways of understanding the world. There seems to be a systematic difference in people's interpretations of the events they participate in: Some people generally attribute events to their own actions, whereas others are inclined to see events as beyond their control. Research indicates that this difference in interpretations is singularly important in understanding how people manage in the social world.

Psychologists generally refer to this trait dimension as *internal-external control* or *locus of control,* following the terminology of Julian Rotter. (In this chapter, the term "locus of control" will be used.) In 1943, Rotter hypothesized that the likelihood of a person's engaging in a given act is a function of two variables: (1) the person's *expectancy* that his or her behavior will bring the rewards available in the situation and (2) the personal *value* of these rewards for the individual.

Rotter's theory is one of a general class of psychological theories that go under the label *expectancy-value* theories. These theories of human behavior are used to predict people's actions on the basis of certain thoughts and feelings relevant to those actions. For example, if the behavior in question involves reading the material assigned by one's history professor, the expectancy-value theorist would need to know what rewards were available—whether completion of the assignment would bring the student a good grade, a gain in useful knowledge, personal growth, or whatever. Then the investigator could predict the likelihood that the student would actually do the reading, based on knowledge of (1) the student's beliefs about whether or not doing the reading would lead to these goals and (2) the value to the student of the goals involved.

The locus-of-control dimension represents the "expectancy" part of Rotter's theory—the relationship between the behavior and its outcomes. The dimension is treated as a personality trait by specifying this expectancy link in a generalized way rather than for a particular situation. Accordingly, locus of control represents the extent to which, in a variety of situations, individuals believe that they have personal control over what happens to them—that control is located within them rather than outside. The more internally oriented people are, the more they believe that events occur as a consequence of their personal actions and are under their personal control; the more externally oriented individuals are, the more they believe that events are unrelated to their personal behavior and are therefore beyond their personal control.

The best-known scale that has been developed to measure locus of control is the Internal-External Control Scale (Rotter, 1966). For each item, the subject must make a choice between an interpretation of an event in terms of internal control and one in terms of external control. The person chooses the statement he agrees with more strongly. The following are some of the pairs of statements used in the scale:

a. Many times I feel that I have little influence over the things that happen to me.
b. It is impossible for me to believe that chance or luck plays an important role in my life.

a. As far as world affairs are concerned, most of us are the victims of forces we can neither understand, nor control.
b. By taking an active part in political and social affairs the people can control world events.

a. In the long run people get the respect they deserve in this world.
b. Unfortunately, an individual's worth often passes unrecognized no matter how hard he tries.

a. In my case getting what I want has little or nothing to do with luck.
b. Many times we might just as well decide what to do by flipping a coin. (pages 11–12)

For items 1 and 2, alternative a is external and b is internal, whereas for items 3 and 4, a is internal and b is external. The score is the number of external alternatives that a respondent endorses from among the larger set of alternatives.

Rotter reported in 1966 that his research indicates that the scale has adequate internal consistency and reliability over time. Furthermore, there is evidence that people's scores on it can be used to make valid and interesting predictions.

Consider resistance to coercion and influence. People differ in their reactions to others' attempts to influence them, as noted at the beginning of this chapter. In predicting how resistant an individual will be to influence, it is helpful to take account of that person's locus of control. Intuitively, it seems reasonable to assume that persons who think they control what happens to them will be less likely to accept the influences of other people than will persons who feel that their fates are controlled by external forces. This idea has been supported in a number of studies (see Lefcourt, 1972, for a review). Internally oriented people conform less than externally oriented ones to group pressures and are less likely to change their attitudes and beliefs toward positions recommended in persuasive communications.

There are some exceptions to this general rule, however; the internally oriented are more influenced than the externally oriented by certain special types of pressures. For example, Ellen Spector Platt (1969) and Steven J. Sherman (1973) have found that the internally oriented are more readily influenced when they actively participate. If internally oriented persons are given the job of convincing others of positions they do not believe in, they will often end up convincing themselves in the process of convincing others. Externally oriented people are much less affected. The greater persuasibility of internally oriented individuals in this situation may stem from the fact that the influence is self-induced.

Locus of control is also a good predictor of achievement behavior. A variety of studies, including that reported by James Coleman and his associates, have shown that an internal orientation tends to be associated with success in school. In fact, according to the well-known Coleman report, locus of control accounted for more of the variability in school achievement among black students than did any other variable. It was a better indicator of academic success than, for example, the geographical location of the school, the quality of the school, or the parents' income. Evidently, internally oriented students seem to feel that they can get ahead by trying, and they devote themselves energetically to improving their conditions. Externally oriented students, on the other hand, seem to feel that their efforts make little difference and therefore do not seem to try very hard (Coleman, Campbell, Hobson, McPartland, Mood, Weinfeld, and York, 1966).

In part, the academic success of internally oriented people may stem from their tendency to change their behavior more readily than do the externally oriented in response to success and failure in all enterprises. Experiments on *level of aspiration* bear this out. In these experiments, each subject performs a series of trials and meets with differing degrees of success and failure. Before each trial the person is asked how he or she

The will is free: Strong is the Soul, and wise, and beautiful: The seeds of godlike power are in us still: Gods are we, Bards, Saints, Heroes, if we will.
—MATTHEW ARNOLD

Figure 4.4 One individual disposition that psychologists have found useful in understanding behavioral differences is the tendency for individuals to attribute the events in their lives either to their own control or to external forces. In the photograph, individuals are shown practicing the rituals of witchcraft, relinquishing their personal powers to the direction of another force. In contrast, the quotation is an assertion that an individual can exercise internal control over his or her destiny.

II SOCIALIZATION: BEING HUMAN

expects to do on the next trial. The expectations of internally oriented subjects reflect their successes and failures more strongly than do the expectations of externally oriented subjects; they raise their expectations after success and lower them after failure more often than do externally oriented people. Apparently, internally oriented persons rely more strongly on their personal experiences as guides to behavior in the future that will ensure them success.

Another reason for the better academic performance of internally oriented persons may be that they seem more willing to delay gratifications—to prefer a later but larger reward to a smaller immediate one. Thus, the internally oriented person perhaps does schoolwork in the hope of a future reward. The externally oriented person, on the other hand, may seek more pleasure in the moment because he or she is not as certain of what the future will hold.

Some of the most interesting applications of the locus-of-control scale have been in understanding social problems having to do with ethnic-group or other social-group membership. Several studies have found greater externality among blacks in the United States than among whites. Also, middle-class children seem to be more internally oriented than lower-class children. These and other findings suggest that groups with more actual access to social rewards are more internally oriented. Thus, these differences in perceptions of control seem to reflect the reality that it is highly difficult for some people to control their own fates. A black person from the ghetto will no doubt find it more difficult to get ahead on his own than will a black resident of a middle-class suburb, regardless of what either one does.

If a way could be found to increase the feelings of personal control among members of minority groups, would their social standing improve as a result? It may seem tempting to suggest that internality is a route to social mobility—that a way for people to get ahead is to believe that they control their own fates. However, recent evidence suggests that this conclusion is oversimplified. Not surprisingly, the relationship between minority-group status and locus of control is apparently more complicated than it originally appeared to be. Patricia Gurin, Gerald Gurin, Rosina Lao, and Muriel Beattie in 1969 suggested that the Internal-External Control Scale, at least when administered to black college students, is better regarded as two scales than one. They labeled the two components *personal control* and *system blame.*

In this revision of the original test, personal-control items refer to the sense of personal control in one's own life. These items agree with Rotter's original conception of locus of control. For example, in one of the personal-control items, the internal alternative, "When I make plans, I am almost certain that I can make them work," is contrasted with the external alternative, "It is not always wise to plan too far ahead because many things turn out to be a matter of good or bad fortune anyhow." In contrast, the system-blame items assess *ideology* about the role of internal and external forces in determining success and failure in the society at large. For example, in one of the system-blame items, the internal alternative, "Leadership positions tend to go to capable people who deserve being chosen," is contrasted with the external alternative, "It's hard to know why some people get leadership positions and others don't—ability doesn't seem to be the important factor."

The study by Gurin and her associates confirmed this line of thinking. Black students who were more internally oriented in their sense of personal

The Ant and the Grasshopper

A grasshopper in the wintertime went and demanded of the ant some of her corn for to eat. And then the ant said to the grasshopper, "What hast thou done all the summer last past?" And the grasshopper answered, "I have sung." And after said the ant to her, "Of my corn shalt thou none have, and if thou hast sung all the summer, dance now in winter."

MORAL: *There is one time for to do some labor and work, and one time for to have rest, for he that worketh not nor does no good shall have oft at his teeth great cold, and lack at his need.* **—AESOP**

control over the outcomes of their own behavior showed superior aspirations and performance, but those who were externally oriented in the sense of blaming the system for institutionalized barriers to achievement had greater career aspirations and showed greater participation in collective attempts to break social barriers to black achievement. Internality of personal control may indeed aid *individual* minority-group members in their attempts to move up socially. But internality of system blame may indicate support for the status quo of society, which would help prevent one's minority group from improving its status as a whole.

This research, in addition to being important for understanding the relationship between personality and social change, also raises questions about the measurement of locus of control. In particular, it raises the question of whether or not researchers should stop treating locus of control as a single general trait about which they can justifiably make conclusions regardless of the social situation or the people involved. There may be many different kinds of control, and if researchers specified the differences, better predictions might be made. This issue of precision versus generality will be addressed again shortly.

The Need for Social Approval

Another personality characteristic with especially important implications for social behavior is the tendency to seek the approval of others. Most people care at least a little about having others like them and approve of them, but people do differ in how much they care: Some people are especially concerned that others regard them favorably.

The strength of the motivation to gain approval has been studied extensively by Douglas Crowne and David Marlowe, who in 1964 labeled

---

"DOWN SO LONG IT LOOKS LIKE UP"

THE VARIABLE OF internal and external control is probably closely related to depression. Depression is one of the most frequent diagnoses of people in mental institutions. The identifying characteristics of the depressed person include passivity, helplessness, lack of motivation to act, dependence, and a feeling of being controlled by the environment. Whereas some people have had more actual misfortune than others, some people may be more susceptible to "downs" than others. What predisposes someone to depression?

An interesting approach to the depression syndrome has been taken by Martin Seligman at the University of Pennsylvania. Using dogs for experimentation, Seligman and his colleagues have tried to create depression in their canine subjects. Although the term "depression" has traditionally been used to describe a human condition, Seligman believes

that he has found an analogous condition in dogs, which he calls "learned helplessness." Seligman has found that he can condition behavior in dogs that is contrary to a dog's best interests: stolid acceptance of bone-chilling electric shock. Dogs who have undergone unavoidable shock do not subsequently avoid shock, even when they are given the chance to escape.

In a typical situation, Seligman placed dogs either in an escape or in a no-escape condition. All the dogs were given a high-intensity shock that lasted for fifty seconds. Half the dogs had to remain in the cage; the others learned to escape. Shock was administered sixty-four times during a single day. Twenty-five hours later the animal was given a second series of ten shocks, but this time every dog could jump a barrier to reach a safe zone. The animals who had previously learned to

---

this variable the *need for social approval*. Crowne and Marlowe's interest in this area of research grew out of their attempt to improve the understanding of how people respond to personality questionnaires. Psychologists had long realized that a person's responses to questionnaire items are influenced not just by the content of the items but also by the person's own *style of responding* to questionnaires. Some people ("yea-sayers"), for example, tend to agree with items regardless of their content, whereas others ("nay-sayers") tend to disagree regardless of content. *Response set* is the term for the tendency to respond on the basis of one's style.

Crowne and Marlowe became interested in another response set—the tendency for people to respond to personality-test items according to their ideas of social desirability. The idea here is that people tend to agree with items that represent "good," or socially acceptable, behaviors and to disagree with items that represent "bad," or socially unacceptable, behaviors. Allen Edwards had already established empirically in 1953 that the more socially desirable the behavior referred to in a test item, the greater the likelihood that people will agree with the item. Crowne and Marlowe's research concerned the fact that people differ in the strength of this tendency to respond in a socially desirable way. They argued that people who consistently respond to questionnaire items in a socially desirable way and thereby present a picture of themselves as very "good" are more concerned with obtaining approval than are other people.

Crowne and Marlowe adopted an interesting strategy for assessing the need for social approval. They developed a special list of statements for their test, the Marlowe-Crowne Social Desirability Scale. The scale consists of thirty-three statements to which the test-taker must answer "true" or "false." Half are socially desirable statements, which individuals might like

Richard Cory

Whenever Richard Cory went down town,
We people on the pavement
    looked at him:
He was a gentleman from sole to crown,
Clean favored, and imperially slim.

And he was always quietly arrayed,
And he was always human when he talked;
But still he fluttered pulses
    when he said,
"Good-morning," and he glittered
    when he walked.

And he was rich—yes, richer
    than a king—
And admirably schooled in every grace:
In fine, we thought that he was everything
To make us wish that we were in
    his place.

So on we worked, and waited for the light,
And went without meat, and cursed
    the bread;
And Richard Cory, one calm summer night,
Went home and put a bullet through his head.

—EDWIN ARLINGTON ROBINSON

escape shock continued to do so, but those who had been captive had learned to accept the shock. Instead of the normal responses of urinating, defecating, and jumping frantically, the dogs who had previously not been able to avoid shock crouched down and waited for the shock to terminate.

In this type of behavior Seligman sees a parallel to human depression, victims of which seem unable to pick themselves up when they are down. He also speculates that depression is likely to occur among people who have experienced a great deal of unpredictable and inescapable trauma, just as his dogs had.

Seligman and his co-workers also tried to cure their animals of the depressive syndrome. They discovered that it was no easy matter. They tried luring the dog out of self-imposed imprisonment by offering it meat, by calling the animal to come over the

barrier, by kicking at the cage, and by removing the barrier to the nonshock area—all to no avail. Finally they forcefully pulled the dog with a leash across the floor of the electrified cage to safety. One dog had to be pulled across fifty times before finally being able to escape shock on its own. All the dogs recovered their capacity to escape shock after undergoing this deconditioning process. The cure for these helpless animals suggests cures for helpless people. Seligman believes that therapy for depressed persons should include having patients find out and come to believe that their own actions can produce the gratifications they desire. Belief in internal control may thus be necessary to avoid depression.

Sources: Adapted from M. Seligman, "Depression and Learned Helplessness," in R. Friedman and M. Katz (eds.), *Psychology of Depression: Contemporary Theory and Research,* (in press).

———, S. Maier, and R. Solomon, "Alleviation of Learned Helplessness in the Dog," *Journal of Abnormal Psychology,* 73 (1968), pp. 256–262.

to attribute to themselves but that happen to be untrue of most people. Consider two such statements in the scale:

I have never intensely disliked anyone.
I don't find it particularly difficult to get along with loud-mouthed, obnoxious people.

The other half of the statements describe behaviors that are socially undesirable, yet probably true of most people. Two of these statements are:

I can remember "playing sick" to get out of something.
I like to gossip at times. (1964, pages 23–24)

If you responded to these statements by indicating that you have never intensely disliked anyone, that you get along with obnoxious people, that you have never "played sick," or that you never gossip, you would be answering in a socially desirable way. You would be projecting an idealized picture of yourself, and this picture would probably be a distortion of the truth. In short, if you told very many of these "little white lies," you would be considered to have a strong need for social approval.

The statements included in the scale were designed to have few implications of abnormality. Crowne and Marlowe wanted the scale to represent not pathology but the need to obtain approval by responding to the environment in a culturally approved and acceptable manner.

The Marlowe-Crowne Social Desirability Scale was developed about 1964, and some of the items now seem quite out of date, particularly with respect to social norms among college students. For example, it is doubtful that it would still be socially desirable at many colleges to agree with the statement that "I am always careful about my manner of dress." The scale may have to be revised every few years to fit changed social norms. However, the original thirty-three items did cohere statistically at the time the scale was constructed; in other words, item analysis suggested that the items were measuring the same attribute. The scale has also proved to be highly reliable over time.

The need for social approval, as assessed by the Marlowe-Crowne Social Desirability Scale, is linked to an interesting set of behaviors, particularly to behaviors indicating receptivity to social pressures. People strongly motivated to gain social approval are more conforming, cautious, and persuasible than are people not so strongly motivated in these directions, and they tend to go along with existing social norms more readily. In experiments, such people were shown to be more conforming in response to situational demands and group pressures and more likely to change their attitudes in response to a persuasive communication.

Furthermore, in other experiments relating to this conforming and submissive attitude, people high in the need for approval were less likely to express anger and hostility under provocation. Other experiments showed them to be more cautious about setting goals in a risk-taking situation, and in word-association tasks they tended to restrict their responses to more conventional, popular, and common associations. For example, women high in the need for social approval were more hesitant than women low in this need to report seeing "dirty" words in a perception task in which they had to report both taboo and neutral words to a male experimenter.

In general, it appears that persons with high levels of this personality trait are playing a careful game, especially in situations in which they may be evaluated. Because they want to be liked, they do what they think others

I have become so popular at my poetry and my styling until anyone associated with me becomes world famous. After they break up with me, they write for top magazines, they are put on top TV shows. I am so popular that movie plays about boxing are outlined around many of my ways. . . . I'm beautiful.
—Muhammad Ali

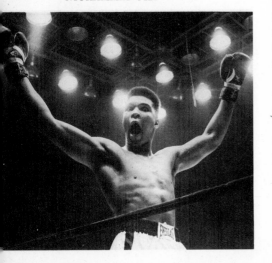

II Socialization: Being Human

expect and want them to do. Through these behaviors, they attempt to present idealized views of themselves.

Unfortunately, those who are most in need of approval seem least likely to get it. Crowne and Marlowe (1964) report a study of members of a fraternity that demonstrated that the higher a person's need for social approval, the less popular he was. Crowne and Marlowe's finding is not surprising, given their other findings. Who would expect great social success for a cautious, conforming person who defensively maintains an idealized image of himself as good and moral? Perhaps all of us need social approval, and the person who has an especially great need generally chooses the wrong tactics to obtain it. This person thus goes without approval and, as a result, the need continues to mount.

Self-Esteem

Nathaniel Hawthorne once said that what a person thinks of himself contains his destiny. Many psychologists have pursued the implications of this statement by exploring people's conceptions of themselves. Knowing what a person really thinks of himself or herself may allow psychologists to make reasonably good predictions about his or her behavior. For example, a person who feels ugly and generally worthless might need to be convinced not to commit suicide. And a woman who sees herself as intelligent and ambitious is more likely than one with a dimmer view of herself to apply for graduate study.

One of the most important aspects of a person's self-concept is the evaluative component. People attach evaluations to themselves; we all see ourselves as good at this and bad at that. A person with a generally positive self-evaluation is said to have high *self-esteem;* someone with a generally poor opinion of himself or herself, on the other hand, is said to be low in self-esteem. The role of self-esteem is so central in determining behavior that it has been studied by psychologists specializing in areas as diverse as clinical, personality, developmental, organizational, and social psychology.

Considering the diversity of approaches to self-esteem, it should be no surprise that investigators have developed a variety of instruments to measure it. Many of these devices are questionnaires. For example, the Feelings of Inadequacy Scale (Janis and Field, 1959) contains the following items:

How often do you feel inferior to most of the people you know?
How often do you have the feeling that there is *nothing* you can do well?
(Hovland and Janis, 1959, page 300)

Other investigators employ a technique known as the *Q-sort,* which requires a person to provide both a realistic self-description and a description of an ideal self that he or she would like to be. Low self-esteem here is defined as a substantial discrepancy between the ideal and actual selves, it being assumed that self-esteem suffers when a person fails to measure up to self-established ideals.

The fact that many different measuring instruments are used in research on self-esteem makes the results particularly difficult to interpret. Different measures of self-esteem do not necessarily correlate highly with one another or have the same meaning. Furthermore, as already shown, respondents to questionnaires sometimes succumb to the temptation to present unrealistic images of themselves. Thus, it may be difficult to know whether a high score on a self-esteem questionnaire represents a genuinely favorable self-image or an attempt to present oneself in a desirable way. For

Figure 4.5 An individual's evaluation of himself or herself, called self-esteem by psychologists, has important consequences for behavior. Persons who feel generally positive about themselves, believing that they are adequate and competent, are likely to attempt more challenges, to relate more effectively with others, and to react with more resilience to failure than are those with low self-esteem. Muhammad Ali and the suicide portrayed here may both have encountered disappointments and frustration that are *objectively* comparable. But their reactions are obviously different.

example, in responding to items on the Janis and Field test described above, the subject must go against a standard of social desirability if he or she states that "there is nothing I can do well."

There are many theories about the development and influence of self-esteem. In terms of the individual's social development, one of the most accepted views is that a self-concept evolves from the individual's observations of the ways in which others behave toward him or her. Charles Horton Cooley in 1902 and George Herbert Mead in 1934 both asserted that the self-concept has social origins. They thought that a sense of self develops by a process of *reflected appraisal,* whereby we learn how other people feel about us and accept their evaluations of us. Cooley's and Mead's viewpoint seems essentially correct; a great deal of research has shown that people are sensitive to the appraisals others make of them. Richard Videbeck (1960), for example, at random told some subjects that they had performed well on tests of their verbal communicative abilities and told others that they had done poorly. Later tests of these subjects' own views of their verbal abilities showed that these views reflected Videbeck's purported evaluations to a large extent. However, more subtle theoretical issues arise in attempting to explain why appraisals by others are more important under some circumstances than others.

Leon Festinger proposed in 1954 that the standards by which we view ourselves are relative in nature. We discover how intelligent, friendly, interesting, and physically attractive we are by comparing ourselves with other people. Who we think we are thus depends on those with whom we compare ourselves. And by the same token, the fact that this comparison process is almost continuous means that one's self-concept can change at any point in life. The fact that this does not always happen in a dramatic

IT HURTS SOME PEOPLE TO BE NUMBER ONE

ALMOST EVERYBODY hates a masochist. (Perhaps that's only fair, given his efforts to be miserable.) But few people understand the masochist. All of us know the person who seems to fall apart on the verge of success. The way in which misfortune continually plagues him is a perpetual mystery, and yet it unfailingly does. Recently psychologists have posited the theory that "failers" are attempting to be "true to self" when they fail. Although the ego gratification they would receive as winners seems to make a positive course of action the most rational, the need to be consistent, stable, and recognizable to oneself and others may pull in the opposite direction those who have suffered past failures.

In order to specify the conditions under which people might prefer to strengthen their low opinions of themselves rather than to improve themselves, Jeanne Marecek and David Mettee conducted a study in which they sought correlations between

self-esteem levels and success at a simple task. One large group of subjects, for example, consisted of college women who had scored in the bottom third on a self-esteem test. In addition to evaluating themselves, the subjects also estimated how certain they felt of their self-ratings. Thus the low self-esteem subjects were divided into two groups according to how certain they were that they had shortcomings. The certainty ratings were given because the researchers expected them to be important indicators of the subjects' willingness to change their self-perceptions.

Subjects were then given a task in which they earned points by matching geometric shapes on a large board. Half the subjects were told that their success was totally a matter of luck, and the other half were told that performance depended on skill. This variation was included because winning

way may reflect many people's tendencies to stick with more or less the same types of friends and associates throughout their adult lives.

Festinger's ideas about the comparative basis of the self-concept were the foundation of an experiment in which Stanley Morse and Kenneth Gergen (1970) led subjects to believe that they were applying for a summer job. As part of the application procedure, each person filled out a number of questionnaires, including a measure of self-esteem. After the applicant completed these forms, a stooge who appeared to be another job applicant entered the room. This supposed applicant had either a very socially desirable appearance (wearing a suit, carrying an attaché case, and so on) or a very undesirable one (wearing a dirty sweatshirt, appearing dazed, and so on). The subject then received more forms to fill out, including a second measure of self-esteem. As it turned out, subjects who had been exposed to the desirable applicant suffered a drop in self-esteem, whereas exposure to the undesirable applicant enhanced self-esteem. Thus, self-esteem *is* relative; people feel inadequate if they must compare themselves to someone whom they consider impressive but confident if they compare themselves to someone they view as a slob.

Given these various influences on self-esteem, how do differences in self-esteem influence behavior? Psychologists have studied self-esteem as a predictor of a variety of social behaviors. As with locus of control and the need for social approval, psychologists have tried to determine whether differences in self-esteem are related to receptivity to social influence. A number of studies (for example, that by Janis and Field, 1959) have shown that people with high self-esteem are more resistant to social influence than are people with low self-esteem. However, in test situations this relationship has not always been obtained. A number of other studies (such as that

by luck would have been less personal than winning by skill. Thus, for low self-esteem subjects the effort to perform at a consistently low rate should not have been as great when it was a matter of luck as when it took skill.

After ten trials, the subjects were casually informed that they were doing well. Marecek and Mettee had predicted that in a second round of ten trials, the low self-esteem subjects who were certain that they were incompetent would resist this "bad news" and would either perform at a lower rate or fail to show the usual increase in success due to the ten-trial warm-up as well as to increasing self-confidence. They would especially fail to do better when they felt that the task involved skill rather than chance.

These predictions were fulfilled. The accompanying table displays the mean change in performance from the first to the second set of trials. The lowest achievers in the second half, who

Average Scores for Improvement in Low Self-esteem Subjects Between First and Second Sessions

CONDITION	CERTAIN	UNCERTAIN
Luck	5.88	4.44
Skill	.65	4.14

changed a mere .65, were those who were certain of their shortcomings when the task involved skill. All the remaining groups improved.

Those who "try harder" seem to be those who harbor the suspicion that they could be "number one." The data also suggest that little can be done for the self-determined loser, except to shake his lack of faith in himself—a difficult task for both the habitual winner and the habitual loser, if for different reasons.

Source: Adapted from J. Marecek and D. Mettee, "Self-esteem, Level of Certainty and Responsibility for Success," *Journal of Personality and Social Psychology,* 22, (1972), pp. 98–107.

by Nisbett and Gordon, 1967) have found that under some conditions an inverted-U relationship between self-esteem and persuasibility prevails, whereby people with moderate levels of self-esteem are more subject to influence than are people with either low or high self-esteem.

William McGuire (1968) suggested that the relationship between self-esteem and receptivity to social influence seems complicated only because self-esteem is related to two psychological processes affecting response to social influence. One process is the individual's ability to receive a message adequately: people with high self-esteem may be better able to receive and understand information. The second process is the individual's tendency to yield to the views of others. As indicated earlier in this chapter, people vary in their persuasibility—the ease with which they are swayed by others. People with high self-esteem, because they have greater self-confidence, may be less willing than those with lower self-confidence to give in. Although experiments testing McGuire's model have had rather ambiguous results, his work represents an interesting method of exploring the ways in which a personality trait such as self-esteem may affect an overt social behavior in complex ways: The complexity of the empirical relationships may result from the fact that the personality variable affects more than one of the underlying psychological processes that control the overt response.

Interestingly, there is evidence of a stronger relationship between self-esteem and persuasibility among men than among women. Alice Eagly (1969) carried out research suggesting that this difference may stem from the fact that in women persuasibility is more a function of acceptance of sex-role pressures than of personality traits such as self-esteem.

Self-esteem also has been studied in relation to interpersonal attraction. Does self-esteem affect the individual's feelings toward other people? Many clinical psychologists, among them Carl Rogers (1951), have stated that favorable self-regard is a necessary condition for positive mental health and thus should be a primary goal of psychotherapy. Rogers feels that the need for positive evaluations from others is a central motivation in human behavior. In studying the relationship between self-esteem and feelings toward others, Rogers found that people with high self-regard tend to be relatively accepting of others. However, some social psychologists have suggested that this may not always be so and that often it is the person low in self-esteem who is more accepting of others. For example, James Dittes (1959) has argued that a person low in self-esteem will have a greater need to be approved by others, will be more threatened by disapproval from others, and thus will show a relatively strong tendency both to like people who accept him and to dislike those who reject him.

Dittes carried out an experiment in which people in a group situation were told that they were either accepted or rejected by other members of the group. Dittes found that to the extent that subjects were low in self-esteem, the subjects showed more liking for group members who they believed had accepted them and a greater disliking for those they believed had rejected them. Elaine Walster (1965) has obtained similar results (which are detailed in an expanded discussion of the effects of self-esteem on attraction in Chapter 6).

These findings seem to contradict the clinicians' hypothesis that people with high self-esteem are more capable of feeling warmth or love for others than are those with low self-esteem. However, Ellen Berscheid and Elaine Walster (1969) suggest an interesting resolution of the two points of view: Clinicians, in contrast to experimenters, generally work with situations in which the individual is not sure whether the other person accepts or rejects him. Under these ambiguous conditions, people with high self-esteem are more likely to assume that others like them; and the more they suspect that others like them, the more they will reciprocate this presumed liking. People with low self-esteem, on the other hand, tend to make no such assumption and may even assume dislike. Thus, in the relative ambiguities of this type of real-life situation, they tend to seem less loving or approving. When the feelings of others are perfectly clear, as experimenters usually strive to make them, those with low self-esteem are more responsive to others' positive feelings.

The Spectrum of Personal Dispositions

So far, this chapter has concentrated on three dispositions of major importance to social psychologists. There are many others as well. The *need for achievement* is one that has received a great deal of attention, particularly from David McClelland (1961) and John Atkinson and Norman Feather (1966). A person with a great need for achievement is especially concerned with successfully meeting various standards of excellence.

Researchers typically measure the need for achievement by analyzing the content of stories that subjects write about pictures in the Thematic Apperception Test (TAT). As a result of their work with this projective technique, investigators have found that the need for achievement is related to social conformity, risk taking, academic performance, and social exploitation of other human beings. Some of the most innovative contributions of achievement motivation to social-psychological knowledge have been in the understanding of societal problems. For example, in 1961 David McClelland suggested that high levels of achievement motivation are a cause of periods of economic progress in a society.

Women's behavior is more difficult to relate to achievement motivation than is men's behavior. The TAT measure, which was developed with male subjects, has often failed to predict successfully the behavior of women. In 1972, Matina Horner suggested that a more powerful determinant of women's achievement behavior may be the *need to avoid success,* because a woman may fear that her success outside the home is likely to result in a loss of the affection and approval of others. Horner holds that in our society women are socially penalized for success in competitive situations. Women therefore learn that in order to succeed socially they must fail at endeavors in which they are competing with men. And the need to avoid success is not, in Horner's view, the same as a lack of achievement motivation. Both men and women may either possess or lack achievement motivation and both can fear or not fear failure, but only women typically fear success as well. The motives to achieve and to avoid success are not mutually exclusive, then; they often coexist in the same individual.

Horner used a variation of the standard TAT in her experiment. The ninety women in the study were given this sentence to complete: "After first-term finals, Anne finds herself at the top of her medical school class." The following completions were scored as indicating fear of success:

Anne is a *code* name for a nonexistent person created by a group of med students. They take turns taking exams and writing papers for Anne. . . . (1970, page 62)

Anne has a boyfriend, Carl, in the same class, and they are quite serious. Anne met Carl at college, and they started dating about their sophomore year in undergraduate school. Anne is rather upset and so is Carl. She wants him to be higher scholastically than she is. Anne will deliberately lower her academic standing the next term, while she does all she subtly can to help Carl. His grades come up and Anne soon drops out of med school. They marry and he goes on in school while she raises their family. (1970, page 60)

In marked contrast is this completion, *not* revealing fear of success:

Anne is quite a lady—not only is she tops academically, but she is liked and admired by her fellow students—quite a trick in a man-dominated field. She is brilliant—but she is also a woman. She will continue to be at or near the top. And . . . always a lady. (1969, page 62)

Additional needs, or motivations, that McClelland and others have considered include the need for *affiliation*—the desire to establish and maintain positive ties with other people—and the *need for power,* or the need to control others. Researchers have attempted to relate these two traits to conformity and other social behaviors.

You will encounter many other personality traits as you read this book. For example, you will see in Chapter 7 that *authoritarianism* is related to racial and ethnic prejudices and in Chapter 13 that *Machiavellianism* is related to social exploitation. As you read about these traits it will be helpful to recall the issues raised in the present chapter.

PUTTING PERSONALITY IN ITS PLACE

The research that has been reviewed regarding locus of control and the need for social approval, self-esteem, and other traits indicates that each of these personal dispositions plays an important role in many social relations.

POWER TO THE PEOPLE
(Or at Least Some of Them)

"POWER HUNGRY"—a frightening, condemning phrase in our language that defines people with an extreme need to be powerful. It is one of our cultural beliefs that people differ in the satisfaction they receive from being powerful. Because people do seem to differ on this crucial dimension, psychologists David Winter and David McClelland at Harvard University set about devising a method with which to differentiate more power-oriented people from those less power-oriented. Not only were they interested in defining the need for power in individuals, they were also interested in discovering how this need would influence the behavior and other personal characteristics of a person. The social ramifications of this type of research are exciting to consider.

Winter, along with his colleague Dwight Green, studied the relationship of the need for power to black activism among students at Wesleyan College in Connecticut. The thirty-eight black students in the study wrote stories about four ambiguous pictures from a projective test, and these were scored for need for power. The subjects were also rated by three judges from Ujamaa, the Afro-American group on campus, for characteristics such as pragmatism, willingness to work within the system, and direct experience with working in the black community. The researchers then correlated need-for-power scores with factors that had emerged from personality evaluations of the projective tests. For example, Northern and Southern blacks responded differently to the pictures. Because their backgrounds seemed to have exerted differing influences on their perceptions, their scores were analyzed separately.

The table shows the relationship between need for power and two behavioral dispositions for Northern and Southern students. Northern blacks who seek power are not so practical, in common terms, but are far more likely than those who are low in power needs to become involved in

II SOCIALIZATION: BEING HUMAN

And many researchers place great value in viewing behavior as being organized by broad dispositions of this type. They are often willing to make predictions about an individual's subsequent behavior on the basis of what they learn about that person from a questionnaire or a projective test that the individual takes once.

If you were to read the original write-ups of some of these individual studies, however, you would notice that the relationships obtained between the personality variables and relevant behaviors are not generally very strong. In most instances, the relationships in published studies are statistically significant—that is, they are unlikely to have occurred by chance. But they generally lack strength much beyond this point, which means that any given trait usually accounts for only a small proportion of the differences in people's behavior. In other words, the personality variables are not in themselves particularly reliable predictors of human behavior, and consequently much of the variability in behavior usually remains unexplained.

These somewhat painful facts about personality research have been given special prominence by Walter Mischel, who in 1968 claimed that the evidence on behalf of the predictive usefulness of most personality traits is, in fact, exceedingly weak. He argues that individual dispositions do not seem to be consistent from situation to situation. Thus, people who are disposed to be happy or cruel or achievement-oriented in one situation do not seem to be so in other situations. That is, traits do not seem to be very general if you look at the same person in different situations. An early indication of this was revealed in 1928, when Hugh Hartshorne and Mark May measured children's honesty in more than a dozen different types of

Correlations Between Judges' Ratings and Motives for Northern-Reared and Southern-Reared Students		
CORRELATIONS	NORTHERN STUDENTS (N = 21)	SOUTHERN STUDENTS (N = 17)
Pragmatism and Need for power	−.33	.58*
Anti-establishment black community work and Need for power	.60**	−.25

*Probability is less than .02
**Probability is less than .01

black-community work that is not associated with the dominant white establishment. The Southern blacks stand in contrast. Those who are high in power needs are less likely to engage in nonestablishment community work. In addition, Winter and Green found the people high in need for power were more likely to be officeholders and considered influential by peers, regardless of geographic background.

The researchers see in black militants a very different activistic orientation than is found among white radicals, with whom black militants may share many goals.

If Black militants tend to be relatively high in [Need for] Power, and white radicals tend to be high in [Need for] Achievement, but low in [Need for] Power, then one could predict that these two groups might have difficulty in collaboration, quite apart from issues, previous history, and present distrust. Blacks would see the main issue as power; whites, as programs. Moreover, Black militants would be keenly sensitive to issues of power, and experienced and knowledgeable about the use and limits of power. White militants, in a paradoxical way, might tend to be exaggerated, ambivalent and fluctuating in their approach to power. (pages 330–331)

It is interesting to speculate on how the need for power influences social movements, conflicts, and various powerful individuals. It is unfortunate, for example, that so little is known about the dispositions toward power of our national leaders.

Source: Adapted from D. Green and D. Winter, "Motives, Involvements and Leadership Among Black College Students," Journal of Personality, 39 (1971), pp. 319–332.

situations. As more fully explained in Chapter 2, there was only a small tendency for children to be consistently honest or dishonest in all the situations; children who were honest in one instance were quite likely to cheat in another. Additional studies reported by Kenneth Gergen in 1968 have shown that people undergo major shifts in their self-concepts as they move from one social group to another. For example, their esteem levels are likely not to remain stable but to fluctuate markedly. People are not so easily classified irrevocably into groups of high and low self-esteem, because they seem to have the potential for both dispositions. When these arguments are combined with the fact that correlations between traits and behaviors of greater than .30 are seldom attained, there is good reason to question the claim that behavior is organized into general traits that can be used to predict actions.

Yet it should not be surprising from a social-psychological perspective that much of the variability in behavior remains unexplained even when traits are taken into account. Most social-psychological research emphasizes not differences between people but the ways in which features of social situations affect behavior. Thus, social-psychological experiments are usually designed to study the effects of situational variables on entire groups. In the opening example of the political rally, for example, most social psychologists would want to compare the general effects of this speech with those of another type of speech or, holding the content of the speech constant, would ask whether the speech would have greater impact if delivered by a black or a white speaker, by a woman or a man, and so on. If there is much truth to the social psychologist's view that such situational factors affect behavior, then personality variables cannot be expected to predict behavior very strongly unless the situation is also taken into account. In some cases, when the effects of the situation are sufficiently extreme, there is no room left for individual dispositions to operate at all. If you increase the heat in a room to 100 degrees Fahrenheit, *everyone* is uncomfortable, regardless of personality. Most experimental effects are hardly this clear-cut, however.

In light of these various arguments, it is time to reexamine the approach to social behavior that emphasizes individual dispositions.

Personality and Situation: Hand in Glove

A good working assumption for most social behaviors is that they are affected both by individual personality factors and by situational forces. The effects of any one personality trait will differ according to the situation, and the effects of a situation will differ according to the individual's personality. In addition, some behaviors may be more dominated by either personality dispositions or situational pressures than are other behaviors. Consider the interaction of both personality and situational influences in relation to each of three personality variables that were discussed earlier in this chapter—locus of control, need for approval, and self-esteem.

Locus of Control.   As the earlier discussion of locus of control implied, socially and economically privileged people—members of ethnic groups that have disproportionate access to objective rewards—are more likely than are less privileged people to view events as being under their own personal control. Racial differences among Americans seem to fit this generalization, because black subjects tend to answer questionnaires and to behave in achievement situations in ways characteristic of externally oriented persons. For example, research has shown that black subjects, more than whites, seem more strongly motivated to avoid failure than to achieve success. This failure-avoidance pattern is especially strong in situations that require competition with whites.

According to Herbert Lefcourt and Gordon Ladwig (1965), if black people are in situations in which they highly expect to succeed, they do not show failure avoidance. These investigators gave black reformatory inmates a particularly racist task: Each inmate competed in a game (with cigarettes as the reward) against a white confederate of the experimenters who won consistently because the game was rigged. Thus, each black inmate experienced continual failure. Because he could quit the game at any time, the experimenters could measure his persistence at the task. Quitting early allowed him to avoid further failure.

The study compared the responses of three groups of black inmates: (1) former jazz musicians who had held membership for at least six months in the reformatory jazz club; (2) inmates who had joined the jazz club but quit after a few sessions; and (3) inmates who had never joined a musical group. The first two groups were told that good jazz musicianship should lead to success in the game.

The first group, the jazz musicians, persisted significantly longer in the competitive task than did the other two groups of subjects, who showed the failure-avoidance pattern—although the three groups did not differ in locus-of-control scores, intelligence, or social-class indicators. Thus, the difference in their behavior appears to be related to their hopes of success. When presented with a situation that yielded greater expectations of success, the achievement-oriented behavior typical of internally oriented persons appeared. Personality dispositions are thus not all-powerful. Whether they influence behavior in the expected ways depends on the situation.

Social Approval. As suggested earlier, people with a high need for social approval may be more conforming, cautious, and persuasible than are persons who are low in this need. Also, a high need for social approval is apparently accompanied by a tendency to present an unrealistically favorable image of oneself. An experiment by Norman Miller, Anthony Doob, Donald Butler, and David Marlowe (1965) suggests some qualifications of these principles and shows that the effects of the need for social approval depend on the situation.

Miller and his associates grouped students into those high and those low in the need for social approval on the basis of the students' scores on the Social Desirability Test. Some weeks later the students participated in an experiment on psychological testing in which they were told that they would receive a number of predictions about their personalities. They were to look at these carefully and to tell the investigator whether or not they felt that each prediction was accurate.

You might on the basis of the earlier discussion expect that people with a high need for approval would generally be more agreeable. Not wanting to disappoint the investigator making the predictions, it could be assumed that, whenever possible, they would indicate that he was correct. However, Miller and his colleagues did not believe that this would happen. They felt that situational characteristics must also be taken into account, especially the characteristics of the investigator making the predictions. In their experiment, therefore, two aspects of the predicting investigator were varied: the presumed level of expertise and the presumed importance to him

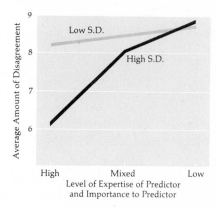

Figure 4.6 Results demonstrating that behavior is influenced by situational factors as well as by chronic needs. Miller, Doob, Butler, and Marlowe (1965) found that subjects with a high need for approval (SD, as measured by the Social Desirability Test) were more likely to agree than low-SD subjects when the other had high expertise and when it was important to that other person that his statements be correct. However, low-SD and high-SD subjects were about equally likely to disagree with the other's predictions when expertise was low and correctness seemed to be of no importance.

that his predictions be correct. Thus, the experimenters presented the investigator either as a psychology student (high expertise) or as an engineering student (low expertise). And to suggest that success was of great importance to the investigator, subjects were led to believe that the predictions had to be accurate in order for the investigator to obtain a needed reward. (For the psychology student the reward would be a good grade, and for the engineering student it would be permission to switch his major to psychology.) No such claims were made about the low-importance investigators. Each subject received predictions from one of these four different types of investigators.

If people who have a high need for social approval tend merely to conform more than other people do, they would most likely agree with a source, regardless of the source's expertise and the importance of the task to that source. If, instead, the need for social approval interacts with a more situation-bound tendency that is sensitive to who is giving the approval and to why he or she is giving it, then persons with a high need for social approval should be especially responsive to the experimental variations of importance and expertise.

The study indicated that people with a high need for approval were affected most by differences in importance and expertise: they agreed more when importance and expertise were high and did not agree when these factors were low. People with a low need for approval, on the other hand, were unaffected by importance and expertise: they showed a moderate level of agreement regardless of the investigator's characteristics. People with a high need for approval were, therefore, *not* uniformly more conforming than were those with a lower need. They were more conforming in the high-expertise and high-importance situation, which incorporated special pressures that made agreement with someone else seem especially appropriate and helpful. Thus, the effect of this personality trait depends strongly on the characteristics of the situation.

Self-Esteem Revisited. Earlier it was shown that investigators have found the degree of self-esteem to be related to the individual's responsiveness to the influences of others. The greater a person's self-esteem, the less responsive to influence. However, there are many limitations to this perspective if various aspects of the situation in which the influence is exerted are taken into account. And predictions may also become much more precise if situational factors such as the characteristics of the communicator, the nature of the communication, who else is listening, and so on are taken into account. Consider, for example, Howard Leventhal and Sidney Perloe's 1962 study. In this study, men received communications that attempted to influence their attitudes toward army life. In one condition the communication was highly pessimistic; it pointed out all the bad things that might happen to the listener if he chose the army as a career. Other subjects read a communication about army life that was highly favorable, emphasizing all the benefits of an army career. When the experimenters examined the relationship between self-esteem scores (which they previously had obtained for all subjects) and subjects' reactions to the pessimistic message, they found that the lower a subject's self-esteem, the more his attitude tended to change. However, when the message was optimistic, exactly the reverse occurred: The subjects who were optimistic about themselves—who were high in self-esteem—were most responsive to the optimistic message, and in this situation their attitudes changed most. How self-esteem is related to attitude change, then, depends on the precise characteristics of the situation.

The understanding of human relations thus improves when the interacting effects of personality and situation are taken into account. In addition, there are several other steps that investigators take to increase the sophistication of social research.

A Taxonomy of Situations

Almost every personality trait interacts in important ways with situational factors. The relationship between people's traits and responses depends to a great extent on what the particular situation means to them. In developing a science, one of the first steps is to establish a *taxonomy*, or categorization scheme, that identifies the relevant entities and tells how they differ. In the study of personality, the beginning of this attempt is to identify clusters of meaningful traits. This is the start of a taxonomy of dispositional "pegs." Also needed, however, is a specification of the kinds of "holes" that those pegs fit into. Thus, those who study personality very much need a taxonomy of situations. Such a taxonomy would enable social scientists to make substantial progress in predicting individual differences in behavior and could potentially increase the scientific validity of social psychology.

There have been some systematic attempts to understand how situational features link up with individuals' traits. For example, Fred Fiedler (1967) studied a personality trait—*leadership style*—and the ways in which it relates to behavior in groups. Fiedler's work will be discussed in detail in Chapter 15, but for now it is important to note that Fiedler discriminated between two major leadership styles. Interpersonally oriented leaders tend to emphasize good relationships in a group; they want high morale, comradeship, and understanding. Task-oriented leaders are disposed toward group success; they simply want to get a job done in the best possible way. Which of these leader types do you think would have greater success in reaching a group goal? Which leader would actually generate greater productivity? Fiedler found that whether an interpersonally oriented leader or a task-oriented leader enhanced group effectiveness depended on the characteristics of the group situation. He then provided a taxonomy of relevant group situations. The principal dimensions on which situations differ in Fiedler's taxonomy are (1) the quality of the social relationships existing between the leader and the members of the group, (2) the ambiguity of the group's task, and (3) the amount of formal power inherent in the leader's position. Neither the relationship-oriented leader nor the task-oriented leader is universally best at encouraging productivity. The style of leadership that is most effective depends on the nature of the group situation represented in terms of the three dimensions. The strength of the evidence supporting Fiedler's model has been questioned by George Graen, Kenneth Alvares, James Orris, and Joseph Martella (1970); nevertheless, his research illustrates a valuable strategy for dealing with personality-situation interactions. It is one of the few systematic attempts to understand how personality traits fit various types of situations.

Self-Perception: Who Am I Anyway?

In addition to considering interactions between personality and situation, there is another useful strategy for improving the predictability of behavior from personality traits. It involves taking account of the person's perception of his or her own personality. Perhaps measured personality traits have not usually yielded very powerful behavioral predictions because it is important not only to measure someone's actual traits but to find out how he or she perceives them.

Suppose that in a particular group situation, a person says to herself, "This is a situation in which someone should exercise leadership." After she has categorized the situation in this way, she is very likely to ask herself if she has what it takes to be a leader in that situation. She might conclude, "Not only is this a situation that demands leadership, but I can be a good leader." The idea here is that people use their various capacities primarily when they regard themselves as having these capacities. The same individual who in one situation sees herself or himself as being capable of leadership in another situation might very well say inwardly, "I'm really not capable of leading in this situation." Thus, a potential for leadership would remain hidden. As it turns out, Chapter 14 explains that persons may be interchangeable in their capacities to fulfill the role of leader.

Predictions made about behavior on the basis of particular personality traits, then, can easily be inaccurate if the person in question does not see the trait as relevant to the situation or believes that he or she does not have that trait in the first place.

Defining Personality: The Politics of Precision

Another way to improve the accuracy of predictions about behavior on the basis of personality involves defining traits more precisely. Most of the traits previously discussed have been defined broadly by investigators. Achievement motivation, for example, often is treated as a general concern with meeting standards of excellence. This broad definition would suggest that a person who is highly motivated to achieve would strive for high standards of excellence regardless of whether he or she was in a classroom,

Figure 4.7 Few feats have been accomplished that have not been products of a high need for achievement. This is reflected in as wide a range of behavior as (*left, center*) the winning of the 1972 Olympic decathlon at Munich by Nikolai Avilov of Russia; (*upper right*) the stunts of daredevil motorcyclist Evel Knievel; and (*lower right*) performance by Van Cliburn, the famed concert pianist.

a bedroom, or doing Zen meditation. In a similar way, traits such as locus of control, need for approval, and self-esteem are defined very generally.

Instead of achievement motivation in general, however, it is more realistic for some purposes to think of specific kinds of achievement motives. A separate consideration of specific achievement motives, such as those for scholarship, sex, meditation, and so on, is useful for certain kinds of predictions. Similarly, a more careful subdivision can be made of the locus of control, self-esteem, and need for approval spectrums in terms of what the individual feels he has control over, what he especially likes or dislikes about himself, and the particular persons from whom he desires approval for his actions.

Given the various levels at which researchers define traits, the matter of prediction can again be considered. Imagine that you are an admissions officer at a major university. Five thousand people have applied, but you can admit only a thousand. You want to admit people who are likely to excel; you do not want to accept someone who will fritter away time at the cost of barring someone who will make a real contribution. You feel you can substantially improve your ability to choose by using a personality measure that would predict the candidates' achievement orientations. Which would be more useful—a measure of general motivation to achieve or one that was specifically designed to test motives for academic achievement? Clearly, someone in the position of an admissions officer would find specific trait measures most useful—particularly those that bear directly on orientation to academic achievement. Yet in most of the research described thus far, investigators have used *general* trait measures in attempting to predict very specific behavior. It is not surprising, then, that the resulting correlations are typically weak if the researcher is trying to predict specific behaviors from a general trait measure.

This tendency toward weak correlations between general traits and specific behaviors is understandable, because researchers measure general traits by compiling answers to a variety of test items. Thus, a person's response to any particular item in the test may be determined by traits other than the one under investigation. As noted earlier, however, such incidental factors vary from item to item and therefore cancel one another out. The researcher ends up with a generally defined trait—precisely *because* he has adopted this strategy of averaging responses across items.

Typically, the researcher then uses this generally defined trait as a basis from which to predict specific behavior. But, as previously noted, any specific behavior is multiply determined, just as responses to any one item in a personality test are multiply determined. Thus, if a researcher attempts to predict students' performances on a particular test in a particular college course as a function of locus of control, he would at best find a weak relationship, because there are other factors that affect their performances on the test; these include the teacher, the other people in the class, the time of day that the class meets, characteristics of the physical meeting place, and how much the student likes the subject matter.

This is not to say that general dispositions never lead to accurate predictions. It really depends on what a person wishes to predict. Generally defined traits are likely to be excellent predictors of generalized behavioral tendencies, although they are generally weak predictors of specific behaviors. Thus, a therapist, for example, might be far more concerned with an individual's general style of behavior than with his performance in any specific situation. This investigator might wish to know whether or not the patient had enough general self-esteem to cope with the different pressures of life. Research in this case might entail making a series of behavioral observations and cumulating the results. General trait measures should be quite successful in predicting general tendencies of this type—more successful, in fact, than more narrowly defined traits.

The strategy of breaking up general personality dimensions into more specifically defined traits is, however, bound to result in greater power to predict specific behaviors, but carried to its extreme the strategy becomes ridiculous. Should performance on a social-psychology exam be predicted in terms of the motive to do well on social-psychology exams? Should performance on a mathematics exam be predicted in terms of the motive to do well on math exams? If motives can be created for every behavior, prediction becomes more precise, but the whole point of studying individual differences is to generate an efficient description for the *multiplicity* of behaviors. The fewest possible dimensions are needed to account for the greatest possible variability in behaviors. And as definitions of traits become increasingly specific, descriptions become less efficient. Researchers could end up with long lists of situation-specific traits. To avoid this result, they will no doubt continue to attempt to predict specific behaviors from rather general dispositions and to improve the strength of the relationships they obtain by making interactive predictions involving features of the social situations that they study.

Each of us develops his or her own theories of personality that, unlike the researcher's personality theories, may go untested. Moreover, the implicit theories to which individuals subscribe contain biases that direct their interpersonal behavior. These implicit personality theories can tell social scientists much about the personality of the amateur theorist as well as about the cultural and situational factors that help to shape his or her theories. Implicit theories are discussed in detail in Chapter 5, and the ways in which these theories can affect the theorist's interpersonal behavior are explained in Chapters 6 and 7.

SUMMARY

Individuals differ dramatically in their social behavior. Psychologists *systematically* study these differences by investigating traits—somewhat stable personality tendencies. Traits are measured via *behavioral indicators*—responses that are taken to represent a trait. An indicator with high *reliability* is one that is stable across time and in different situations. How well an *index*—a behavioral indicator—measures what it is supposed to measure is called the *validity* of the index. Establishing an appropriate index is complicated by the fact that most behavior is influenced by many factors other than the trait psychologists want to measure; therefore, sets of behaviors are better indicators of a trait than are single behaviors. The most commonly used type of index is based on a questionnaire containing a number of statements with which the subject indicates agreement or disagreement; the statements must have undergone *item analysis* to determine their *internal consistency*. Some personality tests measure traits by means of stories elicited in reaction to ambiguous pictures. Another way to study individual differences is by experimental manipulation—contriving situations meant to make people respond in a way that expresses a specific trait.

Several trait dimensions are especially interesting to social psychologists. *Locus of control* refers to a person's tendency to attribute events to his or her own actions (internal control) or to circumstances beyond his or her influence (external control). *Expectancy-value* theories explain locus of control by stating that a person decides to engage in a given action according to the *expectancy* that action will yield certain rewards and the personal *value* of those rewards to the individual. Julian Rotter developed the Internal-External Control Scale to predict a person's locus of control.

Another important trait dimension is the *need for social approval,* generally assessed by the Marlowe-Crowne Social Desirability Scale. This scale is based on the principle that persons with a high need for approval are more likely than others to agree with items that are considered socially acceptable. In general, a person high in need for social approval is conforming, cautious, and persuasible.

A third measurable trait dimension is *self-esteem.* One of the many scales used to measure it is the *Q-sort,* which requires a person to describe an actual self and an ideal self. Research on self-esteem has shown that it depends on the others to whom an individual compares himself or herself. Also, the relationship between self-esteem and persuasibility has been investigated, as has the relationship between self-esteem and reactions to approval and disapproval.

Other trait dimensions studied by social psychologists include *need for achievement* and related traits, *need for affiliation, need for power, authoritarianism,* and *Machiavellianism.*

Knowledge of these personality variables has generally not created strong predictors of human behavior. Most social behaviors are affected by both personality and situational factors; several studies have shown that when researchers take into account both personality and situational factors, their understanding of social behavior improves. Another aid to prediction may lie in the establishment of a *taxonomy,* or categorization scheme, that tells what the important differences are among situations. Behavior may also become more predictable when personality traits are assessed in relation to the person's *perception of his or her own personality.* Traits may also need to be defined more narrowly if they are to be used to accurately predict specific behaviors.

SUGGESTED READINGS

Crowne, Douglas, and David Marlowe. *The Approval Motive: Studies in Evaluative Dependence.* New York: Wiley, 1964.

Gergen, Kenneth, and David Marlowe (eds.). *Personality and Social Behavior.* Reading, Mass.: Addison-Wesley, 1970.

Gordon, Chad, and Kenneth Gergen (eds.). *The Self in Social Interaction,* Vol. 1. New York: Wiley, 1968.

Gurin, Patricia, Gerald Gurin, Rosina Lao, and Muriel Beattie. "Internal-External Control in the Motivational Dynamics of Negro Youth," *Journal of Social Issues,* 25 (1969), 29–53.

Lefcourt, Herbert. "Recent Developments in the Study of Locus of Control," in B. Maher (ed.), *Progress in Experimental Personality Research,* Vol. 6. New York: Academic Press, 1972, pp. 1–39.

McClelland, David. *The Achieving Society.* Princeton, N.J.: Van Nostrand, 1961.

Mischel, Walter. *Personality and Assessment.* New York: Wiley, 1968.

Walster, Elaine. "The Effect of Self-Esteem on Romantic Liking," *Journal of Experimental Social Psychology,* 1 (1965), 184–197.

SOMEWHERE THERE IS A PLACE
AND THERE IS A PERSON
SOMEWHERE.
PLEASE WAIT.

CHAN SEI GHOW

III

ENCOUNTERING OTHERS:
PERCEPTIONS, FEELINGS & THOUGHTS

5

Perceiving Others

PICTURE YOURSELF AT A DANCE. You meet a stranger and exchange hand-shakes and smiles. You dance together and talk for awhile about the dance and about yourselves. You ask questions. Finally the stranger departs. What was this person like? Deep and sensitive? Shy and somewhat boring? A weirdo? You have undoubtedly formed some impression. It takes people very little time to make judgments about one another, even on the basis of the most limited contact. The impressions two people form of one another nevertheless influence the future of their relationship. If a stranger appears deep and interesting, he or she may be a candidate for future interaction. People tend to be particularly understanding of someone who seems shy, to expect a lot from someone who impresses them as intelligent, and to be wary of one who strikes them as aggressive. Because perceptions of others largely determine behavior toward them, it is of major importance to understand how people form and maintain impressions of one another. Thus, this chapter is devoted to person perception—the ways people have of understanding one another, the factors that influence them to form the impressions they do, and the mistakes they are likely to make.

Forming an impression of a person is not a passive process in which the characteristics of the individual are the input and the formed impression is the automatic outcome. If impressions varied only when input varied, then almost anyone meeting the stranger at that dance would have formed the same impression. Such an event is highly unlikely. One individual may judge a newcomer to be "quiet," another might judge the same person to be "dull," and still another person might think the newcomer "mysterious."

147

These various impressions would probably lead to different expectations of the newcomer and to different patterns of interaction as well.

Moreover, people often arrange things so as to guarantee that their assessments of others *become* accurate. Their expectations can be fulfilled if their judgments influence their actions toward an individual in a way that shapes the other's behavior toward them. Consider how a first-grade teacher might tell a friend about his first day of teaching. The account might run as follows:

Met my class today. The first day is always the roughest—you don't know what to expect from any of them. This year's group is a mixed one, as usual—some very cute, bright kids, faces shining with excitement at the thought of school. But there are dumb ones, too, sitting there with blank stares or fidgeting around. You can tell they aren't interested in anything. Runny noses, dirty hands. . . . I feel sorry for those children, I really do. They shouldn't group all those kids together; you've got to treat them differently—with the dumb ones you've got to go slower, put things on their level, revise your teaching programs.

It is clear that the teacher's account is more than purely descriptive. From his individual perceptions—blank stares, dirty hands, shining faces—he has formed impressions. The teacher has gone beyond the facts presented to him and has constructed a set of categories with which to sort and separate the members of the class. His perceptions are ordered and cohesive. Specifically, the teacher has categorized, or *conceptualized,* his class in terms of intelligence, of dumb and bright. Categorization serves a useful purpose for him. Categories provide him with a tidy way of dividing the children into smaller, seemingly more homogeneous groups. These categories will also direct his actions as a teacher. He will expect bright kids to absorb more instruction faster; therefore, he will be inclined to treat them differently from the slower children, who presumably need to be taught more slowly.

Unfortunately for some of his students, the perceptual distinctions the teacher has made may become more and more accurate. Those children labeled dumb will be taught less and will fall increasingly far behind the bright ones. This process, whereby people make true what they perceive to be true, is known as the *self-fulfilling prophecy* (Merton, 1957). Evidence from the classroom indicates its power.

Robert Rosenthal and Lenore Jacobson (1968) used a public elementary school in a lower-class community to test their hypothesis that teachers' expectations of their pupils influence the actual performance of these students. A standard nonverbal test of intelligence was administered to all students. The teachers were told by the researchers that the results of this test predicted which students would show sudden spurts of intellectual development. Each teacher was given the names of a few students who would most probably display rapid intellectual growth within the next year.

In actuality, the experimenters had selected the names of these so-called rapid bloomers at random; the tests did not measure likelihood of rapid blooming; and the students whose names were chosen were no more likely than any others to show sudden development. Thus, the "special" children were different from other pupils in only one respect—their teachers expected more of them. In the lower grades, students who were expected to bloom showed significantly more improvement in IQ scores than did those for whom no such expectations were held. Furthermore, these expectations continued to exert an influence: The increase for rapid bloomers in each grade continued in the subsequent grade.

Rosenthal and Jacobson offer several explanations for their findings. Teachers may have paid greater attention to those children whom they expected to see bloom; they may have been more encouraging and more patient with these children. Besides giving extra encouragement, teachers may have also communicated to these children—both verbally and nonver-

---

In the Eye of the Beholder...

BEAUTY IS NOT SKIN DEEP

DESPITE THE AXIOM "beauty is only skin deep," being beautiful by prevailing cultural standards makes a difference in what others think of you. In support of this idea, Karen Dion, Ellen Berscheid, and Elaine Walster asked college students about the lives of some of their peers. Attractive students were judged as having more socially desirable personalities and as leading more successful and interesting lives than their less attractive counterparts. Once this was found, Dion and Berscheid conducted a study of preschoolers' judgments of friends and found that, in fact, a preschooler's popularity was also related to beauty. Possibly adults in their environment had already transmitted the cultural value to prefer attractive people.

Karen Dion then investigated adult reactions to the misdeeds of second-graders. Photographs of the children were first rated as either attractive or unattractive by a panel of nine judges. The subjects, 243 college females, were asked to give their opinions about a discipline problem in an elementary school. To aid them, they were given a portfolio with a written account of the incident and the name, age, and photograph of the child involved. Subjects either learned that the accusation was very serious (for example, throwing an ice ball at a classmate and cutting him badly) or less serious (as, for example, stepping on a dog's tail). Half the subjects saw a photograph of a cute child; the others, of an unattractive one. The adults were asked to evaluate the likelihood of the child acting badly either in the past or future, the ways in which the child normally behaved, the personality characteristics of the child, and the severity of the punishment the child deserved.

Attractive children indeed tended to be judged differently from unattractive ones for the same behavior, particularly when the reported transgressions were severe. Although punishment was not unfairly given to attractive or unattractive children, good-looking children were assumed to have better personalities, to be better behaved, to be more honest and pleasant, and to be less likely to transgress in the future than were less attractive children.

If these perceptual distortions are widespread, what is their impact on children? Do attractive children come to see themselves as more honest, pleasant, superior in personality, and so on? Do unattractive children actually behave more injuriously than others behave? To what extent do our physical characteristics commit us to a social fate? A general awareness of the answers is vitally needed.

Sources: Adapted from K. Dion, "Physical Attractiveness and Evaluation of Children's Transgressions," *Journal of Personality and Social Psychology,* 24 (1972), pp. 207–213.

————, and E. Berscheid, "Physical Attractiveness and Sociometric Choice in Young Children," University of Minnesota, 1971 (mimeo).

————, ————, and E. Walster, "What Is Beautiful Is Good," *Journal of Personality and Social Psychology,* 24 (1972), pp. 285–290.

bally—that high standards were being set for them. This, in turn, may have improved the self-concepts of the children as well as their motivation to improve. The ways in which these children were perceived, then, may have influenced the ways in which they perceived themselves. If so, these children were victims of their teachers' self-fulfilling prophecies—an example of what Rosenthal and Jacobson call a *Pygmalion effect.*

Although the Rosenthal and Jacobson studies have been subjected to much methodological criticism, Robert Rosenthal (1973) has recently written a comprehensive survey of all the studies dealing with the Pygmalion effect. These experiments were conducted not only in the classroom but also with rats in mazes, counselees in high schools and colleges, and trainees in employment areas. He found that out of a total of 242 studies of the effect of expectations on performance, 35 percent provide evidence of a Pygmalion effect at a significant level (5 percent) that is nearly seven times greater than might be expected by chance. Although 61 percent of these studies do not show significant effects of expectations in either direction, only 4 percent of the cases show significant results in the unpredicted direction. The argument that one person's expectation of another's behavior can be a self-fulfilling prophecy has been substantiated, Rosenthal claims, by the accumulated research.

The importance of these findings for education cannot be overestimated. The results also make it clear that an individual's perceptions of others influence the ways in which he treats them, the ways in which those others see themselves, and the ways in which they relate to the individual in turn. It is extremely important, then, to examine the ways in which people form perceptions and why they view one another as they do.

In this chapter, basic phenomena of person perception will be the focus. The process of *conceptualization*—the ways in which people classify things in their thoughts—will be discussed first. This process has both positive and negative functions: it helps people inject order into their lives, but it may also introduce distortions into their impressions of one another.

Figure 5.1 One person's labeling of another often carries with it certain expectations, and these expectations can then shape the other's behavior. Some psychologists call the phenomenon the "self-fulfilling prophecy"; some call it the "Pygmalion effect," which refers to the sculptor in Greek mythology who fell in love with the ivory statue of a woman (Galatea) he had created and wished it alive. The statue then did become alive, through the good services of the goddess Aphrodite.

Second, the *process of impression formation*—the ways in which people associate and bind together the various elements that make up their impressions—will be discussed. Why, for example, do many people assume that a beautiful blonde is more likely to be dumb than smart? And what do people do when faced with inconsistent information about other individuals? Third, the *attribution of causality*—the process by which a person sometimes believes that others can control their actions at will and at other times believes that they are victims of circumstance—will be discussed. Perceptions of causality have an immense impact on the ways in which people feel about and behave toward one another. For example, society condemns an individual who willfully exploits others but forgives the same man if he did not mean to do it. Finally, the process of *self-perception* will be examined. In particular, the ways in which people make sense of their own emotions will be discussed. How can they be sure that they feel love instead of lust, depression instead of fatigue?

THE FUNCTIONS AND FAILINGS OF CONCEPTS

Although most people may not always be aware of it, they are constantly categorizing or labeling incoming information as they receive it. In fact, most people would probably find it very difficult to exist without doing so. It is through categories that people treat different things as equivalent: A tiger, a bear, and a lion are all "wild animals." People label a smile, a hug, a gift, or a caress all as "friendliness." By grouping things, people simplify their task of dealing with the highly complex world of sensation. Rather than attending to the many differences among animals or to all the behaviors in which others engage, human beings can classify their experiences in groups of similar experiences and think no further. Through this process of labeling, or conceptualization, people avoid being overwhelmed by the immense variability of the stimulus world.

Conceptualization has additional advantages. First, conceptual categories provide us human beings with information about the individual members of a particular category. Knowing that a papaya falls into the category of food tells us something more than the obvious facts of its being shaped like a squash and being orange in color. Because of past acquaintances with objects in the food category, we know that any new object labeled "food" can be safely eaten. Second, a conceptual category pinpoints those qualities that its members share and thus tells us how seemingly different things are related. Meat, bananas, and bread are different in color, shape, texture, and smell; the conception of "food," which encompasses them all, makes explicit their shared quality of edibility. The fact that we can organize things into categories also creates for us a measure of security. Things that are classified are more easily comprehensible, more easily dealt with. Knowing that a round black object with a fuse is a bomb would direct one's action—*away* from it. If people had no concept for "bomb," they would not know how to react. A state of ambiguity is in most cases unsettling, if not frightening. When people have no concept for what they encounter, anything can happen.

Finally, conceptual categories allow people to predict. For example, if a person sees a round orange object the size of a fist, she may categorize it as an orange and proceed to eat it. Because it falls into the category "orange," she can predict with confidence that it will prove good to the taste. By knowing one member of a class or category, she can make predictions about all other members in that group. One concept, that of causality, can give people especially great predictive strength and, by extension, a feeling of security and control. To know that A "causes" B allows one to predict the occurrence of B from the presence of A. And, to the extent that one can manipulate the occurrence of A, one can control the occurrence of B. For example, if a secretary knows that punctuality causes her boss to view her favorably and that slovenliness elicits his disapproval, then she can predict and control his feelings about her through her own behavior.

Conceptualization serves many useful and necessary functions in helping people make sense of the world. However, the process also introduces dangerous distortions into people's perceptions of one another. When a perceiver simplifies the huge influx of stimuli he perceives by grouping those stimuli, he may treat all members of a category as equivalent. When this occurs, the results may be destructive. Simplification may lead the perceiver to assume greater homogeneity than actually exists among the members of a category and to take it for granted that all members are alike. Two types of distortion are particularly interesting. First, the perceiver may be inclined to ignore the *differences* between members of a category. All girls or blacks or WASPs are not the same, even with respect to the general characteristics that define their group. When a person is treated in a particular way simply because he or she falls into a category, most of that person's characteristics have been ignored.

Simplifications can have crippling effects on those who are categorized. Categorization is, for example, the basis of centuries of racial discrimination and oppression in the United States, as will be discussed in Chapter 7.

THE SORCERER'S APPRENTICE

LEARNING TO SEE is a social activity. So are learning to hear, touch, smell, taste, and feel. What our senses tell us long ago lost the battle with the dictates of our social customs. Our capacities for authentically experiencing the world have shrunk since the time we were infants. Then, if taken on a picnic, one watched the ants all afternoon, ate some delicious dirt, enjoyed a dog licking one's face, cried when someone honked a horn, and had a soothing bowel movement.

Learning to experience anew is the goal of sensitivity sessions, Zen Buddhism, and sorcery. Although the last seems most alien to us, a social anthropologist, Carlos Castaneda, has become an intermediary between the "modern" world and that of the occult. Through his Mexican-Indian guide, don Juan, Castaneda grasped major distinctions between two worlds.

I have come to understand sorcery in terms of Talcott Parsons' idea of glosses. A gloss is a total system of perception and language. For instance, this room is a gloss. We have lumped together a series of isolated perceptions—floor, ceiling, window, lights, rugs, etc.—to make a single totality. But we had to be taught to put the world together this way. . . . By teaching me sorcery [don Juan] gave me a new set of glosses, a new language, and a new way of seeing the world. . . . [D]on Juan thinks that what he calls seeing is apprehending the world without any interpretation; it is pure wondering perception. Sorcery is a means to this end. To break the certainty that the world is the way you have always been taught you must learn a new description of the world—sorcery—and then hold the old and the new together. Then you will see that neither description is final. At that moment you slip between the descriptions; you stop the world and see. (page 95)

Societies have been constructed with commonly accepted social perceptions as their bases. Much is gained by society from a stable, well-defined foundation for reality. But people do not often question what they may lose.

Source: Adapted from S. Keen, "Sorcerer's Apprentice: A Conversation With Carlos Castaneda," *Psychology Today,* 6 (1972), pp. 90–102.

The second type of distortion arises because people are inclined to view an individual *only* in terms of his membership in a group and to disregard any qualities not directly related to his position as a member of the category. For example, to label a construction worker a "hard-hat" and to evaluate him only in terms of his occupational affiliation is to ignore the religious, political, and social affiliations that may play important roles in his life. Thus, although concepts are necessary tools that help people to think clearly, they also limit people's perceptions of the world.

Concept Formation: The World in Pieces

The ways in which people divide the world conceptually are somewhat arbitrary. People face immense flux in the world around them, and there are innumerable ways in which the flux may be segmented. Human beings are physically capable of distinguishing between more than seven million different colors; yet in Western culture the visible color spectrum is simplified by using only a dozen or so names (Brown, 1958). Not all cultures use the same number of concepts to divide the color spectrum. The Japanese, for example, use the same word to describe the green of a leaf, the blue of the sky, and the paleness of a complexion; yet what people in the United States call "navy blue" is not in the "blue" category used by the Japanese. Given the wide variation in the ways human beings conceptualize their world and the significance of these concepts for social interaction, it is important to consider how people come to acquire and use their conceptual repertoires.

Several processes seem to operate simultaneously in determining the conceptual capabilities we have as human beings. Only one of these processes is tied closely to actual differences in the real world. To some extent, our concepts are based on the fact that our bodies are genetically wired to respond differently to varying qualities of the stimulus world. For example, light creates a different physiological reaction than does dark, warmth a different response than cold, and so on. These differences lend themselves to our formation of primitive categories, or concepts, at an early age. However, most of our concepts do not rely on such self-evident differences.

A more important process of concept learning takes place through operant, or instrumental, conditioning (see Chapter 2). On the simplest level, when certain actions bring pleasure and other actions only bring punishment, we are inclined to develop concepts that account for the similarities among the rewarded activities and for the ways in which these activities differ from those that bring punishment. For example, turning up the corners of one's mouth typically brings pleasant reactions from others, and turning them down often brings signs of displeasure. In this way, we learn to distinguish between what are called smiles and frowns. As discussed in Chapter 3, perhaps the most powerful effects of operant conditioning on conceptual development take place through the vehicle of language. Even before a baby's first birthday, her parents begin to reward the child for applying particular sounds to various classes of stimuli. For example, certain configurations are termed "cats," and other configurations are "dogs." Later the child learns that people who look certain ways are classified as "safe" and that others who look different are "dangerous." Through this process, the child learns many of the major concepts used by the culture into which she has been born (Brown, 1958).

After a child has gained entry into a linguistic world, her conceptual capacities can mount rapidly. Word combinations and juxtapositions begin to suggest new and different concepts. If the child knows about the category "Southerners" and also knows about "farmers," that child can formulate the concept of "Southern farmer" very rapidly. In addition, a child may derive further conceptual distinctions from the logic that underlies spoken and written communication. After learning that all babies have mothers, when the child sees a Chinese child, she will surmise that there must be a class of people who are Chinese mothers. And she will continue to be heavily influenced by the linguistic medium as an adult. Within the past few years, for example, the mass media—television, radio, magazines, and so on—have taught the American public that there is a mental condition called "stoned," that one aspect of bombs is whether they are "smart," and that in judging a public official the public must be wary of a possible "credibility gap."

Concept Application: Picking Up the Pieces

The concepts available to people vary considerably, depending on their particular life experiences. But even when people share the same conceptual repertoires, they do not always apply those concepts in the same way. In understanding the principles behind concept application, you might imagine for a moment that you are to meet two creatures from outer space—one who is described as "creative, aggressive, and intelligent" and another who is described as "cautious, slow-moving, and placid." Then suppose that you are asked to predict (in the interests of the State) which one will be more trustworthy. Chances are you will be more inclined to label the first creature less trustworthy. In people's relations with others, they seem to have definite ideas about what characteristics "go together." Some writers have described this phenomenon by saying that people have *implicit personality theories*—theories about which personality traits belong together (Schneider, in press), but there is, as yet, no concrete evidence. Everyone may have his or her own implicit theory of personality that permits that perceiver to sort impressions into conceptual categories, but these implicit theories of personality are usually riddled with biases. On the basis of minute pieces of

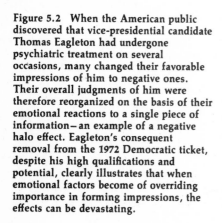

Figure 5.2 When the American public discovered that vice-presidential candidate Thomas Eagleton had undergone psychiatric treatment on several occasions, many changed their favorable impressions of him to negative ones. Their overall judgments of him were therefore reorganized on the basis of their emotional reactions to a single piece of information—an example of a negative halo effect. Eagleton's consequent removal from the 1972 Democratic ticket, despite his high qualifications and potential, clearly illustrates that when emotional factors become of overriding importance in forming impressions, the effects can be devastating.

information about another person, a perceiver may feel he knows "all about" that individual's personality. For example, if the perceiver hears someone characterized as middle-class, a suburbanite, and a housewife, he may assume many details about the woman without putting them to the test. Which details are filled in will depend on who the perceiver is; the outcome may be a favorable or an unfavorable impression. But whoever the perceiver is, he will probably allow his impression to direct his behavior toward her. Herein lies the essential problem of concept application. On what basis are people willing to go beyond the facts at hand to make sweeping conclusions in the process of applying concepts?

Several explanations have been offered to account for the process of concept application. Perhaps the most obvious explanation is that people make their judgments on the basis of past experiences. For example, Southerners whom a person has known may have been politically conservative, or he may have been rewarded for perceiving them as such, and so he assumes that a stranger from the South is probably conservative. Most of the fat people whom people have seen on television are good-humored and funny, so they often assume that all fat people are jolly. This explanation does not, however, offer a fully adequate accounting of the dynamics by which people form impressions. For example, most people have not encountered very many space creatures; yet, if asked, they might feel quite confident in making judgments about space creatures on the basis of very little information.

A second explanation is that people tend to evaluate in an emotional way the few facts about a person that they do have and then to apply this evaluation to the individual as a whole. Thus, if a stranger seems physically attractive and intelligent, and both these traits are emotionally pleasing, a person may be willing to assign all manner of positive attributes to the stranger. The general phenomenon of cognitive balance, which includes the *halo effect* (Thorndike, 1920), has been demonstrated empirically many times. For example, Charles Osgood, George Suci, and Percy Tannenbaum (1957) have shown that someone judged pretty rather than ugly is likely to be rated as nice rather than mean, cheerful rather than melancholy, smart rather than dull, and so on. There are dangers involved in the halo effect; it suggests that love is inevitably blind, that teachers see handsome or beautiful students as brighter, and that promotions in organizations are based on friendship as much as on merit. A negative halo suggests that people fail to see the positive attributes of their enemies, thereby underestimating them or needlessly prolonging enmity.

Clearly, emotions are not always of overriding importance in determining a person's judgments of others. For example, judgments of space creatures could not be based on emotion. One space creature might be described in both positive and negative terms (creative, intelligent, aggressive), which might tend to cancel one another, whereas another creature might be described in fairly neutral terms (cautious, slow-moving, placid). In this case, people's judgments of relative trustworthiness probably would not reflect any single term in the two descriptions. Similarly, in the hypothetical classroom example described earlier in the chapter, the teacher's judgments of "smart" and "dumb" do not seem to follow directly from any single bit of information. Rather, the teacher seemed to have based his judgments on particular combinations of traits: dirty and blank-faced versus eager and bright-eyed. Usually people have at least several pieces of information about an individual, and it seems logical that they base their conclusions on the mix. Exactly how people draw conclusions from the mix is not clear, however. For example, do all the pieces of information about a person weigh equally in the final impression, or do people give more weight to certain types of information than to others? Classic experiments by Solomon Asch (1946) shed light on these issues.

With regard to impression formation, Asch maintained that the whole is greater than the sum of its parts. In other words, any group of characteristics generates an impression different from the impressions formed when each characteristic is presented separately. The specific connotation given to each characteristic varies according to the other characteristics with which it is grouped. The combination of characteristics attributed in a specific instance or to a specific person thus takes on a meaning different from the sum of the meanings of the individual characteristics. For example, a girl who appears to be shy, intelligent, and quiet is not quiet in the same way as one who seems dull, stupid, and quiet. People may tend to interpret the word "quiet" in the first list to mean reserved or hesitant, and they may well take the same term in the second list to mean inarticulate and close-mouthed.

To test his hypothesis that the whole impression is greater than the sum of its parts, Asch presented two groups of subjects with a list of seven character traits. He told his subjects that these qualities described an individual and asked them to write a general description of this person and then to judge him on a series of traits according to the impressions they had formed. In the list of traits that Asch gave the subjects, six of the traits were identical for both groups ("intelligent," "industrious," "skillful," "deter-

---

The Warm-Cold Dimension:

HOT LIPS
OR
COLD FEET

SUPPOSE THAT AT your next social-psychology class meeting the instructor announces that a graduate student will be coming in to lead a discussion for part of the period. Prior to his entry, the instructor hands out an information sheet about the visitor and explains that students' reactions to this type of person would be used later as information about what type of teacher is preferred by the class. The note says the following:

Mr.——is a graduate student in the Department of [Psychology] . . . . He has had three semesters of teaching experience in psychology at another college. This is his first semester teaching [social psychology]. He is 26 years old, a veteran, and married. People who know him consider him to be a rather cold person, industrious, critical, practical, and determined. (page 433)

How would you respond to this visitor as a person, as a teacher, as a discussion leader? What effect would

the prior information have on your evaluations of him?

Harold Kelley, the researcher who conducted some of the most important early studies of person perception, was especially interested in the effects of labeling a real person "cold" as opposed to "warm" prior to the audience's first meeting with him. Research by Swarthmore psychologist Solomon Asch has also indicated that the warm-cold dimension is extremely important in determining how people react to one another. Kelley passed out messages similar to the one above to students in three economics classes at Massachusetts Institute of Technology (MIT). Half of the notes called the graduate student "rather cold" (as in the note above) and half classified him as "very warm." Otherwise, the messages were identical. The student then appeared and led a twenty-minute discussion. The experimenters recorded the amount of student-initiated comments during this period. After the student left, each class member wrote a free-form description of the person

mined," "practical," and "cautious"). The list differed only in describing the person as "warm" to one group and "cold" to the other group. Asch found that the warm-cold variation produced strikingly different impressions. Almost all the subjects who were told that the person was warm assumed that the individual was also very generous, popular, happy, humorous, and successful. On the other hand, when subjects were told that the person was cold, their descriptions of him changed dramatically. This person was seen as stingy, unpopular, unhappy, and unsuccessful, although six of the seven adjectives with which the experimenter described the person remained the same. Single pieces of information, then, can color entire impressions.

Asch also maintained that pieces of information about a person have different levels of importance in determining impressions. He felt that *central organizing traits,* more than other traits, color a total impression. To test his hypothesis that some traits are more central than others, Asch repeated his earlier experiment but this time described the person as either "polite" or "blunt" rather than warm or cold. Asch found that the differences in impressions fostered by varying the traits politeness and bluntness were much weaker than the differences produced by varying the traits warmth and coldness. He concluded that, at least in the context of his experiment, the warm-cold dimension was more central than the polite-blunt dimension.

Asch conducted still another study to test his belief that the exact meaning of any term describing a trait is dependent on its context. He described a fictitious person to two groups of subjects, using different lists

and used an adjective checklist of fifteen traits in describing the discussion leader. The main research question was: What is the impact of the warm-cold variable on the evaluation of the person's actual behavior? A second question was: Were these feelings reflected in the behavior during the discussion? The table shows the results of the trait ratings.

The effects of labeling someone "warm" or "cold" were very striking. Especially for qualities related to personal expressiveness—such as "good-natured," "generous," "humane," and "sociable,"—the quality of warmth was highly significant. Not only did subjects use the warm-cold dimension in the adjective ratings, they also based intricate personality patterns and predictive analyses of the person in the free-form descriptions on this variable. For example, the "warm" person was described as "makes friends slowly but

they are lasting friendships when formed."

There was also evidence that the warm-cold information had behavioral effects: A difference in willingness to participate in the discussion emerged. Of the subjects who received the "warm" note, 56 percent entered the discussion, whereas only 32 percent of the "cold" subjects did so. Thus, the presumed warmth of the leader seemed to control the level of participation; students were apparently unwilling to risk public discussion with the "cold" leader.

This study underscores the importance of having information concerning a person even before meeting that individual. The warm-cold variable seems especially central in coalescing disparate information about someone. It seems that a predisposition toward a person is not easily altered even in the face of contradictory behavior.

Source: Adapted from H. Kelley, "The Warm-Cold Variable in First Impressions of Persons," *Journal of Personality,* 18 (1950), pp. 431–439.

Adjective Check List

LOW END OF RATING SCALE	HIGH END OF RATING SCALE	AVERAGE RATING	
		Warm (N=27)	Cold (N=28)
Knows his stuff	Doesn't know his stuff	3.5	4.6
Considerate of others	Self-centered	6.3	9.6†
Informal*	Formal	6.3	9.6†
Modest*	Proud	9.4	10.6
Sociable	Unsociable	5.6	10.4†
Self-assured	Uncertain of himself	8.4	9.1
High intelligence	Low intelligence	4.8	5.1
Popular	Unpopular	4.0	7.4†
Good natured*	Irritable	9.4	12.0†
Generous	Ungenerous	8.2	9.6
Humorous	Humorless	8.3	11.7†
Important	Insignificant	6.5	8.6
Humane*	Ruthless	8.6	11.0†
Submissive*	Dominant	13.2	14.5
Will go far	Will not get ahead	4.2	5.8

*These scales were reversed when presented to the subjects
†Statistically significant differences between "warm" and "cold" subjects

of terms. One list consisted of the terms "kind," "wise," "honest," "calm," and "strong"; the other list consisted of the terms "cruel," "shrewd," "unscrupulous," "calm," and "strong." Although the last two traits are the same in both lists, the first three in the first list are opposites of the first three in the second list. Asch then asked all the subjects to write down synonyms for the last two traits, "calm" and "strong." He found that although some synonyms appeared in the lists of both groups, there was a considerable number of synonyms that appeared in one group but not in the other. For example, when paired with "kind," "wise," and "honest," the term "strong" suggested that the person was highly principled and would bear up under adversity. On the other hand, when the same word appeared in the context of "cruel," "shrewd," and "unscrupulous," it seemed to connote physical strength and aggressiveness. The quality "calm" also did not function as an independent fixed trait; its meaning was determined by its relation to the other terms.

The significance of the context in which people encounter a trait is clear in the classroom example mentioned earlier: "Quiet," when associated with clean clothes and shining faces, would take on a meaning quite different from the "quiet" associated with dirty faces and blank stares. The teacher labels one child "shy," the other "stupid." The first child will be coaxed and dealt with gently; the second will likely be ignored or taught with painful slowness to accommodate his or her assumed low level of comprehension.

Concept Association: Putting the Pieces Together

Asch's explanation is intriguing, but many social psychologists have been puzzled by it. Why should the whole impression be different from the sum of the parts, and why are some traits so central? Julius Wishner (1960) was concerned with these issues, and his research offers some answers. Wishner used all the trait terms that Asch had employed, but instead of having subjects rate a fictitious person, Wishner had students rate ten different instructors whose introductory psychology classes they were taking. With these extensive data, Wishner was able to determine the relationship between each trait and all the others that the students chose to describe their instructors. For example, he found that if students rated a teacher as warm, she was also very likely to be rated as sociable; however, warm teachers were rated low on persistence. Armed with correlations such as these, Wishner was able to account quite well for the centrality of certain traits. He found that traits were central when they were strongly correlated with the other attributes on which the person was rated. For example, if the perceiver rated a person—real or fictitious—as warm, the perceiver's ratings of her sociability would also be affected; warmth is considered highly correlated with sociability, and thus warmth is central in this case. Bluntness, on the other hand, is not highly correlated with sociability and is therefore not central in evaluating sociability. However, bluntness is correlated with honesty, although warmth and honesty are not highly correlated. Thus, bluntness would be a central trait had terms like honesty been used in Asch's studies. Warmth and coldness might well be a central dimension in forming an impression of a parent, because lovingness and nurturance are generally considered important attributes in parents. Yet warmth might well be peripheral in judging the athletic abilities of a football player, although aggressiveness and passivity might be central.

The implications of Wishner's work go beyond trait centrality. It appears that implicit personality theories operate on the basis of *learned associations.* If you hear the expression "tall, dark, and _____," you immediately know that "handsome" must be used to complete the phrase. Advertisers have taken advantage of the human ability to learn associations. For example, the advertisers of Pepsi Cola knew what they were doing when they associated their product with one of the virtues most highly esteemed by Americans—youth—in the little lyric, "Pepsi, for those who think young." Similarly, if someone mentions Germans, you could probably respond with a long series of adjectives that you feel describe Germans. In other words, as soon as you are aware of one aspect of a person, you suddenly have at your disposal an entire array of associations that may play a major role in your impression of that person.

FORMING IMPRESSIONS: CONTRADICTIONS AND COMBINATIONS

Clearly, people tend to form distinct and integrated impressions of others on the basis of very little information. But how do people form integrated impressions when the pieces of information they have are *contradictory*—when, for example, one piece of information indicates that a person is friendly and another piece of information indicates that she is aggressive? In fact, seldom does all the information about a person fit together into a consistent package. How do people react to inconsistency?

Leon Festinger wrote convincingly in 1957 that human beings cannot tolerate inconsistency. Since that time, many other social psychologists have come to agree with Festinger that inconsistencies arouse cognitive dissonance, which motivates the perceiver to rearrange the inconsistent elements so as to eliminate the inconsistency. (Festinger's theory receives detailed attention in Chapter 9.) If inconsistency is painful, as Festinger maintains, then people should attempt to resolve inconsistencies when they occur. Albert Hastorf, David Schneider, and Judith Polefka (1970) have identified three methods by which people resolve inconsistencies. One method—the *relational* method—involves either changing the meaning of the inconsistent information or adding new traits to relate the inconsistencies in a coherent way. *Discounting,* on the other hand, involves ignoring or reducing in importance part of the inconsistent information. Finally, people can reduce inconsistencies through *linear combining,* so that the final impression is some additive combination of the various pieces of information.

The Asch research demonstrated one important way in which the relational method can resolve inconsistencies. Asch was able to show that the meaning of a word or piece of information is dependent on its context and that the meanings of associated terms shift in relation to one another to create a coherent, unified impression. For example, people might interpret the word "lazy" in the context of "pleasant" and "cheerful" as "easygoing," whereas they might be inclined to interpret the same term in the context of "decadent" and "evil" as "slothful." In both cases, the shade of meaning attributed to the term "lazy" makes this term compatible with the others in the cluster. People tend to change the meanings of concepts, therefore, to resolve inconsistencies. A related way of resolving inconsistencies involves adding new information, or rounding out the picture, so that the seemingly contradictory material makes sense within the larger frame of reference. If, for example, someone describes an individual as both timid and aggressive, the audience may assume that the individual is an ambitious person with low self-regard. His aggressiveness may be an attempt to overcome his timidity so that he can become rich and famous.

A study that Eugene Gollin reported in 1954 provides evidence that many people deal with contradictory material by discounting part of it. Gollin showed subjects a movie in which a young woman acted quite differently in various scenes. Sometimes she appeared kindly and helpful, and at other times she seemed loose and promiscuous. Gollin was careful to choose traits that were not directly contradictory or irreconcilable but that nevertheless did not fit naturally together. Subjects then wrote descriptions of the woman. Three major reactions emerged: Many subjects discounted part of the material and focused on the other part; others assimilated the two characteristics of promiscuity and helpfulness into a unified, coherent image; and still others accepted both parts of the description but made no attempt to combine them. Forty-eight percent of the subjects chose to ignore one part of the description, and the other subjects were equally divided between the other two alternatives. It seems, then, that when pieces of information are not entirely consistent, the tendency is to discount incompatible material.

Because discounting information is a form of sticking one's head in the sand, it is important to consider the conditions under which people are likely to resort to it. Of primary importance appears to be the order in which people learn facts. Another study by Solomon Asch (1946) is illustrative. Asch presented one group of subjects with a list of traits—"intelligent," "industrious," "impulsive," "critical," "stubborn," and "envious"—that become increasingly negative. He presented a second group with the same list of traits but in the reverse order. The impressions subjects formed differed considerably depending on whether they learned about positive or negative traits first. Subjects whose lists began with favorable traits were much more likely than the others to form positive impressions. Asch concluded that early information tends to set a general evaluative tone that colors the ways in which the perceiver interprets subsequent information. This *primacy effect* occurs whenever a person bases his or her impression on the first things that become apparent about another and discounts later information.

Further reflection has led some social psychologists to question the power of the primacy effect. After all, there are cases in which first impressions do not last and in which people are most influenced by what they have just witnessed. In other words, there are also *recency effects,* and whether primacy or recency effects hold sway has important implications for various undertakings, including teaching, propagandizing, and jury proceedings. If the primacy effect occurs more frequently, then a person who seeks to persuade can most effectively present the most important information early in his or her communication. If, on the other hand, early information tends to be forgotten, then the communicator should deliver the most crucial information in the punch line. Political strategists rely on there being a strong recency effect when they plan last-minute media blitzes just before election time.

Social psychologists have conducted many experiments to establish just how general a phenomenon the primacy effect is. Ralph Stewart reported in 1965 that he could prevent a primacy effect by asking subjects to form impressions after each new piece of information. Abraham Luchins (1957) found that warning subjects about the dangers of being misled by first impressions also negates primacy effects and, in fact, may produce a strong recency effect. Norman Anderson and Stephen Hubert reported in 1963 that if they asked their subjects to recall all the information presented to them before forming an impression, primacy effects were completely destroyed. These various findings suggest that special efforts are required to avoid distortions in perception from primacy effects. Otherwise, typical human thinking habits are likely to breed substantial misunderstanding.

Finally, people sometimes resolve inconsistencies through linear combination; that is, they add or subtract pieces of information in arriving at impressions. Social psychologists usually refer to linear combination when explaining how people form final evaluations of one another from information that contains both positive and negative elements. How do people feel, for example, about a person who is both beautiful and aggressive? Does beauty win out? Or is aggression more undesirable than beauty is desirable? Perhaps the answer depends on *who* the person being described is—on whether the individual is male or female, for example. And what happens when someone hears several positive things about another person? Do feelings grow more fond with each new positive fact, or does the individual reach a plateau of positive feeling where new favorable facts make little difference? Social psychologists have used two different models to explain the process by which people combine their impressions—*summation* and *averaging.* The summation model suggests that people form overall evaluations that are the simple sums of individual evaluations. For example, a rating of someone who is beautiful, aggressive, cruel, and generous equals the sum of these traits. Thus, if a person disliked aggression very much and appreciated beauty only moderately, the sum of these mixed feelings would be somewhat negative. The person would feel mild dislike for an individual who was both beautiful and aggressive. The averaging model, on the other hand, indicates that the total evaluation is the average of individual evaluations. Based on this model, an evaluation of an aggressive and beautiful person would be the average of these two traits—also mild dislike in this case.

The distinction between the two models is often trivial, yet they predict very different evaluations in some cases. Consider a case in which someone already has a high regard for a friend and then discovers new favorable characteristics about the friend. The summation model predicts that each new piece of positive information will increase the friend's attractiveness. In contrast, the averaging model suggests that newly discovered favorable characteristics will not make the friend seem more attractive unless these new traits carry a higher evaluation than the already high average. On the other hand, if the newly discovered characteristic rates only medium-high, it will lower the friend's total rating because it is lower than the previously existing average. Thus, new facts that are positive may even reduce the friend's attractiveness if they are less positive than what is already known about the friend. According to the view that people average their evaluations of traits, a new positive fact would reduce the perceiver's regard for that individual if he were a friend and increase it if he were an enemy.

Although psychologists who favor an additive model continue to do battle with those who are disposed to an averaging model, the better part of the evidence seems to favor the averaging model, at least in a slightly modified form. One of the most convincing studies was carried out by Norman Anderson (1968), who showed that people usually average various bits of information to form an overall evaluation. But rather than weigh all the pieces of information equally, Anderson's subjects tended to assign greater importance to highly negative or highly positive traits. Thus, people give a single very bad trait far more weight than mildly positive or negative traits. This makes a good deal of intuitive sense: You are not likely to be attracted to someone who is generous, sensitive, and intelligent if you know that he is a murderer. David Kanouse and L. Reid Hanson (1972) have found that, in general, negative information is more important than positive information in impression formation. Some negative information is totally damaging to an entire evaluation, and no piece of positive information can ever completely redeem a basically negative composite. A salad bowl filled with luscious red tomatoes, light and dark greens, radishes, olives, slices of cheese, and a rotting fish carcass has little more appeal than a salad bowl with just the carcass. Returning to the notion of trait centrality, these findings suggest that negative traits are usually more central than positive traits in determining the impressions people form.

ATTRIBUTING CAUSALITY: THE "WHODUNIT" PROBLEM

Earlier it was noted that concepts help people impose order and meaning on the maze of events in their lives and thus afford them a measure of security, a feeling that things "fit together" and make sense. One concept that perhaps more than any other gives people a feeling of order and predictability is that of causality. People find comfort in believing that things do not just randomly happen; they happen *because.* . . . People tend to feel that if

Figure 5.3 *(Upper left)* people who paid good money for the cure-alls sold at old-time medicine shows assumed that the taking of the medicine caused their cough or warts to disappear, although the potion medically had no power to cure them. And *(lower left)* those in nonindustrial societies who have frogs put on their heads to alleviate headaches credit the frog (cause) for their cure (effect). *(Right)* on the occasions that experts using divining rods did find water, those who had hired the diviner were sure that his use of the rod caused the finding of water. And *(center)* an old person who has been told by a palm reader that he has a long life line probably believes that his longevity is the effect of having that line. Some of these seemingly unrelated causes and effects may, in fact, be related. For example, if one's headache is of the everyday tension variety and if one believes that a frog will cure it, the frog probably can cause the headache to disappear.

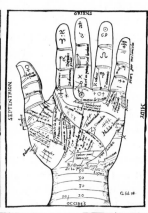

they know the cause, they can influence the outcome. Therein may lie the power, for example, of some organized religions, of many myths and legends, and of science.

People are so eager to make sense of the world in the simplest possible ways that they tend to attribute cause-effect relationships to pairs of associated events even when there is little or no evidence of such relationships. For example, the Belgian psychologist Albert Michotte (1963) showed subjects a film of the following sequence of events: One of two small rectangles moves toward the other, touches it, and stops moving; immediately after being touched, the second object moves forward. Subjects most often described this scene by saying that the first object caused the second one to move or pushed it forward. In other words, they conceptualized the action in terms of cause and effect, and attributed intentions to one of the two rectangles on the basis of insufficient information. The subjects were thereby able to explain the event as well as to describe it. This *causal attribution* also provided them with a much simpler, more concise (if less accurate) way of summarizing the situation than if they had specified that one form had moved toward another and had touched the second form and stopped and that the second form had then immediately moved forward. Along the same line, it is much easier to say that "the Communists caused the Vietnam War" or that "the child is responsible for his failure in school" than to admit that there were many different factors involved.

A major danger in attributing causality is that blame is often misplaced. It is common for representatives of both sides of a dispute—whether the combatants are children or warring nations—to accuse the other of starting the hostilities. Attributing causality is also dangerous when it blinds people to more appropriate causal agents, such as environmental factors that may impinge on the person both from the past and in the present. If educators hold a child responsible for her poor record in school, then they will be inclined to ignore those factors contributing to her failure over which they have some control—failings of the educational system in which she is enmeshed, her teacher's personality, and so on. In the same way, if society believes that criminals are solely to blame for their crimes, it can disregard the factors that led to their criminal behavior, such as poverty, boredom, and the frequency with which violence is peddled by the mass media as a solution to problems of all sorts. To be sure, the world looks far tidier—a less ambiguous and more secure place—with causal attributions. However, the cost of security often involves gross oversimplification.

Oversimplification is not merely bad in its own right. Popular conceptions of causality underlie many of society's central systems for dispensing rewards and punishments. Whether dealing with children, friends, or the accused in a jury trial, society assigns blame and delivers punishment in accordance with its perceptions of causality. Society despises "willful" misdoing and punishes it severely. Similarly, rewards for outstanding behavior largely depend on whether society views the individual as personally responsible for his or her success.

Power and Perceived Causality

One of the first psychologists to take a close look at the process of causal attribution was Fritz Heider (1958), whose theorizing has spanned the past three decades. Prior to the 1940s, the study of perception was largely confined to human perceptions of nonhuman stimuli. The perception of light, form, and color dominated the field. Heider felt strongly that the principles of visual experience were not adequate in accounting for the ways in which human beings perceive one another. For this reason, Heider concentrated on the *phenomenology* of the average person—the ways in which he or she experiences others. One of the major processes in which Heider was interested is the common tendency for a person to see others as having caused their actions.

Heider's initial formulation was based on virtually no systematic research. However, so perceptive was he in dissecting the elements of common experience that most of his theoretical distinctions are still influencing the laboratory efforts of today. In a book such as the one you are reading, with its heavy emphasis on the fruits of systematic research, it is useful to remember the value of insightful theorizing, even when there is little systematic data available. Without insightful theorizing, after all, it is difficult to know what data to collect. Heider's entire elaborate theoretical scheme will not be summarized here. The interested reader might wish to consult the original work (Heider, 1958) as well as recent and highly significant extensions by Edward Jones and Keith Davis (1965) and Harold Kelley (1972).

One of Heider's central concepts is the *power factor*—a person's ability to carry out the activity in question. People tend to see a person's actions as caused by him—to attribute causality to him, in other words—only when they perceive that he has the ability or skill to carry out the action. If a student fails a test, for example, his teacher might be inclined to think that "it wasn't intentional" if the teacher feels that the student did not have the ability to pass the test in the first place. Accordingly, the teacher may be kinder, more forgiving, and less impatient than if the student appeared to be capable of passing the test. Research support for the hypothesis that people tend to place more blame on those who seem capable of better work comes from several sources, among them a study by John Lanzetta and T. E. Hannah (1969). In this study, student subjects believed that they were serving as supervisors over workers who they thought were fellow student subjects. The workers ostensibly had to carry out difficult assignments, and it was the supervisor's job to reward them with money or punish them with electric shocks in such a way as to ensure that their work would be of the highest quality. Half the supervisors received information leading them to believe that one of their workers was a very able, intelligent person. The other half of the supervisors learned that the worker was very low in ability. Both these workers had been instructed to perform very poorly. The question was, which of the two would the supervisor be more likely to punish? If Heider is correct, the failure of the low-ability person would be most forgivable because he had no choice but to fail. When the high-ability person failed, however, the supervisors would blame the failure on the worker's intentions and would react with vengeance. Subjects in Lanzetta and Hannah's experiment did just that.

The finding that supervisors dealt far more punishment to high-ability failures than to low-ability failures raises the question of whether or not it makes a difference *when* a person perceives another as able or skilled. If you have played a team sport, you know that it is not always easy to determine how skillful any one member of a team is at the sport. We all have our moments of glory as well as defeat. Edward Jones, Leslie Rock, Kelly Shaver, George Goethals, and Lawrence Ward (1968) asked whether people seem to have more ability when their performance goes from good to bad or from bad to good. In several experiments Jones and his colleagues arranged it so that student subjects observed what appeared to be another student working at a series of thirty difficult problems. In one condition, the student's performance became increasingly better. He began by missing most of the problems, but by the end of the series he was succeeding on almost every problem. In another condition, just the reverse took place: The student's originally fine performance deteriorated so that he was failing almost completely in the final trials. In a random condition, the student succeeded with some problems but failed with others in no particular sequence. In all three conditions, the student obtained fifteen correct answers, given thirty problems. After observing one of these performances, subjects rated the performer's skill and also recorded their recollections of his performance. The results of the various experiments were consistent and revealing. Subjects who watched the worker's performance decline saw him as far more skillful than either the worker whose performance improved or the worker whose successes were random. In addition, subjects recalled that the worker whose performance deteriorated had obtained more correct answers than he had. Apparently, if a person wishes to create the impression that he or she is intelligent, whether with teachers or employers, it is better to begin strong and then relax rather than to relax first and finish in a spurt of glory. When performance is initially good, people tend to attribute later failures to transient motives or environmental conditions. But when performance is initially bad and becomes increasingly better, people attribute the success to practice or training rather than to ability. This is yet another example of the primacy effect in the perception of individuals.

Internal Versus External Causality

If the perceiver judges that an individual is capable of performing a task, this judgment sets the stage for several additional factors that help the perceiver to decide whether the other individual has acted willfully. Three of those factors are the perceiver's knowledge of environmental forces, the perceiver's motives at the moment, and the perceiver's perspective as actor or bystander.

Among the most obvious factors to consider in judging whether others act willfully are the environmental factors that impinge on them. For example, an individual may seem to have been pushed into actions by social or physical circumstance or to have been influenced by rewards and punishments. As a rule, the greater a person's awareness of environmental influences impinging on another's actions, the weaker the tendency to infer that the other's behavior resulted from his or her own volition.

Social approval operates as an environmental force pushing the individual in a given direction. Edward Jones and Keith Davis pointed out in 1965 that when someone's behavior is *socially approved,* others cannot be certain that it is truly intended. That person's true intentions are masked. By the same token, people are likely to perceive behavior as personally intended if it violates commonly approved norms. A study by Ivan Steiner and William Field (1960) illustrates this line of reasoning. Three-man discussion groups met to discuss the issue of racial integration. In half the groups the experimenter announced that he was having difficulty finding anyone to take the prosegregation side of the argument. He then asked one

of the subjects to help out by taking the prosegregation position. The chosen subject was, in fact, an accomplice of the experimenter. Nevertheless, the experimenter's request did make it appear to the real subjects that an environmental force would be causing a fellow subject's behavior. In the remaining half of the cases, the experimenter neither announced his difficulty nor selected the accomplice to take the position. After the discussion began, however, the experimental accomplice took the same prosegregation position without being asked to do so. After the discussion, subjects rated one another on a variety of dimensions. Of special interest was the extent to which subjects saw the accomplice's expressed opinions as self-determined—that is, as truly his own. As it turned out, subjects were much less certain of the accomplice's true opinions when they felt that he had acted under social pressure than when his unpopular stand had been unsolicited.

As perceivers, we also tend to be influenced by status relationships in attributing causality. If a person has high status, others may assume that environmental factors play less of a role in determining her actions than if she has low status: We tend to assume that high-status individuals do not have to take into account the opinions of those with lesser status and thus are relatively immune to social pressures. For example, teachers, the heads of organizations, and the President of the United States tend to be seen as personally deciding their actions to a greater extent than the people beneath them do. The importance of status in affecting perceptions of causality has been demonstrated by John Thibaut and Henry Riecken (1955). They gave experimental subjects the task of trying to convince another person that their choices of influential materials in an experimental task were good ones. In half the cases the person they were to convince appeared to be much higher in status—older, more mature, and senior in class standing as compared to subjects. In the remaining cases the person to be convinced was a low-status individual—younger, less mature, and lower in class standing than they. After the subjects had attempted to convince one of these persons of the wisdom of their choices, the subjects all learned that they had been very convincing. However, when the subjects subsequently rated the extent to which they felt the reactions they had received were truly intended by their listeners, large differences emerged. The subjects viewed the compliance of the high-status individual as much more internally caused than that of the low-status person. As it happened, subjects also showed a significantly greater amount of attraction for the high-status person. Apparently, then, those with high status are seen as acting more

Figure 5.4 When an individual's behavior is socially expected or approved, others are apt to attribute it to environmental influences rather than to personal causality. Which of these behaviors are you most likely to attribute to the true intentions of the actor— that of Hubert Humphrey (*left*), who is playing ball with these youngsters while being photographed for campaign publicity, or cadet James Pelosi's (*right*), who finished his West Point training despite almost two years of silence and ostracism from his peers?

freely than low-status individuals. As a result, they are more subject to our praise as well as our censure.

In general, the greater a person's awareness of factors impinging on others, the less likely that person is to assign causality to them. If this premise is extended to its logical conclusion, it could be concluded that complete knowledge of impinging factors prevents attribution of personal causality. It may still be argued that people do cause their behavior in the sense that they carry around with them strong learned dispositions that direct their behavior. But from the standpoint of the individual, it is certainly advantageous not to allow events of the past to blind one to more rewarding alternative ways of behaving. And to attribute personal causality to people when they *do* allow their past to rule their present is also to plead ignorance as to the ultimate causes of the dispositions. Learned dispositions result from earlier forces acting on the individual, and to say that the individual willed or caused his or her actions is to misdirect attention, to prematurely conclude the search for the causes of those actions.

The Effects of Motives on the Perception of Causality

One of the most fascinating lines of early research on person perception concerns the effects of people's feelings or motives on their perceptions. As you will recall, most early work on visual perception dealt with reactions

---

MOTIVES NOT ONLY influence the ways in which we perceive the world but what we learn from it and remember as well. Social psychologists, at least since World War II, have been interested in this phenomenon. In 1943 Jerome Levine and Gardner Murphy found that people tend to remember best those messages that agree with their own attitudes. They gave pro- and anti-Communist literature to students who had either pro- or anti-Communist leanings. For several weeks the subjects were tested on their ability to reproduce these passages. Students of both leanings remembered the literature supportive of their own viewpoints best. The figure shows the learning and subsequent forgetting trends of both groups on the anti-Communist readings.

In another study, Ronald Taft tested two groups of boys who were juvenile delinquents, one group black and the other white, on how well they remembered a story about a black baseball player. The story contained many pro- and anti-black statements. Immediately after the first exposure, black subjects were able to remember more pro-black than anti-black statements. When Taft tested the same

black subjects three days later, their ability to recall favorable items about blacks had become even more pronounced. These and other studies point to the widespread tendency for people to see what they want to see. (There are limits to this "truth," however, as Edward E. Jones has shown in additional studies with Rika Kohler.)

Furthermore, when presented with plausible and implausible arguments, subjects tend to remember more plausible statements for their own viewpoints and more implausible statements for antagonistic viewpoints. Apparently, people tend to protect their own attitudinal status quos. They seem to "forget" information that threatens their conceptual status quo, unless there is a good reason not to. Considering these findings, we might justifiably be suspicious of anyone who claims that "the facts speak for themselves."

Sources: Adapted from E. Jones and R. Kohler, "The Effects of Plausibility on the Learning of Controversial Statements," *Journal of Abnormal and Social Psychology,* 57 (1958), pp. 315–320.
J. Levine and G. Murphy, "The Learning and Forgetting of Controversial Material," *Journal of Abnormal and Social Psychology,* 38 (1943), pp. 507–517.
R. Taft, "Selective Recall and Memory Distortion of Favorable and Unfavorable Material," *Journal of Abnormal and Social Psychology,* 49 (1954), pp. 23–29.

LEARNING WHAT COMES NATURALLY

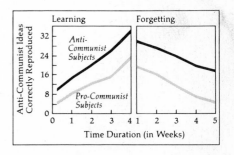

to colors, shapes, light intensity, and so on; the major focus was on charting the relationship between a physical stimulus in the environment and the visual reaction of the observer. Social psychologists like Heider were discontented with such research as it applied to people. They directly challenged the traditional approach by demonstrating in a series of experiments that perceptions of the world are altered substantially by emotional states. This research indicated, for example, that things people like very much seem larger to them (Bruner and Goodman, 1947) and that people often fail to see things that they dislike or fear (Eriksen and Browne, 1956; Rosen, 1954). This departure from traditional perceptual psychology was the focus of heated controversy for more than a decade. When the dust settled, it appeared that the effects of emotion on perceptions have no basis in neurological sensation but derive, rather, from what happens to visual sensations *after* they are relayed to the brain—in other words, from the ways in which people think about the world. People tend to search their environments for information and to apply concepts to this information in ways that are very much influenced by their feelings, motives, and values.

A classic study by Albert Pepitone (1965) demonstrates the potency of these effects. Pepitone gave high-school students an opportunity to win a free ticket to a basketball game. He varied the motivation of the students to win by informing one group that the tickets were for a major college team and a second group that the tickets were for an unimportant high-school game. To obtain the tickets, each student had to win the approval of a panel of coaches that would ask his opinions about various aspects of basketball. The coaches were actually confederates of the experimenter. One of the coaches (Mr. Friendly) was very friendly toward the student throughout the interview; a second coach (Mr. Neutral) was noncommittal in his behavior toward the subject; and a third coach (Mr. Negative) was critical of the student throughout the interview. After the interview, each student was asked to rate the extent to which each of the panel members had been friendly to him and the extent of their power to influence the panel's decisions. These ratings revealed clear distortions in subjects' perceptions of the coaches. Although Mr. Friendly behaved in essentially the same way during all the interviews whether subjects had high or low motivation, the students who were highly motivated rated him as significantly more friendly toward them and more powerful than did students with low motivation. In other words, when they very much wanted the tickets they saw the judge who offered them encouragement as far more approving of them and more likely to influence the panel in their favor than did less-motivated subjects. In addition, regardless of the state of motivation, Mr. Friendly was rated as more influential than either of the other coaches. Thus, subjects perceived the man who seemed most friendly toward them as the most powerful, even when they had no evidence to indicate that he agreed with their opinions about basketball.

Motives have powerful effects on the ways in which people interpret the world, and, as discussed previously, people are fond of interpreting the world in causal terms. When human beings are successful, the most gratifying perception of causality is that they themselves are responsible. Should the same attempt meet with failure, on the other hand, they are more likely to reconstruct their experiences in such ways that they are blameless—namely, by attributing causality to other sources. Rationalizations of this type include "It wasn't my fault—little sister made me do it" and "I just lost my temper—I didn't mean to do it." The human capacity to

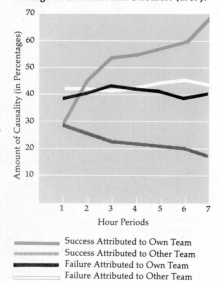

Figure 5.5 We are more likely to take credit for our successes than our failures, as demonstrated by these research findings of Streufert and Streufert (1969).

III ENCOUNTERING OTHERS

interpret the world in causal terms has been demonstrated by Siegfried and Susan Streufert (1969). Student teams worked together in a setting designed to simulate problems in a revolution-torn country. During the several hours in which they took the role of government administrators, they received immense amounts of information and found themselves in the position of being called on to make a great many decisions. During some periods in a schedule that was prearranged by the Streuferts, some teams' decisions met with almost constant success and other teams experienced little but failure. At the end of each hour, all subjects rated the extent to which their outcomes during the previous hour had been primarily a consequence of their own actions, the actions of their opponents, or other factors. As indicated by subjects' average ratings, which are shown in Figure 5.5, the subjects saw themselves as very much responsible for their winnings and their opponents as responsible for their failures.

Similar research (Johnson, Feigenbaum, and Weiby, 1964) indicates that teachers take causal credit for their students' successes but not for their students' failures. Teachers rated whether each student's performance had been due primarily to the child's efforts and abilities or to their teaching skills. Some of the children performed well sometimes and poorly at other times. The ratings revealed that when a child did poorly, the teacher attributed the behavior to the low intelligence or low motivation of the child. However, the teachers saw improvement as a result of their own teaching efforts. It seems that people are most inclined to take credit for having caused things when those endeavors turn out well.

Perceiving Causality: Actor-Observer Disagreements

Individuals vary in their understanding of their environment, and the present discussion must encompass individual differences as well as group trends. Among the differences discussed in Chapter 4 were those between people who saw themselves as internally controlled and those who felt controlled by outside circumstances. In addition, the social roles people play contribute to these differences. Two roles that are associated with differing perceptions of causality are those of the *actor* and the *observer*. Edward Jones and Richard Nisbett suggested in 1971 that this difference between the person carrying out an activity and the person watching is central in determining the perception of causality. This view does much to explain the conflict between those who say "You are to blame, it was your fault, you must be punished" and those who reply "It wasn't my fault, it couldn't be helped, and you have no right to punish me." Conflicts such as these often arise in relationships between parents and their offspring, between society and its criminals, and between the closest of lovers.

Jones and Nisbett's central thesis is that actors are more likely than observers to attribute their actions to situational requirements, whereas observers are more likely than actors to see the same behavior as personally caused by the actors. Jones and Nisbett offered several explanations. First, the actor usually has more information than observers about the events leading up to his behavior. He is in the best position to recall forces that could have influenced him. A second reason for these perceptual differences is that in the heat of action the actor must often pay close attention to the external events impinging on him. A boy trying to impress a good-looking girl may watch her facial expressions very closely for signs of pleasure or displeasure; such cues help him adjust his actions appropriately. For the observer, on the other hand, the most dynamic point of interest is the actor. The environmental factors impinging on him receive less careful attention.

This second explanation has been supported in a variety of studies. In one of them, Richard Nisbett, Craig Caputo, Patricia Legant, and Jeanne Marecek (1973) asked male college students to write brief descriptions indicating their reasons for choosing their major field of concentration and for liking the girl whom they dated most frequently. The students then wrote equivalent descriptions of the preferences of their best friends. Thus, each student wrote descriptions from the perspectives of both actor and observer. All responses were then coded by the investigators into two types. One type of response rationalized behavior in terms of an *environmental situation*—for example, "Chemistry is a high-paying field" or "She's a very warm person." The other type of response referred to *personal causality,* as in "I want to make a lot of money" or "I like warm persons." When describing their reasons for selecting their majors, students attributed approximately equal numbers of choices to situational and personal causes. In contrast, the combined responses with which the students answered for their best friends included three times as many reasons stressing personal causation. In describing their own reasons for choosing their girl friends, students listed environmental factors twice as often as personal

Figure 5.6 Stanley Schachter and other researchers have suggested that we take into account more than the evidence of our physiological sensations when labeling our emotions. For example, any one sensation (such as "butterflies" in the stomach) can be caused by a number of emotions. Thus, people use situational cues in their environment to give shape and perspective to their perceptions of themselves. (Lithograph by M. C. Escher.)

III ENCOUNTERING OTHERS

causes. (Apparently, many students see themselves as "carried away" by members of the opposite sex but as having chosen their majors carefully.) When describing their best friends' reasons for selecting their dates, environmental reasons dropped to approximately 50 percent.

In addition to supporting the Jones-Nisbett hypothesis, these results lend weight to the earlier suggestion that the more a person knows about another individual's situation, the more likely that person is to find environmental causes to explain the other's behavior. Complete knowledge might do away with the concept of personal causality entirely. Thus, the one person everyone knows who is never without an excuse is oneself.

PERCEIVING ONE'S EMOTIONS: LOVE OR INDIGESTION?

Thus far, the main topic has been people's perceptions of one another. Very little has been said about self-perception. Actually, most of what has been discussed is probably as relevant to perceiving oneself as to perceiving others. All people form impressions of themselves. Such impressions are vital parts of their self-concepts. For example, most of us seem to view ourselves as causal agents as long as things are going reasonably well, and all of the factors influencing our perceptions of others' abilities influence our self-perceptions as well. As Daryl Bem asserted in 1967, people seem to use the same kind of evidence and logic in drawing conclusions about themselves as they do in perceiving others (see Chapter 9).

In spite of the usual similarities between perceptions of self and others, there are certain instances in which there are clear differences between the two processes. One of the most fascinating and important of these instances is the perception of a person's own emotional states. Each of us is often faced with a turbulence of experience that is called emotion, and each is the only one who has direct access to his or her emotional experiences. Processes governing a person's perception of others' emotions thus have very limited applicability because the information at an observer's disposal is relatively inadequate.

The problem of how to make sense of emotions is an intriguing one. When our emotions are aroused, they certainly do not enter our experience with labels handily cataloging them. It is difficult for us to know when we are in love as opposed to infatuated or when we are jealous as opposed to angry or frustrated. Furthermore, our definitions of our own emotions fade into one another, turning from anger to despair, for example, or even from love to hate, and vice versa.

Insensitivity to changes in our own feelings can have disastrous effects on our lives. The conduct of our lives vitally depends on the degree to which we understand our emotions. When we classify feelings as love, we may be ready to make all sorts of commitments to others—commitments that we would not dream of making if we had perceived the same feelings as infatuation. And if we identify feelings as hate, we may remain icy toward other people indefinitely. If, on the other hand, we classify the same feelings as anger, the implication is that we may soon warm up again.

Perhaps the major insight into the ways in which we label our emotions has been provided by Stanley Schachter and his co-workers (Nisbett and Schachter, 1966; Schachter and Singer, 1962; Schachter and Wheeler, 1962). Schachter's hypothesis is that our understanding of our emotions is dependent on two major factors. First, there must be some form of conscious *physiological arousal,* or stimulation. Schachter views arousal in itself as quite uninformative; fine discriminations among emotional

SHE'S ALWAYS BEEN CRAZY ABOUT ME BUT I DON'T KNOW— I NEVER THOUGHT SHE WAS VERY MUCH.

BUT I SEE THE WAY GUYS LOOK AT HER ON THE STREET SO I GUESS SHE MUST HAVE A PRETTY GREAT FIGURE.

AND I SEE HOW PEOPLE GATHER AROUND HER AT PARTIES SO I GUESS SHE MUST HAVE A REALLY GREAT PERSONALITY.

AND I SEE HOW HARD EVERYBODY LISTENS WHEN SHE TALKS SO I GUESS SHE MUST BE EXTREMELY INTELLIGENT.

→

SO I GUESS I'M IN LOVE WITH HER.

AND I GUESS I'LL MARRY HER.

AND I'LL GUESS WE'LL BE VERY HAPPY.

SOUNDS LIKE A VERY GOOD DEAL.

states do not seem to appear at the physiological level. At most, human beings seem to recognize rudimentary differences in positive versus negative emotional states. For Schachter, it is *the environment* that provides us with clues about our emotions. We look to the situation in which we are enmeshed. If the situation is the sort that we suppose evokes fear, then we will interpret the arousal as fear; if the situation indicates that anger is the more appropriate feeling, then we will label the same arousal as anger. Whether we interpret our feelings as love, fascination, or simple sexual arousal thus should depend on our interpretations of situational factors, such as where we are, what others have said, and what we have been doing with those others. In all cases the arousal may be the same; only the labels may be different.

In an initial attempt to document these views, Stanley Schachter and Jerome Singer (1962) gave experimental subjects injections of a stimulant (epinephrine). One group of subjects was informed about the properties of the drug and was told that they would soon experience generalized emotional feelings including increased heart rate, a flushed feeling, possible tremors, and so on. A second group was not informed about the drug's effects but was simply told that the drug was a vitamin supplement; no side-effects were implied. After the drug had been administered, each subject was seated in a waiting room in preparation for a supposed study of visual perception. While waiting, each encountered one of two experiences. An experimental accomplice, appearing to be a second subject, began to act in one of the two ways. The researchers viewed the subjects' reactions to the accomplice through a one-way mirror. With half the subjects, the accomplice appeared to be frivolous and joyous; he began by tossing wads of paper into the wastebasket and continued by shooting paper airplanes, building a paper tower, and playing with a hula hoop. With the second group, the accomplice reacted angrily to a request to fill out a questionnaire containing many personal items; he seemed to become increasingly disturbed, and after a final fit of rage he ripped up the questionnaire and threw it away.

All subjects were physiologically aroused by the drug, but the investigators reasoned that those who had *not* been informed about the drug's effects would be far more influenced by the environmental antics of the accomplice. When the experimenters told subjects of the drug's effects, they essentially had supplied those subjects with an explanation for their feelings; these subjects needed to search the environment no longer for an adequate label for their experience. Subjects who thought they had had vitamin shots, on the other hand, would be searching for an explanation for their aroused state and thus would be maximally open to whatever definition of the situation the accomplice provided.

The results showed, as Schachter and Singer had predicted, that the people who had been misinformed about the effects of the drug were most strongly influenced by the confederate's actions. The researchers standing behind the one-way mirror observed that misinformed subjects joined in the accomplice's antics much more readily than did informed subjects— laughing, joining in the games, and otherwise imitating the accomplice. The same pattern emerged when the accomplice behaved badly; misinformed subjects soon became angry, too, and the informed subjects did not join in the tantrum. Subjects' ratings of their own feelings after the experiment paralleled these findings.

This line of reasoning has been applied by Richard Nisbett and Stanley

III ENCOUNTERING OTHERS

Schachter (1966) to understanding the ways in which people experience pain. Subjects in this experiment received a placebo that had no effects. However, half the subjects were informed that the "drug" would cause an arousal reaction similar to that produced by strong electric shock; the other half were told that the drug would produce innocuous symptoms such as itching sensations and numbness of the feet. Later, the experimenter gave all subjects increasingly strong doses of shock and told them that they could terminate the shock when it became too painful to tolerate. The results showed that subjects who thought that the drug was causing their arousal reaction tolerated higher levels of shock than did those who could only attribute their arousal to its actual source—the shock. The ways in which people experience pain thus seem to depend on their understanding of the source of their symptoms as well as on the pain-giving stimulus. Therefore, the perception of pain is apparently only partially based in physiology.

Stuart Valins (1966) extended Schachter's theorizing to perceptions of sexual arousal. Rather than varying the information provided by the environment, Valins altered subjects' perceptions of their inner state of arousal. In an experiment that may have proved more pleasant to subjects than the last few that have been discussed, the experimenter showed Playboy centerfolds to male subjects and asked them to rate the physical attractiveness of each. The experimenter explained that he would be monitoring each subject's heartbeats while the subject was making the ratings. By design, the "heartbeat recorder" emitted sounds loud enough so that the subject could hear what supposedly were his heartbeats. While the subject rated the pictures, the experimenter systematically altered the heartbeat sounds. The experimenter chose some of the centerfolds at random and increased what the subject thought were his heartbeats while the subject was examining the centerfolds. When subjects subsequently rated the pictures, the effects of the planted heartbeats were striking. Those pictures that had been accompanied by increased heartbeats were rated as much more attractive than were the other pictures. What people perceive as sexy, therefore, apparently depends at least in part on the ways in which they read their own bodily signals.

The next two chapters will discuss some of the particular ways in which people perceive one another that have powerful effects on the directions that relationships take. Some ways of perceiving others lead to friendships and loving relationships, which are the focus of Chapter 6, whereas in other cases the outcomes are destructive. The derogatory stereotypes and hostilities that can result when people perceive only the worst in one another are the focus of Chapter 7.

SUMMARY

The impressions we human beings form of one another often shape others' reactions to us and affect others' self-perceptions as well. As a result, an impression sometimes becomes a *self-fulfilling prophecy* when a person's expectations actually help cause those expectations to become fulfilled.

Through the process of *conceptualization*—categorizing or labeling incoming information about others—we all simplify our experiences by sorting them into categories that help us to generalize, to comprehend, and to predict. However, oversimplification may dangerously distort our perceptions.

When we sort one another into categories, we tend to rely on *implicit personality theories* to suggest additional personal qualities that are consistent with the characteristics that we have already perceived. These personality theories may be based on past experiences; may be created by a specialized process of cognitive balance called a *halo effect* (which colors perceptions of one characteristic with the emotions we attach to a related characteristic); or may be composed of certain combinations of traits that we have come to associate.

As Solomon Asch has hypothesized, certain traits derive at least part of their meanings from other traits that the perceiver associates with them. Some traits, called *central organizing traits,* are more crucial to impression formation than others because they have come to symbolize broad categories of qualities. Not all social psychologists agree with Asch. Some researchers, for example, interpret centrality of traits to mean that a trait dimension is central only to a specific cluster of associated traits. For example, an aggressive-passive dimension is probably more central to the role of football player than to the role of parent. Some clusters of traits are *learned associations;* repetition has made certain combinations relatively familiar to all of us.

Facts about people do not always comfortably fit our conceptual categories; impressions sometimes are contradictory or inconsistent. Social psychologists have identified three methods that we use to resolve inconsistencies: the *relational method,* trying to integrate the inconsistent information in some way; *discounting,* acting as if the inconsistency does not exist or is unimportant; and *linear combining,* adding and subtracting new information about a person to an existing impression. Social psychologists disagree about whether, when we face several conflicting facts about an individual, we are influenced most strongly by the first in a series of clues (the *primacy effect*) or by the last of the clues (the *recency effect*). Researchers also disagree as to which of two combining processes we tend to use—*summation,* which involves accumulating the values of a series of traits, or *averaging.* The weight of the evidence supports a modified averaging model, which suggests that people tend not to weigh all pieces of information equally but rather to assign greater importance to highly negative or highly positive traits.

One of the simplest ways for people to make sense of their many impressions is to see events as being directly caused by certain persons or to fit events into cause-and-effect relationships. This *causal attribution* provides people with a sense or order and predictability. However, attributing causality can be dangerous when it leads people to see themselves or others as prime causal agents although environmental factors are at least partially responsible.

The study of phenomenology—the ways in which human beings experience the world—has occupied Fritz Heider for many years. One of his central concepts is the *power factor*—a person's ability to perform a certain activity. People tend to hold another responsible for his or her performance only when that other seems to have the ability or skill to perform successfully. In addition, we generally base our judgments of one another's abilities on early performance; if the performance subsequently slips, we are likely to assume that the individual has transient reasons for performing poorly. On the other hand, when a person begins badly and improves, people tend to attribute the improvement to training or practice, but not to ability. In general, the more we know about other individuals and the pressures that beset them, the less likely we are to see them as personally responsible for their successes and failures. However, we tend to believe that we ourselves are responsible when we are successful and that we are the victims of outside factors when we fail.

The role that a person plays in an event is also important in determining how that person attributes causality. For example, the actor, who is aware of all the behind-the-scenes information that goes into his performance, is more aware of the complex factors that cause his behavior than is the observer, who may only be aware of the performance. Therefore, the observer is more likely than the actor to see the performance as personally caused by the actor.

Awareness of one's own emotions adds another dimension to self-perception. Stanley Schachter and his associates hypothesize that we interpret our emotions according to the situations in which we find ourselves. For example, when we have feelings that could be interpreted either as love or as sexual excitement, we interpret those feelings according to situational cues such as place, time, and the behavior of those around us.

Our perceptions of ourselves and others depend, therefore, on a complex array of personal emotions and values, environmental conditions, and the qualities and actions of those we perceive.

SUGGESTED READINGS

Bruner, Jerome. "On Perceptual Readiness," *Psychological Review,* 64 (1957), 123–152.

Gergen, Kenneth. "The Perception of Others and Oneself," in K. W. Back (ed.), *Basic Issues in Social Psychology.* New York: Wiley, 1973.

Hastorf, Albert, David Schneider, and Judith Polefka. *Person Perception.* Reading, Mass.: Addison-Wesley, 1970.

Schachter, Stanley. "The Interaction of Cognitive and Physiological Determinants of Emotional States," in L. Berkowitz (ed.), *Advances in Experimental Social Psychology,* Vol. 1. New York: Academic Press, 1964, pp. 49–81.

Steiner, Ivan. "Perceived Freedom," in L. Berkowitz (ed.), *Advances in Experimental Social Psychology,* Vol. 5. New York: Academic Press, 1970, pp. 187–242.

Taguiri, Renato, and Luigi Petrullo (eds.). *Person Perception and Interpersonal Behavior.* Stanford, Calif.: Stanford University Press, 1958.

Warr, Peter Bryan, and Christopher Knapper. *The Perception of People and Events.* New York: Wiley, 1968.

6

Interpersonal Attraction

THE NEED TO AFFILIATE is so strong in human beings that when people are deprived of human contact for long, the effects can be startling and painful. The subjective reports of a variety of persons who have been deprived of human contact over long periods bear testimony to the power of human beings' essentially social nature.

Shipwrecked sailors, monks in certain religious orders, and prisoners in solitary confinement, for example, have reported feeling overwhelming anxiety that was far out of proportion to any actual danger confronting them. According to these people, they were unable to control this flood of emotion during their isolation. Although they reported various physical symptoms and psychological effects arising from their anxiety, one of the most common phenomena was a hallucination that other people were with them. For example, Joshua Slocum, who sailed alone around the world, reported that a savior appeared to him during particularly perilous times.

Similar experiences have been reported by laboratory subjects who have participated in sensory deprivation experiments. Students at McGill University who volunteered to take part in studies of the effects of complete isolation and sensory deprivation reported that they felt as if another body were lying beside them in the cubicle they occupied during the experiment (Heron, 1957). In one case, a subject reported that the hallucinated body and his own seemed to overlap, partly occupying the same space.

The need to affiliate is so compelling that it cuts across the immense variability in social customs and social roles that distinguish any one human culture from others. Certain themes characterize the patterns of interaction in all cultures: People everywhere develop friendships, engage in courtship, produce and care for children, and are influenced by family ties. The differences in the ways people engage in these relationships and whom they choose as partners are sometimes so great that they very nearly obscure the similarities among cultures in the basic human tendency to affiliate and to choose with whom to affiliate.

Take the case of sex roles. Women are passive in some societies, as they have traditionally been in the United States, and dominant in others. In the Tchambuli tribe of New Guinea, for example, women shave their heads, prefer one another's companionship, impress the outsider as proud and powerful, and generally run things, according to Margaret Mead (1949). In contrast, their menfolk concern themselves primarily with their own hair styles and with their relationships to the women. Yet, although sex roles, as people in the United States have traditionally known them, are reversed among the Tchambuli, their communities are efficiently managed, the people find satisfaction in one another's company, and children are born and raised. People engage in many of the same basic types of social relationships in New Guinea as they do in North America, but who plays what roles in which relationships sometimes differs dramatically.

The forms that interpersonal relationships take are also affected by circumstantial factors, including environmental influences. For example, most Polynesian and Micronesian social systems have evolved a solution to the consequences of hurricanes and severe storms that wipe out large portions of their village populations with brutal frequency. These people view partners in sex and marriage as much more interchangeable than do most Westerners. No one person is likely to be considered indispensable in a particular role; rather, a variety of persons are considered capable of playing a role such as father or wife (Howard, 1971; Levy, 1969). People in this part of the world are not conditioned to expect their social ties to be deep and irreplaceable. Thus, there are no expectations of "love at first sight" or of finding any *one* person who will inject meaning into one's life. In fact, these inhabitants of the South Pacific consider it unusual for any two people *not* to get along with one another. This outlook has probably also been accentuated by the fact that slow and sparse communication between villages tends to isolate communities; thus, for example, a rather limited selection of persons may be eligible for marriage at any one time in

Figure 6.1 At first glance, most of the research findings in interpersonal attraction have a commonsense flavor to them. The interesting thing about common sense is that it can often account for all possible contingencies and is thus frequently contradictory. Consider these everyday sayings and famous quotations about interpersonal attraction. The chief advantage of scientific sense over common sense is that it tries to specify when and why certain commonsense notions hold and when and why they do not. When you complete this chapter, evaluate how much of it was *really* common sense.

Opposites attract.	*Birds of a feather flock together.*
Absence makes the heart grow fonder.	*Out of sight, out of mind.*
Old friends are best.	*Most friendship is feigning.*
Marriages are made in heaven.	*It's better to marry than to burn.*
Love, like wine, is best when aged.	*There's no fool like an old fool.*
'Tis love that makes the world go 'round.	*Love's a malady without a cure.*
True love never dies.	*Love is like linen, often changed.*

III ENCOUNTERING OTHERS

a given locale, with the result that large age differences between partners in marriage are much more frequent than among inhabitants of urban centers.

Despite the cultural specifics, many common themes emerge. Interpersonal attraction supplies the cement that binds together friends whose relationships vary from casual to deep; lovers; and married couples. Although interpersonal attraction encompasses a wide range of relationships, most social-psychological research in interpersonal attraction has involved more casual relationships. Traditionally, experimenters have found it difficult to predict and manipulate interaction the longer two people have known each other. As a result, deep relationships between lovers or close friends have largely been ignored. Social psychologists have recently taken some steps toward understanding these more complex relationships, however, and these efforts will be attended to later in the chapter.

First, however, some of the more circumstantial factors that get people together—environmental influences—will be explored. Then less random factors—the "other" as perceived by the "self" and the actual behavior of the other—will be discussed. The concept of reward as a global concept that may explain virtually all the reasons people have for choosing their friends, lovers, husbands, and wives will also be considered. And finally, those deeper interpersonal experiences that are most profoundly subject to the innermost desires and unique qualities in each of us will be explored.

As you read about the insights that social psychologists have garnered from their studies of attraction, keep in mind the diversity of forms that interpersonal relations take in different cultures. Nearly all the evidence to be examined in this chapter has been uncovered in studies with subjects who were inhabitants of the United States. If you do not always like what you read about the standards by which people in the United States typically judge attractiveness, then let the evidence of different cultures remind you that there are many, many ways to be a friend, a lover, a husband or wife.

ENVIRONMENTAL INFLUENCES

Most of us feel that we have a great deal of latitude in the friends we choose. The cars, buses, telephones, and spare time available to most North Americans would all seem to ease communication among us and, therefore, to permit us a wide range of individuals from whom to choose companions, friends, and lovers. However, the evidence is that we do not typically exercise this freedom of choice and that, in fact, we typically do not venture beyond the perimeters of convenience in making contact with others.

Physical Proximity: Geography as Fate

The factor uncovered by social-psychological research that is most effective in circumscribing a person's contacts is physical proximity—the distance from one another at which people live or work. In general, the closer two individuals are geographically to one another, the more likely they will become attracted to each other.

The effects of physical proximity on patterns of friendship were demonstrated in a classic study by Leon Festinger, Stanley Schachter, and Kurt Back (1950). These three researchers studied the development of friendships among couples who were living in married-student housing at the Massachusetts Institute of Technology. For the most part, the students did not know one another before moving into the development. Furthermore, the residents had no choice regarding the units to which they were assigned. The housing complex consisted of seventeen separate two-story units, and each contained ten apartments, as illustrated in Figure 6.2. An index of functional distance between apartments was calculated by counting each apartment door as one unit and by adding an additional unit when residents had to go up or down stairs to visit. The researchers also asked each resident to name his or her three closest friends in the housing project. As indicated in Figure 6.2, the closer any two residents lived to one another, the more likely they were to be friends. For example, next-door neighbors were more likely to be friends than were neighbors two doors—a mere thirty-eight feet—away. Those who lived on the same floor were more likely to be friends than were residents living on different floors. In other words, the apartment to which an individual happened to be assigned, the design of a building, and other incidental factors were influential in determining which friendships developed.

One of the most surprising findings indicated in Figure 6.2 is that there is even greater affinity between next-door neighbors than between neighbors two doors apart; the difference between the two distances in the accessibility they permit seems negligible. Robert Priest and Jack Sawyer (1967) suggest that the affinity between two individuals is greater when they live one rather than two doors apart because the *perceived distance*—the number of people rather than of feet that intervene—is less. The fear of awkward encounters may be greater when a person must make a special effort to get to know someone several doors away, whereas the same behavior may seem a casual, even obligatory, response to a next-door neighbor.

Proximity apparently influences the selection of partners in marriage, as well as in more casual relationships. James Bossard (1932) and Alvin Katz and Reuben Hill (1958) report that the probability of marriage increases as the distance in blocks between residences decreases.

One factor that may contribute to the effects of proximity on attraction has been suggested by Jonathan Freedman, J. Merrill Carlsmith, and David Sears (1970). They contend that people try to convince themselves that the inevitable will not be too unpleasant. Therefore, the closer two people live or work to one another, the more motivated they may be to perceive one another favorably. This phenomenon was demonstrated by John Darley and Ellen Berscheid (1967), who gave subjects information about two strangers and then told the subjects that they would meet one of the strangers. Darley and Berscheid found that subjects evaluated the individual they were told they would meet more favorably than they evaluated the stranger they did not expect to meet.

It makes intuitive sense that one must get to know others before liking them and that the closer they are, the more available they are for interaction. Through interaction the other's behavior may become more familiar and thus more predictable; as a result, two such individuals may choose to let their guards down a bit and to encounter each other on a more informal and

Figure 6.2 The pattern of friendships that developed in seventeen two-story student housing units like the one diagramed (*at right*) was dramatically affected by the physical distance at which the residents lived: The closer two students lived to one another (in units of doors between them), the more likely that they would become close friends. Because each student had fewer possible friends to choose from the farther he or she ventured from home (*column 3*), experimenters Festinger, Schachter, and Back (1950) divided the number of actual friends chosen (*column 2*) by the number of possible choices in the entire housing development for each of four units of distance. (The two floors of each of the seventeen buildings yield a total of thirty-four floors in the development; this number is multiplied by the number of possible contacts at each choice distance. For example, the total possible number of one-unit choices on one floor is eight, whereas only two people per floor have neighbors four units removed.) The result is four percentages of people actually chosen as friends at each distance.

	Sociometric Choice and Physical Distance			
Units of Distance	Number of Choices Given	Possible Number of Choices	Percentage Choosing	
1	112	8x34	41.2	
2	46	6x34	22.5	
3	22	4x34	16.2	
4	7	2x34	10.3	

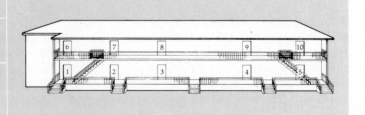

III ENCOUNTERING OTHERS

trusting basis. Evidence that familiarity breeds attraction has been contributed by Robert Zajonc (1968). For example, in one experiment Zajonc showed his subjects photographs from a college yearbook. Some of the photographs were shown to the subjects many more times than others. Of ten faces, each subject saw two faces only once, two faces twice, two faces five times, two faces ten times, and two faces twenty-five times. When Zajonc subsequently asked the subjects how much they thought they would like the people in these ten photographs, plus faces of two people in photographs the subjects had not yet seen, subjects' predictions bore a direct relationship to the frequency with which they had seen the faces: the more times they had seen a face, the more they expected to like its owner. The familiarity hypothesis applies to many experiences, including those of different foods, styles of art, clothing fashions, life styles, values, tools, and weapons. People are often quite resistant to unfamiliar objects and practices at first encounter. However, this resistance may eventually give way to acceptance. To mention one of many examples, modern abstract art was

Figure 6.3 Living arrangements like retirement communities and like the singles' apartments pictured here are an answer to the transience of a society where enduring relationships are increasingly difficult to establish and maintain. Relying on the possibility that physical proximity is the most important single predictor of success in newly developing relationships, these establishments advertise maximum opportunities for social interaction. These arrangements are becoming increasingly popular and often provide the primary source of friendships for residents.

scorned for decades before it became widely popular. Even automobiles faced a great deal of resistance before they became almost universally accepted. Zajonc found that repeated exposure produced more positive attitudes even toward certain Chinese written characters that were flashed on a screen more frequently than were other characters.

Although familiarity usually seems to foster compatibility, there are some cases in which, as the saying goes, "Familiarity breeds contempt." Feuding neighbors and situations that turn the best of friends into the worst of enemies are legendary. For example, people who occupy the same quarters for longer than a few days sometimes find that they can no longer tolerate one another's habits—habits they may have previously overlooked. This phenomenon earned the name "cabin fever" after many reports about North American miners, trappers, explorers, and rangers who tormented or even murdered one another when conditions forced them to live together in isolation for a few weeks, although it was often the case that they previously had been good friends. The same phenomenon may beset family members who "get on one another's nerves" and may partially account for the fact that so many homicides are committed by friends and relatives rather than by strangers.

Freedman, Carlsmith, and Sears identify two conditions in which proximity is not likely to lead to liking. One situation that tends to discourage compatibility arises when two people have conflicting interests, needs, or personalities; in such a case, continued interaction may aggravate the conflict. A second cause of dislike is an initial evaluation of the other that is extremely negative. Under these circumstances, people sometimes seem unable to perceive any positive attributes of the disliked individual, even after repeated contact (Freedman and Suomi, 1967).

Although in most cases people seem to like the things they are most familiar with, they are also sometimes drawn to individuals, places, and things that are *not* familiar. The unfamiliar stimulates scientists, philosophers, and artists to develop new inventions, concepts, and modes of expression; these new developments, in turn, may suffer from the more common, negative effects of unfamiliarity when first introduced to the public. The unknown has also attracted discoverers to unexplored continents and to outer space and appeals to the traveler in each of us. In fact, the appeal of unfamiliar things is often expressed in the saying "The grass is always greener on the other side." Psychologists may someday know the conditions under which familiarity yields boredom.

Interpersonal Space

People maintain preferred distances in their interactions with one another, Edward T. Hall (1966) has hypothesized. These preferred distances protect the personal space surrounding each person, and if it is invaded, that person will probably become uncomfortable and perhaps even hostile toward the transgressor. Preferred distances vary from situation to situation, from relationship to relationship, and from culture to culture. For example, Arabs typically interact at shorter distances than do North Americans. And, as Kenneth Little (1965) reports, people stand closer to their friends than to strangers and are likely to interact at shorter distances at social gatherings than at business meetings. According to Hall, North Americans observe four zones of interpersonal space: public distance, from twelve to twenty-five feet; social distance, from four to twelve feet; personal distance, from eighteen inches to four feet; and intimate distance, less than eighteen inches. Cross-cultural differences in preferred distances have resulted in many misunderstandings between persons of different cultural backgrounds: If a "foreigner" stands too close, the other person may become annoyed.

Although people try to maintain their preferred distances, unusually small distances, when they *are* established, may actually increase the likelihood of friendship. Under special circumstances, people may even shed or suspend their usual expectations regarding social distances. Kenneth and Mary Gergen (1971) noted that in encounter groups people who are in physical proximity are warmer and friendlier to each other than are people who are physically farther apart, even in the same group. This observation led the Gergens to hypothesize that physical proximity may actually trigger friendliness. When they tested this hypothesis, they found that the closer subjects sat to a confederate, the greater their conformity to the confederate's judgments. However, although proximity apparently increased conformity, the Gergens found no evidence that this conformity was a function of attraction; the ratings made by the subjects did not indicate that they were any more or less attracted to their close neighbors. The basis of this apparent paradox may lie in flaws in the techniques of measurement used; the Gergens are currently researching possibilities for measurement techniques that are more sensitive to possible effects that spatial relationships have on feelings.

It remains unclear exactly how spatial relationships affect interpersonal attraction, but personal experiences show that they can. For example, you may have experienced better rapport with classmates when arranged in close-knit circles than when all the students in a class sat at random distances and faced only the instructor. On the other hand, there are situations in which closeness to others can be an aggravation. For example, confinement in a crowded elevator cannot be expected, under ordinary circumstances, to generate many kindnesses.

Temperature and Crowding

There is considerable evidence that uncomfortable environmental conditions affect our emotions and feelings. The irritability that hot weather can provoke and the high frequency of riots during long, hot summers are both

Figure 6.4 People maintain culturally expected distances from one another that vary with the nature of both the situation and the relationship. An observer would almost certainly infer that the two gentlemen pictured at the left-hand side of this photograph are the only persons in the photograph who know one another very well. You can test the effects of interpersonal space by observing the reaction of your closest friend while you keep a distance of five feet the next time you talk. How would you react if a stranger confronted you at a distance of only five inches and struck up a conversation?

familiar occurrences. Several effects of heat on interpersonal relations have also been demonstrated in the laboratory. For example, William Griffitt asked subjects to examine a hypothetical person's responses of agreement or disagreement to questionnaire statements, to form an impression of him, and to predict how much they would like the individual if they were to meet him. In one experiment he had subjects study the responses in either a cool, comfortable setting or in a hot and humid one (Griffitt, 1970). In a second experiment (Griffitt and Veitch, 1971), the investigators varied not only temperature but degree of crowding as well; subjects were placed either in a fairly spacious setting (either hot or cool) or in a small and overcrowded setting (either hot or cool). Hot and crowded subjects expressed significantly less liking for the hypothetical individual

Physical Attractiveness:

WHAT YOU SEE IS WHAT YOU GET

IF YOU PRONOUNCE another person "beautiful" or "handsome," are you stating an objective truth that others would agree with? Or is your evaluation somehow dependent on who you are, where you come from, and what state of mind you happen to be in? Do different persons in fact see attractiveness differently, so that "what you see is what you get"?

Stanley Morse, Joan Gruzen, and Harry Reis reasoned that there may well be large differences in evaluations of physical attractiveness, depending on factors such as the sex, self-esteem, and nationality of the beholder. Accordingly, they compared the preferences of men and women; residents of New York City and white residents of Cape Town, South Africa; and high self-esteem individuals and persons with low self-esteem.

The investigators first administered a self-esteem scale to college students in the two countries and then had them evaluate the attractiveness and sex appeal of male and female persons. They then asked the students how much importance they attached to particular characteristics in judging the attractiveness of members of the opposite sex.

Both men and women considered women more physically attractive than men, and men and women did not appear to differ in their evaluations of the physical attractiveness and sex appeal of other individuals. This finding surprised the investigators, because

they had assumed that males and females would tend to use different standards in judging physical attractiveness. As a result, Morse and his colleagues examined the evaluations that subjects made of each person on nine additional dimensions (such as intelligence and happiness). The ways in which various ratings correlated with one another were noted. Morse found that when men evaluated women, sex appeal and physical attractiveness were the most important items and that they correlated with evaluations made of "intelligence," "fun," and "happiness." When females evaluated men, however, attractiveness and sex appeal were much less important: more stress was placed on "intelligence," "extroversion," "fun," "happiness," and "quietness" rather than on physical attractiveness per se. Interestingly, when men and women evaluated members of their own sex, the pattern was reversed. Men rating other men placed most emphasis on "nervousness," "confidence," "extroversion," "happiness," and "quietness," not on sex appeal and physical attractiveness. Women, on the other hand, were much more concerned with another woman's physical attractiveness and sex appeal and they related these to her "intelligence," "fun," and being "well dressed." The investigators found, in short, that women were more concerned with physical attractiveness when judging another woman than when judging a man, whereas men were very concerned with opposite-sex attractiveness but rather disinterested

than did comfortable subjects. In other words, our reactions to unpleasant physical conditions tend to cloud our perceptions of stimuli, including other human beings, that are objectively unrelated to the source of the unpleasantness.

ATTRIBUTES OF THE OTHER

Although environmental influences facilitate interaction between two (or more) people, there are many other factors that influence their chances of becoming good friends. First, they must decide to interact more meaningfully than they probably would just because they are near each other. The decision to initiate a deeper interaction is based on the attributes the

in same-sex attractiveness. This difference between men and women explains why both tended to regard women as more physically attractive than men.

The investigators also noted which dimensions provided subjects with their most overriding criteria in judging the attractiveness of members of the opposite sex. The experimenters asked the raters how much importance they attached to fourteen characteristics in judging the attractiveness of persons of the opposite sex. Supporting the contention that men and women evaluate attractiveness differently, the investigators found that men placed much greater importance than women on physical characteristics—hair, shape, face, and weight. Women were more concerned with a man's personality and values, placing significantly more emphasis than men on intelligence, independence, manners, sense of humor, and religion. Although students in the United States and South Africa generally agreed on the relative importance of these different items, people with different cultural backgrounds did indeed judge attractiveness differently. For example, South Africans thought that hair, eyes, face, clothes, and manners were more important determinants of physical attractiveness than did Americans, whereas Americans were more concerned with personal qualities, such as intelligence and independence.

And how about the beholder's self-esteem? Does self-esteem also affect how attractive a person is

perceived to be? The findings were rather complicated. In both the United States and South Africa, males and females with high self-esteem considered female persons more attractive than did males and females with low self-esteem. Self-esteem related differently, however, to ratings of men in the two countries. In the United States there was no relationship between self-esteem and the evaluations that males received, but in South Africa women with high self-esteem saw males as more attractive than did low self-esteem women, although men with high self-esteem saw them as less attractive. This suggests that evaluating a female's attractiveness may be of greater psychological significance, in terms of the influence of the self-esteem of both female and male beholders on their perceptions, than is evaluating a male's attractiveness; high self-esteem males may be less willing than low self-esteem males to judge a fellow male as attractive (possibly because of the strong taboo against male homosexuality).

Apparently, your perceptions of others' physical attractiveness are profoundly influenced by your cultural background, your sex, your self-esteem, and the sex and other traits of the persons you judge.

Source: Adapted from S. Morse, J. Gruzen, and H. Reis, "The 'Eye of the Beholder': A Neglected Variable in the Study of Physical Attractiveness?" (unpublished manuscript, New York University, 1973).

initiator perceives in the other. For example, physical attractiveness and the degree to which two (or more) people share similar characteristics—such as attitudes and social background—should both tend to influence the course of a relationship.

Physical Attractiveness

Although many people tend to disown the influence of physical attractiveness on their choice of friends because it seems such a superficial criterion, the empirical evidence suggests that they do, in fact, react differently to physically attractive people than they do to physically unattractive ones. In a recent experiment, for example, Karen Dion (1972) showed female subjects photographs of children who had ostensibly behaved badly. The descriptions of the behavior were identical, but some of the children in the photographs had been said by independent judges to be ugly, and some of them had been judged attractive. The women were much more likely to attribute blame to a child who had been judged physically unattractive and to conclude that the disruptive behavior was typical for that child. In contrast, subjects typically produced excuses for the children who had been judged physically attractive. (Details are related in the topical insert on page 149.)

Keep in mind that the subjects and the independent judges who evaluated physical attractiveness in the studies reviewed in this chapter are probably all inhabitants of the United States and strongly influenced by the standards of beauty that are popular in this part of the world. Even within the United States, standards of physical attractiveness vary a great deal

Figure 6.5 The matching hypothesis, which suggests that individuals seek out others whose physical attractiveness is similar to their own, has provided the basis for most studies of the role of physical attractiveness in heterosexual relationships. The hypothesis has been supported in studies in which subjects have been called on to choose a partner for some interaction, although *ideally*, most subjects express a preference for the most attractive mates possible, regardless of their own attractiveness. Ideals change, however, and these changes in turn apparently influence *who* in reality is likely to be chosen by *whom*. In seventeenth-century Europe, a preference for rounded female forms was reflected in the paintings of Flemish artist Peter Paul Rubens (*left*). In marked contrast is the sparse form of twentieth-century Twiggy, the English model.

among various subgroups. Moreover, even within the guidelines preferred by a particular subgroup, evaluating physical attractiveness can be a highly subjective endeavor that is bound to be influenced by factors like the facial expressions, energy, self-confidence, and bodily carriage of the person being evaluated. These facts do not detract from the meaningfulness of social psychologists' findings regarding attraction. As long as people *agree* that an individual is physically attractive, their behavior toward that person (if other factors are equal) will probably tend to reflect a positive bias.

Most studies of the effects of physical appearance on attraction emphasize heterosexual attraction and the *matching hypothesis,* which states that people choose partners whom they perceive as being of approximately the same physical attractiveness as themselves rather than partners whom they perceive to be much more or much less attractive. This hypothesis has generated inconsistent findings, however. One group of studies has yielded no support for the matching hypothesis. For example, in one study college students were randomly matched for a computer dance (Walster, Aronson, Abrahams, and Rottman, 1966). A post-dance questionnaire indicated that the intelligence and personality of the date did not seem to influence whether or not he or she was liked or dated again. In fact, the only variable that seemed to affect whether the date was liked was his or her physical attractiveness; *everyone* liked the date whom independent judges evaluated as physically attractive regardless of his or her own attractiveness. Other studies have supported the matching hypothesis. For example, in another computer-dating situation, subjects were asked to describe the kind of date with whom each of them would like to be matched (Berscheid, Dion, Walster, and Walster, 1971); the experimenters then led the subjects to believe that they would actually be paired with individuals matching their descriptions. The physical attractiveness of each subject was secretly rated by a panel of judges. The researchers found that the more attractive the individual, as judged by the panel, the more attractive a date he or she requested. And the individuals judged less attractive by the judges' standards requested less attractive dates.

The difference in findings in regard to the matching hypothesis may actually reflect whether or not the individual fears rejection. In cases where subjects preferred dates that were physically attractive by common standards regardless of their own attractiveness or unattractiveness, the subjects evaluated their dates either after meeting them or in a situation in which the subjects knew that they would not meet their choices. Because these subjects were not facing situations in which they might be rejected, they may have decided to aim high regardless of their own deficits. In contrast, in the study by Berscheid and her colleagues that found support for the matching hypothesis, subjects believed they would actually be meeting the people whom they chose; therefore, subjects could minimize their chances of being rejected by choosing to date people whose looks were similar to their own (Berscheid, Dion, Walster, and Walster, 1971).

Additional support is lent the matching hypothesis by Bernard Murstein's (1972) finding that the engaged or steady couples he studied were more similar in physical attractiveness than were randomly matched couples. The physical attractiveness of his subjects was rated both by the individuals themselves and by judges who did not know the subjects. Perhaps the conclusion can be drawn that most people would like to associate with physically attractive individuals, at least in hypothetical situations. However, fear of rejection may reduce those aspirations and increase the inclination to choose partners who people feel will reciprocate their advances. And the more attractive a person feels, the more he or she is likely to feel worthy of an attractive partner.

Similarity: Birds of a Feather

The earliest, and still the most frequent, question asked in the attraction literature revolves around which of the following adages is correct: "Birds of a feather flock together" or "Opposites attract." In other words, does similarity or complementarity facilitate attraction between individuals?

Research has shown that friends are usually more similar in social and economic backgrounds and in attitudes than would be expected by chance. For example, there is abundant evidence that husbands and wives typically share the same race, social class, economic status, educational level, and religion. There have been very inconsistent findings, however, with respect to similarities of personality characteristics. Although some studies have suggested that there is a relationship between personality similarity and attraction, other studies have found this relationship only under some conditions, and still others have found no relationship at all. Furthermore, a few studies have indicated that personality complementarity is more conducive to attraction than is personality similarity.

Social psychologists encounter many difficulties when attempting to determine the relative influences of similarity and complementarity on the attraction process. A major problem is that most studies of attraction, particularly early studies, were unable to trace the effects of attraction directly. For example, researchers compared the scores obtained by friends or married couples on personality and attitudinal measures with those obtained by randomly matched individuals. Researchers did indeed uncover enough evidence that friends' scores are more alike than those of randomly matched individuals to conclude that similarity was in some way related to attraction. But they were still left with the question, "Which occurred first—the similarity or the attraction?" It makes intuitive sense that friends may grow more like one another the longer that a friendship endures. It is also possible that neither friendship nor similarity causes the other and that some third factor, such as proximity, may account for a relationship between similarity and attraction. Recall that the closer two individuals live or work geographically, the more likely it is that they will become friends. In fact, individuals are often brought into physical proximity *because* they are similar in occupation, social class, beliefs, interests, or some other respect. Therefore, proximity rather than similarity may be responsible for some instances of attraction.

In order to clarify the distinction between the causes and the effects of attraction, several investigators have tried studying the development of attraction in individuals who are strangers at the outset of an experiment. In a typical study of this nature, the experimenter matches strangers on the basis of their responses to personality and attitudinal questionnaires and, after a short interaction, compares the degree of attraction reported by subjects who were matched for similarity to the degree of attraction reported by subjects matched for complementarity.

Although an improvement over the old correlational method, which fixed behavior and attitudes in time without revealing their dynamic nature, the methods developed by the investigators whose work will be discussed next have created additional measurement problems. Keep in mind, for example, that to try to predict a person's behavior during a brief interaction on the basis of responses to a paper-and-pencil questionnaire is an endeavor of dubious outcome. The characteristics for which two subjects are matched may not be at all evident to the partners during their brief encounter.

The first clear demonstration that shared attitudes do facilitate attraction was the work of Theodore Newcomb (1956, 1961). For the length of a semester, Newcomb provided rent-free cooperative housing for two separate samples of University of Michigan students in return for their participation in several hours of research per week. All the subjects were sophomore and junior men, and none had been previously acquainted. Before the students arrived in Michigan, they responded by mail to questionnaires measuring their attitudes, values, and personality characteristics. Attractions among house members and changes in attitudes were measured throughout the semester. If similarity is a determinant of attraction, one would expect those house members who had responded similarly before their acquaintance to gradually become friends, and this is what occurred. In the first weeks of the semester, the only variable related to attraction was proximity; roommates and individuals occupying rooms on the same floors were more attracted to each other than they were to other house members. As the semester continued, however, similarity of preacquaintance attitudes became the best predictor of attraction. Thus, Newcomb's research clearly demonstrated that some degree of attitudinal and value similarity is an important determinant of the attraction process, at least in relatively early stages of friendship.

Newcomb studied the influence of attitudes on attraction in a complex situation. His study left many questions unanswered, however. Are people only attracted to others when the objects of their shared attitudes are salient to the relationship? Or must similar attitudes first be important to people as individuals in order to facilitate attraction? Or does similarity in *any* attitude facilitate attraction? These questions are difficult to answer in a situation such as Newcomb's because so many unknown variables influence the relationship.

An approach that is rather different from Newcomb's—one that attempts to eliminate some of the unknown factors that are inherent in complex situations—has been conducted for more than ten years by Donn Byrne and his colleagues. Byrne took the study of similarity and attraction into a laboratory situation so that he could control the salient variables more precisely. He first studied the influence of shared attitudes in the attraction of same-sex individuals, and he held constant other factors that might influence attraction, such as physical appearance, personality, background, interests, and mannerisms (Byrne, 1961). Subjects read responses on attitudinal questionnaires ostensibly completed by another person of the same sex (a stranger) but in actuality completed by the investigators, who tailored the responses to be either very similar, moderately similar, or dissimilar to the subjects' responses, which had been obtained several weeks earlier. The subjects were then asked to estimate how much they would like the author of the responses. Byrne has found, time after time, that the more similar the hypothetical stranger's responses to those of a subject, the more that subject expects to like the stranger. In fact, as Figure 6.6 indicates, attraction increases linearly as the proportion of similar responses increases. This linear relationship between shared attitudes and attraction has been found for children as young as fourth-graders, for college students, Job Corps trainees, surgical patients, alcoholic patients, and, to a lesser degree, even

Figure 6.6 Byrne (1961) has consistently found a linear relationship such as this between the proportion of attitudes subjects believed that they held in common with a stranger and their attraction toward that stranger. Although this clear relationship has been found with a wide variety of subject groups, Byrne's research has been largely restricted to controlled laboratory settings. Factors encountered outside the laboratory have been known to mitigate the tendency for attitudinal similarity to increase attraction.

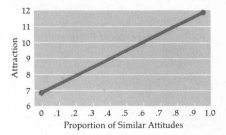

for schizophrenic patients. And the relationship holds, regardless of the significance or triviality of the attitudes and regardless of the physical attractiveness, the race, the status, or the sex of the stranger (Byrne, 1971). Byrne has also extended his research to areas other than attitude similarity; for example, he and his colleagues found a linear relationship between similarity and attraction when studying personality similarity as well as attitude similarity (Byrne, Griffitt, and Stefaniak, 1967).

Byrne has approached the study of attraction in a scientifically controlled way, looking at the influence of individual variables while holding constant as many other variables as he can. As he studies each variable in isolation, he plans to graduate his studies to more and more complex situations. His research has offered impressive evidence that similarity plays an important role in attraction, but to date his experiments have been conducted in rather restricted and artificial situations; the results, therefore, must not be generalized to complex, real-world situations without a great deal of caution. One of Byrne's many critics who points out the questionable generalizability of his results is Bernard Murstein, who in 1971 drew an analogy between Byrne's approach and the sheik who, seeking a fourth wife, was allowed only to observe his prospects' mammary developments:

Under these conditions, it could be reliably demonstrated that whether or not the women were Muslims, or Christians, black or white, brunette or blond, fat or thin, wealthy or poor, toothless or toothsome, the ample, upstanding bosom would be preferred to the meager or bovine pendulant one in a majority of cases. One could probably construct a scale of an ideal breast and calculate choice as a function of departure from the ideal. . . . Few would venture to predict, however, that the woman chosen on the basis of breast would necessarily be chosen if the usual conditions of courtship were allowed to operate. (page 14)

The fact that two individuals have similar attitudes or personality characteristics might be inconsequential if a host of other factors influences their interaction. At best, Byrne's research leads to the conclusion that similarity appears to be of importance in first impressions. Keep in mind, however, that the importance of similarity may be minimized when other factors are introduced. For example, Edward Jones, Linda Bell, and Elliot Aronson (1970) report that subjects responded more positively to a stimulus person who supposedly liked them and held dissimilar attitudes than to an individual who supposedly liked them and held similar attitudes. Apparently people value being liked by a dissimilar other more than by a similar other, perhaps because the approval of a dissimilar other is expected less and therefore seems more complimentary. It will be shown later that similarity can actually reduce attraction in some situations.

Opposite-sex relationships usually command more attention than same-sex relationships do when the topic is similarity and complementarity, particularly of personality characteristics. Unfortunately, this interest has not yet blossomed into systematic investigation as elaborate as Newcomb's or Byrne's. Most of the research has been correlational, investigating similarities between married couples or dating couples, and has yielded inconsistent findings. George Levinger and James Breedlove (1966) and several other investigators have found that husbands and wives *assume* greater similarity between themselves in a wide range of attitudes and behavior than they actually have. Furthermore, Levinger and Breedlove found that assumed agreement rather than actual agreement was correlated with marital happiness. In other words, happily married couples tended to *overestimate* their agreement with each other at least when separately

III ENCOUNTERING OTHERS

describing their attitudes to an outsider, and unhappy couples tended to *underestimate* their similarity. Levinger and Breedlove hypothesized that actual similarity is important only when it involves behavior or attitudes that are instrumental in satisfying the couple's goals. Although this hypothesis was not clearly confirmed in their research, Levinger and Breedlove have uncovered some support for it. If it were the case that only those attitudes and behaviors that are important to the relationship itself need be similar, this would explain many of the inconsistencies produced by heterosexual-attraction research and may also apply to same-sex relationships.

In summary, the case for similarity as an important determinant of attraction is not overwhelming. Although similarities of background, attitudes, and interests appear to play roles in attraction, personality similarity is more complex. In many cases, people may prefer those whose personality traits complement their own over those whose personalities are similar.

The exact role that similarity plays in interpersonal attraction has not been specified either. Similarity may play a greater role during the beginning of a relationship than in a more developed one. Perhaps it serves to get people together; but as a relationship continues, its future may come to depend less on similarities than on other factors, such as common goals; social, sexual, emotional, or economic interdependence; maintaining a stable environment for children; or companionship. And, as already discussed, as the relationship continues and these other things increase in importance, the participants tend to distort the situation, so that they assume that they are more similar than they actually are.

It probably surprises no one that some types of similarity play at least some role in attraction. If you are like most people, you probably feel good when you meet someone who is similar to you. When you want to relax and

Figure 6.7 That similarity of attitudes breeds attraction has long been a popular notion and is one of the primary assumptions of computer-dating questionnaires, as suggested by this excerpt from one such questionnaire. Although experimental research has often indicated a relationship between attitudinal similarity and attraction, the importance of attitudinal similarity can be mitigated. More important mediators of attraction may be the particular attitudes in question and their importance to a relationship, as well as other factors that may take priority in the relationship.

COMPATIBILITY'S PERSONALITY INVENTORY

Please give your first spontaneous reaction to each of the following questions. If you strongly agree with the statement, circle 1; if you agree, circle 2; if you neither agree nor disagree, circle 3; if you disagree, circle 4; if you strongly disagree with the statement, circle 5. Although it may be hard to decide on some questions, be sure to answer all of them.

	Agree		?	Disagree	
1. My parents were fairly religious and so am I.	1	2	3	4	5
2. Religious convictions help produce a home that is harmonious and stable.	1	2	3	4	5
3. I believe in God.	1	2	3	4	5
4. I attend church regularly and would prefer a mate who does the same.	1	2	3	4	5
5. Parents who do not provide religious training for their children are not fulfilling their responsibilities	1	2	3	4	5
6. I believe in the existence of a Supreme Being that controls the fate of mankind.	1	2	3	4	5
7. The breakdown of organized religion is a major problem in our society today.	1	2	3	4	5
8. My religious faith has helped me understand the difference between right and wrong.	1	2	3	4	5
9. A fine moral code can be a good substitute for a religious code.	1	2	3	4	5
10. A person can have high moral standards without being religious.	1	2	3	4	5
11. The portrayal of sex in the movies has gone too far.	1	2	3	4	5
12. I believe that married women who work desert their home for a career.	1	2	3	4	5
13. It is not appropriate to include sex education in the school program.	1	2	3	4	5
14. It is the parents' obligation and responsibility to tell their youth how to dress.	1	2	3	4	5
15. Long hair and beards are a sign of the breakdown in our society.	1	2	3	4	5
16. Current obscenity laws, covering magazines and books, are not strong enough.	1	2	3	4	5
17. Years ago people had more fun than they do today.	1	2	3	4	5
18. I frequently seek new and exciting experiences.	1	2	3	4	5
19. Children must learn when they are very young deep respect for law and order.	1	2	3	4	5

have a good time, you probably call a friend who enjoys the same things you do, and you probably tend to assume that someone who is similar to you also likes you.

When Similarity Hurts.   Several recent experiments have shown that similarity may actually decrease attraction (Mettee and Wilkins, 1972; Senn, 1971; Taylor and Mettee, 1971). For example, in a study by Shelley Taylor and David Mettee (1971), pairs of college women were told either that they had been matched on the basis of similarity or that they had obtained dissimilar scores on a battery of personality tests. These subjects subsequently interacted with one another, and each then rated her attraction to the other. One woman in each pair was actually a confederate of the experimenters and behaved either pleasantly or obnoxiously. The confederate received the most extreme ratings when the subject believed her to be similar—liked more than a dissimilar partner when she was pleasant and disliked more intensely than a dissimilar other when she was obnoxious. When the confederate was believed to be dissimilar, her pleasant or obnoxious behavior did not significantly affect how much she was liked; in either case she was liked to a moderate degree. According to Taylor and Mettee, when people believe that others are similar to them, the characteristics and behavior of those similar others are more salient than if the other individuals seem dissimilar, because similar individuals are perceived as embodying acceptable standards of comparison. Furthermore, when people fear that they share undesirable traits with others, they may be motivated to disavow the characteristics of those others. In a situation such as this, derogation of a similar but undesirable other can reduce the anxiety that is aroused by this possibility.

In summary, the role of similarity in attraction appears to vary in different situations. Whether or not similarity enhances attraction depends, for example, on the type of similarity, on the desirability of the traits involved, on the type of relationship involved, and perhaps also on the stage of the relationship.

Several social psychologists have formulated theories that help to explain the effects of similarity on attraction. Two of these theories are Festinger's social-comparison theory and Newcomb's A-B-X model. Festinger's social-comparison theory is also described in Chapter 10 to help explain social-influence processes.

Social-Comparison Theory.   Leon Festinger hypothesized in 1954 that each of us has a need to evaluate his or her own opinions by comparing them with the opinions of others. We do this to validate our opinions (as well as our abilities, personalities and identities, and ways of behaving) and to adjust our perceptions when they are inaccurate. And sometimes we compare ourselves to others to be able to conform to socially preferred behavior. As explained in Chapter 10, when people deal with information that is ambiguous or contradictory, the temptation is to borrow the opinions of trusted others in forming their own opinions. For example, if you are a women's-liberation activist, you do not seek the opinions of John Birch Society members in deciding, say, which presidential candidate to support in an election year (or whether or not to support a presidential candidate at all). Rather, you would turn to acquaintances or other sources of information that share a world perspective similar to your own, especially as related to the topic at hand. In general, then, the more similar others are to you, the more comfortable you probably tend to be with them as models for comparison and the more rewarding they will be. Thus, if a similar other can satisfy your need for comparison and at the same time assure you that your views are "correct," he or she is probably a candidate in good standing for your liking.

Newcomb's A-B-X Model.   Aristotle said in the fourth century B.C. that "they are friends who have come to regard the same things as good and the same things as evil, they who are friends of the same people and they who are the enemies of the same people."

This same idea has prompted a twentieth-century social psychologist, Theodore Newcomb, to advance an alternate path to understanding the effects of similarity. Newcomb's model is based on cognitive-consistency theory, outlined in Chapter 8, which hypothesizes that people strive for consistency among their feelings, beliefs, and behavior. Inconsistencies produce tension and strain that each of us strives to reduce in some way. For example, we tend to want those whom we like to consistently believe in and to like the same things that we like and, by the same token, for those we dislike not to like the same things that we like. For example, it would probably be upsetting to a male chauvinist to discover that his new girl-friend was a women's-liberation activist who believed that a woman's place is not in the home any more than a man's place is in the home.

Newcomb proposed in 1956 a model that contains three components: person A, A's attitude toward object X, and A's perception of B's (a second person's) attitude toward X. According to the A-B-X model, these three components must be consistent for attraction to flourish. For example, assume that the male chauvinist just introduced (A) believes strongly in male superiority over women (X). If B is his lover, then he must perceive that she also believes in his superiority. Otherwise, his need for consistency is threatened. If, on the other hand, B is someone he dislikes, he would be motivated to perceive that she does not believe in male superiority. And if B is a stranger, then discovering that she believes in male superiority should increase the probability of his liking her.

Newcomb's theory predicts that two people who agree on issues that are important to them both will become attracted to each other because they satisfy one another's need for consistency. And the more important the issues are to the two of them, the more important similarity will be to the relationship.

But what if inconsistency exists? What if the male chauvinist likes his girlfriend, who believes in equality between the sexes? What if, in other words, A and B like each other but differ in their attitudes toward X? Newcomb's theory suggests that the male chauvinist would have several alternatives: he could change his opinion about his girlfriend or about his superiority; he could try to change her attitudes regarding sex roles; he could decide that agreement on the issue of male-female equality is not important to this particular relationship; or he could distort reality and perceive that she actually believes in male superiority. Distortion of reality would explain experimental evidence that friends and spouses assume that they are more similar than they actually are.

The dilemma of the male chauvinist has been described here in very simplified terms. In reality, a relationship is dependent on agreement about many objects, not just one. The more topics that two individuals agree about—and the more important those topics are to the individuals and to the survival of the relationship—the greater the attraction Newcomb would predict between the two individuals.

Similarity is but one way of looking at the means by which personality traits, backgrounds, and attitudes combine to bring two people together or to pull them apart. As will be shown next, another way of looking at these ingredients of attraction has received attention from social psychologists.

Complementarity: Attraction of Opposites

The most widely known theory of complementary needs was proposed by Robert Winch in 1958. Although Winch developed and tested his theory largely in the context of mate selection, he suggested that similar factors operate in other types of relationships as well. Winch hypothesized that people seek out those others who can best satisfy their needs. Winch does not deny that partners in a satisfying relationship may be similar in some ways. He maintains, however, that the relationships with the greatest promise of satisfying the participants' needs are those mutually rewarding relationships that are based on complementary needs in which each of two people, by acting out his or her own needs, simultaneously and effortlessly satisfies the needs of the other. Examples of relationships based on complementary needs fill many legends as well as daily experiences—the domineering husband and his mousey wife (and vice versa), the highly nurturant person who is continually surrounded by dependent friends, and the incessant talker whose most constant friends are good listeners.

Winch hypothesizes that needs can be complementary in two ways: the needs of the two individuals can differ in intensity, as when one person needs to feel dominant and the other is more comfortable when dominated; or the needs can differ in kind, as when one person needs recognition and the other needs to express admiration. Winch tested his theory with twenty-five married couples and found general support for it, but later studies have not at all yielded the same findings.

Clarification of the role that complementarity may play was offered in 1962 by Alan Kerckhoff and Keith Davis, who found evidence of a filtering process operating in attraction, at least in couples. For the couples studied by Kerckhoff and Davis, different factors were important to the progress of the relationships at different points, and complementarity of needs was only important in long-term relationships. In the early stages, social-status variables such as religion and class played the most significant roles; these were later preempted in importance by similarity of values; and these, finally, by need complementarity. Kerckhoff and Davis hypothesized that in the early stage of a relationship the basis of a couple's interaction is the idealized images the two have of each other. The idea of a filtering process makes intuitive sense; however, research reported by George Levinger, David Senn, and Bruce Jorgensen in 1970 suggests that the model will have to be refined if it is to account for all the data.

According to George Levinger (1964), need complementarity may be so intuitively obvious that the problem may be a conceptual one. In some cases, similar needs are actually complementary needs, as when two people possess similar needs in moderate degrees. Also, complementarity is not always mutually beneficial, as may be the case when one individual has a strong need to achieve and the other has a low need to achieve; in this case dissimilarity probably creates more conflict than satisfaction. Still another conceptual complication is injected when individuals are involved in many relationships concurrently, so that different needs may be satisfied by different relationships.

In an attempt to deal with some of these conceptual problems, Milton Lipetz, Irwin Cohen, Jack Dworin, and Lawrence Rogers (1970) defined complementarity as "what in one person satisfies the needs of the other." For example, when spouses were similar in *some* needs, as in the needs for autonomy and affiliation, they were judged complementary, because the similarities would be satisfying to each. Similarity was considered indicative of low complementarity in the case of other needs such as nurturance and succorance, dominance and deference, because similarity of these needs would not be satisfying to both partners; a nurturant person would find a succorant partner more satisfying, and a dominant person would be more satisfied by a deferent companion. Lipetz and his colleagues studied only needs that seemed relevant to marriage. The researchers measured needs both as they characterized the individuals generally (including relationships outside the marriage) and as they applied specifically to the marriage. The investigators found that complementarity of needs as they specifically applied to the marriage was correlated with marital satisfaction, although there was no relationship between satisfaction and complementarity of general individual needs.

Another conceptual problem may make it unproductive for anyone to try to categorize people as being similar or complementary with respect to fixed traits. Psychologists have perhaps too frequently fallen into the trap of trying to fit individuals into clear-cut categories of, for example, "passive" or "dominant," "extroverted" or "introverted." When this leads to over-simplification, it can blind the investigator to the range of behavior that a given individual exhibits in different situations. It may be, after all, that every individual is at different times both dominant and passive, introverted and extroverted, as well as many degrees between the two extremes on any one dimension. Each person may actually be highly flexible in the behaviors of which he or she is capable, for example acting in a relatively dominant manner when necessary and seeming passive when necessary. Even within the context of a particular relationship, the traits exhibited by

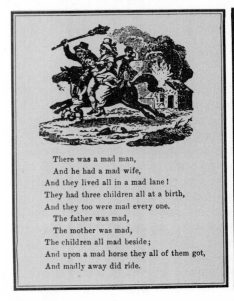

There was a mad man,
And he had a mad wife,
And they lived all in a mad lane!
They had three children all at a birth,
And they too were mad every one.
The father was mad,
The mother was mad,
The children all mad beside;
And upon a mad horse they all of them got,
And madly away did ride.

Jack Sprat could eat no fat;

His wife could eat no lean;

So 'twixt them both

they cleared the cloth,

And lick'd the platter clean.

two people may be quite flexible. Thus, what is most essential to the life of a relationship may be the partners' flexibility and ability to meet one another's needs in a large variety of situations rather than, for example, the dominance of one partner and the submissiveness of the other. The question of overriding importance in a relationship may not be a simple one of single-dimension trait similarity or complementarity but, rather, a question of multi-dimensional trait compatibility.

The available data appear to indicate that both similarity and complementarity operate in attraction. David Marlowe and Kenneth Gergen in 1970 suggested various clarifications of the similarity-complementarity issue. First, similarity of personality must be distinguished from similarity of background, attitudes, values, or interests. Researchers have fairly well established that similarity of the latter variables plays some role in the attraction process, but this type of similarity does not interfere with complementarity operating when personality characteristics are involved. Second, just what needs are complementary must be specified; equating complementarity with dissimilarity is inadequate and misleading. As pointed out by Levinger, many similar needs are also complementary needs. Third, as demonstrated by Lipetz and his associates, different needs may operate in different relationships. Fourth, the situation must also be considered: Similarity and complementarity may play different roles at different stages of a relationship, and other conditions such as the birth of children, the successes of one friend and the failures of another, and similarity of undesirable traits can minimize the influence of similarity on attraction (Jones, Bell, and Aronson, 1970; Taylor and Mettee, 1971). The fifth caution recommended by Marlowe and Gergen concerns perceptual distortion—the tendency for people to perceive their friends and spouses as similar to themselves. To the extent that a tendency toward perceptual distortion exists, the role of complementarity may be concealed from researchers. In addition, other research indicates that some characteristics affect attraction regardless of similarity or complementarity. For example, physical attractiveness, self-rated happiness, intimacy, a moderate degree of dominance, and other characteristics that are usually rated as socially desirable in North American society may attract people to an individual who is relatively well-endowed with these qualities regardless of whether or not they themselves possess those attributes.

THE BEHAVIOR OF THE OTHER

As any of us gets to know someone else, our perceptions of this person are increasingly gathered from what we know of the other's social interactions, including those with ourselves. First impressions are usually based largely on factors such as environmental circumstances, the other's physical attractiveness, and apparent similarities to and differences from oneself. These first impressions typically change with repeated contact. If our contacts with another are continually pleasant, we are likely to perceive the other person as more attractive than before, and if our contacts are unpleasant, the other may begin to seem less attractive. Repeated contact may even affect our perceptions of the other's physical characteristics, so that a long-term friend may grow more beautiful in our eyes and an enemy may come to look more and more sinister.

One type of situation that may change our evaluations of another involves chance occurrences in which fortune or misfortune befalls the other individual. Another situation involves reciprocity, in which another's liking affects a person's tendency to like or dislike that other individual.

The Just World: Where Fates Are Always Deserved

Fortune and misfortune are experienced by all of us, often as a matter of chance. Some social psychologists have turned their attention to the ways in which misfortune affects an observer's liking of the unfortunate person.

How do people respond to an individual who continually meets with misfortune? Are the unfortunate usually attractive because of their sufferings? And if an individual meets with misfortune while trying to help others, is he or she liked more for it? Melvin Lerner and Caroline Simmons (1966) asked just such questions in devising an experiment they described to subjects as a study of the perception of emotional cues. Their subjects were female college students who met in groups and were told to observe the emotional state of an individual and to try to identify the cues that betrayed that state. The individual they were to observe would be performing a learning task and would receive electric shocks for each incorrect response. One of the women, who was actually a confederate of the experimenters, was designated as the individual to be observed. To the subjects, it appeared that this woman had been chosen at random to perform the learning task and that any one of them could as easily have been chosen. The subjects then saw via television that the confederate was apparently experiencing painful electric shocks for her incorrect responses. Although the confederate seemed to react with expressions of pain and suffering, the subjects actually saw only a video tape of the confederate feigning her misery. One group of subjects saw the confederate enter the "learning" room without question or protest. But in another condition—the "martyr condition"—the confederate refused to undergo the shocks, and the experimenter announced that if she did not, the experiment would have to be canceled and the other subjects would lose credit for their participation; the confederate finally agreed to participate, but only "if it is necessary for all of them to get credit." And in a control condition, the confederate received rewards for correct responses rather than punishments for incorrect ones. When the experiment was over, subjects rated their attraction for the confederate.

Lerner and Simmons obtained some very interesting and decisive results. The condition in which subjects rated the confederate as *least* attractive was the martyr condition, in which she was undergoing the shocks to help those same subjects. And she was rated *most* attractive when she received rewards rather than shocks. To explain the common tendency for people to devalue those who suffer for them, Lerner and Simmons formulated what they call the *just-world hypothesis,* according to which our fates are roughly proportionate to our efforts. The belief that human beings are subject to random misfortunes over which they have no control creates an uncomfortable sensation in most of us. To believe in a just world, then, we must believe that those who are unfortunate deserved their misfortune in some way, and we are consequently inclined to denigrate them. This just-world hypothesis makes intuitive sense if it is considered that individuals who have been unusually fortunate can often "rest on their laurels," whereas the low economic or social status of less fortunate people often provides the excuse for their further exploitation, denigration, or use as scapegoats. For example, the unemployed are suspected by many to be "welfare chiselers" if they need temporary assistance, whereas the motives of wealthy farmers who receive many hundreds of times as much money for not growing surplus crops are not suspect.

Perhaps we feel most threatened by random events when we see individuals suffer because they have behaved altruistically; if this is the case, we might tend to "justify" the event by convincing ourselves that the altruistic individuals are unattractive and deserve their fates. On the other hand, random fortune might have the opposite effect. Again, as observers, we might be inclined to seek causes for chance events, but if we assume that good fortune results from special abilities of the fortunate, we might respond to these people with adulation.

Reciprocity of Liking

That liking is reciprocated with liking has long been a popular notion. For example, it was the basis of Dale Carnegie's bestseller, *How to Win Friends and Influence People* (1964). In his book, Carnegie offered advice about how to be liked: "Become genuinely interested in other people; smile; be a good listener; talk in terms of the other man's interest; and make the other person feel important." Psychological experiments have established the soundness of Carnegie's commonsensical prescriptions for social acceptance. For example, James Dittes and Harold Kelley (1956) led student participants in small discussion groups to believe that their fellow group members either liked or disliked them. (The subjects read anonymous evaluations of themselves, ostensibly written by other group members but actually completed by the experimenters.) Dittes and Kelley found that subjects who were led to believe that they were liked were more attracted to the group than were subjects who believed that they were disliked.

Apparently, people are especially receptive to others' acceptance when feeling insecure. James Dittes (1959) conducted another experiment in which subjects whom he encouraged to feel accepted were again more attracted to the group than were subjects who felt rejected, but this time he probed further. Prior to the experiment, he had subjects respond to a self-esteem scale. Individuals who scored low on this scale were assumed to feel more negative about themselves than were those with higher scores. Dittes compared the reactions of subjects who differed in self-esteem to being accepted or rejected. He found that although subjects with high or average self-esteem liked the group better when they were accepted by it, their liking was not significantly greater than when they were rejected. In contrast, subjects with low self-esteem liked the group very much when they were accepted but disliked it very much when they were rejected. Others' regard thus seems especially valuable when one feels insecure about himself or herself.

In the Dittes experiment, it was very clear to the subjects that they were either accepted or rejected. In real life, however, the messages a person receives from others are often ambiguous. When they are feeling insecure about themselves, are people likely to interpret ambiguous messages negatively or positively? Larry Jacobs, Ellen Berscheid, and Elaine Walster hypothesized in 1971 that if low self-esteem prompts negative evaluations, reciprocity of liking may not be effective in sparking attractions between people who are low in self-esteem, because they may not perceive that they are liked. These three researchers tested their hypothesis in an experiment ostensibly conducted to increase the effectiveness of computer-matching programs. The male subjects were given a battery of personality tests and were then asked to place five telephone

Figure 6.8 The just-world hypothesis is useful in explaining people's indifference to the world's many inequities. Although it is difficult for us to understand the seeming injustices of India's caste system, many Americans ignore the problems of poverty surrounding them, assuming that the poor are somehow responsible for their fates. After all, we may believe, this is a just world, so a great deal of misfortune must be deserved.

III   Encountering Others

calls to a hypothetical girl, all under embarrassing circumstances. The subjects were then told that taped recordings of these telephone conversations would be played for a girl from a neighboring college, who would use them to evaluate the subjects. The subjects were also told that in a subsequent session they would receive both a psychiatrist's evaluation of their personality tests and the girl's evaluation of their taped conversations; then the subjects would evaluate the girl. When the subjects returned for the second session, they received either a positive or negative psychiatric evaluation of their personalities; these reports were designed either to temporarily increase their self-esteem or to decrease it. Note that these subjects probably were not all victims of chronic low self-esteem, but some had simply experienced a setback, as all people do at times.

After receiving the psychiatric reports, subjects listened to the girl's evaluation of their telephone performances; some subjects received a highly ambiguous evaluation in which the evaluator would not commit herself to a definite statement. As hypothesized, subjects with lowered confidence liked the girl significantly less than did subjects with inflated self-esteem when her acceptance of them was ambiguous. Thus, although an individual with low self-esteem is more receptive to acceptance from another, that individual is also less likely to recognize when he or she *is* accepted.

Ingratiation: Apple Polishing

Edward Jones (1964) has studied an exception to the rule that people always like those who have unambiguously expressed attraction for them. That exception is *ingratiation*—behavior that is designed by individuals to make themselves seem attractive to others because they have something to gain by impressing those others. There are various tactics ingratiating persons may use: they may present themselves in a favorable light, shower the target persons with compliments, conform to the others' opinions, or do them favors. Many individuals behave in these ways quite sincerely; these behaviors are not ingratiating unless they reflect manipulative intentions.

The hazards of ingratiation have been demonstrated by researchers. One, Hilda Dickoff (1963), reports that people are less attracted to individuals who evaluate them favorably if they suspect ulterior motives than if they do not have reasons to suspect ulterior motives. However, in her experiment Dickoff found that subjects who received unrealistically positive evaluations, even when they highly suspected flattery, were more attracted to the evaluator than when the evaluator was honest in her evaluations. Apparently, flattery *will* get you somewhere—but not as far as when your regard seems genuine.

Because so many determinants of attraction have already been discussed, the reader may be wondering if there is any overall pattern. Are people's reasons for being attracted to one another so fragmented in real life? Many social psychologists have asked themselves the same question, and some of the resulting research is the focus of the following section. Briefly, they have constructed a framework that encompasses most of the data reviewed so far.

REWARD

Reward has become a popular explanation for attraction because it is a broad concept that encompasses most of the other variables that have been known to influence attraction. For example, becoming friends with one's neighbor is, other things being equal, more rewarding than with someone who lives across town, because one does not have to expend as much energy commuting. It is not surprising that we all tend to like those who express attraction for us when it is considered that being liked makes us feel good about ourselves; in other words, being liked is a rewarding experience. The theory of complementary needs is based on the supposition that two people can reward each other merely by acting on their individual needs and that, by expending very little effort, they can achieve a satisfying relationship. The theories of similarity also imply reward. Social-comparison theory maintains that a similar other fulfills people's needs to evaluate themselves and also provides them with supportive feedback—both rewarding functions. Newcomb's A-B-X model suggests that a similar other satisfies a need for consistency and, therefore, is rewarding. In analyzing his extensive research data, Byrne maintained that similarity can be rewarding to people because it assures them that they are behaving appropriately. All research along these lines gives credence to the general idea that reward determines attraction.

There is an impressive array of evidence that reward is important in attraction, that people are attracted to others who are responsible for a satisfying state of affairs. For example, Robert Ziller and Richard Behringer (1960) found that groups of subjects who had previously failed to solve a problem responded more favorably to a newcomer who was capable of solving the problem than did those subjects who had previously been successful. The newcomer had the same skills in both the successful and unsuccessful groups, but he was more rewarding to the failing groups. Gale James and Albert Lott (1964) found that subjects were more attracted to an individual when they received rewards in the person's presence although the individual was not responsible for those rewards. Apparently, positive feelings about a rewarding experience are even generalized to observers who had nothing to do with the reward.

There are two well-known theories of reward, one proposed by George Homans (1961) and the other by John Thibaut and Harold Kelley (1959). Both of these theories view social behavior, including attraction, in terms of rewards received and costs incurred in any interaction. These theories, striking in their parallels to an economic framework, usually are referred to as *exchange theories* and are discussed in detail in Chapter 13.

The concept of reward appears on the surface to be social psychology's answer to the mysteries of interpersonal attraction. However, the concept of reward encounters many difficulties when it is invoked to predict how attraction develops amidst the complexities of real life. For example, it is

III ENCOUNTERING OTHERS

difficult to predict what will be rewarding in a particular situation. Rewards can differ for different people, and the value of any one reward can also vary from person to person. As indicated previously, for example, another's liking and acceptance are more valuable to a victim of low self-esteem than to someone who thinks highly of himself or herself. What constitutes a reward can also change as the context of a situation evolves. For example, praise is a reward, but it loses much of its value when the recipient perceives that the person doing the praising has an ulterior motive. The value of a reward also appears to vary with the degree to which it is expected: the more it is expected, the less value the recipient is likely to attach to it. For example, O. J. Harvey (1962) found that individuals will respond more positively when they are praised by a stranger than by a friend; apparently compliments from friends are expected and therefore do not seem to mean as much as when they come from unexpected sources. Even more to the point, Stanley Morse (1972) found that subjects showed far more agreement with someone who provided them an unexpected favor than with one who provided the same favor when it was expected.

One problem with the reward explanations of attraction is their circularity. For example, reward theories often imply that similarity promotes liking because similarity is rewarding, and it obviously is rewarding or it would not promote liking. Circularity can be avoided if investigators specify in advance what will constitute a reward in a particular situation.

Gain-Loss Theory of Attraction

Three hundred years ago the Dutch philosopher Benedict de Spinoza observed that "hatred which is completely vanquished by love passes into love and love is thereupon greater than if hatred had not preceded it." A very similar idea was put forth by a social psychologist, Elliot Aronson, when in 1970 he suggested that we dislike those who initially like us but later turn against us more than we dislike those persons who consistently dislike us.

People tend to like those who like them. However, the liking felt by one person for another rarely remains constant; on the contrary, people can be expected to gain or lose esteem in the eyes of others. Aronson recognized this inconsistency and suggested that different *patterns,* or sequences, of approval and disapproval are more influential in determining attitudes toward the communicator than is the absolute proportion of approving and disapproving comments. Specifically, Aronson believed that

increases in rewarding feedback prompt a beneficiary to like the communicator more than if the communicator does not vary the reward value of his or her comments. In other words, people may come to like those who have been their enemies more than if they had always been friends. This is an interesting prediction, because people probably receive the greatest number of rewards from those who consistently like them.

In collaboration with Darwyn Linder, Aronson (1965) took his predictions into the laboratory and put them to an elaborate test. Aronson and Linder's scheme called for subjects to interact with the experimenters' confederate on several occasions and to "overhear" a sequence of evaluations by the stooge that were either consistently complimentary to them; consistently negative; the first few positive and the remainder negative; or the first few negative and the rest positive. The results proved striking: The confederate was liked significantly more when her evaluations progressed from negative to positive than when she consistently expressed esteem for the subject. When the confederate's initial liking turned to dislike, she was liked less than when she consistently expressed dislike for the subject.

Why should we prefer individuals who gradually come to like us, when others who have liked us all along have been greater sources of rewards? Aronson suggests four possible explanations. The first is anxiety reduction. If we find that others dislike us, we tend to experience some feelings of anxiety, hurt, or self-doubt. But if these others subsequently come to like us, then we not only experience the usual reward of being liked, our feelings of anxiety are also reduced. Thus, the total reward value of a situation in which others' attraction for us grows is greater than a situation in which others have been attracted to us all along. This line of reasoning would also account for the diminishing value of another who switches from like to dislike, because anxiety is likely to be aroused when we lose the esteem of others. Being disliked is punishment in itself, but when it is compounded with the removal of previous rewards—especially if those initial rewards caused us to drop our usual defenses—the total punishment is greater than if the same others disliked us all along.

Another possible explanation is that the increased liking of others makes us feel competent because we have changed their opinions from critical of us to favorable. Even if we do not deem the others responsible for pleasant experiences of this sort, we may nevertheless come away with the feeling that the interaction has been a satisfying one, and this positive feeling may generalize to the people whose opinions we have changed.

A third possibility is that we assume that people who change their opinions in response to new information are discriminating and discerning. If they are consistently positive or negative, we can minimize the importance of their evaluations by concluding that they are undiscriminating, that they may like or dislike everyone. When, however, others seem discerning, a gradual increase in positive evaluations is particularly appreciated, and an evaluation that becomes increasingly negative is particularly stinging.

The final possibility suggested by Aronson is a contrast effect whereby a positive evaluation after several negative ones *seems* more positive than if it followed several other positive ones.

Since he analyzed the results of his first test of gain-loss theory, Aronson has conducted extensive research to investigate these four possible explanations. As a result, he has concluded that anxiety reduction and feelings of competence are the results of gains or losses in esteem that

Figure 6.9 Subjects in Aronson and Linder's (1965) experiment liked a confederate when she consistently approved of them (++) and disliked the confederate when her comments about them were uniformly negative (−−). More surprisingly, subjects best liked the confederate when her evaluations of them progressed from negative to positive (−+) and least liked the confederate when her opinions of them deteriorated from positive to negative (+−). Thus, people seem to weigh the sequence—specifically, the direction—of evaluations more heavily than the absolute number of compliments bestowed over a period of time.

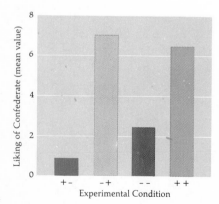

III Encountering Others

influence attraction, whereas neither discernment nor contrast appears to play a role.

Aronson conceived of his work on gains and losses as a means of exploring variations in the subjective reward values of objective rewards. However, the generality of his conclusions has been questioned by some researchers, who say that what holds true in the laboratory in this case may not affect long-term, intimate relationships (Tognoli and Keisner, 1972). Nevertheless, as discussed next, Aronson has extended his gain-loss hypothesis to explaining the durability of many marriages.

Gain-Loss Theory and Marriage

Aronson's gain-loss theory has many implications. One of these, dubbed by his students "Aronson's law of marital infidelity," suggests that a close friend or spouse is a less potent source of rewards than a stranger, because an intimate usually offers an invariantly high amount of esteem and for this reason is probably operating at ceiling level as a source of rewards. Consider Mrs. Suburbia, who after several years of marriage receives a compliment from her husband and reacts with boredom (perhaps thinking to herself, "What else is new?"). Later in the evening the same compliment from a stranger, Mr. Dashing, sends her reeling. She returns home feeling good about herself and about Mr. Dashing. Although Mr. Suburbia and her other close friends are relatively ineffective sources of reward for Mrs. Suburbia, they are the most potent sources of punishment for her if ever they withhold their esteem. Aronson suggests that the tendency for intimates to be relatively ineffective sources of reward but potent sources of punishment may explain why "you always hurt the one you love."

The prospect of "forever seeking compliments from strangers and being hurt by those we love" is a dismal one. Nevertheless, the prospects for a relationship weathering such storms are surprisingly high. Data collected by Aronson and his students suggest a reason: The hurt partner responds to the withdrawal of esteem by escalating efforts to revitalize the relationship. Thus, if Mr. Suburbia becomes jealous of his wife's responsiveness to strangers and suddenly stops lavishing compliments on her, she will renew her efforts to be attractive to him. This effect was demonstrated by Joanne Floyd (1964), who paired children with either a close friend or a stranger and allowed one of each pair to earn trinkets and to share them with the partner. Floyd led some of the children to believe that their partners had treated them generously and others to believe that their partners had been stingy with them. The recipients were then allowed to earn their own trinkets and to share them with their partners. As would be expected, the children were more generous with generous strangers than with stingy ones. But in the case of their friends, the reverse was true: they were more generous with a stingy friend than with a generous one. Perhaps a friend's stinginess suggested that they were losing his friendship, and they therefore used the trinkets to prevent such a loss.

The gain-loss model of attraction can be considered an essentially capitalistic one. According to it, people parcel out various social rewards in response to the ups and downs of a social stock market. The Dow-Jones average of individuals' points remains fairly stable from day to day, but the value of any one person's social stock can fluctuate tremendously. The dividends a stockholder realizes may have little to do with the intrinsic value of another's social output but may have everything to do with the scarcity of social commodities like companionship and affection for which individuals compete. This view of social relations as essentially characterized by principles of exchange and strategy is the topic of Chapter 13. You may want to consider whether human beings are inherently governed by calculating principles, in which case the same themes can be expected to emerge in both capitalistic and more socialistic societies. Or are these styles a matter of conditioning, in which case they can be expected to vary from society to society? Social psychology has as yet neither demonstrated nor discounted either of these possibilities. But if people *learn* attitudes toward cooperation and competition and toward abundance and scarcity, then social-psychological thinking (and possibly your own) is probably heavily influenced by a capitalistic model of the world. The possibility that these attitudes are learned does not necessarily condemn us to capitalistic ways of relating to one another; as explained in Chapter 2, adult human beings are capable of *re*learning and of voluntarily making basic changes in their social outlooks.

DEEP RELATIONSHIPS

Anyone who has participated in a very deep relationship probably suspects that there must be more to attraction than what has been discussed so far in this chapter. For the remainder of the chapter, then, two recent attempts to account for deep relationships will be explored—one, an empirical attempt to distinguish between liking and romantic loving and the other, a theoretical attempt to identify directions for future research by differentiating between the stages that can characterize relationships.

What Is Love?

Love is considered by most of us to be the deepest of relationships and the most intense of attractions, but for the most part social psychologists have not concerned themselves with it. If dealt with at all, love has usually been defined—as Fritz Heider (1958) defined it—as intense liking. However, Zick Rubin (1970) maintains that there are *qualitative differences* between liking and loving. He defines these differences not theoretically but empirically.

Love has many forms, and it is not reasonable to assume that the experience of love is necessarily similar in, for example, man-woman and parent-child relationships or even, for that matter, in dating and married man-woman relationships or in intimate heterosexual and homosexual relationships. Rubin focused on Platonic relationships between people of opposite sexes and on romantic love, which he defined as "love between unmarried opposite-sex peers, of the sort which could possibly lead to marriage."

Rubin began by assembling a large number of statements that corresponded to popular conceptualizations of loving and liking. The statements included items referring to idealization, sharing of emotions, positive evaluations, desire to affiliate, respect and trust, and feelings of being absorbed by the other. He then had several hundred students indicate which of the statements represented their own attitudes toward their boyfriends or girlfriends and which indicated their attitudes toward their Platonic friends. Rubin found that the indicated feelings toward boyfriends or girlfriends could be grouped into three components: affiliative and dependent needs, or attachment; a predisposition to help; and feelings of

Figure 6.10 To what extent are our conceptions of love derived from popular sources such as films, television serials, comic books, and novels? Many of the scenarios featured in popular sources are quite faithful to the romantic ideals of the Middle Ages, which held that love can emerge at first sight, that love can overcome all barriers of race and social class, and that love is a predetermined, all-powerful force. But whereas these ideals originated in the extramarital games of nobles, they now often culminate in marriage. The romantic mythology of the Middle Ages has been Americanized and continues to influence real-life courtship practices. Although romantic love has long been a major focus of the novelist, songwriter, and layman, as portrayed here by classic screen lovers Nelson Eddy and Jeannette MacDonald, it was largely neglected by social psychologists until 1970, when Zick Rubin attempted to empirically identify its components and differentiate it conceptually from Platonic friendships. Until that time, if mentioned at all, romantic love was merely assumed by social psychologists to be intense liking.

absorption with the loved one. In comparison, feelings toward friends seemed to consist of favorable evaluations, respect and confidence, and perceived similarity.

From his data, Rubin constructed loving and liking scales. Sample items from his two scales appear in Figure 6.11. High loving scores tended to come from those among Rubin's subjects who reported loving their boyfriends or girlfriends and who estimated high probabilities of marriage. Furthermore, Rubin found that although subjects indicated liking their "lovers" only slightly more than their Platonic friends, they loved their lovers a great deal more than their friends. And couples whose scores suggested that they were most in love spent the most time making eye contact while waiting for an experiment to begin. Such behavior may indicate that subtlety of communication and a high degree of absorption are characteristic of love.

A Theoretical Analysis of Deep Relationships

With the exception of contributions by Rubin and by two other investigators whose work is about to be considered here, research on attraction has focused almost exclusively on rather superficial relationships. In addition, researchers usually rely on evaluations and avoid directly observing the ways in which people interact in day-to-day relations. This simpler approach is popular among researchers because of the difficulty of studying complex situations. George Levinger and J. Diedrick Snoek (1972) maintain that most of the determinants of attraction that researchers choose to study can probably predict initial attraction and attraction in superficial interactions but are inadequate to account for the dynamics of more involved friendships.

Consequently, these two researchers have developed a conceptual framework that differentiates between deep relationships, superficial relationships, and those that are just beginning to develop. Levinger and Snoek analyzed a broad spectrum of relationships—those between acquaintances, teammates, close friends, spouses, parents and children, employers and employees, for example—in terms of the interpersonal relatedness of the participants. They conceptualized three levels of relatedness, each implying a greater complexity of interpersonal feelings and a deeper degree of involvement than do preceding levels. They also concluded that the level of relatedness tells us more about the basis of a relationship than does the type of relationship. Relationships progress through those levels sequentially. Sometimes they progress to Level 3, but more frequently they remain at Level 1 or 2 or dissolve completely. Figure 6.13 shows the characteristics of relationships at each of the three levels and Figure 6.12 indicates the conditions that are optimum for transition from one level to the next.

Unilateral Awareness. In the beginnings of any relationship, the participants—whether individuals, couples, or groups—possess only a unilateral awareness of one another. A state of unilateral awareness is reached at Level 1 in the relating process. Imagine a couple consisting of Bob and Carol, who are just aware enough of another couple—Ted and Alice—to have formed an impression of them but not to have had any significant interactions with them. Level 1 is the stage of approach, and the probability that Bob and Carol will become aware of and approach Ted and Alice rests on many factors, such as physical proximity, similarity of social status and

Figure 6.11 Sample items from Rubin's loving and liking scales. Rubin has found that liking and loving relationships were each characterized by the three components shown here, and he thus included several items to tap each component.

Liking

1. Favorable evaluation.

I think that_____(my boyfriend or girlfriend) is unusually well-adjusted. It seems to me that it is very easy for_____ to gain admiration.

2. Respect and confidence.

I have great confidence in_____'s good judgment.
I would vote for_____in a class or group election.

3. Perceived similarity.

I think that_____and I are quite similar to each other.
When I am with_____, we are almost always in the same mood.

Loving

1. Attachment.
If I could never be with_____, I would feel miserable.
It would be hard for me to get along without_____.

2. Caring.

If_____were feeling badly, my first duty would be to cheer him (her) up.
I would do almost anything for_____.

3. Intimacy.

I feel that I can confide in_____about almost anything.
When I am with_____, I spend a good deal of time just looking at him (her).

social class, the social environment in general, and personal characteristics like common interests and affiliative needs. At Level 1, Bob and Carol's attraction to Ted and Alice is based on an image formed from minimal information obtained thirdhand or by observation. The body of research on interpersonal attraction does not usually venture beyond this stage of unilateral awareness. It suggests that Bob and Carol's attraction to Ted and Alice at this stage will probably depend on how they perceive Ted and Alice's potential for rewarding them with socially desirable characteristics, compatible interests, or other relatively superficial recompense. However, initial attraction does not necessarily mean that Bob and Carol will choose to affiliate with Ted and Alice. The decision to initiate interaction will also be influenced by current satisfaction with other relationships and by their perceptions of Ted and Alice's accessibility.

Surface Contact. If they decide to move to Level 2 of relatedness, that of surface contact, Bob and Carol and Ted and Alice will begin to interact in a restricted and fairly noninterdependent manner. Their interactions will tend to be constrained by the roles each of them occupies in relation to the others, whether as man or woman, husband or wife, and so on. The more they interact at Level 2, the more likely it is that they will reveal aspects of themselves beyond the dimensions of their roles, although they are not likely to reveal how they feel about themselves or about the relationship. Unlike Level 1, Level 2 allows continual feedback during each interaction and therefore facilitates more realistic appraisals of one another and of the association. Although at this stage Ted and Alice's attractiveness largely depends on the rewards Bob and Carol are realizing from their interactions with Ted and Alice, it still involves the images they attributed to Ted and Alice at Level 1; Bob and Carol still do not know Ted and Alice as unique individuals.

Most relationships are superficial and are likely to remain at Level 2, if they continue at all. If the conditions that facilitated Bob and Carol's

Figure 6.12 In understanding deep relationships, it is important to recognize the varying levels of relatedness between persons. The optimum conditions suggested by Levinger and Snoek (1972) for a relationship to progress in sequence from each level to the next deeper level are listed here in ascending order: Relationships progress from the level of awareness (the stage of approach) to the level of surface contact (the stage of affiliation) to the level of mutuality (the stage at which attachments develop).

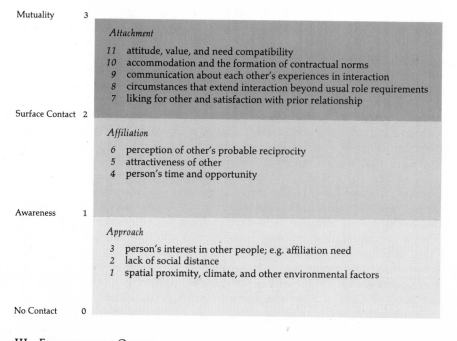

III ENCOUNTERING OTHERS

approach to and affiliation with Ted and Alice continue, and if the relationship is satisfying to both couples, moving to Level 3 is possible.

Mutuality. The transition from Level 2 to Level 3—the level of mutuality—is a transition from affiliation to attachment. Level 3 is characterized by interpersonal depth and interdependence: Each partner's behavior and attitudes are influenced by the other's, resulting in shared behavior, attitudes, and attributes and a feeling of "us" rather than "me" and of "we" rather than "I." It is in respect to this quality of interaction that attraction research is particularly lacking. Mutuality is actually a continuum along which a wide range of behavior is possible. The move toward greater intimacy is generally accomplished by an escalation of self-disclosure. Mutuality will begin to develop if Bob and Carol and Ted and Alice extend their interaction beyond role expectations. This development typically involves a sharp increase in self-disclosure that reveals personal concerns, such as feelings about oneself and one's conflicts. Revealing oneself is delayed until this advanced stage of relating because it requires the risk of becoming more vulnerable. If, however, a person is accepted after a disclosure, his or her self-esteem is increased and the relationship is consequently strengthened.

At Level 3, each individual assumes some responsibility for ensuring a high quality of experience for the others. Accordingly, Bob and Carol and Ted and Alice would each communicate their innermost feelings to the

Figure 6.13 A breakdown of the characteristics of Levinger and Snoek's three levels of relatedness, presented in simpler form in Figure 6.12.

Interpersonal Processes	Levels of Relatedness		
	1 *awareness*	2 *surface contact*	3 *mutuality*
Communication	Unilateral	Confined to role-required instrumental concerns; no self-disclosure.	Self-disclosure concerning personal feelings and the evaluation of outcomes in the relationship.
Common Knowledge	None	Confined to other's public self-presentation.	Much mutually shared information, including knowledge of each other's personal feelings and biographies.
Process of Interaction	None	Stereotypic role-taking; trial-and-error responses to novel situations.	Spontaneous and free-flowing; person understands how other is affected by the interaction and has concern for his well-being.
Regulation of Interaction	None	By cultural norms; untested implicit assumption that other shares same norms.	By joint construction of some unique pair norms, tested and found appropriate by both persons.
Maintenance of Relationship	None	Of little concern; responsibility for maintenance is perceived to be vested in externally derived roles or organizational requirements. Cost of terminating relationship is low.	Person and other both assume responsibility for protecting and enhancing the relationship. Cost of terminating relationship becomes increasingly high.
Evaluation of Relationship	None	Satisfaction on the basis of self-centered criteria; person compares his outcomes with prior experience and with alternate relationships.	Based on mutual outcomes evaluated against joint criteria, reflecting mutual equity.
Attraction to Other	Based on other's reward potential or "image"	Based on person's satisfaction with experienced outcomes, as well as on other's reward potential. Determined considerably by adequacy of other's role enactment.	Based on affection for other as a unique person and on person's emotional investment, as well as on criteria for surface contact.

others—communication that would require trust because such knowledge bestows power over the communicator. Frank communication also stimulates attachment among the participants, assuming that the communication is accepted. In addition, access to one another's innermost feelings makes information available to each participant regarding the effects that his or her own behavior has on others. Mutual agreement and accommodation begin to develop, so that mutually satisfying behavior is maintained and behavior that is superfluous or unsatisfying will tend to be discarded. Levinger and Snoek maintain that similarity of values and interests, especially in areas relevant to the relationship, increase the probability that individuals will be able to reach this state of accommodation. Similarity may also stimulate empathy with one another's experiences, which would give a basis for some of the affection characteristic of deep relationships.

In summary, Levinger and Snoek hypothesize that in deep relationships new factors enter into the attraction process, such as self-disclosure, open communication, trusting, degree of successful mutual accommodation, and empathy. On this level, Bob and Carol and Ted and Alice value one another as unique individuals and act to increase one another's satisfactions.

What Levinger and Snoek have proposed is a *filtering process* that unfolds as a relationship develops and during which different factors influence attraction at different stages. Physical and social proximity are among the earliest determinants; unless these disarmingly random conditions are favorable, the individuals will never meet. If individuals come together after this first and most extensive filtering process, relatively

LOVE OR INDIGESTION, IT'S A LABEL

FEAR, FRIENDLINESS, anxiety, and sympathy—all of these emotions have been objects of psychological inquiry. But nobody has paid much attention to the emotion of passionate love. Liking, valuing, even electronically monitored lust have been poked at and prodded in the psychology laboratory, but passionate love remains a mystery to most of us. With its perverse twists of suffering, frustration, anguish, and powerful if elusive joy, love is not easy to examine and dissect. No theory or research methodology seems to be able to explain it. Ethical considerations may also limit experimenters' manipulations of the behavior of lovers. Who wants to be the one to expose a mask of duplicity or the true conceit of one lover to another?

So the dynamics of love have remained a remarkable mystery—an experience portrayed in legends and media alike as something akin to being struck by lightning. However, two social psychologists, Elaine Walster and Ellen Berscheid, have tried to understand love as a product of physiology. Their ideas are an extension of the work of Stanley Schachter and his colleagues, discussed in Chapter 5, on arousal and cognitive labeling. Schachter concluded that when someone is experiencing emotional arousal, he or she will interpret this feeling according to the social cues that are provided in the environment. Thus, if one sees another angered, the feeling state one thinks he or she is experiencing is also anger, even if the flushed feeling, the edginess, and the increased pulse is actually a drug-produced phenomenon. If the other person seems to be reacting with great joy or euphoria, then the induced arousal will be interpreted as a "high," or elated feeling, and will be labeled as such.

Human beings can also become physiologically aroused without the aid

random requisites for attraction are replaced by more individualistic determinants, such as physical attractiveness; reciprocity of liking; similarity of background, interests, and attitudes; and other factors that can render an association rewarding. Still later, self-disclosure, mutual accommodation, and open communication play important roles in fostering attachment between individuals. If each of these requisites for attraction is met at its appropriate time, the relationship will have a chance to survive the various filters that can discourage relationships. As requisites are met, new requisites preempt them in importance, although former requisites can still play a role: If Ted and Alice were to move away or if their interests or needs were to change in ways that were salient to the relationship, the future of their relationship with Bob and Carol would be uncertain.

There is research data to support the notion of a filtering process. Recall Kerckhoff and Davis' finding that social-status variables were important in the early stages of romantic involvements but were later replaced by similarities of values, which in turn were replaced by need complementarity. In addition, George Levinger (1964) found that, depending on the stages of their relationships with various individuals, college students rated the importance of various characteristics of these individuals differently, according to a filtering process. At first meeting, visible characteristics, such as physical attractiveness, were rated more important than they were rated later on, when characteristics such as the need to give and receive were important.

Relationships that have achieved degrees of mutuality and attachment do not always maintain this level of relatedness. For example, Levinger and

---

of unusual chemical stimuli. A sudden scare, lack of sleep with coffee and cigarettes, a vitamin B shot, many drugs, a monosodium-glutamate "high" from a meal in a Chinese restaurant, an undefined threat to self-esteem—all of these things can create a high level of physiological arousal. At this point the person begins to search for a cause and is vulnerable to the most conspicuous cues in the environment. Should a beautiful person suddenly appear just as arousal is enhanced, the result may be a case of "love at first sight."

Berscheid and Walster suggest that the relationship between arousal and love includes these dynamics:

1. Jealousy, itself an indicator of insecurity, can be very arousing and thus easily attributed by a jealous partner as a sign of great love for the other.

2. Persons who do not believe in sex without love will fall in love more readily if they are sexually aroused than will people who make a cognitive distinction between sex and love.

3. A bachelor of twenty-eight, ready to settle down and anxious about his sexual potency, may suddenly find himself "in love" for the first time in his life.

4. After a long, relaxing sleep, the passion experienced by two lovers the night before may fade considerably.

5. People who think of themselves as "unromantic" will be less likely to label a feeling "love" than will persons who define themselves as "romantic."

Love may truly be based on chemistry—and as Walster and Berscheid suggest, adrenaline may make the heart grow fonder.

Source: Adapted from E. Walster and E. Berscheid, "Adrenaline Makes the Heart Grow Fonder," *Psychology Today,* 5 (1971), pp. 46–50.

Snoek hypothesize that an important determinant of a relationship's success is the degree of investment the partners feel they have in maintaining the relationship. Unless active forces work to maintain the relationship, bonds tend to dissolve. These forces can be either external, as when people feel compelled to honor marriage contracts, or internal, as in a feeling of commitment to others. A large measure of two or more people's energies is necessary to maintain a relationship at an advanced level of relatedness. And, as Levinger and Snoek point out, many relationships are maintained more in response to external pressures than for purposes of internal satisfaction.

Contributions to an understanding of interpersonal attraction such as Rubin's and Levinger and Snoek's have helped to correct the imbalance in interpersonal research that too often ignores the deepest—and thus most important—relationships. However, as noted earlier, social-psychological research is a product of the culture from which it springs. Even the attraction research that delves into the subtleties of deep relationships reflects cultural norms regarding what should constitute a deep relationship and what sort of people should participate together in it.

Societal norms specify, for example, that "lovers" should be one man and one woman. Furthermore, these norms embody a whole set of expectations that partners in a loving relationship usually have of one another. Some of these expectations may be functional in Western society as it exists today (expectations regarding the conditions under which

GETTING INTO SOMEONE

How DO WE BECOME intimate with one another? One approach is to say, "I want to know you better." To know someone better implies receiving information from another. To tell another about yourself is called "self-disclosure." Two theorists, Irwin Altman and Dalmas Taylor, have developed ideas about self-disclosure within the framework of what they term a "social-penetration model." They believe that the more intimate people become, the more willing they are to disclose the information that is most revealing of themselves—the information that makes them feel most vulnerable to one another's negative reaction. The degree to which people penetrate one another's facades is a measure of their closeness. The diagram indicates examples of the levels, or dimensions, of social penetration that relationships can occupy through self-disclosure.

Sidney Jourard and his associates have carried out research on the relationship between liking and self-disclosure. Although correlational data do not allow us to say whether liking precedes or follows disclosure, liking and self-disclosure are closely related. For example, married couples who reported the greatest mutual happiness had higher self-disclosure scores than did less congenial couples; students who revealed the most to their parents also liked them better than did nonrevealers. People of both genders tended to confide the most in their closest same-sex friend. In an experiment in which "liking" and "knowing" were separated, interesting differences were found between men and women. For men, knowing another person well was a paramount determinant of self-disclosure. For women, the emotional response to the person was much more important. Jourard reports that "women are more responsive to their own feelings—that

children should be produced and reared, for example). Many other expectations are clearly superfluous and in some cases even damaging to relationships. The tradition of romantic love leads many persons to expect things of a partnership that they would never expect of any other type of relationship. For example, many persons expect that romantic love will provide them with a reason for living. Furthermore, many women look forward to marriage as a source of economic or emotional security or of freedom from work. Likewise, many men expect a wife to provide, among other things, the services of a full-time maid. Clearly, such expectations often prove illusory. As a result, many intimate relationships dissolve completely, whereas the same individuals might have remained good friends if they had not expected so much (or so little) from one another.

Traditional roles are being questioned by some members of Western society; they are trying to separate the useful from the nonfunctional or unnecessary in role behavior. Alternative ways of relating include equal shares of responsibility in all areas of an intimate relationship; less dependence on one partner for companionship, emotional support, status, self-definition, and physical intimacy; and greater experimentation both inside and outside a particular relationship.

Whether or not researchers will be able to gather data that will illuminate the full range of interpersonal-attraction processes remains an unanswered question. At the deepest levels of intimacy the processes may be extremely complex and subtle. Moreover, it is difficult to obtain people's

is, they vary their interpersonal behavior in accord with their feelings more so than men do. . . . Men trust their brains, their cognition of the other person more than their feelings, as a condition for self-disclosure."

In another study by Dalmas Taylor, Irwin Altman, and Richard Sorrentino (1969), confederates either made themselves agreeable to another person or not agreeable. Subjects revealed the most to the confederates they liked the best. This finding indicates that liking can lead to self-disclosure. The process may be cyclical: Liking brings self-disclosure, which in turn brings more liking.

Sources: Adapted from I. Altman and D. Taylor, *Social Penetration.* (New York: Holt, Rinehart and Winston, 1973).

C. Gordon and K. Gergen, *The Self in Social Interaction,* Vol 1. (New York: Wiley, 1968).

D. Taylor, I. Altman, and R. Sorrentino, "Interpersonal Exchange as a Function of Rewards and Costs and Situational Factors: Expectancy Confirmation-Disconfirmation," *Journal of Experimental Social Psychology,* 5 (1969), pp. 324–339.

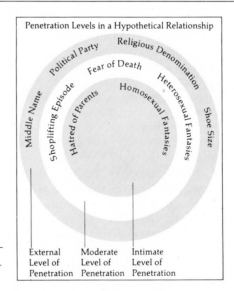

Penetration Levels in a Hypothetical Relationship

Political Party · Religious Denomination · Fear of Death · Heterosexual Fantasies · Middle Name · Shoplifting Episode · Hatred of Parents · Homosexual Fantasies · Shoe Size

External Level of Penetration   Moderate Level of Penetration   Intimate Level of Penetration

cooperation in studying these processes scientifically. However, an understanding of deeper relationships is of paramount importance, because it is just such relationships that are central in the lives of all of us.

The processes of interpersonal attraction do not always result in positive, mutually beneficial relationships. The next chapter will focus on factors that tend to make relations negative and mutually destructive.

SUMMARY

The need for human contact is a powerful force in human social life. When people are deprived of contact with others for long periods, they often become painfully anxious or even hallucinate the presence of others. Although cultures vary greatly in the traditions and social roles that shape specific interaction patterns, certain common themes seem universal: People everywhere acquire friends and lovers, produce and care for children, and so on. Social psychologists have tried to identify some of the reasons for which people choose whom they choose as partners in interaction.

Individuals are most likely to be attracted to those who are closest to them in perceived (if not objective) distance, if only because they are most familiar or most conveniently situated. After a relationship has begun, however, *proximity*, or physical distance, plays a different role. The preferred distance, or *interpersonal space*, maintained between people while interacting is an interpersonal buffer zone that varies according to the nature of the relationship. Social psychologists have found that some conditions of physical proximity, including uncomfortably high temperatures and crowding, produce more irritability than friendliness.

Attraction to others depends also on those others' qualities. The *matching hypothesis* states that people choose opposite-sex partners of approximately the same level of physical attractiveness as themselves; however, it does not hold true when people are not threatened with possible rejection. Although people are attracted to those whom they consider beautiful, when they choose actual partners they avoid rejection by choosing others who are near to what they consider to be their own levels of attractiveness.

Personality variables also play a part in attraction, especially insofar as others are similar or complementary to a person. Similarity of background and social class (as well as proximity and physical environment) are influential in the early stages of attraction because they either facilitate or prevent meeting. Later, both personality and complementarity may influence attraction; these variables fulfill different needs within a relationship or from one relationship to another.

The physical environment and the personality of the other are not the only factors that determine attraction. Sometimes particular characteristics of the other stimulate an individual's attraction to that other person. The *just-world hypothesis* is an attempt to explain the human tendency to be attracted to those who prosper and to find suffering souls unattractive, even when they suffer for us. Those who are blessed by luck must deserve it, we tend to believe, and they thereby become attractive.

Reciprocity—developing a liking for those who are attracted to us— often increases the original attraction. An exception is *ingratiation*, or insincere expressions of admiration. If someone seems to have ulterior motives for behaving in a rewarding fashion, that person's "attraction" will not likely be reciprocated.

Some social psychologists have devised a construct to contain these disparate elements of attraction theory—*reward.* In general, people are attracted to individuals who reward them in some way. The nature of rewards can vary from person to person and can be changed by the context of the relationship; thus, it is difficult to predict when attraction will develop. One means of avoiding the behavioral relativities produced by contexts is to focus on *patterns* of objective rewards and rewardingness that are constant from situation to situation. Elliot Aronson proposed one such predictive tool when he stated that people are not rewarded as much by a steady expression of appreciation as they are by an initially negative evaluation that becomes positive. In other words, the faithful and constant admirer can be boring compared to an admirer who expresses increasing attraction.

Most of the research on attraction has focused on brief, superficial interactions. In addition, research relies on such quantitative measures as the distance between apartments to study a phenomenon that can be difficult to gauge because it varies so greatly among individuals. Consequently, the bulk of attraction research does not necessarily apply to involved relationships.

Several recent attempts have been made to deal with deeper relationships. For example, one researcher compared liking and romantic loving. Two other investigators have conceptualized three levels of relationships—*unilateral awareness, surface contact,* and *mutuality.*

SUGGESTED READINGS

Altman, Irwin, and Dalmas Taylor. *Social Penetration: The Development of Interpersonal Relationships.* New York: Holt, Rinehart & Winston, 1973.

Aronson, Elliot. "Who Likes Whom and Why," *Psychology Today,* 4 (1970), 48–50.

———. "Attraction: Why People Like Each Other," in E. Aronson, *The Social Animal.* New York: W. H. Freeman, 1972, pp. 203–234.

Berscheid, Ellen, and Elaine Walster. *Interpersonal Attraction.* Reading, Mass.: Addison-Wesley, 1969.

Hunt, Morton. *The Natural History of Love.* New York: Knopf, 1959.

Rubin, Zick. *Liking and Loving.* New York: Holt, Rinehart & Winston, 1973.

Walster, Elaine. "Passionate Love," in B. I. Murstein (ed.), *Theories of Love and Attraction.* New York: Springer, 1971.

———, and Ellen Berscheid. "Adrenaline Makes the Heart Grow Fonder," *Psychology Today,* 5 (1971), 46–50.

7
Prejudice

Ralph Hill is middle-aged and balding. He lives in a suburban-looking house—green stucco with a white picket fence surrounding a large, well-tended lawn. He is married, has four children, and drives a Ford station wagon. He makes his living as an executive with IBM.

George Morris, in contrast, is in his early twenties and has long hair. He lives alone in a two-room apartment and rides a motorcycle. He is a student.

IMAGINE THAT YOU RECENTLY MOVED into a place that is located between Ralph's house and George's apartment; Ralph and George are now your next-door neighbors. When opportunities arise for exchanging greetings with your two new neighbors, will you be equally attracted to both? Will you give both of them equal chances to reveal their interests and ideas to you? Probably not. As explained in Chapter 5, we all form impressions of new acquaintances rather quickly and on the basis of the most superficial evidence—clothes, length of hair, facial expression, occupation, and so on. When formed, these first impressions go a long way in determining the extent and nature of our subsequent interactions with others.

As discussed in the preceding chapter, people are most likely to be attracted to others who appear to be similar to them. Thus, if you are a college student in your early twenties and feel comfortable with George Morris' motorcycle, long hair, and living situation, you probably will choose his companionship over Ralph Hill's. In fact, you may be downright cautious in your interactions with Ralph, most comfortable if conversations with him do not touch on topics more controversial than the weather and other innocuous pleasantries. If you take the easy way out with Ralph, however, you probably will never know that he once studied to be a Jesuit priest or that he gave up this formal pursuit in order to marry the woman he still loves. Neither will you find out that, although he works for IBM, Ralph is inwardly dissatisfied with his job and that he is active in Democratic party politics and takes occasional leaves of absence from work to help manage the campaigns of radical candidates. You will not come to understand that Ralph considers his tract house a temporary arrangement and currently is having another house built to his own highly imaginative design. You will never learn numerous other interesting facts about Ralph, including his enjoyment of existentialist literature, his fine collection of still photographs from silent movies, and his interest in deep-sea diving.

On the other hand, you may well be disappointed with George, who, it turns out, has fairly narrow interests compared with Ralph's. Although a student, George is bored with school and looks forward to graduating so that he can begin constructing solid-state components for radios at $13,000 a year beginning salary—his only reason for enduring another two years of college. Upon investigation, you will find that his apartment is completely bare of decoration. In fact, his apartment and motorcycle are both temporary economy measures; he looks forward to the time when he will be able to afford a car as well as a house of his own. You also will learn that most of George's conversations and spare time these days revolve around an obscure religious sect of Oriental derivation, to which he will try persistently to convert you as soon as he begins to relax in your company. Whether or not he succeeds in converting you, he will often become anxious to resume his meditations, to which he devotes hours daily.

Obviously, first impressions can be misleading. And yet we all form them. To the extent that they influence us to avoid or dislike a person before we have done more than scratch the surface—as you might have responded to Ralph Hill—they reflect a prejudice against that individual, or

rather against the group that the person is identified with. Thus, prejudice involves prejudgments, or *stereotypes*, that cause the perceiver to include in a single category a diverse group of individuals; it also involves a predisposition to act in a certain way toward members of that group. For example, the perceiver may assume that if certain persons have a common religion or national origin or facial structure, they must also have a common personality, level of aspiration, or IQ.

This chapter will focus on the most dramatic—and historically the most destructive—of prejudices: racial, religious, and sexual prejudices. Keep in mind, however, that prejudices fill many more corners of our conceptual lives than these categories represent. The groups that we hold prejudices against may be as diverse as "engineering students," "Catholics," "people who talk too slowly," "hard-hats," "Mexicans," and "those with dirty ears." In fact, prejudices fill our lives. They are the bases on which we choose, for or against, and on which we are accepted or rejected by others.

There are positive prejudices as well as negative ones; your initial attraction to George Morris would have constituted a positive prejudice if the subsequent interaction did not yield the rewards you expected. The preceding chapter on social attraction describes some of the processes and results of positive prejudices.

With prejudice defined so broadly, there are no short or simple answers to the questions: What causes prejudice? What are its consequences? And what are the cures? Instead, complicated answers to these questions should be anticipated. In some areas of psychology, multiple theories of a single phenomenon are an embarrassment. The student wants to know which is correct. Was Freud or Rogers or Sullivan or Skinner correct about matters of child rearing, for example? Dissension within the ranks of psychologists makes for interesting arguments but also creates credibility gaps. If psycho-

Figure 7.1 In some societies, including our own, prejudice has resulted in discriminatory behavior as blatant as that shown here. (*Left*) separate drinking fountains for blacks and whites could be found in many places in the South until recently. (*Right*) a South African drive-in theater in which a wall separates blacks from whites. Although such overt means of segregation are now illegal in the United States, segregation is still practiced in many ways. Not only do some white organizations, such as fraternal organizations and country clubs, systematically exclude blacks, some black groups, such as the Black Panthers and other black political groups, also exclude whites.

logists who have spent lifetimes studying these matters cannot agree on answers, where is the layman or student to place his or her trust? The aim of many psychological experiments, therefore, is to test competing theories against one another to see which emerges victorious. In the area of prejudice, however, multiple theories are probably more of an asset than a hindrance.

THE CAUSES OF PREJUDICE

One reason for recognizing that there are many different causes of prejudice is that this makes it possible to account for the facts of prejudice. For example, white prejudice against blacks in the United States seems to spring from a different source than black prejudice against whites, and Hindu-Moslem prejudices in India seem to stem from different issues than male-female prejudices in the United States. One theory probably could not account for these differences.

A second reason for recognizing multiple causes is more philosophical. If it is assumed that any one behavior rarely has but a single cause and that most behaviors are, in fact, multiply determined, then in order to fully understand a phenomenon a wide range of possible explanations must be considered. In the case of prejudice, the study of personality factors or ways of conceptualizing will not suffice as explanation; historical conditions and the role of economic competition, for example, must also be understood. No one of these explanations alone rules out the others—instead, they may all be relevant.

Gordon Allport (1958) conceptualized the various causes of prejudice in the paradigm illustrated in Figure 7.2. He conceived of these causes as falling along a continuum from macroscopic historical causes to microscopic causes that involve personal experience, or phenomenology. The types of causes that he has identified may interact in different ways to produce various forms of prejudice.

Historical Causes

A Marxist theory of prejudice maintains that life is a struggle between the haves and the have-nots and that the haves vilify their victims in order to justify emerging triumphant from *class conflict*. By blaming the people on the bottom for being on the bottom, those who are well-off can walk away

Figure 7.2 Prejudice is caused by many factors, as is most behavior. Allport (1958) has captured this idea in his conceptualization of the factors in prejudice, which range from the most macroscopic or broadly based (such as historical factors) to the most microscopic factors (such as individual, personal experiences). An individual's prejudices may stem from any combination of these factors. Because the nature of prejudice is so complex, it is not surprising that societies have so long encountered difficulties in finding solutions to the consequences of prejudice.

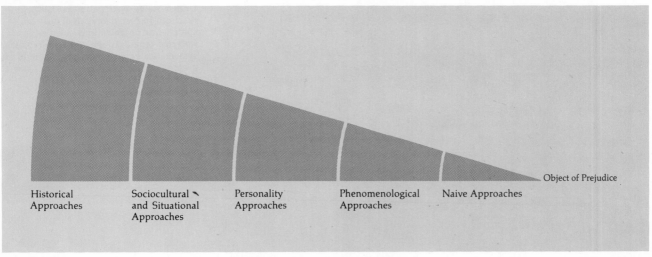

Historical Approaches Sociocultural and Situational Approaches Personality Approaches Phenomenological Approaches Naive Approaches Object of Prejudice

with clear consciences. In the words of Oliver Cox (1948), who adhered to a Marxist viewpoint, "Race prejudice . . . is a social attitude propagated among the public by an exploiting class for the purpose of stigmatizing some group as inferior so that the exploitation of either the group itself or its resources or both may be justified."

Many social scientists at the present time have reservations about a Marxist analysis, primarily because it seems to be based, for the most part, on an ideological position rather than on assessment of the facts. Yet there is some recent research that lends at least partial support to the Marxist analysis. Studies of observers' attitudes toward accident victims show that, rather than pity victims, onlookers often add insult to injury and blame the victims for their own misfortunes (see Chapter 5). The more powerless the onlookers feel and the longer they think the harm will continue, the more likely they are to say that the victims deserved what they got (Berscheid and Walster, 1969). This is not sadism but an attempt to make sense of otherwise unpredictable disasters. Melvin Lerner (1965) suggests that people feel a need to believe that they live in a *just world.* Accordingly, observers at the scene of a disaster cannot tolerate the thought that this is a cruel and unpredictable world in which harm could as easily have happened to them. Instead, they cling to the notion of a just and predictable world and explain the victim's misfortune by saying, in effect, "he deserved it."

Even the perpetrators of harm repond by blaming their victims. Harmdoers can assuage their own guilt by saying that their victims "asked

"The American Dilemma": CREED OR CONVENIENCE?

ABOUT THIRTY YEARS ago a Swedish social analyst, Gunnar Myrdal, wrote a book about black people in the United States. The book became a classic, and the author proved to be a harbinger of the coming crisis in black-white relations in America. Myrdal saw the struggle of the black American in terms of the national ethos, not disconnected from other aspects of social life. Here are some of his introductory comments from his book *The American Dilemma:*

The American Negro problem is a problem in the heart of the American. It is there that the interracial tension has its focus. It is there that the decisive struggle goes on. This is the central viewpoint of this treatise. Though our study includes economic, social, and political race relations, at bottom our problem is the moral dilemma of the American—the conflict between his moral valuations on various levels of consciousness and generality. The "American Dilemma," referred to in the title of this book, is the ever-raging conflict between, on the one hand, the valuations preserved on the general plane which we shall call the "American Creed," where the American thinks, talks, and acts under the influence of high national and Christian precepts, and, on the other hand, the valuations on specific planes of individual and group living, where personal and local interests; economic, social, and sexual jealousies; considerations of community prestige and conformity; group prejudice against particular persons or types of people; and all sorts of miscellaneous wants, impulses, and habits dominate his outlook. . . . (page xlvii)

The American Negroes know that they are a subordinated group experiencing, more than anybody else in the nation, the consequences of the fact that the Creed is not lived up to in America. Yet their faith in the Creed is not simply a means of pleading their unfulfilled rights. They, like the whites, are under the spell of the great national suggestion. With one part of themselves they actually believe, as do the whites, that the Creed is ruling America. (page 4)

How do Myrdal's words sound today? Are we still the same people he described three decades ago, or have we lost the capacity to dream or to make our dreams come true?

Source: Adapted from G. Myrdal, *The American Dilemma.* (New York: Harper & Row, 1944).

for it" and deserved what they got (Glass, 1964). By derogating their own victims, the harmdoers can avoid thinking of themselves as villains. (This topic is dealt with at greater length in Chapter 12.)

If applied to intergroup relations, these findings suggest that the haves, the oppressors, the majority, or the ruling class—be they white Americans in the United States, Englishmen in India, or East Indians in Africa—want to think of themselves as good, upstanding persons. Whether fate has actually been cruel or the haves are actually guilty of exploiting their brethren, the need to justify inequalities exists. Those who benefit at others' expense rectify the imbalance by devaluing and rejecting those whom they oppress. Marxist historical theory thus has some experimental evidence behind it.

Marxist historical theory appears capable of explaining white middle-class prejudice against lower-class blacks; European colonials' prejudice against their African, Asian, and Latin American subjects; Mayflower descendants' prejudices against twentieth-century Italian and Irish immigrants; and perhaps also some men's attitudes toward women.

The Marxist analysis of class conflict is but one type of historical theory of the causes of prejudice. Another theory, Robert Park's (1950), explains ethnic stratification and discrimination in terms of the conditions of intergroup contact. Among the causes this theory encompasses are: (1) the cultural and sociocultural characteristics of the groups before contact, (2) the characteristics of the migration, and (3) the nature of the initial contacts (Barth and Noel, 1972).

To illustrate the effects of these three causes, consider the difference between race relations in the United States and in Latin America. There are racial distinctions in both hemispheres, to be sure, but whereas people in the United States generally make an immediate and crude distinction between "white" and "black," Latin Americans (Mexicans as well as South Americans) have a truer melting pot and consequently recognize more ambiguity. Park's approach can be used to understand why the United States is still in a painful adolescent period emerging from slavery while Latin America has not experienced the same turbulence. Consider the historical conditions on the two continents when slaves were first introduced. Either the sociocultural characteristics of the receiving societies, the conditions of the migration, or the nature of the initial contacts must have been different (Elkins, 1968). (1) The sociocultural characteristics of the host societies were different when Africans first landed on American shores. Latin America had a strong Catholic church that proselytized among the imported slaves, baptized them, conducted religious marriage services, and upheld the inviolability of families. Churches in the United

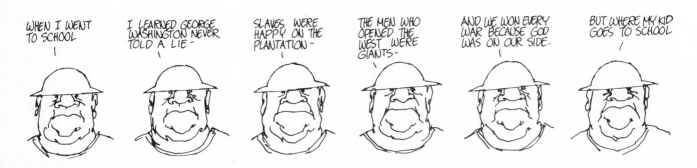

WHEN I WENT TO SCHOOL

I LEARNED GEORGE WASHINGTON NEVER TOLD A LIE—

SLAVES WERE HAPPY ON THE PLANTATION—

THE MEN WHO OPENED THE WEST WERE GIANTS—

AND WE WON EVERY WAR BECAUSE GOD WAS ON OUR SIDE.

BUT WHERE MY KID GOES TO SCHOOL

States, on the other hand, seldom baptized or married slaves, so there was no protection of the family structure. (2) The migration from Africa was equally horrifying for both groups, but (3) the initial contacts were different. Whereas most people in the United States considered slaves as property to be auctioned, in Latin America they were also souls to be counted and saved. In the Spanish colonies, moreover, slaves could buy their own freedom more easily or be set free on special occasions like the birth of a child or the marriage of a daughter in the slave owner's family.

Park's theory, with its inspection of minute details of group contact, points to *some* causes of *some* forms of prejudice. For example, it explains the origins of prejudice against European immigrants in the United States, Asians in Africa, Africans in the United States, and Americans in other countries. It fails, however, to explain prejudice against groups with whom the biased group has had no contact. For example, Princeton men had very negative stereotypes of Turks in 1933 (Katz and Braly, 1933), although none had probably ever met a Turk. Park's theory also fails to explain Eugene Horowitz's (1936) finding that white attitudes toward blacks are more a function of what other whites say than of white contact with black people. Nor does Park's theory describe the causes of sexism, because neither sex has migrated into the territory of the other.

These two historical theories identify some causes of some forms of prejudice. They leave gaps, however, which some of the theories that will be discussed next can fill.

Sociocultural and Situational Causes

The theories discussed in the preceding section were "historical" in the usual sense of the term—their originators examined the grand scheme of things or talked about events of one hundred or more years ago. All theories of cause and effect are historical in another sense of the word—they are based on the assumption that each effect has a history and that somewhere in that history is located its cause. Sometimes social psychologists deal with histories as short as five minutes, and sometimes they deal with a life span. Some causes are rather immediate, as is a recent decline in status or a move to a big city, whereas others are more remote, as when people grow up in an atmosphere of prejudice. Each of these alone contributes to the development of stereotypes and intergroup hostility, and when they appear in combination, as is often the case, their effects seem almost impossible to eradicate.

Downward Mobility. Marxist theory explains why the rich devalue the poor, but there is a sizable body of literature suggesting that those who are

becoming poorer are also becoming more prejudiced. Bruno Bettelheim and Morris Janowitz (1950) report that it may not be social class per se that causes prejudice but rather social *mobility.* Their data show that no matter what social position people start from, if they move down, they become outspokenly hostile (see Tables 7.1 and 7.2). Downwardly mobile persons, the explanation continues, seek reasons for their misfortunes, and rather than blame themselves, their stars, or bad luck, they hit on scapegoats. Scapegoats, by definition, are always innocent victims. They are not to blame for their attackers' downward mobility; they constitute no real threat. It is, in fact, precisely because they are *not* threatening that they are safe targets for hostility. For example, neither black people nor Jews caused the social fall of the people in Bettelheim and Janowitz's study. The real causes were undoubtedly complex patterns in those individuals' economic, social, and personal lives. Thus, for a failing worker to direct his hostility against his boss, his banker, or even his family just increases his risks. He chooses a safer target, therefore, one less able to retaliate.

Realistic Group Conflict. The targets of hostility are not always entirely innocent. There are instances of real group competition, such as Mexican laborers working for lower wages than their Anglo counterparts in Texas, Irish immigrants undercutting the wages of Mayflower descendants in Boston, and black nonunion construction laborers working for lower wages than their unionized white brethren. Competition does produce hostility, as Chapter 14 explains in describing the work of Muzafer Sherif and his colleagues (1961). But economically based group conflict is not a necessary condition of prejudice, because prejudice does not disappear during economic booms. The decade of the 1960s in the United States, for example, was a period of great economic growth and prosperity, but it was also a decade of race riots, antibusing crusades, and presidential commissions investigating white racism (Kerner, 1968). Even in the best of times, when there is no special reason for economic conflict, there is intergroup hostility and prejudice.

Urban Stigma. A cause of prejudice in prosperous times appears to be the uncertainty and insecurity that characterize urban life in particular. Groups

Table 7.1 Attitudes of White Gentiles Toward Jewish Americans

SOCIAL POSITION OF WHITE GENTILES	TOLERANT	STEREOTYPED	OUTSPOKEN AND INTENSELY HOSTILE
Downwardly Mobile	11%	17%	72%
Not Mobile	37	38	25
Upwardly Mobile	50	18	32

Source: Adapted from B. Bettelheim and M. Janowitz, *Dynamics of Prejudice: A Psychological and Sociological Study of Veterans* (New York: Harper & Row, 1950), p. 59.

Table 7.2 Attitudes of White Gentiles Toward Black Americans

SOCIAL POSITION OF WHITE GENTILES	TOLERANT AND STEREOTYPED	OUTSPOKEN	INTENSELY HOSTILE
Downwardly Mobile	28%	28%	44%
Not Mobile	26	59	15
Upwardly Mobile	50	39	11

Source: Adapted from B. Bettelheim and M. Janowitz, *Dynamics of Prejudice: A Psychological and Sociological Study of Veterans* (New York: Harper & Row, 1950), p. 150.

What's in a name, anyway? . . . When I was a kid we didn't have no race trouble— an' you know why? Nobody called themselves Chicanos. Or Mexican-Americans, or Afro-Americans. We was all American. . . . Then after that if a guy was a Spic or a Jig it was his business. I mean it was his business, if he wanted to cling with his own kind. Which most of them did. That's how you get your Harlem and your Chinatown and your Little Italy.

—ARCHIE BUNKER

III ENCOUNTERING OTHERS

that are identified in the public eye with cities thus come to bear a disproportionate share of blame. People in Europe and the United States have identified Jews with urban entrepreneurship and consequently have characterized them as "too clever," "ambitious," "greedy," and generally successful in playing the urban game, according to Gordon Allport (1958).

"The Jews are hated today," wrote Arnold Rose (1948), " . . . primarily because they serve as a symbol of city life." If the concept of the big city has changed—from a place where fortunes are won and lost to a place where purses are snatched and people are mugged—it is not surprising that a new onus has fallen on a new urban group. Many suburban whites now identify urban blacks as the cause of "crime in the streets," even though those blacks who reside in cities are themselves the victims of muggings and must fear for their safety more than suburbanites. Theirs is a case of guilt by association.

Socialization.   Even if we could eliminate all cities, all realistic group conflict, all downward mobility, and all forms of exploitation, prejudice might still persist. There is a sticky quality to cultural traditions that makes them persist long after their *original* causes have vanished. Thus, the East Asian custom of removing one's shoes before entering a house, and above all before entering a kitchen, makes medical sense because it keeps bacteria-infested soil outside on the doorstep. As health and medicine improve in East Asia, it may be expected that fewer people follow this ancient custom, but in fact it persists despite the erosion of the original reasons. It persists because the parents and grandparents of young East Asians still follow the practice and pass it on to their progeny. So also with prejudice—not considered a cultural tradition by most people but, in terms of socialization, acquired through a similar process.

We all live in traditional societies to the extent that we inherit the wisdom of our elders, and along with their wisdom come their prejudices. Thus, Eugene and Ruth Horowitz (1938) found young white children telling them that their parents would disapprove of their having black playmates. Their parents denied having this influence, and their older siblings were no longer conscious of the influence. But the younger children were aware of the rule and of the penalties for violations. In the language of conformity

Figure 7.3 Economic insecurity can breed hostile racial attitudes and scapegoating, as is suggested by the prevalence and intensity of racial hatred traditionally found in some parts of the country. According to sociologist Jerome Skolnick (1969), many white as well as black Southerners have suffered disproportionately from economic insecurity, but the insecure, largely marginal white Southerners—those who are not clearly blue-collar or white-collar workers—have resented assistance programs for blacks most vociferously and have traditionally found their black neighbors easy targets on which to blame their problems. "In the process," according to Skolnick, "the actual sources of the grievances of the marginal white have gone uncorrected. Klan violence represents the thwarted and displaced political protest of whites acting from a context of economic insecurity, threatened manhood, and inability to influence local and national political structures." This photograph was taken in the South in 1932. Nationwide, more than 1,700 black Americans were lynched during the first fifty years of this century.

research, the young children showed *public compliance,* or expedient conformity, whereas their older siblings exhibited *private acceptance.*

Children who grow up in an atmosphere of prejudice conform to the prejudicial norm—at first ritually and later with the conviction that it is the right way to be. Children are socialized into the prejudicial culture of their parents—that is, they encounter numerous forces that induce them to conform to the thoughts and practices of their parents and other informal teachers. (For a fuller discussion of conformity, see Chapter 10.)

Each of us has access to two distinct modes of learning about the world—our personal, individual modes and social, or vicarious, modes (D. Campbell, 1961). Most learning research traditionally has focused on the individual modes—the trial-and-error or perceptual explorations of individual organisms discovering the properties of their respective mazes. When people engage in independent, hermit-like explorations like those often studied by learning theorists in their laboratories, the learning that people do is not as dependent on the advice of others (including past generations) as it is in most real-life learning situations. The moment that people try to learn from the experience of others, however, they become susceptible to (indeed ask for) the advice and influence of others—to their errors as well as their wisdom. Under what conditions are people most

Figure 7.4 A society can, and usually does, transmit a great deal of prejudice to its young. Although prejudice is rarely taught in such an overt fashion as the Ku Klux Klan dogma is being taught to this youngster (*right*), children gradually internalize the prejudices of those around them, learning to be prejudiced through various mechanisms of socialization—observational learning, subtle rewards and punishments, and identification. In fact, these are the means by which children acquire *any* cultural norms, values, and attitudes. These phrases (*below*) are among the many common expressions by which, however innocently, adults teach children to categorize and evaluate various groups.

Coon's age

Jew down

Dumb blonde

Indian giver

Polack joke

Honkie

III ENCOUNTERING OTHERS

susceptible to these influences? Many of the social processes through which people learn are described in Chapter 2, because these processes *are* what social psychologists call "socialization." What follows is a partial list of the conditions, compiled by Donald Campbell (1961), that enhance conformity, or imitation:

1. Experiences and attributes of the person:
   a. The less people know or feel they know about a topic, the more apt they are to conform to others.
   b. The younger people are, and the less well established their own attitudes, the more likely they are to conform to elders' opinions.
   c. The lower people's estimations of their own abilities, the more likely they are to follow others' leads.

According to these principles, children would be expected to be particularly conforming to their parents' ethnic prejudices, because children are by definition younger and are also likely to feel less knowledgeable about and less able to judge social groups. However unfounded the biases of their elders, then, children are not likely to fly in the face of tradition and proclaim that all persons are equal.

2. *Clarity of the situation:*
   The more ambiguous the stimulus, the more a person will conform to others' judgments.

If prejudice represents an unfair and unfavorable prejudgment of an entire group of persons—for example, blacks, whites, Turks, Armenians—the stimulus, or referent, is by definition ambiguous. Subjects who are forced to characterize such groups as a whole may be rightly unhappy with their assignment—they want to know *which* blacks, *which* whites, and so on. It is relatively easy to describe a particular individual as lazy or ambitious, sincere or insincere, but when the only referent is a category name, a person is faced with an ambiguous stimulus, and the inclination will be to adopt any available socially accepted definition of the situation. In light of this, it is not particularly surprising that Daniel Katz and Kenneth Braly (1933) and later Marvin Karlins, Thomas Coffman, and Gary Walters (1969) found highly consistent stereotypes of Turks among Princeton men, who probably had never met a Turk. If in doubt, the principle says, conform.

3. *Attributes of the model:*
   a. The more a model is rewarded in the present for his or her behavior, the more likely an observer is to conform to the model's behavior.
   b. The more a model has been rewarded in the past, the more an observer will conform to that particular model. Thus, models who are perceived as intelligent, strong, successful, or high in status elicit the most conformity.

The evidence supporting these principles shows that adults elicit more conformity in judgment from children than do peers and that older students elicit more conformity than do younger students. Children growing up in a society that has rewarded their elders with social approval or economic gains for discriminating against some category of persons will be inclined to discriminate likewise. The children are in effect learning that if they wish to reap the same social and economic rewards, they must follow the example of their successful elders. This is a rational assumption, and if most of us lived a more noble existence, the influence would be a benign one. However, we live in a society that frequently rewards discrimination, and even if the tendency to imitate high-status others is an optimal solution for the individual, it is not the best solution for society as a whole.

In addition to learning by example, younger generations are taught by the following processes:

4. *Verbal instruction:*
   a. The more the *communicator's* own responses have been rewarded, the more likely his or her communication is to influence another.
   b. The more a *listener* has been rewarded in the past for following the instructions of the communicator, the more influential the communicator's instructions will be.

5. *Reinforced imitative responding:*
   Persons who have been rewarded for imitating or conforming in the past are likely to conform to the same or a similar model in the future.

Principles 4b and 5 help explain why, for example, persons raised in authoritarian homes, where strict obedience is demanded, exhibit more prejudice than do persons who have been raised in more democratic environments. (Authoritarianism is given fuller consideration in the next section of this chapter.) This explanation, however, assumes that authoritarian fathers happen to be more prejudiced, and so the reasoning becomes somewhat circular. But given two homes in which the parents are prejudiced, the home with authoritarian practices is more likely to function as an incubator of prejudices in the children than is the home with democratic arrangements.

Prejudice does not always result from historical, sociocultural, or situational factors. If this analysis were confined to these levels, it would be necessary to conclude that all persons in a given culture at a given time share the same prejudices. However, this is not true. Some people are highly prejudiced toward one or more target groups; others who are faced with the same conditions are far more accepting and tolerant of differences. And still others embrace the usual targets of prejudice simply because it is socially acceptable to do so.

Sociocultural and situational causes of prejudice—downward mobility, realistic group conflict, urbanization, and socialization—explain why urban

Figure 7.5 During World War II, 110,000 Japanese-Americans were "relocated" in concentration camps like the Manzanar Relocation Camp (*below*). The relocation of persons such as this family (*right*) was ostensibly carried out to protect the "internal security" of the United States, although most of the uprooted were citizens of the United States and had done nothing as individuals to arouse suspicion. Whole families were incarcerated, and many lost their possessions and businesses or jobs in the process. The relocation is today generally regarded as a product of wartime hysteria, which intensified discrimination against a stereotyped group.

Jews, blacks, Puerto Ricans, Irish, and other minorities in the United States have been objects of hostility, especially during hard times. They do not explain, however, why the prosperous 1960s were a time of hatred, why Japanese farmers in California were locked in concentration camps, or why colonial Americans drove the American Indians to desperation when there were neither cities nor scarce resources. Just as the historical approaches left loopholes in an understanding of the causes of prejudice, so do sociocultural and situational explanations.

Personality as a Cause

There are at least three approaches to understanding the personality differences that underlie individual proclivities to be prejudiced.

Projection. Sigmund Freud believed that prejudice is a function of the human tendency to project. *Similarity projection* refers to the tendency in all of us to project onto others our own undesirable impulses (especially sexual and aggressive ones, according to Freud)—that is, to see other people doing what we most dread being caught doing. This handy mechanism permits an individual to fight or fornicate because "the other person started it." For example, if a white policeman freely uses violence against black citizens on his beat, he is likely to believe that his violence was required by the violence of the ghetto rather than to attribute it correctly to his own aggressive tendencies. Projection has served people a similar function in assigning sexual intentions. In the words of social psychologist Roger Brown:

> If one can believe that Negro women are inherently sensual and promiscuous, then one can believe that they seduce a man against his better impulses. On the other hand, if anything happens between a white woman and a Negro it must be rape since the woman could not desire the Negro while he is certain to desire her. . . . Negro men have often been lynched for rape. (1965, page 502)

According to the theory of similarity projection, persons who have a marked tendency to describe others as hostile or aggressive betray their own hostility. And individuals who tend to call others lewd or promiscuous reveal their own desires.

On the other hand, *complementary projection* is quite different. If one person calls another sloppy, it is probably because the former is compulsively neat. People who exploit members of ethnic groups for cheap labor are likely to believe that they do so not because they are greedy but because those they exploit are guileless and unqualified. As discussed earlier in this chapter, by rationalizing the harm they have done to others, harmdoers can think well of themselves and continue exploiting their victims.

Both similarity and complementary projection serve to protect people's self-images by enabling them to attribute sexual, aggressive, deceitful, or other intentions to others and thus to justify their own feelings or actions. Although both are plausible causes of prejudice, research suggests that similarity projection occurs more frequently than complementary projection (Campbell, Miller, Lubetsky, and O'Connell, 1964).

Frustration. As developed by John Dollard, Leonard Doob, Neal Miller, O. H. Mowrer, and Robert Sears (1939), the *frustration-aggression theory* postulates that frustration is a sufficient condition for aggression and hostility. Therefore, people can be expected to be hostile and prejudiced toward those who frustrate them. However, if the question of who really frustrates whom is considered, children would be found hating their parents, workers their bosses, students their teachers—in general, underlings their overlords. This direct frustration may happen, but it is certainly not expressed overtly, nor do the sources of frustration need to worry about prejudices of this sort. Instead, danger exists when, for example, children hate other children, ethnic workers hate members of other ethnic groups, and underlings hate other underlings. Most of our daily frustrations come from others on whom we are for various reasons dependent—for example, from a professor, an employer, or members of our own ingroup. Clearly, however, for us to vent our resentment and aggression against those persons would be disastrous. For just this reason, sanctions against ingroup hostility have developed, as have religious injunctions such as "Thou shalt love thy mother and thy father." Superimposed on our hostile impulses toward the sources of our frustrations are strong inhibitions against hurting those who wield the power. Consequently, the aggression seems to be *displaced* onto a target that may be similar to the real villain but is safer. Scapegoating by the downwardly mobile often seems to follow this pattern. (The frustration-aggression hypothesis is detailed further in Chapter 11.)

Some cultures have institutionalized scapegoats in the form of evil spirits. Thus, parents tell their children to wash or pray or do their tasks not "because I said so" but "because if you don't, the witches will get you." Children in the United States no longer speak of witches or evil spirits, but they do know that "the boogeyman can get you." And as they grow older, the boogeyman for white children becomes a black man; for black children he becomes a white man, or simply "the Man"; and for many people in the United States, the boogeymen are "the Communists."

Displacement of aggression explains why people are prejudiced against some groups with whom they have had no personal contact. In fact, the fewer the contacts, the safer the group is as a scapegoat, because the less likely it is to retaliate. Displacement also explains why some groups turn their hatred against themselves. For example, in the Nazi concentration camps the real sources of frustration were the guards, who thwarted the prisoners' every biological and psychological need. However, to strike back at them was suicidal, so the prisoners seemed to displace their aggression onto the only safe targets—other prisoners like themselves.

The Authoritarian Personality. The frustration-aggression hypothesis implies that all persons are candidates for prejudice: Who has not been frustrated in his or her life? But according to another line of research conducted in the aftermath of World War II, it takes a particular type of personality to be prejudiced. It takes a personality that was formed in a home with a dominant and punitive father, so that the children's frustration develops into displaced aggression. But the characteristics are more specific than that. The *authoritarian personality* was defined as fascistic, ethnocentric, anti-Semitic, and politically and economically conservative by post-World War II researchers Theodore Adorno, Else Frenkel-Brunswik, Daniel Levinson, and R. Nevitt Sanford (1950). These four psychologists had developed four attitude scales, known respectively as the *F, E, A-S,* and *PEC* scales, to measure the four characteristics of the authoritarian personality: fascism, ethnocentrism, anti-Semitism, and political and economic conservatism. They found that individuals who scored high on one tended to score high on all four and that persons who scored low on one scored low on all of them. In statistical terms, the four measures were positively intercorrelated, and the composite was used to define an authoritarian personality. (Sample items appear on page 228.)

Having identified this core of symptoms, the researchers inquired into the cause by interviewing respondents about their childhood experiences, particularly their memories of how they were treated by their parents. These recollections revealed that subjects with authoritarian personalities grew up in homes with strict, punishing fathers who demanded obedience and unquestioning loyalty. Thus, the answer to the question "What causes prejudice?" arrived at by Adorno and his colleagues is that strict and punitive child-rearing practices produce authoritarian personalities that are full of hostility and prejudice.

Since this research has been published, it has been thoroughly scrutinized and criticized. The critiques fill an entire book—*Studies in the Scope and Method of "The Authoritarian Personality"* (Christie and Johoda, 1954). The major criticisms are as follows: (1) Perhaps it is not personality structure that makes the scores on the four attitude scales cohere—instead, those scores may reflect norms of people with low incomes and little education. The explanation lies not in their personalities but in their low socioeconomic status (see also Orpen and Van der Schyff, 1972). (2) The researchers collected the data about child-rearing practices through their subjects' recollections—and not even the recollections of the parents but rather those of grown children. Thus, the descriptions do not necessarily reflect what the parents were actually like but rather what their children remembered them as being. (3) The investigators analyzed the interviews about early childhood with foreknowledge of the respondents' attitude-scale scores. Instead of coding the interviews "blind," the researchers knew whose interview they were coding and they thereby opened themselves to the weakness of seeing only what they expected to see. (4) The attitude questionnaires (*F, E, A-S,* and *PEC* scales) also were not infallible. Their primary flaw was that all of the questions were worded in the same way, so that persons who agreed with all of the items received high scores on all the scales. It is therefore possible that what was being measured was not fascism or ethnocentrism; the respondents who scored high may have just been acquiescent. (5) The work implies that only political conservatives can be anti-Semitic, fascistic, ethnocentric, and therefore authoritarian. May there not also be an authoritarian of the left? (6) Finally, it would appear that there is nothing good about the high scorers—the researchers recognized no redeeming virtues. As Roger Brown (1965) points out, the research describes authoritarian personalities as "rigid"; might they not alternatively be described as "stable"? They are called "intolerant of ambiguity"; might that not be considered "decisive"? And they are accused of demonstrating a "conventional idealization of their parents"; might this not be seen as "familial love and warmth"?

Certainly the critics of this work do not want to defend fascism, ethnocentrism, or anti-Semitism, but they do want to prevent another instance of scapegoating. For it is not only the political conservative or the person with little education and a low income who is beset by prejudice and outgroup hostility. If ethnic jokes and other outward expressions of prejudice are acceptable to persons of low socioeconomic status (SES), is it not possible that the poorly disguised "some of my best friends are . . ." expressions of prejudice are the higher SES equivalent? Some researchers have suggested that if the *F* scale were rid of its political bias, left-wing radicals would probably score as high on general authoritarianism as do right-wing conservatives (Rokeach, 1960). Others are not convinced that there is an authoritarian of the left (Brown, 1965). But until the case is settled, social psychologists would do well not to project their own undesirable ethnocentrism onto just one political group; the authoritarian personality may not move in conservative circles alone.

Phenomenological Causes: Thinking Makes It So

The approaches to understanding prejudice discussed so far have located the causes in historical circumstances, in the prevailing social conditions, or in enduring personality structures. The phenomenological approach locates the cause in the immediate present—in the ways in which each of us perceives the world. Our perceptions create our prejudices, according to this approach, rather than our prejudices creating our perceptions.

The ways in which people identify outgroups and discriminate against their members are functions of a particular social consensus—a social fabrication in a particular place and time. Advocates of this position point out that:

The role of shared definitions is crucial in the realm of interethnic relations. Ethnicity is by no means an entirely subjective phenomenon but the social definitions of ethnicity and of appropriate intergroup behavior are highly significant. Numerous physical traits are highly visible, but in any given society few are associated with institutionalized discrimination. An individual is not assigned to a specific ethnic group because he shares certain observable characteristics with other members of the group. He is assigned because there is general agreement (consensus) that he belongs to the group regardless of whether there are actually any physical or cultural similarities. Only by acknowledging the ultimate importance of the shared social definition can we explain the fact that a physically white, obviously Caucasoid person can be classified as a Negro in the United States while a dark-skinned, obviously Negroid person may be classified as "white" (that is, *branco*) in Brazil. When men define themselves as fundamentally alike or different, they act in accordance with this definition regardless of its veracity. (Barth and Noel, 1972, pages 338–339)

The reality of ethnic identity lies, therefore, in people's minds. This approach helps to underline the arbitrariness and even artificiality of ethnic categorization. However, it fails to explain why, for example, people in the United States make a fuss about skin color; why the English and Irish fuss over whether someone is Catholic or Protestant; and why Indians fuss over whether someone is Hindu or Moslem. The approach fails also to explain why each of these nations ignores so many other distinctions. The shape of the nose, length of the forearm, color of the eyes, and so on may sound like silly distinctions to some people, but to a Hindu, the distinction between Catholics and Protestants is just as insignificant.

To understand the causes of each nation's peculiar ways of defining the world, it is necessary to return to an analysis of historical causes of prejudice. Thus, in the United States the majority consensus is that skin color may make a difference because the conditions of black migration and of contact between white property owners and African slaves produced a highly stratified society. In India, on the other hand, the migrant Moslems brought with them customs that were directly opposed to the customs of the native Hindus—Moslems killed and ate cattle, shaved their heads, and grew beards; Hindus worshipped cattle, shaved their chins, and let the hair on their heads grow. If the historical conditions that gave rise to each case of ethnic differentiation were examined, it would be easier to understand why one social group makes distinctions that another ignores.

Why should differences or distinctions in and of themselves create intergroup hostility? If, as stated in Chapter 6, most of us prefer others who are similar to us, what happens if they are different on one dimension, such as race, but similar on another, such as belief? Do we like or dislike such a person? Which similarity means more to us—that of physical appearance or of beliefs? This question has been tossed back and forth between two social psychologists in particular. Milton Rokeach contends that beliefs count most—that we would rather be with a person who thinks as we think rather than with someone who has a similar skin color (Rokeach, 1961; Rokeach and Mezei, 1966; Rokeach and Parker, 1970; Rokeach, Smith and Evans, 1960). Harry Triandis, on the other hand, reports that, at least for some persons and in some situations, racial differences loom larger than do differences in belief (Triandis, 1961; Triandis and Davis, 1965). Upon careful analysis, this apparent dispute begins to disappear. With customs as they are today in the United States, there are personal or intimate situations in which racial differences are more salient than is ideological agreement. This aversion to personal contact with members of other ethnic groups may indeed be a distinguishing characteristic of what could be called a racist society. Although there is not yet any scientifically gathered data, it is probably safe to assume that the United States has more couples who are the same race but vote for different political candidates than it has interracial couples who vote for the same presidential candidates. Triandis did find that the more intimate the proposed social situation, the more his subjects reacted to a potential partner on the basis of race instead of belief. On the other hand, in situations where racial differences seem insignificant compared with philosophical or political agreements, persons choose to affiliate on the basis of belief instead of racial similarity. For example, two Americans from Lincoln, Nebraska—one white and one black—meeting

Figure 7.6 The phenomenological approach places the cause of prejudice in the perceptions of the prejudiced person and prescribes intergroup contact to dispel misconceptions. Contact in which groups cooperate on an equal basis to accomplish a common goal has been found to be most effective. Before blacks and whites joined forces to conduct a civil-rights march in Selma, Alabama, many may have championed civil rights on a theoretical basis as an issue of justice, but they undoubtedly gained increased understanding, respect, and liking for one another through the conditions of their contact.

accidentally in Paris or Tokyo might well be more impressed by their shared cultural background than by their different skin colors.

If belief and race are both important determinants of attraction, why does it still appear that society in the United States is segregated more along racial than along political lines in housing, marriage, schools, and so on? David Stein, Jane Allyn Hardyck, and M. Brewster Smith (1965) provide an answer. They asked white ninth-graders from working-class homes to react to four hypothetical teen-agers who were either similar or dissimilar to the subjects in race and belief. In addition, the subjects were asked to react to a "Negro teen-ager" about whom they had no other information. This study again found belief congruence to be more important than racial differences, but it adds an important postscript. When the subjects had no other information to go on than race, they responded to the "Negro teen-ager" in the same way that they responded to the Negro teen-ager with dissimilar beliefs. In other words, in the absence of information about belief similarity, they assumed *dissimilarity*. Instead of assuming "all other things being equal," they assumed "all other things being different" and reacted accordingly. The assumption of belief dissimilarity is a realistic assumption on issues for which there are sizable differences between the beliefs of blacks and whites concerning, for example, the purposes, causes, effects, and prevention of race riots (A. Campbell and Schuman, 1969). Blacks and whites also differ in the extent to which they blame discrimination for economic inequities (70 percent of the black and only 56 percent of the white respondents agreed that "Negroes miss out on jobs because of discrimination"). On many other issues, however, such as politics, crime, morality, and religion, the population certainly does not split along racial lines, although racially prejudiced people seem to think it does.

Several studies investigating the relative importance of race and belief similarity have found that for *some* people race is more important than for other people (Byrne and Wong, 1962; Goldstein and Davis, 1972; Triandis and Davis, 1965). There appear to be two types of orientations: race-rejectors and belief-rejectors, who differ—because of personality factors—in what they deem most important.

One more explanation of prejudice—aptly called by Allport the "naive" theory of prejudice—deserves discussion here.

Naive Explanations

Naive explanations of prejudice look not at the people with the prejudice but rather at the object of their prejudice to find the cause. According to them, if there is anti-Semitism, it is because Jews are ambitious, materialistic and shrewd; if there is antiblack sentiment, it is because black people are happy-go-lucky, pleasure-loving, and lazy; if whites are unpopular in some circles, it is because they are materialistic, ambitious, and pleasure-loving.

Although few social scientists would dare to espouse a naive view of prejudice, simplistic explanations must be reckoned with. When Dean Peabody (1968) studied the stereotypes—positive and negative—that various groups held of one another, he noticed that different groups were in marked agreement about the characteristics they attributed to each group, although they disagreed as to whether the characteristics were favorable or unfavorable. The particular terms that the different groups chose to describe the same characteristics often were quite opposite in their evaluative significance. For example, members of many groups would agree that the

Japanese are highly productive in the economic sphere and that they outstrip almost all competitors. Yet there are great differences in the ways in which different groups label this characteristic of the Japanese. Their friends may see the Japanese as "industrious," whereas their competitors view them as "economic animals." Robert K. Merton, a sociologist, described this phenomenon in his book *Social Theory and Social Structure* as follows:

> . . . the very same behavior undergoes a complete change of evaluation in its transition from the in-group Abe Lincoln to the out-group Abe Cohen or Abe Kurokawa. . . . Did Lincoln work far into the night? This testifies that he was industrious, resolute, perseverant, and eager to realize his capacities to the full. Do the out-group Jews or Japanese keep these same hours? This only bears witness to their sweatshop mentality, their ruthless undercutting of American standards, their unfair competitive practices. Is the in-group hero frugal, thrifty, and sparing? Then the out-group villain is stingy, miserly, and penny-pinching. (1957, page 428)

Thus, stereotypes often involve unfair *double standards* by which people consider the same characteristic virtuous when displayed by those they like and evil when displayed by those they dislike.

Thus far stereotypes have been viewed as fixed in time, as static products of the cumulative circumstances of history, culture, personality, and possible real group differences. But any of these influences can change. Even history changes: Events constantly are being added to it, and the ways in which people view past events change as well. Social scientists consider it an undeniable fact that stereotypes in the United States are changing. But they are less certain about how to explain these changes. There are at least three possible sources of recent changes in stereotypes in the United States.

Change: Fact, Fading, or Faking?

Given the power of socializing mechanisms—some of which were discussed earlier—by which prejudices are passed from one generation to the next, it is remarkable indeed that stereotypes change at all. However, Karlins,

Figure 7.7 Although a pawn shop and a savings and loan company perform much the same function—that of lending money—people generally regard them quite differently. The savings and loan establishment tends to be associated with the affluent, middle-class interests of its customers and is thus assumed by most people to be respectable, whereas pawn shops are associated with lower-class elements and are therefore not generally trusted by middle-class individuals. In this and many other ways, prejudices lead people automatically to evaluate differently places, behaviors, and people that may be objectively similar.

Coffman, and Walters (1969) report a positive change over three generations of Princeton students. Compared to alumni from the 1930s, Princeton men in 1967 described "Americans" as more materialistic and less shrewd and "Negroes" as more musical and less ignorant. Princeton men still had stereotypes, but they were different from those of the 1930s.

Do the differences found by Karlins and his colleagues reflect a change in *facts,* as proponents of naive theories might say? Were people in the United States actually more materialistic in the 1960s than they were in the 1930s? Or does the change reflect a difference in fads? Has it simply become fashionable to speak of Americans as more materialistic and less intelligent? These are almost unanswerable questions, and they get at what James Jones (1972) calls the crux of racial relations: Are *real* differences the basis of negative judgments, and if so, do they justify the negative judgments? Few investigators have tried to ask, much less answer, this question, because few have dared to define the "real differences" that may exist.

A notable exception is educational psychologist Arthur Jensen (1969), who has tried to demonstrate that IQ is determined primarily by hereditary factors. The implication of Jensen's thesis is that the lower average scores that black Americans receive on standardized tests of intelligence, compared with white Americans, are not the result of poorer schools and employment opportunities but of an inherent deficit in black mentality. His work has been scrutinized with a fine-tooth methodological comb, and critics—among them, Jerome Kagan (1969)—have found many errors in his data sample, his statistics, and his reasoning (see Chapter 3). The apparent difference in average IQ scores is not a *real* difference between racial

WHEN BLACK IS WHITE

IN OUR CULTURE, everyone knows who the "whites," the "blacks," the "reds," and the "yellowskins" are. We habitually label groups who differ in racial and ethnic origins with color names. Each of us also learns connotative meanings of various colors during childhood. For example, we learn early in our lives to value the "light of day" and to fear or dislike the "black of night."

Do our feelings about "white" and "black" spill over into our feelings about white and black people? And what relationship do these attitudes have to our feelings about our own skin colors?

John Williams, a social psychologist at Wake Forest University in North Carolina, has been searching for answers to these questions. In one study he asked students at three colleges to express their feelings about colors, skin colors, and more technical names for labeling people, such as "Caucasian" and "Negro." One group of subjects were white, the other group were black. The data were divided according to several dimensions, including the evaluative, or good-bad, dimension. How differently would people rate linguistically related colors, persons, and ethnic groups?

The figures show the ways white and black students evaluated the three entries on the good-bad scale, for the words "white" and "black" only.

From the figures it appears that all subjects expressed the same relative preference for white color over black. The color white was liked best, and black was rated worst (although the black color was less negatively rated by the black sample). When it came to transferring from a color name to a racial label, however, white subjects rated the two colors very differently than did black subjects. White subjects tended to maintain positive rankings for white entries and negative rankings

groups, the critics conclude, because it would disappear if racial discrimination were to disappear.

An earlier attempt to investigate real differences was made by Richard LaPiere (1936), who examined the relationship between the stereotype of Armenians in California and the reality. He found the two at odds. The stereotypes were false—point by point in error.

Most social psychologists take the view that a stereotype is basically untrue. Stereotypes *are* in error in at least four ways (D. Campbell, 1967): (1) They overestimate the differences between groups and underestimate the variations within groups (implying, for example, that all Germans are industrious and all Frenchmen are sensuous). (2) They carry the assumption that they are accurate, unbiased representations of the world (for example, implying that females *are* submissive rather than that they appear as such because of the perspective of the viewer). (3) Stereotypes carry the implication that the outgroup's behavior is biologically determined (for example, that submissive feminine behavior springs from the glands rather than from social teaching). And (4) negative stereotypes are seen by prejudiced individuals as justifying their hostility rather than causing it. (For example, a person prejudiced against Englishmen may state, "I am right to dislike Englishmen because they are cold." This person refuses to recognize that he thinks of Englishmen as "cold" rather than "correct" because he does not like them.)

As wrong as stereotypes are, they sometimes contain a grain of truth (D. Campbell, 1967)—not very much truth, but a speck. Consider two cases in point: the stereotypes of blacks as musical and of Americans as material-

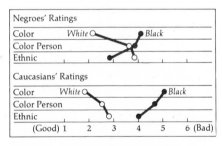

for black entries regardless of whether "black" referred to color, person, or technical class. For black subjects, a "white person" lost the goodness that the color "white" had; a "black person" increased in value over the color black; and a crossover to positive evaluations occurred for "Negro." Thus it appears that both white and black subjects had learned the same connotative meanings for colors. But it also appears that the associative learning relevant to the "people" component of "white people" or "black

people" was strong enough to counteract the associations learned for the colors "white" and "black." Yet only when evaluating the ethnic name "Negro" were black subjects freed completely of the negative connotations of "black."

Black may be beautiful to the liberal and radical contingent, but to the average college student, at least when Williams conducted this study, "Negro" was preferable. As Williams puts it, "White Americans and black Americans will continue to find it very difficult to solve their problems, while Americans (with differing shades of skin color) would have a better chance of doing so."

Source: Adapted from J. Williams, "Connotations of Racial Concepts and Color Names," *Journal of Personality and Social Psychology,* 3 (1965), pp. 531–540.

istic. Princeton students' predominant stereotype of Negroes in 1967 was that they are musical (Karlins, Coffman, and Walters, 1969). The grain of truth lies in the world-wide fame of many black musicians and the popularity of soul music. Although this particular stereotype is essentially positive, it still contains the errors of (1) assuming that all black people are musical and that all are more musical than whites and (2) assuming that black people have natural rhythm, (3) as though that were something innate. How can the predominance of black musical talent in the United States be explained if it is not a biological phenomenon? Quite simply: The entertainment business has been one of the few white-collar businesses in the United States that has not systematically discriminated against qualified black people. Music and (more recently) sports are two professions in which blacks have been permitted to excel. The grain of truth—that many musicians are black—therefore lies in the very same discriminatory pattern that people use to justify the stereotype: (4) Blacks are musical and thus should stick with music.

The predominant stereotype of Americans that Princeton students expressed in 1967 was that they were materialistic (Karlins, Coffman, and Walters, 1969). This, too, is based on some evidence—inhabitants of the United States have more cars, televisions, bathrooms, and money per capita than do the citizens of any other nation. The errors lie in assuming that Americans are a materialistic race and in exaggerating the difference between Americans and more "spiritual" nations. In fact, Americans themselves may be surprised to find that they are no more materialistic than their less-affluent Hindu brethren in India. The chief difference lies again in the opportunities available to the two groups: Many Americans are able to act on their wants and purchase two cars, two televisions, and two bathrooms. Most Indians, on the other hand, are altogether constrained by the economy of their country.

In addition to finding changes in the content of social stereotypes held by different generations of Princeton students, Karlins and his associates report that the stereotypes became more positive for Jews and Negroes and more negative for Americans. Harold Sigall and Richard Page (1971) have questioned the validity of these findings, however. They wonder whether or not the more positive evaluations of minority groups might not represent a little *faking* rather than *fading* of stereotypes and, conversely, whether the more negative evaluation of Americans by subjects might not reflect only an awareness that it is bad form to be too proud of one's own people.

Sigall and Page tested their hunch by leading some subjects to believe that the experimenters could tell what the subjects' *true* attitudes were by means of a special apparatus. While hooked up to the apparatus, the subjects were asked to describe "Negroes," "Jews," and "Americans." The "pipeline"—physiological recording equipment that presumably converted muscular responses into prejudice scores—looked impressive. The pipeline was really a fake; the experimenters had no information about those subjects' true attitudes and were seeking none. Yet the subjects who *thought* that the truth was known expressed significantly more negative attitudes toward "Jews" and "Negroes" and more positive attitudes toward "Americans" than did subjects who had every reason to believe that they could deceive the investigators. The authors concluded that the apparent fading of negative stereotypes of minority-group members in the study by Karlins and his colleagues reflected a faked response, rather than a real change. Apparently today's generation is no less ethnocentric or prone to negative stereotyping than were earlier ones, but it is ashamed of its ethnocentrism.

Today's generation may not have rid itself of its bad habits, but at least it tends to recognize them as such. If recognition is a step in the right direction—if we often end up believing our own performances, as many social psychologists believe (see Chapter 5)—then there *has* been some progress. For those who want to see stereotypes fade more rapidly, there is some comfort in the fact that, as explained in Chapter 2, socialization is a life-long process. In the concluding section of this chapter, some of the means by which society can socialize—or, more precisely, *re*socialize—its members will be examined. But first, the consequences of prejudice should be considered. The consequences are destructive, it turns out, for the perpetrator of racism or sexism or classism of any sort as well as for the victim. The perpetrator is not liberated by acts of discrimination from the desire to continue discriminating and otherwise doing violence to minority-group members. Prejudice apparently is self-perpetuating.

THE CONSEQUENCES OF PREJUDICE

Just as prejudice has multiple causes, so it has multiple effects. Of most concern are the effects on its victims. However, of some concern, too, are the consequences on the perpetrators of prejudice—the "good people" who do the "dirty work" or who have others do it for them.

The Effects on the Prejudiced Person

Sociologist Everett Hughes (1968) traveled to postwar Europe to interview non-Semitic Germans in order to learn the effects of the genocidal campaign against Jews on the rest of the German population. He found that the citizens of Germany were of two minds. Although many of them believed that there had been a "Jewish problem" and felt that something should have been done, they decried the violent and horrifying "solutions" perpetrated by the SS troops and their concentration camps, of which the German public had only been vaguely aware. The Germans that Hughes interviewed thus had dissociated themselves from the grim task they considered necessary and had hired other hands to do the dirty work. This dissociation enabled them to think of themselves as good people who would not condone or commit acts of brutality themselves.

Hughes likened the German public to any public that knows about horrors committed within its prisons. People in the United States, for example, generally agree that there is a "crime problem." Few, however, would condone the degradation and brutality that are vaguely known and rumored to go on inside their country's prisons—acts such as rapes that are permitted in the sheriff's vans on the way to prisons, homosexual rapes permitted in men's and women's prisons, and the beatings and killings of some prisoners within those walls. One solution for the American public is to remain ignorant of these goings-on—a solution adopted by many Germans during the Nazi regime. A second solution, when ignorance is no longer possible, is to think of those prison guards as the agents who do the necessary but dirty work of dealing with "the problem." In this way, the public, who is but one step removed from the brutality, can retain a relatively clear conscience. However, what happens to the agents themselves—the real harmdoers in the system?

The research on harmdoers that has already been reviewed suggests that rather than think ill of themselves, people who perpetuate prejudice and brutality simply devalue and derogate their victims by saying in effect that "they get what they deserve." Even benevolent powerholders, such as organizational supervisors, tend to belittle their subordinates (Kipnis, 1972). In the case of hired agents who do society's dirty work, there is yet another factor that enables harmdoers to emerge with their self-esteem intact. They can lay the responsibility on someone else's shoulders by believing that they are just workers doing their job. Thus, the defense of most of the SS officers in charge of concentration camps was that they were only obeying orders. This defense was not upheld by the jurors at the Nuremberg trials, however. Nor was Lieutenant Calley acquitted of his role in the My-Lai massacre on grounds that he was following orders from above.

Even today people speak of "the Negro problem" or "the race problem" as though the problem lay not in the attitudes of prejudiced people but "out there." This illustrates the need to think of oneself as a good person and not as a prejudiced, brutal, or hateful being. And society conspires to maintain the illusion that the "problem" justifies its prejudices. Occasionally, however, when the evidence is too powerful to permit an acquittal, society reprimands some members for going beyond the bounds of civility. Thus, the National Advisory Commission on Civil Disorders (Kerner, 1968) called the United States a "racist society," because that investigative group could not ignore the evidence.

The Effects of Prejudice on the Victim

Some effects of prejudice on its victims are gross and obvious, like the mass slaughter of Jews in concentration camps, and, to cite a few examples from the history of the United States, the lynching of blacks, the high rates of unemployment among minorities, and the inadequate schooling available to minority groups. In addition, the secondary consequences of occupational

Figure 7.8 Each society has its "problems" and those whom it hires to deal with these problems in whatever way "necessary." Nazi atrocities are perhaps the most striking examples of excesses that can result; however, the harsh and violent manner in which many demonstrators in the United States have been handled also illustrates a possible effect of passing responsibility to workers who are "just doing their job."

and educational discrimination include low incomes, high suicide and infant mortality rates, and relatively high likelihood of arrest and conviction for robbery, loitering, possession of drugs, vagrancy, and so on (Kerner, 1968).

In more need of discussion are the less obvious, psychological consequences of being an object of prejudice. The problem is analogous to that of the perpetrators of prejudice: How can people think of themselves as "good people" when all the world conspires against them?

Self-fulfilling Prophecies. It has already been shown that one cause of prejudice is a social consensus that those who are different from the rest of us are therefore undesirable. The question to ask now is: Does that fabrication become a reality? Does the consensus become a self-fulfilling prophecy? In other words, what are the effects of labels?

One of the most dramatic demonstrations of the psychological effects of prejudicial labels was contributed by Robert Rosenthal and Lenore Jacobson (1968). As discussed early in Chapter 5, by biasing teachers in favor of certain pupils (rather than against them), Rosenthal and Jacobson were able to produce dramatic improvements in the classroom performance and IQ scores of many of these beneficiaries of positive prejudice. The only variable that in fact distinguished the privileged pupils from their classmates was that their teachers were told at the beginning of the school year that these randomly selected children would probably experience "an unusual forward spurt of academic progress." The teachers were not instructed to give the "bloomers" special treatment, nor did the teachers spend more time with the "bloomers," either in or after class. If anything, some teachers felt that they spent more time with the other 80 percent of their students, as though the "bloomers" could be counted on to spurt ahead without encouragement. If not the quantity of time teachers spent with "bloomers," perhaps the quality of attention accounted for their gains. Rosenthal and Jacobson's study does not show the means by which the labels worked; it only shows that they worked. Some other research reported by Rosenthal suggests some means by which teachers produce "bright" and "dull" students.

Using another cover story, Robert Rosenthal (1966) told his assistant experimenters that some of them would be training "maze-bright" rats and that others would have "maze-dull" rats. These animals presumably came from genetically superior and inferior strains, but like the so-called bloomers and nonbloomers studied by Rosenthal and Jacobson, the animals were randomly assigned their labels. The experimenters with the "bright" rats did find, as they expected, that their animals learned significantly better than did the "dull" animals. When interviewed at the end of the study, the experimenters who believed their animals to be bright reported that they felt more satisfied, relaxed, pleasant, and friendly and that they also had handled their animals more. In a related study of equally fake "Skinner-box-bright" and "Skinner-box-dull" rats, Rosenthal found that 47 percent of the trainers who were stuck with so-called dull animals complained about the uneducability of their animals, whereas only 5 percent of the experimenters with "bright" rats voiced such complaints. The trainers of the "dull" animals were so convinced of the stupidity of their subjects that when the random nature of the labels was explained to them at the end of the study, they insisted that no matter what Rosenthal or anybody else said, *their* particular rat was truly dull. Rosenthal reports the amusing results: "Many of these experimenters pointed out that, of course, by random sampling, the two groups of rats would not differ *on the average.* However, they continued, under random sampling, some of the 'dull' rats would really be dull by chance and that their animal was a perfect example of such a phenomenon."

The self-fulfilling prophecy thus has come full circle. Half of the experimenters expected their animals to be dull; those animals did perform poorly; and that was sufficient evidence to the trainers of the inherent dullness of their animals.

Positive prejudice is not generally a problem. The negative effects of unfavorable prejudices present a much greater problem. An important example is provided by educators' prejudgments of children whom they expect *never* to bloom. These prejudgments, communicated however subtly to the children, seem to become self-fulfilling prophecies. The parallel lies not so much with the "bloomers" in Rosenthal and Jacobson's study, who were the beneficiaries of positive expectations, as with the so-called maze-dull rats in Rosenthal's earlier experiment. Indeed, the trainers' comments about the inherent uneducability of their subjects are not unlike comments that teachers sometimes make about "problem" children in their classes or about whole classes of "problem" children. To make matters worse, some entire schools are located in "problem areas"—another name for slums, or inner cities—and many teachers strive to be transferred to schools in more affluent neighborhoods. Teaching in deprived schools is not generally a pleasant experience for teachers, and their resulting feelings of tension probably are not dissimilar from the feelings reported by the trainers of "maze-dull" rats.

What are the consequences for children whose teachers do not expect them to bloom? Recent evidence has been accumulating that shows that black and Mexican-American children do suffer negative consequences at the hands of white testers and teachers. Mexican-American first-grade schoolchildren in one study were taught a manual exercise by either a Mexican-American or an Anglo-American adult. They learned significantly faster when their teacher was Mexican-American (Garcia and Zimmerman, 1972). And this effect did not result from language differences; whether the Mexican-American adult spoke Spanish or English and whether the Anglo-American adult spoke Spanish or English made no difference. *Ethnicity* was all that seemed to matter. Black children, too, seem to respond differently to black and white teachers or testers. For example, when their IQ testers are white, black children's scores drop, but when tested by black adults, their scores soar immediately (Watson, 1972).

In these studies, researchers neither measured nor manipulated the adults' expectations. There is no evidence that the Anglo-American adult had negative attitudes or low expectations of the Mexican-American children (and there was only one Anglo-American adult in each study—a better design would have used a sample of Anglo-American and a sample of Mexican-American adults). Nor were the black or white testers' attitudes toward black youngsters measured. Rather, these studies suggest that investigators can predict which schoolchildren will bloom and which will fail simply on the basis of the teacher's or tester's ethnicity, regardless of that adult's individual expectations or attitudes. Race is such a salient feature in America that it overrides individual differences. In fact, the importance of racial considerations over individual characteristics is the central distinguishing feature of "racist" societies (Jones, 1972). Skin-surface differences between examiners and their examinees seem to create so much stress that neither the adult nor the child succeeds at the task (Watson, 1972).

A more recent experiment by Pamela Rubovitz and Martin Maehr (1973) has revealed that white teachers may in fact respond differently to black and white students. Their results were based on the behavior of white undergraduate students enrolled in a teacher-training course as they taught a lesson to four students—two white and two black. The investigators led the teachers to believe that one black and one white student were gifted whereas the other two students were average. As would be expected on the basis of the research already discussed, teachers responded differently to the students on the basis of these labels. But even more alarming was the different treatment received by black and white students. Black students were praised less, given less attention, ignored more, and criticized more than were white students. Even more shocking, the gifted blacks received the least attention, the least praise, and the most criticism. The white teachers in the experiment were all young, inexperienced, and had little previous contact with black people—a factor that may help account for their extreme biases. However, most of them expressed liberal beliefs. Rubovitz and Maehr also administered the dogmatism scale developed by Milton Rokeach to their student teachers; Rokeach (1960) hypothesized that individuals who score high on this scale can be either left-wing or right-wing authoritarians (discussed earlier in this chapter). Rubovitz and Maehr found that those liberal teachers who scored high on the dogmatism scale were the most extreme in their differential treatment of black and white students.

Neither nonprejudiced whites nor Spanish-speaking Anglos nor non-chauvinist males can change the fact that blacks, Mexican-Americans, and women do more poorly in the presence of someone not of their "own kind." Matina Horner demonstrated in 1971 that whereas both men and women fear failure, women also fear success. Also, women suffered a lower sense of self-esteem than did males—a factor that can be assumed to have self-fulfilling effects, thereby depriving many women of the successes that could boost their self-esteem. (Horner's work on fear of success in women is discussed at greater length in Chapter 4.) The chapter now turns its focus to the effects of keeping women "in their place."

Sex Roles. Sandra and Daryl Bem in 1970 described the subtle sex-role distinctions whereby society has taught woman to know her place. They propose the following description of a married life-style as one that is reasonable and enlightened—certainly a far cry better than the usual arrangements that existed between married persons in bygone generations.

Both my wife and I earned Ph.D. degrees in our respective disciplines. I turned down a superior academic post in Oregon and accepted a slightly less desirable position in New York where my wife could obtain a part-time teaching job and do research at one of the several other colleges in the area. Although I would have preferred to live in a suburb, we purchased a home near my wife's college so that she could have an office at home where she would be when the children returned from school. Because my wife earns a good salary, she can easily afford to pay a maid to do her major household chores. My wife and I share all other tasks around the house equally. For example, she cooks the meals, but I do the laundry for her and help her with many of her other household tasks. (pages 97–98)

If a relationship between a man and a woman is truly egalitarian, so that the woman's "place" equals that of the man, it should be possible to switch the pronouns "he" and "she" without losing the sense of equality, suggest the

A father and his son were involved in a car accident in which the father was killed and the son was seriously injured. The father was pronounced dead at the scene of the accident and his body taken to a local mortuary. The son was taken by ambulance to a local hospital and was immediately wheeled into an operating room. A surgeon was called. Upon seeing the patient, the attending surgeon exclaimed, "Oh my God, it's my son!"

Can you explain this? (Keep in mind that the father who was killed in the accident is not a stepfather, nor is the attending physician the boy's stepfather.)

The answer appears on page 251.

Bems. In other words, the positions occupied by male and female should be interchangeable. Are they?

Both my husband and I earned Ph.D. degrees in our respective disciplines. I turned down a superior academic post in Oregon and accepted a slightly less desirable position in New York where my husband could obtain a part-time teaching job and do research at one of the several other colleges in the area. Although I would have preferred to live in a suburb, we purchased a home near my husband's college so that he could have an office at home where he would be when the children returned from school. Because my husband earns a good salary, he can easily afford to pay a maid to do his major household chores. My husband and I share all other tasks around the house equally. For example, he cooks the meals, but I do the laundry for him and help him with many of his other household tasks. (page 98)

Whereas the woman in the first paragraph seemed lucky because her husband had compromised his aspirations and agreed to help her with the housework, by prevailing cultural standards the man in the second paragraph sounds "hen-pecked." Unless your concepts of sex roles are highly unusual, you probably felt that the woman in the first paragraph was given a break by having her office at home where she could care for the children; the man in the second paragraph, on the other hand, probably seemed restricted by having to take care of the children at home, because home has traditionally been the "woman's place."

Low Self-esteem.   Because women have occupied a subordinate position for so long, even they have adopted the prevailing sex-role ideology, and it is not uncommon to find women who are prejudiced against other women. Philip Goldberg (1968) asked women to judge scholarly articles written either by "Joan T. McKay" or by "John T. McKay." The women who read Joan's articles gave them significantly lower ratings than did the women who read John's. In reality, the articles were identical; only the author's names differed. As explained in Chapter 2, many more women than men, at least traditionally, have harbored desires to be of the other gender. Low esteem for one's own group identity is characteristic of minority groups and is one of the grounds for calling women a minority group in spite of their slight numerical majority (Muhr and Bogart, 1972).

Studies of black children's racial preferences and identification before people began saying "black is beautiful" also revealed low self-esteem. Black children in 1947 showed not only an awareness of racial differences but also a preference for whiteness (Clark and Clark, 1958). The experimenters used two brown-skinned, black-haired dolls and two white-skinned, blonde-haired dolls and asked the children to choose the doll that (1) "is a nice doll"; (2) "looks bad"; (3) "is a nice color"; and (4) "looks like you." The majority chose a colored doll as looking like themselves, but 50 percent also chose a colored doll as the doll that "looks bad." On the other hand, they chose white dolls as the "nice doll" (59 percent) and as the doll with the "nice color" (60 percent). Black college students of that era held correspondingly negative views of blackness. In fact, their stereotypes of "Negroes" in 1941 were very similar to the stereotypes held by white students (Bayton, 1941). Do these findings reflect a kind of self-hatred? Certainly the black college students did not think of *themselves* as "superstitious," "lazy," "happy-go-lucky," or "ignorant." Rather, they listed the characteristics they associated with *lower-class* Negroes. In a second experiment, James Bayton and his colleagues Lois McAlister and Jeston Hamer (1956) asked black and white college students to describe both upper- and lower-class blacks and whites. The results, indicated in Table 7.3, revealed that derogatory stereotypes of "Negroes" were primarily stereotypes of lower-class people, regardless of race. Thus, it was lower-class people that subjects saw as "happy-go-lucky" and "lazy" rather than blacks or whites specifically.

Why, in the absence of other information, had both black and white students assumed that to be "Negro" was to be lower-class? Apparently, this assumption reflected the reality that in 1947 the chances were that a black person was a lower-class person: 65 percent of the black population had incomes under $3,000 per year, whereas only 23 percent of the white population was that poor (Jones, 1972).

Whether prejudice is directed against blacks or women or other minorities, then, it tends to lead victims to expect the worst of one another on the basis of the same superficial characteristics with which persons outside the minority group justify their prejudices. Apparently, prejudices often assume the form of culture-wide mythologies that lower the self-esteem of victims and bias the perspectives of others as well. When this happens, minority-group members are both agents and victims of prejudice. The efforts of some minority groups to expel their own prejudices against themselves through consciousness raising are discussed later in this chapter.

THE CURE AND PREVENTION OF PREJUDICE

The terms "cause" and "consequence" suggest a medical model in which prejudice is a social disease with specific causes and consequences, or symptoms. This analogy can be pursued to see what is meant by a "cure." In the language of preventive medicine, the solution is clear: Remove the causes and there shall be no more prejudice. To be sure, eliminating the various historical, economic, cultural, personal, and phenomenological roots of prejudice is not an easy task.

Social and Economic Reform

The historical sources of prejudice cannot be removed. It is a fact that some groups have been oppressed by others, and that fact cannot be erased. Clearly, however, people can influence what happens tomorrow, which in

Table 7.3 Stereotypes by Race and Class

| RATER | BLACK | | | | WHITE | | | |
	Upper Class		Lower Class		Upper Class		Lower Class	
Black	Intelligent	61%	Loud	55%	Intelligent	48%	Physically dirty	36%
	Ambitious	35	Superstitious	44	Ambitious	28	Ignorant	34
	Progressive	25	Very religious	35	Progressive	27	Rude	33
	Neat	24	Lazy	28	Sophisticated	26	Lazy	19
	Ostentatious	23	Ignorant	26	Tradition-loving	21	Loud	18
White	Intelligent	53	Superstitious	66	Intelligent	59	Happy-go-lucky	20
	Ambitious	51	Lazy	39	Ambitious	49	Materialistic	20
	Ostentatious	29	Physically dirty	34	Materialistic	45	Ignorant	19
	Industrious	28	Unreliable	34	Pleasure-loving	33	Lazy	19
	Courteous	27	Musical	30	Industrious	25	Loud	19

Source: Adapted from J. Bayton, L. McAlister, and J. Hamer, "Race-Class Stereotypes," *Journal of Negro Education,* 25(1956), pp. 76–77.

turn will become history. If the human race is able to engineer the course of current events so as to eliminate exploitation of some groups by others, it may succeed in eliminating a major cause of prejudice for future generations. Important steps in this direction could include establishing minimum (and maximum) income levels, instituting compensatory educational programs, and redressing the imbalance in occupations that are stratified by sex and race (Martin and Poston, 1972). It is not necessary to begin by working on the attitudes of prejudiced persons, in other words. If the social and economic mountains can be moved instead, then the attitudes probably will take care of themselves, for reasons that will be explained in the concluding section of this chapter.

People who resist social and economic reforms often warn that reforms will produce a "backlash" of resistance and hostility. However, backlashes are characteristic only of situations in which the dominant majority feels that the reforms jeopardize their economic status. In planning and presenting their programs to the public, reformers therefore need to make it clear that their reforms will not jeopardize, for example, the social or economic standing of the white working class. In fact, a large supply of unemployed laborers keeps wages low, and fuller employment should benefit both groups. The mathematics of wages and labor are matters for economists to analyze, but the social-psychological advice remains clear: So that history will no longer provide food for prejudice, it is important to create maximum opportunities for all without generating new downwardly mobile groups.

The naive theories of prejudice that were discussed earlier confuse the effects of prejudice with its causes. Thus, for example, a naive theory

HIGH SELF-ESTEEM IN BLACKS

ONE OF THE BASIC premises of the psychology of race relations has been that blacks living in the United States must be low in self-esteem. Exposed daily to humiliations, defeat, and disparagement, surely blacks must learn at an early age that they are "no good." Even most black scholars and revolutionaries have characterized black self-esteem as low.

Morris Rosenberg of the National Institute of Mental Health and Roberta Simmons of the University of Minnesota studied self-esteem in black and white children in the public schools of Baltimore, Maryland. The self-esteem of 2,625 randomly selected third- through twelfth-graders in twenty-six schools was tested. This is the most definitive study comparing self-esteem in blacks and whites ever conducted. The most startling finding of the study was that, overall, *black children have as high if not higher self-esteem than do white children, regardless of their basic life conditions.*

Here are some of Rosenberg and Simmons' other findings:

1. Black children consider themselves as good looking as white children do.

2. Children of both races are quite happy with their looks.

3. Black children are as likely as white children to say that their parents have done "very well" in life and that their fathers' jobs have high prestige, in spite of the fact that their fathers usually occupy a lower socioeconomic position in the community.

4. Children of black parents who are separated or never married have self-esteem scores that are as high as the scores of other black children. This is not true of white children or of blacks at primarily white schools.

5. Black secondary-school children, including those who make an average mark of D in school, are likely to say that they are "pretty smart" and that they believe that their parents would agree. This is less true of white children, whose evaluations of their own intelligence tend to correspond to their grade-point averages.

espoused by some people contends that women are discriminated against by men because there are innate, sex-linked differences in temperament between men and women and because women's temperament—less stable than men's—makes them less satisfactory employees; proponents of this theory fail to take into account the fact that in most jobs these differences in temperament are irrelevant. The White Citizens' Council of segregationists in the United States and the proponents of apartheid in South Africa make similar claims—that black people are innately inferior to white people and thus are overrepresented among the poor and the unemployed. A naive view treats the *effects* of prejudice as though they were the *causes*. To eliminate the causes of prejudice among adherents to naive theories, then, it will be necessary to eliminate the effects. If more women are hired for demanding jobs, if black people become less poor in relation to white people, for example, the grounds for these stereotypes will disappear.

Child-Rearing Practices

The personality theories discussed earlier suggest that there is something beyond the state of the economy that contributes to prejudice. Some reveal the importance of democratic as opposed to authoritarian child rearing, for ethnic majorities as well as minorities. White Protestants who score low on the *F* scale hold few prejudices against other ethnic groups, and black persons with low scores on the same scale exhibit group pride rather than self-disparagement. Democratic child rearing is, therefore, an important ingredient in societal integration (Noel, 1964). However, child-rearing

6. Black children are as likely as white children to expect to go to college and are somewhat more likely to want to than are whites.

7. As many black children as whites want to be "very rich" and "very famous," to be "highly successful at their work," and "to do better than their parents."

Rosenberg and Simmons concluded that ghetto living may not deflate black children's self-esteem, because in comparison with blacks who are in frequent contact with whites they grow up in a fairly protected environment. Most of the people around young ghetto dwellers are similar to them in economic level, parental relationships, and race. These black children may thus be sheltered from the abuses of white society. Rosenberg and Simmons have also reported indications that blacks' self-esteem erodes in the pressure of white company. Secondary-school black children, especially those at predominantly white schools, tended to suffer the most in loss of self-esteem. For them, the values and punishments of the white world undermined the safety of the black way of life. These researchers have also shown that white children who do not "make it" in the competitive white world suffer self-esteem damage much as black children do.

Diminishing self-esteem will continue to be a consequence of being black in America as long as inequities persist, because blacks living in the United States cannot help but come into contact with majority white standards of beauty, wealth, and happiness. Rosenberg and Simmons' findings also suggest that white America may pay a price for its competitiveness—a price that is measured in this case as lower self-esteem scores for white children than for their black peers.

Source: Adapted from M. Rosenberg and R. Simmons, *Black and White Self-esteem: The Urban School Child.* (Washington, D.C.: American Sociological Association, 1971).

practices can be quite resistant to change. It is precisely those families that raise children in an authoritarian manner that may be least likely to be exposed to the educational and mass-media influences that can teach them the importance of democratic child-rearing practices. Thus, any mode of child rearing tends to perpetuate itself through a circular process in which the same practices are passed from one generation to the next.

Intergroup Contact

Although one might expect a psychologist to think that if people's attitudes are improved, they will come to behave more decently, many social psychologists would say just the opposite: If people's behavior is improved, their attitudes will follow suit. As Chapter 9 explains, when people cannot change their actions to match their beliefs, they often change the attitudes instead. Thus, the Equal Rights Amendment to eliminate sexual discrimination and Supreme Court rulings to eliminate racial discrimination may be *causes* rather than effects of attitude change. If attitudes do follow behavior, it is imperative for human beings to think about what kinds of relations they want to shape, so that the shaping will be conscious and purposeful rather than inadvertent and random.

One condition that is vital in establishing positive intergroup relations is *contact.* Several studies have indicated the usefulness of intergroup contact in housing, schools, and jobs. As a consequence of integrated arrangements, white residents tended to stereotype their black neighbors less (Kramer, 1950); white and black schoolchildren felt less social distance between one another (Koslin, Koslin, Cardwell, and Pargament, 1969) and expressed a greater desire for personal contact with people of different races (Singer, 1964); and white workers expressed a greater willingness to work with black colleagues on an equal basis (Harding and Hogrefe, 1952).

Contact can engender hostile relations between groups as well as friendly ones. For example, black children in some newly integrated schools have suffered diminished academic self-respect (Weber, Cook, and Campbell, 1971); Israeli children of Near Eastern origins living temporarily with families of European origin seemed to develop feelings of inferiority (Sapir, 1951); and both black and white children in at least one integrated school continued to express a preference for segregated classes (Koslin, Koslin, Cardwell, and Pargament, 1969). Interethnic contact in and of itself is thus no guarantee of improved intergroup relations.

Whether school integration increases or decreases children's prejudices apparently depends on the racial attitudes of their parents and friends, according to Ernest Campbell (1958). Classroom integration does not enhance racial attitudes if pupils return every night to homes in which prejudice prevails.

There are many factors that can contribute to positive intergroup relations. Situations that have required *cooperation* between groups in order to achieve shared goals have been responsible for the most dramatic decreases in prejudice (Harding, Proshansky, Kutner, and Chein, 1969). As Chapter 14 explains, hostilities erupt easily when two groups compete rather than cooperate.

In the case of relations between the races, contact between people of unequal status has existed in the United States for at least 200 years. And, in the case of relations between the sexes, contact between people of unequal status in the United States predated the arrival of Europeans in

America and continues in the present. If relations between the sexes and between the races are to improve it is imperative that members of these groups have *equal status* in their relations. Human beings cannot expect to reduce prejudice without ironing some of the real inequalities out of the social fabric. Contacts in which blacks occupy inferior positions in relation to whites only serve to reinforce traditional stereotypes. For example, when the contact is between a white housewife and her black maid, the black woman may try to please the white woman by acting out the deference that she assumes the white woman expects. The result will probably serve to confirm the white woman's stereotype of blacks as not too bright and best suited for menial work and at the same time to fuel the resentment and hostility the black woman feels for her white oppressors.

Optimum conditions for positive intergroup relations also include opportunities for *informal contact* in which each party can observe the other outside the constraints of formal social roles. Only in informal situations can people come together primarily as individuals rather than as members of particular groups, and only then can they experiment with unprescribed patterns of relating to one another.

Role Playing

Any group-fabricated consensus that separates the population into rival groups on the basis of skin color or other superficial distinctions generates role behavior that conceals both the differences among the members of any group and the similarities among people in all groups. A solution is for prejudiced persons to put themselves in their victims' shoes. Role reversals can be made by people occupying any pair of positions, including male and female, black and white, and handicapped and physically normal. For example, normal college students who played the role of disabled persons, traveling around campus in wheelchairs for an hour, experienced significant changes in their attitudes toward handicapped persons (Clore and Jeffery, 1972). In just one hour they learned to empathize with handicapped persons and became much more attracted to the experimenter, who was in a wheelchair and appeared to be disabled.

An Iowa schoolteacher made an equally powerful demonstration of the effects of role playing by dividing her class into blue-eyed and brown-eyed children and discriminating against those with brown eyes one day and against those with blue eyes the following day. The results (which are recorded in the film *Eye of the Storm*) were dramatic indeed: The children quickly adopted inferior and superior social roles on the basis of no greater real difference than eye color. Although her experiment has received some criticism for teaching discrimination, her results suggest instead that the children learned what it feels like to be discriminated against. If you have someone do unto you as you have done unto others, these experiments suggest, you will change your ways, or at least your attitudes.

Another cure, which the phenomenological approach suggests, involves teaching people about the powerful self-fulfilling effects of role expectations and about the noninformative nature of role performances. Education of this sort might succeed in disrupting some of the destructive social consensuses held by some groups about others. The self-fulfilling effects of role expectations illustrate how a group consensus may *become* true, not because it reflects the nature of the other but because it creates characteristics in the other. And because people *do* tend to behave as they are expected, this behavior tells the perceiver nothing more about the person than that he or she is behaving according to expectations. Similarly, role behavior reveals nothing about the unique qualities of the individual. If, for example, a man running for president speaks as a president would be expected to speak (instead of as a violinist or football player might speak), it is not possible to know anything about him personally other than that he can sound like a president when called on to do so (Jones, Davis, and Gergen, 1962). Is he really like that when he is not playing a public role? Or does he have a frivolous or reckless streak, too? In this case, the deceptive nature of the official role may have disastrous consequences if it results in the election of the man whose temperament is least suited for the job of national leader.

A possible means of reducing the occurrence of role behavior involves teaching people to think of sex roles, racial roles, religious roles, and even age roles as being just as constraining in nature as is the role of president. Thus, if a woman appears feminine, a black person noncompetitive, or a professor sober and responsible, it is not easy to learn about the individual behind the role. Role behavior consists of performances that are at best routine and uninformative and are at worst deceptive or destructive. The implied cure, then, involves *not* taking role behavior as evidence that, for example, women *are* submissive, black people noncompetitive, or profes-

Figure 7.9 Role playing is often an effective way to increase tolerance, understanding, and empathy between groups. In this interracial group, white policemen and black militants met with the ultimate goal of increasing cooperation and reducing tensions in the community; role playing was one technique used to achieve that end. The members of each group "exchanged races" by wearing a white or black mask and playing the role of a member of the other race. In this way, each person had the opportunity to directly experience the behavior, attitudes, and self-concept generated in members of the other group by the roles society assigns.

sors dry and professorial but rather thinking of role behavior as nothing more than a performance put on at the implicit request of the audience.

Consciousness Raising

Some of the most dramatic evidence of prejudice in the United States dates from the 1930s and 1940s, and many of the studies cited in this chapter were conducted during those decades. Whether the more positive attitudes toward outgroups that have been revealed in more recent studies reflect facts of changing status relationships between groups or gradual fading of old prejudices or a little faking on the part of the subjects, things have changed. Black schoolchildren in 1969 in Lincoln, Nebraska, no longer considered white dolls "nicer." The majority preferred black dolls, demonstrating that they have learned that black is beautiful (Hraba and Grant, 1970). Nebraska's children are not unique; other studies have shown similar results, as well as higher self-esteem scores for black children (Ward and Braun, 1972), often higher than the self-esteem scores of their white counterparts (see the topical insert on pages 244 and 245).

Black college students, too, have acquired new ways of looking at themselves and at their black brothers and sisters. Rather than blaming black people for their poverty, they are blaming the systematic discrimination that has prevailed in the United States for centuries (Gurin, Gurin, Lao, and Beattie, 1969). However, although they feel that the source of the problem lies outside black people, they feel that the source of the solution lies within. Thus, the same students who blame the system are also those who support collective action—civil-rights activities where possible and riots where necessary (Forward and Williams, 1970). This change in the thinking of black militants forced some psychologists to revise their tests and theories. As explained in Chapter 4, researchers previously found it possible to classify people as having either an internal or external orientation. The new black activists, however, apparently were the first in modern America to fit neither one nor the other of these categories. Their analysis of the *problems* that black people in the United States face suggests an external orientation, because they blame the system rather than themselves. On the other hand, their approach to a *solution* reflects an internal orientation, because they believe that the answer lies in taking things into their own hands rather than in waiting for the system to change itself. Previously, a person was thought to have *either* an internal or an external orientation, but not both.

A sense of internal control for successes and external control for failures enables members of other minorities that have been victims of discrimination to hold themselves and their group in high esteem in spite of what the rest of the world may think. Consciousness-raising groups work on this principle. By demonstrating to women, for example, that their fear of success (as well as failure), their traditional submissiveness, and their excessive concern with what other people may think of them are natural consequences of the treatment women have received, women's-liberation groups help their members attribute their weakness to the stars (or to their husbands or to their surroundings) rather than to themselves. At the same time, these groups encourage members to change their situations, because it is within the power of women to do so. It is not woman's nature to be more submissive than men but rather her traditional treatment that has made her so.

Many stigmatized people have succeeded in rejecting society's negative evaluations and expectations of them by joining forces and providing one another with the support needed to reorganize their self-concepts and to replace negative labels with positive ones (Goffman, 1963). Relief from outgroup expectations is provided by women's groups and communes, black students' activities buildings, and men's-liberation groups—all environments in which members can confront their self-images with new definitions and concepts of self and society.

The ways in which people acquire, organize, and change their attitudes—whether toward themselves or society, whether toward people, objects, or events—are discussed in Chapters 8 and 9.

SUMMARY

When a person assumes either favorable or unfavorable things about others on the basis of superficial characteristics, that person holds a prejudice. The most striking and dangerous forms of prejudice are those that denigrate large groups of people—races, nationality groups, or genders, for example.

Several theoreticians have attempted to explain the causes of ethnic, racial, and class prejudice in terms of *historical causes*. Marx, for example, saw prejudice as arising from *class conflict:* Those in the dominant classes, he said, ease their consciences about their treatment of the suppressed classes by characterizing these classes as inferior. There is evidence that people do indeed tend to justify the fates of victims. Another historical theory, that of Robert Park, explains intergroup prejudice in terms of the *conditions of intergroup contact*.

Insights from historical theories like those of Marx and Park can be supplemented with insights from theories that examine more immediate *social and situational causes* of prejudice. For example, one theory says that downwardly mobile groups develop prejudices because they need scapegoats to account for their slide. Other theories point to economic competition for jobs and to the characteristics of modern urban life as producers of prejudice. Socialization also helps to account for prejudice; children who grow up in an atmosphere of prejudice conform to prejudicial norms.

Additional sources of prejudice are based in the *personality* configurations and processes of many prejudiced persons. For example, the Freudian mechanism of *projection* explains how people attribute to other groups the undesirable characteristics that they fear in themselves. *Frustration-aggression* theory postulates that people *displace* the aggression they feel toward those who actually frustrate them onto targets that perhaps resemble the real sources but are safer. Some researchers have identified a cluster of personality traits, which together constitute an *authoritarian personality;* these psychologists contend that persons with authoritarian personalities are the most likely to be prejudiced, although analyses of their data have left questions as to the validity of this conclusion.

Still other investigators report *phenomenological causes* of prejudice and suggest that shared social definitions affect individuals' perceptions of others. These investigators disagree, however, about whether people prefer others who are of similar racial backgrounds or those who share similar beliefs. For example, one experiment revealed that similarity of belief was more important than race in choosing a friend but that when given no information other than a potential friend's race, the subjects assumed that people of another race held beliefs dissimilar to their own. But some researchers contend that race supercedes belief in certain situations, as in intimate relationships.

Investigation of *naive explanations* of prejudice—explanations that place the blame for prejudice on the victims—reveals that *double standards* operate in stereotypes. In other words, prejudiced individuals view the same characteristic—say, thriftiness—as laudable in the people they admire and as reprehensible in those they dislike. Although some studies seem to indicate that stereotypes are becoming less negative, the evidence of other studies shows that the stereotypes remain much the same but that people do not articulate them as strongly as in the past, because they have come to believe that prejudice is wrong.

Prejudice has bad effects on its perpetrators as well as on its victims. In addition, victims of prejudice and discrimination often become victims of self-fulfilling prophecies; they come to believe that the labels attached to them must be true. As a result, they often suffer from lack of self-esteem and even come to devalue their fellow victims.

It is possible to eliminate prejudices. One way is by means of social and economic reforms; for example, if well-paying jobs were available to blacks, the stereotype of the "lazy Negro" might disappear. Another means is through more democratic child-rearing practices. A third way is through intergroup contact under conditions that stimulate cooperation and in which the status of the groups is relatively equal.

Answer to the riddle on page 241: The surgeon was the boy's mother. Many have difficulty solving this simple riddle, which is an indication of the impact of sex-role stereotypes in our society. Present the riddle to others. Keep track of the length of time it takes them to solve the riddle, as well as their age, sex, education, and any other variables you feel may be related to the stereotyping of sex roles.

SUGGESTED READINGS

Allport, Gordon. *The Nature of Prejudice.* New York: Doubleday, 1958.

Friedan, Betty. *The Feminine Mystique.* New York: W. W. Horton, 1963.

Goldschmid, Marcel. *Black Americans and White Racism.* New York: Holt, Rinehart and Winston, 1970.

Grier, William, and Price Cobbs. *Black Rage.* New York: Bantam, 1969.

Griffin, John H. *Black Like Me.* New York: New American Library (Signet), 1962.

Jones, James. *Prejudice and Racism.* Reading, Mass.: Addison-Wesley, 1972.

Rush, Sheila, and Chris Clark. *How to Get Along With Black People: A Handbook for White Folks (And Some Black Folks Too).* New York: Third World Press, 1971.

8
Social Attitudes

BEFORE READING THIS CHAPTER, pause for a moment to consider the things that have been most important to you during the past few days—the things that have moved you to action or have frozen you in your tracks. Chances are that most of them are charged with a good deal of emotion. Your close friends, a lover, parents, a teacher, a college degree, money, freedom, God, and so on—you may have invested your feelings in them all. You care, and because you care you are willing to devote many hours of your life—hours of hope and worry and planning—to these persons, things, or ideas. For the social psychologist, many of these emotional investments take the form of *attitudes,* and as you can well imagine, the study of attitudes occupies a central place within the discipline. Any study of human interaction that does not include the participants' attitudes has missed an essential ingredient. To understand attitudes is to understand many patterns of human behavior, whether they characterize an intimate pair or an entire society.

To be more specific, attitudes are usually viewed as relatively enduring dispositions in our responses to various aspects of the world, including persons, events, and objects. The study of attitudes is not so much concerned with temporary mood states or flights of feeling as with regularities in people's social behavior. Three components of attitudes can be singled out for study. One was already touched on in the mention of emotional investments: Attitudes invariably have an *affective* component. To explore a person's attitudes toward college fraternities, for example, would mean taking into account his or her general feelings toward them: are they good or bad? The second major component is *cognitive.* One's feelings are usually tied to some form of thought or perception. One person might feel positive toward fraternities because they can provide a close circle of friends in the midst of impersonal surroundings; another might dislike fraternities because they are elitist in character. Third, attitudes usually have a *behavioral* component. If a person feels positively toward fraternities or sororities and his or her thoughts are consistent with these feelings, then this person should be prone to act in support of them. This action might include joining a sorority or fraternity, voting for their continuation in a college-wide referendum, speaking positively about them to others, and so on. Theories about attitudes and the research that social psychologists have conducted in studying them vary in their relative emphasis on these three components, but each is built on one or more of the components.

The concept of attitude has been a central one in social psychology. In 1935, Gordon Allport wrote that "the concept of attitude is probably the most distinctive and indispensable concept in contemporary American social psychology." This view is widely shared by social psychologists today.

This chapter will begin with a consideration of attitude measurement—the ways in which attitudes are assessed. Then the inconsistencies that sometimes occur in people's feelings and behavior will be discussed. Another major topic of concern is the source of attitudes: To what extent are attitudes forged by experience? To what extent are they shaped by parents, peers, and society at large? Because there are so many objects in the world about which we form attitudes, it is important to consider ways in which attitudes are organized in our minds. It is likely that principles of organization work to provide at least some degree of clarity and sensible, consistent behavior. These issues are discussed in this chapter.

Figure 8.1 People often think of attitudes as consisting only of beliefs and feelings, but attitudes also have a behavioral component. Attitudes can influence actions very subtly; they can affect even the type of material we read and the people we choose to associate with. The more strongly we hold our attitudes, the more overtly we are liable to express them. The authors of these graffiti (*opposite*) may have preferred anonymity to public exposure, unlike the antiwar marcher (*right*), who is committing herself on a one-to-one basis, and the soap-box speaker (*below*), who apparently is attempting to reach as many people as possible with his ideas. Their choices of media for self-expression suggest that the persons who wrote the graffiti may not hold their attitudes as strongly as do the two persons who are attempting face-to-face persuasion.

HOW CAN ATTITUDES BE MEASURED?

Given the cardinal significance of attitudes in daily life, it is important that they be accurately assessed. The study of attitudes is only as strong as the measuring devices on which findings are based. Without adequate mea-

sures it cannot be determined that an attitude exists or that it was formed in a particular way. A complete discussion of attitude measurement is beyond the scope of this textbook. However, it will prove useful to discuss briefly several major types of measures, their virtues and their shortcomings.

Constructing an Attitude Scale: The Thurstone Method

In 1928 Louis Thurstone asserted unequivocally in the *American Journal of Sociology* that "attitudes can be measured." It was Thurstone's belief that one could elicit *opinions* that are *verbal expressions of attitudes*. Thus, attitudes could be measured indirectly through expressed opinions. In considering the problem of how to measure opinions, Thurstone realized that any measure would be subject to error. For example, the respondent could always misperceive the meaning of a particular statement, the questioner could fail to understand the meaning of the respondent's answers, and so on. It was Thurstone's hope that scales could be constructed that were unambiguous to respondents and that would allow respondents to answer in ways that could be interpreted unambiguously.

Thurstone viewed attitudes as varying along continua—from low to high, good to bad, and so on. Thus, to say someone has an attitude toward the legalization of marijuana is to assert that the person could be placed on a continuum of opinions about the legalization of marijuana ranging from complete endorsement of its legalization to complete opposition to it.

The simplest way to ascertain an attitude about legalization of marijuana might be to ask an individual if he or she favors legalization—the response might be in the form of "yes" or "no" or some intermediate response. The yeses and noes would be fairly easy to categorize and could be placed at opposite extremes of the dimension. In addition, one could conceivably measure the intensity with which the answers were given. But if the person did not respond with simple yeses and noes but gave less easily codable responses, the attitude-measurement problem would become more acute. For example, if someone responded, "Marijuana is no more

harmful than alcohol," the attitude toward marijuana might appear to be somewhat positive. And if someone else responded, "Smoking marijuana leads to hard drugs," this person's attitude toward legalization might seem more negative. But neither statement can be categorized with absolute certainty.

Thurstone suggested the following procedures in constructing attitude scales:

1. Define the attitude variable to be measured (say, legalization of marijuana).

2. Collect a wide range of opinions about the attitude variable from a large number of respondents. In the case of marijuana, these might include:

    Marijuana should never be legalized because it destroys the minds of teen-agers.

    It leads to harder drugs.

    It has no harmful effects.

    It should be treated like alcohol or cigarettes.

    It should be free on demand.

3. To produce a smaller list of opinion statements, edit the opinions according to these criteria:

    a. Statements should be brief.

    b. They should be stated so they can be endorsed or rejected by the reader.

    c. They should be relevant to the reader's attitude about the issue.

    d. They should be unambiguous.

    e. They should represent the whole range of opinions possible about the attitude variable.

4. A quantitative value for each statement is calculated by placing it on a card and having judges sort the stack of cards into eleven piles ranging from most negative (score of 1) to most positive (score of 11). For example, the statement that marijuana destroys the minds of teen-agers might be given a score of 1 by a judge, and the statement that it should be free on demand might be scored 11. Each statement is then given a score based on the opinion of the majority of the judges. (Ideally, Thurstone felt, as many as 300 judges should be used in this task.)

5. Select a shorter list of approximately twenty-five opinion statements about which judges show strong agreement that represent an evenly graduated scale from most negative to most positive. These final statements compose the attitude scale. (1928, page 552)

Having thus constructed an attitude scale, one must then ask: How is an attitude measured with it? The procedure is very simple. The reduced list of statements is presented to a group of subjects. The subjects are then asked to indicate (perhaps with a plus sign) all the statements with which they agree and (with a minus sign) all those with which they disagree. The final score is the average scale value of all the statements that an individual has endorsed. The larger the score, the more positive the person's feelings toward the attitude object.

The procedures used by Thurstone were complex and required great human resources. For the most part, this kind of work is done only by social psychologists who specialize in attitude-scale construction. Most social psychologists construct attitude scales employing only rudimentary forms of these procedures, or else they use well-known scales that have already been rigorously constructed and tested.

Summated Ratings: The Likert Method

Although Thurstone's method was the first comprehensive effort at attitude-scale construction, a procedure developed in 1932 by Rensis Likert has exceeded it in current popularity. The assumptions that shaped Likert's method were very similar to those proposed by Thurstone; Likert also emphasized that each statement should be (1) clear, concise, and straightforward. Also, the set of statements should (2) represent a wide range of opinions and (3) reflect a single attitude variable.

Likert's procedures differ from Thurstone's in several important respects. On Likert's scale judges are provided with a large initial pool of items to which they respond in one of five ways: *strongly approve* (or *agree*), *approve, undecided, disapprove,* and *strongly disapprove* (or *disagree*). An arbitrary score of 1 is given to the strong approval response, a score of 2 to the mild approval answer, and so forth, with a score of 5 reserved for extreme disapproval or disagreement. This group of initial items is then reduced to only those items that evoke a wide range of responses. For example, the earlier item stating that marijuana should be treated like alcohol or cigarettes should yield a wide range of responses. Some people will heartily endorse it; others will strongly disagree; and still others will be neutral. The item is therefore a very good one in its capacity to discriminate among people. Furthermore, people who agree with this item are also likely to agree with another item stating that the harmful effects of marijuana have been overrated; those who disagree with the first item are likely to disagree with the second as well. Responses to the two items are therefore consistent; if a sufficient number of items can be found that have similar properties, a successful Likert scale could emerge. A scale on which responses to all items are highly correlated is said to be *internally consistent*—a major criterion of scale construction.

The items selected are used to assess attitudes. Responses are scored with the same five-point scale from "strongly approve" to "strongly disapprove," and the total attitude score is the sum of the scale values. In a recent study of athletes, James Jones (1972) used several Likert-type items to construct a sports attitude scale. Figure 8.2 shows several of the statements used in this scale. The scale consisted of the summated ratings of twenty-two items. The lower the summated score, the more positive the respondent's endorsement of beliefs and slogans glorifying athletics.

In practice, investigators often select items on the basis of their own best guesses about the range of opinions to be reflected, item clarity, and other criteria. Dispensing with the initial judgments, they administer the items directly to subjects and create the scale on the basis of subsequent analysis of the responses. This technique is perhaps the most popular attitude-measurement technique used by social psychologists.

Unidimensional Scaling: Seeking the Vital Thread

One problem with the Thurstone and Likert scales is that the investigator can never be sure when they are really tapping a single underlying dimension. For example, you might agree with the statements that marijuana has harmful effects and that it can lead to harder drugs. However, your reasons for your answers may be very specific in each case and may have nothing to do with your generally positive feelings about the drug. Each scale item may thus be measuring a slightly different disposition, and summing these different dispositions is not wholly merited. To avoid this problem a number of investigators have tried to develop unidimensional scales—attitude scales that more convincingly tap single underlying attitude dimensions.

One of the first attempts at unidimensional scaling was carried out by Emory S. Bogardus in 1928. In particular, Bogardus sought to measure *social distance*—the degrees and grades of understanding and feeling that persons experience regarding each other. How much distance do people wish to maintain between themselves and particular others? Do they want full integration? Are these others acceptable for membership in their families? Or do they want these others to remain as far away as possible, so that they would perhaps not even be permitted to visit the same country in which the respondents resided? Bogardus felt that measuring social distance "charts the character of social relations."

Bogardus' technique is simpler than that of Thurstone. Bogardus was primarily interested in racial or ethnic relations and the extent to which psychological barriers influence those relations. The technique is simply to identify a particular racial or ethnic group and to ask respondents to check which of seven relationships they would be willing to engage in with members of this group. Results of a study using Bogardus' scale are in Table 8.1. For example, if a respondent is willing to accept a person into the most intimate relationship (kinship by marriage) a score of 1 can be assigned; a 2 might be given if the person is willing to admit members of the racial group into his or her social club; and so on. A score of 7 is given the respondents who inject the most distance between themselves and others—those who would entirely exclude members of a race from the country. Scores are

Figure 8.2 On a Likert scale, subjects indicate the degree to which they agree or disagree with each item. For the Likert-type items shown here, a low sum (4 is the lowest possible for this set of items) indicates a strong attitude favoring traditional glorification of sports; a high sum (20 is the highest possible here) represents a strong attitude disapproving glorification of sports.

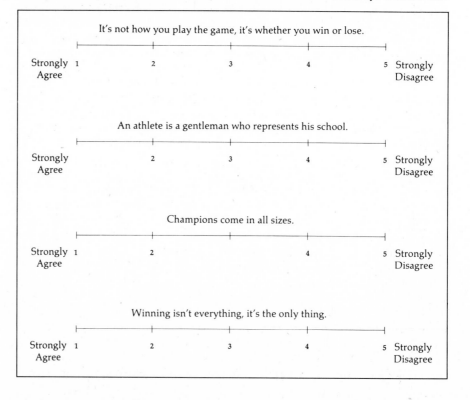

III Encountering Others

computed by averaging an individual's responses. The higher the score, the greater the desired distance—and presumably, the greater the amount of prejudice. It was Bogardus' belief that his measurement of social distance could accurately predict the pattern of behavioral relations that characterizes interactions between members of different ethnic or racial groups. Subsequent research has lent some validity to Bogardus' belief. However, because it relied too heavily on Bogardus' suppositions and not enough on sophisticated measurement tools, the scale is not widely used today.

Vast improvements in unidimensional scaling were made by Louis Guttman (1944, 1950). Guttman's basic idea is very simple. If we like A more than B and B more than C, then we should also like A more than C. This logic should hold, for example, in the case of the Bogardus social-distance scale. If an individual accepts a racial group into close kinship through marriage, it is fair to assume that all of the items suggesting greater distances would also be endorsed. Similarly, if a person does not want a racial group in the country, then none of the closer relationships should be acceptable to that individual.

Although all the scales described so far assume unidimensionality of attitudes, the Guttman procedure requires more extreme unidimensionality. If the number of reversals (A > B, B > C, but C > A) exceeds 15 percent, the researcher must revise the items so the inconsistencies fall below that percentage. If this criterion is met, the scale has an additional advantage over other scales: Knowledge of a respondent's score on the scale allows the investigator almost complete knowledge of all the respondent's answers to the items. To put it another way, all respondents who receive the same total score will have achieved that score in roughly the same way. With the Thurstone and Likert methods one can never be sure. A person who is truly neutral in his or her feelings about marijuana might obtain the same total score as another person who, in great conflict, strongly agrees with many items and strongly disagrees with others. However, the Guttman criteria are unfortunately difficult to meet.

The Semantic Differential: Evaluation Invaded

You may have felt that the measures discussed so far relied too much on expressions of cognitions and did not tap respondents' feelings directly enough. One popular attitude-measurement technique that largely avoids this problem is the semantic differential. This technique was developed by Charles Osgood, George Suci, and Percy Tannenbaum (1957) in their

Table 8.1 Responses to Bogardus' Scale for Measuring Acceptable Relationships (Social Distance)*

ETHNIC GROUPS	1 CLOSE KINSHIP BY MARRIAGE	2 PERSONAL CHUMS IN SAME CLUB	3 NEIGHBORS ON SAME STREET	4 EMPLOYMENT IN SAME OCCUPATION	5 CITIZENSHIP IN SAME COUNTRY	6 VISITORS ONLY TO SAME COUNTRY	7 EXCLUDED FROM SAME COUNTRY
English	93.7%	96.7%	97.3%	95.4%	95.9%	1.7%	0.0%
Americans (Native White)	90.1	92.4	92.6	92.4	90.5	1.2	0.0
Norwegians	41.0	56.0	65.1	72.0	80.3	8.0	0.3
Indians	8.1	27.7	33.4	54.3	83.0	7.7	1.6
Jews (German)	7.8	2.1	25.5	39.8	53.5	25.3	13.8
Negroes	1.4	9.1	11.8	38.7	57.3	17.6	12.7
Hindus	1.1	6.8	13.0	21.4	23.7	47.1	19.1

*Based on sample of 1,725 white Americans
Source: Adapted from E. Bogardus, *Immigration and Race Attitudes* (Boston: D. C. Heath, 1928), p. 25.

efforts to measure the meaning of interpersonal experience. A semantic-differential scale consists of a concept followed by rating scales anchored by pairs of bipolar adjectives, such as good and bad, hot and cold, easy and hard, and so on. Figure 8.3 shows a sample semantic-differential scale.

As you can see, one could use any number of adjective dimensions to rate any one concept. Nine dimensions are used in Figure 8.3, but why not ninety? Extensive research has shown that most of the dimensions can usefully be grouped in three distinct categories. Many dimensions, such as good-bad and happy-sad, seem to reflect generalized *feelings* people have for a concept—their like or dislike of it. These dimensions, then, compose a measure of basic *evaluation*. A second group of interrelated dimensions, including strong-weak and easy-hard, make up a measure of perceived strength or *potency,* as the investigators termed it. A third basic dimension is termed *activity* and includes adjective pairs such as fast-slow and young-old. Numerous applications of this technique have been made in attitude research, although most attitude researchers are concerned with the evaluative dimension of the semantic differential alone.

Beyond the Rating Scale

The level of sophistication and refinement in the early days of measurement was somewhat limited, and the paper-and-pencil measures just discussed reflect these limitations. For example, people are sometimes aware of the purpose of a study and do not reveal what they do not wish to be known. As Eugene Webb, Donald Campbell, Richard Schwartz, and Lee Sechrest (1966) have argued, social psychologists need *unobtrusive measures* that do not create suspicion—what Milton Rosenberg (1956) has termed *evaluation apprehension.* There are also important differences between what people say they feel and what they are actually willing to commit themselves to in terms of future behavior. The assessment of attitudes has been broadened as researchers' knowledge and skills have improved. No longer do researchers rely solely on verbal responses to formal questions.

Researchers in recent years have been supplementing attitude ques-

Figure 8.3 The semantic differential, used to measure attitudes, is based on the principle that concepts have subtle connotative meanings that are difficult to describe. Researchers use it in attempting to measure these connotative meanings in an indirect way by asking individuals to quantitatively rate specific concepts on various dimensions, such as those shown in this example. For example, one could use these dimensions to measure various connotations people attach to statements such as "Marijuana should be treated like alcohol and cigarettes" and "Winning is everything."

	Rating							
	1	2	3	4	5	6	7	
cruel								kind
active								passive
hard								soft
wise								foolish
good								bad
weak								strong
calm								excitable
beautiful								ugly
slow								fast

III ENCOUNTERING OTHERS

tionnaires with what Elliot Aronson and J. Merrill Carlsmith (1968) call *behavioroid* and *behavioral* measures of attitudes, designed to avoid some of the limitations of standard paper-and-pencil measures. A behavioroid measure is a test of action that falls short of overt behavior but involves more than a pencil mark. A typical example of a behavioroid measure is when a subject commits herself or himself verbally to some future behavior, although the behavior itself is never measured. A behavioral measure, on the other hand, actually assesses the individual's overt actions in ongoing relationships. Asking a person to make a commitment to a voting preference would provide a behavioroid measure; assessing the individual's voting pattern or monetary contributions to political causes or candidates would provide a behavioral measure.

Behavioroid Measures: A Case of Prejudice. Melvin DeFleur and Frank Westie (1958) devised a behavioroid measure of racial prejudice and nonprejudice. The attitudes of white college students toward blacks were initially assessed with standard paper-and-pencil questionnaires. Part of the interview consisted of viewing photographic slides showing interracial pairs of males and females. After the interview session, the experimenters attempted to measure the racial attitudes of their subjects by examining their commitment to later actions.

Subjects—all of whom were white—were told that another set of slides was being prepared. The behavioroid measure consisted of their responses to the question of whether or not they would be willing to be photographed with a black person of the opposite sex. Various levels of prejudice could be tapped in this way. Some subjects said they were unwilling to be photographed; according to this measure, they were the most prejudiced subjects. Those who agreed to be photographed with a black person

Figure 8.4 Because an individual's verbal assertions and behavior are often inconsistent, a broader measure of attitudes is needed than standard scales alone yield. Assessment of the behavioral component of the attitude is preferable. The dress and organized actions of Ku Klux Klan members (*below*) are behavioral indicators of attitudes, but such measures are often difficult for researchers to obtain, and behavioroid measures are frequently employed instead. Rather than measure the overt behavior itself, behavioroid measures tap attitudes by seeking a commitment to behavior, such as that reflected in this individual's bumper sticker (*left*).

indicated on a "standard photographic release form" the uses to which they were willing to allow the photographs to be put—uses varying from other laboratory experiments to a national publicity campaign advocating racial integration. Subjects who consented to these uses were said to be least prejudiced. The release forms were never used for these purposes, but from the commitments and refusals expressed via these forms, the experimenters inferred the subjects' actual inclinations to interact with blacks.

As you can see, behavioroid measures permit experimenters greater confidence in their attitude assessment, because subjects are actually forced to commit themselves to probable behavioral acts. But is it possible to completely disregard the subjects' attitudes as measured by the rating scale? Twenty-two percent of those who were *prejudiced* according to the paper-and-pencil measure were unprejudiced behaviorally; their words, but not their actions, showed prejudice. Conversely, 40 percent of those who were unprejudiced on paper were behaviorally prejudiced; their words were sweet and their actions bitter. To put it another way, approximately 60 percent of all DeFleur and Westie's subjects showed differences in their responses to paper-and-pencil and behavioroid measures of attitudes.

It is tempting to discount words and trust actions only, but it is actually dangerous to do so. Actions in this and other situations may be influenced by a variety of factors, only one of which is underlying prejudice. The chance for national publicity may have appealed to the egos of many subjects, and their volunteering may be a better indication of vanity than of prejudice. Still others may have felt guilty about their prejudiced responses to the questionnaire and wanted to reduce guilt feelings—a response that is explored further in Chapter 10. Thus, to use a single behavioroid indicator alone is an important risk in assessment. Multiple measures are always preferable to single measures, regardless of type. The inconsistencies in prejudice found in this experiment also raise the question of whether or not underlying attitudes are consistent with behavior—whether or not, in other words, we do as we say.

Behavioral Measures.   Imagine that a student group is working on a list of nonnegotiable demands to submit to their school administration. Before the students are ready to present formally their demands, however, the administration preempts the student group by granting the demands. A recently developed theory (Brehm, 1966) suggests that the students would respond to the administration's move by devaluing the demands, thinking them less imperative or central than before, and perhaps generating a set of stiffer demands. This theory, which is discussed at greater length in Chapter 10, predicts that if people's freedom of choice is threatened, they will change their attitudes in an effort to regain that freedom. Furthermore, the more important they believe that the situation is, the more likely that this *psychological reactance* will produce attitude change.

The originator of this theory, Jack Brehm, developed a behavioral measure of attitudes as one means of testing his proposal. He and his colleague Ann Cole (1966) conducted an experiment that they described to their subjects as dealing with "first impressions." One of the experimenters asked pairs of students to evaluate each other. Following these evaluations, the experimenter placed a pile of papers in front of one of the students and asked him to stack the papers in ten piles of five each. The experimenter then privately recorded whether or not the other student helped and, if so, how long before he did so. The behavioral measure of attitude toward the student was positive if the subject helped and negative if he did not. The subject before whom the papers were placed was actually an accomplice of the experimenter. Prior to the evaluations, he either had or had not done an unsolicited favor for the real subject. (The favor was giving the subject a cola and refusing to accept money for it.)

You might assume that the subject would feel obligated to reciprocate the favor and to help stack the papers as a return favor. But Brehm and Cole made the startling prediction that the recipient of a favor would be least likely to volunteer help; they reasoned that the prior favor implied an obligation to reciprocate and thus threatened the subject's freedom to evaluate the accomplice objectively. In order to reassert his freedom, a subject who had received a favor would remain withdrawn. This tendency would be especially strong, reasoned the investigators, when the freedom being restricted was important to the subject; when it was relatively unimportant, the favor might then be reciprocated in the usual way.

The results are indicated in Table 8.2; subjects were less likely to help the accomplice if he had done them a favor than if he had not when the experiment was introduced as a very important project for the National Science Foundation. On the other hand, when the study was described as a project of a graduate student in sociology, the favor tended to be repaid. Both the importance of the study and the favor had strong effects on the subjects' attitudes toward helping the accomplice, as measured by their willingness to help. However, the subjects' later evaluations revealed that *neither* the importance of the study nor the favor had any systematic effect on their first impressions of the accomplice. The behavioral measure proved all-important.

The various measurement techniques—their descriptions, advantages, and disadvantages—are summarized in Table 8.3.

SAYING IT IS NOT DOING IT

Several instances have been shown in which behavior does not go hand in hand with expressed views—when, in other words, we do one thing and say another. Verbally prejudiced subjects do not always prove to be behaviorally prejudiced; in Brehm and Cole's study, negative responses to a helper showed up as failure to reciprocate a favor but were not reflected in impression ratings. Most of us assume that to know a person's expressed feelings is to be able to predict his or her behavior. But behavior does not always conform to feelings, or vice versa. Consider the individual who is white and liberal, who attacks racism verbally, but who does not want to

Table 8.2 Number of Subjects Who Helped the Confederate Stack Papers

	IMPORTANCE OF PROJECT	
SUBJECTS WHO:	*Graduate Student in Sociology (Low)*	*National Science Foundation (High)*
Received No Favor		
Helped	9	7
Did Not Help	6	8
Received Favor		
Helped	14	2
Did Not Help	1	13

Source: Adapted from J. Brehm and A. Cole, "Effect of a Favor Which Reduces Freedom," *Journal of Personality and Social Psychology,* 3 (1966), p. 424.

live next door to a black family. Consider *any* form of hypocrisy. What is the relationship between public behavior and internal feelings?

Early researchers studied verbal attitudes so that they could predict behavior in social settings. For example, Bogardus stated this goal clearly in commenting on his social-distance test, claiming that the test "would indicate *what* changes in attitudes and opinions the natives [Americans] would need to undergo in order to give the immigrants a square deal . . . and where racial conflicts are likely to take place." However, the results of a classic study reported in 1934 by Richard LaPiere raised serious questions about the unguarded optimism of Bogardus' view.

LaPiere traveled across the United States twice and up and down the Pacific Coast—a total of ten thousand miles—with a Chinese couple. They were received in 66 hotels, auto camps, and tourist homes and were served in 184 restaurants. They were refused service only once. Six months after his visits, LaPiere sent copies of a questionnaire to the same establishments the trio had visited, asking, "Will you accept members of the Chinese race as guests in your establishment?" Of the eighty-one restaurants and forty-seven hotels that replied, 92 percent replied that they would not accept Chinese customers; the remainder checked: "Uncertain, depends upon circumstances." Even in the mid-thirties, when certain kinds of racism were more overt than they are today, the written replies did not reflect the behavior of the respondents.

As a result of his study, LaPiere cautioned social scientists in their use of attitude questionnaires, suggesting that "it would seem far more worth-

Table 8.3 Measuring Attitudes

MEASURES	SUBJECT MUST:	ADVANTAGES	DISADVANTAGES
Scaling (paper & pencil)			
Thurstone attitude scale	agree or disagree with statements	easy to respond to; gives good reading of score relative to a group	both hard and costly to construct; results are often inconclusive
Bogardus social-distance scale	approve or disapprove graded hypothetical situations	question directly relevant to behavior under study	verbal statements and behavior do not always match
Likert summated ratings	evaluate statements on five-point scale	easiest scale to construct	same as above; hard to know what a single score means
Guttman scalogram analysis	agree or disagree with graded statements (should be internally consistent)	theoretically the purest scale	hardest to construct; may be impossible for important variables
Osgood, Suci, & Tannenbaum semantic differential	choose points between bipolar adjectives on relevant dimensions	easy to construct; norms exist for comparison	same limitations as any paper-and-pencil measure
Behavioroid			
commitment, volunteering	agree to perform task; volunteer for a task	closer to behavior than paper-and-pencil and easier to use in research than behavioral measures	more costly in time and effort than paper-and-pencil measure; may still show results different from behavioral measures; may be subject to experimenter influence (see Chapter 1)
Behavioral			
performance	actually perform task or part of it	direct applicability to behavior under study	generally most costly measure to obtain; results may be contaminated by experimenter or special situational effects

while to make a shrewd guess regarding that which is essential than to accurately measure that which is likely to prove quite irrelevant." Social scientists have often considered the study of verbally expressed attitudes a shortcut to predicting behavior. However, LaPiere's research shows that scientists cannot well afford the shortcut. Critics of the early research have emerged, and with some justification. For example, it is possible that the proprietors may not have recognized the couple as Chinese or that they did not wish to irritate the white man, LaPiere, who was traveling with them. The responses to LaPiere's letters were probably written by the owners of the establishments. However, the Chinese couple was dealt with by desk clerks and waitresses. It is also possible that "management policy" in this unusual instance of interracial contact was unknown by those in the lower echelons. Since this early study, however, dozens of researchers have used more sophisticated methods that have brought similar results.

The idea that covert attitudes and overt behavior should not be assumed to be synonymous has been expressed with more and more frequency in recent years. In 1972, Robert Abelson in an article entitled "Are Attitudes Necessary?" suggested that internal attitudes and public behaviors may be under very different kinds of control and that, as a result, there may often be little resemblance between the two. Abelson insists that psychologists should consistently test for an association between the internal state and the corresponding behavior, and not simply assume that the two are consistent. On the other hand, a study that fails to find consistency between covert attitudes and overt behavior should not automatically be taken to indicate that little or no correlation exists between the two.

In LaPiere's study, what is the verbal attitude, and what is the attitude object? The attitude can be identified as the *stated* intention not to accommodate Chinese people. "Members of the Chinese race" is the attitude object. LaPiere assumed that the innkeepers behaved toward the attitude object in a manner that was inconsistent with their stated intentions. If the

Figure 8.5 Social psychologists have found that it is risky to predict behavior solely on the basis of verbal expressions of attitude. Whether the speaker is an individual or an institution, saying something is often unrelated to doing it, as the appeal to polluters on this factory facade testifies.

innkeepers both wrote the letters and confronted the customers, their behaviors may not have been inconsistent. Is the inclusive category "members of the Chinese race" the same attitude object as Mr. and Mrs. Chu, a specific Chinese couple standing in front of the innkeepers? There is good reason to believe that they are not. This couple may have seemed far more Westernized, far more respectable and prosperous, than the stereotype of Chinese travelers that prevailed among white North Americans at that time; the presence of the Chus' companion could have reinforced this impression of respectability. Thus, where findings of inconsistency are encountered, it is initially important to ask if the attitudinal and behavioral objects are really comparable.

It is also important to realize that we never observe internal attitudes—only external behaviors. Attitudes expressed verbally may be influenced by a wide variety of factors, only one of which is the person's underlying feelings. What a person says depends on who is asking the question, the use to which the respondent thinks the information will be put, memories, and so on. Caution is therefore necessary whenever "true" attitudes are identified on the basis of the attitudes that people choose to express. Thurstone felt that we are all condemned to interpret verbal as well as nonverbal expressions before we can arrive at any understanding of one another's attitudes. In this light, the usefulness of multiple measuring devices is obvious. When verbal as well as other forms of expression can be tapped, generalizations will be more valid than when any single measure is used by itself.

The use of multiple measures can allay suspicions that people's underlying feelings toward an attitude object are not consistent. As Donald Campbell (1963) has suggested, what appear to be inconsistencies may often be pseudo-inconsistencies. If someone requests a favor you do not want to grant, you will be more likely to grant the favor if the two of you are standing face to face than if you are talking over the telephone. But the different expressions in these situations do not necessarily show conflict in underlying attitudes or in various modes of behavior. As explained in Chapter 10, the shorter the physical and psychological distance between people, the more reluctant they usually are to cause one another discomfort. This is not to say that people never harbor inconsistent attitudes. To be sure, they do. But what seems to be inconsistent to the observer may not really be so.

Although these various considerations help to explain discrepancies in various forms of attitude expression, it should be realized that such discrepancies constitute exceptions rather than the rule. That is, researchers have found relatively high degrees of consistency in the various actions of most people. To balance the discussion, consider the data obtained by Morton Deutsch and Mary Collins (1951) in an extensive study of race relations. The authors studied biracial interactions in two kinds of interracial housing projects: (1) where blacks and whites were assigned to living units without regard to race and (2) where blacks and whites were assigned to separate sections. The fully integrated projects—Koaltown and Sacktown—were in New York City, and the internally segregated projects—Bakerville and Frankville—were in Newark. Deutsch and Collins obtained their data through long and intensive interviews with housewives in their apartments. Table 8.4 suggests that, unlike LaPiere and others, Deutsch and Collins found a very high degree of congruence between the attitudes that were expressed verbally by their subjects and behavioral indicators of

Figure 8.6 Direct contact with the objects of our attitudes can foster positive relationships. Accordingly, after a series of student demonstrations involving police intervention, several universities sponsored basketball and other games in which teams were composed of "heads" and "feds." Such events provided informal contact in a friendly, sportsmanlike atmosphere to encourage the development of harmonious relationships between the groups. Because the players' concepts of the teams they were playing were more favorable than their concepts of "heads" or "feds," reciprocal attitudes and relations both improved.

III ENCOUNTERING OTHERS

the housewives' attitudes. In integrated projects, where there was frequent interracial contact, verbal expressions of attitudes were very positive and relations were friendly. In contrast, both verbal expressions and behavior tended to be negative in segregated projects. The residents' verbally expressed feelings were thus reasonably good predictors of their behavior.

As explained in Chapter 7, which tells how prejudice can be reduced through intergroup contact, many social psychologists have concluded on the basis of studies like that of Deutsch and Collins that opportunities for informal and cooperative contact are among the most potent conditions fostering positive relations between individuals or between groups. By considering behavioral expressions of attitudes as well as verbal expressions, then, researchers have been able to provide more dependable predictive information about pressing social problems.

Thus, there is reason to suggest that verbally expressed attitudes and those expressed in other ways are closely related in many social contexts. However, the notion that verbally expressed attitudes are foolproof indicators of predispositions to behavior is not warranted. Verbal expressions are sometimes under quite different pressures and constraints than are behavioral expressions. When verbal expressions of attitudes reflect these pressures and constraints, they are likely to be weak predictors of behavior.

ORIGINS OF ATTITUDES

What is your attitude toward the legalization of marijuana? Patients' rights in mental institutions? Traditional family roles? Jane Fonda? Your school's basketball team? Your roommate? You could probably make a statement about your attitude toward each of these issues. If you stopped to ask

Table 8.4 Interracial Contact Patterns and Attitudes of White Housewives Toward Negroes in Four Housing Projects

TYPES OF CONTACT WITH AND ATTITUDES TOWARD NEGROES	INTEGRATED PROJECTS		INTERNALLY SEGREGATED PROJECTS	
	Koaltown	Sacktown	Bakerville	Frankville
Casual Contact				
As Neighbors in the Building	60%	53%	0%	0%
Outside on Benches	46	64	7	21
Shopping in Stores, on Streets Around Project	12	13	81	60
Neighborly Contact (Visiting, Helping, Clubs, and so on)				
None	61	28	99	96
Once or More	39	72	1	4
Type of Relations				
Friendly	60	69	6	4
Accommodative	24	14	5	1
Mixed	7	11	2	3
None	5	0	87	88
Bad	4	6	0	4
Feelings Expressed				
Liking, Friendship	42	60	9	5
Mixed, Reserved	30	12	12	27
Avoidance, Dislike	28	28	79	68

Source: Adapted from M. Deutsch and M. Collins, *Interracial Housing: A Psychology of Interracial Social Relations* (Minneapolis: University of Minnesota Press, 1951), pp. 53–83.

yourself where these attitudes came from, you would probably feel that they grew directly from the nature of the attitude object itself, as perceived by you. You are for or against marijuana because of what you feel the drug does to people. You are for or against Jane Fonda because of her politics and style. You may root for your school's male basketball team because they are the "good guys" and represent your school. But research suggests that the belief that attitudes reflect the actual state of reality is not always justified. People may experience events in exactly the same way; however, their attitudes may show marked disagreement. This research also suggests that our attitudes are shaped and reshaped daily in subtle and significant ways.

In general, it may be said that we develop our attitudes in a social context. That is, our attitudes about any issue or person are likely to be

CHAINS THAT COMFORT

My very chains and I grew friends
So much a long communion tends
to make us what we are.

IN THESE CONCLUDING lines of "Prisoner of Chillon," Lord Byron comments on the propensity of human beings to accept and even come to love what they must endure. Is there psychological proof that attitudes truly can make palatable a seemingly unbearable existence?

William McGuire, a Yale University psychologist, began studying this problem more than a decade ago. He particularly wanted to know whether or not things that become more probable are better liked. In order to study the relationship of an outcome's probability on its desirability, he used logical syllogisms of this familiar type: (1) All men are mortal (major premise); (2) Socrates is a man (minor premise); therefore, (3) Socrates is mortal (conclusion). Using issues of student interest, McGuire constructed twenty-four propositions about eight topics and scattered them with filler material throughout a questionnaire. He then asked high-school and college students who were untrained in Aristotelian syllogisms to rate the likelihood and desirability of each of the propositions. One week later the experimental subjects were given a strong persuasive message concerning the increased likelihood of the minor premise occurring. For example, one case was constructed as

follows: (1) Any form of recreation that constitutes a serious health menace will be outlawed by the City Health Authority; (2) the increasing water pollution in this area will make swimming at the local beaches a serious health menace; therefore, (3) swimming at the local beaches will be outlawed by the City Health Department. The minor premise (2) was the focus of the persuasive message, and in this case it was argued that swimming would become a health menace.

The subjects were again given the questionnaire to fill out. McGuire was interested in discovering what the effects on desirability ratings of the minor premise would be when its probability was raised. Also, what would be the effects on the conclusions? Would an increase in the probability of a related premise affect the desirability of the conclusion?

For almost all of the issues, *increasing the likelihood of something increased its desirability.* This tendency encompassed the logically related conclusions as well as the minor premises, but to a smaller degree. Although it is not clear what the effects of wishful thinking are on probability estimates, this research shows that we tend to welcome the inevitable (or at least to find it more welcome).

Source: Adapted from W. McGuire, "A Syllogistic Analysis of Cognitive Relationships," in M. Rosenberg, C. Hovland, W. McGuire, R. P. Abelson, and J. W. Brehm (eds.), *Attitude Organization and Change,* Vol. 3. (New Haven, Conn.: Yale University Press, 1960), pp. 65–111.

shaped and molded by the people around us—both those who are close to us, such as friends or family, and those who speak to us through the media, including newspapers and movies. All are purveyors of attitudes and it is within this context that most attitudes appear to be shaped. There are exceptions, but the main focus in this chapter is on the means by which our social environment creates attitudes. First, however, a major exception to these social shapers of attitudes should be considered.

Direct Contact: Seeing Is Believing

The feeling, thinking, and acting components of attitudes can be formed and changed as a result of direct contact with an object. Consider the number of new attitudes you form during a day, a week, a month. Every time you meet a new person, hear a new recording, go to a concert, or read a book, you are exposed to a situation in which the formation of an attitude is possible. Attitudes are inevitable consequences of moving about in an environment, thinking and feeling and acting in response to what you encounter there.

You may recall here the research evidence indicating that direct contact between individuals of different races is a potent facilitator of positive racial attitudes. The study by Deutsch and Collins is one of the most frequently cited examples of research that has supported this direct-contact hypothesis of interracial tranquility. Table 8.4 shows that white people who lived in integrated housing projects, where there was direct contact with black people, expressed more positive attitudes about blacks than did the white populations of the segregated projects, where direct interracial contact was minimal.

One should not conclude, however, that all attitudes based on direct contact are going to be positive. For example, if a person viciously insults you every time you are in direct contact with him or her, no amount of contact is going to make you like that person. Research has established that positive relations come out of interactions occurring under conditions conducive to cooperation rather than to competition or hostility (for example, Sherif, 1966); this research is explored in detail in Chapter 14.

However, in general it appears that direct contact, provided that it is gratifying, can engender positive attitudes. Lack of contact, on the other hand, sets the stage for the rapid development of negative attitudes. Additional evidence regarding this problem suggests that contact does not even have to be gratifying to produce positive attitudes. Simple exposure to a person or object, regardless of its characteristics, can produce uniformly positive evaluations. (This evidence is discussed at length in Chapter 6.) Briefly, Robert Zajonc (1968) of the University of Michigan hypothesizes that " . . . mere repeated exposure of the individual to a stimulus is a sufficient condition for the enhancement of his attitude toward it." Zajonc's subjects tended to report increasingly positive evaluations of nonsense syllables and Chinese characters as the subjects were increasingly exposed to them. Zajonc has shown that Americans tend to evaluate most positively those words in the English language that are in most common usage.

The finding that exposure breeds liking has many implications. Stanley Milgram (1970) has written about the "familiar stranger"—the other person an individual sees regularly but never interacts with. For example, two people who catch the same train every morning may find that their feelings of closeness and familiarity breed a friendliness that eventually evolves into interaction, especially if the two happen to meet outside the usual place.

Figure 8.7 Our attitudes toward most objects are learned indirectly, through the eyes of others. Yet, indirectly learned attitudes are usually as strong as if they had been acquired through direct experience. This woman apparently prefers to keep her education about others indirect, although ironically a sign on her premises implores, "You can't love God whom you have not seen and hate your brother whom you have known."

("Say, aren't you the guy who takes the 8:13 train out of Biloxi Station every morning?")

However, the effects of exposure cannot alone explain all the attitudes we form. The impressions we form of others when we first meet them, and the pleasure or pain we receive from them during our first encounters with them, may have extremely powerful effects in enhancing or negating the influence of mere exposure. When evaluating others, human beings often rely on categories that replace direct experiences (see Chapters 5, 6, and 7). We see whom we expect to see, rather than the person who is really there.

Indirect Learning: A Hit or Miss Proposition

Most of us have never directly encountered most persons or objects about whom we hold attitudes—the North Vietnamese, the Greek dictators, the President, members of Congress, Paul Newman, and so on. When we form attitudes in the absence of direct contact, our experiences are actually with various representations of the object, through photographs and verbal descriptions, in books and magazines, on posters and television. These can never accurately reflect the real character of a person or object.

We in turn apply our own mental representations in thinking about an attitude object. Keep in mind that representations usually also act as filters with which we focus on those features of objects that are important to us at the time. Much is lost as a result of our biased perceptions. These filters sometimes screen out information that would deepen our understanding of events and of one another. In addition, impressions of others probably grow more distorted as they are passed along to other people who have had no direct experience with the attitude objects. As research shows (Allport

---

Two Cases of Community Values:

GRAVEL ROADS AND SAND CASTLES

In the 1870s a group of missionary families of the Mormon faith settled at the base of a mountain in western New Mexico. Struggling with the bare land, the poor rainfall, the drought, disease, and disillusionment of trying to convert the Indians, they and their descendants have remained in the village of Rimstone until today. Forty miles across the mesa is situated a similar village of approximately 250 people. The citizens of Homestead straggled in during the Depression years en route to California. Because these two towns are so similar in physical and economic resources, one might expect that the people within the two towns would come to share the same values over time.

Evon Vogt and Thomas O'Dea studied the similarities and differences in values between the two communities. They found that both groups shared the pioneer values of hard work and endurance. However, these investigators discerned distinct differences in the handling of two problems that affected the well-being of the whole community: repairing the roads and building a new gymnasium.

One summer the state roads in the area were being graveled. The Mormon community and the Depression town both decided to take advantage of this road crew's presence to repair the towns' roads. The Rimstone people handled the situation in the usual fashion. The problem was discussed at the church meetings, a householder meeting was called, and everyone agreed to contribute $20 per household to meet the cost of the road work. In Homestead this type of cooperative plan was rejected. Instead, several individuals who owned stores on the main street each contracted separately with the construction firm to have a load of gravel placed in front of each store. This left the rest of the village streets a sea of mud during rainy weather.

Another major problem involved the building of a new gymnasium. The

and Postman, 1947; Schachter and Burdick, 1955), rumors grow more and more distorted as they spread. Thus, indirectly learned attitudes appear to rest on shaky ground.

Most Americans have attitudes toward China. But for the vast majority, the attitude object is really a distillation of photographs, descriptions, words, and film, rather than the actual character of the nation. Because most of us are dependent on indirect representations, we experience an attitude object such as the People's Republic of China in ways that are determined by others, including media managers, politicians, political activists, and military leaders. This process of *indirect learning* is the basis of what sociologists and anthropologists call *cultural transmission*—the passing on of dispositions from one generation to the next or from one cultural context to another. Among the attitudes passed from generation to generation, for example, are political ones, as when children vote for the party of their parents' choice *because* it is their parents' choice. Another source of indirect learning is *propaganda*—the efforts of government officials, media managers, politicians, advertisers, and business managers to promote attitudes that are supportive of their institutions' desired goals through mass mind management. Formal education may be the most potent source of indirect learning for most Americans—a possibility that is explored further in Chapter 16. Formal education dispenses legends as well as truths and does not always make clear which is which.

Functionalism: The Importance of Self-Gratification

Each of us harbors a wide range of wants—from simple creature desires for food and warmth to the more complex needs for love and autonomy. These

plans were presented to both towns in 1950. In both cases the state was willing to pay for building costs if the community would provide the labor. The Mormon community acted in a way that was comparable to the road-building problem. First the church council was involved and then the community at large. It was decided that each able-bodied man would contribute fifty hours of labor or $50 to the school project. Work was begun in 1951 and, after a row of classrooms was added to the initial gymnasium, was completed in 1953.

In Homestead the plan was rejected by the families on the basis that "I can't be up in town building a school; I've got my farm to tend." When additional money was provided for labor, the foundation was dug, adobe bricks were made, and members of the community worked on a strictly cash basis of $1 an hour for labor. When the money ran out, the building stopped. Three years later 10,000 adobe bricks lay in piles turning to rubble in the wind and rain. No gymnasium was ever built.

In these examples and in others as well, the researchers showed the effects of value differences in these two towns. The cooperative orientation of the Mormon community had great survival value for the Mormon town. The individualistic entrepreneurial approach of the Homesteaders seems self-defeating in comparison. Yet each town continues to go its own way. Little mixing or intermarriage goes on. Neither town seems to be able to learn any new values from the neighbor's experiences. Because value systems are strongly intertwined networks, it may be almost impossible to change details without altering the whole framework, even when survival is at stake.

Source: Adapted from E. Vogt and T. O'Dea, "A Comparative Study of the Role of Values in Social Action in Two Southwestern Communities," *American Sociological Review,* 18 (1953), pp. 645–654.

wants vary widely from person to person, but they are important shapers of behavior nevertheless. Our quests for self-gratification also have an immense influence on our attitudes. As a general rule, the persons, events, objects, and so on that gratify our desires come to be positively valued; those that hinder our search for gratification are negatively valued. Our attitudes toward persons, events, objects, and so on are thus determined by their functional value to us.

Perhaps the most extensive treatment of this position has been provided by Daniel Katz and Ezra Stotland (1959). In the resulting *functional approach* to attitude development they isolate several important ways in which attitudes are gratifying to people. Not only do attitudes reflect the generalized rewards and punishments we experience in our daily strivings; they are also generated by some very specific quests. Two of these deserve special mention here because they are closely related to other discussions in this textbook. The first is the need for *ego defense.* Each person harbors certain insecurities about himself or herself and about the environment and would prefer to escape information that would only intensify these insecurities. Thus, a person who is anxious about his or her abilities may form negative attitudes toward those who seem threatening. For example, a supervisor who finds that one of her subordinates is more skilled than she herself is may develop a strong dislike for the subordinate. Katz and Stotland also feel that people possess a basic desire to understand, or to *acquire knowledge.* Thus, sources of information that enable them to reach valid conclusions are highly valued. For example, a teacher who enables his students to feel that they understand the world in a richer and more sophisticated way should enjoy the positive regard of his students. One important implication of this position is that a source who gives us information supporting our tentative beliefs about the world will be more highly valued than one who unconvincingly challenges those beliefs. We should thus value those who tell us that our convictions are correct and devalue those who suggest that we could be wrong. (This issue will be discussed later in the context of cognitive dissonance.)

A great deal of research supports the functionalist position on attitude formation. One of the most ambitious attempts to tighten the theory and to examine it systematically has been carried out by Martin Fishbein and his colleagues (Anderson and Fishbein, 1965; Fishbein and Hunter, 1964). A series of experiments has led Fishbein to conclude that one's attitude toward a specific person (or object or event) will depend on the strength of the belief that the person will help or hinder one in reaching a valued goal. For example, an individual who strongly values world peace should be especially positive toward a president who develops a plan for world peace. Fishbein argued further, however, that we usually have *many* beliefs about how a certain attitude object may help or hinder us, and the effects of these beliefs on our attitude can be added to or subtracted from. For example, we may also believe that the same president adopts unfair campaign tactics or uses strong-arm techniques to secure congressional support; these beliefs could subtract from an otherwise positive attitude toward him. Although Fishbein's research has lent strong support to this type of analysis, there are limitations, a few of which are discussed in Chapter 5. That chapter shows that feelings about another person do not add up in a simple fashion as we acquire more and more information about that person. Rather, we seem to weigh information in different ways and tend to average its effects in reaching a final evaluation. Thus, although Fishbein has contributed substantially to an understanding of the formation of attitudes through multiple beliefs, modifications in the theory are necessary.

Classical Conditioning: Black Is What You Make It

Russian physiologist Ivan Pavlov demonstrated a process by which many animals learn to make specific responses to particular cues that are associated with (but not the same as) the objects that originally produced the responses (see Chapter 2). Psychologists have since demonstrated that a "conditioning" process may be responsible for much attitude formation.

Psychologists have demonstrated that attitude formation in human beings is subject to a process of conditioning that is similar to that by which Pavlov's dogs learned to salivate when presented with a sound or a light. A typical procedure is to pair a conditioned stimulus, perhaps a nonsense syllable, with an unconditioned stimulus, usually electric shock, so that the unconditioned response, or aversive arousal, is generalized from the shock to the nonsense syllable (Razran, 1961). Typically, the nonsense syllables that subjects evaluate as neutral at the outset of an experiment take on negative connotations after consistently being paired with an electric shock. The affective component of attitudes is the component most frequently called into play in these studies, so that the combined data demonstrate affect learned by association.

One interesting demonstration of the classical conditioning of social attitudes, through the use of semantic-differential techniques, was conducted by Mark Zanna, Charles Kiesler, and Paul Pilkonis (1970). These researchers recruited fifty female subjects, ostensibly to conduct a physiological study aimed at "developing a more sensitive and instantaneous physiological measure than the old standard ones of heart rate." The women were forewarned that they would be shocked a random number of times at predetermined intervals in the experiment and that they would be signaled when the intervals were beginning and ending. For one group of women, the onset of shocks was signaled by the word "light" and the termination of shock intervals was signaled by the word "dark." These signal words were reversed for a second group of subjects, and a control group heard only the signals "begin" and "end."

To discover the true effects of these procedures on subsequent evaluations of the words "light" and "dark," the researchers made a significant effort to measure the effects of the conditioning outside the original laboratory; in a separate experiment in another part of the building, a different experimenter administered a different test to the same subjects in which the terms "light" and "dark" were embedded. The results of this second procedure indicated that all groups of subjects evaluated "light" more positively than "dark." This preference for "light" suggests that the subjects had prior attitudes toward the words "light" and "dark." However, the contrast between the evaluations of "light" and "dark" were most exaggerated when "dark" signaled shocks and "light" signaled relief. The difference between the evaluations of the two words was smallest when "light" signaled shock and "dark" indicated relief. Thus, "light" was evaluated more positively than usual when it had been paired with a positive event and less positively than usual when it had been paired with pain. In addition, these conditioned responses also generalized to associated words. Although "white" was uniformly evaluated more positively than "black," the difference was smallest when "light" had indicated the onset of shock.

The negative associations many people have with the word "black" may inadvertently contribute to the stereotypes with which white people disparage black people.

Things Go Better With Coke: Inadvertent Conditioning

The experiment by Zanna and his colleagues provides evidence that attitudes are sometimes formed when people come to associate objects with pleasant or unpleasant events. This finding suggests, for example, that we might not like people with whom our only contact is in hot, crowded subways and that we will be particularly drawn to those ideas we encounter in courses taught by attractive, entertaining teachers. This idea is especially intriguing, because it suggests that a certain randomness and arbitrariness will always characterize the formation of attitudes; objects combine with reinforcing and punishing events almost infinitely.

The applicability of conditioning techniques in increasing the effectiveness of virtually *any* message also presents alarming possibilities. It permits people to manipulate situations so that others will form attitudes, not because of the characteristics of the attitude objects themselves but because of the contexts in which the attitude objects are presented. Irving Janis, Donald Kaye, and Paul Kirschner (1965) have demonstrated the power of the context in which an attitude object is encountered. They asked subjects to read a persuasive communication, giving some of the subjects soft drinks to enjoy with their reading material. The subjects given soft drinks were more persuaded by what they read than subjects who were not.

ATTITUDE ORGANIZATION

Social psychologists use the term "attitude" to refer to a person's affective, cognitive, and behavioral dispositions toward a person or object or idea. People are capable of forming attitudes toward virtually every person, thing, or idea that can be represented to them. For example, oneself, other

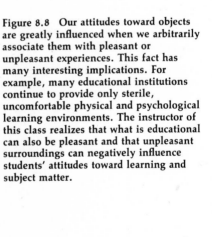

Figure 8.8 Our attitudes toward objects are greatly influenced when we arbitrarily associate them with pleasant or unpleasant experiences. This fact has many interesting implications. For example, many educational institutions continue to provide only sterile, uncomfortable physical and psychological learning environments. The instructor of this class realizes that what is educational can also be pleasant and that unpleasant surroundings can negatively influence students' attitudes toward learning and subject matter.

people, ethical principles, events, physical objects, and so on all can be referred to as attitude objects. John Robinson and Phillip Shaver (1969) have published a survey of attitude tests that summarizes the major types of attitude questionnaires currently available. They found that existing questionnaires tend to fall in the following attitude categories:

1. life satisfaction and happiness
2. self-esteem
3. alienation from others
4. authoritarianism or dogmatism
5. sociopolitical attitudes
6. values
7. general attitudes toward people
8. religious attitudes

As you can see, there is very little of what we think or do or feel that does not fall into one of these categories. But if virtually all our thoughts, feelings, and actions are functions of our attitudes, then there must be some form of organization by which an individual can link these diverse experiences so that he or she can lead a coherent existence. People may be motivated to create such organizations so that, for example, their thoughts, feelings, and behavior do not lead them to form different attitudes about the same object and so that their attitudes about different objects do not incline them to take conflicting actions, think conflicting thoughts, or feel conflicting emotions. For the remainder of this chapter, major principles of attitude organization will be explored.

Figure 8.9 presents a general model of attitudes experienced as feelings, thoughts, or actions toward an object. The object can be any (or a combination) of the different people, places, things, and so on represented in Figure 8.9. Thus, the attitude objects to which you attend may include your roommate, your father, and yourself. As you can see in Figure 8.9, the nature of organization demanded by so many attitude objects can be tremendously complex. Not only do you have relationships with objects; those objects enter into relationships with one another as well. Thus, you may not evaluate independently your attitudes toward a person and an issue; your attitude toward the person may be influenced by your attitude toward the issue, or vice versa.

Suppose the issue were the legalization of marijuana and the person were your father-in-law. Let us assume also that your attitude toward prohibition of marijuana is negative. You think that making criminals of people because they use a relatively harmless drug is unjustified and inhumane and that marijuana should be legalized immediately. You campaign for political candidates who support legalization. Thus, in every sense, your attitude toward the prohibition of marijuana is negative. You greatly admire and respect your father-in-law. You are married to his son, and you enjoy family gatherings with him. In every respect, then, your attitude toward your father-in-law is positive.

It is entirely possible that your father-in-law has an attitude toward marijuana that is different from yours. He may even approve of penalties for marijuana use as much as you disapprove of them. This discrepancy is likely to lead to conflict between the two of you. In such a situation you would probably feel an undesirable tension, and to rid yourself of it you may change your attitude toward your father-in-law, your attitude toward

Figure 8.9 A model of attitudes. Our attitudes consist of feelings and thoughts about all of the classes of stimuli shown here, as well as actions directed toward those stimuli. Even though the objects of our attitudes are diverse, our attitudes are not independent of one another, but are complexly intertwined.

Person

Feelings

Thoughts

Actions

Objects

Persons

Places

Things

Events

Values

Principles

Decisions

the use of marijuana, your attitude toward yourself, your attitude toward your husband, or your attitudes toward the candidates you have supported. In some way, you would probably manage to weave the various interrelated attitude objects into a coherent whole.

Social psychologists have spent a great deal of time attempting to identify the organizational principles used by human beings to make sense of such complexities. Broadly speaking, the attitude-organization theories developed to date can be subsumed under the general designation of consistency theory. Thus, although many different theoretical approaches have been developed, most theorists assume that attitudes are organized in such a way as to reduce unfitting, inharmonious, or conflicting elements. In this way one's mental life is smoother and less complicated. When disharmony exists within our heads, life seems unpleasant and we are motivated to change things. The organizational task that we all face, therefore, is to

Overhauling Opinions: BACK TO BASIC VALUES

THINK OF SOMETHING you have a strong opinion about. Women's liberation? Civil rights? Imperialist aggression? Restoration of the death penalty? Government secrecy? What would someone have to do to make you change your mind without feeling coerced? And how long would someone have to try? Would you guess less than an hour? Milton Rokeach, an American psychologist, believes that it is possible to get people to adjust their strongly held opinions after working with them in educational situations for about an hour. In fact, he claims, he and his colleagues have done it.

Neither threats nor promises are involved. Instead, a person is made to feel dissatisfied with himself or herself. The researchers produced such dissatisfaction by showing people instances in which their attitudes were inconsistent with their values. The researchers made a clear distinction between attitudes and values. An attitude they defined as an organization of interrelated thoughts and feelings that relate to a specific object or situation (what was called an opinion at the start of this discussion). A value they defined as either a desirable state of existence or a desirable way of acting. They viewed a person's many attitudes as being founded on a few basic values that

transcended situation-specific considerations.

In their experiment Rokeach and his colleagues asked two groups of college students to rank eighteen values that related to a desirable end-state (called terminal values) in the order of personal importance. Then the participants were asked to write down their attitudes toward civil-rights demonstrations. One group was then dismissed, and it became the control group for the experiment.

The experimental group was then shown how earlier groups had ranked the eighteen values, and the experimenters specifically pointed out that freedom had been ranked first and equality eleventh. It was suggested that students tend to be much more interested in their own freedom than in other people's freedom, which is what equality represents. The participants were then invited to compare their own rankings with the rankings of the earlier groups. They were then shown correlations between rankings of freedom and equality and positions on civil-rights issues: People unsympathetic to civil rights tended to rank freedom high and equality low, whereas those who are sympathetic ranked both high. Again the correlations were interpreted: People unsympathetic to civil rights are saying that they care about their own freedom but not other people's, and people sympathetic are showing their concern

achieve consistency in our attitudes. Several attempts to understand consistency in attitude organization will be explored here.

Balance: Keeping Our Feelings in Order

In 1958, Fritz Heider published a book entitled *The Psychology of Interpersonal Relations* in which he discussed an organizational principle he called *balance.* Recall the hypothetical relationship between your attitude toward your father-in-law and your attitude toward the legalization of marijuana. The situation according to Heider's notion of balance is diagrammed in Figure 8.10, a common form in balance theory.

Because you are opposed to penalties for marijuana use, the link between you and the penalties has a negative value. This is entered as a minus sign in Figure 8.10. And because you and your father-in-law really get along quite well, the link between you and your father-in-law is posi-

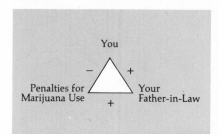

Figure 8.10 According to Heider (1958), a person would strive to relieve the imbalance of attitudes represented here. Multiplying the signs representing these attitudes, which mathematically produces a minus, reveals imbalance.

---

for other people's freedom as well. The group were again invited to compare their rankings and their civil-rights positions with those of their peers.

Almost half the students became aware of inconsistencies in their value and attitude systems. Some found that they had put a high value on freedom but a low value on equality. Others found that, although they cared about civil rights, they had ranked equality low—indicating a stand based more on social acceptability than on principle.

Then students rated their degree of satisfaction with themselves on an eleven-point scale. Finally, they used the scale to indicate their degree of satisfaction with their ranking of each of the eighteen values.

Tests conducted three to five months later showed considerable value and attitude changes in the experimental group. Higher values were put on freedom and equality, and more favorable attitudes were expressed toward civil rights. The self-satisfaction ratings done at the end of the experimental session turned out to be excellent predictors of the value changes: The lower a subject's self-satisfaction was, the greater the resulting changes tended to be.

The experimenters had difficulty believing that the single, brief

experimental session would bring about such dramatic changes. They thus conducted two more series of experiments using subtler measures of behavioral effects, such as responses to letters inviting membership in the National Association for the Advancement of Colored People (NAACP). This testing covered the period from three weeks to seventeen months after the experimental sessions. Again, the results supported the conclusion that the students in the experimental group experienced significant changes in their attitudes and values, whereas members of the control group—who did not have the opportunity to compare their values and attitudes with those of their peers or to hear the experimenters' suggested interpretations of their meanings—did not. Fifteen to seventeen months after the test, fifty-one people from the experimental group but only eighteen people from the control group responded favorably to the NAACP letter; the experimental and control groups had originally been of the same approximate size.

Source: Adapted from M. Rokeach, "Persuasion That Persists," *Psychology Today,* 5 (1971), pp. 68–71, 92.

tive. And, finally, the link between your father-in-law and penalties for marijuana use is positive, because your father-in-law thinks those penalties necessary and thus favors their continuation. If you multiply the signs for all three links, you get a minus sign. The minus sign is a mathematical representation of an uncomfortable state of psychological affairs, which Heider calls *imbalance.* When imbalance exists, says Heider, psychological pressures are brought to bear to set the organizational apparatus right, or to restore balance. The individual can restore balance by changing the minus sign to a plus sign (by, in this case, becoming a proponent of marijuana penalties) or by changing either of the plus signs to a minus (by convincing your father-in-law that marijuana should be legalized or by growing to dislike your father-in-law).

Balance theory deals with two central relationships—*liking relationships* (L) and *unit relationships* (U). The liking aspect refers to the positive or negative evaluation of a relationship between any two attitude objects and is represented by plus and minus signs. All the examples discussed so far have dealt with liking. Unit relationships, on the other hand, exist to the extent that two or more things form a unit. When, for example, people are related as husband and wife or as father and daughter, the two are a unit.

Still other units are created by the actions of individuals. For example, if a person *causes* an event, then the person and the event may form a unit in the minds of others. Consider the following situation. In 1973 Americans became absorbed by certain political activities that had occurred during the presidential campaign of the previous year, particularly the bugging of Democratic campaign headquarters in the Watergate complex. If you had

Figure 8.11 As the Watergate scandal was breaking in 1973, Victor Voter did his best to maintain a balance between his attitudes toward Nixon and Watergate. Victor finally decided that he could feel comfortable only when he regarded Nixon and Watergate as linked, for better or worse, in what Heider (1958) would call a unit relationship. Victor's growing contempt for the emerging scandal eventually triumphed, and his regard for Nixon plummeted.

felt that the President of the United States knew of these activities, you ascribed a causal unit relationship between the President and certain illegal acts (a plus). If you disapproved of these activities, you would have had a negative (minus) attitude toward them. Assuming that you liked President Nixon (a plus), this relationship between attitudes would have caused you discomfort. Mathematically, the product of the two positive attitudes and the one negative attitude is a minus, indicating imbalance.

The imbalance could have been reduced in one of three ways. You could have decided that you dislike Nixon, changing the sign representing that relationship to a minus. In this case, the product of the plus sign representing the relationship between President Nixon and the illegal activities and the minus signs representing your attitudes toward the President and the illegal activities would be a plus:

$$(+) \times (-) \times (-) = (+)$$

You could also decide that the illegal activities were justified and change the sign for that relationship to a plus, in which case the plus sign for the unit relationship (President Nixon and the illegal activities) and the plus signs representing your attitudes toward the President and the Watergate activities would produce a plus:

$$(+) \times (+) \times (+) = (+)$$

Or you could dissociate President Nixon and the illegal activities, deciding that they did not actually form a unit, and change that sign to a minus. In this last case, the minus sign representing the unit relationship, the minus sign representing your attitude toward the illegal activities, and the plus sign representing your attitude toward the President would yield a plus:

$$(-) \times (-) \times (+) = (+)$$

In any of these cases, the product of the signs for the relationships between you and the President, you and the illegal activities, and the President and the illegal activities would be a plus, indicating balance. The course you take depends on the strength of your attitudes toward any of the elements of the triad; the strongest attitudes would be least likely to change. Keep in mind also that balance theory cannot accurately predict the actions you would take to resolve the imbalance.

Psychological Implications: Search and Resistance

Heider's theory has provided the basis for several more complex consistency models (Cartwright and Harary, 1956; Rosenberg and Abelson, 1960). Each of these models points to interesting features of psychological balance. One of these models evolved because Robert Abelson (1968) was intrigued with the way in which balance needs either set in motion a search for new information or close us off from additional facts. For Abelson a basic unit of cognitive organization is termed an *implicational molecule,* which is a self-contained set of statements that, taken together, is psychologically consistent. It is important that all the elements within these molecules fit together. If a molecule is incomplete, or if there is a nonfitting element, the molecule will require cognitive reorganization.

The three most striking characteristics of implicational molecules are that (1) they tend toward completion, (2) completed molecules are resistant

Figure 8.12 Implicational molecules, hypothesized by Abelson (1968) to be the basis of cognitive organization, are self-contained units consisting of information about particular objects. Each unit must be complete and consistent with others for psychological comfort. If one part is not, the perceiver will seek new information to make the unit complete and consistent. If you heard that Jim sent Amy flowers, which she loves, the molecule would be consistent but incomplete; you might tend to assume that Amy thanked Jim or try to learn whether or not she did. But if you heard that Jim sent flowers to Amy, whom he hates, you would probably seek information to explain this inconsistency. You might be satisfied if you discover that Amy is allergic to flowers.

to change, and (3) molecules with nonfitting elements produce pressure to relieve the inconsistency.

The following sentences represent an incomplete molecule:

1. Jim sent Amy flowers.
2. Amy was surprised.

The above sentences suggest the following action to complete the molecule:

3. Amy thanked Jim.

Whether or not sentence 3 is added verbally, the temptation is to complete the molecule begun with sentences 1 and 2 by recruiting something like sentence 3. Suppose you are faced with the following incomplete molecule:

1. Jim loathed Amy.
2. Amy loved flowers.

To make these two elements consistent, a sentence like the following might be expected to provide the missing link:

3. Jim did not send Amy flowers.

However, suppose that the following were actually the case:

3. Jim sent Amy flowers.

This is a nonfitting element that makes the three elements difficult to organize around a single implicational principle. However, a fourth sentence like the following can complete the molecule:

4. Amy had hay fever.

This factor completes a four-sentence implicational molecule that is organized around a principle that might be defined as duplicity. If you felt a "need to explain" the surprising third sentence, you were experiencing the pressure to search out elements that would reduce the inconsistency in the implicational molecule.

When a molecule is fully self-contained and complete, it takes a jolting rearrangement of facts to alter one's view. A complete implicational molecule is highly resistant to change. Imagine what it would require to alter the molecule of statements that capsulizes your attitude toward, say, Adolf Hitler. (Attitude change is discussed in more detail in Chapter 9.)

Cognitive Dissonance: A Preliminary Peek

Research support for Heider's model and for various derivations of it has been extensive. Nevertheless, many psychologists have felt that the theory is too limited. It may be too exclusively concerned with the affective aspect of attitudes and not sufficiently attentive to the cognitive domain. Our dispositions toward the world are tied together with more than emotional glue. Specifically, people also seem to value logical consistency among their various ideas. As early psychologists like William James (1890) and Prescott Lecky (1951) argued, people resist the pairing of two conflicting ideas about the world. If people believe that automobiles are dangerous polluters of the environment, they probably would not like to entertain the notion that automobiles are not polluters, much less a more extreme notion—that automobiles are actually beneficial to the environment. Similarly, if one dislikes a person, it makes little logical sense to do that other person a favor.

This distaste for inconsistencies in logic has been captured by Leon

Festinger (1957) in the term *cognitive dissonance.* According to Festinger, when simultaneously considering two cognitions or thoughts that imply the opposite of each other, one is thrust into a state of dissonance. Because this state is painful, the tendency is to attempt to rid oneself of it. The methods that people use to reduce dissonance are highly intriguing. (A thorough discussion of dissonance is part of Chapter 9.) It is important to realize that one fundamental way in which attitudes are organized is in terms of logical consistency. For Westerners, at least, a sense of internal harmony depends on the degree to which all of a person's attitudes logically imply the others.

When Inconsistency Helps

Some theorists have criticized the consistency theories for ignoring the human penchant for variety. For example, Daryl Bem (1970) has this to say about the hypothesis that the need to eliminate inconsistencies is the central motive in attitude organization:

I don't believe it. At least not very much. In my view, a vision of inconsistency as a temporary turbulence in an otherwise fastidious pool of cognitive clarity is all too misleading. My own suspicion is that inconsistency is probably our most enduring cognitive commonplace. (page 34)

A theory that has people trying to eliminate all the inconsistencies in their lives overlooks the fascination people often have for mysteries, puzzles, surprise endings, scientific problems, and incongruous juxtapositions. Rather than seeking the simplest, most congruent, and most familiar state of affairs, we often seek the excitement of novelty, surprise, and mystery.

Any theorist who argues that either consistency or variety is *the* basic motive of human behavior is sure to be deluged with solid examples of the opposing tendency. To see consistency as the sole motive is to ignore many of the creative contributions of artists, writers, scientists, philosophers, and explorers. And to see nothing but the search for variety is to commit a comparable oversight. It appears, then, that individuals reach their own personal compromises between their needs for consistency and variety. For example, people often find ways to exercise needs for novelty without disturbing the consistencies they cherish most. They can brighten otherwise monotonous lives by becoming absorbed in crossword puzzles or mystery stories. If they cannot solve the puzzles or mysteries, their lives are not significantly disturbed. If they *are* successful, they feel competent at resolving inconsistencies. The reward in this case is a sense of competence that may not otherwise be found in the day-to-day routine (White, 1959).

D. E. Berlyne (1967) suggests that everyone has an optimum level of tension, or arousal. Whenever a person finds the level of tension rising above that ideal level or dropping below it, the motivation to restore equilibrium arises. When inconsistencies push tension above the individual's optimum level, the tendency probably will be to attempt to reduce it. On the other hand, when the individual is so understimulated that boredom results, a search for stimulation through variety may ensue. If minor triumphs over inconsistency are rewarding enough, individuals may experience *arousal jags,* in which they repeatedly seek arousal above their optimum thresholds so that they can have the pleasure of reducing it. Such may be the appeal of roller-coaster rides, LSD, and pornographic movies.

An important feature of all organizing principles is that they help people diminish to a manageable level the amount of information processing that they must do. Human life is such a complex fabric of experiences

Figure 8.13 Consistency theories, based on the assumption that the optimum psychological state is one of harmony and tranquility, have been criticized for ignoring the many ways in which people seek arousal, novelty, and variety.

that people often find it useful or even necessary to simplify and categorize their experiences. Cognitive organization is necessary for people to perform even the simplest tasks. It begins in infancy and continues through many years of formal schooling.

Although this ability to organize our cognitions is invaluable, there is sometimes the danger that our simplifications will constitute significant distortions in our perceptions of reality. In fact, the organizing principle of simplification is the basis of all stereotypes—positive and negative (see Chapter 7). You may be able to recognize various methods by which you and your acquaintances reduce the complexities of your environment. Perhaps you can identify ways in which simplification has been helpful and ways, as well, in which it has been destructive. If you do not always like the organizing principles people use, keep in mind that one of the most striking features of attitudes is that they change. The many ways in which attitudes change is the focus of Chapter 9.

SUMMARY

Basic to the study of social psychology are attitudes, which underlie all human social behavior. Attitudes, relatively enduring dispositions, have three components—*affective* (feeling), *cognitive* (thinking), and *behavioral.*

One of the first steps in studying attitudes is measuring them. The central assumption in attitude measurement is that attitudes can be measured indirectly through expressed *opinions,* although opinions are not always accurate reflections of attitudes. Attitude scales were developed to measure, from low to high, degrees of opinion on specific topics. The most popular technique of constructing attitude scales is the method of *Likert scaling.* This method allows subjects a spectrum of five responses, from strongly approve to strongly disapprove. Yet another consideration in attitude measurement is *social distance,* a measurement of degrees and grades of understanding between people. A technique has been developed to determine the validity of these scales; it detects needs for revamping of scales when results are inconsistent. The *semantic-differential* scale, another popular device for measuring attitudes, requires the subject to rank items on qualities from, for example, hot to cold and aggressive to passive.

Recently, researchers have supplemented their attitude-measurement techniques with *behavioral* and *behavioroid* measures. Behavioroid measures reflect an individual's expressed commitment to behave in a certain way, whereas behavioral measures reflect actual performance of those behaviors. At times, however, behavioroid measures do not accurately reflect the behavior that an individual will actually engage in; it is important, therefore, to be aware of the underlying reasons a person may have for his or her responses to a behavioroid measure. For this reason, it is often safest for social psychologists to make use of more than one measure.

In this ambiguous world, people's attitudes toward specific issues do not always agree; each person's attitudes are dependent on his or her prior experiences. Direct contact with the object of an attitude is one source of information. Another source is experience with representations of the object, such as photographs and verbal reports. Indirect learning, sometimes called *cultural transmission,* is the passing on of impressions from one generation to the next or from one cultural context to another. The need for self-gratification, proposed by functionalists, is also assumed to influence a person's attitude development, especially through his or her desires for *ego defense* and the desire to *acquire knowledge.* A conditioning process, which associates attitude objects with subjective experiences, may also be responsible for some of the attitudes that people form. For example, an attractive, entertaining teacher may indelibly interest students in subject matter.

Although everyone harbors a confusing array of attitudes, we each attempt to organize them into a consistent whole. One organizational principle, proposed by Fritz Heider, is that of *balance.* In a triadic relationship of attitude objects, the evaluation of a relationship between any two is represented by a plus sign (positive relationship) or a minus sign (negative relationship). These are *liking relationships.* In a *unit relationship,* one attitude object consists of two or more related elements, such as husband and wife. When positive and negative evaluations are totaled, an overall plus sign indicates balance and an overall minus sign indicates an uncomfortable state of imbalance. An elaboration on Heider's original balance theory suggests the existence of *implicational molecules,* which are self-contained, psychologically consistent sets of statements. If a molecule is incomplete, or if there is a nonfitting element, the molecule will require cognitive reorganization.

Some theorists believe that inconsistency, as well as consistency, is important because inconsistency accounts for much human creativity and interest in problem solving. Each of us has an optimum level of tension, or of arousal. If the level of tension drops below or rises above the ideal level, we are motivated to restore equilibrium. If inconsistency is rewarding enough, we may even seek an *arousal jag,* which prolongs the pleasure of reducing inconsistency. In any case, attitude organization helps us to reduce the complexities of the environment and may be, like many other things in life, both helpful and destructive.

SUGGESTED READINGS

Abelson, Robert (ed.). *Theories of Cognitive Consistency: A Sourcebook.* Chicago: Rand McNally, 1968.

Fishbein, Martin (ed.). *Readings in Attitude Theory and Measurement.* New York: Wiley, 1967.

Greenwald, Anthony G., Thomas Ostrom, and Timothy Brock (eds.). *Psychological Foundations of Attitudes.* New York: Academic Press, 1968.

Kiesler, Charles, Barry Collins, and Norman Miller. *Attitude Change: A Critical Analysis of Theoretical Approaches.* New York: Wiley, 1969.

Triandis, Harry C. *Attitude and Attitude Change.* New York: Wiley, 1971.

9

Attitude Change

ALL OF US ARE AGENTS of attitude change. As we relate with our friends, families, and lovers, we try to make ourselves intelligible. Furthermore, it is usually important to us that these others see the value of our commitments, appreciate our opinions on various issues, and share our sentiments about other people. In order to achieve these ends, we become agents of attitude change. At the same time, other people daily attempt to alter our own attitudes. Friends, family, and lovers act in this capacity; and politicians, teachers, and advertisers depend for their livelihoods on their abilities to alter attitudes. Thus, each of us is both an agent and a target of attitude change. And the more we know about the process, the greater our personal effectiveness and freedom is.

The preceding chapter set the stage for this discussion. For example, in order to identify an attitude and know whether it has changed, researchers must have reliable measures. It also is helpful to know how people acquire attitudes if predictions about their change are to be made. And finally, knowledge about how attitudes are organized is indispensable to changing them. This chapter begins, therefore, with a discussion of the principal approaches taken by psychologists to the problem of changing attitudes.

LEARNING IN ATTITUDE CHANGE

In 1953, Carl Hovland, Irving Janis, and Harold Kelley published *Communication and Persuasion,* the first in a series of volumes sponsored by the Yale Communication Research Program. Although they studied many controversial issues relevant to propaganda during the Cold War, the growing influence of mass media, school desegregation, and so on, the investigators conceived their project as "basic research"—in this case, concerned with the influence of words and symbols on individuals.

The theoretical orientation that guided Hovland, Janis, and Kelley was *learning theory.* They considered attitudes to be internal, implicit responses that motivate each of us to approach or avoid given objects, persons, groups, or symbols. These researchers further suggested that attitudes have *drive value,* that they propel behavior. From this perspective, attitudes are relatively stable states that energize human behavior and that affect the ways in which human beings organize their experiences. Unless outside influences intervene, these attitudes become represented in routine habits of thinking, feeling, and behaving. But outside influences are likely to disturb a person's unjustifiably consistent attitudes toward many objects. When external events do influence an individual, learning has occurred. The process by which learning occurs is often *persuasion.* The persuasion situation has four principal components, as shown in Figure 9.1.

The studies reported by Hovland and his colleagues in their many volumes represent important efforts to investigate these components systematically in order to identify the optimum conditions for changing attitudes. These components will be considered in more detail next.

Communicator Credibility: Whom Can You Trust?

How much of what people hear do they believe? To what extent does their belief in what they hear depend on how much they trust the communicator?

Figure 9.1 There are four principal components of persuasion, according to Hovland, Janis, and Kelley. The way that the components combine in a particular instance determines the favorability of the situation for attitude change. The components are: the communicator, or characteristics of the speaker or writer; the message, including its content, style, and organization; the channel, or medium through which the message is presented; and the audience, or target of the communication.

The Communicator   The Message   The Channel   The Audience

These questions were among the first addressed by Hovland, Janis, and Kelley. Their expectation was based on common sense, and they assumed that the more trustworthy and expert the communicator appeared to be, the more persuasive he or she would be. The prototype for studies of communicator credibility was conducted by Carl Hovland and Walter Weiss (1951).

Hovland and Weiss created four persuasive communications: they proposed that antihistamine drugs should be sold without a doctor's prescription; that atomic-powered submarines could feasibly be built at that time; that the steel industry was to blame for the steel shortage; and that television would force movie theaters out of business by 1955. When the experimenters presented these arguments to their subjects, the researchers credited the communications to one of two sources, one source having high and the other low credibility. For example, in the high-credibility condition, the argument for atomic submarines was attributed to J. Robert Oppenheimer, a respected American physicist; in the low-credibility condition, the source was said to be the Russian newspaper *Pravda.*

Subjects' attitudes toward these issues were assessed by questionnaire before and after they read the persuasive communication. The experimenters also asked subjects to evaluate the presentation for fairness and objectivity. Any differences in judgments between sources of high and low credibility were due entirely to associations the subjects had with those sources, because the actual content of the communications was identical.

The results were exactly as one would expect. More subjects judged that the high-credibility source had made a fair presentation than thought the low-credibility source fair. Oppenheimer was a persuasive source, and *Pravda* had somewhat less persuasive appeal to Hovland and Weiss' American subjects; 96 percent considered Oppenheimer's argument fair, whereas only 69 percent considered *Pravda's* agrument fair. Similarly, subjects considered the conclusions of the high-credibility source more justifiable than the conclusions of the low-credibility source. Again, there was a striking difference between Oppenheimer and *Pravda.* Opinion change followed the same pattern, with greater change occurring when the source was deemed highly credible.

Although the high-credibility communicator produced greater attitude change in the *immediate* situation, this effect eventually disappeared. Messages from low-credibility sources became increasingly believable over time, producing a *sleeper effect.* Hovland and Weiss concluded that people at first associate the contents of a message with its source but that content and source eventually become disassociated, the source being more quickly forgotten. Thus, the long-range impact of a message depends on its *content,* whereas short-range effectiveness depends on the credibility of the communicator.

Characteristics of the Message

The studies of communicator credibility led the Yale group to conclude that content and source are independent or become so over time. The next questions these researchers focused on concerned the features of the content, or the message per se, that affect persuasiveness. One question they asked was whether communications are more effective if they provide conclusions for the audience or allow the audience to draw its own conclusions. Carl Hovland and Wallace Mandell (1952) presented subjects with arguments about the stability of American currency. Conclusions about the necessity of devaluation were drawn explicitly in one communication and

Figure 9.2 Although a communicator's credibility has short-term effects on attitude change, her or his personal influence disappears with time, according to research findings reported by Hovland and Weiss in 1951. Any long-term effect a persuasive communication has on attitudes is primarily a result of the content of the message.

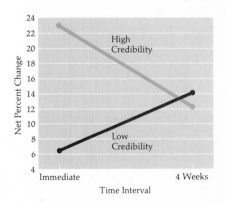

were left for the audience to draw in the other. The results suggest that people are significantly more easily persuaded when they do not have to draw their own conclusions. The researchers hastened to caution that their results do not indicate that all communicators would do best to draw conclusions for their audiences; instead, the investigators suggested a variety of factors that might decrease the effectiveness of drawing others' conclusions for them. For example, highly educated and intelligent audiences may be better equipped to draw conclusions and, in fact, may be insulted if the communicator draws them a picture. Chapter 10 reveals that people tend to resist overt attempts to persuade them.

Is a message more persuasive if only one side of an argument is presented or if both sides of the argument are discussed? On one hand, by presenting both sides the communicator runs the risk of providing the audience with a rebuttal to the position the communicator is advocating. On the other hand, the apparent bias of a one-sided presentation may diminish the communicator's credibility. During World War II, Carl Hovland, Arthur Lumsdaine, and Fred Sheffield (1949) exposed groups of soldiers to communications arguing that Germany's surrender would not result in a quick end to the war. One group of subjects was given only arguments that predicted a long, continuing war with Japan. A second group was given the same arguments in addition to arguments predicting that Japan's weaknesses would result in an early end to the war. The soldiers' beliefs about the length of the war after Germany's surrender were measured both before and after this communication. Whether or not the soldiers were persuaded by these communications seemed to depend on the initial positions taken by the soldiers. Soldiers who initially opposed the communicator's conclusion were more persuaded by two-sided arguments than by one-sided arguments. However, soldiers who initially agreed with the communicator's position were more persuaded by one-sided arguments than by two-sided arguments. This result suggests that if a communicator is on your side, you do not want that person to expose the opposing arguments. It may be that when your position is firm, you would prefer to avoid arguments that could undo your resolve. On the other hand, if a communicator takes a position opposite to yours, then representing your side of the argument makes him or her more effective in persuading you. Apparently, presenting both sides makes a communicator seem more objective, but only when the audience does not agree with the communicator's position.

Organization of Arguments. When a professor returns your paper with some good comments as well as some less flattering ones, in which order would you prefer receiving these comments? Would you like to be told all the good things about the paper and then be informed of its inadequacies? Or would you prefer to be confronted with its inadequacies and then to be told its strong points? Which of the two sequences would most likely lead you to accept your teacher's recommendations? Similarly, if you were a lawyer, would your arguments to the jury be more persuasive if you presented the strongest evidence first or waited until a climactic moment late in the trial?

The order in which arguments are presented and the effects of this order on persuasion are topics of *The Order of Presentation in Persuasion* (Hovland, 1957). To summarize the chief results of this volume, the most effective sequence of arguments depends on other factors. If people become committed publicly to one position before hearing the opposing arguments, there is a tendency for them to reject arguments that challenge that decision. And if a communicator presents a communication with contradictory arguments, then those arguments that are presented first seem to carry more persuasive weight. However, William McGuire (1957) also found that when desirable conclusions precede undesirable ones, *all* the conclusions are accepted more strongly than when undesirable conclusions are presented first. McGuire suggested that by learning desirable conclusions first, people are made attentive and are positively reinforced, so that they learn more. Furthermore, this rewarding state of affairs affects subsequent conclusions favorably, even when they are less desirable. When in a mood to agree, people will tend to be more vulnerable to any argument. The time interval between the presentation of two sides of an argument as well as the time interval between the communication of these messages and subsequent action also appear to be influential. In an experiment that simulated a jury trial, Norman Miller and Donald Campbell (1959) varied the interval between the pro and con arguments (the prosecution's versus the defendant's cases, respectively) and the time interval between the presentation of the last argument and the subjects'—the jury members'—delivery of the verdict. The results showed that the jury's decision was definitely affected by these variations in time intervals. A related discussion of how the issue of presentation order applies to attitudes about individuals appears in Chapter 5.

Persuasion Through Fear. The image of the perpetual fires of Hell is a compelling one that conjures thoughts of hot, burning flames forever sapping the body and consuming the mind. Dante recorded his visions of such an Inferno, and these images have since fueled the sermons of many a clergyman. Other agents of socialization, including parents, have been known to rely on scare techniques. If you suck your thumb, warts will grow on your nose. If you play with your penis, it will fall off. Even as an adult, you have been admonished that "speed kills," that sitting in a draft will give you a cold, and that if you do not have a college degree, you will not find a good job. All of these threats are issued in an attempt to persuade you to behave differently. But do threats further the communicator's purpose or hamper it? Does content that aims to persuade by arousing fear cause people to pay closer attention to a message or to turn away in disgust or in a desire not to believe the extent of the danger?

Figure 9.3 People have long sought to persuade one another through fear, as this fifteenth-century painting by Hieronymus Bosch testifies. Social-psychological research has suggested, however, that extreme fear may be an ineffective persuasive technique and in fact may motivate an audience to totally reject the message.

From the learning-theory standpoint, the motivational effects of fear on the learning of a message and on acceptance of its recommendations is of particular interest. The Yale research group suspected that fear is a motivator that will generate a need for anxiety reduction. If the recommendations in a message serve to reduce anxiety, they will be accepted. But if the message generates more anxiety than the recommendations can reduce, the recommendations may be rejected and some other means of fear reduction sought.

In a classic study of fear arousal, Irving Janis and Seymour Feshbach (1953) prepared three versions of a fifteen-minute illustrated lecture on the importance of proper dental hygiene in avoiding tooth decay. The lectures provided information about the causes of tooth decay and recommended proper oral hygiene. One version of the lecture was aimed at arousing maximum fear of tooth decay, another version made a moderate appeal to fear, and a third version made only a minimal appeal. The strong appeal suggested that improper care could be very dangerous because tooth decay could spread to other parts of the body and could lead to other ailments, such as paralysis, arthritis, kidney damage, and partial blindness. The strong appeal also used personalized language, addressing the viewer directly as "you" rather than speaking of people in general, and featured a slide show of diseased gums and decayed teeth in vivid color. The moderate appeal was characterized by impersonal language and black-and-white photographs; it did not emphasize the painful and extremely dangerous consequences that tooth decay sometimes has. The minimal appeal used x-ray pictures and photographs of completely healthy teeth only.

Janis and Feshbach randomly assigned high-school freshmen to the three conditions. Each subject filled out a questionnaire and one week later, immediately after being exposed to one of the lectures, filled it out again. As expected, the strong appeal produced the greatest concern about decayed teeth and diseased gums. The students were clearly unsettled by this highly fear-producing message. However, from the standpoint of oral hygiene, the most frightening appeal did not produce the best results. On the contrary, Janis and Feshbach found that the *minimal appeal* was actually most effective in equipping subjects to resist subsequent counterpropaganda. For example, minimally aroused subjects were more inclined to resist claims

---

*The Effects of
Future Appraisal:*

HUMBLE PIE PREFERRED TO PRAISE

STUDIES OF ATTITUDE change are usually concerned with issues that are not very personal to the subject: capital punishment, water fluoridation, police activities, a cure for the common cold, or the likability of spinach, for example. To what extent do these studies apply to attitudes toward oneself? Although there is good reason to believe that many of the same processes affect attitudes toward the self, the study of self does involve complexities. It has frequently been shown, for example, that information that is gratifying to the person is much more likely to be accepted than is information that is detrimental to self-esteem. This helps to explain the popularity of a flatterer in social life, especially if the flattery is subtle.

A study by Alice Eagly and Barbara Ackson indicates, however, that we do not always accept the good things that people say about us. Subjects originally were asked to rate their own creativity. They were then given a test of creativity, and later they were told by the experimenter that they were far more creative than they had said they were. Half of these subjects were also told that they would be tested again for creativity. The remaining half believed that this task was behind them and that they would not be tested further.

The question was, what effect would expectations of further evaluation have on self-ratings of creativity? The results showed that those who were not going to be retested let the positive message sink in; they came to believe that they were more creative as a result of the evaluation received. Those who had yet to clear another hurdle remained cautious and did not elevate their self-appraisals on the basis of the new information.

It is not precisely clear why those who expected another test hesitated in accepting the praise they had received; they may simply not have trusted themselves to appear so creative the second time around. However, the study does go on to suggest that it may be difficult to change the self-attitudes of another person through praise if he or she expects the source of praise to remain. If so, these findings strike a pessimistic note to those therapists, teachers, and others who believe that giving positive reassurances to those who need help improving their self-esteem is a powerful therapeutic device. In ongoing social encounters, can we ever be sure that we are free of future appraisal?

Source: Adapted from A. Eagly and B. Ackson, "The Effect of Expecting To Be Evaluated on Change Toward Favorable and Unfavorable Information About Oneself," *Sociometry,* 34 (1971), pp. 411–422.

that all but one brand of toothbrushes were ineffective in preventing tooth decay, whereas the most fearful subjects did not tend to resist such a claim. Furthermore, minimally afraid subjects actually followed the recommendations made in the communication more closely than did those subjects who were most afraid of tooth decay.

These results fit well the learning-theory model of fear-motivated attitude change. A little fear induced change, but too much fear caused subjects to ignore the recommendations.

The generality of Janis and Feshbach's findings was challenged by Howard Leventhal in 1970. Although he allows that people often reject messages that arouse extreme fear and that they may even be unable to comprehend terrifying messages, Leventhal asserts that, in general, the more fearful a communication, the more attitude change it produces. Leventhal has performed a great many experiments on persuasion through fear and finds that, in most instances, fear-arousing communications are *more* effective than are those that arouse little anxiety. Leventhal maintains that the results of the original Janis-Feshbach study were somewhat unique and that, with very few exceptions, the more fearful a communication, the more persuasive it is.

Personality and Persuasibility

Some people are apparently easier to persuade than others, whatever the message and whoever the source. As discussed in Chapter 4, differences among people present a problem to social psychologists who seek clarity in understanding attitude change—some people change, and others simply do not. In very few studies of attitude change do all subjects change their attitudes in the same direction. Some subjects do not change at all, and others change in the opposite direction from most. Some individuals establish for themselves reputations of being gullible or stubborn, and people often assume that the ability to be persuaded or convinced is a stable aspect of an individual's personality.

Carl Hovland and Irving Janis (1959) edited a volume of studies aimed at learning which dispositions render people easily persuasible or resistant to persuasion. The usual format for studies of persuasibility is to present subjects with persuasive communications and to measure their attitudes before and after exposure to those messages. Some subjects who showed generalized attitude change on all topics seemed to have a general tendency to be persuaded, independent of specific issues. This general tendency is termed *persuasibility,* which researchers have investigated using the techniques of personality assessment discussed in Chapter 4. A variety of personality measures was used by Hovland and Janis, including questionnaires, inventories, ratings by teachers and peers, and self-ratings, all employed to construct composite personality profiles. These results suggest that there are systematic personality differences between people who are easily persuaded and those who are not.

A finding that appeared to lie behind all of Hovland and Janis' results was that males who were self-confident had positive self-images and were less persuasible than those whose feelings of self-esteem were low. Apparently, to be persuaded about something is to admit that another person has more facts, more convincing arguments, greater expertise, or superior command of the issues. Most people are persuaded sometimes by someone. But to be consistently persuaded on most issues by most people is to be persuasible—at least among males in our society. Females are, in general,

Figure 9.4 Caspar Milquetoast provides an extreme example of an individual whose mind is easily changed regardless of issue or circumstance. Psychologists have found that man tends to be most easily persuaded when his esteem is low but that low self-esteem seems to reduce woman's susceptibility to influence.

more easily persuaded than men—a finding that has emerged from several studies (Marlowe and Gergen, 1969). However, females who are low in self-esteem are *not* more persuasible; rather, as Kenneth Gergen and Raymond Bauer (1967) have demonstrated, self-demeaning women seem alienated from and reject those who attempt to influence them. Apparently, then, self-esteem *can* be an important factor contributing to persuasibility, although its effects perhaps tend to be different for women and men.

On Becoming One's Role

During the Democratic primary circuit of the 1968 national election, the target of Democratic and Republican contenders alike was Lyndon Johnson and his Vietnam policy. The Vice-President, Hubert Humphrey, supported the President, as his role demanded. Then Lyndon Johnson surprised everyone by deciding not to run for a second term as President. Johnson's decision threw the race wide open, and Mr. Humphrey's hat was among those thrown into the ring. Many observers, believing Humphrey to be a liberal and a pacifist, expected him to dissociate himself from Johnson's policies on Vietnam and to disclaim his proadministration behavior as a necessary part of his *role* as Vice-President. That did not happen. Humphrey's statements about the war did not change substantially after he was "freed" from his role. One possible explanation of Humphrey's behavior is that he had privately believed all along that the war was a just war. Another explanation of why he did not dissociate himself from the war may be that he considered this stand the best political strategy he could employ to avoid both alienating supporters of Johnson and appearing too liberal in contrast to Richard Nixon during the campaign. But a third possibility is that through his role playing he came to believe what he said.

Saying Is Believing. People believe what they hear more readily when they actively participate in the saying of it. Irving Janis and Bert King (1954) demonstrated this human proclivity by comparing attitude change in subjects who themselves had articulated messages with attitude change in subjects who had listened to other people articulate the messages. Janis and King asked each subject to give an informal talk based on a prepared outline to two other subjects. During the talk, the student was to play the role of a sincere advocate of the point of view represented in the outline. Each of the three students in a group presented a different message (for example: television will cause more theaters to go out of business; the meat supply will be cut by 50 percent within two years; or a completely effective cure for the common cold will be found within two years), so that each subject actively delivered one communication and passively listened to the other two. Subjects experienced sizably more attitude change toward the advocated position when they actively participated in the communication. In contrast, fewer than half as many subjects experienced attitude changes when they played a passive role in the communication.

In order to comply with the experimenter's request to play an active role, Janis and King's subjects may have found it necessary to improvise good arguments and thereby may have persuaded themselves; after all, people cannot expect to convince others any more thoroughly than they can convince themselves.

On the other hand, feelings of satisfaction from having performed competently may have had the effect of reinforcing the ideas communicated, so that the conditions under which a message is encountered are more important than the persuasive power of the arguments in determining the extent of attitude change. In a second experiment, Bert King and Irving Janis (1956) varied the degree to which subjects needed to improvise and varied the degree to which subjects could feel satisfied with their performances. Subjects tape-recorded their speeches either by reading a prepared talk, which required little improvisation, or by talking extemporaneously after reading silently to themselves from an outline—a condition that demanded much more improvisation in presenting the arguments. The experimenters varied their subjects' satisfaction by rating their recorded speeches either favorably or unfavorably. Improvisation led to greater attitude change than satisfaction; 50 percent more subjects who improvised changed their minds in the direction of the position advocated than did those who read the talk. Subjects' attitudes were not affected by the degree of satisfaction the evaluations gave. Apparently, a communicator can increase the effectiveness of a message by enlisting the active participation of the audience. Advertisers who write jingles that viewers repeat to themselves long after the commercials are over have capitalized on this human willingness to engage in self-persuasion. So have cheerleaders, teachers, religious leaders who have developed ceremonies that require the active participation of their followers, and political leaders who depend on anthems and loyalty oaths to arouse patriotism and group feelings.

Notice that the results of Janis and King's second experiment show that *attitude change may follow behavior change* as well as precede it. People often assume that attitudes must be changed before behavior can be expected to change; this reasoning is frequently invoked by white segregationists when they advocate delaying integration. In contrast, Janis and King's finding suggests that those who are interested in bringing about social changes may be able to do so more quickly by encouraging or compelling people to behave as desired rather than by attempting to manipulate their attitudes. For example, Jack Brehm and Arthur Cohen (1962) have pointed out that legislating desegregation (contrary to what segregationists often claim) may have more powerful consequences than conducting an information campaign and hoping that people will be persuaded by it to change their actions.

Research on role playing has continued during the past decade and has reconfirmed many times the finding that people tend to believe their own

Figure 9.5 Audience involvement is an effective persuasive technique and is used by many societies, which obtain the participation of their young in routine patriotic activities. American children (*right*) pledge allegiance to the flag and Chinese young people (*left*) read *Quotations from Chairman Mao*.

performances. The emotional aspect of role playing in particular seems to affect attitude change.

Fearing Is Believing.   Many attitude-change studies have been criticized because they have dealt with issues of relatively little importance to subjects. For example, Janis and King's topics were peripheral, including uncontroversial topics such as finding a cure for the common cold and whether the United States would gain or lose movie theaters in the future. Irving Janis and Leon Mann (1965) confronted the problem head-on by investigating attitude change *and* behavior change in response to messages about a topic that was important to all their subjects—cigarette smoking. Despite their desires to quit smoking, all of Janis and Mann's subjects had found themselves totally unable to reduce their cigarette consumption. Communications designed to change these attitudes generally do not work. Even appeals to fear, such as those that emphasize the danger of lung cancer and its consequences, are often unsuccessful (Janis, 1967; Leventhal, 1972). The experimenters decided to force their subjects to confront smoking problems by role playing the traumatic experience of having cancer.

All twenty-six women that Janis and Mann selected were between the ages of eighteen and twenty-six and were moderate to heavy smokers, consuming at least fifteen cigarettes daily. After the experimenters assessed their subjects' attitudes toward smoking with questionnaires, they assigned some women to role play a cancer victim and asked others to passively listen to a tape recording of a role-play subject without themselves participating. Each woman was asked to imagine that the experimenter was a doctor to whom she had gone for treatment of a bad cough. The scenes to be enacted were during her third visit to the doctor when she received the results of the x-ray and other medical tests. The experimenters gave the women in the role-playing group the following sketches of five scenes and asked each to act out the scenes as realistically as she could.

SCENE 1:   *Soliloquy in waiting room:*
A woman is worried about her diagnosis and experiences conflict about whether or not to smoke another cigarette.

SCENE 2:   *Conversation with physician as he gives diagnosis:*
The experimenter tells the woman that he will be frank and honest and unfortunately has bad news. She has a small malignant mass just under the right lung (shows actual x-ray) and an operation is needed as soon as possible. There is a moderate possibility of successful surgery.

SCENE 3:   *Soliloquy while physician phones for hospital bed:*
The woman expresses her feelings about the bad news.

SCENE 4:   *Conversation with physician about arrangements for hospitalization:*
The physician asks the woman for information about medical coverage and family background and tells her that she will be in the hospital about six weeks.

SCENE 5:   *Conversation about causes of lung cancer:*
Physician talks about the patient's smoking history and asks if she is aware of the link between smoking and lung cancer. He discusses the urgent need to stop smoking.

The results were dramatic. The role-playing experience influenced subjects to mobilize their attitudes as well as their actions to decrease their cigarette smoking. Specifically, role-playing subjects changed more than passive subjects toward (1) believing that smoking causes lung cancer, (2) fearing personal harm from smoking, and (3) intending to quit smoking. And when asked two weeks later about their smoking habits, subjects who had played the role were smoking an average of 10.5 fewer cigarettes a day than they had been two weeks earlier (down from 24.1 to 13.6 cigarettes, on the average). In contrast, the drop in cigarette consumption among subjects who had not played the role was less than half the drop reported by those who had (4.8 fewer cigarettes smoked a day). Apparently, the fear elicited by the thought of death from cancer was magnified by the experience of role playing and goaded Janis and Mann's subjects into greater vigilance in curbing their smoking.

And the results lasted. Janis and Mann conducted their original sessions in July 1963. Two follow-up surveys of the same women were made in March 1964 and in January 1965 (Mann and Janis, 1968). In addition to the group that had played the role and the group that had not, a third group of women from the same school, a control group, received no treatment—neither role playing nor tape recordings. Follow-up interviews of all the subjects were conducted by telephone, so that they were divorced from the original experimental setting. The smoking patterns of the three groups during the eighteen months that followed the role playing are shown in Figure 9.6. Cigarette consumption dropped approximately three cigarettes daily per subject in all three groups after the Surgeon General's report linking smoking to lung cancer was published in February 1964. As illustrated in Figure 9.6, the effects of role playing persisted for at least eighteen months, and at the end of that time, role-playing subjects were smoking about as many cigarettes per day as they had been just after the role-playing experience. The Surgeon General's report apparently reinforced the effects of the role playing and kept cigarette consumption at relatively low levels. The effects of the warning endured longest when subjects had either played the role or listened to the recording of a role-playing subject, whereas the effects of the warning gradually dissipated (although not completely) in subjects who had neither played the role nor listened to the recording.

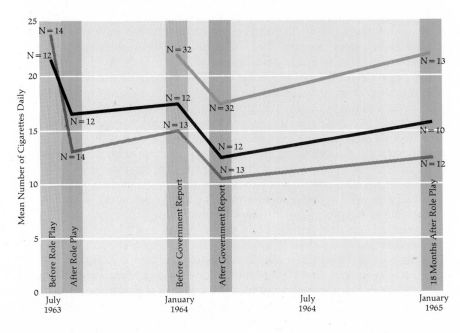

Figure 9.6 Role playing the experience of having cancer can have long-term effects in dramatically reducing cigarette consumption, Mann and Janis reported in 1968. The Surgeon General's report on the harmful effects of smoking was equally effective in reducing the short-term smoking habits of role players, subjects who passively listened to the role play, and those in a control group who were exposed to neither. But the Surgeon General's report had the most eduring impact on the role-playing group.

These findings provide dramatic evidence that role playing can have power-ful effects on attitudes as well as on behavior and that these effects are not limited to opinions about topics that are of little concern to subjects.

Social Judgment: Frames of Reference

Consider a situation in which two people judge the temperature of a pail of water. The actual temperature is, say, 65 degrees. The measure of their attitudes is simple: Each person reports that the water is either very cold, cold, moderately cold, moderately warm, warm, or very warm. Each person puts a hand in the water, and the reactions are surprising. One subject reports that the water is moderately warm and the other says it is moder-ately cold. Prior to putting their hands in the water, the subject who thought the water rather warm had stuck his hand in 30-degree water and the other subject had just touched 100-degree water. The two subjects had thereby acquired different frames of reference, and their judgments were consequently affected. Because researchers do not always know the frames of reference subjects use, they are not always aware of the judgmental predispositions that affect their subjects' responses and thus their attitudes.

When Muzafer Sherif and Carl Hovland edited the final volume of the Yale attitude-change program in 1961—a volume titled *Social Judgment*—they discussed the judgmental factors that affect attitude change and par-ticularly the individual's responses to the communicator's attitudes.

According to Sherif and Hovland, the same argument from a com-municator will not be perceived in the same way by all who are exposed to it. People make judgments that researchers must take into account if they are to understand attitude change. In particular, people make judgments about incoming messages on the basis of their previous experiences. These experiences need not even be by way of direct contact with an attitude object; some of the most extreme opinions that people hold they acquire through religious, moralistic, or ideological instruction and are based on faith rather than direct contact. For example, Christians believe in the divinity of Jesus without having met the man, people acquire attitudes toward heroin without having experienced it, and schoolchildren come to believe in objects called atoms that they cannot see. Although they may be difficult for the believer to test, beliefs such as these have nevertheless prompted believers to proselytize, fight, and die for their views.

When a belief is firmly held, it may provide a basis for judging a wide variety of objects. Thus, if the belief that God punishes sinners is central to the thinking of an individual who calls himself a Baptist, he may reject objects as diverse as coffee, card playing, the writings of Shakespeare, and Methodists. According to Sherif and Hovland, the statements or objects that an individual accepts or rejects can be represented as a psychological reference scale. The items on an attitude scale that are acceptable fall within a *latitude of acceptance,* and those that are not acceptable fall within a *latitude of rejection.* Sherif and Hovland, with their colleagues, have studied the ways in which personal reference scales reflect what is and is not acceptable to people. Consider the following study.

Alcohol was still prohibited in public places in Oklahoma in 1956. A referendum was held then to enable Oklahoma voters to remain dry or to join the rest of the nation in legalizing liquor. During the campaign preced-ing the referendum, Carl Hovland, O. J. Harvey, and Muzafer Sherif (1957) selected both favorable and unfavorable arguments regarding prohibition from newspapers. From this rather lengthy set of statements, judges chose nine statements that were representative of the controversy. These statements ranged from very much opposed to the sale of liquor—the "dry" position—to very much in favor—the "wet" position. The most extreme statements were the following:

The dry position: Since alcohol is the curse of mankind, the sale and use of alcohol, including light beer, should be completely abolished.

The wet position: It has become evident that man cannot get along without alcohol; therefore there should be no restriction whatsoever on its sale and use. (page 246)

The researchers instructed subjects to read the nine items and to rank them from least to most objectionable. They found that the latitude of rejection for people who held the most extreme views—either for or against prohibition—tended to be significantly greater than for those who held more moderate views. In other words, those with moderate views had what might be called a higher tolerance quotient than did extremists; moderates accepted a wider range of statements than did extremists. Furthermore, when a person was subsequently presented with an additional statement that was relatively moderate but nevertheless opposed to a subject's own position, that person tended to judge the item as being *more extreme* than it actually was. For example, when subjects heard a moderate wet speech, those who adhered to the driest position judged the speech as much wetter than did subjects who agreed with the speaker's stand. And those adherents to the driest position also judged a moderately wet message as wetter than it actually was. Therefore, whether the stimulus is a pail of water or a speech, judgments are highly dependent on a person's frame of reference.

Hovland, Harvey, and Sherif also found that attitude change followed different patterns according to subjects' prior points of reference. The greatest changes of opinion occurred when the position advocated in a communication was closest to that already held by the subject. Subjects heard one of three fifteen-minute taped speeches: one speech advocated an extremely dry position and was judged B on the scale from A to I; another speech advocated an extremely wet position (H on the scale); and another

Figure 9.7 Our perceptions of situations are always influenced by our individual frames of reference. It is not surprising, then, that two individuals can perceive the same situation differently or that one's perception of it varies as particular circumstances vary. Charlie Chaplin's audience, for example, may almost have believed that he found his shoe appetizing during the gold-rush days in which a starving Charlie was stranded in a snow storm with no other food available.

speech offered a moderately wet position (F on the scale). The dry speech was played for a wet as well as for a relatively neutral audience; and the moderately wet speech was played for wet, dry, and neutral subjects.

This study yielded two particularly striking findings, as indicated in Table 9.1. First, relatively neutral subjects were most influenced by extreme speeches (either wet or dry), which apparently predispose people to resist contrary communications. Second, the extreme wet communication produced less attitude change among dry subjects than did the moderate wet communication. Apparently, the closer the advocated position to a subject's original position, the more effective it is likely to be. Thus, for example, it is not surprising that Archie Bunker rarely changes anyone's opinions despite his frequent efforts to do so. In fact, the flagrant exaggerations of reality that he weaves into his diatribes often persuade his audiences to adopt opposite viewpoints.

Any attitude involves judgment. All researchers who study attitude change have utilized methods that require subjects to make judgments. These judgments differ, because each person's frame of reference is based on a different set of experiences. Anyone who wants to understand the available evidence regarding attitude change should be aware of the range of prior experiences that can shape judgments.

COGNITIVE FACTORS IN ATTITUDE CHANGE

Although the learning approach has traditionally dominated social-psychological thinking about attitude change, psychologists interested in attitude organization have contributed many additional insights into the processes by which attitudes change. Their research has dealt with two related concepts: cognitive consistency and cognitive dissonance.

Cognitive Consistency

Chapter 8 explains that cognitive consistency is an organizing principle that helps people find order amidst the complexities of their experiences. This organizing principle also helps people change their attitudes to *restore* consistency when inconsistent or incongruous information disrupts their states of equilibrium. People tend not to be satisfied with conflicting or ambiguous experiences; instead, their attitudes tend to change until their attitudes again form a consistent configuration.

Changes of Heart That Bring Peace of Mind.   One of the earliest and most precise statements of the consistency-striving process in attitude change was formulated by Charles Osgood and Percy Tannenbaum (1955). Chapter 8 describes the semantic-differential technique developed by Osgood and his colleagues. These investigators assumed that both the source and the

Table 9.1   Percentage of Subjects Changing to More Positive Opinions

SUBJECTS	COMMUNICATIONS		
	Wet	*Dry*	*Moderately Wet*
Dry	27.5% (69)*		31.6% (114)
Neutral	52.2 (92)	40.2% (87)	
Wet		24.0 (25)	

*Number of total subjects

Source: Adapted from C. Hovland, O. J. Harvey, and M. Sherif, "Assimilation and Contrast Effects in Reactions to Communication and Attitude Change," *Journal of Abnormal and Social Psychology,* 55(1957), p. 249.

message have values to each individual in the audience, and they arbitrarily demarcated the range of possible evaluations as falling between +3 and −3. They predicted from their model that whenever people experience a discrepancy between the values they place on sources and the values they place on the concepts espoused by those sources, pressures build up that eventually compel them to "homogenize" the two values by bringing them closer together. For example, if your attitude toward Henry Kissinger could be characterized as a relatively positive +2 and your attitude toward an all-out war between the United States and the Soviet Union is −3, then it would be predicted that Kissinger's endorsement of war with the Soviet Union would prompt you to change your attitudes toward both Kissinger and war with the Soviet Union. Specifically, Kissinger could be expected to fall in your esteem and the concept of war with the Soviet Union could be expected to lose some of its horror. By thus realigning your attitudes, you could reduce the discrepancy between your attitudes toward Kissinger and war with Russia and thereby feel more comfortable with your thoughts.

Conflicting values do not always meet halfway when the discrepancy between them is resolved. Some values are more firmly held than others. Thus, if your horror of the prospect of all-out war between the United States and the Soviet Union outweighs your affection for Kissinger, then your evaluation of Kissinger might dive while your view of all-out war

Figure 9.8 When people are incredulous about what they hear or see, as many of the onlookers here appear to be, their attitudes are not likely to undergo change. Incredulity is taken into account in the attitude-change model devised by Osgood and Tannenbaum (1955).

remains as negative as ever. The research data Osgood and Tannenbaum have produced suggest that, in general, preferred sources diminish in value when they endorse disliked concepts and disliked sources gain something when they denounce disliked concepts.

Another factor that sometimes checks attitude change in the face of inconsistent attitudes is *incredulity* when there is too large a discrepancy between source and message for the audience to assimilate. When the audience is incredulous about what it hears or sees, attitudes are not likely to change—at least not for the moment. If you heard that the President had endorsed eliminating all penalties for the use of marijuana, you might think something like, "Surely the President would not have endorsed legalization of marijuana! I had better wait for more informed reports."

One of the most interesting implications of this theory is that the attitude-change process works on both the source and the concept. In other words, if someone you admire supports something toward which you are bitterly opposed, your admiration for that person will be lessened *and* your bitter opposition may be softened. The converse is also implied: A person you dislike can become endeared to you by advocating a position with which you agree, but your feelings toward the position may suffer.

Protecting One's Attitudes. Robert Abelson suggested in 1959 that four strategies could be used by an audience to diminish the discomfort generated by incongruous information. Consider a situation in which a highly positive source endorses a highly negative concept. To use Abelson's own example, suppose that you are a devout Roman Catholic who has just

WHEN PROPHECY FAILS

ABOUT FIFTEEN YEARS AGO on a frosty night, a small group of people huddled together in a clearing awaiting deliverance from world catastrophe. They waited for a spaceship that they believed was coming to rescue them. The news of this arrival had been received by their leader, a woman who had been given the duty of transmitting written messages sent to her from the Guardians of outer space. These messages, often dealing with spiritual matters such as reincarnation and interspace communication, had finally predicted that the world was going to end in a cataclysm. Only the true believers, wherever they might be, would be saved!

Most of the twenty-five to thirty believers were upper-middle-class, well-educated members of the community or were college students. The night of the predicted disaster was a school vacation, so the collegiate followers were instructed to wait at home for the spaceship that would pick them up.

During the weeks prior to the disaster date, the group clung firmly together and vacillated between cordiality and reluctance to disclose their knowledge to outside agents, be they members of the press, curiosity seekers, or potential followers. Those who would be saved were already determined. Nevertheless, three new followers were accepted; although they seemed normal enough in most respects, their names would be very familiar to most students of social psychology: Leon Festinger, Henry Riecken, and Stanley Schachter, now three of the most prominent leaders in the field.

The group of believers was doomed to have its prophecy fail. What would happen to them, many of whom had quit their jobs, spent their savings, given away cherished possessions, and in innumerable ways given signs of commitment to the messages of the Guardians? This was the burning

learned that the Pope endorsed LSD. You might react with one of the following strategies:

Denial: The easiest strategy is to deny the incongruous relationship. The denial in this case might be phrased as follows: "No, the Church disapproves of unnatural interference with normal bodily processes. I don't believe the Pope would do this." This reaction is synonymous with the response Osgood and Tannenbaum called incredulity.

Bolstering: This strategy leads the person to seek additional evidence to bolster the stronger of two conflicting evaluations. For example, the devout Catholic might recall all the things the Pope has done that the individual approves of.

Differentiation: This strategy involves splitting the negative element into a "good" and a "bad" part and linking the venerated source only to the "good" part. (For example, "LSD is good for medical treatment in some cases of schizophrenia, and the Pope endorses *that* use.")

Transcendence: This strategy involves subsuming the whole dilemma within a larger scheme that explains the contradiction. ("The Pope is infallible. Therefore, he has good reasons for what he says.")

These strategies are ways by which, when confronted with the inconsistencies that other theories predict will produce attitude change, people are able to resist change and neatly resolve the discrepancies.

Cognitive Dissonance

Consistency theories have generally been quite successful in predicting changes in attitudes. Behavior also can change for purposes of maintaining consistency with attitudes or other actions. For example, if a person's

question for the infiltrators. For two months prior to the date the catastrophe was due and for one month after, the three investigators surreptitiously gathered as much evidence as they could about members' feelings, acts of commitment to group beliefs, and efforts to convert others to their way.

The actual time of deliverance was filled with great tension, confusion, and dismay as the members waited for the spaceship. The arrival time was changed and postponed; finally, after tension had mounted to the breaking point, the announcement came: The world had been saved! Through the spiritual faith and strength of this little band, the danger of holocaust had been prevented! Joy broke out. A new phase of group life began. Henceforth, the faithful who had waited together began a dynamic program of press conferences, photo sessions, a song fest, and other activities and projects. Any skepticism among members prior to that time had completely evaporated. The researchers found,

however, a great difference between lone believers who had spent the night in vigil without the social support of the fellow members and those who had waited together. These lone members were much more likely to turn their backs on the group afterwards.

Although the great upsurge of group activity following the failure of the prophecy seems contrary to normal expectations, it is predictable from Festinger's theory of cognitive dissonance. The idea that members' commitment was to a foolish ideal would be too dissonant to tolerate. Thus, with the help of friends, they supported the notion that they had been saved by their beliefs. Dissonance was reduced by increased commitment. Their great night of trial was a test that gave them the knowledge that they were not fools but courageous saviors of the earth.

Source: Adapted from L. Festinger, H. Riecken, and S. Schachter, *When Prophecy Fails.* (Minneapolis: University of Minnesota Press, 1956).

attitude toward the President changes in the negative direction, that individual is subsequently less likely to vote for the President's reelection or to contribute to his campaign. Unfortunately, the relationships between attitudes and actions are not always so simple. If you are like most people, you may often be so completely absorbed in action that you do not fully understand why you are behaving in just the way you are; at such times it is only afterward that you look back and reflect on the meaning of what you have done. Sometimes people look back in embarrassment or horror, only then expressing regrets such as, "How could I have lost him like that when I love him so" or "I guess I must have said that for the sake of argument." These statements represent a particular type of inconsistency—that between attitudes and behavior. Inconsistency between attitudes and behavior has received enormous attention from researchers, but keep in mind that the theory of cognitive dissonance of which it is a part is broad enough to extend as well to inconsistencies between different attitudes and to inconsistencies between behaviors. Cognitive-dissonance theory has had a profound impact on both the theory and research methods that characterize social psychology.

In 1957 Leon Festinger wrote a book titled *A Theory of Cognitive Dissonance* in which he laid out the rudimentary forms of a theory that has generated a vast amount of research, of argument and counterargument, of theoretical development and counterdevelopment, and of methodological shifts in research strategy. Social psychology has changed a great deal since 1957, and much of the change can be directly traced to Festinger's theory—to elaborations of and reactions against his work.

According to Festinger's theory, two cognitive elements "are in a dissonant relation if . . . the obverse of one element would follow from the other." Such is the case, for example, when a person knows that he is

Figure 9.9   Making a choice between two equally attractive alternatives is one of many instances that may arouse cognitive dissonance. Because all the positive attributes of the rejected young lady are inconsistent with this young man's decision, he must devalue them to reduce his dissonance. Reevaluating the chosen young lady more positively completes his dissonance-reduction process.

III   Encountering Others

among friends but nevertheless feels afraid. These cognitions are dissonant, according to Festinger, because it does not follow logically that a
person should be afraid (one cognition) when in the company of friends (a
second cognition).

A basic premise of dissonance theory is that discrepant cognitions
produce an uncomfortable psychological state—*dissonance*—that people are
motivated to reduce or eliminate. Consider the discrepancy between attitudes and behavior that Hubert Humphrey faced as a result of his stint as
Vice-President. For decades, he had been an articulate spokesman for
international disarmament and other liberal causes. As Lyndon Johnson's
Vice-President, however, he found that his role demanded that he support
the hawkish Administration policy regarding United States' involvement in
Vietnam. At some point, perhaps long before Johnson's decision not to run
for reelection freed Humphrey from the constraints of his role, Humphrey
must have felt a need to reduce the dissonance between his basic antiwar
beliefs and the hawkish position to which he had conformed as Vice-President. He had already behaved as a hawk regarding Vietnam, so that this
behavior was difficult to change. Thus, he could not easily reduce the
dissonance through behavior change; to denounce the policy he had supported would have added to the dissonance. One additional option was to
change his basic attitude—that is, to assume a more positive attitude toward
the war in Vietnam. As it happened, he remained a staunch defender of
United States involvement in Vietnam, even when his role no longer
demanded a hawkish position and when many of his old supporters would
have preferred that he disown Johnson's policy.

The basic premise that people strive to reduce dissonance among their
cognitions has placed dissonance theory in the vanguard of social-
psychological work on attitude change. Dissonance research has focused on
two main areas—the free-choice situation and forced compliance.

Freedom to Choose. We all make decisions as a regular part of our daily
lives. At least we think we do. B. F. Skinner (1971) asserts in his book
Beyond Freedom and Dignity that most of our decisions are actually made
for us by relentless influences in our environments. Regardless of the
sources of our decisions, we nevertheless *think* we make many of them.
Consequently, we feel responsible for the outcomes of our decisions in
varying degrees.

The earliest study of the effects of free choice in resolving dissonance
was conducted by Jack Brehm (1956) in preparation for his doctoral thesis.
He recruited female college students, ostensibly for a market research
study. The manufacturers, so the subjects were told, were planning new
sales campaigns and wanted to assess the product preferences of college
students and of other consumer groups as well. Each subject was told that
she would be recompensed for her time with a gift from one of the manufacturers. Eight products, each worth between $15 and $30, were placed in
front of the subjects: an automatic coffeemaker, an electric sandwich grill, a
silkscreen reproduction, an automatic toaster, a fluorescent desk lamp, a
book of art reproductions, a stopwatch, and a portable radio. Each woman
inspected the items and rated each item on an eight-point scale ranging
from "definitely not at all desirable" to "extremely desirable." The subjects
were subsequently reminded that each would receive one of the items as a
gift. The experimenter explained that, to ensure that everyone would receive a gift she liked, each student would choose between two of the eight

products. Which two products a subject chose from was determined by the experimenter, so that either both of the products were very attractive to her, based on the ratings she had already completed, or one product was very attractive and the other was considerably less attractive. Brehm assumed that a choice between two very attractive products would arouse greater dissonance than would a choice between a highly attractive item and one with considerably less appeal. In fact, Brehm suspected that a choice between two products of highly divergent attractiveness would require no real decision at all. After the women had chosen their gifts, they were asked to read research reports on the products. After reading the reports, the subjects evaluated the eight products again. Table 9.2 shows Brehm's results. As predicted, subjects who chose between two attractive items experienced the most dissonance reduction; they seemed to have a greater need to believe that they had made the right decisions than did subjects who had made less difficult choices. Apparently, for the person who has made a difficult decision, "If I chose it, it *must* be good." On the other hand, dissonance-free subjects showed little tendency to reevaluate more positively the products they chose and to devalue the items they rejected. Many studies since Brehm's have confirmed the conclusion that people tend to glorify the options they choose, especially when the choice is difficult. When there appears to be little choice, people seem to feel little responsibility for the effects of their actions and thus do not feel pressured by dissonant cognitions to change their attitudes. In Brehm's study, a subject's cognition that she had chosen one of two highly desirable items was dissonant with her cognition that she had really wanted both of the items; because her decision was expressed in an irreversible action, her only way of reducing the dissonance she felt was to alter her attitudes toward the items. Brehm's study is thus a classic demonstration that actions can produce attitudes, that at least to some extent people become what they do and come to believe passionately that what they have done is right.

Forced Compliance. As B. F. Skinner asserts (1971), people may not be nearly as free as they think. A variety of external pressures shapes everyone's behavior. People cherish an *illusion of freedom,* according to Skinner, because they disregard the tremendous influence of environmental factors. Dissonance researchers have used this illusion very subtly to demonstrate dissonance-reduction processes. The best example of this type of environmental engineering is the forced-compliance paradigm.

In 1957, Festinger postulated that when people are *forced* to behave publicly in ways that contradict their private beliefs, little dissonance will be

Table 9.2 Reevaluation of Products (Brehm)

| CHOICE | CHANGES IN EVALUATION* | | TOTAL DISSONANCE REDUCTION† |
	Chosen Product	Rejected Product	
One Attractive Product	+.11	0	.11
Two Attractive Products	+.38	−.41	.79

*The figures in the table represent the difference between a first and second rating on a scale from 1.0 (not at all desirable) to 8.0 (extremely desirable).

†Because reduction in dissonance may be accomplished both by raising the desirability of the chosen object and by lowering the desirability of the unchosen one, the totals here represent the algebraic difference in change of ratings (plus and minus signs are disregarded).

Source: Adapted from J. W. Brehm, "Postdecision Changes in the Desirability of Alternatives," *Journal of Abnormal and Social Psychology,* 52(1956), p. 386.

created and attitudes will not change. When, on the other hand, people are influenced to engage in the same behavior in ways that allow them to feel that the choices are theirs, dissonance is aroused. As a result, attitudes will fall in line with actions.

Leon Festinger and J. Merrill Carlsmith (1959) performed what has become a classic experiment. Their findings have since been replicated many times with many types of subjects and with many group tasks. They had subjects perform a very boring task for two hours. After two hours of putting round pegs in round holes and square pegs in square holes, each subject was requested by the experimenter to tell the next subject that the experiment had been fun and exciting. He promised half the subjects $1 for telling this little lie and claimed that the person who was supposed to perform this function in the experiment had failed to show up. He also told them that the decision to "help out" in the experiment was up to them, but the experimenter's anxious manner made it difficult for subjects to refuse. In this and in other forced-compliance situations, the experimenter must apply just enough pressure so that people still feel that they have a choice. The experimenter offered each of the remaining half of the subjects $20 for telling the lie. Although they were given the same "choice" as the other half of the subjects, these subjects probably found it substantially easier to tell the lie. After all, who could refuse to tell a small lie for $20?

After telling the lie to the person they believed would be the next subject, the subjects were referred to the psychology department office, where evaluations of experiments and of experimental subjects were being conducted. Presumably, these evaluations were in no way connected with the experiment. The subjects were asked to evaluate, among other things, the degree to which they had enjoyed the experimental task. Subjects who had been paid $1 reported enjoying the task substantially more than did subjects who had received $20. In fact, on a scale of +3 to −3, the task rated −.73 among subjects paid $20 and +1.36 among subjects paid only $1. In

Figure 9.10 According to Festinger's cognitive-dissonance theory, people who are forced to behave contrary to their beliefs will not experience dissonance and consequent attitude change, whereas individuals who are induced to do so, believing the choice is their own, will modify their attitudes to be consistent with their behavior. Festinger's theory, developed in 1957, would therefore predict significant differences in the attitudes of draftees and of West Point cadets toward the strains, restrictions, and arbitrary rules of army life, although neither draftees nor cadets would likely choose these circumstances if actually given a choice.

other words, subjects who were paid $1 to tell a lie came to believe the lie more than did those who told it for $20.

According to dissonance theory, to say something you do not believe for no good reason is painful and dissonant. And because you cannot deny that you told the lie, you must change your attitude. Thus, subjects paid only $1 "decided" that the task had not been so boring after all. Subjects who were paid $20, on the other hand, were not saying something for no good reason; on the contrary, they had a very good reason for saying something they did not believe. Their behavior was therefore consistent with their desires; there was little or no dissonance to reduce, and so they

THE PEACEKEEPING PROPERTIES OF COMMITMENT

It stands to reason that if you do not much like a group of people and the people in that group do not much like you, you will avoid them if you can. The opinions of the group's members will not affect your attitudes very much, either; you will not feel that you must conform to their ideas. But what if you are attracted to the group and want to remain in contact with it? Or what if you do not like the members very much but feel that you have little choice but to stay in contact? (This sometimes occurs during military service, at school, in work situations, and in some family situations.) If the group does not agree much with you, will you pretend to change your mind just to keep the peace? Or is it likely that instead of just outwardly complying you will really change your mind?

Clearly, social approval from a group and initial agreement with its commonly held attitudes can be great spurs to changes in an individual's attitudes, but in a significant number of instances people also undergo genuine changes of mind in groups that offer them no social approval, as long as group opinion seems united against them. Imagine that your gym volleyball team, of which you are a low-ranking member and to which you do not feel a great deal of attraction, decides that showering after a game is uncalled for, whereas you feel that it is definitely called for. What would be the likely outcome of this disagreement? A major factor in

predicting the attitudinal changes people will undergo is whether or not they feel *commitment* to a group and expect that they must or for some other reason will continue to work with the group, according to Charles Kiesler, James De Salvo, Sara Kiesler, Michael Pallak, and Mark Zanna.

Kiesler and his associates have done numerous studies—with college men, college women, and teen-age boys—to test their hypotheses about conformity to group opinions. In a typical experiment, subjects are incorrectly told that the experiment is designed to see how well groups of strangers can work together on various tasks. In one, the task was to rank objects, including paintings; in another, it was to predict baseball-team standings in a pennant race. Subjects were then asked to size up the group privately. They then performed the task required. Subsequently, on some pretext, each person was given a phony rating of himself or herself ostensibly made by the other members of the group. Some were given high ratings, and others received low ratings. All were told that group opinion favored other rankings. They were then asked to rerank the items although the group would never see the new rankings. The experiments showed that the less others like us, the less we like them and that the less we like them, the less they affect our opinions.

However, this turned out not to be true of people committed to the group—subjects who had expectations that they would meet with it at least could afford psychologically to admit to themselves that the tasks were really rather dull.

Notice that Festinger and Carlsmith's result is just the opposite of the learning-theory prediction of attitude change under these conditions. The learning-theory approach discussed earlier emphasizes the reinforcing effects of rewards and therefore suggests that the $20 reward would produce greater attitude change than would the $1 reward. Notice as well that the behavioral component in this study—verbal expression of an attitude one does not hold—is similar to the one in the role-playing studies in the Yale attitude series. Festinger himself noticed this similarity and, in fact, reinter-

once more. Both committed and uncommitted persons who were led to believe that they were well liked tended to change their opinions in the direction of group opinion, which is the expected effect of social approval. But the least-attracted committed people changed their opinions almost as much, whereas the least-attracted *un*committed people changed theirs hardly at all. In other words, as long as you expect to go on working with a group, your opinions—private as well as public—are likely to change to conform to the group's. Thus, if you initially dissent from the consensus of your volleyball team not to shower, you are likely to think of reasons to forgo showering after volleyball. Furthermore, the change will probably be a lasting one.

Interestingly, if the dissident persons in Kiesler's experiments discovered an ally in the group *before* changing their opinions, they tended to stick by their opinions. But if they found out after conforming, the information had little effect—except that they tended to resent or dislike the would-be ally.

Kiesler and his colleagues emphasize that commitment makes the kind of difference discussed above only when there is little attraction to or actual dislike for the group. He theorizes along these lines: If you are not committed to a group and feel out of harmony with it, you can reject the group and break off with it or you can devalue it by deciding that its opinions are of no particular consequence. But you cannot do either if you are bound to continue with the group; you must make your peace with it and with your

idea of yourself as a person who acts out of conviction.

Commitment, then, leads to a somewhat longer-range view of interactions than lack of commitment. Outwardly complying with a group's opinions without changing your mind is something you can get away with in the short term but not the long. Other experiments by Kiesler and his colleagues suggest that individuals who have become committed to one another—married people, say, or close associates—are less likely than uncommitted people to tolerate behavior from one another that seems to violate social norms. They are more likely to call the other's attention to such behavior and to suggest change than to ignore it. But familiarity does not necessarily explain the willingness to point out a partner's social errors: in the experiments that suggested these conclusions, commitment was created by pairing strangers who thought that they were involved in ranking various occupations.

Sources: Adapted from C. Kiesler, "Attraction to the Group and Conformity to Group Norms," *Journal of Personality,* 31 (1963), pp. 559–569.

————, "Conformity and Commitment," *Trans-Action,* 4 (1967), pp. 32–35.

————, and J. De Salvo, "The Group as an Influencing Agent in a Forced Compliance Paradigm," *Journal of Experimental Social Psychology,* 3 (1967), pp. 160–171.

————, S. Kiesler, and M. Pallak, "The Effect of Commitment to Future Interaction on Reactions to Norm Violations," *Journal of Personality,* 35 (1967), pp. 585–599.

————, M. Zanna, and J. De Salvo, "Deviation and Conformity: Opinion Change as a Function of Commitment, Attraction, and Presence of a Deviate," *Journal of Personality and Social Psychology,* 3 (1966), pp. 458–467.

preted in terms of dissonance theory Janis and King's finding that people come to believe a message more after reading it out loud than after listening to it in silence. Role-playing subjects, Festinger asserted, would have found it dissonant to publicly say (for no good reason) things they did not believe and thus would come to believe the persuasive communications they delivered; to do so constitutes self-persuasion.

A second forced-compliance study amplifies the lessons of the Janis-King experiment. In this study, Elliot Aronson and J. Merrill Carlsmith (1963) exposed children to a room in which there were many toys. After playing with the toys for a while, the children ranked them from most desirable to least desirable. The children were then put into one of two situations. In one situation, the experimenter left the room, threatening to "be very angry with you and take away all the toys" if the child played with his or her second-favorite toy. In the other situation, the experimenter also left the room and forbade the child to play with the second-favorite toy, but he threatened the child with no greater punishment than "I would be annoyed." After a brief period during which the children were free to play with any toy but the forbidden toy, the experimenter returned and had them rerate all the toys. What Aronson and Carlsmith wanted to know was how a child would rate what had previously been the second-favorite toy. Their results were conclusive and have been replicated in many studies. If the command not to play with a toy is enforced with a *severe* threat, there is relatively little change in the ranking of the forbidden toy. But if the threat is a mild one, children tend to diminish the attractiveness of the forbidden toy; dissonance has been aroused because of a discrepancy between liking the toy and not playing with it. A severe threat apparently provides ample external justification for not playing with the toy, but the mild threat does not. Because children in the mildly threatening situation have less justification than if threatened severely for not playing with the toy, they can justify avoidance of the object by changing their attitude toward the toy, diminishing its attractiveness. The implication is: If you want your children to develop their own internal constraints, avoid severe threats of punishment.

Dissonance Arousal and Reduction: A Closer Look

The preceding discussion of free choice and forced compliance has been a brief introduction to cognitive-dissonance theory. Dissonance theory has generated an enormous amount of research, and all of it revolves around two core concepts—arousal and reduction. Dissonance is *aroused* by the simultaneous presence of two or more discrepant cognitions. And because dissonance is an aversive experience, the individual is motivated to *reduce* the discrepancy between cognitions. This process of reducing dissonance apparently is responsible for the high degree of attitude change that typically results when actions are dissonant with attitudes. Dissonance-free situations—whenever decisions come easily—do not appear to stimulate attitude change. These processes of dissonance arousal and dissonance reduction deserve closer examination.

Dissonance Arousal. Free-choice and forced-compliance situations are the two most popular and successful means experimenters have of arousing dissonance. In both these situations, the experimenters manipulate subjects in such a way that they "feel" as though they have freely chosen a course of action that turns out to be discrepant with their prior attitudes. A young subject of Aronson and Carlsmith's might have expressed the dilemma by saying, "I like that toy (or I thought so), but I'm not playing with it."

Dissonance apparently tends to be aroused when we behave in ways that are discrepant with our attitudes without having very good reasons for doing so. An experimenter tries to arouse dissonance by creating or capitalizing on two dissonant cognitions in subjects. The following list summarizes some of the ways, besides the lie-telling and free-play situations, by which researchers have aroused dissonance. Notice that experimenters invoke a wide range of situations, topics, behaviors, and attitudes to arouse dissonance.

1. College women undergo initiation rites before being accepted into a discussion group on the psychology of sex. Women who must read aloud obscene words and descriptions of sexual intercourse experience more dissonance when they later find that the discussion is dull and boring than do women who are subjected to a milder initiation (Aronson and Mills, 1959).

2. Subjects are asked to give a negative evaluation of a confederate they believe is another subject, although they have actually formed a pleasant impression of him. Subjects either are given no choice in the matter and experience little dissonance or can freely choose whether or not to read the negative evaluation and pay the price of high dissonance (Davis and Jones, 1960).

3. Students write an essay favoring the side of the police in a student-police campus incident. Dissonance is higher among students paid $.50 than among those paid $5 (Cohen, 1962).

4. College women choose between two manufacturers' products (toaster or stop-watch, lamp or radio, and so on). The two from which they select are either *both* very desirable (high dissonance) or one is desirable and the other considerably less so (low dissonance) (Brehm, 1956). This study is detailed on pages 303 and 304.

In his original formulation, Festinger (1957) implied that any apparently discrepant cognitions should arouse dissonance. Over the years, it has been a popular exercise to imagine situations in which discrepant cognitions do not seem to imply dissonance and thereby to embarrass the theory. The research on dissonance theory has produced both stable, clear results as well as equivocal, inconsistent results. Theorists have recently concluded that discrepancies of a particular kind, and not just any two discrepant cognitions, arouse dissonance. For example, Aronson (1969) characterizes this kind of discrepancy in the following statement: " . . . although we were not fully aware of it at the time, in the clearest experiments performed to test dissonance theory, the dissonance involved was between a self-concept and cognitions about a behavior that violated this self-concept." Thus, Aronson suggests that what was dissonant in the Festinger and Carlsmith experimental set-ups was not a subject's cognitions that the task was dull and boring and that he or she had nevertheless told someone that it had been fun and interesting; rather, the discrepancy lay between the cognitions "I am a decent, truthful human being" and "I misled a person, I have conned him into believing something that just is not true, he thinks I believe it, and I will have no chance to set him straight because I probably will never see him again."

Elizabeth Nel, Robert Helmreich, and Elliot Aronson (1969) have uncovered evidence that, as Aronson predicted, attitude-behavior discrepancy arouses dissonance only if it somehow alters or challenges the person's self-concept. They varied the degree of dissonance—while holding constant the degree of discrepancy between attitudes and behavior—by varying the amount an audience agreed with subjects' dissonant statements. The experimenters preselected female college students who gave strong *negative* responses to the item, "There should be no legal restrictions on the use of marijuana for people over 21." This item had been one of many, covering many topics, in a small opinion survey.

After each subject had spent about ten minutes answering the questionnaire, which the experimenter said was aimed at assessing values toward controversial issues, each subject was interrupted by a second experimenter who asked her help in recording a video tape about marijuana. The second experimenter told each woman that she was studying attitude change. The role of the subject in this research would be to persuade an audience that among people over 21 marijuana use should not be legally restricted. Thus, each subject performed a behavior that was quite discrepant with her attitude. In addition, each subject was led to believe that the video tape would be viewed by one of three audiences. Although all subjects were told that their audiences would be composed exclusively of students, each woman was told that her audience would either favor legalization, oppose it, or be uncommitted.

Each subject received an outline of arguments that she could use, taped her speech, and was paid $.50 or $5 for her participation. Afterward, the subjects returned to the first experiment and filled out the rest of the survey, which repeated the question about marijuana as it had appeared on the original questionnaire. By comparing subjects' attitudes toward marijuana before and after the video taping, the experimenters found that the most attitude change occurred among subjects who espoused attitudes that were discrepant with their own and that, furthermore, dissonance was greatest—and stimulated the most attitude change—when the audience was neutral.

Apparently, when the audience already had made up their minds about the issue, subjects felt little responsibility for their discrepant actions and therefore had little reason for bringing their attitudes into line with their actions. In contrast, when the audience sounded less resistant to persuasion, subjects seemed to feel more accountable for their actions and therefore to be prompted by dissonance to align their attitudes with their actions —in this case, to soften their attitudes toward marijuana use. The pressure on subjects to change their attitudes increased, of course, when they were paid relatively little to perform the odious task of endorsing marijuana use.

Judging from Nel, Helmreich, and Aronson's study, Festinger's original formulation—that dissonance results anytime actions and attitudes are discrepant—may be inadequate. Early dissonance theory would have led to the prediction that discrepancy will arouse dissonance and thus motivate attitude change regardless of the audience's composition. On the contrary, Nel, Helmreich, and Aronson conclude that dissonance is most likely to be aroused when the consequences of compliant or free behavior are discrepant with the individual's own self-concept. And it seems that our self-concepts are powerfully dependent on the actual or imagined effects of our actions; the knowledge that one has performed a discrepant act apparently is far less threatening than is the possibility that one might mislead others.

Dissonance Reduction. According to cognitive-dissonance theory, dissonance arousal implies dissonance reduction. Dissonance arousal suggests a state of physiological upset, conflict, or tension that the victim will seek to reduce. In his original statement, Festinger proposed that people have at their command three ways of reducing dissonance:

1. They may change their cognitions of their own actions—that is, mentally interpret those actions in order to see them as more consistent with previous actions and attitudes.
2. They may change their cognitions of the environment in order to recall their actions as more constant than the actions actually were.
3. Or they may add *new* cognitive elements—this cannot eliminate dissonance entirely, but it can swamp the dissonant elements with more consonant cognitions and thereby diminish the effects of the dissonant elements.

In general, people find it very difficult to change the facts of behavior. Consequently, they rarely change their cognitions of behavior. And because it is not possible to completely eliminate dissonance by adding consonant cognitions, people are likely to use this mode only for maintaining the status quo—not for reassessing and reorganizing values and other attitudes. In fact, the one form of dissonance reduction that is easy for people afflicted with dissonance to summon is that of changing one's cognitions of salient

The Fox and the Grapes

A fox looked and beheld the grapes that grew upon a huge vine, the which grapes he much desired for to eat them. And when he saw that none he might get, he turned his sorrow into joy, and said, "These grapes are sour, and if I had some I would not eat them."

MORAL: *He is wise which faineth not to desire the thing the which he may not have.*

features of the environment. As a result, whenever a dissonance experiment is conducted, the researchers predict that their subjects' evaluations of environmental elements will change. Thus, experimenters expect subjects to change their attitudes toward toys they do not play with, toward tasks that turn out to be dull, and even toward other people who are dull.

One of the earliest challenges to dissonance theory was made by the learning-theory approach to attitude change, represented by Irving Janis and a team of his colleagues at Yale. They attacked the original Festinger and Carlsmith study, which seemed to show that attitude change increased when incentives diminished. The learning approach would predict the opposite—that maximum attitude change should follow the greatest incentive or reward.

Recall that in Festinger and Carlsmith's forced-compliance study subjects performed a dull task for about two hours and then were asked to tell a waiting subject that the task was fun and exciting. Subjects were paid either $1 or $20 to tell this small lie. Subsequently, in a disguised post-test, subjects who performed the task but did not tell the waiting subject anything about it rated their enjoyment of the experimental task −.45 on a scale of +3 to −3. In contrast, ratings were −.05 for highly paid subjects and +1.35 for low-paid subjects. This result supports dissonance-theory predictions; the difference between the control subjects and the $1 subjects is presumed to reflect the degree of attitude change produced by subjects' attempts to reduce dissonance. However, learning theorists predict that the greater the reward, the more effort subjects will expend in role playing the counterattitudinal position and, therefore, the more likely they will be to persuade themselves of the view they espouse. A learning approach, then, would predict greater attitude change among those subjects who were paid $20 than among those paid $1.

Irving Janis and J. Barnard Gilmore (1965) suggested that high reward did not produce attitude change in Festinger and Carlsmith's study because $20 was too much pay for the task involved: " . . . there are grounds for wondering if the extraordinarily large reward of $20 might have unintentionally generated some degree of suspicious wariness about being exploited by the experimenter or some degree of guilt about being 'bought' to lie to a fellow student."

To test their supposition that an unusually large incentive may inhibit attitude change—by implying that the experiment is being conducted under questionable auspices—Janis and Gilmore asked Yale undergraduates to participate in a brief survey. The experimenters described their project to all subjects as a national survey of students' attitudes toward science and math. But they varied the purpose of the survey by telling some subjects that the survey was being conducted under the auspices of a publicly sponsored national research organization and other subjects that the survey was being sponsored by a new publishing company that was seeking information for an advertising campaign. All subjects were then asked to write short essays proposing that a year of physics and a year of mathematics be added as requirements for all college students. The experimenters supplied the subjects with arguments and had them write their essays *before* being paid either $1 or $20 and filling out a questionnaire measuring their attitudes toward the topic they had written about. Control subjects, on the other hand, were told they would write their essays later, so that they did not role play support for physics and mathematics requirements before being paid and filling out the questionnaire. Thus, any variations in attitude change the questionnaire revealed among control groups would have been results of the varying rewards and could not have resulted from dissonance created by role playing counterattitudinal positions.

The identity of the study's sponsor seemed to make a difference only among subjects who role played support for physics and mathematics requirements. Attitudes changed when their essays would be used by a relatively benevolent-sounding sponsor; they did not change when the sponsor's intentions were admittedly commercial. The importance of the sponsor's intentions and credibility as portrayed to a subject are, therefore, important in determining how acceptable that subject will find the sponsor's opinions and requests—just the prediction Janis and Gilmore made. But their results bore no evidence that the magnitude of reward affected attitude change. And because the main issue was whether incentive or dissonance reduction produces attitude change, this study was not conclusive. Stronger results have been obtained by Alan Elms and Irving Janis (1965), who selected an attitude issue about which subjects may have felt much more strongly than they did about physics and mathematics requirements. Their study was quite similar to Janis and Gilmore's, but the issue was sending American students to the Soviet Union and the sponsor was either the Soviet Union (unfavorable) or the United States (favorable). All subjects were asked to write a favorable essay and were paid $.50 or $10. Acceptance of the proposal was maximum under conditions of overt role playing, favorable sponsorship, and large reward. This finding supports the learning point of view.

The two studies described above, as well as many others, suggest that incentives and the dissonance aroused by inadequate incentives can affect the course of attitude change. In fact, dissonance reduction and monetary rewards may be two types of incentives that motivate attitude change. If so, then it is not surprising that these two forms of incentives interact. Apparently, people are motivated to realign their attitudes by the need to reduce dissonance, provided the discrepancies involve their self-concepts. But when a discrepant situation does not call the self-concept into play, various incentives—including monetary rewards—are generally effective in stimulating the desired attitude change.

The cognitive-dissonance theory of attitude change rests on the assumption that dissonance arousal is an aversive state that motivates dissonance reduction through attitude reorganization. There have been a number of attacks on dissonance theory from many perspectives; the findings of learning theorists have already been examined. Learning theorists have established the power of monetary incentives when the self-concept is not sufficiently challenged by a discrepant act to produce the incentive of dissonance. But perhaps the most successful attack on dissonance theory has centered on the theory's core notion that arousal and reduction of dissonance are the mechanisms of attitude change. The leader of this attack is Daryl Bem.

SELF-PERCEPTION THEORY: WHAT AM I DOING HERE?

An alternative to the cognitive-dissonance explanation of attitude change has been contributed by Daryl Bem (1965). He agrees with the findings dissonance theorists have produced but denies their theory. In particular, Bem has denied the central dissonance assumption that discrepant actions produce psychological conflict, which motivates attitude change. To replace the role of psychological conflict, or dissonance, in motivating change, he has put forth an alternate explanation of how actions change attitudes. The following statement forms the core of Bem's approach to attitudes:

Individuals come to "know" their own attitudes, emotions, and other internal states partially by inferring them from observations of their own overt behavior and/or the circumstances in which this behavior occurs. Thus, to the extent that internal cues are weak, ambiguous, or uninterpretable, the individual is functionally in the same position as an outside observer. . . . (page 2)

Recall that attitudes are measured by inference from some form of behavior such as checking one item on a scale, making a verbal statement, or behaving overtly. An observer can infer a person's attitude by looking at that individual's behavior and the circumstances under which it occurs. Bem's point is that we do exactly the same thing in understanding our own personal attitudes. The average person, like the average social psychologist, infers attitudes from behavior—including his or her own attitudes.

Consider the bored and lying subjects in Festinger and Carlsmith's study. Consider, in fact, the viewpoint of any observer who sees someone endure a boring task, hears that person exalt the experience to someone else, and knows that the person was paid $1 to do so. In guessing the real attitude of the subject toward the seemingly dull task, the observer can disregard the possibility of financial motivation; compensation was a mere $1. The lack of financial motivation somehow suggests that the subject's real attitudes are responsible, thereby freeing the observer to assess the attitude directly. In this situation, the observer will probably assume that the other person's attitude and behavior are consistent. In contrast, if the subject has been compensated $20, the observer might conclude that the financial incentive is sufficient to explain the behavior; thus, the observer will tend to look no further for inferences about the subject's private views.

Bem believes that people regard their own behavior much as an observer would. Individuals who are offered $20 to perform a relatively easy task, such as talking with another subject for a minute or two, may ask no questions of themselves. In the Festinger and Carlsmith $1 condition, subjects might surmise that because the environment provides no sufficient incentives for their actions, their actions must reflect their true attitudes toward the task, which they consequently recall as more interesting than it

Figure 9.11 Bem (1965) suggests that we infer our attitudes from our own behavior. It is possible that the chronological sequence of self-portraits shown here, which were painted by Vincent Van Gogh during the period of time from 1887 to 1889, reflect the artist's self-perceptions of his own maladaptive behavior; in fact, during the time period when Van Gogh painted these self-portraits, he was becoming increasingly disturbed and victim to radical mood changes. Wilkins reported in 1971 that some psychotherapists are applying Bem's approach to clinical situations by encouraging patients to cognitively examine and reevaluate their fears and anxieties. By encouraging patients to cease their behavioral expressions of anxiety, for example, these therapists have found that patients often experience a subsequent decrease in cognitively experienced anxiety.

actually was. Thus, Bem concludes, subjects did not *change* their attitudes to reduce an unpleasant motivational state, they *inferred* their attitudes from their behavior and the circumstances in which it occurred. People often make inferences about their attitudes by observing their own behavior. Thus, Hubert Humphrey may have felt no conflict between his attitudes and his actions as vice-president; he may simply have assumed, for example, that the Vietnam War was justified because he had supported it.

To demonstrate the uniformity of the perceptions of self and observers, Daryl Bem (1967) replicated the Festinger and Carlsmith study, using subjects rather than accomplices as observers. Seventy-five college students participated in a study that was designed, the experimenter claimed, to "determine how accurately people can judge another person." The subjects heard a tape recording of a college sophomore, Bob Downing, stating that he had participated in an experiment involving two motor tasks, which he described in detail. Control subjects rated Bob's attitude toward the task. The experimental subjects were told that Bob had accepted an offer of either $1 or $20 to tell the next subject that the tasks had been fun. Bem's subjects then heard Bob telling a girl in the waiting room that the tasks had been fun and enjoyable. When Bem had his subjects estimate Bob's attitude toward the tasks, their estimates as observers were identical to the evaluations of the tasks that Festinger and Carlsmith's liars had made. When the price was $1, observers estimated Bob's attitude to be more favorable toward the tasks than did observers who had been told that Bob had received $20 or those who had been told nothing about monetary incentives.

Simulations by Bem and other psychologists, which encompass a variety of tasks, attitudes, and subjects, constitute a significant challenge to the dissonance-theory explanation of Festinger and Carlsmith's findings. However, several investigators have in turn challenged Bem, charging that his procedures were not equivalent to Festinger and Carlsmith's because he failed to provide his observers with one salient piece of information about Bob that Bob would have about his own attitudes—namely, Bob's attitudes prior to the experiment. In a series of studies, two teams of researchers gave observers the premanipulation attitudes of the "subjects" and found that their observers could no longer predict the effects of distasteful actions on those who perform them (Jones, Linder, Kiesler, Zanna, and Brehm, 1968; Piliavin, Piliavin, Loewenton, McCauley, and Hammond, 1969). Daryl Bem and H. Keith McConnell (1970) countered with a study in which they demonstrated that real subjects who perform dissonant actions cannot recall their own initial attitudes at the time of the final assessment. Rather, subjects seemed to *misremember* their original attitudes toward the monotonous tasks and to see their postmanipulation attitudes as the same attitudes that motivated them to do the tasks. Bem and McConnell interpret the experience of misremembering as different from attitude change.

The issue has not been resolved, and the argument continues. Self-perception theory can explain a large number of experimentally generated findings. But dissonance theory still seems to most social psychologists to be the best explanation of how actions shape attitudes in situations that involve strong personal opinions and self-concepts.

The controversy should not be allowed to obscure the fact that dissonance researchers have demonstrated two very important generalizations: Choice between objects or between courses of action is usually followed by enhanced evaluation of the chosen alternative and devaluation of rejected alternatives. And when people do things that they do not want to do (or do not do something that they would like to do) for inadequate reasons, they tend to bring their attitudes into line with their behavior.

The next chapter examines some of the specific means by which parents, educators, peers, political propagandists, advertisers, and other agents of social influence attempt to sway people. Their efforts are not always successful, and Chapter 10 also discusses the factors that increase or decrease the likelihood that a given communication will be accepted.

SUMMARY

Most research on attitudes is central to the topic of attitude change. One approach to attitude change is through *learning theory,* which considers attitudes to be internal, implicit responses that are subject to the principles of learning. Attitudes are relatively stable, but when outside influences are inconsistent with attitudes, learning may occur and attitudes may change. Whether or not learning takes place depends on a variety of factors that fall into four categories: the *communicator,* the *message,* the *channel,* and the *audience.*

One of the most important aspects of the communicator is his or her *credibility.* Credible communicators produce greater attitude change than do noncredible communicators, although the effects of credibility can be reduced when only the content of a message and not the source persists in memory over time. Regarding the message, the organization of arguments and order in which they are presented are also important in their effects on attitudes. *Fear* is a technique often used to change attitudes, but under certain conditions it backfires. If the message contains a *minimal* appeal to fear and suggests methods by which those in the audience can effectively reduce their anxiety, then the audience is likely to accept it; too much anxiety may result in rejection of the message. Regarding the audience, some people are much easier to persuade than others are. For example, the most easily persuaded males tend to be low in confidence or self-esteem. Also, taking an active role in expressing opinions often alters attitudes more than does being passively persuaded. One reason for the convincing effects of playing a role is people's desire to change their attitudes in order to make their attitudes consistent with their actions.

Various experiences also help to shape *frames of reference*—learned standards by which people judge their experiences. Social psychologists, in representing attitudes on a psychological reference scale, delineate a *latitude of acceptance* for acceptable statements or objects and a *latitude of rejection* for unacceptable statements or objects. Apparently, people who are moderate in their attitudes toward an issue have greater latitudes of acceptance than do extremists at either end of the scale. Extremists seem to harbor a particularly strong tendency to resist contrary communications and to misperceive the contents of those communications.

Cognitive-consistency theorists see attitude changes as a function of the organization of attitudes. People strive to maintain consistent relationships between attitude objects. Inconsistent ideas produce what Leon Festinger terms *cognitive dissonance*—an uncomfortable psychological state that people try to reduce or eliminate. In the process of reducing inconsistencies, human beings tend to devalue a communicator when that person endorses disliked concepts. Likewise, disliked communicators gain value when they denounce disliked concepts. When a high degree of discrepancy exists between the values the audience places on the communicator and on the message, the audience can reduce its discomfort in four ways: *denial* (based on *incredulity,* which is produced by too large a discrepancy between source and message), *bolstering* (finding additional evidence to support the source or the message), *differentiation* (splitting the negative cognition into a "good" part and a "bad" part and linking the respected source to only the "good" part), and *transcendence* (explaining the dilemma as part of a larger scheme).

When people seem to have little choice or are forced to comply, they feel little responsibility for their actions and do not feel pressured by dissonant cognitions to change their attitudes. The *illusion of freedom,* therefore, is an important component of attitude change when actions are discrepant with initial attitudes. Dissonance-free situations—whenever decisions come easily—do not appear to stimulate attitude change. Recent research on dissonance suggests that behavior arouses dissonance primarily when it is inconsistent with or challenges the individual's self-concept.

One alternative explanation to dissonance theory states that just as an observer infers what other people think from what they do, individuals often infer their own attitudes from their own actions. However, dissonance theory still seems a valuable explanation for the ways in which actions shape attitudes in situations that involve strong personal opinions. In addition to this explanation, it has yielded two concrete generalizations: When people feel that they have chosen freely, they are likely to regard the chosen object more favorably than the one they reject; and when they feel that they have been forced to choose one object over another, people are less likely to enhance the value of the chosen alternative. And when they cannot adequately justify their actions, they often change their attitudes to be consistent with their actions.

SUGGESTED READINGS

Aronson, Elliot. "Mass Communication, Propaganda, and Persuasion," in E. Aronson, *The Social Animal.* New York: W. H. Freeman, 1971, pp. 47–88.

Bem, Daryl. *Beliefs, Attitudes, and Human Affairs.* Belmont, Calif.: Brooks/Cole, 1970.

Cohen, Arthur. *Attitude Change and Social Influence.* New York: Basic Books, 1964.

Festinger, Leon. *A Theory of Cognitive Dissonance.* Stanford, Calif.: Stanford University Press, 1957.

Zimbardo, Philip, and Ebbe Ebbesen. *Influencing Attitudes and Changing Behavior.* Reading, Mass.: Addison-Wesley, 1969.

NOW I HAVE KNOWN you
And knowing you

Now i
HAVE KNOWN ME
CHAN SEI GHOW

IV

INTERACTING WITH OTHERS: LIFE & DEATH TOGETHER

10
Social Influence:
Advice & Consent

Senator Short votes for a bill that would permit the president to give weapons to an underdeveloped country—a bill that he actually feels is unwise.

Nancy Nichols refuses to wear the sturdy new winter coat her mother has purchased for her but insists on wearing a thin and tattered cape from a band uniform instead.

Sergeant Murphy shoots thirty bullets into a band of Asian villagers, although the action makes him violently ill.

Ron Jacobs grows a dashing beard during his vacation in the Rockies, but in spite of his fondness for his new visage shaves it off before returning to the office.

Mary McCanney forces herself to guzzle beer at a fraternity party although she privately loathes beer.

NONE OF THESE PEOPLE SEEMS to be acting very logically, and most of us may feel that we would not do the same things under similar circumstances. However, these varied behaviors are responses to similar forces—forces of social influence—and we are all constantly subject to their effects. Because of the immense power of social influence in guiding human behavior, social psychologists have long been drawn to the topic. In this chapter their major paths of inquiry are traced.

Many years ago, experimental psychologists discovered what they came to call the *autokinetic phenomenon.* When they seated subjects in an entirely darkened room and exposed them to a stationary pinpoint of light, for reasons still not entirely understood, the subjects reported seeing the light move. And when the light was turned off and then on again, the subjects reported seeing it move again, although not necessarily

321

in the same direction or for the same distance as they reported seeing it move the previous times.

A social psychologist, Muzafer Sherif (1935), used this procedure to investigate the effects of social influence. Sherif believed that human beings in situations without norms quickly construct their own, and he employed the autokinetic phenomenon to demonstrate the process by which social norms develop.

Sherif exposed each subject to a pinpoint of light several times. After turning the light on each time, he asked the subject to tell him how far the light had moved. After a while the range of the subject's judgments stabilized; each subject reported a small, fixed range within which the light moved. For example, the subject might first have reported that the light moved two inches, then twelve, then five; later, he was more likely to report, say, five inches, then four, then six, and so forth. In essence, the subjects established their own norms.

SOURCES OF SOCIAL INFLUENCE

After demonstrating that subjects individually construct their own norms for the apparent movement of the stationary light, Sherif sought to discover what would happen if two conflicting norms clashed. He thus selected groups of two or three subjects who already had established dissimilar norms. When two or three subjects were put together in a darkened room and announced their judgments one after the other over a series of trials, Sherif found them influencing one another. For example, if one subject had established a norm of nine inches and the other had established a norm of

Our normal expectations about reality are created by a social consensus. We are taught how to see and understand the world. The trick of socialization is to convince us that the descriptions we agree upon define the limits of the real world. What we call reality is only one way of seeing the world, a way that is supported by a social consensus.

—CARLOS CASTANEDA

Figure 10.1 When faced with ambiguity and no available objective reference points, human beings attempt to construct their own realities. The construction of reality is usually attempted by seeking the opinions or observing the behavior of others and seems to provide the impetus for a good deal of social influence. The quotation gives expression to this phenomenon. This theme can also be seen in the work of M.C. Escher, including this lithograph (*right*).

IV   INTERACTING WITH OTHERS

three inches, their norms were likely to converge eventually at about six inches. Sherif's study suggests that, failing to perceive a stable and unambiguous reality, people *construct* a reality and, moreover, that they use one another as points of reference in constructing that reality.

The Need for Social Comparison

On the basis of Sherif's work and that of other researchers, Leon Festinger (1954) has developed a theory of social-comparison processes that seeks to account for the convergence of opinions within a group. The theory states the conditions under which discrepancies of opinion within a group will stimulate members to reduce the discrepancy. Festinger postulates that we are all driven to evaluate the correctness of our opinions. According to Festinger, we are not content with our own opinion of the President, of a movie we have seen, or of a friend; we want to find out if we are *right.* In effect, Festinger assumes that every person is an amateur scientist who seeks to test his or her opinions against reality.

Festinger believes that everyone—scientist and layman alike—prefers objective tests when objective standards are available. But when objective and unambiguous standards are not available in reality, people will seek to evaluate the correctness of their opinions by comparing them to the opinions of others. The need for norms apparently is so compelling that people will seek out the opinions of others, even when the availability of only ambiguous, subjective standards renders such a test irrelevant.

Festinger further assumes that, given the unavailability of objective points of comparison, the tendency to compare one's opinions with those of others decreases as the difference between their opinions and one's own increases. We do not seek to compare our opinions with those of other people who are very unlike ourselves, but are rather much more at ease comparing opinions with a relatively similar other. For example, if you consider yourself a member of the counterculture, you probably will not be tempted to compare your attitudes toward work with those of a fraternity or sorority member, because a more similar other—one who comes closer to sharing your basic aims and values—is almost certainly available. To discuss your opinions with a dissimilar other would result in less certainty and conviction than you had before—an undesirable outcome if it is true that people want assurance from others that their opinions are correct.

Festinger hypothesized that, given the three conditions just described—the drive to evaluate one's opinions, the tendency to evaluate them by comparison with others when objective standards are unavailable, and the tendency to select similar others for comparison—people seek to reduce discrepancies of opinion between themselves and those they choose as points of comparison. Consequently, pressures toward uniformity of opinions inevitably arise when people interact for long in groups of two or more. These pressures impel individual members to change their attitudes toward those of others in the group and also to attempt to convince other members to move closer to their own.

Festinger's theory accounts for the social-influence process found in Sherif's study of the autokinetic phenomenon; subjects wanted to be correct in their opinions about the movement of the light, but lacking an objective test, were influenced by (and in turn influenced) the judgments of the others in the group.

But the need to evaluate opinions is not the only variable at work when people influence one another. Social psychologists have learned a great deal about social-influence processes from their studies of conformity and obedience. These two phenomena are examined next to see what they can teach about social influence.

Conformity

You have volunteered to take part in a psychological study of perception. You and seven other subjects are seated in front of two cards on which there are lines of varying lengths. On one card is a "standard" line and on the other card are three lines. You are asked by the experimenter to compare the standard to the lines on the other card and, when called on, to tell him which of the three lines is equal in length to the standard.

The experiment proceeds without incident. All subjects agree that the standard is clearly equal in length to the second of the three lines. For a second set of cards, the choice is equally obvious. On a third set, the choice seems clear at first, but now you cannot be sure. You had thought that the second line was equal to the standard, but one after another of the other subjects, who are called on before your turn comes, indicates that the first line is equal in length to the standard. The first line had seemed to you at least three-fourths of an inch shorter than the standard. But why should the other students see it differently? Are you sitting at a bad angle? Are the others all correct and you wrong? Finally, it is your turn. Will you stand alone as a minority of one, or will you go along with the unanimous majority? If you go along with the majority, as most subjects actually did, you will have conformed.

The situation just described was used by Solomon Asch (1956) in his classic demonstration of conformity. All the "subjects" but one were confederates of the experimenter, instructed to give wrong answers at predetermined times. It is true that most of us conform to a great many popular standards. But it is surprising that we conform on matters about which we are asked to be honest and in which the evidence is clear, even though others have reported seeing the matter differently. Yet Asch found that subjects in his experiment went along with the incorrect majority on 32 percent of the trials in which the confederates gave wrong answers. Furthermore, the *incidence* of these errors did not vary significantly with the *size* of the errors that the majority made.

After the completion of the experiment, Asch conducted extensive interviews with both independent and yielding subjects. Among independent subjects Asch found that the basis for independence could reside in any of several sources. Some subjects based their independence on a thorough confidence in their own perceptions, which enabled them to resist group pressure; for others, independence from group norms was a result of being withdrawn from the others; and many subjects were independent despite considerable doubt.

The erroneous judgments reported by yielding subjects seem to reflect three basic ways in which social influence by the majority was accepted by the minority: through *distorted actions, distorted judgments,* and *distorted perceptions.* Many subjects—victims of their own distorted actions—were aware that their perceptions differed from those of the others and, moreover, were confident of the accuracy of their perceptions. But they nevertheless made conscious decisions to conform anyway. For example, one subject who had consciously betrayed the evidence of his perceptions explained his decisions to conform this way: "I figured, What's the sense of

Figure 10.2 These two cards are examples of those shown to subjects during Asch's (1956) conformity experiments. Subjects were asked to judge which of the comparison lines was similar to the standard. The task was actually easy; individuals not subjected to group pressure chose the correct line in more than 99 percent of the trials. However, individuals subjected to group pressure conformed to the incorrect judgments of the "unanimous" majority 32 percent of the time.

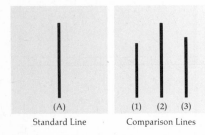

(A)

Standard Line

(1) (2) (3)

Comparison Lines

IV Interacting With Others

my giving another answer [not that of the majority]? If they are wrong, then I'll be wrong too, and if they're right, I'll be wrong." Another subject simply stated: "I agreed less because they were right than because I wanted to agree with them." Still another subject's remark reveals the humorous implications of a conformist imperative: "If I knew we were supposed to disagree, I would have."

But the effects of wanting to conform may not always be as superficial as this last statement suggests. Subjects who erred because of distorted judgments had lost confidence in the accuracy of their own perceptions and had assumed that the majority was right and they were wrong. Some subjects reported straining to adjust their perceptions to the majority judgments. The determination to conform may have actually resulted in altered perceptions. Subjects who yielded to majority influences often dramatically underestimated the number of their errors in the postexperimental interviews, reporting only one or two of an actual ten or twelve errors or altogether refusing to admit that they had made any errors at all or that they had been influenced by the majority. Apparently, a few subjects were completely unaware of any discrepancies between their perceptions and majority opinions.

Asch's findings suggest that there are qualitatively different types of conformity. His findings of distortions at the levels of action, judgments, and perceptions correspond to Herbert Kelman's (1961) distinctions between three processes of social influence: *compliance,* in which people allow themselves to be influenced in order to elicit some favorable action from the agents of influence; *identification,* which involves adopting others' standards because those standards have become associated with relationships that are satisfying in their own right; and *internalization,* or acceptance of influence because it is consistent with the individual's existing value system. According to Kelman, internalization is the least superficial and the most durable of these three types of social influence.

Kelman (1961) has also made a cruder distinction between *public conformity* and *private acceptance.* In the context of Asch's experiment,

Figure 10.3 The observed reactions of two of Asch's subjects—one who did not yield to the incorrect majority and one who did.

Independent

After a few trials he appeared puzzled, hesitant. He announced all disagreeing answers in the form of "Three, sir; two, sir." At Trial 4 he answered immediately after the first member of the group, shook his head, blinked, and whispered to his neighbor, "Can't help it, that's one." His later answers came in a whispered voice, accompanied by a deprecating smile. At one point he grinned embarrassedly and whispered explosively to his neighbor: "I always disagree—darn it!" Immediately after the experiment the majority engaged this subject in a brief discussion. When they pressed him to say whether the entire group was wrong and he alone right, he turned upon them defiantly, exclaiming: "You're probably right, but you may be wrong!" During the experimenter's later questioning, this subject's constant refrain was: "I called them as I saw them, sir."

Yielder

This subject went along with the majority in eleven out of twelve trials. He appeared nervous and somewhat confused, but he did not attempt to evade discussion at the close of the experiment. He opened the discussion with the statement: "If I'd been first I probably would have responded differently." This was his way of saying that he had adopted the majority estimates. The primary factor in his case was loss of confidence. He perceived the majority as a decided group, acting without hesitation: "If they had been doubtful I probably would have changed, but they answered with such confidence." When the real purpose of the experiment was explained, the subject volunteered: "I suspected about the middle—but tried to push it out of my mind." It is of interest that his suspicion did not restore his confidence or diminish the power of the majority.

subjects sometimes conformed for the sake of going along with the majority and at other times could not recognize their conformity as such.

Asch has conducted many variations of his initial conformity study. He obtained one of his most provocative findings when he planted one confederate among seven true subjects. Ironically, the confederate's incorrect responses were greeted with laughter by the group. Group members little suspect their dependence on each other. The laughter of the true subjects gave way to respect when as few as three confederates, instructed to disagree, were placed in the group.

Richard Crutchfield (1955) has improved on the technique Asch developed and has demonstrated that it is possible to test conformity among several subjects at the same time. In a typical Crutchfield experiment, five subjects sit in neighboring booths. They can neither see nor hear one

THE
GREENING
OF THE
BLUE

MOST RESEARCH ON conformity tends to show the power of majority-group pressure on a pitiful minority. The steam-roller effects of majority rule are investigated and regretted. But perhaps equally treacherous is the power of a small minority over the majority, especially over a benign, trusting, unsuspecting majority. Three French social psychologists created a situation in which a tenacious, vocal, and deft minority managed to reshape a perceptual norm that the majority had adhered to for about fifteen years.

Groups of four female subjects, plus two confederates, participated in a study that was ostensibly concerned with measuring perceptions of light intensity and color. After pretests that precluded the possibility that any of the subjects had visual difficulty, the subjects were required to name the color of each of thirty-six slides, all of which had been selected from the blue dimension of the color spectrum. Whereas virtually all of the subjects in the control group called all of the slides blue, the confederates were able to exert a strong influence on the perceptions of the subjects. Both of the confederates called all of the slides green. At least a third of the subjects named at least one of the colors green. In some experimental groups, as many as 57 percent of the subjects responded that one or more slides was green. In other groups, no one mentioned green but the confederates.

At first glance it would appear that groups in which no one was swayed by the two confederates had more confidence or greater clearheadedness

than did the other groups. However, evidence to the contrary was revealed in a second experiment that seemed to subjects to be unrelated to the first. In this second experiment, another experimenter entered the room and requested that the subjects privately engage in a color discrimination test. Each subject saw sixteen disks from the blue-green zone of a spectrum presented in random order a total of ten times each.

Compared with subjects who had not undergone the "greening" experience, the subjects who had undergone it named many more colors green than blue in the second experiment. Curiously, the subjects who did not declare any slides green in the first experiment were more likely to change their perceptions and see green where others saw blue than were those who had gone along with some of the confederates' green choices. When suppressed, any inclination to call colors green during the public session seemed to have an effect that was delayed until choices could be made privately.

Even when they had publicly resisted an incorrect opinion, a majority of subjects were influenced to label colors differently than they had been labeling the colors since childhood. How much less difficult it must be for a determined majority when the attitude objects are not physical but ideological.

Source: Adapted from S. Moscovici, E. Lage, and M. Naffrechoux, "Influence of a Minority on the Responses of a Majority in a Color-Perception Task," *Sociometry,* 32 (1969), pp. 365–380.

another. An experimenter projects slides with a variety of designs in front of each of them and asks for judgments. They are told that the responses of their fellows will be indicated by lights in each booth, and each is told that he will be the last to respond. Each watches four lights go on in his booth and he assumes that the lights indicate the choices of other subjects. But the indicated choices are in fact made by the experimenter, who is operating a master control panel. Using this technique, Crutchfield has been able to enlarge upon Asch's insights into conformity. One of the most interesting things Crutchfield has done is to extend Asch's findings into the area of attitudes, including attitudes toward the self. For example, when Crutchfield questioned military officers privately, all said that they believed they would make good leaders. But when questioned again under the conditions Crutchfield had devised to test conformity, 37 percent conformed to the humble "self-reports" of their fellow officers and denied that they believed they would make good leaders.

The Crutchfield technique was used by Read Tuddenham and Philip MacBride (1959) to see just how far conforming subjects would go in accepting opinions endorsed by a unanimous majority. The experimenters found that extreme conformists would endorse statements as absurd as the following:

1. The United States is largely populated by old people, 60 to 70 percent of the total population being over 65 years of age.
2. Male babies have a life expectancy of 25 years.
3. Men are, on the average, eight to nine inches taller than women.
4. People in the United States eat, on the average, six meals a day. (page 260)

Stanley Milgram (1961) used Asch's technique to explore the possibility of cross-national differences in conformity. He hypothesized that the French would prove less conforming than Norwegians—a hypothesis that flowed quite naturally from Milgram's observations of the differences in everyday social behavior between members of the two nationalities. Here are some of his informal observations:

I found Norwegian society highly cohesive. Norwegians have a deep feeling of group identification, and they are strongly attuned to the needs and interests of those around them. Their sense of social responsibility finds expression in formidable institutions for the care and protection of Norwegian citizens. . . .
Compared with the Norwegians, the French show far less consensus in both social and political life. The Norwegians have made do with a single constitution, drafted in 1814, while the French have not been able to achieve political stability within the framework of four republics. . . . The extreme diversity of opinion found in French national life asserts itself also on a more intimate scale. There is a tradition of dissent and critical argument that seeps down to the local *bistro*. (page 51)

Milgram conducted his study in Paris and Oslo, using appropriately matched samples of students in both cities. Subjects judged the lengths of acoustic tones rather than of lines, and in five separate variations of the study, the French were consistently less conforming than the Norwegians. It was not unusual for a French subject to curse his apparent fellow subjects for their stupidity in conforming!

Milgram's research puts to rest objections that laboratory findings about conformity deal only with casual judgments about which subjects care too little to put up any kind of fuss. In four of Milgram's variations, subjects believed that the experimenter was working for the aircraft industry, trying to develop signals that pilots could more easily detect. But subjects continued to conform and to deny the evidence of their own senses, even when they believed their judgments were, quite literally, a life-or-death matter.

Milgram believed that, just as the study of conformity could yield insights into cross-cultural differences, the study of obedience might also reveal cross-national differences.

Obedience

Adolf Eichmann and Lieutenant William Calley, among others, have defended acts of brutality on grounds that, in effect, they had "just obeyed orders." Most people may loathe these actions and feel confident that *they* would never commit such atrocities. But research data suggest that this confidence is largely unwarranted. What would *you* do in the following situation?

You have been summoned to participate in a study of the effects of punishment on learning with another subject, who is a pleasant middle-aged man. The two of you draw slips of paper from a hat to determine who will be the teacher and who will be the learner. You are designated the teacher, and the experimenter explains that your job will be to teach a series of word pairs to the learner. You watch the learner being strapped into an electric-chair apparatus (to prevent excessive movement on the part of the learner, the experimenter explains). You watch an electrode being taped to the man's wrist and electrode paste applied to his skin (to prevent blisters and burns, the experimenter tells you). The experimenter explains that the electrode is attached to a shock generator in an adjoining room. You are to administer a shock to the learner by pressing lever switches on the fearsome-looking shock generator each time the learner makes a mistake in recalling the word pairs he must memorize. There are thirty lever switches on the shock generator, labeled from left to right in 15-volt increments from 15 to 450 volts. The lever switches are also labeled with verbal descriptions of the intensities of shock, ranging from "Slight Shock" to "Danger: Severe Shock"; the last two lever switches on the extreme right are labeled "XXX." The experimenter instructs you to move one 15-volt level higher on the shock generator each time the learner gives a wrong answer. He assures you that "although the shocks can be extremely painful, they cause no permanent tissue damage." The experiment begins, and the learner indicates each response by pressing one of four switches in front of him that lights up one of four quadrants atop the shock generator.

After the learner's first mistake you raise the voltage from 15 to 30 volts; a third mistake you punish with a 45-volt shock; and so on. As the experiment progresses, the shocks become increasingly severe. After you press the 300-volt switch, you hear the learner pound on the wall in protest; from this point on his answers no longer appear on the panel in front of you, and eventually even the learner's protests cease and he falls completely silent.

If you look to the experimenter for guidance, he instructs you to consider no answer a wrong answer and to increase the voltage accordingly. If you protest that the experiment should be discontinued and the learner's condition investigated, the experimenter repeatedly tells you to continue with your task, making statements like "the experiment requires that you continue" and "you have no choice, you *must* go on."

You may think it impossible that you would ever follow such commands when your obedience was apparently injuring a fellow human being.

But if you are like 65 percent of Milgram's (1963) subjects, you would indeed follow the experimenter's instructions until you had pressed the switch administering the highest possible voltage. In actuality, all of the subjects played the role of teacher in the study, because the learner was in fact Milgram's accomplice and received no shocks. The typical subject did not relish his obedient actions. Many of Milgram's subjects became quite upset during the experiment. Consider, for example, the reactions of one subject as reported by an observer:

I observed a mature and initially poised businessman enter the laboratory smiling and confident. Within 20 minutes he was reduced to a twitching, stuttering wreck, who was rapidly approaching a point of nervous collapse. He constantly pulled on his earlobe, and twisted his hands. At one point he pushed his fist into his forehead and muttered: "Oh God, let's stop it." And yet he continued to respond to every word of the experimenter, and obeyed to the end. (page 377)

Other subjects responded with fits of nervous laughter, bit their lips, sweated profusely, or dug their fingernails into their flesh after the learner began pounding in protest. But many of these same subjects nevertheless continued to increase the voltage level. Some reported after the experiment that, although they had wanted to stop, they continued the punishment because the experimenter "wouldn't" let them stop.

Milgram designed this experiment to study the phenomenon of obedience to legitimate authority. His subjects obeyed voluntarily; no threat of reprisal discouraged them from leaving at any point during the experiment. The experimenter's ability to exact so much obedience apparently must be attributed to his status as a legitimate authority in the laboratory setting. Milgram's findings have been replicated in subsequent experiments.

Obedience is a phenomenon of central importance—social life as we know it would almost certainly crumble without it. Numerous organizations depend on obedience for their functioning (see Chapter 16). But obedience can serve forces of evil as well as forces of good: It was the rise of Nazism in Germany that inspired Milgram's obedience research. He speculated that fascism was particularly likely to arise in countries in which people are especially obedient. Milgram's original plan was to conduct a cross-national study of obedience in two countries—Germany and the United States—because he expected obedience to be more prevalent in Germany. When Milgram began his research, however, he found his American subjects so much more obedient than he and his colleagues had suspected that to extend the research to Germans seemed beside the point.

After demonstrating the basic phenomenon of obedience, Milgram conducted a number of experimental variations. One of the most provocative findings yielded by these later studies concerns subjects' psychological distance from their "victims." In 1965, Milgram reported varying the teacher's psychological (and physical) distance from the learner in order to

Figure 10.4 Photographs from Milgram's (1963) obedience experiment, in which two-thirds of his subjects administered apparently painful shock to another individual because they were instructed to do so. *(From left to right)* the "shock apparatus"; the confederate is supposedly connected to the apparatus; the procedure is explained to the subject; this particular subject, refusing to administer any more shocks, rises angrily in protest; after the experiment the subject is introduced to the confederate, who, he learns, has not really been in danger. From the film *Obedience*, distributed by the New York University Film Library.

discover how distance affects the tendency to obey commands. In the condition of greatest distance, teacher and learner were seated in separate rooms, as the subjects in Milgram's original study had been. Milgram increased the psychological distance still further by eliminating the cries of the learner. Thus, the teacher received little feedback about the effect his actions were having on the learner. In the condition of least distance, the teacher was seated next to the learner, so that they were in full view of one another. The teacher believed that the learner would receive shocks only when he held the learner's hand against the shock plate. When the learner in this close condition refused to hold his hand against the shock plate, the experimenter instructed the teacher to force the learner's hand against it.

Milgram found that subjects were less obedient as physical, visual, and auditory contact with the victim increased. This finding might help explain why, in modern times, decisions can be made to drop atom bombs that will destroy entire cities, to engage in mass executions, and to open fire on demonstrators. For example, compared to an infantryman engaged in hand-to-hand combat, it is much easier for a computer-directed-bomber crewman eight miles above the earth to keep his mind off the personal damage he is inflicting. It might be easier still for the heads of the armed forces, who are thousands of miles away from the combat, to feel removed from the destructive effects of their decisions; easier still for the commander-in-chief alone at his desk. But Milgram found that even in the condition of greatest proximity between subjects and stooges, many subjects (30 percent) continued to escalate the shocks up to the maximum voltage at the command of the experimenter.

Milgram also studied the effect of the experimenter's distance from the teacher on obedience. The willingness of subjects to obey increased as the experimenter placed himself closer to the subject. When the experimenter left the room after giving initial instructions and communicated with subjects thereafter by telephone, obedience dropped from 65 percent to 22 percent; when the experimenter sat but a few feet from subjects throughout the experiment, obedience was three times as high. Thus, most of us seem better able to resist the commands of an authority when we need not

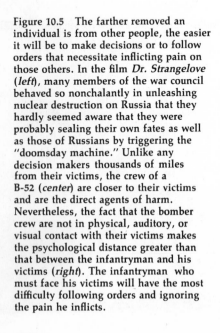

Figure 10.5 The farther removed an individual is from other people, the easier it will be to make decisions or to follow orders that necessitate inflicting pain on those others. In the film *Dr. Strangelove* (*left*), many members of the war council behaved so nonchalantly in unleashing nuclear destruction on Russia that they hardly seemed aware that they were probably sealing their own fates as well as those of Russians by triggering the "doomsday machine." Unlike any decision makers thousands of miles from their victims, the crew of a B-52 (*center*) are closer to their victims and are the direct agents of harm. Nevertheless, the fact that the bomber crew are not in physical, auditory, or visual contact with their victims makes the psychological distance greater than that between the infantryman and his victims (*right*). The infantryman who must face his victims will have the most difficulty following orders and ignoring the pain he inflicts.

confront him—at least in situations in which the disobedient individual does not expect the relationship with the authority to be a long one.

A criticism of Milgram's early studies is that the high incidence of obedience may depend on the experiment being conducted under the auspices of Yale University or some other prestigious institution that is associated with scientific endeavors. Why, a critic might ask, should subjects suspect that anything really harmful could result from a study carried out at Yale? To test the possibility that the site of the experiment had affected the results, Milgram repeated the study in Bridgeport, Connecticut. He rented an office in a seedy downtown office building, lettered "Research Associates of Bridgeport" on the door, and conducted the experiment exactly as he had conducted it in New Haven, where Yale is located. He found that subjects recruited in the Bridgeport area were fully as obedient as subjects participating in the study at Yale.

Alan Elms and Stanley Milgram (1966) became interested in the personalities of those who obey and those who defy authority. Foremost among their findings was a difference between obedient and disobedient subjects in the scores they obtained on a personality scale measuring tendency toward authoritarianism (see Chapter 7). Some other investigators have been unable to replicate these results, but the possibility remains that individuals who possess particular personality characteristics, such as those linked with authoritarianism, may be habitually obedient. It follows that individuals who are habitually disobedient may possess certain characteristics that predispose them to deviance. Whether or not such a predisposition exists is discussed in greater detail in the following section. But first, some of the social forces that may discourage deviance before it is ever expressed will be examined. As will be shown, group pressures toward conformity are compelling deterrents to deviance in most cases.

DEVIANCE

We all walk a tightrope of social expectations. We are surrounded by norms—and at any moment we can slip in the eyes of society and become "deviant." Our deviance may not take a harmful form. For example, a

woman who becomes highly successful as a lawyer, or a gifted artist living in seclusion, may be considered deviant by certain social subgroups. They may make substantial contributions to society but may nevertheless pay the price of social criticism. Why is there so much conformity in society? Why do we toe the line?

Insights into these issues can be gained by asking how to account for the conformity demonstrated by Asch, Crutchfield, Milgram, and many other researchers. Why do people find it so difficult to say, "I see it differently"? It has already been suggested that people conform partly out of a desire to be correct and that what is "correct" is largely determined through social comparison. It is also possible that people feel a desire not to be too different. They may feel that they will be rejected if they obstinately persist in beliefs or behavior different from that of the group. Are their fears of rejection justified? An experiment by Stanley Schachter suggests that deviants may have cause for their fears.

Behavior Toward a Deviant: Baa Baa Black Sheep

In 1951, Schachter conducted a classic experiment on group behavior in the presence of a deviant. He set up discussion groups in which he planted confederates instructed to behave in predetermined ways. The discussion topic was chosen to ensure that virtually all the real subjects would agree with one another. The confederate was "programed" so that his initial

---

Children as Property:
THE PARENTAL PREROGATIVE

PEOPLE TRY TO CHANGE one another's attitudes and values routinely, but society takes their means into account in deciding whether or not their attempts are morally and legally legitimate. What is the social and legal position regarding extreme attempts to change people's minds by isolating them from their reference groups and strongly attacking their belief and value systems? Society generally does not consider what it calls brainwashing to be "fair play," even in wartime situations; it is regarded as an enemy act. Such treatment is seen as an interference with a person's free will, or, more broadly, with his or her "freedom"—something most of us value greatly.

Now imagine yourself walking down the street. Two strangers rush up to you, force you into a waiting car, and speed away with you. They take you to a strange house or motel, lock you in a room, treat you somewhat roughly, and yell at you, telling you that your behavior is evil and motivated by the devil. They argue with you and question you, hoping to persuade you that your mistaken behavior is in conflict with your religious beliefs.

They plead with you to return to your family's way of doing things. You are deprived of sleep and of a chance to think, to talk with your friends, to leave the room, or to relax. Would you apply the term "brainwashing" to this situation?

Maybe this situation seems so bizarre that you cannot imagine yourself in it. Perhaps it is bizarre, but according to news reports, hundreds of young people in the United States have been subjected to this treatment. According to Ted Patrick, one of the key figures in the abductions and a former aide to California Governor Ronald Reagan, 600 young people have been successfully "deprogramed" of their former activities, beliefs, and behavior. What was their behavior? Not, as you may imagine, drug taking, radical or subversive political activities, deviant sexual behavior, gambling, crime, cheating at school, or any illegal activities—or even anything that the society at large judges improper or undesirable. Rather, the behavior held to be motivated by the devil is religious behavior—firm adherence to a religious dogma. The undesirable behavior is not devil worship but participation in one of sixty-one fundamentalist,

opinion would be considerably different from the opinions of the subjects. Schachter found that, after discussion began, group members quickly turned their attention to the deviant and spent much of their time trying to change his mind. Schachter further compared group behavior toward a deviant whom group members believed they had influenced with group behavior toward a deviant who obviously had decided not to conform. He found that groups of subjects continued to exert pressure on deviants whose opinions began approaching theirs, whereas they eventually stopped pressuring the deviant who would not change.

The group liked the deviant who allowed himself to be influenced much more than it liked the recalcitrant deviant. In fact, the sheep who returned to the fold was liked as much as was another accomplice who agreed with the group from the outset of the discussion. And the recalcitrant deviant was not merely passively disliked; when committee assignments were made, he was given the dullest tasks.

A distinct pattern of group response to deviance emerges from Schachter's work. First the group turns its attention toward the deviant and exerts pressure on him to change his opinion. If the group finds the deviant intractable, it will not continue to pressure him indefinitely. Rather, the group will stop communicating with the deviant—partly, perhaps, as punishment and partly because other, more rewarding, matters demand its attention. This pattern primarily characterizes highly cohesive groups dis-

pentecostal, and Oriental sects.

The kidnapped adherents, "Jesus freaks," are all young people, most of them in their late teens or early twenties. And their kidnappers? In most cases, evidently, the kidnappers are working at the parents' request; in some cases, the kidnappers are the parents. To your way of thinking, does the fact that the abductors include the parents of the kidnapped persons affect the justifiability of their actions? The abductors see themselves as "rescuing" young people from sects that have "psychologically kidnapped" them. In other words, they see their own actions as benevolently motivated, strenuous attempts to save "children" from misguided behavior.

What about the law? What position do you think it takes with regard to treatment of this nature? The individual rights and civil liberties of the person subjected to this treatment are clearly jeopardized. Yet because the people are young and their inquisitors may include their parents, state and federal laws are ambiguous. In fact, the "deprogramers," as they call themselves, claim that they have had police cooperation. In at least one case, though, a woman from Texas was

forced by authorities to free her son because he was twenty-one years old.

This account leaves several questions: What are the rights of young people with respect to freedom of belief and action? How old must a person be before the law clearly acknowledges that he or she has such rights? How much do definitions of "brainwashing" and other frowned-on techniques of persuasion depend on *who* is doing the persuading? How far can parents go in trying to influence their children's behavior and beliefs, especially if their offspring's behavior, although not in strict conformity with social standards, is not illegal or demonstrably harmful?

What is your verdict on these issues? How does the treatment the victims of these abductions received compare with efforts to rehabilitate or punish refractory prisoners in jails and penitentiaries? With attempts to win captured war makers over to the other side? To win the "hearts and minds" of embattled Asian villagers? With attempts to mold the attitudes and behavior of young children?

Source: Adapted from "Kidnapping for Christ," *Time* (March 12, 1973), pp. 83–84.

cussing topics relevant to the groups' functions. For less cohesive groups, and for those discussing topics less relevant to group purposes, there is less evidence of a decline in communication to the deviant.

In short, the group will soon reject a recalcitrant deviant and—psychologically, at least—expel him from the group. It may well be that fear of rejection is what motivates some of the conformity already discussed. Conformity may be motivated, as well, by fear of humiliation or of looking foolish. Thus, if subjects in Asch's original conformity experiment were afraid to speak their minds because of possible laughter and ridicule, it may well have been a realistic fear. In fact, Asch's subjects themselves responded in precisely this fashion when a lone confederate disagreed with seven subjects; his error was greeted with raucous laughter. Fears of being wrong, of being humiliated, of being disliked, and of being assigned inferior roles could have motivated the conformist tendencies that have been demonstrated in so many experiments. Keep in mind, however, that the effects of these fears on conformity have not been documented with research data; there is as yet no solid evidence for knowing whether or not fears of this sort produce conformity.

Behavior of the Deviant: Delivering the Wool

Social psychologists have gained insight into some of the factors that precipitate people's conformity. They also know something about the psychology of those who regard themselves as deviant from a group—different from their peers in some important way. Some of this knowledge comes from many studies by Jonathan Freedman and Anthony Doob (1968). These investigators wanted to study people who feel deviant in a general way from others. The knowledge that they were deviant had to be important to subjects—not something they could dismiss as trivial. The researchers thus gave subjects (for the most part, college students) a series of personality tests but told them nothing about the content of the tests. The subjects took a first test and then handed it in to the experimenter. While the experimenter was supposedly scoring the test, the subjects took a second test. When they handed in the second test, subjects were given the results of the first test. At the same time, they were given a third test. This procedure was repeated several times.

In a typical experiment, the information given to one-half the subjects indicated that they had scored very similarly to most students. The in-

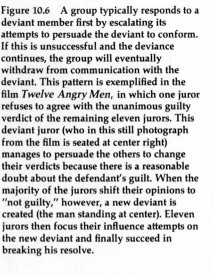

Figure 10.6 A group typically responds to a deviant member first by escalating its attempts to persuade the deviant to conform. If this is unsuccessful and the deviance continues, the group will eventually withdraw from communication with the deviant. This pattern is exemplified in the film *Twelve Angry Men*, in which one juror refuses to agree with the unanimous guilty verdict of the remaining eleven jurors. This deviant juror (who in this still photograph from the film is seated at center right) manages to persuade the others to change their verdicts because there is a reasonable doubt about the defendant's guilt. When the majority of the jurors shift their opinions to "not guilty," however, a new deviant is created (the man standing at center). Eleven jurors then focus their influence attempts on the new deviant and finally succeed in breaking his resolve.

formation given to the other subjects indicated that they were different from most students, although the specific respects in which they differed were not revealed to them. To learn what effects feeling similar or different had on subjects' subsequent behavior, Freedman and Doob examined responses to a questionnaire. This questionnaire consisted of several innocuous true-false items from a personality test and was constructed so that subjects could compare their responses to those of their peers. Subjects were instructed to read the typical answer to each item and then to indicate agreement or disagreement with that answer. Freedman and Doob defined conformity as the number of "typical" responses with which a subject agreed. They found that deviants were less likely than nondeviants to conform to majority opinions. One interpretation of these results, offered by Freedman and Doob, is that the deviants did not conform because they had already been told by the experimenter that they were different from other students. Disagreement with majority opinions simply supported that judgment.

Further research by Freedman and Doob (1968) suggests that the extent to which a deviant is responsive to influence by others depends on who these others are, whether or not the participants anticipate a future relationship, the nature of the deviance, and how easy it is to give up one's deviant position. Apparently, then, a great deal hinges on the specifics of the situation and on the type of influence exerted. From a scientific point of view, this conclusion is discouraging. However, from the point of view of

Figure 10.7 The label "deviant" does not reflect the nature of the behavior itself but merely indicates that the behavior is different from the current norms of the majority in a particular society. Consider the wide range of behavior portrayed here, all defined as deviant by the prevailing society. (*Top left*) Hare Krishna adherents; (*bottom left*) Yossarian, the main character of *Catch-22*, who sits naked in a tree to protest the craziness of the military establishment in which he is an involuntary participant; (*bottom center*) Copernicus, a Pole who shocked his contemporaries in the fifteenth century by declaring that the sun, rather than the earth, was the center of the solar system; and (*right*) a woman suffragette in the early twentieth century.

humanity, such a conclusion may be encouraging; apparently, the deviant is not as eager to rejoin the group under any and all conditions as might have been expected. Prior status as a deviant may actually confer strength in resisting influence in some social situations.

RESISTANCE TO SOCIAL INFLUENCE

The fact that modern society is divided on many issues suggests that there are many forces operating against conformity. Some likely forces will now be examined. Asch's studies of conformity have yielded some insights.

Asch (1956) found that by planting a single confederate instructed to give a correct opinion among a group of confederates instructed to give false judgments, he could induce in a single subject considerable resistance to the influence of a misleading majority and thereby drastically reduce the frequency of conformity. Apparently, people require only minimal social support to resist social influence that goes against their personal judgments.

A second source of resistance to social influence, especially in complex Western societies, is the multiplicity of groups among which individuals can seek support. If one set of people does not agree with an individual on issues that are important to that individual, he or she can usually find acceptance in other groups that have more congenial opinions. The possibility of shifting group allegiances is implicit in, for example, Festinger's social-comparison theory. In emphasizing that the drive for self-evaluation requires satisfaction, Festinger suggests that if no one in a particular social group satisfies the drive a tendency will arise to move out of that group and into another. The deviant thus tends to reject the group as surely as the group tends to reject the deviant (Festinger, 1954).

It is important to remember, however, that disagreement does not always lead a dissident member to abandon the group. There are drives other than the need for self-evaluation that a particular group may satisfy. And there are many factors that may restrict a person's movement out of a group. Consider a person who finds himself enrolled at a university where the prevailing ethos is antagonistic to his own beliefs; it may not be easy to transfer to a school with a more congenial atmosphere. Or, consider those who aspire to change their social or economic standing but who are prevented from shifting groups because of their sex, race, physical disability, educational background, or other status.

A third source of independence and diversity—reactance—deserves extended consideration. One social psychologist has proposed that it is a basic motive.

Reactance: Getting Your Back Up

Whatever philosophers and theologians think about the issue of free will versus determinism, it is a fact that most of us in Western society *feel* free. (See Chapter 9 for a detailed discussion of these feelings.) Jack Brehm (1966) has studied people's reactions to interference with this feeling of freedom. He has theorized that "if a person's behavioral freedom is reduced or threatened with reduction, he will become motivationally aroused. This arousal . . . is directed against any further loss of freedom and . . . also . . . toward the reestablishment of whatever freedom had already been lost or threatened." Brehm calls this motivational state *psychological reactance*. Although reactance may sound similar to a simple response to frustration, it is different. Frustration results when a person is blocked from achieving a goal. Reactance is something more. Suppose a person decides to go to the

Figure 10.8 Social-psychological research suggests that being labeled a deviant has consequences for the individual's future behavior, including that person's increased resistance to social pressure.

"Big Deal!"

movies. Suppose she is then told that she *must* go to the movies. There is no reason for the person to feel frustrated but, according to Brehm, she *will* feel reactance because her freedom to change her mind has been blocked.

Reactance results in an increased desire to act contrary to the force that is constricting one's freedom. Thus, if someone feels that she is being *prevented* from doing something, she will want to do it *more* than before; if she feels she is being *forced* to do it, she will want to do it *less* than before. This line of reasoning makes intuitive sense when people's responses to numerous behaviors that are either enforced or forbidden are considered. Thus, for example, Harold Kant and Michael Goldstein (1970) found that frequenters of "adult" bookstores report childhoods that were significantly more sheltered from pornographic materials than did nonfrequenters. Ironically, then, the efforts of antipornographers, liquor and drug prohibitionists, and those who enforce other moralities may sometimes have the self-defeating effect of making the behaviors they condemn more attractive to those they try to protect.

An attempt at social influence will provoke reactance only when an individual *perceives* that it will interfere with his or her freedom. If a communicator appears simply to be supplying information and arguments in order to help the audience make up its own mind, then little, if any, reactance should be aroused. But if the information and arguments are *perceived* as attempts to limit the audience's freedom by changing its attitudes, then reactance might very well result. Reactance may be manifested in a number of ways. The audience may simply hold stubbornly to its original position. Or it may express more confidence in the correctness of its position. Or the audience may react by changing its opinion in the direction opposite to that espoused by the communicator and thereby become more extreme in its position than ever.

Jack Brehm devised a test of his hypothesis that if one *incidentally* learns another's position, then that other person will be better able to produce attitude change than if one is told that learning the other's position will lead to attitude change. He first gauged subjects' opinions on a variety of issues. He then gave the subjects a second copy of the same questionnaire that showed someone else's opinion for each item. The opinions agreed with those of subjects for some of the items but disagreed for others. In a low-threat condition, subjects were told merely that they were being exposed to the opinions of "another student" so that they would be better able to predict the other student's positions on two issues. Subjects in the high-threat condition were told, as well, that they were expected to show opinion change toward the other student's positions—a condition that Brehm predicted would cause subjects to feel threatened with diminished freedom to choose their own positions and, therefore, would cause them to experience and to manifest reactance. The results supported Brehm's reasoning.

Brehm has conducted a wide variety of studies supporting the notion of reactance. The conclusion that people—at least those in the United States—do not like to be told how they ought to think seems well supported. This tendency toward reactance may, therefore, constitute yet another factor that protects people from uniformity of thought.

Despite the prevalence of this desire to protect one's freedom, people are far more malleable in some situations than in others. Subjects in psychological experiments are sometimes especially malleable, perhaps because these situations are of brief duration and give a subject little time to

Figure 10.9 In a clever ruse to avoid a chore, Tom Sawyer made use of the principle that Brehm (1966) has since termed "reactance." Tom first convinced his friends that white-washing the fence was an enjoyable activity but then refused to allow them to join in the fun unless they paid him. From the perspective of Brehm's theory, Tom's friends were willing to pay for the privilege of working because they could thereby buy back their freedom to partake in a desirable activity from which Tom had temporarily excluded them.

think and to marshal his or her resources against influence. Subjects may not be able to think of the reasons they have for holding an opinion and therefore may yield to influence in the crucible of the experiment even though the influence may not endure for long after they return to the environmental influences that created their original beliefs.

An individual's least-challenged attitudes paradoxically often seem to be the ones that are most vulnerable to influence. It is as if people build defenses against attacks on their beliefs; thus they become seemingly immune to future attacks on those beliefs. But if subjects were more in the habit of immediately rising to the defense of the opinions researchers want to change, these attitudes might not be so vulnerable to researchers' influence attempts. The work of the social psychologist who demonstrated the applicability of a medical analogy to the dynamics of persuasion will now be discussed in some detail.

Inoculation Against Persuasion

William McGuire (1964) has demonstrated that people can be inoculated against persuasion, much as they can be inoculated against bacteria. Just as inoculation with a weak form of bacteria may stimulate a person's body to form defenses and thereby to become immune to later, more virulent forms of the disease, a challenge to a person's beliefs may arouse psychological defenses that render the individual less vulnerable to persuasion than when a belief goes unchallenged.

To put this supposition to the test, McGuire needed to study beliefs that had not been challenged before—that had, in other words, not been inoculated against challenges. For this reason, McGuire settled on cultural truisms—beliefs that are rarely challenged during the usual course of events. These truisms include such beliefs as: "It is a good idea to brush your teeth after every meal if at all possible." When such beliefs are first challenged, the individual may be overwhelmed. Such was often the case when, for example, McGuire exposed subjects to an essay on "Some Dangers of Excessive Tooth Brushing," which claimed: "Biochemical studies . . . indicate that most tooth decay occurs while the food is still in one's mouth, so that the brushing comes too late to do much good" and warned that "constant tooth brushing can . . . produce mouth cancer." McGuire suggests that the vulnerability of unchallenged beliefs results because such truisms have evolved in relatively aseptic environments in which people have not been stimulated to examine or defend these beliefs in any great detail.

McGuire suspected that people's beliefs can be made more resistant to change by challenging and subsequently resupporting those beliefs. More precisely, McGuire predicted that arguments *supporting* a truism—what McGuire calls "supportive defenses"—would be less effective in buttressing a person's initial belief than arguments *attacking* the truism followed by counterarguments *refuting* the challenging argument and reinforcing the original belief—"refutational defenses." McGuire bases this prediction on the notion that subjects exposed to a supportive defense will not feel their belief threatened and so will be relatively unmotivated to think through their reasons for maintaining the belief and to buttress it with counterarguments. Subjects exposed to a refutational defense, on the other hand, will be stimulated by the initial challenge to their belief to recall the reasons for their belief and to generate new reasons.

One of McGuire's studies was conducted in two one-hour sessions, one week apart. In the first session, one-half the subjects were exposed to arguments supporting a truism, and the other half were exposed to arguments against the truism, followed by a refutation of the arguments against the truism. One week later, both groups of subjects were exposed to new attacks on the cultural truisms. McGuire found that the attacks of the second session were least effective in the case of subjects who had already experienced a challenge to their beliefs. In other words, subjects who had been inoculated were least persuaded by the second round of attacks. McGuire's data from this and other of his studies of inoculation show that a belief that has never been attacked is much more susceptible to social influence than is a belief that has been protected by inoculation.

Consider the implications of McGuire's work for the issue at hand—whether or not people can be expected to succumb readily to social influence. Certainly, the beliefs most likely to be attacked in daily life are those that are most controversial. And, nearly by definition, controversial beliefs are precisely the beliefs that people have had the most experience defending.

The implications of McGuire's work for child rearing and for education at all age levels are striking. His findings suggest, for example, that parents who seek to instill a particular set of beliefs in their children would be well advised to expose them also to the opinions they most want to discourage. Parents can thus refute the unwanted opinions while their children are still at home, and their children will resist those opinions when they encounter them later on. When it is recalled that one-sided attempts to persuade can also cause an audience to resist a message through psychological reactance, the attempts of moralists to "protect" people from information about sex, drugs, and other "evils" seem self-defeating.

TECHNIQUES OF SOCIAL INFLUENCE

In Arthur Miller's *Death of a Salesman,* a classic American drama, a salesman commits suicide largely because he no longer is influential. Dale Carnegie's book *How to Win Friends and Influence People* is a compendium of manipulative techniques by which people like the salesman in Arthur Miller's play can get others to do what they want. The long-lasting popularity of Carnegie's book shows how potent these techniques are.

And yet the manipulative strategies that Carnegie prescribes are not always the most influential techniques. There certainly are times when an outstretched hand or a pat on the back does *not* win people over but is more likely to make them resentful.

How does the agent of social influence actually exert influence? Clearly, the agent must do more than simply state an opinion and express a wish that the target person accept the opinion. What are some of the techniques that will increase the probability that an agent's influence attempt will be successful? A number of relevant variables have been explored in the preceding chapter on attitude change. At this point several additional techniques of influence in face-to-face situations will be discussed.

The Power of Expressed Confidence

In order to examine the spontaneous behavior of people attempting to change one another's minds, Harvey London (1973) has devised the following method of study: Two students participate as subjects in a study that they believe is being conducted to determine how juries make decisions.

Each student receives a booklet and retires to a corner of the experimental room to read it and to arrive at his or her own verdict in the case. The booklets are nearly the same, but not quite. Both booklets include a factual summary of a law case, which describes a dispute between a plaintiff and a defendant in which there is some justice on both sides. The only difference between the booklets is that one contains a legal analysis arguing very powerfully for the plaintiff and the other contains an analysis arguing powerfully for the defendant. The subjects are not aware that they have read different legal analyses. After collecting the booklets and checking subjects' verdicts (which usually are the same verdicts that their booklets endorsed), the experimenter seats the two subjects at a table in the center of the room. He informs the subjects that they disagree and that, because he is interested in how juries make decisions, he would like them to act as a two-member jury, discuss the issue, and arrive at a unanimous decision.

London distinguished between two types of subjects—*persuaders* (those whose verdicts did not change in discussion) and *persuadees* (those whose verdicts did change). He wanted to learn what the persuaders had done to influence the persuadees. Initially he eliminated some sources of potentially irrelevant influence by matching each pair of subjects for similarity of age, sex, race, and social class. Prior to discussion, persuaders and persuadees had been about equally convinced of their respective positions, and examination of taped recordings of the discussions did not reveal that persuaders possessed greater ability to deal articulately with points of logic than did persuadees. What, then, made the persuaders more persuasive?

In examining the recorded discussions, Harvey London and his colleagues began to notice a difference in style between the persuaders and the persuadees (London, Meldman, and Lanckton, 1971). Two subjects might make similar, if opposing, substantive points, but they expressed them in contrasting ways. Persuaders tended to use words expressing confidence, whereas persuadees tended to use words expressing doubt. For each subject, the investigators subtracted the words expressing doubt from the words expressing confidence to derive an overall *expressed-confidence score.* They found that most persuaders obtain significantly larger expressed-confidence scores than do persuadees. The difference between a typical persuader's expressed confidence and a typical persuadee's expressed confidence was substantial as early as the first third of the discussion. This finding suggests that if an observer could determine the relative confidence and doubt expressed by the participants a few minutes after a discussion begins, that observer might be able to estimate which of the participants would persuade the other.

Both persuaders and persuadees expressed diminished confidence during the final third of the discussions. It is not surprising that the persuadee's expressed confidence wanes as he or she becomes increasingly persuaded and gives up. But why should the persuader's forcefulness decrease? One possible explanation is that the persuader wants to let the persuadee down easily. If they continued to express a great deal of confidence after they had begun to prevail, persuaders might make the persuadees antagonistic and recalcitrant; perhaps such behavior would create the reactance Brehm describes. The persuader may decrease his or her forcefulness in order to preclude this kind of resistance. This possibility was investigated in an experiment in which a communicator's level of expressed confidence was manipulated by planting an accomplice in each two-member jury (London, McSeveney, and Tropper, 1971). When an accomplice expressed a great deal of confidence—more than that expressed by a typical persuader—subjects became angry and were less persuaded than when an accomplice expressed about as much confidence as a typical persuader. Thus, it appears that expressed confidence is effective as an agent of persuasion, but only up to a point. Beyond that point the expression of confidence generates resistance, which is possibly the result of reactance.

Much of the research on techniques of social influence focuses on pressure emanating from the source of influence toward the target person whose attitudes or behavior the source wants to change. However, one line of research has recently focused on how a source can get a person to comply *without* resorting to the usual social pressures. Two of these modes of influence—the foot-in-the-door technique and guilt—are discussed next.

The Foot-in-the-Door Technique

Jonathan Freedman and Scott Fraser (1966) have studied a technique named after a practice used by salesmen—the foot-in-the-door technique. A salesman will first try to get a customer to comply with a small request, such as allowing the salesman to enter the customer's home, after which the salesman will have an easier time getting the customer to comply with a large request, such as buying the salesman's product—or so proponents of the technique claim.

Freedman and Fraser devised two studies in order to determine the effectiveness of the foot-in-the-door technique. In one study, housewives were approached and asked to comply with a small request—to answer questions about the kind of soap used in their homes. Later, the experimenters contacted each of the housewives again and made a larger request: they asked permission to have several men come to the subject's home and

Figure 10.10 The foot-in-the-door technique is employed to solicit an individual's cooperation with a small request as a first step in obtaining compliance with a larger request.

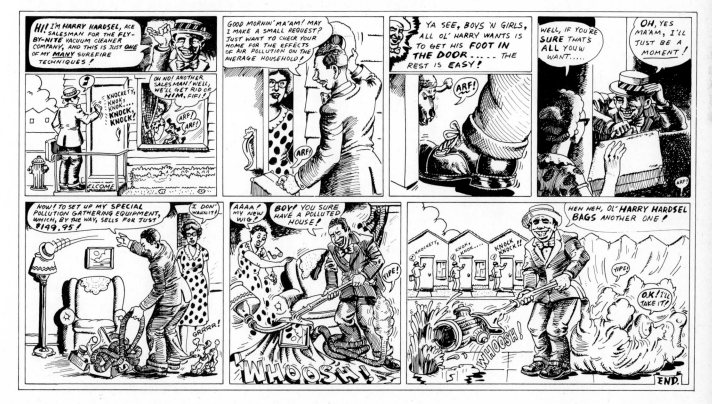

spend two hours listing and classifying all household products. In the control condition, the experimenters did not precede the large request with a smaller request; only the large request was made. Freedman and Fraser found that compliance with the early request did make a difference: significantly more subjects agreed to the large request when it was preceded by acquiescence to the first request. In another experiment, Freedman and Fraser were able to get large numbers of people to put a big sign urging safe driving in their front yards by using the foot-in-the-door technique; without it, they got little compliance.

As a result of the research they and others have conducted, Freedman and Fraser believe that the foot-in-the-door technique works because the first act of compliance changes the target person's self-perception. Freedman and Fraser suggest that after a person has complied with a small request, "he may become, in his own eyes, the kind of person who does this sort of thing, who agrees to requests made by strangers, who takes action on things he believes in, who cooperates with good causes." In the preceding chapter, it is pointed out that people may form self-perpetuating impressions of themselves by noting their own behavior, much as other observers might. A change toward a more generous self-concept makes a target person more susceptible to subsequent requests. However, there are also conditions under which this technique is resented: If the foot in the door is too large, reactance may well result.

Guilt and Compliance

Guilt is another factor that may alter attitudes and behavior in the absence of external social pressures. It is commonsensical that a person who feels guilty is more likely to comply with a request coming from the source of his or her guilt than a person who feels no guilt. The belief that people can

TWO STEPS TO MASS PERSUASION

MOST OF THE RESEARCH in this chapter has centered on social-influence processes in small groups. But what about the large-scale efforts of advertising, mass media, and political campaigns in which masses of people are urged to conform in adopting certain goals? Those whose job it is to promote a product, a candidate, or an ideology often attempt to create artificial needs in people, whether the need be for foot powder or for a leader who will vanquish a "sinister" if helpless opponent.

One of the most interesting hypotheses regarding mass persuasion suggests that it relies on face-to-face communication—particularly of the "two-step," or two-stage, variety. The basic idea involved in the two-step communication flow is that messages from the mass media exert their greatest influence via their impact on a relatively small group of opinion leaders. These leaders then spread the message among their friends and associates. By providing these others with information and social support and by exerting social pressure on them, these opinion leaders create attitude change in the groups in which they have potent interpersonal relations.

A study of election behavior in 1940 first revealed the possibility of a two-stage process—a stage involving influence between the mass media and opinion leaders and a stage involving influence between opinion leaders and their followers (Lazarsfeld, Berelson, and Gaudet, 1948). Since then, studies of voting behavior, style setting, movie going, and drug usage have expanded and refined the original formulation. Opinion leaders have been found to be demographically similar to those they influenced, more tuned in to mass media, and selected for leadership if the situation called for leadership.

Methodological problems often

expiate guilt through certain kinds of action is a notion that is deeply ingrained in many religious and moral systems; it has been an important form of social control in Western civilization.

The idea that people will act to expiate guilt has been put to many tests, including two conducted by J. Merrill Carlsmith and Alan Gross (1969). In a format resembling Milgram's obedience experiment, Carlsmith and Gross instructed subjects to throw a switch whenever a "learner" made a mistake. In one experiment, Carlsmith and Gross told half the subjects that the switch sounded a buzzer that would inform the learner of his mistakes; the other half believed that closing the switch delivered an electric shock to the learner. When the learning experiment was over, the learner—the experimenters' accomplice—asked the subject to participate in a telephone campaign to save the redwoods in northern California. Carlsmith and Gross found that subjects who thought they had hurt the fellow subject (and who, according to the hypothesis, felt guilty) were much more likely to comply with the accomplice's request than were subjects who had no reason to feel guilty. However, the concept of guilt is not the only means by which the result can be explained. For example, subjects may have felt *sympathy* for the person they shocked rather than guilt for having shocked him.

Carlsmith and Gross (1969) tested for sympathy as a cause of compliance in a second study. This second study was quite similar to the first, but some subjects were led to feel sympathy for the learner rather than guilt for having caused him pain because they did not deliver the shocks but witnessed them being received. Sympathy did not generate compliance with a request from the victim. In fact, subjects in the sympathy condition complied even less than did control subjects, who felt neither guilt nor sympathy.

Throughout this chapter, the power and techniques of persuasion and,

plagued this research because the population of leaders and followers would snowball to proportions beyond the investigators' scope or resources. One study carried out by Elihu Katz was effective in isolating and in controlling these problems and as a result offers the most clear-cut demonstration of a two-step flow in communication.

The subjects were all doctors in four Midwestern cities, and the central question was which doctors would prescribe a newly accepted drug to their patients. All of the doctors were interviewed concerning their attitudes, backgrounds, the drugs they prescribed, and professional reading habits. In addition, the doctors were asked which three colleagues they most often "talked shop" with, which three they most often sought advice from, and which three they saw socially most often. At the same time, the investigators kept a complete audit of all drug prescriptions filled at all local drug stores; with these records they could monitor the medical circle's acceptance of the new drug.

Katz's major finding was that the rate of adoption of a new drug was strongly related to the social integration of the doctors in that medical community. More influential in promoting adoption than type of education, income of patients, age, or reading habits was the doctor's being named a friend or discussion companion by colleagues.

As long as the band is playing, it is important to ask with whom one is dancing and who is leading.

Sources: Adapted from E. Katz, "The Two-Step Flow of Communication: An Up-to-date Report on an Hypothesis," in H. Proshansky and B. Seidenberg (eds.), *Basic Studies in Social Psychology.* (New York: Holt, Rinehart and Winston, 1965), pp. 196–209.

P. Lazarsfeld, B. Berelson, and H. Gaudet, *The People's Choice,* 2nd ed. (New York: Columbia University Press, 1948).

to a lesser extent, the defenses that people mobilize to resist social influence have been discussed. But social influence is not in itself a force for good or evil. Rather, it is a tool with which some people carve relatively happy and fulfilling existences for themselves and with which others only destroy. The same techniques of persuasion are mobilized by Republicans and Democrats, by Communists and anti-Communists, by religious fanatics and atheists, by those who would sell liquor and those who discourage its use.

Paradoxically, social scientists who are repelled by such phenomena as Nazism (and who have had the courage and imagination to put social science to work generating information that may prevent recurrences of brutality on the scale committed by the Nazis) are among those who have found it useful to exert total control in their laboratories. It seems, then, that whether the arena is a laboratory or the world, social influence is a *means* of persuasion; the *end* to which it is applied is of necessity left to the discretion of the persuader—in effect, to each of us.

SUMMARY

The autokinetic phenomenon—the perceived movement of a pinpoint of light that is actually stationary—caught the attention of a social psychologist, Muzafer Sherif. He was interested in how members of a group influence one another when they lack solid norms to guide their opinions. Sherif used the autokinetic phenomenon to test the influence of one person's perceptions of the light's movement on another person's perceptions. Mutual influence occurred, and the conclusion was reached that people construct the world largely on the basis of social agreement. Sherif's work provided one basis for Leon Festinger's *social-comparison theory,* which delineates some of the basic conditions that foster *conformity* in groups. Festinger assumed (a) that each of us feels a need to evaluate the correctness of his or her opinions; (b) that in the absence of an objective test of reality, we seek out others with whom to compare our opinions; and (c) that we tend to prefer similar others for comparison.

Solomon Asch, in a classic study, pitted a lone subject against a group of people secretly instructed to disagree with the subject. Asch found that subjects conformed with the incorrect majority in 32 percent of the trials in which the confederates gave wrong answers. Such a tendency to conform can have political implications. The tendency to obey an authority figure is also fraught with political implications; for example, in Nazi Germany obedience to an authority figure led an entire population to permit acts that very few of them would have committed on their own. Stanley Milgram conducted a series of classic *obedience* studies. In what was supposedly a learning task, about two-thirds of Milgram's subjects obeyed an *authority* figure (the experimenter) and delivered what they believed were very painful shocks to a learner—despite the pleas of the learner and their own better judgment.

Those who do not conform or obey—*deviants*—elicit strong responses from the group with which they disagree. As demonstrated by Stanley Schachter, a group will try mightily to convert deviants to the group's opinions and will welcome them with open arms if they do finally agree with the group. But they who persist in heresy will find themselves actively rejected by the group. Knowledge of these strong group pressures may well contribute to conformity. But, as Jonathan Freedman and Anthony Doob have demonstrated, deviants who believe that they are in some substantial way different from those who are around them can be quite resistant to attempts to influence their opinions.

We often lose our desire for certain objects or activities if told that we *must* have those objects or do those things. According to Jack Brehm, this *psychological reactance* is one of the mechanisms that helps people resist influence. The feeling that one is free to make choices may become more important than the choices themselves. Consequently, if we believe that the purpose of a communication is solely to sway our opinion, we are more likely to react against that communication than when the communication conveys no persuasive intent. In fact, persuasive communications can backfire, causing us either to strengthen our stand or to change it in the direction opposite to that intended.

One researcher, William McGuire, has explored ways of *inoculating* people against the attempts of others to change their opinions. Beliefs can be bolstered against attempts at persuasion by familiarizing the person with counterarguments against his or her beliefs and then with the shortcomings of those arguments. McGuire's subjects who first had been required to devise counterarguments were more resistant to persuasion than were subjects who were not required to devise counterarguments. Apparently, then, those beliefs that have never been questioned are the most susceptible to influence.

Harvey London and his colleagues have shown that confidence, expressed in subtle ways from the start of a verbal interchange, adds greatly to the persuasiveness of a message. London has been able to predict who will persuade whom in a two-person confrontation by comparing the verbal confidence expressed by each person.

Another way of inducing people to change their beliefs is the *foot-in-the-door technique,* which uses a small and acceptable request to prime a person for a larger request. In addition, favors can sometimes be secured from people by causing them to feel *guilt.*

SUGGESTED READINGS

Cohen, Arthur. *Attitude Change and Social Influence.* New York: Basic Books, 1964.

Freedman, Jonathan, and Anthony Doob. *Deviancy.* New York: Academic Press, 1968.

Kiesler, Charles, and Sara Kiesler. *Conformity.* Reading, Mass.: Addison-Wesley, 1969.

London, Harvey. *Psychology of the Persuader.* Morristown, N.J.: General Learning Press, 1973.

McGuire, William. "Inducing Resistance to Persuasion: Some Contemporary Approaches," in L. Berkowitz (ed.), *Advances in Experimental Social Psychology.* New York: Academic Press, 1964, pp. 192–227.

Milgram, Stanley. "Behavioral Study of Obedience," *Journal of Abnormal and Social Psychology,* 67 (1963), 371–378.

Wheeler, Ladd. *Interpersonal Influence.* Boston: Allyn and Bacon, 1970.

Zimbardo, Phillip, and Ebbe Ebbesen. *Influencing Attitudes and Changing Behavior.* Reading, Mass.: Addison-Wesley, 1970.

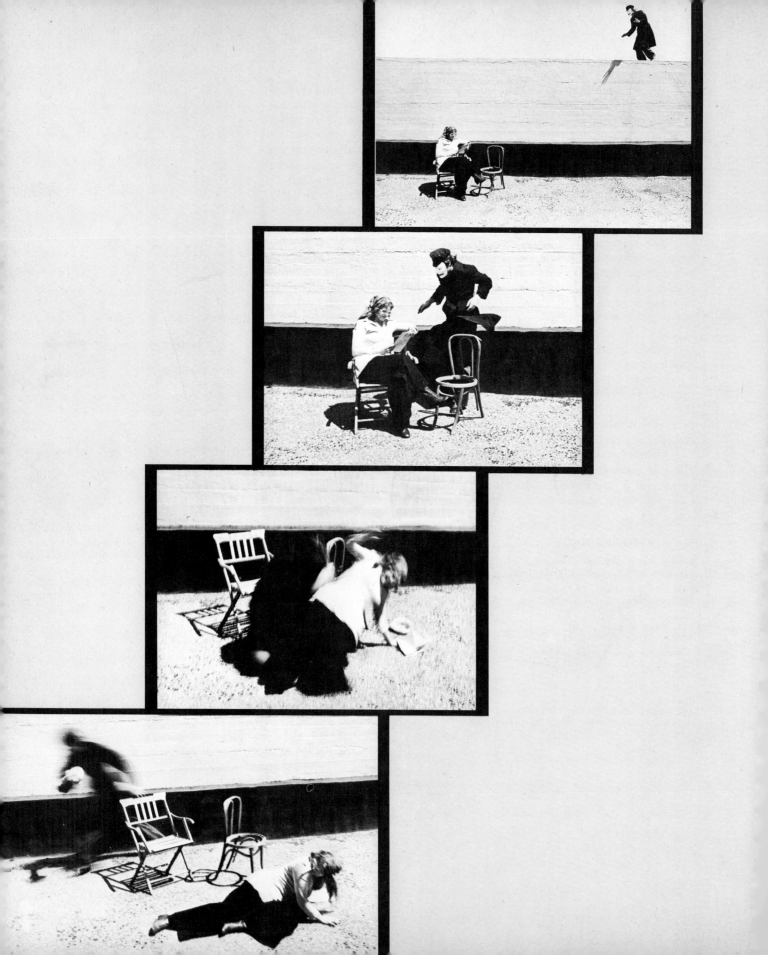

11
Aggression

America has always been a relatively violent nation. Considering the tumultuous historical forces that have shaped the United States, it would be astonishing were it otherwise. (*National Commission on the Causes and Prevention of Violence,* 1969)

EVEN IN A NATION ACCUSTOMED TO considerable turbulence, the past decade or so has seemed remarkably violent. The course of national politics has been greatly altered by the assassinations of John Kennedy, Robert Kennedy, Martin Luther King, and Malcolm X and the wounding of George Wallace. Mass murders claimed the lives of nine nurses in Chicago and fourteen passers-by at the University of Texas. Newspapers and television carry daily accounts of robberies, assaults, and muggings. And these events we learn about are but a small fraction of the total number of violent incidents; less dramatic crimes are either reported on back pages or neglected by the media altogether. Still other acts of violence not even the police hear about. It is no wonder that "law and order" has become a central issue in national elections.

But violence is by no means unique to the United States. During the past few years, Irishmen have slaughtered other Irishmen, Indians and Pakistani have perpetrated mass murders on each other, and black Ugandans have assaulted Indian Ugandans. Nor is violence unique to the present. Any history book recounts dozens of bloody battles, and if sufficient detail is included, episodes of looting, pillage, and rape will be found as well. Complaints of terror in the streets and longing for personal safety were frequently voiced in Renaissance Florence and Elizabethan London as well as in contemporary Philadelphia. This is small solace to victims, but it

347

nevertheless indicates the pervasiveness and seriousness of human aggression and violence, even in seemingly diverse societies.

Social scientists, long interested in the problem, have recently increased their efforts to understand the processes underlying violence and aggression and the means by which people can control and reduce such behavior. In this chapter some of the resulting work is examined.

WHAT IS AGGRESSION?

The task of defining aggression is not an easy one. Consider the following actions and try to evaluate them according to whether or not they are aggressive. Then try to formulate your own definition.

1. A driver screams at an old man who is slowly crossing the street against a red light.
2. A baseball player scores a home run.
3. A boxer knocks out his opponent in the eighth round.
4. A farmer slaughters a chicken and prepares it for dinner.
5. A husband and wife argue over who is to throw out the garbage.
6. A policeman clubs a robber on the head as the robber is escaping from the site of a crime.
7. A woman dislikes Jews and avoids them.
8. A disappointed lover slashes his wrists.
9. A chemist accidentally blows up her laboratory; her assistant is killed in the explosion.
10. An assassin takes a shot at the President and misses.
11. A teen-ager attacks a stranger, kills him, and flees.

Figure 11.1 Results (*opposite*) of a survey by Stark and McEvoy (1970) show the frequency of physical violence in the United States according to race, sex, geographic region, income, education, and age. A representative national sample of more than 1,000 adult Americans was interviewed about the extent to which they were victims or perpetrators of physical violence. The data challenge many popular conceptions about who is prone to physical violence. For example, blacks apparently are not a particularly violent subculture; approval of slapping one's spouse increases with income and education; and the middle class is apparently as prone to violence as are the poor, perhaps more so. In light of this finding regarding socioeconomic status, the fact that violence by poor persons comes to the attention of law-enforcement agencies more frequently than does violence by middle-class persons suggests that middle-class persons have greater access to professional counseling and have more privacy in which to settle disputes. The only common stereotype supported by Stark and McEvoy's data is that of women as being less approving of violence, less likely to be victims of violence, and less likely to perpetrate violence than males are.

These examples introduce a number of issues. One concerns the *target* of the aggressive act: The baseball player who scores a home run would not be viewed as an aggressor by many people, yet his swat may closely resemble the strokes of the policeman who uses his club on a thief. A second issue is *legitimacy:* People are more likely to label the policeman as aggressive if they believe his assault is unjustified rather than a necessary duty. Closely related is the important question of *intent:* If the chemist did not plan to demolish the laboratory, then she is not thought of—legally or more generally—as an aggressor. Finally, whether *damage* actually occurs or is only attempted must be considered: Is an assassin aggressive if he hits his target but not aggressive if he misses?

As you might expect, there are several definitions of aggression. But the one that most people agree on amounts to this: *Aggression includes real or planned acts of physical or verbal abuse directed by one human being at another.* Aggression may therefore be closely related to violence, which often involves great force, especially physical force, used against others.

No actual harm need occur for an act to be aggressive. The assassin who misses his target as well as the college student who thinks he is delivering electric shocks to another student in an experiment in which the shock box is not connected have acted aggressively. Although it is often difficult to know how and why a person plans to act, the alternative would be to consider as aggressive only those acts that resulted in harm. From the social scientist's point of view, this solution would rule out experimental studies of all but the least severe forms of aggression; for both ethical and practical reasons, scientists cannot run laboratories in which actual injury is a routine part of experimentation. Thus, if they are to study aggression in

IV INTERACTING WITH OTHERS

controlled situations, planned as well as real harm should be included in a definition of aggression.

The idea of abuse is also important in defining aggression, because it distinguishes between aggressive and assertive behavior. There are times when it is virtually essential to take a stand and be assertive. Thus, if a motorist finds herself trapped in an alley between two large trucks whose drivers have decided to renew an old friendship, she might reasonably suggest that they move their vehicles. Although her behavior could result in an aggressive episode if the truckers took offense, the motorist's initial request would be classified as assertive rather than aggressive.

INNATE AGGRESSION: IS IT NATURE'S WAY?

Psychologists have devoted considerable attention to innate mechanisms that may be related to aggression. Some have concentrated on instinct in their formulations, attributing people's penchant for violence to their "human nature." Investigators have aimed more specific efforts at discover-

Physical Violence*	Race		Sex		Region				Income			Education				Age				National Average
	Black	White	Male	Female	East	Midwest	South	West	To $5,000	$5,000-$9,999	$10,000+	To 8th grade	Some high school	High-school graduate	College	To 30	31-50	51-65	65+	
Percent who:																				
Have been slapped or kicked by another person:	18	13	13	12	15	15	9	17	12	16	14	11	15	12	17	16	14	15	6	13
Have slapped or kicked another person:	22	18	22	13	17	19	14	23	14	19	20	15	20	16	20	18	21	17	10	18
Have been punched or beaten by another person:	17	12	19	4	16	10	8	9	11	13	13	14	9	13	12	10	15	10	5	12
Have punched or beaten another person:	20	13	21	4	15	12	7	20	7	16	15	9	19	11	13	15	14	10	4	13
Could approve of a husband slapping his wife's face:	25	20	25	16	22	18	16	26	14	22	23	16	23	17	25	26	23	15	11	20
Could approve of a wife slapping her husband's face:	27	22	26	19	24	21	18	25	18	24	24	19	22	18	28	33	20	18	13	22
Have been threatened with, or actually cut with, a knife:	11	8	12	3	8	5	10	11	9	8	8	7	10	6	9	11	7	7	7	8
Have been threatened with a gun or shot at:	9	6	10	2	6	4	7	9	6	7	7	9	6	7	5	9	5	8	4	6
Have had to defend themselves with a knife or a gun:	14	4	10	2	10	3	5	5	5	5	8	4	7	5	6	9	6	4	2	6
Own firearms:	27	43	50	32	24	45	50	46	34	41	47	40	39	41	43	38	47	40	36	41

*Childhood incidents and experiences in military combat have been eliminated.

Source: Adapted from R. Stark and J. McEvoy, "Middle-Class Violence," *Psychology Today,* 4 (1970), 52-54, 110-112.

ing exact biological influences on aggressive behavior. This section of the chapter first examines evidence of biochemical influences and then turns to theories that define innate tendencies in nonphysiological terms.

Biological Mediators: Stocking the Arsenal

One striking example of biochemistry's role in aggressive behavior was found in a study of laboratory rats by Douglas Smith, Melvyn King, and Bartley Hoebel (1970). Some of the rats used in the experiment were initially killers that killed almost immediately any mice placed in their cages. Others were pacifists: given the opportunity to kill, they consistently refrained from attacking. The investigators believed that a biochemical agent that mediates killing was present in the brains of both groups but was activated in one and not the other. They therefore anesthetized all the animals and implanted miniature tubes in their brains. As expected, they found that when they injected certain activating drugs (such as carbachol and neostigmine) through the tubes into a certain part of the brain—the lateral hypothalamus—previously peaceful rats became killers. On the other hand, rats that ordinarily killed mice on sight were inhibited from killing when injected with a different drug (methyl atropine).

These researchers also found that the activating or inhibitory effects did not occur if they inserted the tube even one millimeter away from the

Figure 11.2 Unlike human combat, fighting in nonhuman species is rarely geared to killing one's opponent. Many species have found ways around physical combat that still permit the settling of disputes. Many researchers have studied aggressive behavior in animals, both in the laboratory and in the wild, in attempting to find out whether or not aggression is in part innate.

hypothalamus; that only certain chemicals would produce the effects; and that the stimulating or inhibiting effects on aggressive behavior lasted only for the few hours in which the drug was pharmacologically active. At present, researchers do not know if these drugs would have the same effects on human beings as they do on rats. It is likely, though, that there are at least some parallels.

Brain malfunctions may be responsible for at least some aggressive acts committed by humans. Perhaps best known is the case of Charles Whitman, the Texas resident who barricaded himself in a tower and for ninety minutes shot with a high-powered rifle at everything that moved. He wounded twenty-four people, killed fourteen, and even hit an airplane. Whitman's autopsy revealed a brain tumor the size of a walnut, located in a portion of the hypothalamus known as the amygdala. Moreover, personal notes that Whitman left behind reveal that he suffered painful headaches and at times experienced uncontrollable urges to be violent. To some extent, then, human beings' capacities for aggression may be influenced by biological malfunctioning, and this conclusion has led some investigators, particularly ethologists, to conclude that human aggression is instinctual.

Ethology: Preprogramed Violence

In explaining human violence, ethologists have relied heavily on making analogies to the aggressive patterns of other animals. Seen within this perspective, man is unique among animals in both the frequency with which he kills members of his own species and the relative absence of immediate instrumental goals, such as acquisition of food, sex, or territory.

One leading ethologist, Konrad Lorenz (1966), explains the human penchant for aggressive behavior in evolutionary terms. He reasons that animals that are equipped with deadly weapons—poisonous fangs, sharp talons, powerful teeth and jaws—either develop inhibitions against killing members of the same species or become extinct by annihilating one another. Lorenz has observed, for example, that many of nature's potential killers have developed ritualized acts of surrender, so that a battle almost never ends in the death of the weaker participant.

The wolf turns his head away from his opponent, offering him the vulnerable, arched side of his neck; the jackdaw holds under the beak of the aggressor the unprotected base of the skull, the very place which these birds attack when they intend to kill. . . .
When the loser of a fight suddenly adopted the submissive attitude, and presented his unprotected neck, the winner performed the movement of shaking to death, in the air, close to the neck of the morally vanquished dog, but with closed mouth, that is, without biting. (pages 132–133)

Lorenz believes that human beings, by contrast, are less well-equipped by nature for aggression and thus never developed inhibitions against aggression that occur as automatically and dependably as do the wolf's or jackdaw's. In recent centuries, however, man has rapidly developed deadly weapons—but he still lacks inhibitory mechanisms that are strong enough to match his destructive potential. According to this analysis, humans are almost certainly doomed to join other unsuccessful species who failed to survive because of aggression between members of the same species.

Fortunately, there is also some reason for hope, even according to Lorenz's arguments. If people are ingenious enough to develop weapons of mass destruction, there seems no inherent reason why they cannot learn to inhibit their aggressive impulses as well. Although humanity may not have time enough to rely on slow-working evolutionary processes for salvation from its own destructive potential, the possibility exists that people can use language and other forms of communication to shape human evolution.

Animals as diverse as fish, worms, gazelles, and lizards stake out particular areas and put up fierce resistance when intruders encroach on their territories. Many species distribute odorous secretions over their individual turfs so that other animals will be aware of their territorial prerogatives. For example, a wolf or wild dog marks its domain by urinating around the perimeter. Ethologists refer to these actions as manifestations of *territoriality*.

Noting that humans also can be extremely aggressive when defending their homes and personal property, Robert Ardrey (1966) has postulated that people may be territorial animals whose aggressive actions arise from the same instinctual base that motivates their nonhuman counterparts.

Figure 11.3 Are people territorial animals? History offers innumerable instances of human aggression in defense of home and land. For example, the Berlin Wall (*left*) was built to keep East Germany "intact." The Great Wall of China (*right*) offered protection against invasion by northern "barbarians." However, the overwhelming evidence points to social factors as more important sources of human aggressiveness than instinct is.

We act as we do for reasons of our evolutionary past, not our cultural present, and our behavior is as much a mark of our species as is the shape of a human thigh bone or the configuration of nerves in a corner of the human brain. If we defend the title to our land or the sovereignty of our country, we do it for reasons no different, no less innate, no less ineradicable, than do lower animals. The dog barking at you from behind his master's fence acts for a motive indistinguishable from that of his master when the fence was built. (page 5)

Ardrey invokes numerous examples: juvenile gangs fighting to protect their turf, neighbors of similar ethnic backgrounds "joining forces" to keep

out those of different skin color or religion, and nations warring over contested territory. But not all human beings exhibit similar inclinations toward aggression or have similar attitudes toward property. There are tribes of human beings that do *not* fight over property or material goods; others simply do not practice any form of aggression (Montagu, 1968). Clearly, then, Ardrey overstates his case. Environmental and social sources of aggression loom as vastly more important than does instinct, as is pointed out many times throughout this chapter.

FRUSTRATION AND AGGRESSION

One of the best-known explanations of human aggression was proposed more than thirty years ago by a group of psychologists and anthropologists at Yale University. The *frustration-aggression hypothesis* (also discussed in Chapter 7) contains two basic claims: *frustration always leads to some form of aggression,* and *aggression never occurs without prior frustration* (Dollard, Doob, Miller, Mowrer, and Sears, 1939). The original statement of this hypothesis emphasized innate connections between frustrating events and subsequent tendencies to aggress against the people responsible for the frustration. Later versions placed greater emphasis on learning. The hypothesis thus occupies a place somewhere between instinctual theories and the environmental emphasis most contemporary researchers favor.

John Dollard and his associates defined frustration as an interference with responses directed at some goal. Suppose, for example, that James hears an ice-cream truck coming down his street. He wants ice cream and may first try to get the necessary money from his mother. If she refuses, he will be deprived of the ice cream and thus will be frustrated. In this situation, the response is defined in terms of all the steps leading to the desired refreshment. The goal is consumption of the ice cream; the boy's mother, by making it impossible for him to attain the goal, is the frustrater. According to the frustration-aggression hypothesis, James will be encouraged to aggress against her.

Yet, for obvious reasons, actual physical aggression against one's mother might not be desirable. In this case, the Yale group hypothesized, aggression can take many forms: muttering under one's breath, imagining sequences of revenge, or making believe that the frustrater died, for example. Thus, the aggression engendered by frustration does not have to be direct or even observable.

The second part of the frustration-aggression hypothesis—that frustration invariably precedes aggression—has proven especially vulnerable to criticism. Even brief reflection can suggest many situations in which aggressive behavior occurs for reasons far removed from any source of frustration. Hired assassins murder individuals whom they have never met, and children use painful wrestling holds on their playmates in imitation of televised brawlers. Or consider the plight of a male college student, age nineteen, who is dating a twenty-one-year-old coed. He takes her into an expensive restaurant and orders in his most sophisticated tone of voice two double scotches, only to be asked by the waiter for identification. Although decidely frustrating, this situation seems far less likely to elicit physical or verbal abuse than an embarrassed silence.

To meet criticisms of the original version of the frustration-aggression hypothesis, Neal Miller (1941) modified it to read that frustration instigates many forms of behavior, only one of which is aggression. Although this is probably a far more realistic assessment, it lacks the dramatic quality of the earlier formulation and therefore has received far less attention. Still, a great deal of evidence has surfaced suggesting that frustration is at least one important elicitor of aggression. Consider the following findings.

Roger Barker, Tamara Dembo, and Kurt Lewin (1941) allowed children to play with a number of attractive toys in a playroom. Other children were taken into a small adjacent room from which they could see the toys but were not allowed to enter the room and play with them. The situation was clearly a frustrating one for the young observers. As expected, when later exposed to the toys, children who previously had been prevented from playing with them engaged in a great deal of destructive activity, smashing some of the play things to the ground and breaking others. Those who had not been frustrated played constructively and quietly.

Carl Hovland and Robert Sears (1940) correlated the number of lynchings of Southern blacks with indices of economic prosperity during the period between 1880 and 1930. When the price of cotton had been high and farmers were prosperous, few lynchings occurred. In contrast, recessions and depressions seemed to be associated with high frequencies of lynchings. Hovland and Sears interpreted this finding to mean that when times were bad, people became frustrated and vented their frustration through murder.

Neal Miller and Richard Bugelski (1948) led a group of young men to believe that they were going to be taken out for a night on the town. Instead, when the time came, they were merely given a difficult and boring test. Both before and after the disappointment, the subjects answered questionnaires concerning their attitudes toward Mexicans and Japanese. Their post-disappointment scores indicated a significant increase in negative attitudes and a corresponding decrease in the positive traits they attributed to Japanese and Mexicans, even though these ethnic groups had in no way been involved in the frustration.

Why would a person generalize from the actual source of frustration and take out aggression on irrelevant targets? Neal Miller (1948) attempted to explain this type of behavior in terms of fear of retaliation, convenience, and similarity of the victim to the aggressor. In the above example the young men presumably were angry at the experimenter. But because they feared the experimenter's possible retaliation, they redirected their antagonism to the convenient and safe target of hypothetical Japanese and Mexicans. Psychologists often refer to this phenomenon as *displacement*, and it is epitomized by the familiar story of the frustrated businessman returning home from work and verbally attacking his unsuspecting wife when he is really angry at his boss. Displacement also has been demonstrated in laboratory experiments with animals. For example, Miller (1948) trained two rats to act aggressively toward each other whenever they were shocked. Although there was a doll present in their cage, the rats almost always attacked each other rather than the inanimate object. When one of the rats was removed from the cage, however, the remaining one then attacked the doll, thereby displacing its aggression onto the only convenient target at hand.

ATTACK AND AGGRESSION

Although frustration appears to be one potent source of aggression, it is not the only source. Abuse from others—either verbal or physical—can also spark aggressive behavior. And apparently the cues that precede or accompany an act of aggression determine for the attacked person the particular meaning of the aggression. For example, what an attacker *says* about his actions may distort the victim's perception of his or her own pain and as a result change the intensity of the victim's counterattack.

Verbal Attack

An experiment by Russell Geen (1968) suggests that frustration may not even be the most powerful stimulus to aggression. He compared the effects of verbal insult and two kinds of frustration on undergraduates' willingness to give painful electric shocks to another student. The situation involved an experimenter, an actual subject, and a confederate of the experimenter who posed as another undergraduate. Subjects who were exposed to *task frustration* were asked by the experimenter to put together a jigsaw puzzle. The task was described as a kind of intelligence test but actually was unsolvable. Other students were subjected to *personal frustration* when

---

HUMOR ISN'T ALWAYS FUNNY—at least not for psychologists who study its forms and functions. One view of humor that is popular with psychologists stems from Freudian theory. It centers on the idea that mirthful expressions release otherwise suppressed feelings of hostility. To test the hypothesis that how hard one laughs depends on who is being laughed at, psychologists Dolf Zillman and Joanne Cantor decided to give two forms of the same jokes and cartoons to two different groups of people. In one form subordinate members of society were in a position of dominance in the joke, and in the other the superior had the upper hand. The investigators showed these to two groups of people who varied in apparent social status: the subordinate group was composed of college students, and the superior group consisted of male Metroliner train passengers en route from New York to Washington, D. C. Would students laugh more when subordinates dominated superiors in a comic situation? Would businessmen from the Metroliner laugh more when the reverse was true?

An example from a large collection of items that are concerned with subordinate-superior relations in the home, school, and office is shown.

Zillman and Cantor found that covert hostility to those in different status positions did indeed seem to be expressed in greater appreciation of the humor of jokes in which a subject's own group was dominant. The table gives the average scores showing who thought what type of dominance expressed was funny. The higher the score, the greater the appreciation of humor directed at the particular victim of domination.

Thus, for example, businessmen thought it funnier when the professor threw the pie in the student's face than when the reverse occurred, whereas students found the student's pie throwing more humorous.

Knowing what amuses a person tells one a lot about that individual's personality and view of others, according to the results of this study. Laughter is a delightful human response and sometimes also a delighted response that belies hostility.

Average Scores for Appreciation of Humor

SUBJECTS	STUDENT THROWS PIE	PROFESSOR THROWS PIE
Students	46*	33
Businessmen	37	47

*Numbers represent statistical results obtained from scores on humor-appreciation measures.

Source: Adapted from D. Zillman and J. Cantor, "Directionality of Transitory Dominance as a Communication Variable Affecting Humor Appreciation," *Journal of Personality and Social Psychology*, 24 (1972), pp.191–198

Humor & Hostility:
THE LAUGH THAT KILLS

their progress in figuring out a jigsaw puzzle that *could* be solved was interrupted several times by the confederate so that they could not complete it in the time allotted. Still others were given the solvable task but were victims of verbal *insult* by the confederate, whose attacks seemed entirely arbitrary. Control-group members were presented with the solvable puzzle and allowed to complete it.

All the subjects subsequently viewed a prize-fight sequence from the movie *Champion*. After viewing this filmed aggression, each subject was placed in a situation ostensibly of teaching the confederate to solve a problem by means of an impressive-looking box containing electronic equipment. The experimenter informed the subjects that they could teach the task to the confederate by pressing either one button that signaled a correct response or any of ten buttons that would deliver shocks of different intensities when the confederate was wrong. The confederate then made a prearranged sixteen errors on thirty trials. Students who had been frustrated either by the task or personally by the confederate delivered stronger shocks than did subjects in the control group. This finding confirmed the prediction of the frustration-aggression hypothesis. However, those subjects who had been verbally insulted delivered the strongest shocks of all.

In a more recent study of the effects of verbal attack, William Gentry (1970) exposed individuals either to insult, frustration, insult *and* frustration, or *neither* insult *nor* frustration. As Geen had found, persons who had been insulted subsequently delivered more intense shocks than did members of any other group. These results do not allow us to conclude that insult always provokes more aggression than frustration does. With milder insult and stronger frustration, for example, the findings might well be reversed. The results do, however, demonstrate that verbal attack can have potent effects in provoking aggression.

Physical Attack

Given the power of verbal attack in eliciting aggression, it is not surprising that direct physical attack also causes aggressive behavior. In animals, the phenomenon of shock-induced aggression has received considerable attention. When Lawrence O'Kelly and Lynde Steckel (1939) applied painful electric shocks to otherwise friendly rats, these animals almost immediately assumed defensive postures and fought among themselves until

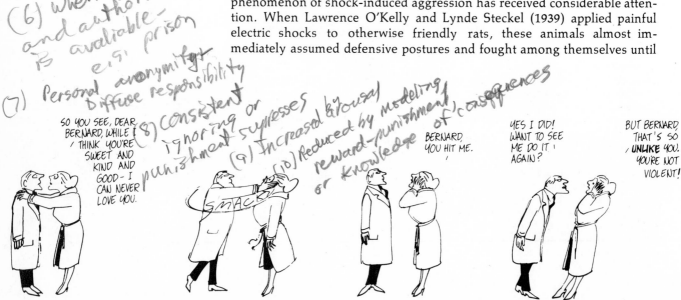

the shocks ended. Given electric shock in the absence of another animal, monkeys will attack inanimate objects such as tennis balls (Azrin, Hutchinson, and Sallery, 1964).

Human aggressive responses, however, are much more complicated under ordinary circumstances. They are determined by the individual's perception of the attacker's intent and the propriety of retaliation as well as by physical pain. A study conducted by James Greenwell and Harold Dengerink (1973) indicates the importance of the interpretation placed on painful events. Subjects learned that they were competing with an opponent; the one who was quickest to respond to a stimulus could deliver an electric shock to the other. Before each trial the participants were to inform each other what strength of shock to expect in case of defeat. In fact, the experiment was rigged. There was no opponent, only a confederate. And the experimenter determined whether the subject would receive or deliver shocks and provided each subject with feedback concerning the strength of shocks according to a predetermined schedule.

In keeping with the animal studies cited earlier, Greenwell and Dengerink found that following trials on which subjects had lost (and therefore received shocks), the subjects usually increased the level of shock that they planned to deliver on the next trial. Furthermore, if the shocks they received remained at a constant level but the feedback they received was falsified to indicate that the level had increased, subjects tended to increase the levels of shock that they planned for their partners. On the other hand, those who received progressively more severe shocks but were told that the shocks were of constant intensity did not, in turn, increase the intensity of shocks supposedly being delivered to their opponents. Thus, aggression is influenced not only by the actual severity of physical attack but also by the attacked individual's *belief* about its harshness. Evidence such as this underlines the importance of the *interpretation of the situation* in any comprehensive definition of aggression.

INSTITUTIONAL AGGRESSION

Although this chapter so far has concentrated on the aggressive actions of individuals who have been frustrated or attacked on a one-to-one basis, personalized aggression is not at all the only type of violence existing in our society. A great many aggressive acts are committed by people who are

merely "doing their jobs" or who find themselves in violent situations because of their jobs and then become angered and commit aggressive acts. Consider the following two descriptions:

At least nine-tenths of the casualties were perpetrated by the police and citizens by stabbing and smashing in the heads of many who had already been wounded or killed by policemen . . . it was not just a riot but "an absolute massacre by the police . . ." a murder which the mayor and police . . . perpetrated without the shadow of necessity. (Kerner, 1968, page 213)

. . . individual policemen were not to blame for their actions and probably could have controlled themselves had they not been "ordered into action by Mayor Daley."

A study group under contract to the President's National Commission on the Causes and Prevention of Violence issued a report yesterday that was highly critical of the Chicago police. It said that the police had conducted indiscriminate attacks and that these attacks amounted to "what can only be called a police riot." (*New York Times*, December 3, 1968, page 28)

Although the above descriptions bear many similarities and may seem to be accounts of the same event, the situations described actually occurred more than one hundred years apart. The first riot (a description of which appears in Otto Kerner's *Report of the National Advisory Commission on Civil Disorders*) actually occurred in the context of Civil War New Orleans when police and special troops battled with newly emancipated blacks. The second passage refers to the 1968 Democratic convention in Chicago. In both cases, it seems that the aggression employed by law-enforcement agents to restore order far exceeded that contributing to the initial disorder. Yet, at least in the case of the convention, the event caused a great deal of sympathy and support for police actions. In wartime, society makes heroes of those who are especially effective in their violence, rewarding them with publicity, medals, and invitations to the White House. Clearly, perceptions of whether or not a given aggressive act is legitimate can tremendously influence its acceptance by society.

Passing On the Misery

Bruno Bettelheim noted in 1943 that more acts of violence have been committed in the name of obedience than ever have been motivated by rebellion. The Nazi concentration camps, the central metaphor for evil in

Figure 11.4 Violence is socially acceptable in some situations but not in others. When football quarterback Joe Namath made the play captured in these photographs, he expected rough treatment from other players. But what would be the reaction of Joe and any onlookers if he received the same treatment off the field?

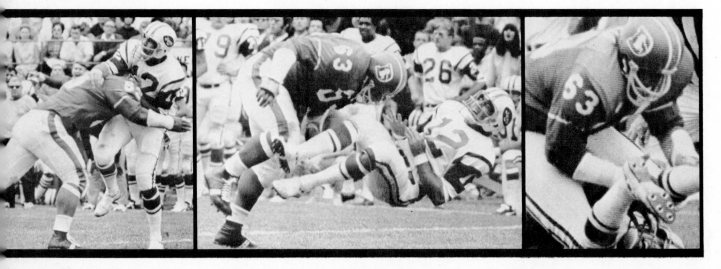

IV INTERACTING WITH OTHERS

the twentieth century, provide especially compelling evidence for Bettelheim's contention. In addition to frequent beatings, stabbings, shootings, and genocide in the gas ovens, the prisoners endured daily hardships, including inadequate food, minimal clothing, and exposure to heat, rain, and freezing temperatures seventeen hours per day, seven days per week. Imprisoned in two of the most notorious camps for several years, Bettelheim himself interviewed other prisoners about their reactions to life in the camps as a means of "maintaining his sanity" (Bettelheim, 1943). He describes his fellow prisoners as a mixed group including Jews, political opponents of the Nazis, Jehovah's Witnesses, homosexuals, and others whom the regime wanted either to intimidate or destroy.

There were great variations in individual reactions to their plight, but Bettelheim observed that a relatively small group of prisoners—members of the middle class who had not been involved in political activity—were particularly vulnerable to the physical and verbal torments.

They found themselves utterly unable to comprehend what had happened to them. . . . They had no consistent philosophy which would protect their integrity as human beings, which would give them the force to make a stand against the Nazis. They had obeyed the law handed down by the ruling classes, without ever

---

HOW SOFTLY DID TEDDY WALK?

FAMED FOR HIS SAYING, "Walk softly and carry a big stick," Teddy Roosevelt spent much of his career in militant activity. Two social psychologists, Michael Harrison and Albert Pepitone, have wondered recently whether or not having a potent weapon at one's disposal increases the frequency and intensity of one's aggression. By studying filmed conflicts between policemen and demonstrators, Harrison and Pepitone noted that armed policemen engaged in more acts of brutality than did unarmed policemen. To put their observations to a more stringent test, they brought male subjects into an animal-training laboratory and instructed them in how to shape a rat's behavior using electric shock. One-third of the subjects served as controls, who could train their animals by using two buttons, one labeled "mild" and the other labeled "slightly painful." One-half of the other subjects could also use a button labeled "moderately painful," and the other half had a third button labeled "extremely painful." All subjects with three shock-intensity alternatives were told not to use the highest-voltage buttons in their training efforts.

All subjects were told that they should be able to train the rat in six minutes using mild shock. This was actually not possible, and the pressure mounted as the clock ticked away for twelve minutes. What did the three groups do to "shape up" their rats? The control group, with only two buttons, gave the fewest and mildest shocks. Subjects with "extremely painful" buttons gave the most and the stiffest shocks of all, although they did not actually use the strongest-shock button. And the middle-range group gave an intermediate number and intensity of shocks.

Why are the most powerfully armed persons likely to be most cruel? Pepitone and Harrison speculate that very potent weapons make other punishments seem mild and ineffectual in comparison and that prohibiting use of the most potent weapons increases the rationale for using the milder weapons.

The results of this study seem to indicate that Teddy Roosevelt's strategy would be difficult to carry out. Apparently, little sticks are more desirable than big sticks in the hands of guardians of the peace.

Source: Adapted from M. Harrison and A. Pepitone, "Contrast Effects in the Use of Punishment," *Journal of Personality and Social Psychology*, 23 (1972), pp. 398–404.

questioning its wisdom. And now this law, or at least the law-enforcing agencies, turned against them, who always had been its staunchest supporters. . . . They could not question the wisdom of law and of the police, so they accepted the behavior of the Gestapo as just. What was wrong was that *they* were made objects of a persecution which in itself *must* be right, since it was carried out by the authorities. The only way out of this particular dilemma was to be convinced that it must be a "mistake." (Bettelheim, 1943, page 426)

Of additional interest was the behavior of long-time prisoners—those who had been prisoners in the camps for several years and had, in a certain sense, adjusted to the conditions. Bettelheim noted that it was common for these prisoners to copy the guards' every action: the way they walked, their language, even their abuse of other inmates. One game that the guards played was to beat a group of prisoners and to bet on who could withstand the punishment for the longest time. Some long-time prisoners adopted this same activity as recreation among themselves. Others collected scraps of guards' old uniforms and sewed them onto their own clothing so as to closely resemble their captors, despite the fact that they often were severely punished by the guards for doing so. At first impression, such behavior seems nothing short of incredible. But in the light of studies like the one conducted by Albert Bandura, Dorothea Ross, and Sheila Ross (1963b), which is described later in the chapter, victims' *identification with the aggressor* becomes slightly more believable, although no more easily understandable. This study, and numerous others like it, have demonstrated that individuals imitate the actions of successful aggressors whom they condemn on a verbal level.

When tried at Nuremberg following World War II, those responsible for the concentration-camp atrocities claimed that they were only obeying orders. Because the tribunal considered this defense to be insufficient justification, it convicted and executed or imprisoned for life many former

Figure 11.5 Violent acts in the name of obedience to authority are often rewarded, as demonstrated by the awarding of medals to this highly decorated South Vietnamese major (*left*) and to World War II hero Audie Murphy (*right*), who later became a popular film star. Although the soldier quoted on the opposite page may not have enjoyed his job as much as the major and Murphy may have, he nevertheless obeyed the orders of his superiors because he feared the consequences of disobedience.

IV Interacting With Others

Nazis. Although in no way implying that punishment is not warranted under such circumstances, a series of experiments by Stanley Milgram (1963) has demonstrated that under certain circumstances most individuals will inflict harsh pain on innocent persons in order to follow instructions.

Reactions to Authority: "Just Doing My Job"

In the preceding chapter, it was noted that 65 percent of Milgram's subjects obeyed the commands of an experimenter to deliver increasingly severe shocks to a man in an adjoining room who they believed was a fellow subject. They did this even though the man pounded on the wall, presumably in pain and begging the subject to stop, and then fell completely silent. No physical efforts were made to prevent subjects from leaving if they got up or refused to push the shock buttons; the experimenter limited his prompting to verbal commands that they continue.

The learner's indications of pain were somewhat effective—nine of the forty participants stopped after hearing the pounding on the wall. But for a large majority of subjects, the experimenter's insistence overcame any misgivings they had about what they were doing. Twenty-six of forty subjects continued until they had pressed the switch that administered the most intense shock.

Although most subjects continued, it was clear that they were very uneasy about the situation. Profuse sweating, trembling, groaning, and nervous laughter were common. Many requested permission to stop, and many expressed fear for the learner's health. Nevertheless, the authority represented by the experimenter was sufficiently compelling that his demands overcame any inhibitions the subjects had against harming another human being.

A later study revealed some cause for optimism: By providing subjects with social support for disobedience, Stanley Milgram (1965) found that he could dramatically reverse the blind obedience that nearly two-thirds of his subjects had demonstrated when pitted alone against the experimenter. In this study, two confederates shared the teaching task with the subject. When the learner first pounded on the wall, one confederate announced that he would not continue further and resisted all of the experimenter's efforts to dissuade him. After the second pounding on the wall, the other teaching confederate followed the lead of the first and sat down on the other side of the room. If the subject was still participating, he assumed the entire teaching task, as he had in the first experiment.

In sharp contrast to the initial findings, only four of forty subjects who witnessed the nonconforming models continued to the end. After the second confederate left, only fifteen subjects continued, and most of them stopped on one of the later trials. Thus, given the misgivings that subjects were almost certainly experiencing, the influence exerted by the two disobedient models liberated subjects from the compulsion they otherwise felt to obey the experimenter's orders.

Deindividuation: The Faceless Villain

The authority of the individual who commands others to be aggressive is not the only element within the institutional context that can encourage brutality. Some institutional situations are particularly conducive to unrestrained, impulsive aggression because these situations engender feelings

"I told them to stop," he said. "They didn't, and I had orders to shoot them down, and I did this. I shot them, the lady and the little boy. . . . I was reluctant, but I was following a direct order. If I didn't do this," he argued, "I could stand court-martial for not following a direct order."

—SOLDIER AT SONG MY, SOUTH VIETNAM

of anonymity and thereby lead to abdications of personal responsibility. What results is a weakening or reduction of both the social constraints and the inner restraints that normally guard against impulsive acts of aggression. This process characterizes groups as diverse as rioters, the policemen who are deployed to quell riots, partygoers, and lynch mobs. In all of these cases, factors such as uniformity of roles or clothing discourage people from perceiving one another's individuality. The result is what Leon Festinger, Albert Pepitone, and Theodore Newcomb in 1952 termed *deindividuation,* as opposed to *individuation,* which is characterized by consciousness of individual differences and feelings of personal responsibility.

Philip Zimbardo and his colleagues Craig Haney and Curtis Banks (1973) set out to see how well-adjusted Americans would respond to one of the most depersonalizing of situations—that in which people are assigned either the role of "prisoner" or the role of "guard." The investigators converted the basement of the Stanford University psychology building into a mock prison. The prison included three-man cells, with only mattresses, sheets, and pillows; a "yard" for exercise and recreation; and an unlit closet for solitary confinement. From seventy-five male volunteers, they selected the twenty-one who appeared most mature, most stable, and least involved in antisocial behavior and assigned them randomly to be guards or prisoners. To enhance the realism of the situation, they secured the cooperation of the Palo Alto police department: Officers drove to the prisoners' homes, charged them with suspicion of armed robbery or burglary, "arrested" them, and delivered them to the station for fingerprinting and preparation of identification files. The prisoners were next taken to the mock prison, where they were stripped, sprayed for lice, and forced to stand naked and alone in the prison yard. They were then issued shapeless smocks to be worn as uniforms, placed in their cells, and ordered

Figure 11.6 Zimbardo's prison simulation powerfully demonstrated the consequences of deindividuation that are characteristic of many institutional settings. These photographs, taken during the experiment, begin to capture the aggressive and sometimes sadistic manner assumed by "guards" and the passive, self-deprecating behavior exhibited by "prisoners," who experienced severe psychological and physical reactions to their treatment. In actuality, both "prisoners" and "guards" were college students selected for their maturity and stability and randomly assigned to their respective roles.

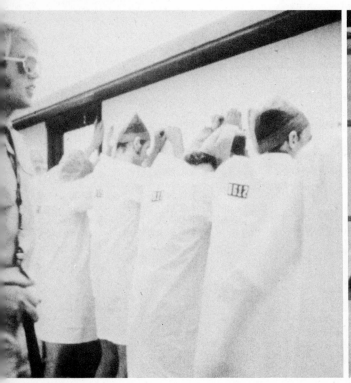

to remain silent. After this, the prisoners stayed in their prison twenty-four hours a day. Their schedule included exercise, meals, and free time.

The guards, on the other hand, worked in three eight-hour shifts and went home when not on duty. Physical violence toward prisoners was strictly forbidden. Guards, like prisoners, were dressed impersonally.

During the first five days, four of the ten prisoners had to be released as a result of fits of rage, crying, and acute anxiety. A fifth was released because he developed a rash that covered large portions of his body. Their instructions allowed guards a high degree of latitude in the postures they could assume toward prisoners; in practice, however, the guards' actions ranged from tough-but-fair to excessively cruel. Virtually no friendliness or helpfulness toward prisoners was observed. The guards stretched the ten-minute line-up periods that had been established for counting prisoners into two-hour interrogation sessions that featured verbal insult and abuse. They did this on their own initiative—no instructions the investigators had given them could have predisposed them to this sort of cruelty.

None of the investigators foresaw how easily their subjects would fall into these roles, nor how traumatic and destructive these temporary roles would be. The researchers originally planned an experiment that would last fourteen days, but they called it off after six days in order to prevent what they felt might be permanent psychic damage to their subjects. Whereas during the initial stage of the study both prisoners and guards indicated general unhappiness with the situation, by the sixth day, when the study was terminated, only the prisoners were glad it was over. The guards appeared to have become sufficiently involved in their work that they were reluctant to relinquish their positions of power.

Even among individuals selected for their emotional stability and altruistic orientations, then, prison life may elicit considerable aggression.

Figure 11.7 Situations that engender feelings of anonymity have been found to lead to the abdication of personal responsibility and increased, as well as indiscriminate, aggression. When riot police march in large groups, wearing similar clothing and covering their faces with riot visors, they may not feel the pressures associated with personal identifiability and accountability.

Thus, the brutality rampant in modern prisons may be as much a function of the *situation*—or, more precisely, of prevailing conceptions of the situation among even those who have never set foot in a prison—as it is a function of any predispositions to violence that may characterize those who are imprisoned or those who choose careers as guards.

Riots, lynchings, and other instances of mass violence represent additional situations in which individuals are likely to commit aggressive acts that they ordinarily would not engage in. All these situations have some features in common. In 1969 Philip Zimbardo employed the term "deindividuation" to explain the phenomenon of mass violence. The prerequisite conditions for this phenomenon, according to Zimbardo, include *personal anonymity* and *diffuse responsibility* as major components. He hypothesized that these conditions result in the weakening of social controls that are based on guilt and shame and, furthermore, that the resulting violence would tend to be irrational and impulsive in execution and in choice of victims.

To test this hypothesis, Zimbardo structured an experimental setting so that one-half of the subjects performed in the dark, were never spoken to by name, and wore bulky overcoats and hoods. Zimbardo intended these conditions to minimize subjects' sense of personal identity and responsibility. The other half of the subjects remained in their normal attire during the experiment and were in a well-lit room, were spoken to by name, wore name tags, and received instructions that emphasized the individuality of their reactions. All listened to two tapes—one of a pleasant and the other of an obnoxious woman. The subjects were instructed to administer shocks to each woman, who they thought was in an adjoining room, in accordance with their reactions to each. Subjects were also informed that they must deliver some shock on every trial but that the intensity would be determined by how long they depressed a button. The subjects participated in groups of four, but no subject could see what any of the others were doing.

Zimbardo found that subjects who wore bulky overcoats and hoods and who were not called by name administered shocks that on the average lasted almost twice as long as did those of the other subjects. In addition, the deindividuated subjects' shocks revealed little correlation with their evaluations of their victims, whereas the duration of the shocks administered by members of the more individuated group correlated highly with their opinions of the women who supposedly were receiving the shocks. This result supports two aspects of Zimbardo's theory. First, removing the burden of individual responsibility apparently tends to make people more willing to aggress. Second, in deindividuating situations, aggressors tend to be more indiscriminate in their choice of victims; legitimate as well as undeserving foes are chosen. Evidence derived from the mass media also supports this latter point. For example, during riots in the United States, the stores of both white and black merchants, those who are considered exploiters as well as those who are not, have frequently been destroyed with equal abandon by angry inner-city residents.

Figure 11.8 Situations that foster feelings of anonymity also foster both abdication of personal responsibility and reduction of inhibitions against aggression. Many forms of institutional violence are the result of (and historically have resulted from) feelings of anonymity, as indicated in this fourteenth-century etching of a public executioner in Paris.

EFFECTS OF REWARD AND PUNISHMENT

Instances of aggression and violence are not exclusively the products of human beings' innate characteristics, of institutional contexts, or of the immediate situations in which people find themselves. These factors have cumulative effects on all of us. The consequences of our past actions, aggressive or otherwise, affect how we behave today. Do we behave well or badly, repay aggression with aggression or with forgiveness, respond to our frustrations with hostility or with reflection?

The outcomes of each of people's past aggressive actions probably have been either rewarding or punishing to them. If their actions were effective and went unpunished, the likelihood that they would resort to similar actions in the future increases. This was certainly true in most parts of the South where whites were rarely tried for or convicted of the murder or lynching of blacks. Thus, the type of response to verbal or physical abuses—whether people are rewarded or punished for engaging in such abuses—influences whether people commit further aggression.

Reward

Given the effectiveness of reward in numerous social situations (see Chapter 2), it is not surprising that reward influences aggression as well. Richard Walters and Murray Brown (1963) clearly demonstrated that rewarding a child for aggressing against a toy Bobo doll usually results in subsequent aggression against other children. The doll was constructed so that its eyes and a flower in its button hole lit up when anyone punched it in the stomach with sufficient force. Boys were either rewarded with a glass marble following some punches but not others (partial reinforcement) or reward was simply intrinsic—the enjoyment they could obtain by punching the doll and illuminating its eyes and lapel flower. All of the boys subsequently were allowed to play a series of games involving physical contact with a naive peer. The children who had been partially rewarded for aggression against the Bobo doll showed significantly more hitting, kicking, kneeing, elbowing, and other aggressive acts than did boys who enjoyed exclusively intrinsic rewards.

Gerald Patterson, Richard Littman, and William Bricker (1967) have studied the *development* of aggressive behavior in a natural environment. They entered a nursery school and observed sixty class meetings, each lasting two and one-half hours. In the course of their observations, they witnessed 2,583 aggressive incidents among the children and in each case recorded the aggressor, the victim, the form of the aggressive act (whether hitting, verbal insult, or some other form), and its consequence. They had hypothesized that when a child is praised for his or her aggression or wins his or her objective, the next act of aggression he or she undertakes will tend to be against the same victim and to assume the same form. On the other hand, if the aggressive act is met either by counteraggression or by the victim regaining a toy or territory, the child's next aggressive act will either be directed at a different victim, will assume a different form, or both. These two predictions both were confirmed. Furthermore, children who were passive when they entered the nursery school learned that counteraggression usually met with success; they therefore became increasingly ready to resort to action when aggressed against. Patterson and his associates concluded that children learn both to be aggressive and to respond forcefully when attacked because in doing so they are rewarded directly or indirectly by adults and peers.

These findings raise an interesting question: Can classroom aggression in young children be reversed by changing reinforcement contingencies? In a particularly interesting naturalistic study, Paul Brown and Rogers Elliott (1965) observed the aggressive patterns of twenty-seven male nursery-school children for one week and then requested that the teachers not attend to any but the most severe aggressive actions. (It was intended that the teachers' nonattention would, in the terminology of learning theorists, extinguish the bad behavior.) In addition, Brown and Elliott asked the teachers to reward cooperative and other desirable behaviors. Within fourteen days, both verbal and physical aggression decreased substantially. Several weeks later, the experimenters returned and found that the incidence of physical aggression had returned to the earlier level, although verbal aggression had continued to decline. They therefore again recommended nonattention to fights and other disruptions; as indicated in Table 11.1, this second round of efforts at extinguishing aggressive behavior produced even greater reductions in both forms of aggressive behavior than before. This study carries special promise because, following the extinction periods, two of the most violent boys in the class "became friendly and cooperative to a degree not previously thought possible."

Reinforcement of aggression is seldom accomplished through a conscious effort on the part of parents, teachers, and other socializing agents, but it nevertheless occurs. Attention per se is a rewarding experience, and human beings of all ages go out of their way to obtain it. But if attention is not usually given to children unless they are acting out some form of aggression, it is likely that they will learn to rely on aggressive acts to gain attention. Brown and Elliott's observations provide dramatic evidence that aggression can be deconditioned by ignoring aggressive behavior.

Punishment: The Two-Edged Sword

The effects of punishment apparently are far more complicated than those of reward. Whereas some authorities—parents, educators, political and religious leaders, and so on—have claimed that only the threat of punishment deters many individuals from acting more aggressively (Walters and Thomas, 1963), others have contended that punishment only temporarily suppresses aggression and that as soon as the threat becomes less imminent, the suppressed behavior will recur (Estes, 1944).

In some situations, punishment apparently can eliminate aggressive responses, although the effects may depend on the regularity with which it is applied. For example, Jan Deur and Ross Parke (1970) observed first-, second-, and third-grade children playing a game that involved putting on boxing gloves and hitting a toy clown in the stomach. They reinforced some children by giving them a marble after half of their punches and punished them by sounding a loud buzzer after the other half of their punches. The researchers also informed the children that marbles meant that they were

Table 11.1 The Influence of Teacher Behavior on the Aggressive Behavior of Nursery-School Boys

TIMES OF OBSERVATION	CATEGORIES OF AGGRESSION*		
	Physical	Verbal	Total
Pre-treatment	41.2	22.8	64.0
First treatment	26.0	17.4	43.4
Follow-up	37.8	13.8	51.6
Second treatment	21.0	4.6	25.6

*Average number of incidents.
Source: P. Brown and R. Elliott, "Control of Aggression in a Nursery School Class," Journal of Experimental Child Psychology, 2 (1965), p. 106.

playing the game well and that buzzes meant that they were playing poorly. After two minutes of this inconsistent feedback, half of the children received neither rewards nor punishments (extinction) and the remainder were punished by the buzzer for all subsequent punches. Punishment worked more quickly than extinction did in persuading the children to stop playing the game.

There was another important finding, however. Youngsters who had received the combination of 50 percent reward and 50 percent punishment on their first several trials were far more resistant to the schedules of both continuous extinction and continuous punishment than were children who had been treated more consistently. Thus it would appear that it was the inconsistent practice of both rewarding and punishing aggression that produced behavior resistant to extinction and minimally affected by punishment. This finding suggests a somewhat distressing analogy. In most families and schools, children who aggress sometimes are rewarded (for example, they succeed in taking the toy away from their playmate or they are told that they are brave for winning fights) and at other times punished (for example, they are called bullies, or their playmates successfully defend their possessions). If Deur and Parke's findings are generally applicable, inconsistencies of this nature may lead to considerable resistance to later punishment, possibly resulting in incorrigibility.

Clearly, then, both in the laboratory and in naturalistic settings, the consequences of aggression substantially influence both its frequency and the form it takes. Reward is an effective shaper of aggressive acts, and systematic extinction in combination with rewards for desirable (nonaggressive) behavior appears to be particularly effective in controlling excessive aggression, at least among children. Punishment, on the other hand, also has some suppressive influence on aggression. However, a problem

Figure 11.9 Children learn many aggressive behaviors through modeling, or imitation, of others' behavior. Young Jordanians (*left*) between the ages of eight and sixteen carry machine guns and live ammunition when accompanying their elders in raids on Israeli territory. An American youngster (*right*) learns how to use a gun just as daddy does.

that often accompanies the use of punishment should not be overlooked: It often provides compelling examples of the very behavior that it is employed to eliminate. A great many punishing acts, such as yelling or spanking, require the punisher to behave aggressively himself or herself. Thus, modeling can also increase aggressive behavior; this process is described fully in Chapter 2. Does the modeling process contain additional implications both for increasing and for reducing aggressive behavior?

MODELING OF AGGRESSIVE BEHAVIOR

There are at least two ways in which the modeling of aggressive acts is connected with aggressive behavior. First, violence can be taught by means of example; observers show a remarkable inclination to repeat the violent performances of others. Second, viewing violent models who gain rewards for their violence or go unpunished may communicate the message that it is acceptable for the viewer to use aggressive responses in a similar fashion. In each case, the probability increases that the observer will behave in an aggressive manner.

In a now-classic study by Albert Bandura (1965), one group of children saw an aggressive model rewarded for smacking a Bobo doll with a club; one saw him punished; and one saw him receive neither reward nor punishment for his behavior. Children who saw the model punished subsequently exhibited less aggression than did those in the other conditions, although when encouraged to recall the model's actions, they were able to reconstruct the model's techniques accurately. Bandura warned that even when aggressors are punished, they may still be instrumental in teaching observers novel ways to aggress as well as pushing prevailing standards of behavior in the direction of overt aggression. Even if observers do not approve of the model's intentions, the aggressive actions may be reenacted by those same observers when the situation suits them.

The discerning reader may have noted that in the strict sense of the definition this last study is not directly concerned with aggression because the target is an inanimate Bobo doll. However, a study conducted by Albert Bandura, Dorothea Ross, and Sheila Ross (1963b) has revealed that children also imitate aggressive acts on human targets. These investigators showed nursery-school children a television program in which a boy named Johnny is playing with some toys and refuses to let another boy, Rocky, play with him. Rocky proceeds to hit Johnny with a baton, lasso him with a hula hoop, shoot darts at his cars, and defeat him in such a manner that the aggressor winds up with all the toys. At the end of the sequence he departs with Johnny's hobby-horse under his arm and a sack of Johnny's toys over his shoulder.

When the children who saw this scene were asked to evaluate Rocky's conduct, most of them indicated disapproval. But when the experimenters placed them in a somewhat analogous situation, those who had seen Rocky's victory performed in a dramatically more aggressive manner than did those who either had seen the same sequence with a different ending (in which Johnny successfully counterattacked) or who had not seen a movie at all. The effect was personified by the actions of a four-year-old girl who had expressed severe disapproval of Rocky's behavior during the movie but, when placed in the analogous situation, imitated many of his actions. Indeed, after vanquishing the original owner of the toys, she turned to the experimenter and inquired, "Do you have a sack here?" Thus, the influence of witnessing a successful aggressive model apparently overrides observers' stated opinions about the model's behavior.

The Medium Is the Message

Another determining factor in the effectiveness of models is the media through which they are presented. For example, Albert Bandura, Dorothea Ross, and Sheila Ross (1963a) compared the effects of showing the same content as a cartoon, on film, or as a live drama. The subjects who watched either the live performance or the film saw an experimenter beating a Bobo doll with a mallet, hitting it, kicking it, and verbally berating it with statements such as "Sock him in the nose," "Hit him down," and "Pow!" The cartoon presentation featured similar actions, but the protagonist was dressed as a black cat and typical cartoon music was included.

After presenting one of these versions, the experimenters frustrated the youngsters by inviting them to play with a collection of highly attractive toys and then informing them that these toys were being reserved for other children and that they therefore would have to be content with the toys that were in the next room. These toys included some that the subjects had encountered earlier, such as Bobo dolls and mallets, in addition to various toys that were not well adapted to aggressive play.

Members of all three groups engaged in more aggressive play than did members of a control group, who had not seen any of the presentations. As it turned out, the cartoon and the film appeared to be more effective than the live presentation. This finding suggests that the violence reported by the media might be especially influential in promoting aggressive behavior among young children. In fact, a topic of great contemporary interest concerns the effects of media violence on children's social behavior.

The Effects of Televised Aggression

Many children receive almost continuous exposure to television; Aletha Hudson Stein, Lynette Kohn Friederich, and Fred Vondracek reported in 1972 that their sample watched television an average of thirty hours per week. A large portion of this exposure is to violent behavior; George Gerbner (1972) found that an average of more than seven of every ten programs contained at least one violent episode. And, as already noted, violent actions are related to subsequent imitation of them. Therefore,

Television portrays a world in which "good guys" and "bad guys" alike use violence to solve problems and achieve goals. Violence is rarely presented as illegal or socially unacceptable. Indeed, as often as not, it is portrayed as a legitimate means for attaining desired ends. Moreover, the painful consequences of violence are underplayed and de-emphasized by the "sanitized" way in which much of it is presented.

—NATIONAL COMMISSION ON THE CAUSES AND PREVENTION OF VIOLENCE

investigators have devoted much effort to documenting the effects of televised violence on children's interpersonal behavior. Two of these studies, discussed below, illustrate the kind of work being done and the typical findings.

Faye Steuer, James Applefield, and Rodney Smith (1971) presented eleven video-taped television episodes, each lasting ten minutes, to two groups of preschool children. One group watched programs taken from Saturday morning television that included one or more incidents of violence. Programs such as these are geared specifically to children and typically consist of numerous cartoon shows and filmed dramas as well. The other group of children saw shows taped from the same time period that did not include any violence.

Each school day, both before and after watching the programs, the investigators observed the children in order to measure the amount of aggression that occurred. They defined aggressive acts as hitting, kicking, choking, or throwing objects at other children. As it turned out, a substantially greater number of aggressive acts were committed by those children who had watched the violent programs, as indicated in Figure 11.10. The finding that watching a ten-minute violent program on each of eleven school days made children significantly more aggressive is especially striking because the investigators matched their young subjects so that prior to the exposure they were all equally aggressive.

Some psychologists have argued that violent programs may increase the level of observed aggression not because they are violent per se but because they are generally more exciting and therefore increase viewers' general arousal (Klapper, 1968). An experiment reported by Dolf Zillman in 1971 revealed evidence of this possibility. Adult subjects viewed one of three films: an educational film, a filmed prize fight, or an erotic film. Afterwards they interacted with an experimental confederate in a situation in which they were encouraged to punish the confederate. The results showed that the amount of punishment delivered was not related to the amount of aggressive content in the film but rather to the excitement value

Figure 11.10 The comparative effects of televised violence and nonviolence on the behavior of two of five pairs of preschoolers studied by Steuer, Applefield, and Smith (1971). The subjects were initially matched for similar levels of home television viewing, observed at play with other children for ten sessions, and then observed for an additional eleven sessions that were each preceded by viewing of ten-minute television programs that either did or did not have violent content. Of the five pairs studied, the two pairs represented here showed by far the most dramatic differences between responses to televised aggression and responses to televised nonaggression. A third pair of youngsters showed a much less dramatic difference, and the remaining two pairs showed almost no differences. The range of responses revealed in these data points to the possibility that responses to televised violence are to a large extent governed by individual dispositions and therefore can be expected to differ markedly from person to person.

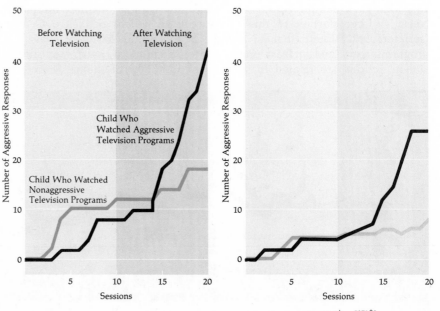

Fig. 11.14 – SOP182

IV INTERACTING WITH OTHERS

of the film. Thus, an erotic film can be just as potent a stimulant to aggression as is an aggressive one.

It has become evident during this discussion that modeling exerts powerful effects on aggressive behavior—whether the observer is a child or an adult, whether the model appears in person, on film, or on television, and whether the behavior being modeled is aggressive or otherwise arousing in its effects on the observer. We appear, to a marked degree, to do what we see others do. By the same token, each of us may at times be a potent model for others. Thus, one means of reducing aggression is to inhibit our own aggressive behavior. In doing so, we contain our own violent impulses and inhibit others as well from aggressive acts.

REDUCING AGGRESSION

Most of this chapter so far has been concerned with theories of aggression and the conditions under which aggression occurs; this last section will explore some of the means of reducing aggression that are available to parents, educators, civil authorities, and social engineers of all types.

Catharsis

What psychologists call the *catharsis hypothesis* is perhaps the best-known theory on reducing aggression. According to this approach, by bringing unconscious impulses to the surface—whether through fantasy or displaced action—people can render these impulses harmless. Thus, boys who participate in school sports may become less likely to vent their aggressive impulses on their families and friends, for example.

Partial support for this theory has been provided by Seymour Feshbach. In 1955 he hypothesized that "fantasy expression of hostility will partially reduce situationally induced aggression." As a test, Feshbach exposed one group of college undergraduates to verbal insults and then allowed them to fantasize revenge against their attacker; he insulted a second group and did not allow them time to fantasize; and he allowed a third group that had not been insulted to fantasize.

Feshbach measured aggression by means of a sentence-completion test on which subjects could attribute whatever qualities they wanted to the individual who had attacked them. The three groups did not differ in their answers to the questions as a whole. However, when Feshbach examined answers to a subset of questions that he believed to be particularly revealing of aggressive impulses, he found that insulted subjects who had been given an opportunity to fantasize indicated less aggression than did insulted subjects who had had no time to fantasize.

More recent studies, however, provide relatively strong evidence against the catharsis hypothesis. Shahbaz Mallick and Boyd McCandless (1966) gave third-graders who either had or had not been frustrated by a clumsy and inconsiderate confederate the opportunity to shoot a dart gun at a picture of live individuals, to shoot the gun at a target, or to do arithmetic problems. According to the catharsis hypothesis, shooting the gun at the picture of the people would be expected to have reduced aggression the most. Instead, no differences were found in the number of shocks later administered to the confederate, regardless of whether or not subjects were allowed to shoot the dart gun. In a second part of the same experiment, Mallick and McCandless gave some frustrated and some nonfrustrated third-graders an opportunity to shoot the dart gun at a picture of a child the same age and sex as the one who had frustrated them; other children who had or had not been frustrated either were engaged in social conversation or were told that the confederate was tired and crabby and probably would have been nicer under other circumstances. This reinterpretation proved an effective means of reducing the number of shocks later delivered to the confederate, whereas shooting a dart gun was ineffective. The authors concluded that at least when children can aggress only against inanimate objects, catharsis does not occur.

The generality of Mallick and McCandless' findings has been extended by Richard DeCharms and Edward Wilkins (1963). These investigators studied male college students who were insulted by a confederate. Some were given an opportunity to respond to the insult; others heard another individual berate the confederate; and still others had no opportunity to see the confederate punished. According to the catharsis hypothesis, those who had an opportunity to attack or to hear another do so should subsequently be less aggressive against the confederate. Instead, they became more aggressive. Thus, the best that can be said about the catharsis hypothesis is that if catharsis occurs at all, it is not a highly general reaction; the conditions under which it occurs remain unspecified.

Modeling

Exposure to nonaggressive models, on the other hand, appears to be a far more potent means of reducing aggression than is catharsis. As shown previously, Stanley Milgram reported in 1965 that subjects were markedly less willing to follow an experimenter's instructions that they aggress after they had observed two confederates refusing to do so. Robert Baron and C. Richard Kepner (1970) also reported that subjects who were exposed to a nonaggressive model after being insulted behaved less aggressively than either those who saw an aggressive model or those who witnessed no model. Given the power of aggressive models to elicit aggression, it is not surprising that nonaggressive models exert comparable effects in reducing aggression.

Criticism of aggressive models also appears to be successful in reducing subsequent violence in some situations. For example, Robert Baron (1972) found that those subjects who heard one confederate criticize another for aggressive behavior subsequently delivered less intense shocks than when they observed no censure. However, although censure did affect the intensity of shocks, it did not affect the duration of shocks that subjects administered. In a related experiment, Ladd Wheeler and Seward Smith (1967) found that criticism of aggressive behavior was effective, but only when the critic was of high status (in this case, a naval officer) rather than a peer (an enlisted man).

Use of Reward and Punishment

It was noted earlier in the chapter that reward and punishment can serve to increase aggression. By the same token, reward and punishment can be used to reduce aggressive activity. Although this point should be clear from the previous discussion, Richard Pisano and Stuart Taylor (1971) have expanded its implications in an interesting way. They investigated the effects of different coping strategies that individuals could employ to countermand aggression directed at them. Subjects ostensibly were playing a game in which they had a single opponent; the purpose of the game was to react to a signal as quickly as possible. Before each trial, the participants were to signal their opponent as to the level of shock that the opponent could expect if he reacted more slowly than they. If subjects were faster, they would be spared the shock but would be informed of the intensity of the shock they would have suffered had they lost.

In reality there was no opponent; the subject won and lost on a predetermined one-half of the trials, and the levels of shock supposedly set by the opponent actually were controlled by the experimenter. One strategy the investigators utilized was a *pacifist* approach; regardless of the subjects' actions, they received the least intense shocks possible on every trial. A second approach was that of *punishment* in which the opponent invariably delivered the most painful possible shocks to the subjects. A third strategy was a *matching* strategy; the opponent adopted whatever level of shock the subject had set on the previous trial.

Of the three approaches, the matching strategy was by far the most effective in reducing shock intensities. In contrast, when the opponents continually selected the most intense shocks, subjects chose increasingly high shock levels to match the ones that they were getting. The peaceful approach was not as counterproductive as the warlike strategy, but neither did it succeed in reducing the initially high levels of shock chosen by the subjects. The study suggests, then, that rewarding low shock levels and punishing high ones (through matching) is more effective than noncontingently rewarding (through continuous low-intensity shock) or noncontingently punishing (through continuous high-intensity shock) aggressive acts. In effect, turning the other cheek does not seem to be an effective means of reducing another's aggression. This is not to say that pacifism is never effective in taking the teeth out of others' aggression. To mention but one example, Mahatma Gandhi and his followers were able to change the course of Indian history dramatically through nonviolent resistance. However, the effectiveness of pacifism depends to a great extent on the circumstances under which it occurs and the meaning it holds for both victim and aggressor. This topic is taken up again shortly.

Victim Pain

In an era of push-button warfare and urban depersonalization, people often escape the knowledge of the *consequences* of their aggression. The target is "somewhere out there"—some stranger or someone unlike the aggressor. Should perpetrators of violence learn the extent of the pain they cause others, perhaps they would be less aggressive.

Robert Baron (1971a) required subjects to deliver electric shocks to another person. He created variations in victims' pain by means of a machine that he told subjects measured physiological reactions and thus provided an index of the victim's discomfort. The meter registered relatively more intense pain when some subjects pushed the shock buttons than when others pushed the same buttons. Regardless of whether or not they had been angered previously, subjects who received information that the confederate was in pain tended to reduce the strength of their attacks. In fact, the greater the magnitude of pain cues, the greater the decrease in strength and duration of shocks subjects thought they were delivering. Thus, angered subjects were not elated when they saw that they were causing their foe considerable discomfort and took measures to relieve the victim's suffering. By means of somewhat different techniques, other researchers, such as Harvey Tilker (1970), have found that cues that the

Figure 11.11 Laboratory research suggests that observing a victim's pain inhibits further aggression toward that victim. Can these findings be generalized to "real-world" situations? If national leaders were confronted with first-hand evidence of the violent consequences of their decisions, would the world be more peaceful?

victim is undergoing distinct discomfort tend to inhibit an aggressor, at least in laboratory settings. Subjects have even reduced the intensity and duration of their shocks when their victims were different from the subjects in attire, current occupation, and attitudes (Baron, 1971b).

These findings add significantly to the earlier discussion of pacifism. They suggest that at least one condition under which a pacifistic strategy will reduce aggression is when the pain a pacifist undergoes is manifest—when neither aggressors nor observers can ignore the consequences of violence to the victims. Additional factors that influence individuals to help the victims of misfortune are discussed in Chapter 12.

SUMMARY

Although it might seem to be easy to distinguish actions that are aggressive from those that are not, this distinction begins to blur if one asks who the *target* of the act is, how *legitimate* the act is, and what the *intent* behind it is. Aggression in this chapter is defined as any real or planned act of physical or verbal abuse that one human being directs at another.

Aggressive behavior may be influenced by innate factors. Biochemical functions or malfunctions appear to be important sources of aggression. However, there is little evidence that instinct underlies human aggression.

One of the best-known theories of aggression is the *frustration-aggression hypothesis.* Initially its proponents theorized that aggression always follows frustration. More recent research, however, has shown that frustration is only one of a number of factors that can lead to aggressive behavior. Under certain conditions, physical and verbal attack may be more potent than frustration in causing violence. The individual's *interpretation of the situation* also influences his or her reaction to attack.

Despite the negative value our culture places on many aggressive acts, in some cases, such as military and police actions, violence is applauded. Also, orders by authority figures to do violence are often able to overcome an individual's inhibitions against violence, especially if this authority confronts a lone individual. *Personal anonymity* and *diffused responsibility* are additional sources of license to commit acts of aggression or violence.

Just as the consequences of one's past actions influence his or her present behavior, so do aggressive tendencies arise from one's past experience. For example, as research has shown, if the aggression of schoolchildren is rewarded in some way, it is likely to increase; if it is ignored, however, aggressive activity is likely to become less frequent. The role of punishment in deterring aggression is more complicated. Punishment mixed with reward makes aggressive behavior difficult to extinguish.

Viewing aggressive models can stimulate aggressive acts. Those who see models rewarded for violent actions are more likely to imitate them than are those who see them punished. But those who see the model punished may still learn forms of aggression for use in other situations. A model can encourage aggression, whether the model appears on film, on a televised program, or is actually present, although a filmed or video-taped model apparently can sometimes be more effective than a live one.

Aggression can be reduced as well as encouraged. One way may be through *catharsis*—giving vent to hostile feelings—although catharsis does not seem to be effective in all circumstances. More reliably, a model who refuses to behave aggressively may encourage other individuals to behave nonaggressively. When threatened with aggression, an individual will discourage it more quickly by responding with submission or by punishing the aggressor with an even higher level of aggression. Another way to reduce aggression, research findings suggest, is to allow the aggressor to witness the victim's pain. Findings such as these may prove useful in society's efforts to reduce violence and aggression.

SUGGESTED READINGS

Bandura, Albert, and Richard H. Walters. *Social Learning and Personality Development.* New York: Holt, Rinehart and Winston, 1963.

Berkowitz, Leonard. *Aggression: A Social Psychological Analysis.* New York: McGraw-Hill, 1962.

Buss, Arnold H. *The Psychology of Aggression.* New York: Wiley, 1961.

Kaufmann, Harry. *Aggression and Altruism, A Psychological Analysis.* New York: Holt, Rinehart and Winston, 1970.

Kerner, Otto. *Report of the National Advisory Commission on Civil Disorders.* New York Times editors. New York: Dutton, 1968.

Larsen, Otto (ed.). *Violence and the Mass Media.* New York: Harper and Row, 1968.

Lorenz, Konrad. *On Aggression.* New York: Harcourt, Brace & World, 1966.

Schlesinger, Arthur M., Jr. *Violence: America in the Sixties.* New York: New American Library, 1968.

12
Prosocial Behavior

Kitty Genovese is attacked by a knife-wielding assailant in a residential neighborhood of New York City. As thirty-eight of her neighbors watch, the assailant makes three separate attacks on her. No one comes to her assistance or even calls the police, although the killer takes more than half an hour to murder her.

A young woman is set upon by her estranged husband, who stabs her repeatedly. A fellow student rushes to her aid and strikes the attacker with a chair while other students throw books at the assailant. The man is disarmed and the victim recovers from her injuries.

A woman is abducted and raped. She manages to escape from the car of her assailant and runs nude along a busy freeway, calling for help and trying to flag down cars. No one stops, and the rapist eventually recaptures her and drags her back into his car.

A sniper is firing from a tower at the University of Texas. Despite obvious danger of death, several people leave their refuge to bring the wounded to safety.

A seventeen-year-old boy is stabbed in the stomach while riding home on the subway. Eleven other riders watch as he bleeds to death; none comes to his assistance, although his attackers have left the car.

Two young boys wading in a fast-moving stream are overcome by the current. A nearby picnicker dives into the water and pulls one to safety. While attempting to save the other, he and the boy both drown.

WHY IS IT THAT HUMAN BEINGS vary so much in their response to crises that endanger others? It is easy to answer that "some people" care about their fellow beings and "other people" do not. Undoubtedly, most people would be tempted to feel that they are among the "some" but that they know lots of the "others." Yet, when this question is considered more closely, the answer becomes more complex. What would *you* do if confronted with one of the situations described at the beginning of the chapter, in which danger threatens and you must decide in a split second whether to act or not?

Most of us have experienced situations in which we have not acted when we felt that we should. Many feelings can prevent people from acting on their judgments of what they "ought" to do—feelings such as uncertainty that they are competent to help, fear of making a spectacle of themselves, depression, and inertia. The picture of nonintervening bystanders that emerges from interviews with witnesses to such tragedies as the Kitty Genovese slaying is not one of people who are simply callous misanthropes. Rather, these bystanders are everyday citizens who for various reasons, including the presence of other potential aiders and the identity of the victim, construe the situation as one not requiring *their* action. If one is to understand, then, what inspires and what blocks helping, it is important to suspend for the moment the desire for simplistic some-people-do-and-others-don't interpretations of altruistic acts and to examine instead the various factors that influence a given person to help or not to help in a particular situation.

The domain of prosocial behavior is broader than the crisis reactions offered in the examples above. Acts that may be considered prosocial include a wide range of behavior—from saving a person who is drowning to helping someone carry his packages, from donating a kidney to donating a penny, from the heroic to the merely thoughtful. The common denominator of these acts is their apparent selflessness, the voluntary doing of "good" for another person without apparent gain for oneself.

Dennis Krebs (1970), in a recent review of writings on altruism, has identified three aspects by which conventional wisdom defines prosocial acts: A prosocial act is performed voluntarily by an actor; the actor intends for the act to benefit another person or group of persons; and the act is performed as an end in itself and not as a means to fulfilling an ulterior personal motive of the actor. People have espoused selflessness and concern for others for thousands of years, and altruism is one of the most universally accepted ethics. Almost every culture embraces a norm that specifies that concern is good and that selfishness is bad. The unwritten rule in most societies is that when the cost is not too great and another person is in need, one should do all that one can to aid that person. Some societies have even legislated the conditions under which sanctions require one member to aid another member.

The universality of some norm of social responsibility indicates that this standard has functional value, that it operates to facilitate social life. Furthermore, there is evidence (Hebb, 1971; Trivers, 1971) to suggest that altruistic behavior is instinctual and directed toward the survival of the species. If prosocial behavior does indeed serve to protect the species from extinction, the process of evolution may have produced an inherited concern for others.

Despite the pervasiveness of the helping norm and the possible biological basis for prosocial concern, societies have varied in the degree to which they emphasize altruism. Talcott Parsons (1951) has suggested that societies (and individuals) have either an individualistic or a collectivistic orientation. An individualistic culture or person emphasizes personal concerns about self-fulfillment, achievement, and expression. A collectivistic orientation, on the other hand, is concerned with social responsibility, interdependence, and mutuality among people.

THE CURRENT SIGNIFICANCE OF PROSOCIAL BEHAVIOR

Current social-psychological interest in prosocial behavior stems from both cultural and scientific factors. Cultural factors include reactions to the depersonalization inherent in mass society and to the breakdown of previously accepted behavioral standards governing our society—factors that are contributing momentum in many sectors of society toward the values of community and interdependence.

This culture's religious and humanistic traditions, which call for mutuality and concern for others, are in conflict with its capitalistic, competitive features, which place great emphasis on individualism. The current era

Figure 12.1 Altruism is an ideal norm advocated in most societies, past and present, as exemplified by the pledge doctors take to help others; an engraving depicting the story of the good Samaritan, who aided others; and the behavior of a modern New Yorker assisting an epileptic.

> *I solemnly pledge myself to consecrate my life to the service of humanity.*
> *I will give to my teachers the respect and gratitude which is their due;*
> *I will practice my profession with conscience and dignity;*
> *the health of my patient will be my first consideration;*
> *I will respect the secrets which are confided in me;*
> *I will maintain by all means in my power the honor and the noble traditions*
> *of the medical profession; my colleagues will be my brothers;*
> *I will not permit considerations of religion, nationality, race, party politics,*
> *or social standing to intervene between my duty and my patient;*
> *I will maintain the utmost respect for human life, from the time of conception;*
> *even under threat, I will not use my medical knowledge contrary to the laws of humanity.*
> *I make these promises solemnly, freely, and upon my honor.*
>
> —THE DECLARATION OF GENEVA (based on the Hippocratic Oath)

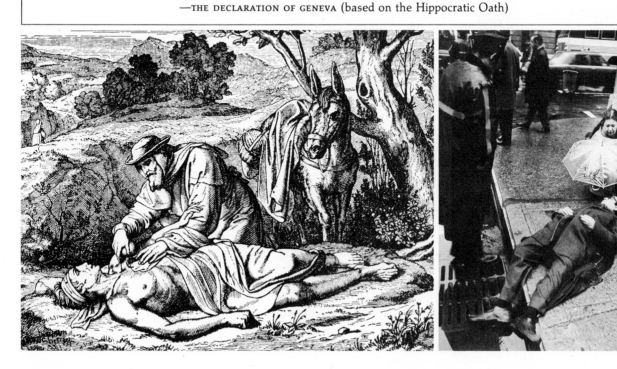

seems to be characterized by a strong reemphasis on religious and humanistic values. Many people have become conscious of the alienating, dehumanizing effects of an increasingly complex and technological urban society, and on many fronts a commitment to creating structures that foster a sense of collective identity and shared concern for one another is emerging. This commitment to a collectivist orientation has assumed a variety of forms and has affected much of society. For example, collectivist alternatives to competitive society have taken the form of urban and rural communes, religious communal groups, the joining together of ghetto parents to operate cooperative day-care centers, and middle-class involvement with sensory awareness and growth-oriented group experiences. With this commitment to collectivist concerns comes renewed interest in norms of helping and concern for others.

There are also factors more specific to psychology as a scientific discipline that create the current interest in prosocial behavior. For example, the investigation of prosocial behavior offers a framework in which to study important psychological processes such as guilt, sympathy, and compliance. In addition, there are few psychological processes that are as intrinsically interesting or as important in their influence on all of us as is selfless behavior.

Of the three defining characteristics of prosocial behavior—it is other-oriented, it is intrinsically motivated, and it is volitional—each represents an area of current interest in American psychology. First, most psychological theories have tended to conceptualize human behavior as egoistic—emphasizing the self-interested and drive-reducing aspects of human functioning. Prosocial behavior is particularly interesting because of its seeming independence from the usual notions of reinforcement. And second, many psychologists are currently seeking a conceptual framework that can adequately deal with actions that are governed by processes of volition and self-regulation rather than by the social situation (Kanfer and Philips, 1970; Kimble and Perlmuter, 1970).

Although there is increasing theoretical interest among psychologists in understanding behavior that is other-oriented, psychologists have often been content to leave to philosophers the problem of whether behavior is truly motivated by concern for others or by anticipation of personal gain. Psychologists have paid insufficient attention to the intentions, or motives, that govern this type of behavior, concentrating instead on antecedents that lie in the immediate social context. They are now concerning themselves with the entire act and investigating the actor's intentions behind prosocial behavior. Dennis Krebs (1970) has written: "Motivational specification is particularly important in relation to a moral behavior such as altruism. . . . Fortunately, due to the constraints of experimental situations, the range of ulterior motives in laboratory studies is usually limited and the motivation behind the behavior in question quite apparent."

Given the abundant evidence that people do not always act altruistically, despite the social utility of unselfish actions, it is important to investigate the conditions and principles that govern the occurrence of altruism in particular situations.

As mentioned above, most cultures have advocated some norm of prosocial concern. A norm is a standard of action that specifies what behavior is expected, or "normal," and what behavior is abnormal. Every society has rules that define appropriate behavior for its members. Sanctions, implicit and explicit, promote adherence to social norms. These

Figure 12.2 All societies encourage some forms of prosocial behavior, and it is not uncommon to observe altruism in forms that are almost institutionalized. National charity organizations and community-action groups are examples. A New Orleans community organization (*below*), consisting of ghetto youths wishing to help their peers, calls itself "Thugs United." Telethons (*opposite*) sometimes engage the services of celebrities to help raise money for causes such as muscular dystrophy. Do charity benefits such as this telethon actually encourage altruism through modeling? Do people tune in to the antics of the celebrities without being significantly affected by the charity appeals? Or do most viewers perhaps watch such shows to be absolved of responsibility because others appear to be taking care of the problem in question?

IV Interacting With Others

sanctions range from mild disapproval to incarceration or even more severe forms of censure, depending on the threat to the established social order posed by the offenses. (Norms are also discussed in Chapters 13 and 14.)

If it is truly normative in Western culture to show concern for others and to help others whenever possible, it is relatively easy to understand the horror people express when they read of failures to lend aid to others who are in danger. But if helpfulness is a norm, why are people surprised and approving when others *do* act altruistically? If "norm" defines expected behavior—normal behavior—then one might anticipate the system of rewards by which Western society attempts to encourage dramatic examples of adherence to a prosocial norm—medals for people who run into burning buildings to save parakeets, for example—but not the mild surprise anyone might feel at seeing someone stop on the freeway to help a stranded motorist fix a flat tire.

Allan Teger (1970) has suggested that the norm of helping, although frequently endorsed verbally, is actually an *ideal* norm—neither a true expectation of behavior nor even a particularly morally compelling force. As an ideal norm, the prosocial ethic is an expression of the fact that people value socially responsible behavior. It is a standard that carries the social power of what Fritz Heider, in 1958, called *ought force.* In this chapter, the focus will be on the forces that determine whether an individual will actually do what society says he or she ought to do in a particular instance.

THE INFLUENCE OF OTHERS

In this section, the ways in which the actions and characteristics of other people affect an individual's altruistic behavior will be considered. Perhaps the simplest of these diverse influences from others is modeling—learning to perform prosocial acts by watching another person perform such an act. This discussion will focus on the relative effects of what people say and what they do. It will also examine the factors that influence a bystander to intervene in an emergency. The discussion of interpersonal influences on prosocial behavior will close with a consideration of the ways in which altruism is governed by the characteristics of the potential recipient.

Doing Unto Others as Others Do

One of the central themes of this book is that the ways in which others respond to a situation profoundly affect the manner in which any one person responds. One way in which others affect a person is simply through that person's observation of their actions in various circumstances (see Chapter 2). In regard to prosocial behavior, their actions can remind an individual of what it is that he "ought" to do, can give him new patterns of behavior in situations that he has not confronted before, or can inform him of possible consequences of alternate actions.

In addition to encouraging prosocial behavior, prosocial models are likely to support or extinguish the observer's prior convictions about the importance of prosocial behavior. Salomon Rettig (1956) questioned college students about the degree to which their altruism had been fostered by religious conviction and about the amount of reinforcement they had received for prosocial actions. He then examined these data in relation to the students' scores on an altruism scale. He found that the longer students had attended college, the less significant generalized religious reinforcement

became in prompting altruistic behavior and the more significant prior situational reinforcement became. The one variable that proved to be related to altruism for *all* groups of students, however, regardless of how long they had been in college, was the degree to which their parents had engaged in altruistic behavior. When parents served as altruistic models, children were more inclined to be altruistic. Thus, the influence of religious conviction decreases and that of reinforcement increases with years in college, but the effects of parental modeling remain strong and stable.

David Rosenhan (1970) found a similar pattern among people who had given enormously of their time and resources in the civil-rights movement of the late 1950s. Rosenhan found that when he examined the modeling influences of their parents he could distinguish easily between these people and those civil-rights workers who had given but minimal amounts of time. Those who had given most generously had parents who were themselves socially concerned; those who gave less, on the other hand, were brought up by parents who seemed less than fully committed to prosocial action.

Naturalistic studies such as Rettig's and Rosenhan's indicate that altruistic models play a significant role in eliciting altruistic behavior from observers, but they do not provide the kind of precision that comes from controlled laboratory investigations. The importance of behavioral models in producing prosocial behavior has also been demonstrated in the laboratory by researchers who studied behaviors as diverse as aiding in a search (Ross, 1970), volunteering to be in an experiment (Rosenbaum and Blake, 1955), donating to charity (Harris, 1968), and fixing a flat tire (Bryan and Test, 1967). The evidence of both naturalistic and laboratory settings seems to establish that an altruistic act by one person can substantially increase the chances of subsequent altruistic acts by others.

Model-Observer Similarity. There is evidence that the effect of a model depends on who the model is, as well as on what the model does. Harvey Hornstein, Elisha Fisch, and Michael Holmes (1968) have investigated the question of whether or not *any* model can increase the likelihood of observer altruism. Their basic procedure involved leaving several open envelopes on the sidewalks of Manhattan. From each envelope protruded a man's wallet containing money. Also in each envelope was a brief note explaining that the writer had found the wallet and was returning it to the owner. In other words, each finder was led to believe that the writer of the note had first found the lost wallet but had lost it again before he was able to return it. The experimenters stationed observers where they could note when an envelope was picked up and record characteristics like sex and estimated age of the person who retrieved it. The experimenters measured altruistic behavior by the number of wallets that people, following the example of the model who had written the note, returned intact with the money they had found.

Hornstein and his colleagues reasoned that a model who seemed quite dissimilar from the observer would not have as strong an effect on the observer as would a model who was similar. As they had little control over the kind of person that would find and pick up the envelope, the researchers faced the problem of making the model seem dissimilar to the finder. They chose, therefore, to vary the similarity between observer and model by creating the impression that the model was from a different cultural background. One set of notes accompanying the wallet was composed in broken English and explained that the writer was a visitor to the United States.

Another set of notes, on the other hand, was composed in normal English prose. For example, one of the normal notes stated, "I found your wallet which I am returning. Everything is here just as I found it." The contrasting note from the dissimilar model said, "I am visit your country finding your ways not familiar and strange. But I find your wallet which I here return. Everything is here just as I find it."

The results showed that the similar model prompted more finders to return intact wallets than did the dissimilar model, as shown in Table 12.1. Almost two-thirds of the finders returned the wallet when the model was similar to them, but more than half failed to do so when the model was dissimilar. However, if the similar model complained of the inconvenience (the negative condition in Table 12.1), the enhanced altruism was completely eliminated—unlike the effects of the positive and neutral notes.

There seem to be cross-national differences in people's attitudes toward dissimilar others. For example, Roy E. Feldman in 1968 asked passers-by for directions in one study; in another, he asked strangers to mail a letter (on the pretense that he was waiting for someone and could not leave); and in other studies merchants or taxi drivers were "accidentally" overpaid to check on their honesty. When he assessed the various reactions of more than 3,000 people, he discovered that, for example, Athenians tended to treat foreigners better than they treated compatriots. On the other hand, Parisians and Bostonians tended to treat compatriots better than they did foreigners.

Some progress has been made in clarifying the role of the model in altruistic behavior. Some models are effective and others are ineffective as producers of altruistic behavior in observers, and there exists at least one condition under which an altruistic act may not increase the chances of an identical act by another person. Perhaps the next thing to investigate is the effects of different components of the modeling process itself.

Do as I Say but Not as I Do. Most studies of modeling have used behavioral models of one sort or another. Some researchers (for example, Harris, 1968; Rosenbaum and Blake, 1955) have utilized verbal cues as well, but few attempts have been made to compare the relative effectiveness of behavioral and verbal models. To measure the effects of *behavioral modeling*, Joan Grusec and Sandra Skubiski (1970) had elementary-school children observe an adult model donate to charity half of his or her winnings from a game.

Table 12.1 Returns of Wallets

CONDITION	TOTAL RETURNS	TOTAL NOT RETURNED*
Similar model		
Neutral note	12	8
Positive (courteous) note	14	6
Negative (complaining) note	2	18
Dissimilar model		
Neutral note	4	11
Positive (courteous) note	5	10
Negative (complaining) note	6	9

*Includes *no return* and *returned but not intact.*

Source: Adapted from H. Hornstein, E. Fisch, and M. Holmes, "Influence of a Model's Feeling About His Behavior and His Relevance as a Comparison Other on Observers' Helping Behavior," *Journal of Personality and Social Psychology,* 10 (1968), p. 225.

When the purpose was to discover the effects of *verbal modeling,* the model did not play the game but strongly endorsed the idea that winnings should be shared equally with charity. No model was witnessed by the control group.

The results indicated that behavioral modeling elicited larger donations from the children than did verbal exhortations. In fact, only under fairly specific circumstances was verbal modeling more effective than no model at all—only when the potential donor was female *and* the model had previously established a warm, nurturant relationship with the subject.

What do these results suggest to parents the world over, who from time immemorial have urged their children to do as they are told and not as they see others do? The parents of daughters may be able to rely somewhat on verbal modeling, if Grusec and Skubiski's findings are any indication. But must the parents of sons expect that their verbal appeals will have little success in effecting altruistic behavior—as was the fate of verbal appeals to male schoolchildren in Grusec and Skubiski's study? Perhaps not. James Bryan and Nancy Walbek (1970) found that verbal exhortations do have an effect on observers, regardless of their sex. Their child subjects observed films of a model who either donated winnings to charity or refused to donate and who simultaneously made either neutral statements or statements sanctioning sharing or refusing to share. The subsequent behavior of these children indicated that their tendency to share was affected by behavioral but not by verbal modeling of generosity. However, when each child was asked to record a statement telling the next child what to do, the child's

Figure 12.3 Research suggests that the experience of watching people like this elderly woman donate blood will have a greater effect in encouraging this youngster to be altruistic than would verbal lectures about the medical needs for blood. If verbal lectures are not accompanied by actions, this pattern is also imitated by children—their talk and not their behavior becomes altruistic.

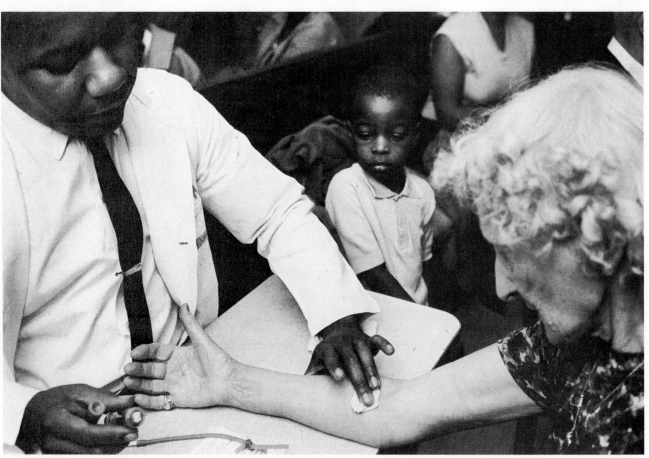

IV INTERACTING WITH OTHERS

statement typically reflected the influence of the original model's verbalizations: The children advocated more sharing when the model had advocated either sharing or refusing to share than when the model had made neutral statements. It is as if *any* statement about sharing—greedy or generous—calls forth the norm of altruism. Thus, the children's statements were virtually unrelated to what they had seen and reflected, instead, only what they had heard. Apparently, behavioral modeling influences an observer's behavior, whereas verbal modeling influences his verbalizations.

These results do contain a message for parents: If parents only want their children to *say* that people should help others, it is probably sufficient that they just tell them so. But if they want their children to actually help others, the parents must act altruistically rather than simply talk about it. To their surprise, Bryan and Walbek found that modeling of hypocrisy—that is, in this case, refusing to share while verbally sanctioning sharing—works in very much the same manner as does the modeling of other behaviors: The modeled behavior produces more of the same. Providing inconsistent models of behavior and spoken opinion seems to increase the probability of exhortations that conflict with actual behavior. Bryan and Walbek's discovery that children will refuse to share but verbally endorse sharing, just as their model had done, is reminiscent of Rosenhan's finding that white civil-rights workers in the 1950s were likely to fully commit themselves to the civil-rights cause only if their parents had demonstrated an equal commitment to altruistic behavior.

The modeling of altruism has also been shown to be affected by other variables, such as the cost of helping (Wagner and Wheeler, 1969), the rewardingness of the model (Hartup and Coates, 1967), and vicarious reinforcement (Presbie and Coiteux, 1971). The modeling of other than altruistic acts is discussed in Chapters 2 and 11.

Bystander Intervention in Emergencies

Prosocial behavior can take a wide range of forms, as is evident in the preceding section on modeling. However, one form of prosocial concern in particular has evoked a great deal of public interest and is of great significance to us as members of the human community: the willingness, in emergencies, of people to break out of their roles as bystanders and to come to another's assistance. Precipitated by such incidents as the Kitty Genovese slaying and the subway slaying mentioned at the beginning of this chapter, a series of studies have been conducted in search of the conditions that determine whether people will respond to one another's distress. The research on *bystander intervention* has grown out of the extensive efforts of two social psychologists, John Darley and Bibb Latané.

Darley and Latané (1968) were struck by the failure to respond demonstrated by the witnesses to the Genovese killing. Here was a situation in which thirty-eight people witnessed the slaying of a woman, and no one acted to save her. Even if a person might like to imagine that he or she would spring instantly into action and, heedless of danger, run to the aid of the victim with brave shouts of "damn the torpedoes," the fact that no one confronted Kitty Genovese's murderer will probably not come as any real surprise. Even the most idealized notion of helping does not require the chance bystander to face a knife-wielding killer, but what is surprising and seems so incomprehensible is the failure of the bystanders to do anything at all during the thirty-minute assault. No one organized the neighbors to go

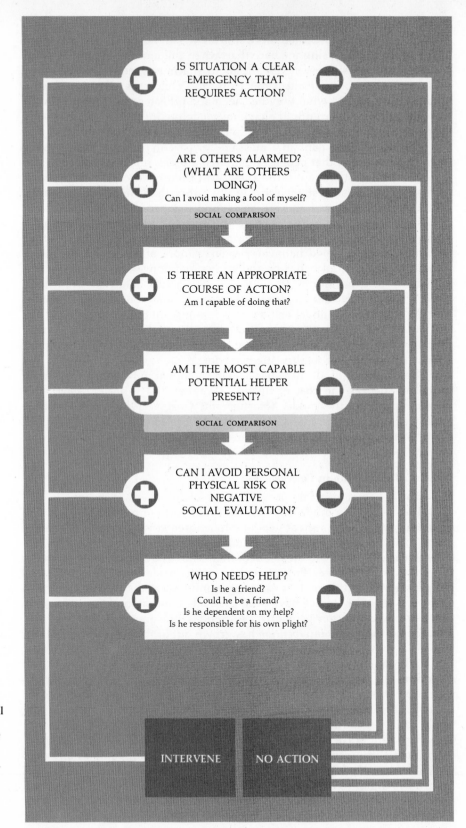

Figure 12.4 Whether or not an individual intervenes in an emergency is mediated by a complex array of factors that involve the bystander's perceptions and assessment of the situation. The process is depicted here in schematic form. A "yes" answer to any question allows the bystander to proceed to the next level in the process. If all answers are "yes," the bystander is likely to intervene.

out and help; the police were not summoned; no one even called an ambulance or checked the victim after the assailant left.

Darley and Latané were impressed by the witnesses' apparent lack of social responsibility. They were also struck by the weak explanations for the bystanders' inaction offered by the newspapers: The effects of living in a megalopolis, increased alienation, apathy, and other assorted explanations seemed incomplete explanations of why people fail to intervene to help others; these same factors fail to account for any number of prosocial acts that *are* performed by city dwellers. Darley and Latané discounted these general cultural factors and looked instead to those situational factors that are specific to emergencies.

Defining Emergencies.   Darley and Latané felt that emergency situations are characterized by several unique features that make the participants susceptible to atypical social processes. The most distinctive feature of an emergency is that it involves threat or harm. There are but few positive outcomes for action in an emergency; on the other hand, there is great potential for negative consequences. Thus, the best possible outcome of an emergency is a return to the status quo. An additional factor is that emergencies are such rare events and differ so widely that people tend not to be well prepared for them. Emergencies are also unforeseeable; they emerge suddenly and unexpectedly, and they require immediate action. Failure to act quickly usually leads to a deterioration of the situation.

If an individual is going to intervene in an emergency, he or she must make not one but a series of decisions. And this decision-making process may or may not lead to a decision to intervene. Darley and Latané have tried to isolate some of the factors that affect these decisions.

Because most emergencies are, at least initially, ambiguous events from an observer's point of view, the definition of the situation as one requiring action—by anyone—is the first step in the intervention process. If the situation is not defined as an emergency, then obviously no action is required and the decision-making process stops. Because the situation is ambiguous, and because one risks making a fool of oneself by acting inappropriately, the presence of other people who do not appear alarmed will tend to produce a social definition of the situation as one not requiring any action.

Even if the observer defines the situation as an emergency, another decision must be made about the appropriate course of action. People are generally cautious about taking responsibilities; they fear getting blamed if anything goes wrong. The presence of more than one bystander causes the perceived responsibility to be diffused among the observers. As a result, each bystander feels *less personally responsible* for the situation than if he or she were alone. Because the thirty-eight witnesses to the Genovese slaying were in separate apartments, relatively certain that their neighbors were aware of what was happening, each could rationalize that the situation did not directly require his or her personal action.

To test these two ideas regarding the effects of others on bystander intervention, Darley and Latané performed several experiments in which they confronted subjects with simulated emergencies.

Social-Comparison Processes.   In one of their studies, Latané and Darley (1968) summoned their subjects ostensibly to participate in a market research study. While the subjects thought they were waiting for the experiment to begin, they heard what sounded like someone falling and being injured in the adjoining room. All the while, however, the experimenters were watching to see if responses to this possible emergency differed according to whether the subject was waiting alone, with a stranger, or with a friend.

From the standpoint of all subjects, the situation was ambiguous; it was not clear to them exactly what had happened. Because of the uncertainty of the situation, the experimenters predicted that whenever another person was present, a desire for *social comparison* would prompt a subject to use the other's reactions to interpret the ambiguous cues. The experimenters reasoned that people do not wish to commit themselves until they are reasonably sure that a particular course of action is appropriate. When alone, each person has only himself or herself to rely on to define a situation. The presence of others adds complexity to the definition process, and when the others are not responding with alarm, the individual may assume that no emergency exists. Furthermore, Latané and Darley suspected that people in emergency situations tend to keep their responses at a minimum until a consensus is reached about the seriousness of the situation. They expected that strangers would hesitate longer before helping a third person than would friends, because the risk of appearing foolish would seem greater among strangers than friends.

The results confirmed Latané and Darley's expectations. Subjects in the company of a passive, unconcerned stranger were substantially less helpful than were subjects who waited with a friend. The most helpful of all were those subjects who waited alone.

Diffusion of Responsibility. A different experiment conducted by Darley and Latané in 1968 involved subjects who thought they were to participate in a discussion group. To better understand the effects of an experience like this, consider it from the viewpoint of a subject arriving for the experiment.

When you arrive, the experimenter directs you to a booth. You sit alone but are able to communicate via intercom with other participants in the group. The experimenter tells you how many other participants are in the group. As the discussion gets underway, the other participants describe, via the intercom, their reactions to college and to city life. Suddenly, one of the other students, who has already mentioned that he had been anxious and upset during his first few months at college and that he is subject to seizures, begins to stutter, and his breathing becomes labored. He complains that he is "having a bit of trouble." His speech becomes more and more incoherent, he says he needs help, and then there is silence. The experiment requires you to stay in your booth, and you cannot talk to anyone because the intercom opens only into the victim's booth. You have no idea where the experimenter went. Chances are, you have never before confronted a situation such as this. What would you do?

If you respond as did most of Darley and Latané's subjects, the fewer the participants you believe are listening to the commotion over the intercom, the more likely you will be to respond, and to respond quickly, to the emergency. Hence, you will respond most rapidly when you believe yourself to be the sole witness to trouble. Figure 12.5 shows the response patterns of Darley and Latané's subjects.

The results of these two experiments are consistent with two related hypotheses offered by Darley and Latané to explain why the presence of others inhibits bystander intervention. In the first place, passivity in others

Figure 12.5 In a study of bystander intervention by Darley and Latané (1968), the results of which are summarized here, the subjects were told that they were members of small discussion groups. Some subjects thought there were two people in the group, others believed there were three, and still others, six. The subjects, seated alone, were told that they could speak to the others when their microphones were switched on, and they heard the others, one at a time, when the others' microphones were on. Actually, the subjects heard tapes that had been devised by the experimenters. One tape was that of the victim, who seemed to be having a seizure. The results revealed that both the presence and number of bystanders affect diffusion of responsibility. More people acted—and acted faster—when they thought that they were the sole source of help or thought that there was only one other person who could help than when they thought that several others shared the responsibility with them.

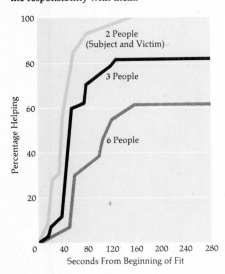

IV Interacting With Others

generates a tendency to define ambiguous situations as nonemergencies. Secondly, even when there is no opportunity for communication among bystanders (as in the second experiment), there is a tendency for the presence of others to diffuse responsibility for taking action. (Some of the more destructive effects of diffused responsibility are discussed in more detail in Chapter 11.)

Although other bystanders were present throughout both experiments, the results cannot be explained by the diffusion-of-responsibility hypothesis in both cases. Recall that in the first study willingness to intervene differed according to whether a stranger or a friend was present. This difference seems to indicate that somewhat different social definitions were operating; the same number of bystanders were present under both conditions in the first study, but responsibility was not equally diffused. Apparently, then, the results reflected a difference between the passive reaction of a stranger and the trusted reaction of a friend.

Several additional studies have lent support to Darley and Latané's hypotheses regarding bystander intervention but have also suggested some conditions under which the presence of others may have but a limited effect on emergency intervention. For example, although Charles Korte (1971) and Leonard Bickman (1971) both have shown that feelings of responsibility in an emergency can diffuse among bystanders, their results also suggest that no diffusion of responsibility occurs when other bystanders are somehow unable to come to the aid of the victim. Subjects responded as quickly as if they had been alone when they knew that the only other person who could be aware of the emergency was in another building (Bickman's study) or strapped down (Korte's study). This evidence suggests that the decision process involves assessment not only of the *number* of people present but also of their potential as interveners.

In still another study, Shalom Schwartz and Geraldine Clausen (1968) adopted the experimental procedure Darley and Latané had developed, with the exception that one group of subjects was led to believe that another member of a discussion group was medically competent to deal with the accomplice's apparent seizure. The least intervention was volunteered by those subjects who believed that there was someone present who was more appropriately trained to handle the situation. Thus, it seems that the likelihood of intervention is affected not only by the number of other bystanders but also by their relative capacities to be of assistance.

Rounding Out the Picture. Studies of the factors that inhibit bystander intervention indicate that an emergency is a complex social situation that requires the bystander to make a number of immediate decisions. But the complexities of an emergency situation also make it quite difficult to arrive at the necessary decisions. Because we are all influenced by others, the decision-making process is complicated by the presence of other bystanders who give discrepant or ambiguous cues as to the appropriate response. However, many of the researchers whose work is described in this chapter feel that it is misleading to facilely assume that those bystanders who fail to intervene are unconcerned. As a matter of fact, it is the subjective impression of many experimenters that those subjects who fail to react to the sounds of distress seem to be more disturbed by the episode than are subjects who intervene.

The episodes described so far were ones in which there was no threat of danger to the bystander, save that of acting inappropriately. If the bystander's own safety is also at stake, the decision-making process becomes still more complex.

To determine the effects of personal risk, Harvey Allen (1972) studied bystander intervention in a nonemergency situation. The experiment took place on a subway train in which one confederate sat next to a subject and gave false information to another confederate who had asked directions. The measure of intervention was how often subjects corrected the misdirections. Before the confederates exchanged the misdirections, however, the experimenters varied the demeanor of the information-giver by having him behave in either a sarcastic, a physically threatening, or a neutral manner when yet another confederate tripped over his feet. Therefore, before having an opportunity to intervene, subjects had a chance to form some opinion about the potential risks of acting in a way that could antagonize the information-giver. Allen found that those subjects who had seen the information-giver as physically threatening intervened the least. Subjects were more willing to intervene when the confederate had been merely sarcastic rather than physically threatening and were most helpful when he had made a neutral response. Of particular interest is the fact that this relationship between the information-giver's characteristics and the likelihood of a bystander correcting his error held even after the information-giver had departed.

It seems, therefore, that bystanders make an initial assessment of a situation and a decision about what to do that is resistant to change even after the threat is removed. This apparent intransigence may also result from bystanders' desire to avoid appearing inconsistent—to themselves as well as to others.

The definition of a situation as to whether or not it requires the bystander's own action and the subsequent decision about whether or not to act on that definition are complicated by both real and imagined consequences of taking the action. In addition to fear for personal safety, the fear of negative social evaluation is often salient in emergency situations. Consider, for example, the agonies of indecision expressed by one of Charles Korte's student subjects when he was confronted with the sounds of an asthmatic attack:

I am wondering if this is a put-on job and I am the only subject. Is this part of the experiment, not seeming to breathe? I'll bet it is. If not, the other two can take care of him. Am I willing to risk someone's life just to prove I'm right? I guess so—no legal obligation, of course. Should I just feel stupid or guilty the rest of my life? (1971, page 153)

The particular circumstances faced by this person were engendered by an experimental situation, but it is easy to imagine the same sort of process taking place under normal circumstances. In fact, Ervin Staub (1970) found that the older a child gets, the more reluctant he or she is to intervene in an ambiguous situation for fear of doing something inappropriate. It seems that we human beings are taught early in life that losing face is one of the worst things that can happen. When asked why they failed to intervene during various emergencies, witnesses indicated that they were afraid they had misconstrued the situation, were afraid they would somehow make things worse if they intervened, or hoped that someone better equipped to deal with the situation would come along.

In discussing the factors affecting whether or not people will attempt to help their fellow human beings, the social definition of emergencies, the diffusion of responsibility, and fear of consequences have been explored.

IV INTERACTING WITH OTHERS

An additional variable involves the effects of living in a complex urban environment: City dwellers do indeed seem more inured to suffering than do their rural counterparts. John Darley (1970) places much of the blame on the daily confrontations urbanites—and particularly the urban poor—face with unresponsive bureaucracies, inadequate public facilities, and uncaring public officials. He feels that constant exposure to these frustrating encounters produces in the individual a pervasive feeling of helplessness in controlling what will happen to him or her as well as to others. When presented with an emergency, a person who has developed this *low control of effects syndrome* will tend to feel that anything he or she does will be to no avail and, furthermore, may actually have detrimental consequences. Perhaps some of the current social movements mentioned at the beginning of the chapter, to the extent that they create a sense of collective concern and instill a sense of personal effectiveness, will help counteract feelings of helplessness that can disable people.

The Recipient: The Face of the Fortunate

Whether circumstances encourage or discourage prosocial concern depends in part on who the person in need is. Clearly, most people do not feel equal concern toward everyone; friends and family usually receive preferred treatment over strangers or brief acquaintances, especially when cost or risk to the benefactor is involved. Close personal ties are not, however, the only assets of potential recipients that prompt willingness to render assistance. This section will examine what social psychologists know about who is likely to receive help.

Friendship, almost by definition, refers to a relationship in which the participants can expect to render and receive aid when it is needed. Because this altruistic element in friendship seems so obvious, researchers have not

Figure 12.6 Urban dwellers are usually blamed for indifference in emergency situations. Darley (1970) has hypothesized that urbanites' continual encounters with unresponsive bureaucracies and officials in all areas of their lives result in feelings of helplessness. The urban poor, relegated to slums (*left*), are most likely to be susceptible to this "low control of effects" syndrome. Even though they may fare no worse financially than rural poor (*below*) and in fact may have more opportunities open to them, the complexities of city life render them more dependent on bureaucracies.

devoted much experimental attention to helping patterns among friends. The evidence that does exist, however, is not unequivocal. Although Jack Sawyer (1966) found that friends harbored the most mutual altruistic concern and that antagonists harbored the least, studies with child subjects indicate that children, at least, do not necessarily prefer friends over strangers when distributing rewards (Floyd, 1964; Wright, 1942). When the experimenters analyzed their subjects' verbalizations, however, they discovered that generosity to strangers was often motivated by a desire to make new friends or to obtain retribution for the past selfishness of friends. In any case, these findings do not provide a very compelling explanation for the sacrifices and other altruistic gestures by friends that dot both legends and real interpersonal experiences. Most of us may be more concerned about appearances and more superficially considerate around those we do not know well, and we may tend to take our friends for granted when bestowing small favors. But when large sacrifices are demanded, it is for our friends that most of us are willing to commit ourselves in a real way.

Another characteristic of the recipient that may elicit altruism is *dependence.* Leonard Berkowitz and his colleagues conducted a series of studies based on the expectation that need, or dependence, would elicit assistance (Berkowitz and Connor, 1966; Berkowitz and Daniels, 1963). The researchers required "workers" to construct paper boxes or envelopes for a "supervisor"; they varied the level of dependence by portraying some supervisors as utterly dependent for their rewards on their workers' output and others as less or not at all dependent. As expected, productivity increased concurrently with the level of the supervisor's dependence on the workers, even when the individual workers thought that the supervisor would not know how much each had produced—a factor that discounted fear of negative evaluation as a motive. Elizabeth Midlarsky (1968) also found that experimental subjects volunteered more help to a partner with broken eyeglasses than to a less dependent recipient, even when the act of helping resulted in electric shocks for the benefactor.

The assumption that dependence generates help has not received universal support, however; even acute need may not prompt assistance in all instances. Male subjects demonstrated more willingness to help finance the preparation of a thesis when the money was requested by a volunteer—a condition of low dependence—than when the request came from the beneficiary's partner—a condition of high dependence (Schopler, 1967; Schopler and Bateson, 1965). An interesting feature of these studies is that they involved situations in which any one of several people could have helped the person in need; therefore, subjects could have rationalized that someone else would help. As the research on diffusion of responsibility makes clear, because someone is in dire need does not guarantee that others will come to his or her aid. Dependence may evoke altruism only when the potential benefactors feel that attention is focused on them. But even this condition is not always sufficient to elicit aid, as prolonged suffering in places like Biafra, Bangladesh, and Bedford Stuyvesant attests. Clearly, then, other factors than need are involved in promoting altruistic concern.

One factor that seems to mediate the effects of dependence is the perceived origin of that dependence. At one extreme, when people appear to have gotten themselves into a jam, or seem to have "made their own beds," the obligation to help is not very compelling. For example, John Schopler and Marjorie Matthews (1965) found that male college students, when given an opportunity to help a peer at cost to themselves in a money-earning situation, were more likely to help when they perceived the other person as having been made dependent by the experimenter rather than by his own decisions. Findings such as these suggest that dependence is not a unitary phenomenon but, rather, one that is often infused with the prior personal judgments of both the observer and the dependent person. This process will be discussed in more detail later in this chapter; when the effects of altruism are examined, it will become obvious that judgment about whether or not another person is deserving often is made only *after* the perceiver has made a decision about whether or not to help.

THE EFFECTS OF PSYCHOLOGICAL STATE

It has been shown that the presence, actions, demeanor, and personal characteristics of other people can profoundly affect an individual's tendency to behave prosocially. In keeping with the thrust of the chapter, this section will continue to consider situational determinants. But now the psychological state of the benefactor rather than the social situations that influence altruistic behavior will be emphasized. *Transitory psychological states,* such as guilt or happiness, can each affect observers' responsiveness to others. These states sometimes result from the observer's own thoughts or actions; at other times, the actions of others produce them.

All of us have experienced, at one time or another, the exhilaration that accompanies successful completion of a difficult task. When success comes our way, we feel that the world, for once, is indeed just and can do us no wrong. This state of mind can produce intense feelings of good will toward our fellow human beings. Do these benevolent feelings affect subsequent behavior, or are they confined to an internal reaction to previous events? When we perceive ourselves as generous, are we inclined to be kinder toward others, or are we merely deluding ourselves? These questions have provided the focus for a rapidly growing body of psychological research.

Success and Failure: Bouquets and Brickbats

Alice Isen's (1970) work is illustrative of research into the comparative effects of success and failure. She asked teachers and college students to take a battery of perceptual and motor tests, ostensibly to learn the relationship between these skills and creativity. At random, she told some subjects

At length I recollected the thoughtless saying of a great princess, who, on being informed that the country people had no bread, replied, "Let them eat cake."

—JEAN JACQUES ROUSSEAU

Figure 12.7 People's needs and dependence often generate indifference rather than altruism in others, even when help would be easy to give. This situation is hardly restricted to twentieth-century American society, as indicated by the remark of Marie Antoinette, the wife of French king Louis XVI, when crowds of other French men and women were clamoring outside her sumptuous quarters for bread.

that they had done extremely well and others that they had done quite poorly. Still other subjects received no feedback on their performance or did not perform the tasks at all.

Isen found that subjects who believed that they had been successful subsequently donated more generously to a school fund *and* more frequently volunteered assistance to a person struggling with an armload of books than did subjects who believed that they had failed or who had received no feedback. However, recipients of negative evaluations did not show significantly less tendency to help out than did subjects who had received no feedback. Neither group showed a special interest in being generous.

This study indicated that the experience of success does indeed increase altruistic behavior toward others. However, success produces a complicated aggregate of reactions in most people. Increased generosity in Isen's experiment may have derived from any of several sources, including a positive feeling that can accompany success, which Isen referred to as the "warm glow of success"; a feeling of competence that can follow success; an enhanced expectation on the part of potential benefactors that they will receive rewards in the future; or from a combination of these factors.

Mood State: Glows and Glowers

Alice Isen and her colleague Paula Levin (1972) set out to see if they could induce a positive mood in subjects by some means other than the inordinately complex experience of success. They decided to have one experi-

WHERE DID ALL THE GOOD GUYS GO?

ALTHOUGH THIS CHAPTER places great emphasis on the impact of situations in producing or inhibiting altruism, we all know people who seem especially kind and helpful to those in need. In contrast, we also know others who never seem to help anybody. Is it possible that there are some people who, regardless of the situation, are more likely to come through with help than others are?

Psychologists Kenneth and Mary Gergen and Kenneth Meter studied the relationship between personality and helping behavior. The subjects were seventy-two college students enrolled in a personality course. As part of their class activities, these students took ten different personality tests, including tests of self-esteem, dominance, affiliation, and self-consistency. A few days after administering the tests, the professor handed out a mimeographed sheet from the psychology department indicating that voluntary help was much needed for five different types of tasks. These activities involved counseling troubled students at a local high school, helping to collate and assemble the class' test data, and assisting other professors in carrying out research either on deductive thinking or on unusual states of consciousness. In actuality, the investigators had produced the notice and had purposely varied the helping activities requested so that they could address the question of whether or not a person who volunteered to help with one of these tasks would also volunteer to help with the others. If some people are basically more helpful than others, then there should be a particular set of personal characteristics distinguishing the helpful person from others.

Correlations were computed between each of ten traits and each of the five prosocial behaviors, with the male and female groups separated in order to help develop a more accurate set of statistics. In all, more than one-fourth of the 100 correlations were significant beyond chance, thirteen for males and sixteen for females. Interestingly, only five of the correlations between

menter approach students in a library and give them each a cookie. In a seemingly unrelated encounter, the second experimenter subsequently asked the students who had received cookies, as well as some who had not, if they would help her out by being in her experiment. As it turned out, there were more volunteers among the students who had received cookies than among those who had not.

These findings seem to establish that a positive mood leads to increased helpfulness. It could still be argued, however, that the researchers had merely uncovered an instance of modeled altruism, that the students' generosity had not resulted from positive mood at all. So Isen and Levin set out to eliminate any possible influence of modeling in a second study. This time, they arranged for some people to find a dime in a telephone booth; these people, the experimenters reasoned, would be made happier by their unexpected profits but would not have been exposed to an altruistic model, because nobody *gave* them the dimes. More people who found dimes did indeed subsequently help the experimenter pick up papers she had spilled than did people who had not found dimes.

You may feel at this point that the effects of giving someone a cookie or leaving a dime to be found in a phone booth are not matters of great import. Most psychologists would agree that knowledge of the effects of cookie-giving per se is not particularly interesting. What is significant is the fact that these very simple manipulations distinguish between two quite important psychological processes—reaction to success and reaction to positive feelings. The Isen and Levin study has established that people are more

personality traits and helpfulness that were found in the male sample were also found in the female group. This finding indicates that if there are indeed people who habitually do good, their personal qualities are quite different depending on whether they are male or female. The idea of a generalized altruist is made even less credible when reversals are taken into account—that is, when personality traits are positively related to some types of volunteering and negatively related to others. For example, in the case of volunteering for research on deductive thinking, women who score high on a sensation-seeking scale tend to want to volunteer for this research, whereas men who have high scores on the same test avoid volunteering for deductive-reasoning research.

One of the most relevant traits for the giving of help might seem to be nurturance. The nurturant person is defined as giving warmth, service, acceptance, and as being generally helpful. In fact, counseling high-school students of the same sex does correlate significantly with nurturance for both sexes. However, nurturance does not correlate with any other form of helping. This may be because the only option to help other people by interpersonal means was this task. The data show further that for both sexes high sensation-seeking scores correlate with offering to help with research on unusual states of consciousness. Certainly this type of helping would be gratifying to a sensation seeker.

The results of this study indicate that some types of people are likely to be more helpful in some situations; other types will emerge as the "good guys" in other situations. *When* people help depends heavily on how the situation happens to interact with their personal dispositions at the time. There seem to be very few all-around good Samaritans among us.

Source: Adapted from K. Gergen, M. Gergen, and K. Meter, "Individual Orientations to Prosocial Behavior," *Journal of Social Issues*, 28 (1972), pp. 105–130.

altruistic during a positive than a negative mood state, whether the mood is aroused by successful performance on an examination or by a pleasant interaction with another person. Positive mood is not, however, necessarily the only component of the success experience that can increase helpfulness. In fact, feelings of competence also seem to promote altruistic behavior (Kazdin and Bryan, 1971; Midlarsky and Midlarsky, 1972).

Although the conclusion that positive moods increase altruism is warranted, there are further contributions to an understanding of the effects of mood on altruism that will now be examined. For one thing, not all positive mood states arise from such gratuitous windfalls as finding a dime in a telephone booth or receiving a cookie from a stranger. Some positive mood states are cognitively mediated, such as the memory of a week when everything seemed to go right, the recollection of a particularly happy time during one's past, or quiet meditation while walking through the woods. Second, the possible effects of *negative* moods on altruistic behavior have not yet been discussed. It has been shown that failure in the laboratory has typically not rendered subjects any more or less altruistic than control groups, although this effect may be due to other components of the failure experience that cancel out the effect of melancholy. Bert Moore, Bill Underwood, and David Rosenhan (1973) have investigated cognitive components of mood states as well as the effects of bad moods.

These investigators asked children to recall events from their own lives that had made them particularly happy. Other children were asked to recount events that had made them particularly sad. Each child was then asked to think briefly about one of the experiences and about how it had made him feel. Children in the control groups either waited quietly or were asked to do an innocuous counting task. The results of this study are summarized in Figure 12.8. As the experimenters had expected, children who had remembered happy events were subsequently more generous in sharing their money with other children than were subjects who had had neutral experiences. Moreover, children who had thought about sad events gave significantly less of their money than did those in control groups. Thus, internal as well as external events can help determine whether or not people behave altruistically.

Here the research into mood states and altruistic behavior stands: Positive moods, whether generated by external or by internal events, lead to increased altruism. Furthermore, negative moods can inhibit altruism. Clearly, then, success is not the only kind of experience that can result in good will; altruism is fostered by a more general positive mood, too.

Guilt and Sympathy

One of the most widely espoused norms regarding altruism in our society is that of restitution—the notion that one should help people whom one has injured. As indicated by the evidence about bystander intervention, however, widely espoused norms are not always mirrored in actual behavior. But even assuming for the moment that guilt produces a desire to make restitution to the injured party, is this effect restricted to the injured party or does guilt produce a sort of generalized impulse to be helpful that extends to others? A generalized urge to be helpful might, at least on some occasions, result from the desire on the part of the benefactors to reassure themselves that they are indeed the good people that they like to think of themselves as being. But if a generalized tendency toward helpfulness occurs, would it

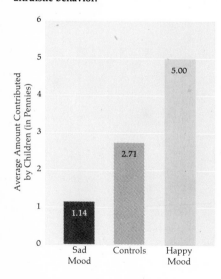

Figure 12.8 Children who reminisced about sad events were subsequently less generous in sharing their money with other children than were control subjects, who had had neutral rather than sad experiences. Those who reminisced about happy events, on the other hand, were more generous than were control subjects. The results are those of Moore, Underwood, and Rosenhan (1973), who investigated the influences of moods on altruistic behavior.

IV Interacting With Others

likely be produced exclusively by guilt, or might it simply result from witnessing someone being wronged—whether or not the observer is the wrongdoer? Is there some sense of fair play, some desire to ensure justice, that—quite apart from any feelings of personal responsibility—promotes increased helpfulness?

Edna Rawlings (1968) sought answers to these questions. Student subjects observed a co-worker receiving shocks; some were led to believe that they were responsible for the co-worker's suffering (guilt condition), and others merely watched (observer condition). The co-workers of control subjects did not receive shocks. These students were subsequently given an opportunity to make a personal sacrifice that would benefit a third person, who was neither the guilty party nor the victim. The results showed that both guilty students and observers were more helpful than were control subjects, but guilty and observing subjects did not significantly differ in their willingness to help. This finding would seem to indicate that guilt-produced altruism does generalize to persons other than those wronged and, furthermore, that altruism may be prompted merely by witnessing an injury for which the observer is not responsible.

Restitution. Rawlings demonstrated that guilt can promote charitability toward persons other than those the guilty party has injured. But what about restitution—reparation by the guilty to the injured party? It seems reasonable to assume that if guilt increases helpfulness toward noninjured persons, it should produce an even stronger sense of helpfulness toward the person wronged. But Jonathan Freedman, Sue Ann Wallington, and Evelyn Bless reported in 1967 a series of studies that only partially support this conclusion. They arranged for some of their subjects to accidentally spill a carefully arranged set of index cards, apparently causing the unidentified

Figure 12.9 Feelings of guilt created by hurting others can increase altruistic behavior, not only toward the injured party but toward others in general. Guilt may be one of the factors motivating these American soldiers to distribute candy to South Vietnamese children.

owner additional hours of tedious work. These subjects were then given an opportunity either to help the owner or to help an uninjured person by volunteering to be in his experiment. Oddly enough, there was no significant difference between guilty and nonguilty subjects (control subjects) in their willingness to help the owner of the cards. However, more guilty than nonguilty subjects were willing to help a person *other* than the owner. Thus, it would appear that guilt does indeed produce increased helpfulness, but not toward the victim!

A subsequent study, using the same situation, resolved this apparent paradox. Freedman, Wallington, and Bless found that more guilty than nonguilty subjects *were* willing to help the owner of the cards, but only if they did not have to meet him. When subjects had to face their victim, there was again no difference in helpfulness between guilty and nonguilty subjects. It seems, then, that the effects of guilt in promoting altruism can be negated by distress at having to meet the victim.

In 1972 Vladimir Konecni further clarified the issue of when a person will help his or her victim. He found that a person who has wronged another *in the other's presence* is more altruistic than someone who has not—whether the altruism is directed toward the injured party (specific guilt, resulting in restitution) or toward a different person (generalized guilt). Apparently, interacting with the injured party can hold no terror to a person who has already wronged the victim to his or her face. But Konecni also discovered that people who had witnessed a misfortune that had been caused by someone who did not stop to help, or even to apologize, were more likely to volunteer help to the victim than were people who had themselves injured either this or another victim. This finding indicates that perceiving an injustice produces an even stronger incentive to be altruistic than does guilt.

Rawlings' results underscored the power of guilt more than Konecni's did, but in Rawlings' study the recipients of help were not the ones who had been wronged. Rawlings established that the desire to be helpful increases after seeing an injustice; Konecni added the knowledge that helpfulness increases still further if the potential benefactor did not himself injure the victim. In other words, people apparently have a generalized desire to maintain a just world and a more specific desire to help the victims of injustice. It would not be surprising to learn, therefore, that someone is inclined to make a more generous donation to a charity after viewing a television documentary about the victims of war in Bangladesh, and this particular form of generosity would be even less surprising if the charity involved helping the Bengalis.

Guilt or Image Repair?   The effects of guilt and sympathy on altruism seem to have been elaborated rather satisfactorily by the line of research just described, but one nagging question remains: Are the effects of guilt on altruism really attributable to an internalized feeling of guilt, or are they merely results of having been *observed* transgressing? In other words, a desire to repair one's flagging image in the eyes of others rather than feelings of guilt may be responsible for the increased helpfulness. This suspicion seems unfounded, however, when Ruth Fisher's (1971) report is considered: Unwitnessed transgression motivates donations to charity that are every bit as generous as those prompted by witnessed transgression. It seems safe to conclude, therefore, that the effects of transgression on altruism are actually at least partially due to feelings of guilt and not necessarily to a quest for image repair. This final observation serves to solidify the conclusions about the effects of guilt and sympathy that have already been examined.

THE EFFECTS OF ALTRUISM

As already explained, people's behavior toward one another is affected by a variety of circumstances. Often analyses of psychological research stop at this point—with statements that certain conditions lead to certain behaviors. However, altruism is a topic that is important to all of us, and the effects of our decisions about whether or not to behave altruistically should be understood. These effects have a bearing both on the ways in which we behave in the future and on those who benefit or suffer as a result of our decisions. In this way, we may begin to understand why some people are particularly likely to help those in need and why others seem unaffected by the needs of other people. As shown in the following section, one prosocial act tends to lead to others, and failing to help may lead to feelings about the victim or the situation that make subsequent prosocial behavior less likely. It will also be shown that people who receive help are sometimes less than completely grateful for their benefactors' efforts.

Reciprocity: Balancing the Seesaw

If there is a norm regarding altruism that is more widely espoused than that prescribing that a harmdoer compensate his victim, perhaps it is the norm compelling the recipient of help to return that favor if the occasion should arise. Indeed, Alvin Gouldner suggested in 1960 that the latter norm is a universal component of moral codes and that reciprocity is a force that contributes to the maintenance of a stable social structure. People questioned by Donal Muir and Edwin Weinstein (1962) about social obligations did indeed subscribe to a norm of reciprocity, which they applied both to themselves and to others. Gouldner, however, was careful to distinguish between a *verbal* norm of reciprocity, which Muir and Weinstein seem to have demonstrated, and *behavioral* reciprocity. The norms people preach are sometimes only weakly related to the norms they practice.

Does the norm of reciprocity guide people's actions as well as their verbalizations? Modeling data discussed in Chapters 2 and 11 certainly give

The Lion and the Mouse

Upon the roaring of a beast in the wood, a mouse ran presently out to see what news: and what was it, but a lion hampered in a net! This accident brought to her mind, how that she herself, but some few days before, had fallen under the paw of a certain generous lion, that let her go again. Upon a strict enquiry into the matter, she found this to be that very lion; and so set herself presently to work upon the couplings of the net; gnawed the threads to pieces, and in gratitude delivered her preserver.

Without good nature, and gratitude, men had as good live in a wilderness as in a society.

MORAL: *There is no subject so inconsiderable, but his prince, at some time or other, may have occasion for him, and it holds through the whole scale of the creation, that the great and the little have need one of another.*

—AESOP

an affirmative answer. More directly concerned with altruism, however, was the finding that children were more likely to share crayons with another child if that child had previously shared candy with them (Staub and Sherk, 1970).

But what are some of the variables that affect reciprocated altruism? For example, is a large favor more likely than a small favor to stimulate help in return? There is some evidence that at a verbal level people are concerned with the size of an original favor, as indicated in Muir and Weinstein's data mentioned earlier. But are verbal statements regarding the effects of large favors supported by actual changes in tendencies to behave altruistically? H. Wilke and John Lanzetta (1970) found evidence that a direct process of exchange may govern reciprocity of altruism: the more help that one of their subjects offered another, the more help the second subject was likely to reciprocate when the original benefactor was in need.

However, the results of a study by Dean Pruitt (1968) indicate that the exchange may be influenced more by the size of the sacrifice than by the objective amount of material assistance. Pruitt had subjects play a game in which two people alternately received money and decided in what proportions to share the sums with each other. Pruitt was interested in the effects of different types of sharing by the first player on subsequent sharing by the other. He found, not too surprisingly, that a person who gave a large percentage of a fixed amount of money tended to receive more money in return than did a person who gave only a small percentage of the same amount. But he also found, as indicated in Figure 12.10, that people who gave a large percentage of a small sum (80 percent of $1) tended to receive more money than did those who gave a small percentage of a larger sum (20 percent of $4). Yet the actual sums of money yielded by the two percentages were identical. The subjectivity of these subjects' assessments suggests that the concept of exchange is not one that can be defined in absolute, material terms. Even more striking was the discovery that people who gave a fixed percentage (20 percent) of their money tended to receive more money in return if they had been given only a small sum of money ($1) to share than if they had been given a larger sum ($4), even though the amount of money shared was actually less for the person with the smaller sum. In other words, the level of reciprocity is determined by the degree of sacrifice implied by the first helper's gesture rather than by the absolute value of the original gift. The reciprocity norm, as well as the conditions under which it is likely to fail, is discussed further in Chapter 13. There it becomes apparent that the reciprocity norm is not necessarily the most powerful norm governing behavioral exchanges.

When Reciprocity Fails

It is not always the case, however, that receiving a favor increases a person's generosity. Research has revealed several factors that may counteract tendencies to reciprocate.

Perhaps the most obvious circumstance that can inhibit reciprocity is one that leads the recipient to believe that his benefactor had little choice but to do him the favor. The recipient may not consider a favor to be altruistic at all if it does not appear to have been performed voluntarily. And an act that does not appear to be altruistic cannot be expected to precipitate acts of reciprocity (Goranson and Berkowitz, 1966). A favor may actually decrease reciprocity toward the benefactor if the beneficiary receives that

Figure 12.10 It is not the size of the gift that determines the beneficiary's reciprocated generosity but the size of the sacrifice involved, according to these results of a study by Pruitt (1968). Benefactors who gave a large percentage of a small sum (80 percent of $1) were likely to receive greater rewards from beneficiaries than were those who gave a small percentage of a larger sum (20 percent of $4), although both amounts were actually the same. (The amount of reward was represented by chips that were worth 1.5 times as much as the equivalent amount held by the benefactor.) The beneficiaries also seemed to feel that 20 percent of $1 was a larger sacrifice than 20 percent of $4, even though the actual amount received by them was smaller.

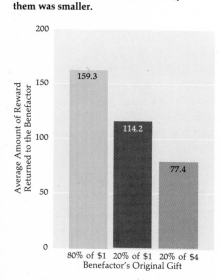

IV Interacting With Others

favor in an inappropriate situation, as John Schopler and Vaida Thompson (1968) found when they offered subjects flowers under awkward circumstances. Another factor that can actually reduce reciprocity operates whenever people receive favors that restrict their freedom of action. As described in Chapter 8, subjects in such a situation volunteered less help to a favordoer than did unobligated subjects (Brehm and Cole, 1966).

The conclusions that altruism can increase a beneficiary's helpfulness toward the benefactor, and perhaps toward others, and that this reciprocity can be eliminated or even reversed in certain circumstances have emerged from studies of the effects of altruism on the beneficiary's subsequent behavior. But the *benefactor's* subsequent behavior can also be influenced by his or her own altruistic performance. For example, in a study detailed in Chapter 10 because it demonstrated the foot-in-the-door technique, Jonathan Freedman and Scott Fraser (1966) asked subjects to perform a relatively effortless act of altruism. These subjects were subsequently more likely to perform a more demanding act of altruism than were people who had not been requested to make the initial sacrifice—regardless of whether or not the two requests were made by the same person and whether the two tasks were similar or dissimilar. Thus, it appears that merely performing an act of altruism produces a certain commitment to prosocial action that increases the disposition to perform subsequent prosocial acts.

The Repercussions of Failing to Help

A staggering proportion of the residents in any institution for the aged, the crippled, or the mentally disturbed never receive a visitor, even though relatives and friends often live in surrounding communities. These people are victims of their own suffering, or, perhaps more accurately, of others' avoidance of the sight of their suffering. It seems that failure to help only ensures continued failure to help, whether the initial failure to act results from choice or from impotence. And this plight is not limited to persons who are confined in institutions; it may afflict all of us in our times of greatest need.

As became clear in the discussion of dependence, the mere fact that someone is in need does not guarantee that people will rush to his or her assistance; in fact, a needy person may elicit the opposite reaction if the need is too intense or too frequent. Apparently, people do not like to be reminded of others' discomforts too forcefully or too frequently. At times, invocations of moral obligations may only make matters worse. For example, if the cost is too great, if the potential benefactor is too depressed, or if there do not appear to be any vehicles for rendering effective assistance, the potential benefactor may resent feeling obligated to help.

One result of negative feelings toward the needy is that cognitive or behavioral strategies are usually employed to avoid thinking about their needs. The decision not to deal with the suffering of others may not be intentional; it probably is not the case, for example, that people say to themselves, "I've got to think of a way to quit feeling bad whenever I see a blind person." Nevertheless, people do use various means, conscious or unconscious, of avoiding their own unpleasant feelings regarding suffering. The solution often chosen by friends and relatives of inmates in various institutions involves simple avoidance of the victim; the relative of a rest-home patient may find life too busy for visits or may come to believe that he "doesn't recognize us anyway" or that "it just upsets him." Similarly, most

Americans, as soon as they are able, structure their lives so that they do not often confront the abject poor, the infirm, or the oppressed. Perhaps we all avoid confronting the reminders of injustice and of others' needs for assistance in order to preserve sanity in a world that is full of injustice and need.

In addition to physical avoidance of suffering, there is a cognitive process by which people sometimes justify their failures to alleviate suffering by justifying the suffering itself. In order to preserve their notion of the world as a just and equitable place, people often tend to perceive those who are in need as somehow deserving their fates. (The process by which people hold unfortunate others responsible for their misfortunes is explored in Chapter 5.) Research on dependence, discussed earlier in this chapter, has also revealed that when people have opportunities to help others but fail to do so, they are more likely to perceive those victims as having voluntarily gotten themselves into harmful situations.

The idea that people are motivated to perceive the world in consistent terms is one of the most pervasive in social psychology. Cognitive-dissonance theory (described in Chapters 8 and 9), balance theory (also explored in Chapter 8), and exchange theory (see Chapter 13) all hinge on a general motivational tendency among people to construe the world in coherent, logical ways. When events or cognitions are ambiguous or contradictory, the tendency is to reconstruct the elements to form a more consistent whole.

A manifestation of this desire for consistency that is particularly important in its implications for altruism is the desire to believe in a just world, where the good are rewarded and the bad are punished, according to Melvin Lerner (1970). His just-world hypothesis, also discussed in Chapter 6, suggests that when a person sees others in need and yet fails to offer help, that observer will be motivated to perceive the victims as "bad" or as in some way deserving of their fates, thus rationalizing his passivity towards them. The obverse would also be expected: Victims are more highly esteemed by a benefactor after he has helped them.

Evidence to support Lerner's theory is suggestive rather than direct, but what data exist support the theory. In two separate experiments, Dana Bramel (1969) and Ellen Berscheid and Elaine Walster (1969) found that subjects who had caused others pain or difficulty tended to rate their victims as less attractive and as more deserving of suffering than did subjects who

Figure 12.11 Because intense suffering makes most of us feel uncomfortable, we often react by turning away, employing behavioral and cognitive strategies to rationalize our failure to help and to justify further indifference. Consequently, some of the most needy groups within the population, such as the poor, the mentally or physically handicapped, and the aged often find themselves abandoned by those who are capable of alleviating their suffering.

had not inflicted suffering on those they rated. Another study (Lerner and Simmons, 1966), described in detail in Chapter 6, contributes evidence that people tend to rate even victims whom they have not had a chance to harm or help as deserving of suffering: Subjects were most rejecting when they believed that the victim had volunteered to continue the punishments so that they (the experimental subjects) would receive credit for participating in an experiment without having to take the test and the shocks. Lerner explains these responses to an innocent victim as follows:

When the person becomes aware of a victim who is clearly innocent of any act which might have brought about the suffering, he is confronted with a conflict. He can decide he lives in a cruel, unjust world where innocent people can suffer or that the only people who suffer in this world are those who deserve such a fate. (1970, page 227)

To have to witness suffering, even when it is for the observer's benefit, seems to be a sufficiently negative experience under some conditions to arouse antagonism rather than pity. Through this response to misfortune, human beings are able to simplify their world a great deal. They need not agonize over the undeserved sufferings of those they like; the people who suffer simply become the people they do not like.

Paradoxically, derogation of victims seems to be both a *result* of confronting a situation in which the individual fails to act altruistically when he feels he ought to and a *cause* of the failure to act. When a situation permits action and the individual fails to act, his failure motivates derogation, which in turn makes it even easier to refrain from action. The uses of this sort of response to suffering are dramatically evident in the case, for example, of enlisted men who witnessed officers torturing Vietnamese civilians and, because of fear of negative sanctions, failed to intervene. As a result of the failure to intervene, a person who is faced with a conflict such as that between witnessing suffering and fear of the torturer's authority may come to derogate the victim; he may thereby be even less likely to intervene when he sees one of his peers performing a similar act.

If people dislike those they fail to aid, what evidence is there that they like those they do aid? Lerner and Simmons provided some subjects with an opportunity to alleviate the suffering they were observing by changing the victim's learning assignment from a punishment procedure to a reward procedure. When subjects were able to alleviate the victim's suffering, they

rated her more positively. Judson Mills and Ronald Egger (1972) also report that people who alleviated others' miseries were more positively disposed toward them than were subjects who could only watch helplessly.

Receiving Help: The Ecstasy and the Agony

Most of us expect some sort of gratitude from the recipients of help and kindness. Yet help does not always elicit gratitude. The amputee selling pencils on the street may feel little love for the people dropping dimes in his can. And the people of developing nations, wary of the strings attached to aid, seem remarkably restrained in their expressions of gratitude for wheat shipments, dams, and generators. In field interviews with fifty officials from over a dozen nations, Kenneth and Mary Gergen (1971) discovered widespread animosity among recipients of aid toward their benefactors—even when the benefactors were attempting to use the aid to build bridges of good will. One of the major problems expressed by recipients was the position of dependence in which aid placed them.

Although people may express initial gratitude for the physical assistance that temporarily alleviates their suffering, they do not necessarily like to be reminded of their dependence on benefactors. Dependence not only can be a blow to self-esteem but it often serves to reduce the recipient's freedom, as well. Brehm and Cole, in the study mentioned earlier, found that beneficiaries rated their benefactors as less attractive when a favor had reduced their freedom than when the favor had not reduced their freedom.

Another possible explanation for negative feelings toward benefactors was hinted at in the Pruitt study described earlier. Recall that this study revealed that a large amount or even a large proportion of goods may not be as effective in ensuring the beneficiary's gratitude (as indicated by his willingness to reciprocate) as is the beneficiary's subjective appraisal of how much of a sacrifice the gift represents.

Most forms of charity do not represent much of a sacrifice, whether the beneficiary is a beggar, a Third World country, or a welfare recipient. A well-dressed passerby, the United States government, and most other sources of charity give so small a proportion of their goods that the beneficiary's existence is not substantially altered. Moreover, the beneficiary may perceive that the benefactor's motives may not be benign (Tesser, Gatewood, and Driver, 1968). Thus, Third World leaders may feel that the aid they are given carries with it implicit expectations that they reciprocate with political and economic favors.

Many benefactors give aid with regularity. International aid programs, charities, religious institutions, alumni, and so on may give on a constant and continuing basis. However, as research by Stanley Morse (1972) has shown, aid that is expected or anticipated is little appreciated by the recipient. Unexpected aid—the surprise gift—is far more likely to make friends.

Still another source of resentment of aid is the recipient's inability to reciprocate; aid that does not allow reciprocation may produce enemies—it is embarrassing for recipients to be unable to pay their debts. (Some of this research on foreign aid is detailed in Chapter 15.)

In the discussion of prosocial behavior, it has been shown that a variety of situational factors can profoundly affect the tendencies of people to aid one another. With remarkable regularity, conformity to the norm of helpfulness is dependent on the social situations in which people find themselves. These factors affect not only their behavior but also the ways in which they perceive and feel about one another. Bear in mind, however,

*You praise my self-sacrifice,
  Spoon River,*

In rearing Irene and Mary,

Orphans of my older sister!

*And you censure Irene and
  Mary*

For their contempt for me!

*But praise not my
  self-sacrifice,*

*And censure not their
  contempt;*

*I reared them, I cared for them,
  true enough!—*

But I poisoned my benefactions

*With constant reminders of
  their dependence.*

—E.L. MASTERS

IV INTERACTING WITH OTHERS

that the experimental evidence that has been accumulated is but a starting point in understanding the full range of human prosocial concern. Prosocial behavior covers a widely divergent range of activities that may be affected by many different factors. Therefore, generalizations must be made carefully. For example, whereas mood may increase or decrease a person's tendency to be charitable to others, it may have no bearing on how he or she would respond in an emergency. Or the presence of others may reduce the individual's tendency to intervene in an emergency but increase the probability that he or she will comply with a request.

The diversity of behavior that may be considered prosocial becomes apparent if acts like those of the Berrigan brothers are considered. Daniel and Philip Berrigan were two priests who entered a draft-board office and destroyed draft records as a protest against the United States' involvement in the Vietnam War. If judged according to the letter of the law, their act was antisocial but, inasmuch as it placed human life above the dictates of a specific government, it was considered by them to be a high-risk prosocial act. Many other revolutionaries and martyrs—regardless of the extent to which one agrees with their goals—feel themselves motivated by altruistic concern. Right-wing activists who participate in illegal paramilitary activities also see themselves as serving a prosocial function by protecting the naive citizenry against "alien" or "subversive" elements that they believe the federal government is too weak or too left-wing to deal with. Thus, although people may have different—even conflicting—goals, their motives may be remarkably similar. A left-wing radical and a right-wing reactionary, a policeman and a thief, a Catholic missionary and an atheist may be equally motivated by prosocial concern. The differences between them lie primarily in *whom* they are trying to help and in *how* they believe they can best aid those in need.

There are countless examples of great and small sacrifices that people make for one another. Although the factors discussed in this chapter do much to shape the forms that prosocial behavior takes and to determine when it occurs, most of us express prosocial concern in some form. It is up

Figure 12.12 To be prosocial, behavior need only be voluntary, beneficial to others, and an end in itself. Although the goals of prosocial actions are often similar, the ways in which these goals are accomplished can differ considerably. Robin Hood helped the poor—a goal of many altruists—by giving them goods stolen from the wealthy—a method that might be deplored by certain other altruists.

to each of us to adapt the insights provided in this chapter to our own circumstances. As has been discovered under several guises in this chapter, each prosocial action that a person undertakes is likely to generate still other prosocial acts—by the original benefactor, by the beneficiaries, and by uninvolved observers as well. To some extent, then, each of us is able to decide what sort of human community we will live in. The fact that our actions are often not geared to produce the most satisfying community life possible is explored in depth in Chapter 13.

SUMMARY

Almost every culture has norms that encourage prosocial actions—actions that are defined as voluntary, beneficial to another person or group of people, and performed solely for themselves and not for personal gain. But not all cultures place the same emphasis on altruism. Individualistic cultures emphasize personal fulfillment, achievement, and expression; collectivistic cultures stress interdependence and mutuality. The norm of helping, although widely espoused, is actually only an ideal with "ought" force, or influence on what we as potential benefactors believe we should do.

Altruistic behavior is affected by other people, especially models. An important factor in the influence of a model is his similarity to us; the similar model is more likely than the dissimilar one to influence our own responses to a person in need of help. However, *behavioral modeling* and *verbal modeling* are distinctly different in effect. For instance, a hypocritical model who talks about altruism but does not actually help is likely to evoke that same inconsistent response in an observer.

John Darley and Bibb Latané have conducted a variety of studies on *bystander intervention* to learn the conditions that determine whether one person will aid a distressed other. The potential helper must first decide that the situation requires someone's action. Then the proper course of action must be decided. Finally, the bystander must decide that he is in a position to offer appropriate aid without great harm to himself.

It is often difficult for the observer to determine the seriousness of an emergency. In such cases, we often use *social comparison,* comparing our reactions to those of others present, in interpreting the danger. However, this process often impedes a decision to help. Other factors that influence bystander intervention include the perceived *potential* of other bystanders to help; the physical threat to the bystander; the fear of losing face by acting inappropriately; and the *low control of effects syndrome,* which invests contemporary man with a cynical view of his personal effectiveness against general dehumanization.

People who need help are not all equally successful in eliciting a particular individual's help. When the need is great, we are more likely to assist our close friends than we are to assist total strangers. In addition, a person's *dependence* on someone's help can elicit altruism, although if the person seems responsible for his own plight, the benefactor may be less likely to help.

Altruism is affected not only by *social situations* such as those described above; it is also affected by *transitory psychological states.* One such state is produced by prior success in a seemingly unrelated task, which may create a feeling of competence or general good will. The good feeling produced by success appears to increase altruism.

Altruism often arises from guilt or sympathy and a desire to compensate the injured for their pain, but guilt can generalize from those a person has wronged to other victims he or she has not injured and from a personal act of wrongdoing to an act for which the observer is not responsible.

The norm of reciprocity encourages us to return favors, and research shows that we practice what is preached. But reciprocity may be blocked if the favor seems to be a very small sacrifice, to be involuntary, to be inappropriate, or to be restrictive of our freedom.

If we perform one prosocial act, we are likely to do others to maintain our altruistic image; but if we fail to help once, we are likely to fail again. We may fail to help if the need is too intense or too frequent, because reminders of suffering are unpleasant. We may either avoid these reminders or come to believe that those who suffer deserve their fates. If we are forced to confront the victims of injustice, we may develop a great dislike for those victims. But if we are able to help, the dislike often disappears.

In the same way that the sight of suffering makes us uncomfortable, the needy may be uncomfortable with their dependence on the help of others, perhaps resenting it. Research indicates a variety of factors that can cause recipients of help to react negatively to their benefactors.

Prosocial action can take many forms and can spring from a variety of motivations. But, because one prosocial act often leads to another, we can all facilitate the spread of altruistic behavior.

SUGGESTED READINGS

Bickman, Leonard, and Thomas Henchy (eds.). *Beyond the Laboratory: Field Research in Social Psychology.* New York: McGraw-Hill, 1972.

Bryan, James, and Perry London. "Altruistic Behavior by Children," *Psychological Bulletin,* 73 (1970), 200–211.

Darley, John, and Bibb Latané. *The Unresponsive Bystander: Why Doesn't He Help?* New York: Appleton-Century-Crofts, 1970.

Krebs, Dennis. "Altruism—An Examination of the Concept and a Review of the Literature," *Psychological Bulletin,* 73 (1970), 258–302.

MacCauley, Jacqueline, and Leonard Berkowitz (eds.). *Altruism and Helping Behavior.* New York: Academic Press, 1970.

13

Exchange & Strategy in Social Life

YOU ARE INVITED TO PLAY A GAME. If you win, you will receive wealth, fame, freedom—almost anything you wish. If you lose, however, you may become impoverished, lose your health and any hope of future happiness. A round of the game is played whenever two or more players meet and exchange moves. A move consists of either acting out or refraining from acting out some type of behavior, verbal or otherwise. You must play each round very carefully, for others' moves can place you in a very poor position. For temporary periods you may join with others to form a team, but in the final accounting you are on your own. There are rules of the game, but they are often quite inexact or ambiguous, and you must watch carefully to be sure that you are not breaking them. If you break rules you risk punishment, which may vary in severity from mild embarrassment to forced removal from the game. Sometimes removal is only temporary (a few years), but in other cases you may be executed for violations. Very clever players are able to violate many of the rules to their own advantage, and most players look for ways of doing so. Whenever another player gains something in a round, the rest of the players may lose accordingly. What do you say to the invitation? Would you like to play? Or rather, would you like to see how you are already playing?

This description represents the model of social interaction that will be revealed in this chapter. The approach is more formally known as the *behavior-exchange model*, and you will soon understand why this particular name was chosen. The model has received careful study by social psychologists for almost two decades. To the extent that the model validly represents

actual social interaction, the stakes may be nothing less than life or death. However serious the implications of this model may be, it is hardly the first time that psychologists have depicted human beings as selfish, manipulative strategists or have depicted social life as a battlefield. Freud, too, saw the human being as a complicated beast whose behavior was the unwitting outcome of the inner battle between irrational, rational, and moralistic forces. Whereas Freud saw the battle primarily as an internal one and people as chiefly irrational, the behavior-exchange model views the battle as primarily interpersonal and people as quite rational indeed.

The notion that human behavior tends to follow the behavior-exchange model may now be an unwelcome lodger in your boardinghouse of ideas about the world. But it will be worthwhile to stifle your displeasure for a time. If you get to know this boarder a little better and get to understand his behavior, you may be surprised at the amount of human behavior that is illuminated by his mode of social interaction. If, in the end, you find you cannot comfortably inhabit the same house together, then send him packing. Theories are only approximations of reality, and alternative models of social interaction may better enhance your understanding of interaction in the real world. However, you should also be careful not to dispense with a theory solely for emotional reasons before you have examined whether or not it reflects the actual state of social life.

This chapter first examines the basic suppositions of the behavior-exchange approach and several important implications of the model. After looking at basic assumptions, the model will be applied to a variety of common social situations. Situations in which people abide by the rules of the game as well as situations in which people break the rules and exploit others unfairly will be examined. Although this chapter will draw primarily from the writings of social psychologists, it will also make occasional mention of the model's family ties to sociology, anthropology, psychiatry, political science, and other disciplines as well.

BEHAVIOR EXCHANGE

At birth, the individual human being's behavior is motivated by a number of biologically based needs. Required are food, water, air, possibly physical touch, and so on. But, as discussed in Chapter 2, the person will not remain long in this "biologically thrown" condition. Parents, siblings, teachers, peers, and the mass media quickly mold his or her desires in a variety of ways. In addition to the biological—or primary—needs, the individual develops a series of learned—or secondary—motives. He or she begins to desire high grades, attractive clothes, money, equality, and so on. Given this range of human motivation, a major supposition can be put forth: *At each moment people so act as to provide themselves maximum fulfillment of their needs.* To put it another way, people behave at all times so as to gain as much pleasure as possible and to reduce pain to a minimum. This supposition is hardly new; it is as old as pre-Christian philosophy and has played an essential role in theories of human behavior from the ancient Greek philosopher Epicurus to B. F. Skinner. Often it is termed the *hedonistic* view of human behavior, or *hedonics.*

Although the hedonistic view will be congenial to many readers, there are two sorts of reservations that some of you may have at this point. On the one hand, you may protest that this view is mistaken because it does not account for many aspects of human behavior. For example, hundreds of thousands of people are starving in the United States, and if the hedonistic theory applied universally, they would be filling themselves with food. What prevents these people from satisfying their desire for food? And why is it that people sometimes do not say the things they most want to say? Or why do people give up their lives in martyrdom for others? Actually, cases in which human beings deny their own desires pose little problem to the hedonist explanation of human behavior. Starving people may not steal food because the cost of taking it (which might be social ostracism or a jail sentence) might exceed the pain of starvation. If people fail to express their feelings when they most wish to, then the cost of embarrassment must exceed their desires for openness. And martyrs must have learned to value their fellow human beings, God's will, or the thought of themselves in the memories of others more than their own lives. Therefore, all these behaviors may be adopted in order to maximize pleasure and minimize loss.

The second reservation about the hedonistic view of behavior is more problematic. If *all* behavior is guided by a desire to minimize loss and maximize gain, how does this knowledge help in predicting behavior? As discussed in Chapter 1, scientific theories are useful only if they specify the conditions under which one event occurs as opposed to another. Accordingly, the hedonistic assumption can be converted from raw form into a sophisticated theoretical tool. If psychologists agree that people generally seek maximum pleasure and minimum pain, then they are in a good position to make predictions, assuming that they can establish which behaviors bring pleasure, which bring pain, and in what degree. If they know what value people usually associate with each of the various alternatives facing them, they can also predict which options people will choose.

Social Approval as a Reinforcer

An essentially hedonistic model may make a good theory, but does it adequately account for social motivation in the real world? Consider one very important example. If you stop to think about your own needs, you will probably realize that you have a strong need for the approval of others, whether in the form of their love, appreciation, or respect. The well-known clinical psychologist Carl Rogers (1961) has suggested that the need for approval is one of the most powerful of human needs, sometimes even more potent than the need for food or safety. From Rogers' point of view,

Figure 13.1 The hedonistic view that people are primarily motivated to maximize pleasure and minimize pain has played a major role in attempts to explain human nature since the time of the ancient Greeks. This etching depicts the triumph of Bacchus (Dionysus), the god who "invented" wine and orgies.

. . . Today I'll haste to quaff my wine
As if tommorrow ne'er should shine;
But if tommorrow comes, why then—
I'll haste to quaff my wine again.

—ANACREON

when a person is unable to gain others' regard, he or she is likely to develop neurotic symptoms. Psychiatric patients, he feels, are usually people who do not receive sufficient acceptance from others. The psychiatrist Erich Fromm (1968) has added that unless the person receives others' regard, he or she will be unable to give love to others. Furthermore, social theorist David Riesman (1961) has asserted that people are more sensitive to the approval of others in the present era than people ever were before. Many other thinkers who have pinpointed the importance of the need for social approval could be added to this list.

These various speculations about the human need for social approval pave the way for psychologists to predict actual behavior. If people are so generally in need of the approval of others, they should be very responsive to cues of acceptance and rejection in social relations. They should behave in ways that elicit this acceptance from others and avoid behaving in ways that elicit rejection from others, even if rejection or acceptance is communicated through very subtle cues.

William Verplanck (1955) was one of the first psychologists to investigate the possibility that human beings are motivated to maximize social approval and minimize disapproval. Seventeen students in one of Verplanck's seminars were the experimenters in this study. Each experimenter casually engaged another person in a conversation in an everyday setting, such as a dormitory or cafeteria. Throughout the conversation, each experimenter silently recorded how many opinions the other person stated. During the first ten minutes of the conversation, the experimenter expressed neither agreement nor disagreement with any opinion the other person expressed; this period yielded a base line for each subject's rate of opinion expression. During the next ten minutes—the reinforcement period—whenever the subject expressed an opinion, the experimenter indicated agreement by nodding, smiling, or saying "you're right." During the final ten minutes of the conversation—the extinction period—the experimenter either ignored the opinions or showed mild disagreement. Although not

Figure 13.2 Particular situations can arouse the need for social approval in each of us, and the nature of our social interactions is affected accordingly. This need can be especially acute in adolescents, who typically depend heavily on peers for standards of behavior and social support.

IV INTERACTING WITH OTHERS

free of methodological problems, the results from twenty-four of these conversations strongly suggest that positive regard is a potent motivator of human behavior. In all twenty-four cases, the rate of opinion expression increased during the period when opinions were reinforced from what they had been during the base-line period. And during the extinction period, only three of the twenty-four cases failed to show the predicted decline in opinion expression.

Verplanck's classic study has triggered a long line of research attempting to trace in more precise terms the effects of subtle forms of positive regard in shaping behavior. For example, research has revealed that social approval can be a powerful tool in the hands of psychotherapists. Therapists typically instruct their patients to say anything that comes into the patients' minds; hesitant speech is often interpreted by a therapist as an indication that the patient is disturbed or anxious about his or her thoughts. The therapist may be particularly attentive at these moments.

The therapist is not a passive agent who simply listens at these moments and contemplates the patient's meaning, according to Joseph Matarazzo, George Saslow, Arthur Wiens, Morris Weitman, and Bernadene Allen (1964). Rather, these investigators suggest, the therapist is an intrusive agent who often modifies the patient's verbal output through very subtle signs of social approval. With these thoughts in mind, the investigators arranged to have applicants for civil-service employment interviewed in systematically different ways. The examiners conducted the forty-five-minute job interviews in three fifteen-minute intervals, which were base-line, reinforcement, and extinction periods. Two investigators each interviewed twenty job applicants. In contrast to Verplanck's study, the behavior they attended to was not opinion expression but instead included any talking whatsoever. The investigators supplied reinforcement only by nodding their heads. The investigators attempted to be as consistent as possible in their behavior, except that in the reinforcement period, each nodded his head whenever the applicant was talking.

Verplanck had given the student experimenters considerable flexibility in indicating agreement, and many unwanted biases could thus have contributed to his results. By restricting approval to the simple act of nodding the head, Matarazzo and his colleagues gained a high degree of control over extraneous sources of bias. The results of this experiment were in essential

Figure 13.3 While conversing, people tend to be sensitive to one another's subtle nonverbal behavior—nodding, facial expressions, posture, and other cues that might suggest one another's reactions. Approval, or disapproval, of the other's words is often subtly conveyed through these nonverbal means. It is interesting to speculate what Lyndon Johnson's facial expression here was meant to convey to Richard Nixon, his successor to the presidency, and whether Nixon's pat of Johnson's hand was a friendly, approving gesture or a patronizing, disapproving one.

agreement with Verplanck's findings. The applicants' rate of talking significantly increased during the reinforcement period and decreased dramatically during the extinction period. The interviewers' simple nod of the head thus seemed to have a marked impact on the applicants' self-expression. Clearly, then, even silence from a psychotherapist affects a patient's tendency to reveal his or her inner thoughts. For that matter, it is safe to assume that all of us, by our expressions of social approval, exert some influence on the openness of those around us.

Do these studies actually demonstrate the impact of social approval rather than that of some other factor? Perhaps a nod of the head simply indicates to a speaker that the listener understands and thus encourages the speaker to proceed more rapidly. Agreement with his or her opinions may also give a speaker a feeling of being correct; and with an increased sense of correctness, the speaker may feel encouraged to continue.

Needs for social approval vary in two important ways that are discussed in other chapters. Chapter 2, in which socialization is discussed, and Chapter 4, in which individual differences are explored, suggest that people differ sharply in their needs for approval. Based on their past learning, some people seem generally to rely on social approval more than others do. On the other hand, as indicated in Chapters 2, 11, and 12, people's needs and desires are strongly influenced by the particular situations in which they find themselves. It is reasonable to expect, then, that situations that temporarily increase individuals' needs for approval will alter their sensitivity to social approval accordingly. The present discussion will now consider in detail each of these two ways—individual and situational—in which needs for approval vary.

Individual Needs. As explained in Chapter 4, researchers who measure differences in the need for approval find that those whose scores indicate a great need for approval are more conforming than are those with apparently lower approval needs. And individuals with high needs for approval are also more responsive to subtle signs of approval than are those with low approval needs, according to Douglas Crowne and Bonnie Strickland (1961). These two investigators conducted a study that was similar in format to the verbal conditioning studies that Verplanck initiated. Student subjects responded to questions for twenty-five minutes. An experimenter reinforced some subjects for uttering plural nouns by nodding affirmatively and uttering "mm-*hmm*" after each plural noun. Subjects who had previously scored high on the Crowne-Marlowe social-desirability measure were far more responsive to reinforcement than were low scorers. During the first five minutes, both groups uttered nearly the same number of plural nouns, but as the reinforcement continued, the plural-noun output of subjects with high approval needs began to increase dramatically. Those with a low need for approval, on the other hand, remained relatively stable in their use of plural nouns. And the susceptibility of subjects with a strong need for approval and reinforcement was not a function of their preference for plural nouns. When the experimenter responded to the use of plural nouns with a stony "uh-uh," the effects of reinforcement were reversed: Those subjects with strong approval needs emitted fewer plural nouns during the twenty-five minutes of nonreinforcement than did those with lesser needs.

Apparently, as Crowne and Strickland found, learned needs for approval can increase people's responsiveness to approval cues from others.

But what about situationally induced needs for approval? Do circumstances create temporary needs, and, if so, do these needs operate in the same way as do more chronic needs?

Situational Needs. A study by Elaine Walster (1965) answers both these questions affirmatively. During the initial phase of her experiment, she told female college students either that they had done very well on a personality test or that they had done poorly on the test. She intended this information to alter temporarily the needs of the subjects for approval. She reasoned that those who had suffered a blow to their self-confidence would be more desirous of another's approval than would those whose confidence had been increased by positive feedback. After each woman had taken a test that established the effects of the information on her self-confidence, a very attractive young man (actually the experimenter's accomplice) entered and asked the whereabouts of the experimenter. He engaged each woman in conversation and asked her out for a date. Walster reasoned that if a person is in great need of approval, then he or she would be inclined to view more positively someone who provides the needed approval. Thus, she measured the responsiveness of her female subjects to social approval by subsequently asking them to rate their attraction toward the male accomplice.

The results confirmed her prediction: Women who previously had been deprived of approval by receiving discouraging feedback subsequently rated the confederate as more attractive than did women whose needs for approval had been temporarily sated.

Walster subsequently informed all the participants of the details of the study and of its significance. Nevertheless, the ethics of this procedure have been questioned (Rubin, 1970). You may well ask whether or not, in this experiment, the means justified the end—namely, arriving at the conclusion that self-satisfaction serves as insulation against flattery.

The evidence reviewed so far indicates that needs for social approval operate in a manner not dissimilar to the operation of biological needs. Researchers can differentiate among people in a quantitative way with respect to their learned, generalized needs for approval. In addition, needs for approval wax and wane depending on the availability of approval in given situations. From these findings about social approval, it seems reasonable to assume that other learned needs operate in similar fashions. Thus, the discussion of hedonic motives that was problematic earlier in this chapter can now become more concrete. Researchers have been able to differentiate among various qualities and quantities of pleasure that different people seek as well as the types and intensities of pain that they attempt to avoid. And researchers have also examined the relationship of people's needs or desires to their actual behavior. An image of the behavior-exchange individual is beginning to emerge.

The Interaction Matrix: How We Are Ensnared

So far, only the lone individual seeking to gratify his or her own needs, both biological and learned, has been considered. Clearly, such a view is short-sighted, for it leaves out the essentially social character of human life. We are all dependent on others for the fulfillment of vital needs.

Consider the case of Arlene, a senior in college who faces the difficult decision of what to do after graduation. There are two major possibilities open to her, and these are indicated in Figure 13.4. She can take a job with

Figure 13.4 The intrinsic payoffs Arlene feels she would receive by accepting a job with her father's business firm as compared to those she would receive by joining a rock band. She can anticipate the satisfaction she would intrinsically derive from each job by subtracting the costs of either choice from the rewards. The intrinsic values to Arlene of the two alternatives are arbitrarily represented here as points on a scale from −10 (extreme anguish) to +10 (extreme pleasure).

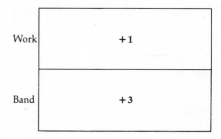

Work	+1
Band	+3

her father's business firm. Or, because she happens to be an outstanding singer, she can try to succeed in the rock scene. Figure 13.4 also indicates the degree of *intrinsic* satisfaction that Arlene would obtain from each of these activities. This intrinsic satisfaction is represented by a hypothetical twenty-point scale, with the most pleasureful extreme at +10 (supreme ecstasy) and the most painful extreme at −10 (supreme anguish). Each number entered in the figure is computed by subtracting the pain from the pleasure involved in either going to work for her father or singing in a band. Thus, the pain of going to work for her father would include the drudgery of a standard work week filled with tasks of low interest value and her feeling that she had given up all sorts of exciting alternatives. Arlene might attach a value to these combined costs of −6. The intrinsic pleasures, on the other hand, might include feelings of financial security and independence and the hope of a position of authority. These intrinsic pleasures might add up in Arlene's mind to +7. Subtracting the −6 from the +7 leaves +1; in the figure this is the value attached to the job option her father has offered her. Thus, Arlene might anticipate that she would experience slightly more pleasure than pain as a result of working for her father's company, but not very much more. On the basis of a similar mental calculation, Arlene might conclude that she would experience more intrinsic pleasure if she joined a rock group. There would be the pain of early starvation and the fear of failure—a total of, say, −4. But there would also be the intense pleasure of singing and high hopes of success at a highly valued activity, and Arlene might value these combined assets at +7. The total hedonic payoff entered in the band-option segment of Figure 13.4 is thus +3.

But Arlene is not alone in her world, and the pleasure she would derive from either of the two options would be further influenced by the reactions of others to her choices. To keep matters simple, consider the reactions of one other person in Arlene's life—Bill, her boyfriend—and limit Bill's possible responses to two: approval and disapproval. Because Arlene cares very much about Bill and values his opinions, his opinions constitute additional payoffs—either positive or negative. In this case, the source of the payoffs is *extrinsic*—that is, the payoffs derive not from the activity itself but from another's response to it. Bill's approval of Arlene's choices would increase their payoff value to her, and his disapproval would decrease it. Assume that his approval would add two points of pleasure (+2) and his disapproval would decrease the value of either choice by a similar amount (−2). To the intrinsic payoffs represented in Figure 13.4, therefore, it is possible to add and subtract the extrinsic payoffs of Bill's opinions. As indicated in Figure 13.5, if Bill approves, working for her father and breaking into the rock scene as a singer increase in Arlene's value to +3 and +5 respectively; if he disapproves, the values of these alternatives drop to −1 and +1 for Arlene.

At this point it is necessary to focus on Bill's situation in more detail. Specifically, separate his intrinsic from his extrinsic rewards and enter them in the matrix. What are his actual preferences, and why? As it happens, Bill has secured a graduate-school fellowship from a nearby university. If Arlene takes the job with her father's company, she can remain close by and the chances of their staying together—a prospect for which Bill has high hopes—will be maximized. If Arlene joins a struggling rock band, on the other hand, their life together will be disrupted and life will be very sad for him. Thus, Bill is torn between urging Arlene to take the job her father has offered her—an outcome that would bring Bill much intrinsic pleasure

Figure 13.5 Arlene's payoffs for each work choice, given Bill's approval or disapproval. She estimates that Bill's approval would increase her payoffs on the hypothetical scale by approximately two units of pleasure, whereas his disapproval would decrease her payoffs by two units of anguish. Bill's reactions provide the extrinsic source of Arlene's payoffs, and their value is added to her intrinsic payoffs, shown in Figure 13.4.

		Bill	
		Approve	Disapprove
Arlene	Work	+3	−1
	Band	+5	+1

—and urging her to pursue a singing career, an outcome that would bring Bill a good deal of intrinsic pain.

At the same time, Bill wants Arlene to be happy. On an extrinsic level, then, Bill would derive pleasure from supporting Arlene's desires and pain from standing in her way. In combination, Bill's strong intrinsic desire for a happy future with Arlene and the extrinsic pain he would feel at standing in her way might result in a total value of +3 for his approval of Arlene's decision to go to work for her father and a +2 for his disapproval of her decision to join a band. For him to approve of her singing would bring slightly more pain than pleasure (−1), and to disapprove of her going to work for her father would definitely be painful (−4). These values are represented in Figure 13.6.

As you scan the matrix, several conclusions seem apparent. Whereas Arlene would definitely have chosen a career in rock music if left to herself, she does not feel totally free to make a decision based exclusively on her own intrinsic desires. A career in music may cost her her relationship with Bill. In effect, these factors lead her to make an exchange. Almost all the decisions that all of us make have this complex character. We are constantly involved in exchanging our actions for the behavioral reactions of others with whom we interact.

The payoff matrix also reveals the behavioral options that are optimally rewarding for the parties under the circumstances. If people attempt to maximize their rewards, then the cell of the matrix that represents maximum returns for both parties should be preferred by both. In this case, Arlene's choice of working for her father and Bill's approval would yield the greatest reward to them both. Other matters aside, then, it is possible to predict that this will be the result of the exchange between Arlene and Bill.

You should keep in mind that the discussion of Arlene and Bill's situation has been limited to only two behavioral alternatives. If the matrix had been expanded to include the total range of possible solutions to their dilemma, the conclusion that Arlene would go to work for her father might not have been the outcome. There are probably other considerations that would influence Arlene's decision besides Bill's feelings, Arlene's relationship with Bill, and the intrinsic merits of the two types of work. An expansion of the matrix might also reveal other exchanges that could possibly have offered greater pleasure to them both.

We do not always succeed in maximizing joint outcomes, however, nor are we always willing to settle for less than the maximum intrinsic rewards available to us. This discussion will now focus on a number of hurdles that block maximum fulfillment of our needs, and it will also elaborate on some of the ways in which people go about getting their own way at the expense of others.

In the discussion of Arlene and Bill's interaction, what John Thibaut and Harold Kelley (1959) call an *interaction matrix* was set up. Ideally, an interaction matrix indicates each participant's hedonic payoffs for engaging in a range of behavior exchanges.

A clearer understanding of what an exchange model involves can be derived from the formulations of Thibaut and Kelley (1959). Basically, their model centers on four aspects of any interaction. First, the participants exchange certain *rewards,* whether these be companionship, sex, help with one another's homework, physical attractiveness, or other assets. At the same time, certain *costs* are incurred by each participant: these might involve failure of the partner to live up to the individual's expectations;

Figure 13.6 Bill and Arlene's total hedonic payoffs for engaging in each of two behavioral alternatives. Arlene's payoffs, which are affected by Bill's wishes, are the same as those presented in Figure 13.5. As shown here, Arlene's decision will in turn affect Bill's payoffs, because he is torn between his desire to continue the relationship with her (an intrinsic reward) and the extrinsic satisfaction he would derive if Arlene pursued the career that would make her happiest.

	Approve	Disapprove
Work	Bill +3 +3 Arlene	−4 −1
Band	−1 +5	+2 +1

time, energy, and other resources spent as a result of the interaction; and possible benefits from other activities that the individual has sacrificed for the sake of this particular relationship. The difference between the total cost and rewards represents the *outcome* of the interaction—a third concept in Thibaut and Kelley's model. If this outcome is positive, the individual has profited from the relationship; if negative, an overall loss has been suffered. (The rewards and punishments in Thibaut and Kelley's model are equivalent to the payoffs exchanged by Arlene and Bill.)

Clearly, human beings do not always evaluate their relationships in totally objective terms. As explained in Chapter 6, if the satisfactions are great enough, feelings of friendship or love may develop, and these may lead the participants to make sacrifices for one another that they do not necessarily expect one another to match. Whether or not a relationship continues depends not on the absolute level of the outcome but on how it compares with the outcomes of past relationships, with previous interactions with the same partner, or with what the individual perceives is being realized by others. These considerations provide the individual with a *comparison level*—a fourth concept that is central in the exchange model developed by Thibaut and Kelley. The individual must feel that the outcome of an interaction exceeds this comparison level before evaluating it positively. Two people may receive exactly the same treatment from another, but their differing comparison levels may bring happiness to one and pain to the other.

You may be thinking by this point that this is all very well as an academic exercise, but so what? Why is it valuable to think in terms of an exchange model? The model has much to reveal, both of scientific and personal interest. In fact, most of the remainder of this chapter will be spent discussing various kinds of relationships that an exchange model elucidates. However, before embarking on these more detailed excursions, it is important to consider two more general implications of the interaction-matrix model described here.

The Power of Predictability. You meet someone who has just moved in across the hall, who is to sit next to you in class, or who has asked you out. Immediately you wonder: "How will we get along together?" "Is this relationship going to be a good one or a 'bummer'?" Questions such as these are asked by everyone, from the foreman who wonders how productive a newly formed crew will be to the bride and groom who ponder their fate as a married couple. If we think in terms of the possible exchanges that can be made, we can make some reliable predictions about the course of relationships. First assume that in most instances people act according to a *minimax strategy*, wherein each participant seeks to minimize loss and maximize gain. The strategy requires a participant to try to shape the other's behavior to his or her own advantage. And because each is trying to make it unrewarding for the partner to inflict pain and rewarding for the partner to provide pleasure, the result is a state of *interpersonal accommodation* (Kelley, 1968). If there are cells of the matrix in which mutual satisfaction is possible, the relationship should prosper.

Joseph Sidowski, Benjamin Wyckoff, and Leon Tabory (1956) tested the hypothesis that groups, including couples, seek interpersonal accommodation. Some subjects were led individually into a cubicle where the experimenter attached electrodes to their left hands. In front of them were two push buttons and a point counter. The experimenters instructed them that their goal would be to use the buttons to make as many points as possible. They could push either button as often as they wished, and, depending on which button they happened to press at a particular time, they would receive either points on their counter or shocks from the electrodes. In each instance, a second subject was in an adjoining chamber and faced the same circumstances. Both subjects were told that the other was there and that the combination of their moves would somehow produce points or shocks, but they were not told what moves or combinations would produce what outcomes: By pressing the right-hand button, the person in the first chamber provided a point for the person in the second chamber. Pressing the left-hand button gave the second subject a shock. At the same time, if the second subject pressed the right-hand button in his or her chamber, the first subject received a shock. Pressing the left-hand button,

---

THIS CHAPTER emphasizes the motivating influences of past and present rewards on human behavior. The future, too, can hold rewards that have motive force. Some investigators, like psychologist David Phillips, believe that hopes for the future can stave off even death.

Phillips reasoned that birthdays would be especially exciting events for famous people, bringing them public interest, gifts, and other exciting consequences. Thus the motivation to live out the next birthday might be especially strong in a famous person. The average expected death toll per month of the 348 famous Americans Phillips studied was twenty-nine. When he checked the death rates for his sample in the month prior to each person's birthday, the death toll was sixteen.

Phillips assumed that if the low death rate in the months preceding birthdays reflected a desire on the part of his subjects to delay dying until their birthdays had passed, an unusually high death rate should be expected during the month following the individuals' birthdays. This assumption proved well founded. For the first three months after each of the birthdays, an average of thirty-eight died—nine deaths more than the predicted average.

Death patterns also rise and fall before and after significant dates in United States history, such as dates that mark presidential elections and holidays. Exactly fifty years after the Declaration of Independence was signed, both John Adams and Thomas Jefferson died on the Fourth of July. Jefferson's last words were reported as follows by his physician:

About seven o'clock of the evening of that day, he awoke, and seeing my staying at his bedside exclaimed, "Oh, Doctor, are you still there?" in a voice, however, that was husky and indistinct. He then asked, "Is it the Fourth?" to which I replied, "It soon will be." These were the last words I heard him utter.

Another famous American who seemed to have struck a bargain with destiny was Mark Twain. He is quoted as predicting, as follows, the circumstances of his own death:

I came in with Halley's comet in 1835. It is coming again next year, and I expect to go out with it. It will be the greatest disappointment of my life if I don't go out with Halley's comet. The Almighty has said, no doubt: "Now here are these two unaccountable freaks; they came in together, they must go out together." Oh, I am looking forward to that.

Twain died April 21, 1910—thirteen days before the comet appeared.

These cases yield striking evidence that people can exercise a remarkable degree of control over their own bodies, even to the point that death may defer.

Source: Adapted from P. Koenig, "Death Doth Defer," Psychology Today, 6 (1972), p. 83.

WHEN DEATH DOTH DEFER

however, delivered points to the first subject. Thus, subjects had the choice of cooperating or engaging in reciprocal retribution. This situation is depicted in Figure 13.7. The relevant minimax strategy was obvious: Each subject desired to gain points and avoid shock and so would try to construct rules that would maximize gain and minimize losses.

The experimenters had hypothesized that the behavior of the pair would move in the direction of mutual gain—in the direction represented by the upper-left cell in Figure 13.7. In other words, the experimenters predicted that the subjects would increasingly accommodate each other by delivering points rather than shocks.

Within five minutes after each of twenty pairs of subjects began interacting, both participants in every pair had increased their rates of delivering points to their fellow subjects and had decreased their rates of shocking them. This trend continued for fifteen minutes, after which a high level of rewarding responses became stable. Further research showed that these same results could be secured even when subjects knew of the social nature of the exchange (Sidowski, 1957).

These results suggest that people tend to move toward exchanges that are maximally satisfying to all participants. However, if this were the entire story, all relationships should be satisfying. Clearly this is not the case, and the model suggests why. Consider a three-alternative situation in which you are enthusiastic about classical music, find folk music okay, and loathe rock music. You have a friend who finds the classics a bore, tolerates folk music, but really finds his soul in rock. The interpersonal-accommodation hypothesis predicts that when you are together you will tend to listen to folk music, because it has the highest mutual payoff for the two of you together. However, according to the hedonistic assumption, both of you would find the situation rather unsatisfactory because it is not maximally fulfilling for either of you. Thus, in attempting to maximize your pleasure, it is probable that both of you would seek out other partners, at least for purposes of listening to music.

This type of process is further explained in the discussion of need complementarity in Chapter 6. You may recall that friendships, marriages, and romantic involvements usually have the best chances of success when the participants greatly need what each other has to offer. This line of thinking suggests that if each person's preferred activities were known, it would be possible to predict the ways in which his or her relationships would develop. Whenever an activity providing one member of a pair (or group) with maximal pleasure also provides the other(s) with maximal satisfaction, and vice versa, the relationship should be a success. Unfortunately, prediction is rarely so simple. Two very important additional elements must be considered.

If life is a marketplace where people exchange their pleasures and pains for the best available price, then any given relationship must be evaluated in relation to the market as a whole. (The similarity of this social marketplace to an economic stock market is noted on pages 203 and 204.) This point may not yet be clear from the discussion in this chapter, because the *dyadic*, or two-member, relationship has been the focus in this chapter. However, it must be noted that whether or not even two people find a given relationship satisfying will depend not only on their payoffs *within* that relationship but also on the payoffs available in *competing* relationships. The competition that is most threatening to a relationship is an outside partnership that would provide higher overall reward for the same activity. If you are a

Figure 13.7 When given the choice between cooperation and reciprocal retribution represented in the matrix, subjects studied by Sidowski, Wyckoff, and Tabory (1956) chose to cooperate, especially when the noncooperative alternative involved exchanges of strong rather than weak shocks between twenty pairs of subjects. The graph shows the proportion of points (cooperative responses) given by partners out of the total number of responses (both cooperative and noncooperative) in both the strong-shock and weak-shock conditions.

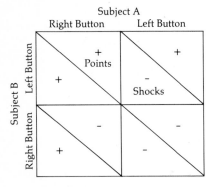

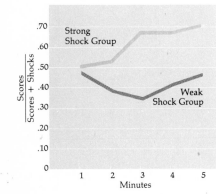

young woman, you may enjoy the loving tenderness of your boyfriend, but if that same loving tenderness can also be provided by someone who is wealthier, more handsome, or more novel and exciting, an early breakup with your boyfriend might ensue. Thus, perfectly satisfactory relationships can dissolve. By the same token, mutually dissatisfying relationships often persist for long periods, as many married people know, because there seem to be no alternatives that offer higher payoffs.

When Predictability Hurts.　　There is a second qualification to the rule that people seek relationships that are maximally fulfilling. People usually are unable to explore the entire matrix of possibilities for human relating,

Figure 13.8　In Thibaut and Kelley's behavior-exchange model, whether or not a relationship continues depends not only on the absolute satisfactions derived from the relationship but also on the payoffs the participants believe to be available from alternative, competing relationships. An excessive example is provided by Henry VIII, sixteenth-century king of England, who was in the habit of disposing of his current wife as he became aware of the charms of another woman.

are unwilling to explore them, or are simply unaware that the possibilities exist. Any group of persons, any couple, has the potential to engage in almost any type of behavior with one another—from putting one another to death to providing great ecstasy. In spite of this vast potential, people generally confine themselves to extremely limited ranges of activities with the other people or groups with which they interact. With friends, people tend to relate in one set of ways, with their families in another, and with lovers, in still another. Seldom do two or more interacting people sample from the vast range of untried possibilities, perhaps because individuals are largely unaware of these possibilities. Because of the rapid way in which people go about forming impressions of one another (discussed more fully in Chapter 5), they may feel that only a few types of exchanges are likely to be rewarding. In addition, people wear the blinders of tradition. They do not bother to think past the types of exchanges that people *usually* have with "a friend," "my family," "my husband" or "my wife." Those who are more adept at exploring the available matrix of possibilities are more likely to find deeply satisfying exchanges and to find more of them than do less adventurous souls.

You are probably beginning to see the possibilities for making reliable predictions about the successes and failures of relationships. It becomes increasingly possible to make accurate predictions as you become more aware of the exchange values that various activities have for each participant. But in order to accurately predict the degree of success of a relationship, you must also take into consideration other factors, such as the

Figure 13.9 Gambling in Las Vegas casinos (*below*) can be contrasted with gambling in the streets (*right*) in that the interpersonal exploitation in Las Vegas is institutionalized and depersonalized, whereas in games between friends, exploitation must take place on a one-to-one basis.

availability of third parties who can provide greater pleasure at less cost and the capacities of the participants to explore the matrix of possibilities. In addition, as several other chapters explain, the relative values of various possible exchanges for any one participant shift with changes in situational factors like the present status of the other participant and the behavior of others toward that person.

EXPLORING THE MATRIX OF HUMAN RELATIONS: THE GAME PLAN

Thus far, some of the fundamental characteristics of behavior exchange have been explored in this chapter, as well as some of the important implications of this model of social interaction. In the remainder of the chapter, the behavior-exchange approach will be used to explore several important aspects of human relations: the ways in which human cooperation can be enhanced; some important means by which people of all cultures seem to take care of conflict on an informal basis; the human desire for equity in relationships; the ways in which people control others in order to increase their own gains; and, finally, some individual differences in people's tendencies to manipulate one another.

Cooperation Versus Exploitation: Thou and You

The basically antagonistic state of human relations as seen from the standpoint of the exchange approach has generated among social psychologists a strong interest in studying conflict. It seems quite clear that in an age of nuclear weaponry the human species is not likely to survive unless it finds ways to reduce human conflict. From the perspective of the exchange approach, one of the major sources of conflict stems from the individual's tendencies to seek gain at others' expense. The central research question therefore has been to pinpoint factors that reduce (or increase) these exploitative tendencies. How can we reduce exploitation and increase cooperation among people?

Imagine yourself in the following position. You are an experimental subject placed in a room by yourself. In front of you are two buttons, one red and the other black. You are to play a game with a partner whom you have never met and who is in an adjoining room. As a result of the way you play the game, you can win or lose money. The game is set up as follows. There will be a series of trials in which both you and your partner will press one of the buttons, each without knowing the other's choice. Depending on the particular combination of buttons you both have chosen on a trial, you will either win or lose. Before the game you learn exactly what the payoffs will be for the various combinations. These payoffs are shown in Figure 13.10. If you press a black button on the same trial that your partner chooses black, you will both receive eight cents. However, should you decide to press black when he chooses red, he will come away with a dime and you will only receive a penny. Similarly, if he presses black when you press red, he receives one cent to your ten. Finally, should you both choose red on the same trial, you will both receive only two cents each.

Which of the buttons would you tend to choose? For most people, this is not an easy choice. Consider the dilemma carefully. If you want to win as much money as possible, then you may assume that the clear choice is the red button, which represents your only chance to win ten cents a trial. However, if you stop to consider your partner's desires, you may realize that he (or she) may also want to win as much money as possible and thus

Figure 13.10 We are often faced with the dilemma of whether to assume a competitive or a cooperative posture in our interpersonal dealings. Shown here are the payoffs, dependent on the joint choice of both players, in a hypothetical interpersonal-bargaining game. A push of the red button betrays a desire to reap most of the rewards and to deprive one's opponent of a fair share; a push of the black button represents a cooperative attitude of sharing the rewards and faith that the other player will also cooperate. If both players cooperate, they both win (although slightly less than if only one of them competed). But if both players compete, both tend to lose.

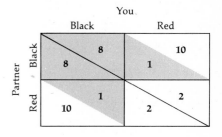

may be moved as well to push the red button. If so, you both will come away with meager winnings. You therefore conclude that the best thing to do is to cooperate by pushing black. In this way, you can both obtain moderately high winnings on each trial. And, after all, cooperation is preferable to exploiting your partner. Or is it?

What if your partner does not cooperate? If you cooperate and he does not, his earnings may be ten times as large as your earnings. Thus, you may fear feeling foolish for having cooperated. You realize that your partner may take advantage of you and reduce your gains to a penny per trial while he walks away with a dime. So perhaps the red button is a safer option after all. And so it goes.

Researchers often refer to this type of experimental situation as *interpersonal bargaining*. This particular bargaining game pits tendencies toward cooperation against those toward exploitation. If you both cooperate, you both do very well. But in most cooperative situations, you must trust others to contribute as much as you. If you exploit others for your own gain, you may obtain maximum material rewards. Yet, as is the case in real life, if all of us exploit, we all tend to lose.

What do people actually do in a situation such as that just described? J. Sayer Minas, Alvin Scodel, David Marlowe, and Harve Rawson (1960) presented both male and female Ohio State students with a dilemma that differed from that already described only in that the subjects' goal was to achieve points rather than money. The subjects chose the exploitative route almost two-thirds of the time, choosing the red button on approximately 62 percent of the trials. Males and females did not differ in this respect.

If you are a humanist, this finding will be very disappointing; it seems to substantiate the view that people care about little else than their own gratification. Yet if you were a mathematically oriented game theorist, you might be surprised that subjects did not make the exploitative choice on *all* the trials. In their classic work *Theory of Games and Economic Behavior*, John Von Neumann and Oskar Morgenstern (1944) point out that there are rational strategies (which can be computed) that yield "best" solutions.

Figure 13.11 Life is filled with interpersonal-bargaining situations that call competitive strategies into play because one person's gain is another's loss. In the screen characterization shown here, W. C. Fields plays a poker player planning his strategy. Researchers have found that they can encourage either exploitative or fair-minded responses by varying the relative payoffs of competitive and cooperative options.

These are the *minimax solutions* mentioned earlier. If you consult Figure 13.10 once again, you can see that the minimax solution is to press the red button—the exploitative rather than cooperative option. This choice permits greatest winnings (ten cents as opposed to eight) and minimizes losses (two cents as opposed to one), and is thus the most "rational" solution.

However, as revealed by the Ohio State study and many others (for example, Rapoport and Orwant, 1962), people do not always opt for the most *mathematically* rational solution. Nevertheless, this finding should not obscure the fact that individuals play their games in ways that are rational to *them*. The mathematical solution can simply lead to unproductive outcomes, because it recognizes extrinsic factors alone (for example, the amount of money or points to be gained) and does not take into account

---

YOU CAN TRUST THE TRUSTING

FOR CENTURIES PEOPLE have played out their fortunes on floors and tables. Imaginary empires (and sometimes also real fortunes) have been won and lost in Monopoly, war, go, and chess. Because games of skill and chance are microcosms of the "real" world, psychologists have been eager to explore human behavior through game strategies.

A common game that can be used to explore many facets of human behavior is a betting game in which both players' scores depend on the combination of their choices. Consider the matrix of wins and losses devised by Morton Deutsch. Assuming you are Player 1, controlling keys A and B, what choice would you make playing against a fellow student if the possible payoffs are those represented in the matrix? Your opponent will see your choice before he chooses. Will you trust him or not?

If you choose A and he chooses X, you both win $9, but if he chooses Y, you lose $10 and he wins $10. But if you choose B and he chooses X, he loses $10, whereas you gain $10. You both lose $9 by choosing B and Y.

Deutsch suspected that whether you choose A or B depends a lot on how trusting you are as a person. He believed that a relationship exists between trusting and being trustworthy and that these two behaviors are associated with personality scores obtained on the *F* (for fascism) scale (described in Chapter 7). A few weeks before they

were given the betting task, the subjects were given the *F* test.

In the first half of the study subjects were in the position of Player 1 and were allowed to choose their option first. This choice would be announced to the co-player, who would then make his choice. Because players were vulnerable to exploitation in this situation, they had to decide whether or not to trust the other player. In the second half of the study, subjects became Player 2. They were told that their partner had just pushed the A (trusting) choice. Each subject then had the option of pushing X and winning $9 for each player or of pushing Y and thereby winning $10 and creating a $10 loss for the opponent.

Deutsch found considerable support from these data for his hypothesis that high scorers on the *F* scale were both less trusting and less trustworthy and that low scorers were the reverse. Mid-range scorers were middling in their game behavior.

Apparently, the qualities of trust and trustworthiness are related. Thus, the people who constantly fear they are being "done in" seem to be the people most likely to do you in first!

Game Stategy and F Scale Scores

GAME BEHAVIOR	F SCALE SCORE		
	Low (N=14)	Medium (N=30)	High (N=11)
Trusting and trustworthy	85.7%	33.3%	18.2%
Suspicious and untrustworthy	0	43.4	81.8
Suspicious but trustworthy	0	13.3	0
Trusting but untrustworthy	14.3	10.0	0

Source: Adapted from M. Deutsch, "Trust, Trustworthiness and the *F* Scale," *Journal of Abnormal and Social Psychology*, 61 (1960), pp. 138–140.

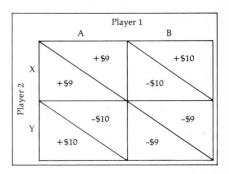

the psychological realities of two players who are responding to one another's choices.

So far, this discussion has neglected the factors that encourage or reduce exploitation in the bargaining arena. Thus, seven factors that affect people's tendencies to exploit or not to exploit one another will now be discussed in some detail.

Extrinsic Payoff. Although extrinsic rewards and punishments are not the only factors that shape human behavior, extrinsic factors do influence the likelihood of exploitation, or so laboratory research suggests. When researchers have increased monetary rewards for cooperation and decreased them for exploitation, their subjects generally have become more cooperative. For example, J. Sayer Minas and his colleagues (1960) followed up their original study of Ohio State students by altering the matrix depicted in Figure 13.10 to resemble that in Figure 13.12. As you can see, the minimax strategy has shifted from pressing the red button to pressing the black one, which indicates cooperation. Before, maximum gains and minimum losses were yielded by the red button; but now the black button provided these outcomes. Students' inclinations to exploit one another changed accordingly. The altered matrix, which favored cooperation rather than exploitation, generated a 50 percent rate of exploitation, whereas the exploitation rate had been 62 percent when the payoffs fostered competition.

The 50 percent rate of exploitation generated by conditions that favored cooperation seems particularly high: Why, if the black button could satisfy humane desires for cooperation *and* economic needs, should anyone choose to exploit others? The investigators concluded that people do not wish to maximize their gains so much as they wish to win *more* than others. They want to *maximize the differences* between themselves and others. This tendency to maximize differences has since been demonstrated more directly (Umeoka and Shnotsuka, 1965a, 1965b). These findings present a nightmare for those who dream of a more cooperative world. It is difficult to find ways of socializing people to value cooperation so that they will be inclined to work for community gains rather than for exclusively self-centered prosperity. If it is the case that human beings strongly desire to obtain more than others, the chances for cooperative arrangements seem very dim. Further research in socialization may reveal ways of reducing the human passion for winning more than others. Another possibility is that human beings may discover factors that are powerful enough to override excessive greed in most situations.

Future Relationships. As society becomes increasingly mechanized, mobile, and specialized, relationships grow briefer in duration. It would not be unusual for a person to live in a small apartment one year and in a suburb halfway across the country the year after that. Both benefits and costs accrue from the resulting transience in human encounters. One of the unfortunate results is that short-term relationships seem to enhance exploitation. When people do not have to face one another, as explained in Chapters 10, 11, and 12, they may not feel accountable for their actions. Situations that permit "hit-and-run" encounters invite the participants to take advantage of one another. This effect was demonstrated in an experiment by David Marlowe, Kenneth Gergen, and Anthony Doob (1966). Their subjects participated in a standard bargaining experiment. Some subjects were informed that they would meet their partners after the trials

Figure 13.12 A payoff matrix that increases the likelihood of cooperative responses in interpersonal-bargaining situations. Maximum gains and minimum losses can be realized if both participants choose the cooperative response (the black button). Compared with matrices such as that in Figure 13.10, which yields one-third cooperative responses, this payoff matrix increases cooperation to one-half of responses.

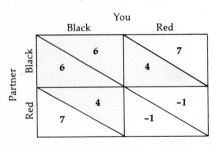

IV INTERACTING WITH OTHERS

had been completed and would then be able to talk about the game and one another's actions. Other subjects learned that they would remain anonymous, that they would never meet their partners. The results of the thirty-trial game revealed far more exploitation among subjects who were banking on anonymity than among subjects who expected to confront partners.

Although these results suggest that people are least likely to exploit those with whom they expect to interact, further aspects of the study reveal limitations of this conclusion. Some subjects received information leading them to believe that their partners were egotists. Other subjects came to believe that their partners were very humble. These differing personality types produced strikingly different effects depending on whether or not subjects anticipated future relationships. If the students expected to meet a humble individual, they were very careful not to exploit him. The embarrassment caused by hurting a weak person apparently would be relatively acute. However, when they expected to meet an egotist, exactly the opposite occurred: Subjects were more exploitative than when they did not expect to meet this type of person. Apparently, when people anticipate meeting others who are likely to be dominant and overbearing, as an egotist might be, they are tempted to take measures to ensure the respect of these domineering others.

The evidence suggests that if people want to increase cooperation, they should develop more tightly-knit and self-contained communities, where people can reasonably expect long-range interdependence. But evidence also suggests that each of us can reduce the chances of others exploiting us simply by not being overbearing ourselves.

Keep in mind that the picture of exploitative and cooperative inclinations that has been painted may be significantly modified by the type of social character that prevailing socialization practices encourage.

Motivational Set. Socialization (see Chapter 2) has profound effects on whether or not people come to value cooperation in human relations.

Figure 13.13 It is easier to exploit an individual with whom you expect to have no further interaction than one whom you expect to confront again. This social-psychological finding would probably not surprise this tourist, who is being victimized by a high-pressure sales pitch for cheap novelty souvenirs at highly inflated prices.

However, the socialization process is not the only factor that determines whether or not people choose to cooperate with one another in specific situations. Researchers have found that it is also possible to create temporary motivational sets toward cooperation. For example, Morton Deutsch (1960) gave subjects one of three sets of instructions before conducting a bargaining experiment—either *cooperative*, which told subjects to be concerned for their partners' welfare as well as their own; *individualistic*, which emphasized that the only goal of the game was to win money for oneself and to disregard the partners' outcomes; and *competitive*, which informed subjects that the primary goal of the game was to win more money than their partners. The differing motivational sets that these three types of instructions created had a dramatic impact on the choices that the players made during the game. Subjects in the cooperative condition made 89 percent cooperative choices, compared to 35 percent cooperative choices in the individualistic condition and 12.5 percent cooperative choices in the competitive condition.

Although Deutsch's findings may seem quite obvious to you, the implications raise complex questions for the future. Through what mechanisms can people create motives for cooperation? In Russia, posters at strategic locations remind workers that they are striving together for the good of all. In China, all workers wear the same uniforms—a constant reminder that they are all in it together. Do relatively superficial devices such as posters and clothing have any effect in instilling a cooperative spirit? This question will not be definitively answered until more evidence is gathered, particularly the evidence that may result from systematic studies of populations such as that of China, where cooperation seems a much more integral part of the social framework than, say, in the United States.

The Core of Communication. A major reason why interdependent and close-knit communities suffer the least from exploitation is that they offer ideal conditions for effective communication. When people can communicate with one another, negotiation reflects mutual understanding of the special needs of all parties. Some of the benefits that communication can earn the participants were revealed by the Deutsch study just described. Some of the subjects in each of Deutsch's three experimental conditions were allowed to speak with their partners before choosing whether or not to cooperate. When communication was allowed, exploitation decreased dramatically. As discussed in Chapter 7, lack of communication is highly detrimental to race relations or relations between any two groups that have a history of stereotyping each other.

Others' Cooperativeness. There is reason to believe that exploitation will diminish significantly when others are cooperative. Cooperation should generate more cooperation. This conclusion would follow from the discussions of modeling in Chapters 2 and 11 and is in keeping as well with norms of equity, which will be discussed shortly.

Research on this topic gives little reason for optimism, however. In a typical bargaining study, the experimenters gave subjects false reports of their partners' choices (Bixenstine, Potash, and Wilson, 1963). These choices varied such that some subjects found themselves playing with highly cooperative partners and others with very competitive partners. In the cooperative condition, partners supposedly made 83 percent cooperative choices in the thirty-trial game; in the competitive condition, on the other hand, subjects found their partners making 83 percent competitive choices. Surprisingly, this immense difference in partners' cooperativeness had no effect on subject's own levels of exploitation. Later, Edwin Bixenstine and Kellogg Wilson (1963) could elicit cooperation from subjects only by exposing them to drastic amounts of cooperation (95 percent). Research such as this unfortunately is limited by the particular setting used for a study, by the values in the payoff matrix, and by the participation of subjects who have been shaped by lifetimes in dog-eat-dog economic and academic systems. Hopefully, future research will reveal conditions that can more easily elicit cooperation and reduce exploitation.

The Effects of Threat. Numerous limitations have plagued bargaining researchers. Not the least of these is that the participants are offered very few behavioral alternatives—typically the choice is between pressing a red or a black button. An additional alternative of great interest to psychologists is the use of threat. When people can threaten others with punishment for behavior they want to discourage, what is the effect on their relationships? Can they hope to work together for mutual gain, or does the availability of threat undermine relationships? Parents often find threats useful in shaping their children: "If you don't stop this instant, you'll be spanked." And diplomats say: "If you help our enemies, you will be destroyed."

Although threats sometimes secure the desired results for the moment, there is some reason to believe that at least under some conditions, the long-term effect of threats may be less pleasing. For example, Morton Deutsch and Robert Krauss (1960) engaged pairs of subjects in a game in which each player was in charge of a fictitious trucking company—either Acme or Bolt. Their chief aim was to carry goods to a destination. For each trip completed, the subjects received sixty cents minus operating expenses at the rate of a penny per second. The object was for subjects to reach their destinations as rapidly as possible.

Each subject received a road map (the basis of Figure 13.14) indicating that each player had two alternate routes, one short and the other long. The short route consisted of a one-lane segment to be shared by both players. If both players attempted to cross this segment at the same time, they would meet head-on, be unable to advance, and lose money as the seconds ticked away; to proceed, it would be necessary for one or the other to back down and let the rival pass first. Thus, cooperation was necessary for mutual benefit. The players could also take the longer routes and be assured of reaching their destinations; however, they would sacrifice valuable operating expenses by doing so.

Subjects played the trucking game under various conditions of threat. In the bilateral-threat condition, both Acme and Bolt controlled gates (as indicated in Figure 13.14) that either could use to prevent the other from passing through the one-lane segment. In the unilateral-threat condition, only Acme controlled a gate, thereby gaining an obvious advantage. If both Acme and Bolt reached the lane at the same time and Bolt refused to back down, then Acme could prevent Bolt from ever using the single lane. In the no-threat condition, neither player had a gate. The experimenter did not allow communication between any two players.

The major experimental question was whether the availability of threat would increase or decrease the players' winnings. And, if only one party had threat capability (as is almost always the case in parent-child relations, in international relations between rich and poor nations, and in dictatorships), did only the threatener benefit, or did the threatener tend to share the benefits with the other party?

Table 13.1 indicates the average monetary payoffs won by subjects under all three conditions. Interestingly, only when neither player had a threat option did either player profit from the game. The combined winnings for both players when neither was in a position to threaten the other averaged more than two dollars. When both parties had the power of threat, however, both players lost heavily. And when threat was available only to Acme, poor Bolt suffered considerably, losing an average of almost three dollars. However, although Acme suffered less when it controlled the means of threat, it ended up losing money. Acme would have been better off had it not been able to threaten its rival. The results suggest, then, that real-world negotiators would reach far more productive solutions if they would not fall back on threat to enforce their wishes. However, it is important to exercise caution in making such generalizations, because real-world negotiations typically allow communication among participants, whereas Deutsch and Krauss did not.

Furthermore, there is evidence that the mutually defeating conflict Deutsch and Krauss found is lessened when the participants are playing for

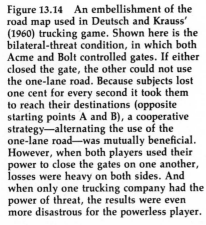

Figure 13.14 An embellishment of the road map used in Deutsch and Krauss' (1960) trucking game. Shown here is the bilateral-threat condition, in which both Acme and Bolt controlled gates. If either closed the gate, the other could not use the one-lane road. Because subjects lost one cent for every second it took them to reach their destinations (opposite starting points A and B), a cooperative strategy—alternating the use of the one-lane road—was mutually beneficial. However, when both players used their power to close the gates on one another, losses were heavy on both sides. And when only one trucking company had the power of threat, the results were even more disastrous for the powerless player.

Table 13.1 Average Winnings and Losses Under Various Threat Conditions

PAYOFFS	NO THREAT	ACME THREAT ONLY	BILATERAL THREAT
Acme's	$1.22	−$1.19	−$4.07
Bolt's	0.81	− 2.87	− 4.69
Total	2.03	− 4.06	− 8.76

Source: M. Deutsch and R. Krauss, "The Effect of Threat Upon Interpersonal Bargaining," *Journal of Abnormal and Social Psychology,* 61 (1960), pp. 181–189.

important stakes. Philip Gallo (1966) had subjects play the trucking game for real money rather than for imaginary money, as Deutsch and Krauss had done. Gallo found that subjects playing for real money cooperated five times as often as did subjects who were playing for imaginary stakes. Apparently, people are willing to suppress their mutually defeating competitive inclinations in conflict-of-interest situations when they feel that they have an important investment in the outcome—when, in other words, they sense that it is in their best interests to suppress these inclinations.

Does Power Corrupt? The threats and punishments to which people resort in a competitive situation are influenced by the *magnitude of power* that they can wield, according to findings reported by William Smith and Walter Leginski (1970). These investigators had male college students play a bargaining game in which the goal was to agree with an opponent to adopt one of several possible contracts. The participants could resort to bids, threats, and fines in their bargaining. The two bargainers in each pair stood to gain from different contracts. There was actually only one real subject in each pair; the programed opponent delivered a predetermined sequence of demands, threats, and punishments. The power of the artificial opponent was in all cases lower than that of the subjects.

Smith and Leginski found that the greater individuals' magnitudes of power, the greater are their expectations for the success of their outcomes, as judged by their resistance to compromise. High-power subjects expected the opponent to yield to their demands without having to resort to threat. At first they were reluctant to use their power. After it became apparent that the opponent would not yield, however, they increased the frequency and intensity of their threats and punishments. It appears, then, that the greater the power individuals have at their disposal, the more likely that they will resist compromise and resort to threats and punishments.

Further indications that power can corrupt have been reported by David Kipnis (1972), for example. He found that power corrupts a powerful person's view of the less powerful and demeans the less powerful in the process. For example, subjects who had more power than others stepped up efforts to influence the less powerful. They also regarded the less powerful as being at the mercy of others. They wanted to minimize their contacts with the less powerful subjects. And they also devalued what less powerful persons did, although this devaluation of others did not seem to boost their own self-esteem.

Most exchanges are probably between persons with unequal power. The effects of uneven distribution of power have been particularly damaging in the case of relations between men and women and between members of different racial, ethnic, and religious groups. These particularly destructive effects on the oppressed as well as on their oppressors are the focus of Chapters 7 and 11. In addition, the willingness or failure of observers to aid the victims of injustice affects the likelihood of further injustice, as discussed in Chapter 12.

Patterned Interaction: Its Functions and Failings

As emphasized several times in this volume, it is helpful to be able to make reasonably accurate predictions about the results of our actions. Unless there were implicit rules governing social exchange, we would probably live in constant fear of being exploited by everyone around us, and we would never know from moment to moment how to fulfill our needs. On a simple level, consider two persons approaching each other on the street. How do they arrive at a mutually satisfying exchange of greetings? Should they bother to recognize each other? Would a simple nod of the head suffice? Should they stop and exchange intimate information? Would you find it odd if one person suddenly began tap dancing while the other began reciting poetry?

The most significant question raised by an example such as this is: How do the relatively wide ranges of potential actions narrow and become stabilized into particular behavioral repertoires? In the present case it is clear that the situation must be *mutually defined*. The situation just described would most likely be categorized as an incidental meeting of two

THE RECIPROCITY WHEEL

LOVE, MONEY, THINGS, status, services, and information—these are all important resources in human social life. But can they all be encompassed by a single theory of exchange?

Consider some of the problems: Some resources are concrete—goods, for example; other resources are symbolic—smiling, for example. Some payoffs are particularistic—it matters who gives them, as is the case with love; others are universal—the source matters less, as is true with gifts of money or information. And giving of some resources, such as money or goods, depletes the holdings of the giver, whereas giving of other resources, such as love or information, does not impoverish the giver.

Uriel Foa notes that it is important to understand tangible as well as intangible resources (such as affection, sympathy, and dedication) in order to understand social behavior. But he feels that a theory is nevertheless needed that can explain exchanges of all sorts of human resources. Foa has developed a system for classifying interpersonal and economic resources, despite the fact that different resources follow different rules of exchange. His system is based on two dimensions: concreteness-symbolism and particularism-universalism. Plotted on a graph, the six resources mentioned at the beginning of this discussion take on a circular configuration. The characteristics of each resource type places it closer to some of the remaining types than to others. Money, for example, is flanked by information and goods and is furthest from love. Love is closest to status and

services. Information is closest to status and money and furthest from services. And so on.

Foa tested his classification scheme by having eleven people, who were not familiar with the categories in Foa's model, categorize messages on cards into as many different categories as they thought were needed. The deck contained three representative messages for each of the six resource classes—a total of eighteen messages. Without knowing about the classes represented in Foa's model, subjects tended to group the six resources similarly to neighboring categories in the model—usually love with status and/or goods with money. In another experiment, people were asked to judge which of the same messages were the most similar and the most dissimilar to one another. No other messages representing the class to which the received message belonged were included. People were most likely to group resources from neighboring classes; and in choosing dissimilar messages, they unwittingly drew most choices from a far class of resources.

Interestingly, when subjects were asked what they would most like to receive in six hypothetical exchanges from a friend to whom they had given a particular resource, there was one resource chosen most frequently in exchange for each resource they had received. Furthermore, the frequencies with which resources were chosen were directly related to the nearness in terms of Foa's model of the received resource to the desired resource. (For example, love tended to be associated

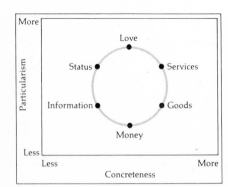

IV INTERACTING WITH OTHERS

persons in a public place rather than, say, a private rendezvous of clandestine lovers or a conference between teacher and student.

Given a mutually agreed definition, certain behaviors become more likely. Chances are, the two people meeting on the street have been in similar situations before and have learned that certain behaviors are appropriate in these circumstances, whereas others are not. Furthermore, each person assumes that the other has also had similar experiences. These various prior experiences and assumptions tend to lead to a mutual definition of a situation and to suggest a set of salient actions to both participants. Some theorists speak of these mutual definitions as sets of rules determining what behavior is appropriate in various types of situations. The rules specify what is and is not allowed. Such rules are usually

more with status than with material goods or money.) But when people were asked what they would like to receive from friends (rather than being asked to pick the most similar resource), people showed no tendency to choose resources from the same class. For example, if they gave goods to friends, they nevertheless wanted love in return. Foa concluded that the appropriate type of exchange is determined by the type of social institution—friendship, in this case—more than by the intrinsic values of resources exchanged.

Foa then set up an experiment that involved exchange of aggression rather than giving and overt behavior rather than verbal responses. People were to work with a partner, in actuality a confederate of the experimenters who frustrated each subject by taking away one of the six resources. From each subject in one group, the confederate took away love by complaining about having to work with the subject; from each subject in another, he took away status by criticizing the subject's performance; from each subject in still another, he took away his services by giving the subject a shock; and so on. Each subject could aggress by taking away from the confederate the resource closest to or furthest away from the one he had taken away from the subject. Most people chose to retaliate by depriving the tormentor of the most similar resources possible.

Foa, having thus uncovered some support for his model, applied his theory to behavioral patterns. In particular, Foa noted that the urban environment is particularly suited for exchanging universalistic rather than particularistic resources. People in urban settings therefore tend to be short-changed with respect to love and status. Lack of opportunities for exchanges of such resources result in a relaxation of informal controls on social behavior. A person who violates a social rule loses status in a small town or rural setting whether or not the infraction leads to legal trouble, but in cities it is often quite possible to avoid censure and escape a great deal of responsibility.

In general, social institutions in American society are specialized with respect to the resources they exchange. This is in marked contrast to institutions in societies that are based on more intimate communities in which specialization is less pronounced. Foa notes, for example, that it is common for Thai workers, but not for American workers, to discuss personal problems with their bosses.

What if only the most distant resource is available? Foa suggests that the intensity of response will be much higher and that the resulting satisfaction will be much lower. Thus, a person needing love but settling for money may never be satisfied no matter how much money he or she amasses. And someone deprived of status who can retaliate only by destroying goods may do a good deal of damage (whether by vandalizing, rioting, conducting an overly zealous police search, or some other activity) but still end up feeling frustrated.

Source: Adapted from U. Foa, "Interpersonal and Economic Resources," *Science,* 171 (1971), pp. 345–351.

called *norms*—standards of behavior that a particular group accepts and expects—and are shared by most members of a given cultural group.

After two people have applied a particular definition to a situation, they must arrive at *definitions of themselves and each other* with respect to that situation. For example, you probably would greet a "friend" differently from a "stranger." You might not greet an "enemy" at all. Within the category of friends, you might stop and chat with your roommate but only smile at the person who sits next to you in a class. Among strangers, your behavior toward a dignified-looking man might differ markedly from your behavior toward a person whom you surmise is an underclassman. Thus, within a given situation, norms vary for differently defined types of persons. Theorists often refer to a definitional type as a social *role*—the pattern of behavior that characterizes (and that others expect of) a person who occupies a particular status or position in a social situation.

It is enlightening to think of this stabilizing process in terms of the theater. Before the action and dialogue can transpire, the setting must be determined, and the actors must be given specific parts to play. In order for a mutually satisfying exchange to take place, the actors must arrive at essentially the same scene in the same play at the same time and must be cast in complementary roles. A scene between a superior and an inferior would not be successful if both actors assumed the role of the superior. The fact that most exchanges do seem to occur rather smoothly attests to the existence and power of social norms and roles.

Both norms and roles serve to define the context of an interaction and to restrict the range of behavior that is likely to occur within that context. Norms and roles thus become structural pillars of the social environment. They lend stability and organization to the realm of social relations, creating a relatively efficient system for the maximization of individual satisfactions. In contrast, imagine the difficulties of living in a totally unpredictable social world where, for example, the President sometimes behaved like a sailor enjoying his first night on land in three months or a stranger sometimes approached you in a public place and began quizzing you about your personal life and giving you unwanted advice.

Interesting demonstrations of norms in action and of their unspoken power have been contributed by Harold Garfinkle (1967). Garfinkle assigned his students the task of violating the norm that prescribes dealing with people at face value. The students were to act as though others were deliberately trying to conceal their real motives. Garfinkle reports the following results:

[A]cute embarrassment swiftly materialized for the two students who attempted the procedure with strangers. After badgering a bus driver for assurances that the bus would pass the street that she wanted and receiving several assurances in return that indeed the bus did pass the street, the exasperated bus driver shouted so that all the passengers overheard, "Look lady, I told you once, didn't I? How many times do I have to tell you!" She reported, "I shrank to the back of the bus to sink as low as I could in the seat. I had gotten a good case of cold feet, a flaming face, and a strong dislike of my assignment." (Garfinkle, 1967, page 52)

Note that the bus driver reacted with outrage at having his motives questioned and that the student who had violated the norm experienced intense embarrassment. Thus, the pain suffered by both the deviant and the victim as a result of violating a social norm attests strongly to the power of norms over behavior. In another assignment, Garfinkle asked students to take on an inappropriate role in a familiar setting. The assignment was to

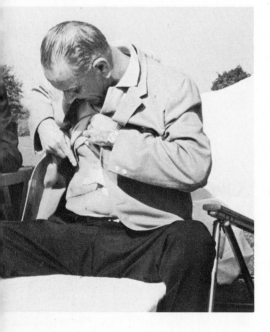

Figure 13.15 Norms and role definitions have considerable effects on our behavior as well as on our expectations in social situations. Many people reacted negatively to then-President Lyndon Johnson's display of a surgical scar, a clear violation of behavioral norms supporting presidential dignity.

enter their own homes as if they were boarders. Thus, they were to avoid being personal, to remain polite, and to speak only when spoken to. Garfinkle vividly summarizes the experiences of the students:

Reports were filled with accounts of astonishment, bewilderment, shock, anxiety, embarrassment, and anger, and with charges by various family members that the student was mean, inconsiderate, selfish, nasty, or impolite. Family members demanded explanations: What's the matter? What are you being so superior about? Why are you mad? Are you out of your mind or are you just stupid? One student acutely embarrassed his mother in front of her friends by asking if she minded if he had a snack from the refrigerator. "Mind if you have a little snack? You've been eating little snacks around here for years without asking me. What's gotten into you?" One mother, infuriated when her daughter spoke to her only when she was spoken to, began to shriek in angry denunciation of the daughter for her disrespect and insubordination and refused to be calmed by the student's sister. (Garfinkle, 1967, pages 47–48)

Both norms and roles vary widely in their capacities to influence behavior. For example, some norms are nearly universal, such as the propensity of all humans for bipedal locomotion and for verbal communication. Other norms apply to some cultures but not to others; these include certain marital practices, food preferences, and religious beliefs. Different subcultures within a culture may also adopt characteristic styles of dress, speaking, and leisure activities. Specific norms even develop within a dyadic, or two-person, relationship. As two people spend more and more time together, they learn which activities yield mutual satisfaction, and they therefore work to stabilize these mutually satisfying behavior patterns.

Because normative behavior in any type of social system, from dyads to entire cultures, are those behaviors that we can assume *have typically yielded maximum satisfaction* in the past, members of that system tend to value and support their continuation. People thus tend to rely heavily on the "bird in the hand" if it has always given them pleasure and hesitate in chasing after those in the bush. People often preserve normative behavior by imposing sanctions against deviations from the norm. These sanctions may take many forms, including a disapproving glance in a dyad, the use of ridicule within a small group, and a society's threat of fines, imprisonment, or execution. In each case, members of the system threaten to withdraw satisfaction from the deviant.

Most cultures, subcultures, small groups, and even dyads exhibit some degree of *role differentiation*. That is, roles become different from one another in function. This differentiation is an inevitable consequence of interaction, because a satisfactory exchange usually requires complementarity between the roles of the participants. As norms develop, people often adopt complementary roles. For example, a husband and wife may develop a pattern in which the husband first offers his opinion concerning, say, finances and the wife then accepts his decision. However, this pattern may give way to one in which the wife dominates when the couple makes decisions regarding some matter other than finances, such as furniture. These patterns may become part of the mutual definition of this couple's respective roles: the husband as business manager and the wife as interior decorator. This example is highly sexist, as role differentiation in marriages often is. Marriages do differ, however, in the extent to which husband and wife share in decision making. But in many ways, subtle and unsubtle, husbands still typically assume far more decision-making power than do their wives. Even if both spouses work, for example, the husband's job or career typically determines where the couple will live and if and when they

Figure 13.16 A broad spectrum of people in any society find different societal norms restrictive to some degree. The consequences of self-exposure for this man were probably quite different from those for the President's "offense" (*opposite*).

will move. Role differentiation also occurs in larger groups, in which role behavior may emerge that distinguishes, for example, a leader from a follower, a healer from a scapegoat, and so on.

In any relationship, after a person's role becomes established, he or she is expected to behave as an occupant of that role in all situations to which that role applies. As is often the price paid by those who deviate from norms, people who exhibit behavior that is inappropriate to their roles risk some form of social punishment. However, standards of conduct are quite relative, varying with the offender's identity. For example, the minister whose community discovers that he has a lover faces severe social censure and the probable loss of his job, whereas an artist may actually be expected to have a lover.

Besides giving the social environment a stable quality, norms and roles also define *power relationships*. Each actor quickly assesses the power or status of another and treats him according to the appropriate norm. Shared expectations about appropriate behavior are useful to most of us because they often prevent all-out competitive battle for the available sources of satisfaction. Norms frequently require the powerful to give help and comfort to the weak. If the master does not oblige his servant, the servant may be obliged to rebel against him. Given human exploitative tendencies, norms and roles may shield many people from a constant, unbridled Darwinian struggle for survival.

Although some norms and roles may be necessary and useful, they also restrict those they protect. Have you ever felt like skipping, shouting, or dancing in a crowded public place but refrained because you anticipated social disapproval? Perhaps there was a time when you wanted to engage your parents in a serious discussion but found that they still thought of you as a small child whose thoughts regarding serious "adult" matters were unimportant. More generally, in a culture with many subcultures, the dominant group may impose its norms on subordinate groups for whom those norms may not apply. In this way, society's role expectations are oppressive to particular individuals and groups. The traditional positions of women and blacks in the United States offer some glaring examples.

But no matter who we are, almost all of us are to a large extent imprisoned by norms and roles. There is much evidence—that reported by D. E. Berlyne (1960), for example—to suggest that human beings, and other animals as well, seem to possess a need for novelty, for change, and for exploration. Satisfaction of this need is not facilitated by norms and roles. In fact, one might liken the influence of norm and role expectations to a powerful and conservative political force that strives to maintain those behavior patterns that have been successful in the past and to resist all threats of change.

As you can see, norms present us all with a continual enigma. They restrain, control, and bore us. And yet we also seem to demand a consistent, stable, and predictable environment. Norms and roles help satisfy the need for stability, and this prevents both societies and individuals from abandoning them. Contradictory needs, such as those for stability and for change, can often be found to exist simultaneously within societies as well as within individuals.

The Reciprocity Norm: A Universal Script?

Although norms do much to maintain order and provide security in society, some are more effective and more pervasive than others. One of the most powerful norms, and one that may well be universal, is the reciprocity norm. (The importance of this norm in eliciting altruism is discussed in Chapter 12.) In its barest form, the reciprocity norm is embodied in the expectations most of us have that other people will return good for good and evil for evil. When people derive positive outcomes from exchanges, we expect that in return they will reward their partner in the exchanges; if they do not do so, we may become disappointed or upset. Similarly, when people derive negative outcomes from exchanges, we feel that they have the right, and sometimes even a moral obligation, to return these outcomes in kind. "Do unto others as you would have them do unto you," "an eye for an eye, a tooth for a tooth," and "tit for tat" are all popular ways of expressing the reciprocity norm.

Sociologist Alvin Gouldner (1960) has postulated that the reciprocity norm is a prerequisite for organized society. Without this norm, all forms of trust would be undermined and there would be little reason for people not to exploit one another at every turn. The reciprocity norm thus furnishes a sort of universal script that guides relationships.

The power of the reciprocity norm is not difficult to demonstrate empirically, as becomes apparent in the discussion of reciprocity in Chapter 12. However, some unexpected implications of the reciprocity norm have also been revealed. For example, in Chapter 12 it is explained that reciprocity is more a function of the size of the first sacrifice in an exchange, as perceived by the beneficiary, than a function of the absolute value of the gift. Another unexpected implication of the reciprocity norm was articulated by J. Stacey Adams (1965), who formulated a model of equity in human relations that stems directly from the principle of reciprocity. According to Adams, people want to feel that what they receive is equal to what they give. In other words, people need to feel that the resources they expend for others are equal to the resources those other people expend for them. Adams also believes that in many cases people are unsure about what constitutes equity. For example, how much pay should a gifted artist receive for a painting that cost him very little in time and effort? And what is a reasonable gift for someone who has found and returned a lost wallet? In situations such as these, Adams observes, people are likely to turn to other people for proper definitions. Through this process of social comparison, which is explained in greater detail in Chapters 6 and 10, people try to find out what others have given and received under similar circumstances.

One type of situation in which people commonly judge the appropriateness of their rewards through comparison with what others have received is that in which workers exchange their labors for pay. Money, after all, is a representation of worth that changes almost constantly and is at all times dependent for its relative value on the ups and downs of the marketplace. Thus, workers, and their taskmasters as well, may have some difficulty establishing just what constitutes fair pay for a given type, quantity, and quality of work. The only means of arriving at standards of fair pay may, therefore, require comparisons of people doing equivalent work—comparisons of their performance and also of the pay they receive for their trouble.

If workers do indeed compare their treatment to that received by other workers, they should desire pay that is equivalent to their labors. Furthermore, in deciding what constitutes equitable pay, they should look around them to see how much workers are being paid. If they find that others are receiving more money for the same work input, they should either slough off and do less work, complain, or strike. These consequences of underpaying workers have been demonstrated by James Vaughan Clark (1958) and by Irving Lane and Lawrence Messé (1971).

A more startling prediction generated by Adams' model of equity is that workers who are paid *more* than they feel is equitable will also feel stress. And the model also predicts that, if given an opportunity, overpaid workers will upgrade the quantity or quality of their work until it is commensurate with their pay. To learn whether or not overpaying people would improve their performance, J. Stacey Adams and Patricia Jacobson (1964) systematically overpaid subjects for doing a difficult proofreading job. These researchers told some workers that they were not really qualified to do the work. They also told them that they would nevertheless receive the same high wage that qualified workers earned, even though they did not have the status of qualified workers. Other subjects received the same wage but were told that they were fully qualified. The implication for workers who thought they were qualified was that they were being paid equitably. By examining the work done by the two groups, Adams and Jacobson learned that those subjects who felt that they were being overpaid did far superior work: They located more errors in the material they were proofreading than did subjects who assumed that they were receiving equitable pay.

These results have not gone unchallenged, however. Other investigators, such as Edward Lawler (1968), have expressed reservations. For example, the subjects whom Adams and Jacobson called unqualified may have taken the task on as a challenge to their literacy and self-esteem. It may also be true that people have ways of talking themselves into believing that they deserve all the rewards they receive. Specific reasons why reciprocity can fail are discussed in Chapter 12. And, as shown in detail earlier in this chapter, bargaining-research results showing that people are not typically inclined to return cooperation with cooperation suggest that the reciprocity norm is not necessarily the most powerful norm governing human exchanges, at least not in contemporary American society.

Tactics of Self-Presentation

People are faced with innumerable alternatives for action at any given moment. Social norms narrow this range of possibilities dramatically. Yet, even with this narrowed spectrum of individual relationships, most people still face a broad range of behavioral alternatives within the diversity of informal contacts they do cultivate. In turn, the specific ways in which people maneuver among these alternatives largely determine the actions of others toward them. By managing behavior as an actor manages a stage performance, people both control and maximize their outcomes.

One of the most significant ways in which individuals manipulate their social environments is through self-presentation—that is, through conveying special images of themselves to others. Whether they come across as dominant or submissive, scholarly or athletic, naive or sophisticated, and so on, makes a great deal of difference in the reactions of other people to them. These images operate in much the same way as roles. By adopting a specific definition of self at the outset of a relationship, people actively contribute to their partners' definition of situations. Because two people in an interaction must often adopt complementary roles in order to achieve a satisfactory exchange, when one has adopted a specific self-definition, the other's choices are reduced to roles that are complementary. In other words, the first person has helped to cast the second person in a role. Alan Weinstein (1967) has called this process *altercasting*. To be sure, altercasting is a two-way process, although some people are more skillful or influential at it than others.

Political campaigns are particularly dramatic examples of self-presentation. Take senatorial candidate Will Stump as he appears at the Centerville rally. (Specified in parentheses are the various components of the image he creates.) The first impression Stump creates at the rally is that he is neatly but not extravagantly dressed (implying that Stump is dignified but not aloof). He begins his talk with a few examples of Centerville humor and a word of praise for local officials (such behavior implies that Stump has a sense of humor and is attuned to life in Centerville). He depicts his opponent in the campaign as either indecisive or wrong on all major issues (which implies that Stump firmly holds the right opinions). He quotes a few ambiguous statistics relating to economics or crime and then interprets them to support his views (implying that he is well-informed on major issues and backs up his opinions with the *facts*). In closing, he utters a few lines exalting the need for moving the country in a positive direction (which implies that Stump possesses the broad perspective of a true statesman; Stump is eloquent). Surrounded by a partly orchestrated and partly spontaneous display of enthusiasm, Stump steps down from the podium to shake the outstretched hands of the eager crowd (to convey the impression that he can mingle with the people and share his greatness with them in a simple, human way).

Political dramas such as these are standard fare in the theater of life;

Figure 13.17 Most of us are aware that political campaigners consciously convey images of themselves that they believe will maximize their chances of success. But how often are we aware of our own attempts at self-presentation?

political actors reenact the same repertoire again and again. Most people are aware of the underlying motives of the campaigning politician. But it is possible to analyze many everyday interactions involving self-presentation in this somewhat cynical fashion. Notably, Erving Goffman (1955, 1959) has made a career of examining common experiences from this perspective. For Goffman, the world of social behavior is truly a stage and every person, a performer. Behavior constitutes performances that the actors tailor to specific audiences. To succeed in social interaction, an individual must be skilled in the dramaturgical techniques of both creating and maintaining impressions.

Goffman's orientation is highly compatible with the behavior-exchange viewpoint that is outlined in this chapter. Goffman recognizes that acquiring all the information about the context of an interaction is of great predictive value to an individual. When an individual is fully informed about a situation "he could know, and make allowances for, what will come to happen and he could give the others present as much of their due as is consistent with his enlightened self-interest," Goffman observed in 1959. However, because full information is frequently unavailable, individuals must often rely for predictive material on appearances—for example, cues, hints, and expressive gestures. Similarly, they mold their appearances to some degree to control what information they convey to others. Appearances may or may not faithfully represent reality, but, given the elusive nature of reality, the observer often must act on the basis of appearances. It thus becomes essential for the performer to include in his or her performance some indication that the appearance is not deceptive. If the observer were to sense deception, the performance would be discredited, much to the embarrassment of everyone concerned.

A performer initially establishes his or her role in an interaction—in Goffman's terms (1955), a performer presents a specific *face*. It can be expected, according to Goffman, that the performer's behavior throughout the interaction will be consistent with that face. A person is said by Goffman to *be in face* or to *maintain face* whenever he presents an internally consistent face that is accepted and supported by others. The person who presents an inconsistent or inappropriate face, on the other hand, is *out of face*. Goffman uses the term *face-work* to describe actions taken by a person to repair his image by avoiding or correcting situations that threaten the face he wants to present. There seems to be a tendency not only to protect one's own face but to protect others' face as well. As a minor example, when someone stumbles over a doorstep, momentarily losing face, not only does he or she try to cover up the clumsiness as much as possible, but others may pretend not to have seen the mistake. Face-saving such as this, Goffman feels, is an essential force holding society together. It supports the norm system and allows people to live together adaptively.

Two experiments that demonstrate face-work will now be examined. In the first experiment, Bert Brown (1968) had subjects play the trucking game, described earlier, that was designed by Deutsch and Krauss. The subjects played against a stooge who systematically exploited them for the first ten trials. Half of the subjects were then told that their performance looked foolish, whereas the other half were told that they looked good because they had played fairly despite their being exploited. The first group thus experienced loss of face. All the subjects subsequently played ten more trials of the game during which they could either retaliate at great monetary cost to themselves or not retaliate and increase their winnings. Retaliation

Figure 13.18 Self-presentation, or trying to convey a particular image of oneself, is one of the most significant ways to influence the social environment so that it will yield maximum outcomes. By presenting ourselves at the outset of a relationship as, for example, dominant, crafty, accepting, or helpless, we partially determine the other's behavior toward us. Self-presentation is a technique we all use to some extent, some more deliberately and skillfully than others. What image is this young man trying to convey?

IV INTERACTING WITH OTHERS

is a measure of corrective face-work, because by retaliating, a person saves face by standing up to and challenging the one who has caused the loss of face. As predicted, the humiliated subjects were significantly more likely to retaliate than were the subjects who had not lost face.

As part of a later study, Andre Modigliani (1971) arranged the experimental situation so that subjects failed on their part of a group task. Each subject was then approached by the leader of the task group (actually a confederate in the experiment) who either belittled or praised the subject's performance. Modigliani felt that belittlement would embarrass subjects and that, if given the chance, they would engage in face-work to change others' definitions of the situation. He then gave all subjects an opportunity to engage in face-work during a discussion of the task situation with their group leader. This discussion was observed by an experimental assistant who categorized each subject's statements. When a subject offered excuses for bad performance, derogated the task, or denied failure, the statements qualified as face-work. As it turned out, the greater the embarrassment, the more ambitious the attempts at face-work.

These two studies demonstrate the usefulness of face-work in maintaining self-esteem. The research about to be discussed shows, however, that most of us do shift our self-definitions for many reasons. This research suggests that even those whom a person feels he knows well are likely to seem strange and alien to him if he sees them under unfamiliar circumstances. The teen-ager who is known by her friends as happy-go-lucky may seem taciturn and gloomy to her mother; a deep, sensitive friend may be an unaware oaf in the eyes of his wife. The impressions that most of us form about other people (discussed at length in Chapter 5) are likely to lead us to quite mistaken conclusions outside the situations in which we usually encounter those other people. In a sense, social life may seem a giant charade in which we all adopt masks and seldom truly meet. Before drawing this cynical conclusion, however, it is best to look at more research.

As already explained during the discussion of differences in the effects of anticipating future relationships, people seem to be more exploitative of egotists than of humble persons. Kenneth Gergen and Barbara Wishnov (1965) have also found that when an individual confronts a conceited egotist, he or she is inclined to become egotistical as well; however, when the other person is self-critical, the observer, too, begins to dwell on his or her own shortcomings.

David Schneider and Andrew Eustis (1972) explored subjects' reactions to people who differ in the amount they reveal. They found that subjects express much higher levels of self-esteem when they meet someone who is highly revealing than when they meet someone who is more reluctant to speak. Apparently, people wish to gain the liking of the open person and therefore present positive images of themselves.

Kenneth Gergen and Margaret Gibbs Taylor (1969) found that the activities people engage in with one another also influence the ways in which they present themselves to one another. When working on a task that demands efficiency and productivity, for example, subjects alter their self-definitions to emphasize their strong points in the work situation; when the task involves getting along together as well as possible, however, subjects tend to present themselves as being deficient in task-related qualities, apparently to emphasize their "human" qualities.

Joel Cooper and Edward Jones (1969) found that subjects alter their public images in dramatic ways in order to avoid appearing similar to a person they feel is obnoxious. For example, they give up positions that they had fully espoused a short time earlier.

These results certainly support the idea of social life as a charade. A person's public countenance may thus seem to be in constant flux and to contain many inconsistencies. However, in several experiments, Kenneth Gergen (1968, 1972) has explored the subjective experiences of subjects as they went through their public transformations. He found that most subjects felt that they were presenting true and accurate pictures of themselves from moment to moment. Apparently, individuals are capable of expressing high levels of self-esteem at one moment and low levels at the next; likewise, they may appear dominant and powerful in one setting and weak and submissive in another. Yet, in all settings, people usually *feel* that they are being honest and appearing authentic. The implication is that we all have many potential ways of being that are often inconsistent and unrelated to one another. At any particular moment we are aware of only a small number of these ways and are thereby able to feel true to ourselves. We are convinced by our momentary thoughts and actions that we truly are what we seem to be. (These powers of self-persuasion are also described in Chapter 9). In effect, we tend to believe our own performances.

People rapidly shift their public identities like chameleons in order to gain pleasure and avoid pain. However, people do not often *intend* to be manipulative. They are not generally aware of their shifts in appearance nor of the possibly manipulative effects of these shifts. Yet there is also a great deal of blatant deceit in human relations. It is this more extreme type of manipulation that is discussed next.

The Plot Thickens: Ingratiation

Perhaps the most important investigation of deceitful manipulation has been conducted by Edward Jones (1964). Jones was especially interested in the ways in which people curry one another's favor. If someone can gain another's liking or favor, he or she increases the likelihood that the other person will provide all manner of rewards on a long-term basis. People often engage in subtle forms of lying to gain these rewards.

Behavior that people adopt for tactical purposes, for increasing their attractiveness to one another, is *ingratiation*. Jones identified three major

Figure 13.19 Ingratiating tactics (such as flattery, presenting oneself in a favorable manner, and opinion conformity) are often used by one or more parties in a social interaction to make themselves more attractive and thereby increase the rewards they are likely to reap from the interaction. Here, Mae West and W. C. Fields demonstrate some of the tactics of ingratiation.

CUTHBERT J. TWILLIE: *Whom have I the honor of addressing, Milady?*

FLOWER BELLE LEE: *They call me Flower Belle.*

TWILLIE: *Flower Belle! What a euphonious appellation! Easy on the ears and a banquet for the eyes.*

FLOWER BELLE: *You're kinda cute yourself...*

TWILLIE: *Ah! What symmetrical digits. Soft as the fuzz on a baby's arm.*

FLOWER BELLE: *But quick on the trigger.*

TWILLIE: *Yes—Yes. But, may I?*

FLOWER BELLE: *Help yourself.*

tactics of ingratiation. A compliment—*flattery*—is particularly effective when it concerns features of the target persons that they value but are uncertain about, such as looks, intelligence, or prowess. As pointed out in Chapter 6, flattery can be a very effective tool in gaining others' esteem. Ingratiating persons can also employ *opinion conformity* (discussed in Chapter 10 as well). If they agree with the target person when they have said something controversial, they can solicit the target's gratitude. As a third strategy, ingratiating individuals may employ some form of *self-presentation*. For example, Edward Jones, Kenneth Gergen, and Keith Davis (1962) have shown that people of relatively lower power in a relationship will often boast in order to gain the regard of their superiors. Superiors, in contrast, may deliberately play down their virtues while relating socially to their juniors. Their virtues are already implicit in their rank; if they are to gain the regard of their subordinates, therefore, they must make themselves more approachable, more human. It is a striking phenomenon that when social roles are complementary and thus interdependent, the two participants may tend to emulate one another in a sort of pacification ritual.

One study of ingratiation reveals several ingratiating tactics simultaneously. Edward Jones, Kenneth Gergen, Peter Gumpert, and John Thibaut (1965) conducted the study to learn what happens when a person is failing and needs a positive evaluation from a superior. The researchers felt that whether or not such persons will resort to ingratiation depends first of all on how open to ingratiation tactics they perceive their superiors, the targets of ingratiation, to be. It seems that people are more likely to direct ingratiation at targets who are willing to change their behavior than at targets whose judgments appear frozen. For example, ingratiating tactics may get you better grades in a humanities course where the teacher's feelings about you may strongly influence his or her evaluation of your performance on essay tests. But it is unlikely that ingratiation would be very effective in a mathematics course in which your grade is dependent on your responses to problems with unambiguous solutions. Furthermore, Jones and his colleagues felt that the specific tactics of ingratiation that people use are tailored by them to fit the values of the target person. For example, someone entering into a debate about legalization of abortion would not use the same tactics in influencing religious conservatives as he or she would in trying to convince an advocate of women's rights.

In another part of this study, a task supervisor appeared to value either task efficiency, exalting virtues such as hard work and rationality, or social compatibility, espousing humor and friendliness. Given what this chapter has already said about ingratiation, can you predict which tactics subjects would find most appropriate in ingratiating themselves to targets in either of these cases?

The experimenters assigned subjects the task of judging the effectiveness of various advertising slogans and told them that their performance would be judged by a task evaluator. Subjects could earn as much as ten dollars for a good performance. During a practice session, all the subjects were made to feel incompetent at the task. From their viewpoint, then, success would be difficult to achieve.

Half the subjects then learned that the task evaluator would use his own discretion in evaluating their performance; their task evaluator thus was potentially open to influence by them. The rest of the subjects were told that the evaluator had already determined the correct answers; their evaluator thus was not open to their influence, because no amount of ingratiation could alter his judgments. Within each of the two conditions—open and closed—described above, half of the subjects overheard their evaluator stressing the importance of task efficiency to the experimenter and the other half heard about the importance of cooperation and friendliness in the job situation.

Subjects next had an opportunity to ingratiate themselves with the task evaluator both by conforming to the evaluator's opinions and by tailoring their images to win his approval. Two weeks prior to the experiment, subjects had recorded their opinions on various aspects of student life. During the experiment itself, they had a chance to communicate their own opinions to the evaluator. Opinion conformity was measured as the extent to which subjects changed their opinions to agree with the evaluator's. In addition, the subjects also filled out a series of self-ratings that related both to productivity (such as "efficient," "hard-working") and to social solidarity (such as "friendly" and "warm"). The experimenters assumed that the extent to which subjects stressed those virtues valued by the evaluator would reflect the degree of their eagerness to ingratiate themselves (by altering their images through self-presentation).

As predicted, subjects behaved in the most ingratiating ways when they believed that they could influence the task evaluator's judgments of them through ingratiation. When they could, they jumped at the chance to influence the evaluator. However, the type of tactic they chose depended on

Figure 13.20 Machiavellianism, a manipulative approach to social interaction, can be measured with the Machiavellian scale, a short version of which appears here. The sixteenth-century Italian philosopher-prince Niccolò di Bernardo Machiavelli (*opposite*), after whom the scale was named, advocated power and strategy over ethics as the preferred means of getting ahead in politics.

A Test
Are You Machiavellian?

	Disagree a lot	a little	neutral	Agree a little	a lot
1) The best way to handle people is to tell them what they want to hear.	1	2	3	4	5
2) When you ask someone to do something for you, it is best to give the real reasons for wanting it rather than giving reasons which might carry more weight.	1	2	3	4	5
3) Anyone who completely trusts anyone else is asking for trouble.	1	2	3	4	5
4) It is hard to get ahead without cutting corners here and there.	1	2	3	4	5
5) It is safest to assume that all people have a vicious streak and it will come out when they are given a chance.	1	2	3	4	5
6) One should take action only when sure it is morally right.	1	2	3	4	5
7) Most people are basically good and kind.	1	2	3	4	5
8) There is no excuse for lying to someone else.	1	2	3	4	5
9) Most men forget more easily the death of their father than the loss of their property.	1	2	3	4	5
10) Generally speaking, men won't work hard unless they're forced to do so.	1	2	3	4	5

Check the point on the scale that most closely represents your attitude. To find your Mach score, add the numbers you have checked on questions 1, 3, 4, 5, 9, and 10. For the other four questions, reverse the numbers you checked—5 becomes 1, 4 is 2, 2 is 4, 1 is 5. Total your 10 numbers. This is your score. The National Opinion Research Center, which used this short form of the scale in a random sample of American adults, found that the national average was 25.

the perceived orientation of the evaluator. When dealing with the kind and friendly evaluator, subjects attempted to gain his approval through conformity. They systematically changed their views to match his. Subjects did not bend, however, in the face of a taskmaster. When the evaluator stressed productivity, subjects adopted self-presentational strategies. They described themselves as rational, efficient, and productive—in striking contrast with subjects who faced a nurturant evaluator. Apparently, then, people are eager to use tactics of ingratiation when it will do them any good. As explained in Chapter 10, ingratiation may backfire if the ingratiator's intentions become conspicuous. Nevertheless, people often seem to tailor their specific strategies to what they surmise are the preferences of those individuals whom they hope to influence.

Enter the Machiavellian, Stage Right

Ingratiation tactics are many, subtle, and relatively easy to employ. All that people need to ingratiate themselves is a certain talent for deceit and a willingness to exploit others. Almost all of us have used ingratiation tactics at various times, perhaps to get the family car on Saturday night or to convince a professor to raise the grade on a term project. But hypocrisy also takes more extreme forms. Some people have developed social manipulation into an art. You probably know someone who always manages to borrow money, who gets you to overcome an initial reluctance to do favors, who in the words of a popular song "builds you up just to let you down."

This type of person has been the object of study for two researchers—Richard Christie and Florence Geis (1970). Following the inspiration of the Italian philosopher-prince Niccolò di Bernardo Machiavelli, they used the term *Machiavellianism* to describe the manipulative approach to social interaction. In his classic volume *The Prince,* Machiavelli proposed certain means of succeeding in politics; he emphasized the efficacy of power and strategy over ethics. Christie and Geis compiled a set of statements from Machiavelli's volume and rephrased them in common language. They rephrased half of the statements to express meanings that are polar opposites of the meanings intended by Machiavelli. The experimenters then asked subjects to indicate their agreement or disagreement with the statements.

They considered Machiavellian those responses that were in agreement with statements expressing Machiavellian sentiments, such as "The best way to handle people is to tell them what they want to hear," and those reponses that were in disagreement with un-Machiavellian statements, such as "One should take action only when sure it is morally right." From responses to twenty items like these, they identified subjects as being relatively high or low in Machiavellianism. This scale has proved to be reliable over time and seems to measure stable personality traits.

In a range of experimental settings, persons scoring high on the Machiavellian scale exhibited more successful manipulative tactics than did their low-scoring counterparts. To illustrate the successful use of these tactics, Christie and Geis have developed a bargaining game they call the con game. The object of the game is for *two* players to agree to split between them the sum of ten dollars given to them by the experimenter. The complicating feature of the game is that there are three players in the group! Thus, if player A offers B an even split—player C could counter the offer by agreeing to let B have $6 while he only took $4. Player A might then see that he would be cut out by this exchange and offer C a fifty-fifty

A prince being thus obliged to know well how to act as a beast must imitate the fox and the lion, for the lion cannot protect himself from traps, and the fox cannot defend himself from wolves. One must therefore be a fox to recognize traps, and a lion to frighten wolves.
—NICCOLÒ MACHIAVELLI, *The Prince*

split. C would then counter, and so on. A situation such as this demands skill at persuading others and ruthlessness as the winning combination of traits. Christie and Geis consistently found that persons who scored high on the Machiavellian scale are the most successful players at the con game. They win far more money playing the game than do persons who are low in Machiavellianism. And the greater the stakes, the more successful the high scorers are at the game.

Besides being good barterers, high scorers are also more convincing liars than are low scorers, according to a study by Ralph Exline, John Thibaut, Carole Hickey, and Peter Gumpert (1970). And when Florence Geis, Robert Christie, and C. Nelson (1970) instructed their subjects to distract another subject during a task, they found that high scorers manipulated more, were more innovative in devising distracting tactics, and enjoyed their role more than did low scorers.

This research has enabled Christie and Geis to offer a rather detailed description of the Machiavellian type of person. Above all, the Machiavellian is able to remain emotionally detached from other persons and from ideological positions. This detachment allows him to exploit others and to shift his opinions whenever expedient; it also shields him from susceptibility to social influence by others. The Machiavellian is not necessarily vicious, but he is always opportunistic. And, unfortunately for the rest of us, the Machiavellian recruits others into his ranks. Because he frequently is successful at obtaining more than his fair share in exchanges, others may be tempted to emulate the tactics that bring him so much success. In addition, the victims of his manipulations usually pay the price of trusting others less. And after several encounters with Machiavellian techniques, the cynicism a less deceptive person develops may lead him to adopt manipulative tactics in self-defense; perhaps he would justify his actions with the view that "the best defense is a good offense."

FACING SOCIAL CONFLICT

The importance of our general inability or refusal to seek new ways of living together on the planet cannot be overestimated. There continues to be much conflict among sisters and brothers, parents and children, lovers, citizens, and nations. We should not cherish hopes of more constructive problem solving without asking ourselves which personal or national interests we, as individuals, would be willing to forfeit for the sake of maximum mutual benefit. Nevertheless, the question remains: Given the ingenuity human beings have displayed in maximizing their creature comforts, why have they not yet found better ways of resolving their conflicts? Social psychologists have been particularly interested in human cooperation and conflict. An immense amount of research has gone into understanding the obstacles that prevent people from cooperatively resolving conflicts and what might be done to solve this dilemma. One approach to the problem has centered on the exchange properties of behavior that have been described in this chapter. The implications are sobering.

The number of resources available to people as they go about seeking pleasure and avoiding pain are often limited. There is a finite amount of money, property, food, clothing, formal education, and cultural artifacts of various sorts, and as these resources are distributed throughout the population many people receive fewer advantages and resources than they need (or feel that they need). If each person desires as much as he or she can have (up to the point of satiation) at the lowest cost to him or herself, then everyone is in competition for certain existing commodities. The human condition has thus encouraged a competitive posture. The outlook that people bring to their encounters, at least in Western urban centers, consequently may seem to be dominated by a *psychology of scarcity* rather than by a psychology of abundance. (The similarities of interpersonal-attraction processes to a marketplace that is subject to principles of capitalism are noted during the discussion of reward theories of attraction in Chapter 6.)

From this vantage point, it may be somewhat easier to understand why the human race has had so little success in curbing conflict over the years. When vying for what they assume are scarce commodities, people (in the United States, at least) are essentially at one anothers' throats, either figuratively or literally. Thus, reducing conflict must be a continuous process. To quell conflict in one social, economic, or political realm and hope for peace is naive. As long as conflict threatens so many areas of human interaction, people must constantly be searching for means and methods of ensuring the good of all.

Many of these methods are discussed in the pages of this book. One major solution that frequently can be useful in curbing human conflict is to instill in people a positive attitude toward others' satisfaction and a loathing for their suffering. Thus, others' happiness can contribute to a person's own happiness. This is essentially the problem of moral development (discussed in Chapter 2). Another solution to conflict is to use punishing agents, such as police and armed forces, to prevent gross exploitation. The problem then becomes one of preventing these punishing agents from indulging in gross exploitation themselves. The discussion of aggression and violence in Chapter 11 is relevant to this type of solution. Still a third alternative is to create social conditions that enhance people's desire to help one another. For example, in discussing what social psychologists refer to as the *contact hypothesis*, Chapter 7 suggests that social conditions are conducive to hostilities when they promote competition and are conducive to harmony when they encourage cooperation among the participants. The discussion of prosocial behavior in Chapter 12 suggests additional conditions that foster tranquil rather than hostile exchanges. As you may conclude from reading these chapters, human ignorance still outweighs human knowledge when it comes to engineering peaceful coexistence. And existing political means of applying this knowledge places society even further behind in engineering peace. Almost any issue of any newspaper bears overwhelming testimony to this human dilemma.

In Chapters 14 through 17 the focus of this book turns to groups, and the topics of conflict and harmony, competition and cooperation, reemerge many times in those chapters. Relations between groups are apparently governed by many of the same processes as are interpersonal relations.

SUMMARY

Life is a game, according to the *behavior-exchange model* of social interaction. This model presupposes that all human beings try to experience as much pleasure and as little personal pain as possible. In their attempts to maximize pleasure and minimize pain, people often modify their true opinions or misrepresent past actions to present themselves in a socially desirable light, because social approval brings pleasure. Research has revealed some ways in which particular pleasures and pains can be quantified and ways in which these quantified dimensions can be used to predict behavior.

Individuals' own needs and satisfactions are not, however, the sole determinants of their actions; not only do they derive *intrinsic* rewards from the fulfillment of their own needs, they also derive *extrinsic* satisfaction from others' responses to their actions. An *interaction matrix* is a tool to show the relative values of intrinsic rewards and extrinsic rewards in any given situation to the participants in a social relationship.

In an attempt to maximize pleasure and reduce pain, two persons in a relationship will work toward a state of *interpersonal accommodation*, or mutual satisfaction. The relationship may dissolve, however, if other relationships can provide the participants with greater satisfaction of their individual needs. Because most people have a limited range of expectations (based on role definitions) for each of their relationships, they often do not garner as many rewards as might exist in a relationship.

This frequent inability to act outside of role constraints often creates conflicts, one major source of which is the individual's tendency to seek gain at others' expense. Researchers use experimental gaming situations to study *interpersonal bargaining*, the pitting of tendencies toward exploitation against tendencies toward cooperation. If the participants cooperate, both succeed; if one does not trust the other and exploits him, the exploiter will win; but if both exploit, both will lose.

A major barrier to cooperation is the human desire not only to win but to win more than others. Given this motivation, it is difficult to produce cooperation. Nevertheless, five factors that can foster cooperation are: expectation of future contact with the individual; high social value placed on cooperation; communication between groups or individuals; visible cooperation of others; and an absence of threat in interactions.

To a large extent, the danger of exploitation is reduced by stable and predictable patterns of interaction, which are produced in the following way: First, the situation should be *mutually defined* to narrow the range of acceptable behavior; that is, norms must be defined. Then the individuals involved must arrive at *definitions of themselves and each other* in that particular situation; in other words, they should define their *roles*. After a person's role becomes established, he or she is expected to behave as an occupant of that role in all situations to which the role applies. Among other effects, norms and roles define *power relationships* and prevent many all-out competitive battles. But they can also limit and restrict individuals.

One norm is that of *reciprocity*, which dictates that we return good for good and not harm those who have been good to us. It is a powerful norm, perhaps with universal applicability. Research shows its many applications as well as its limitations.

Self-presentation through role behavior has been studied extensively by Erving Goffman. After a person has established a role in an interaction, he or she is motivated to maintain that role or, when it is weakened, to repair the image by face-work. People work to *maintain face* not only for themselves but for others as well. Laboratory research has demonstrated that although people often change their roles or images, these alterations are not always intentional or meant to deceive others; rather, people tend to believe that their own performances are consistent.

Purposeful manipulations of self-image are called *ingratiation* when they are meant to increase a person's attractiveness to powerful others.

Flattery, opinion conformity, and self-presentation can all be used in ingratiation, and all have been demonstrated in laboratory research.

Extremely manipulative people can be said to be high in *Machiavellianism*, a term that derives from the Italian political theorist who advocated power and strategy with little regard for ethics. A Machiavellian is ruthless and opportunistic; is able to lie with facility and to remain emotionally detached from other people and from ideological positions; and is likely to betray the trust of others through manipulative tactics.

SUGGESTED READINGS

Blau, Peter. *Exchange and Power in Social Life*. New York: Wiley, 1964.

Christie, Richard, and Florence Geis. *Studies in Machiavellianism*. New York: Academic Press, 1970.

Gergen, Kenneth. *The Psychology of Behavior Exchange*. Reading, Mass.: Addison-Wesley, 1969.

Goffman, Erving. *Relations in Public*. New York: Basic Books, 1971.

Homans, George. *Social Behavior: Its Elementary Forms*. New York: Harcourt, Brace, & World, 1961.

Jones, Edward. *Ingratiation*. New York: Appleton-Century-Crofts, 1964.

Krasner, Leonard, and Leonard Ullman. *Research in Behavior Modification*. New York: Holt, Rinehart and Winston, 1965.

Thibaut, John, and Harold Kelley. *The Social Psychology of Groups*. New York: Wiley, 1959.

ASKING theiR ROAd ...
SEVEN yellow
BAMBOO HAts
ALL tuRNed togetheR

ANONYMOUS

V

BEHAVIOR IN GROUPS:
PLANNED & UNPLANNED

14

Informal Groups

BACK IN THE MIDDLE 1940s, I SPENT some time in the army as a private. I hated it. I was not badly treated; I did not see combat; I was never in danger of any kind; but I just hated it. I hated the things we were required to do, the conditions under which we were required to live, the people with whom I was forced to associate.

Then the time came when we had to travel from Virginia to Hawaii. It was a ten-day trip by train and ship. Only a relatively small number of soldiers were going, and most were eighteen year olds with limited background and education. Seven of us, including myself, were older men with college degrees. We seven clung together. There was nowhere to go and no one with whom to interact except ourselves. There was nothing much to do, but we played bridge, talked, reminisced, told jokes. I never played bridge very much before that trip or since. I never even liked it very much; but it seemed the most remarkable and fascinating game in the world for those ten days. I couldn't have enough. And those six other guys—the nicest, sweetest, best guys in the world. We loved each other. We were like brothers. Everything was so warm and comfortable that I was actually *happy.* In fact, I don't know offhand when in my whole life I was so continuously happy over so long a stretch of time. And in the army!

Occasionally, I remember, we would discuss the possibility of trying out for officer-training school. As officers, life would be easier, but we would undoubtedly have to stay in the army longer. We all thought we would remain privates and push for discharge. Of the seven of us, I was far and away the most vehement in supporting the private-and-discharge alternative.

Then one time the other six came to me, all together, and told me they had decided to opt for officer training. The advantages were simply too attractive. Wouldn't I join them? I was astonished. How could they be so foolish? So weak? I refused. I tried to dissuade them. They put the pressure on, argued, pleaded, listed the advantages. To the end I resisted and finally in black despair I cried out, "Go ahead, leave me. Desert me. To hell with all of you."

Then they broke down laughing and explained it was a put-up job. They just wanted to see if I could resist group pressure, and there were bets on as to whether I would or not. I tried to laugh, too, and boasted that I was immovable in my convictions. But I wasn't. I have never forgotten the despair of those moments and how near I came to agreeing to be an officer rather than have them leave me.

Eventually, we reached Hawaii and separated. It may have seemed to me on that wonderful trip that we were soul mates who would remain together forever, but the fact is that since I left the army—so long ago—I have never been in contact with one of them. (Asimov, 1972)

Within ten days, a group of six individuals became important enough to a highly intelligent man—writer Isaac Asimov—to cause him happiness and despair. Why did this group of men so profoundly affect his emotions and behavior? Have you ever reacted similarly in a group?

All of us live most of our daily lives in various types of groups. Consider how you function—and how much of your time you spend—with your friends, peers, and neighbors; in committees and classes; and in social, academic, community, political, religious, work, and perhaps therapy groups. Some group experiences are as intense as the army private's, some are superficial; some are permanent, others are temporary. In spite of a wide range of situational differences, many of the groups you belong to are characterized by informal patterns and structures that have meaning apart from the groups' specific functions.

This chapter will consider why individuals join groups, why members of groups behave and think similarly to one another in many respects, and how members develop particular patterns of relationships with one another in the course of their interaction. The chapter will also explain the function of group leaders and how informal relations lead to group cohesiveness—the "we" feeling of a group. The final discussion concerns the relationships that develop in the encounter-group situation.

THE MAKING OF A GROUP

What distinguishes the groups we belong to from mere aggregates of individuals, such as people riding in an elevator or waiting at a bus stop? There are two distinguishing features: First, individuals in a group are *interdependent* in one or more ways. Interdependence may mean that the

Figure 14.1 The informal relationships discussed in this chapter exist not only in informal friendship groups but also in more formally organized groups, such as this turn-of-the-century high-school basketball team. Within formal groups, informal norms, roles, group spirit, and conflict often operate as powerful influences that enhance or interfere with a group's functioning as a whole. And just as informal groups often emerge within formal groups, informal groups often undergo increasing formalization of their structures and activities.

behavior of each member influences the others or that the same event influences each member. Interdependence also implies some type of interaction—verbal, physical, or emotional. Second, individuals in a group *perceive the existence of the group* and their own membership in it. Individuals riding in an elevator, then, would generally not qualify as a group. Although there might be interaction among a few individuals, there would be little interdependence among them, and they would generally not consider themselves a group. If the elevator were to become jammed for a period of time, however, this aggregate of people may *become* a group. On one dimension of interdependence, all the individuals in the elevator would be influenced by the same event. They would probably then interact as a group by discussing their common predicament and offering one another support and suggestions. At the same time, their perceptions of themselves as a "group" in trouble would likely develop. Not infrequently, individuals who meet in this kind of emergency situation form a group that continues to meet after the crisis has passed.

These two characteristics—interdependence of members and perception of the existence of the group—hold true for all groups, large and small, formal and informal.

Formal Versus Informal Groups

It is important to understand the distinction between formal and informal groups. These categories are not mutually exclusive: Informal groups may exist within formal ones. Essentially, the formal group is highly structured and thus more easily analyzed. In a community action group, for example, there may be positions such as chairman, fund raiser, coordinator, representative to the town council, active members, financial supporters, and infrequent visitors. Within this formal group, there may also be informal groups based on shared outside interests, on special activities like political involvement and cultural interests, on shared friends, or on other factors. Informal relations have powerful effects on the effectiveness of even the most formal groups. (Formal organizations are discussed in Chapter 16.)

Fulfillment of Social Needs

Every group you belong to uses you, and in turn you use your fellow group members. Although you probably do not think of yourself as being used by or as using others, you are nevertheless gaining some type of reward from them. The more successful that group members are in satisfying one another's needs, the more satisfied that each is with the group and the more likely it is that the group will continue.

As Marvin Shaw (1971) and others have found, everyone has several social needs—such as needs for affection, approval, love, security, prestige, achievement, and stimulation—which usually require association with other people for satisfaction. For example, one reason for your participation in particular groups is your attraction toward its members (see Chapter 6). But you may also participate in a group to enjoy its activities or to share its values and goals. You may join one group for intellectual stimulation, another because members play tennis or ride bicycles, and still another because the members wish to raise funds for a worthwhile cause. People join a variety of groups to satisfy goals lying outside any one group's boundaries.

Group participation, then, can yield many rewards. These rewards can have their basis in the attractiveness of those with whom the individual is

Figure 14.2 People often feel a need to evaluate their behavior, reactions, opinions, and abilities against those of other persons when no objective standards are available. The need for social comparison is at least one motivating force behind a wide range of behavior, including affiliating with others, participating in discussions, playing competitive games, taking examinations in school, and answering popular quizzes. The Perfect Husband, Perfect Wife Quiz, taken from *Radical Therapist*, is a takeoff on such quizzes. You can find out if you are a "perfect" wife or a "perfect" husband by scoring yourself on each item as follows: 0 = "never," 1 = "sometimes," 2 = "an average amount," 3 = "usually," and 4 = "regularly." The perfect score on eight items is a total of 32.

Perfect Wife Quiz

1. Do you allow your husband an appropriate amount of the family income, to spend as he chooses, without accounting?   0 1 2 3 4

2. Do you still "court" him with an occasional gift of flowers; by remembrance of birthdays and anniversaries; by unexpected attentions?   0 1 2 3 4

3. Are you cooperative in handling the children, taking your full share of responsibility and also backing him up?   0 1 2 3 4

4. Do you make it a point never to criticize him before others?   0 1 2 3 4

5. Do you share at least half your recreation hours with him?   0 1 2 3 4

6. Do you show interest in and respect for his intellectual life?   0 1 2 3 4

7. Do you show as much consideration and courtesy to his relatives as you do to your own?   0 1 2 3 4

8. Do you enter sympathetically into his plans for social activities, trying to do your full share as a hostess in your own home and, when a guest in the homes of others, trying to make him appear to the best possible advantage?   0 1 2 3 4

---

interacting, in affiliation itself, or in characteristics of the particular group with which an individual is involved.

Social Comparison: Who Am I? The drive to evaluate personal opinions was discussed in Chapters 6 and 10. But people need to evaluate more than their opinions. They continually question the adequacy and appropriateness of their behavior, abilities, and emotional reactions: Am I a good student? Am I intelligent? Am I personable? Did I behave appropriately at the party? How should I react the next time someone insults me or the next time I receive a compliment? Do I look silly playing soccer? Am I getting enough out of life?

Because our complex world offers few objective standards for dealing with such concerns, we are often uncomfortable and uncertain. Some comfort comes from learning how others react to similar situations; a kind of reality is established when we find that we react as others do. Getting social evidence that we are responding appropriately and correctly gives us one reason to seek out others. Thus, affiliation with others is rewarding.

An experiment conducted by Jerome Singer and Vernon Shockley (1965) demonstrates how this hypothesized drive to compare ourselves with others can influence affiliative behavior. Singer and Shockley had female subjects complete an experimental task and led them to believe that they would be given another task. Half of the women had received feedback about their performance on the experimental task; the other half were given no information. Then the experimenters told the women that they would have to wait while the second part of the experiment was set up and gave them the opportunity to wait alone or together. Singer and Shockley found that more of the women who had received no information—and were therefore uncertain about their earlier performances—chose to wait together. The women who had received feedback had an objective standard for evaluating themselves and did not show the need to affiliate with others.

The Need for Cognitive Clarity. Stanley Schachter (1959) suggests that the drive for cognitive clarity is related to, but broader than, the drive for social comparison. The need for cognitive clarity also motivates people to affiliate with one another. Suppose that one day your most conservative, traditional professor, who usually lectures uninterrupted for the full class period, were to enter the classroom in mod clothes, sit on the desk, and casually open a discussion about the social issues involving the use of alcohol and marijuana. One could probably predict that after the class hour groups of students who had never before spoken to one another would gather together in an attempt to discover the professor's motives and intentions. Is it an experiment? Is this the way he really is? Has someone finally reached him? Is this the way the class will be conducted from now on? In an ambiguous situation we seek out others' ideas to obtain cognitive clarity and thereby reduce ambiguity.

The need for cognitive clarity in affiliative behavior was demonstrated in an experiment by Stanley Schachter and Harvey Burdick (1955). These investigators created a puzzling situation in a girls' school: During the first hour of classes, the principal went to several classrooms, pointed to one girl in each, and said, "Miss——, get your hat, coat, and books and come with me. You will be gone for the rest of the day." He gave no explanation for this unprecedented order. Schachter and Burdick noticed that the need for cognitive clarity kept the rest of the girls in close contact for the greater part of the school day, discussing what had occurred and what might be happening. Apparently, one reason people affiliate with one another is to clarify ambiguous situations that they encounter.

Reducing Anxiety: Someone to Cling To.   Imagine that you have signed up for an experiment in order to satisfy a psychology class requirement. You report to a laboratory containing formidable-looking electrical equipment. You and the other subjects, none of whom you know, are met by a somber man in a white coat and horn-rimmed glasses; he introduces himself as Dr. Gregor Zilstein of the neurology and psychiatry department of the medical school. He tells you that you will participate in an experiment testing the effects of electric shock. After a seven- or eight-minute lecture on the importance of the research, Dr. Zilstein ominously tells you that you will receive a series of electric shocks and that they will be intense and painful but will do no permanent damage. You are told that you will be hooked up to equipment that will measure your physiological responses to these shocks. You and all the other subjects in the experiment are then told that there will be a ten-minute wait while the equipment is set up; you may wait alone in a comfortable room with books and magazines or you may wait in one of the empty classrooms with some of the other subjects. At the request of the experimenter, each subject writes down a preference. Would you choose to wait alone or with your peers? If you responded as have most subjects in this situation (all of whom have been women), you would be more inclined to wait with others if you foresaw pain than if you did not.

This situation was used by Stanley Schachter (1959) in a series of classic experiments to study the effects of fear on affiliative behavior. He compared the affiliative behavior of highly fearful women, who expected intense shock, with that of low-fear women, who expected mild shock that would produce only a tingling sensation. Schachter found that highly fearful subjects chose to wait with one another significantly more often than did the women who had little cause for alarm. Stress, then, is one condition that increases affiliative behavior.

Schachter's initial experiment turned the old adage "misery loves company" into a testable hypothesis but left two questions unanswered: Why is it that people want to be with others when they are afraid? And do fearful people want to be with just anyone or only with people who are also afraid? Schachter explored the second question by using only subjects who were highly afraid in an experimental situation similar to that just described. Half the subjects were given the same choice as the original subjects had: they could wait alone or with others who anticipated the same painful experience. The other half of the subjects had to choose to wait alone or with others who were *not* expecting shock but waiting to see their advisers. Schachter found a significant difference in the degree of affiliation in the two groups: Subjects who could wait with others in the same predicament were more likely to affiliate with one another than were those whose potential companions were in a different situation. Misery does not like just any company—only miserable company.

Why do fearful people want to be with others who are in the same position? Schachter had five hypotheses. He first considered three possibilities: that fearful subjects, by talking with others in the same predicament, wanted to gain cognitive clarity about the situation; that they hoped to get their minds off their unpleasant fates; or that they hoped to convince others to leave and, with their support, escape from the situation. Schachter

---

Perfect Husband Quiz

1. Do you try to make the home interesting, attractive, cheerful, a place of rest and relaxation—devoting as much thought and study to that as you would to a job "downtown?"   0 1 2 3 4

2. Do you encourage your wife to go out frequently with her women friends, though it means leaving you home alone?
                                0 1 2 3 4

3. Do you serve meals that are enticing in variety and attractiveness?   0 1 2 3 4

4. Do you handle household finances in a businesslike way?   0 1 2 3 4

5. Do you keep yourself attractive (though not offensively so!) in appearance, in order that your wife may be proud to have everyone know you are her husband? 0 1 2 3 4

6. Are you a "good sport," cheerful and uncomplaining, punctual, not nagging, not insisting on having your own way or the last word, not making a fuss over the trifles or requiring her to solve minor problems that you should handle alone? 0 1 2 3 4

7. Do you bolster your wife's ego by not comparing her unfavorably with more successful women but making her feel that she is the most successful woman you ever met?   0 1 2 3 4

8. Do you prevent your mother and other relatives from intruding unduly, and show courtesy and consideration to her own relatives?   0 1 2 3 4

ruled out these first three hypotheses by allowing highly fearful subjects to wait together in a room but not allowing them to talk to one another. He found that highly fearful people chose to wait together, in support of their need for affiliation, even though communication was forbidden.

Schachter's two remaining hypotheses have been more fruitful in explaining why highly fearful subjects choose to be with others who share their fear even when they cannot communicate with them. One possible explanation is that subjects experience a *need for social comparison;* the subjects may have wanted to wait with others in the same situation to evaluate the appropriateness of their own fear. And they could have accomplished social comparison merely by observing the calmness or tenseness of others. The other possibility Schachter considered was that the subjects may have hoped to derive direct *fear reduction* by affiliating with the others; their fears might have been reduced, for example, if the other subjects had volunteered nonverbal gestures of support and comfort, such as smiles and glances. Subsequent research has supported both these hypotheses.

An experiment conducted by Harold Gerard and Jacob Rabbie (1961) has demonstrated the power of social comparison. These investigators reasoned that if social comparison accounted for anxious subjects' desire to affiliate, then affiliative behavior would be less likely if the subjects already knew how others were reacting to the situation. They attached electrodes to all subjects, and the electrodes were ostensibly connected to a dial that would show the subjects an accurate index of their emotionality. One group of subjects received information only about their own emotional level. Other subjects saw their own readings and the readings for three fictitious persons, who registered approximately the same emotional levels as did the real subjects. Subjects in a third group received no information about either their own or others' emotional levels. The subjects who had knowledge of their own and others' emotional reactions proved to be significantly less likely to prefer waiting with others than were subjects who had no information or who knew only their own emotional states. Thus, removing uncertainty about the appropriateness of their reactions reduced the desire to affiliate. These results provide compelling evidence that anxiety tends to motivate people to seek the company of others whose responses they can compare with their own.

The presence of other people also has an anxiety-reducing effect, as Stanley Kissel (1965) and other researchers have found. Using physiological measurements of anxiety, Kissel found that he could reduce an individual's anxiety with the mere presence of another person. The other person need not even be in the same anxiety-provoking situation if he is someone the individual already knows.

It appears, then, that stress increases affiliation because people in the company of others are able to evaluate the appropriateness of their reactions and to reduce their anxieties.

NORMS AND SIMILARITY AMONG MEMBERS

Even in the brief glimpse of the group life of seven soldiers on a cross-country train, it was apparent that those seven men were similar in several ways. All of them were older than most of the other recruits; all were college graduates; all were eligible for officer training; all agreed on the ultimate decision not to become officers; and all found satisfaction in similar

Figure 14.3 When faced with fear and anxiety, people commonly seek the company of others. Social psychologists have found that others can both provide comparison points against which to evaluate one's own reactions to distressing situations and reduce the amount of anxiety or fear that one feels. In this five-century-old woodcut by Albrecht Dürer illustrating the day of judgment, one can see people, rich and poor, old and young, gathered to give each other what comfort can be had in the face of the ultimate fear.

V Behavior in Groups

activities. In formal groups, selective membership rules may be responsible for this kind of similarity. But in groups like the informal one established by the soldiers, it is most likely that the friends were drawn together because of the similarities in their backgrounds and attitudes— among the most powerful determinants of interpersonal attraction known (see Chapter 6).

In any case, members of a group become increasingly similar as they arrive at group norms. Norms are explicit or implicit agreements that dictate acceptable and expected behavior and attitudes for members. Group norms do not usually cover the entire spectrum of members' behaviors, attitudes, and values, however. The nature and scope of norms vary from group to group and depend on what the members consider to be important and relevant to the functioning of the group. A group of teen-agers, for example, may develop norms governing how its members should dress, talk, and interact with parents, teachers, and nongroup peers; what they should do in their spare time; and how they should generally perceive the world. The norms of a group of women college students, on the other hand, may specify what constitutes acceptable social and academic behavior; the conditions under which it is acceptable for one member to date another's boyfriend; attitudes about career and marriage; and the degree of intimacy they will share. A group of husbands may develop norms about job performance, acceptance of their wives' careers, and sharing family responsibilities. And norms for a Wednesday-night discussion group may govern topics of conversation, visitors to the group, and whether or not members arrive on time.

Informal groups within organizations often develop norms about the rate at which members should work and how they should carry out their tasks. The overly industrious office or factory worker may even become the victim of informal social penalties if he or she greatly exceeds the output of fellow workers and thereby demonstrates to supervisors that they have not been working to capacity. Even a transient informal group at a party may develop a temporary set of norms about the type and level of conversation, the degree to which the members may become personally and emotionally involved, and the degree of physical contact. A group's norms may range from the very specific to the very general.

How Norms Develop: The Glass Is Blown

According to Leon Festinger (1950), two factors account for the emergence of norms within a group. One factor is the desire of members to *validate their beliefs* when the physical environment does not provide validation. Members often strive for agreement on issues that are relevant to them as a group. Thus, to the group of soldiers on the train, beliefs about God and marriage may have been irrelevant. But beliefs about the army were central to the group's activities and concerns; they therefore spent a good deal of time talking about the army and trying to validate their shared beliefs about the advantages and disadvantages of becoming an officer.

The second factor responsible for the development of group norms is the necessity or desire of the members to *maintain the group*. If members have no way of knowing what to expect from one another and cannot agree on a mutually satisfying way to function, they will have little motivation to remain within the group.

Not all group norms create uniformity within a group. Some norms establish diversity because they apply only to particular group members.

Mrs. Guinea answered my letter and invited me to lunch at her home. That was where I saw my first fingerbowl.

The water had a few cherry blossoms floating in it, and I thought it must be some clear sort of Japanese after-dinner soup and ate every bit of it, including the crisp little blossoms. Mrs. Guinea never said anything, and it was only much later, when I told a debutante I knew at college about the dinner, that I learned what I had done.

—SYLVIA PLATH

For example, the behavior expected of the group leader is usually different from that expected of other members. People may expect leaders to take initiative, to be innovative, to be the principal organizers, and to mediate conflicts. A group's members may consider leadership behavior inappropriate when it comes from anyone other than the person they have designated as their leader, and the would-be leader may even be rejected by the group. Similarly, the behavior expected of new members differs from that expected of established members. New members may be expected to conform more rigidly than senior members to group norms, to take less aggressive roles, and to carry out the less attractive group functions.

How Norms Operate: Bottled Up

After a group's norms have been formed, its members have a vested interest in making sure that everyone adheres, especially to those norms on which the group's functioning depends. Implicit in a norm is the range of deviation that members will tolerate. Group members will agree, tacitly if not explicitly, that their most important norms should be strongly enforced. For example, a group of college students who like to share ideas may not permit a member to use others' ideas to write his or her own papers; they may strictly enforce restrictions against such behavior because they feel that mistrust would disrupt the smooth flow of ideas in their group and impede its functioning. On the other hand, a great deal of deviation from

Figure 14.4 What is labeled "deviant" is often more dependent on the situation and the status of the deviant individual than on the behavior per se. A topless dress created by famed designer Rudy Gernreich was received warmly when modeled at a high-status fashion show (*right*). But a San Francisco dancer-actress (*left*) was arrested for wearing a similar dress on an airplane bound for Los Angeles. Depending on the group in which the wearer found herself (the fashion-show crowd or the airline passengers), the same type of behavior brought praise or punishment.

less central norms may be tolerable; for example, norms concerning the time and place to talk may not be as central to this group of students.

Just as acceptance is the consequence of adherence to norms, rejection is the consequence of deviance. Rejection ranges from mild disapproval to ostracism. As Chapter 10 explains, other group members will take great pains to persuade the deviant to conform. But if these others surmise that the deviant will not yield, their efforts at communication rapidly decrease and rejection follows.

The extent of a group's rejection depends not only on the importance of the norm the deviant member violates but also on the status of the deviant. Thus, high-status members often have more freedom to deviate than do lower-status members, providing their behavior is not detrimental to the group. But, as James Wiggins, Forrest Dill, and Richard Schwartz (1965) note, if deviation does turn out to be detrimental, the higher-status deviant must pay higher group penalties than a lower-status deviant.

Reference Groups: The Secret Standard

Those groups to which a person belongs physically are *membership groups*. Everyone is also a part of various *reference groups* with which he or she identifies; membership in a reference group is psychological. Whether a group serves solely as a membership group or as a reference group for its members will have important consequences for the influence it has over those members. A person may comply with the norms of a membership group only when necessary—for example, when he is being observed. In contrast, he uses a reference group as a standard with which to compare himself, and he internalizes reference-group norms as his own; he therefore tends to conform to them whether or not he is watched by the group.

Often a person's religious group, family group, occupational groups, and close friendship groups serve as his reference groups. Membership groups can also act as reference groups, as when a member of a basketball team spends a great deal of time in other sports activities with fellow team members and internalizes such team norms as a competitive spirit or the enjoyment of physical activity. At times, a group to which someone does not belong may become a powerful reference group for him. Many teenagers, for example, model themselves after the "in group," in hopes that they will be noticed and accepted by its members. In a similar fashion, immigrants or the children of immigrants are often more blindly accepting of the symbols and traditional ideology of the culture they aspire to join than are the country's settled inhabitants. Thus, paradoxically, the aspiring nonmember is often a group's most outspoken and uncompromising advocate of its ideology.

One famous study, conducted by Theodore Newcomb (1943), studied the effects of reference groups on the student body of Bennington College in Vermont. He studied changes in the political and social values of the women from their entrance into the college through graduation. Bennington was unique: A small, isolated, self-contained institution, it was known to be extremely liberal and active in public issues, but it enrolled students from upper-class, conservative homes. Newcomb found that as freshmen the students held the conservative attitudes and values of their parents and home communities; most of them, however, gradually became more liberal as they progressed through their college careers. Interviews with the women indicated that as freshmen they still identified with their families and home communities; later, however, they began to use Bennington as their reference group.

Not all the students in Newcomb's study identified with the Bennington community. Some continued to treat it as merely another membership group. One of these students, interviewed by Newcomb, reported: "All that's really important that's happened to me occurred outside of college, and so I never became very susceptible to college influences." Another treated it as a *negative* reference group, actively rejecting it and using it as a standard against which to contrast personal attitudes: "I wanted to disagree with all the noisy liberals. . . . So I built up a wall inside me against what they said."

GROUP STRUCTURE: THE MYTH OF SPONTANEITY

Do people in informal groups interact spontaneously? Research indicates that spontaneity is highly limited in groups. Even in informal groups, stabilized patterns of relating develop as interaction proceeds, and each member comes to have a place in relation to every other member. The resulting *informal structure* partly governs the way in which each member interacts and functions. When members establish patterns of relating to one another, these patterns determine to a large extent the nature of their future interactions.

Established interaction patterns are basic parts of the norms a group develops. A few members may be involved in a power struggle; others may form a particularly close-knit subgroup; several may perform predictable functions like compromiser, task leader, or scapegoat; and all may assume more-or-less stable positions in a status hierarchy in which top members receive deference from the others.

People Patterns and the Sociogram

Think of the groups that you belong to and try to identify their structures. Typical group positions are easy to identify and may bring to mind roles that members of your groups occupy—leader, joker, deviant, and the silent member, to name a few. There are different aspects of group structure: group positions; the personal relationships between individual members, such as power relationships and trusting relationships; and the rank of each member on a particular dimension, such as power, popularity, status, or amount of resources. The various relationships and rankings that any one member occupies are related and interdependent; for example, one's power, status, popularity, and influence in a particular group are highly interrelated (Shaw, 1971). Positions, the relationships among them, and the norms that prescribe the behavior that is appropriate in these positions and relationships are all aspects of group structure.

One technique that social psychologists find useful in analyzing group structures is the *sociogram* (Moreno, 1934). Researchers using this device ask all the members of a group to name those people with whom they would like to interact on a given occasion or for a specific purpose. For example, the members may be asked with whom they would like to go to a party, to share political ideas, to spend vacation time, or to complete an organizational task. Their choices can then be graphically plotted, as are the responses of the ten group members represented in Figure 14.5, who were asked with whom they would like to spend free time. This sociogram shows that Jim is the most popular—six others want to spend free time with him, whereas he himself prefers only three of these fellow members. In fact, Jim, Jack, Ralph, and Paul apparently form a closely knit group. It may be that they spend time together often. In contrast, Pete seems to be a loner; he neither chose anyone else nor was chosen by anyone. However, he might show up quite differently on a sociogram had the group members been indicating those with whom they would like to do a research project. If this were the case, Pete would appear to be task- and achievement-oriented but not concerned with socializing. Bob and Mike, on the other hand, pair off by themselves. They seem to form their own group. No one else wants to spend spare time with them, and they want to spend their time together.

Sociograms can show a great deal about any one person's status in a group and can help to predict how that individual is likely to communicate with the others. But a sociogram must be built to indicate a specific activity, and the questions used to build it must be asked carefully. Asking people with whom they would *like* to spend spare time, for example, may yield very different results from asking them with whom they *do* spend time. And asking them with whom they would like to go to a party may yield very different results from asking with whom they would like to share ideas.

The Whys of Group Structure

Although the structure that a group develops tends to perpetuate itself, with effort it is modifiable. Members who are not satisfied with their positions in the group often try actively to change either their relative positions or more basic features of the structure. Often, too, certain situations—for example, the need for different resources or a change in members' resources—encourage a group to alter particular aspects of its structure. For example, if an underground newspaper suddenly decided to organize a fund-raising campaign, a previously low-status member might assume the leadership role and command a great deal more status and influence than before if she is the only member with expertise in the new situation.

Personality. The form that a group's internal relations takes is probably never entirely distinct from the traits and idiosyncrasies of its members. The power of personality in shaping group relations was demonstrated in

Figure 14.5 Sociograms can be helpful in understanding various aspects of a group's structure. Structural patterns vary according to the type or activity of the group; this particular example was based on the responses of group members when asked with whom they would like to spend free time. Reciprocal choices are indicated by double arrows, and one-way choices are indicated by arrows pointing from chooser to chosen.

an experiment conducted by Joel Aronoff and Lawrence Messé (1971). These investigators formed five-member groups of individuals who had particularly high needs for safety; who had feelings of insecurity, incompetence, dependence, and mistrust; and who had unusually strong needs for order and predictability. Aronoff and Messé also grouped people who tended to value opportunities to increase their self-esteem and who expressed the desire to establish their competence and to command respect. The investigators gave each of the groups a series of tasks to complete and coded the interactions of each individual into categories such as "gives opinion," "gives orientation," "integrates past communication," and "asks for opinion." Aronoff and Messé found that in safety-oriented groups, task-related activity was concentrated in a few individuals and responsibility was commanded by relatively few members. In contrast, the high-esteem groups developed more egalitarian structures characterized by the equal distribution of responsibility. Aronoff and Messé concluded that both safety-seeking and esteem-seeking groups developed structures that were compatible with the needs of their members. Because safety-seeking in-

Social Structure on a Street Corner:

THE UNSEEN SOCIETIES

MANY INFORMAL GROUPS owe their existence to the fact that people are in the same place and circumstances at the same time. For example, informal groups form in many cities, where people in certain socioeconomic categories are cut off from many of the material privileges enjoyed by the mainstream society and also from social and political power. These informal groups unite members in common activities, provide support, regulate behavior, provide role models, and generally develop viewpoints that help members to interpret events. Much of the social life in ghettos and slums takes place "on the street" rather than in private homes, clubhouses, and bars. The street corner is the gathering place and the home base for groups composed of poor city dwellers, especially young members of minority groups.

A classic study of one male "street corner society" was conducted in the late 1930s by sociologist William Whyte. This investigator became a participant-observer in a subsociety located in an Italian slum in a large Eastern city. He described the social structure of the area, which he called "Cornerville"—its social clubs and their members; its politics and politicians; its rackets, or illegal

businesses, and its racketeers.

The street-corner clubs were formed according to sex, ethnic group, age, and geography. Young Italian boys living on the same street "hung around" together. Social status within these groups initially depended on physical power—who could beat up whom—but as the members of a particular group grew into their twenties and beyond, and the "kids' gangs" became "clubs," leadership abilities and other factors also came into play. Doc, for example, was the leader of the Nortons and was widely respected first for his physical and then for his leadership abilities. He commented: "I was a tiger when I was a kid. I wasn't afraid of anybody. Most kids when they fight just push each other around, but I had a knockout punch in my right. . . . It wasn't just the punch. I was the one who always thought of the things to do. I was the one with half a brain."

Unlike formal groups, in informal groups leadership positions are not officially obtained or even named, and it is possible for leaders not to realize that they are in fact leaders. Angelo, for example, was the leader of a group that never made a move without him. Yet Doc commented: "No, Angelo doesn't know he's their leader. If you told him that he'd be ruined. He wouldn't know what to do."

dividuals are particularly insecure, anxious, and dependent, they feel more secure when directed and guided than when taking the initiative in groups; thus, they develop hierarchical group structures in which most members need not feel burdened by responsibility. High-esteem individuals, on the other hand, because they are anxious to demonstrate their competence, are reluctant to sit back and take directions from others and are likely to take initiative; they are therefore more likely to develop egalitarian structures in which everyone can have a share of the action and responsibility. History supports this finding: Power has often become concentrated in the hands of dictators in times of social insecurity—as when economic desperation grew in Germany until a leader emerged, Adolf Hitler, who could solve the Germans' immediate problems. Nations in turmoil seem to be fertile ground for the concentration of power in authoritarian hands.

After reviewing the relevant literature, Marvin Shaw (1971) identified other examples of the influence that individual members can have on a group's developing interactional patterns. He suggests, for example, that women tend to be less assertive in their group interactions than men—not

Leadership in these street-corner cliques brought with it responsibility, and if a leader's behavior was inappropriate or uncaring, he might lose his position. Doc was acutely aware of his responsibilities and felt that he had violated his role by withdrawing from a local election in which he was widely supported by members of many clubs. He had withdrawn because he had no job—it was during the Depression—and could not treat his boys properly. Money was shared to some extent in the clubs; leaders, in particular, were expected to be beneficent. In shame, he all but abdicated his position by failing to show up most of the time. But his personal popularity pulled him through this crisis, because his club members retained their faith in him and loyalty to him.

Group membership had a large influence on the structure of the member's social relationships. The most binding relationships were between men and not between men and women. The philosophy of the all-male memberships is summed up in the statement: "A girl you can meet anytime. . . . It takes years to make a friend."

Group acceptance could have dramatic effects on the self-esteem and consequently the behavior of any

member, not just of the leader. Whyte discusses an incident in which Doc ministers to a club member whose shaky and worsening standing was bringing him to a crisis. Bowling was an important club activity. Important members were expected to do well and were supported and cheered, whereas members who tried to bowl "above their heads" were heckled and undermined. Long John was a low-ranking member who became a very good bowler—and bragged about it. His performance dropped suddenly, partly because the group was critical; he was then heckled mercilessly. He confided to Doc that he could not sleep because he felt as though he were suffocating. Doc, after some probing, traced the fear to a childhood incident. Whyte suggested that Doc could help him regain his emotional balance by bringing him into a locally influential social circle, centering on and headed by Spongi, a racketeer who ran a betting parlor and a crap game. Doc did, and it worked. Doc and a friend also began to support Long John in the bowling alley—and eventually he won first prize in individual competition.

Source: Adapted from W. Whyte, *Street Corner Society; The Social Structure of an Italian Slum,* 2nd ed. (Chicago: University of Chicago Press, 1955).

surprising, considering that the female sex role as it is taught in the United States is a passive one (see Chapter 2). Shaw also suggests that high group morale seems to be associated with groups of people-oriented and well-adjusted individuals. Anxious individuals tend to set, and be satisfied with, relatively lower group goals, and they shift opinions more frequently. Moderately assertive individuals, on the other hand, participate more and conform more to group norms, influence group decisions to a greater degree, and tend to promote group cohesiveness (which will be discussed at length later in the chapter).

Situations Shape the Structure.   Personality is only one determinant of the complex structure in a group. According to Dorwin Cartwright and Alvin Zander (1968), the particular combination of group members and their interactions with one another make each group structure different from others, as do situational factors in general. For example, the physical and social environment create differences among groups; a member may behave and be reacted to differently in different groups. The moderately dominant person will tend to be more assertive in a group of shy individuals than he ordinarily would be; an individual who alone possesses some information or skill needed by the group will play a more central role than he would if other members also possessed that skill; the most centrally located members in an apartment complex often become central figures in the interactional patterns that emerge; and, to take an example that reflects the norms of the larger society, when a group needs a secretary, it rarely assigns a man to that position if the group has any female members.

Cartwright and Zander also suggest that *efficiency* is a factor that encourages a structure in which members assume different functions. The larger the group and the more specific its goal, the more important efficiency is, as is evident in the discussion of formal organizations in Chapter 16. Even in small informal groups, individuals are likely to be happiest if the group functions smoothly without much duplication of effort.

LEADERSHIP

A position of power—the leader's—almost always emerges in any group. Even in a formal group, where leaders are usually appointed or formally elected, informal leaders may arise who actually have more influence over the group than do the formal leaders (see Chapter 16). Members of an informal group are aware of the hierarchical structure of their group even though they may not talk about it. They usually agree, for example, on who the leader is. The leader is simply the person with the most influence in the group. He or she is likely to give suggestions and directions that are the most acceptable to other members, to intervene the most in group dissension, to initiate and receive the greatest number of communications from the greatest number of group members, to give and have more opinions, to do the most to increase the group's morale, to give approval and disapproval to others' actions, and to represent the group in interactions with outside groups. In their studies of the leaders of informal groups researchers have used a variety of approaches, three of which are described in the following sections.

Are Leaders Born?

For a long time, research on leadership centered on traits or personal characteristics that "made" a leader. Researchers assumed that leaders were "great men" who would assume leadership in any situation. The results of this approach were disappointing. Reviews of such research—by Richard Mann (1959), for example—suggest that there is little consistency in the traits that appear to be characteristic of leaders. Generally, leaders tend to be more intelligent than nonleaders (but not much more intelligent), and they tend to be better adjusted than nonleaders are. Leaders also tend to be more verbally fluent than nonleaders are.

But these tendencies are the only ones that consistently characterize leaders. In fact, leaders do not seem to be radically different from other group members. They are not much more intelligent than their followers, their ideas are not perceived by other group members as particularly deviant, and they share the group's values and ideals.

The Structural Approach: The Right Place at the Right Time

Because research into unique personality traits of leaders has not revealed consistent findings, social psychologists have often turned to a *structural approach,* which views leadership as one of many positions in a group that any member can fill. Just who the leader is at any particular time depends on who can best help the group to satisfy its current objectives. Leadership is situational and is likely to change as group objectives change. One example might be the underground newspaper that decided to embark on a fund-raising campaign. The leadership skills required when the group's objectives were newspaper writing and production were different from those needed when their objective became fund raising. In an example discussed later, groups of preadolescent boys switched leaders when their primary concern changed from camping activities to defeating rival groups.

Any member of the group is a potential leader. This was demonstrated by Alex Bavelas, Albert Hastorf, Alan Gross, and W. Richard Kite (1965). Their experiment—often called the "mouse-that-roared" study—suggests that any member can be *made* into a leader. Bavelas and his colleagues created several groups of four men each to discuss three human-relations problems. During the discussion of the first problem, the experimenters obtained a base measure of each subject's participation and later had each member rate the others' leadership abilities, effectiveness in guiding the discussion, amount of participation, and quality of ideas. Before their second discussion, subjects were told that they would receive feedback on their individual contributions to the discussion. When a subject's participation (or lack of it) was judged to be a valuable contribution to the solution, a green light would appear on a panel in front of him. A red light would appear when his participation (or lack of it) hindered the group's arrival at a solution. Each member would see only his own feedback. In reality, the experimenters reinforced the contributions of "target subjects," one of the least talkative and lowest-status members of each group; they discouraged the participation of the other group members.

Can relatively low-status members who have contributed little to a group be made into leaders? Apparently they can be. After the second problem was discussed, Bavelas and his colleagues found dramatic increases in both the target subjects' contributions and the group's perceptions of these reinforced subjects as leaders. They were rated by other members as being significantly higher the second time on all four leadership indices—leadership abilities, effectiveness in guiding discussion, amount of participation, and quality of ideas. Even the postures of many of the target subjects changed during the course of the feedback session; they stopped slouching and began sitting attentively upright. Furthermore, some of the changes in their behavior, as well as the groups' perceptions of their leadership abilities, carried over to the third discussion, during which no feedback was given. Although in the third session the target subjects' participation and status in the groups declined somewhat, these subjects still participated significantly more often than they had in the original sessions. Thus, it appears that any member, even a low-status one, can become a leader if he perceives that he can contribute more to the group than can other members.

The structural approach to leadership focuses on the leadership role rather than on the particular person who happens to occupy that role. Several attempts have been made to identify just what the leadership role includes and if its requirements can be satisfied by any one individual. Studying various groups, Andrew Halpin and B. James Winer (1952) identified two major types of leadership behavior: giving *consideration,* or showing mutual trust, friendship, respect, and warmth for other group members; and initiating *structure,* or constructively helping the group toward its goal. Somewhat similar categories were suggested by Robert Bales (1953), who identified two behavioral orientations basic to the leadership function: *task orientation* (leading the group toward its goals) and *group-maintenance orientation* (building the morale and socioemotional cohesiveness of the group). Bales maintains that although some leaders may be able to carry out both these functions effectively, two different individuals emerge as leaders in many groups—the task specialist and the socioemotional specialist, who is concerned with the interpersonal relationships and morale of the group.

In groups with both a task specialist and a socioemotional specialist, the two leaders generally complement one another; which one assumes more importance depends on the type of group. Often, especially in an informal group, the socioemotional specialist is more important because the group is not particularly task-oriented, and the skills of the socioemotional specialist are likely to be needed in spite of situational changes.

The structural approach has been criticized. Edwin Hollander and James Julian (1969) feel that the structural view is too narrow and that research stimulated by this approach has usually neglected the characteristics of the individual leader altogether. A leader's traits are nevertheless important insofar as other members perceive them to be relevant to the situation. Additionally, the individual leader's competence (Hollander, 1960) and his interest in group members and group activity (Hollander and Julian, 1969) influence the ways in which group members respond to his attempts to influence them. Furthermore, the structural view has revealed little about followers, although the characteristics of followers certainly influence the latitude of influence that is available to a leader. In all probability, the needs of the followers influence the type of leader they will get. It is unlikely, for example, that individuals who are high in self-esteem, such as some of Aronoff and Messé's subjects, would accept a highly authoritarian leader, whereas an authoritarian style may be welcome in a group of people who seek primarily safe group experiences. According to Hollander and Julian, the structural approach falsely treats the leader and situation separately, although the leader is not only a shaper of the situation but is also shaped by the situation. Any approach that considers the leader separately from other factors overlooks aspects of the situation that may be important—aspects such as the group's objectives, resources, structure, size, and history. Therefore, the structural approach, devised in

Figure 14.6 The process approach to understanding leadership takes a more complex view of leadership than just the leader's personality or role. Leaders are seen as integral parts of ongoing situations in which they, their followers, and situational conditions are complexly intertwined. Lawrence of Arabia's role in Arabian history is one illustration of leadership as process. His initial interest in Arabian customs and culture no doubt shaped his behavior and tactics, and it is likely that it was these acquired characteristics that enabled him to exert such a great influence in the Arabian revolution.

reaction to the trait approach, has its own shortcomings: Some researchers believe that it does not adequately consider the leader's personality.

Leadership As Process: Onward, Upward, and Downward

A new view of leadership—one that takes into account the complex relations among leaders, other group members, and situations—is presently developing (Hollander, 1969). Social psychologists are realizing that the trait and structural approaches emphasize two inseparable aspects of leadership. Leadership is not a static position but an ongoing process in which the person who is leader plays a formative part; leader, followers, and situation interrelate. The process is in part a transaction between leader and followers: Leaders carry out particular functions expected of them by their groups in return for greater status, recognition, esteem, and influence. These rewards, however, are contingent on their meeting the group demands. The leadership process is therefore a two-way influence relationship, and a conception of the leader as a person who simply directs others is misleadingly simple. The leader's behavior and status to a large degree depend on the expectations of the followers and vary with the demands of the broadly defined situation.

Edwin Hollander (1958) has suggested that leaders accumulate *idiosyncrasy credits* that they may spend during the course of leadership. He tested his hypothesis in the context of five-man decision-making teams, one member being his accomplice. The accomplice, having insight into the task facing the group, made generally better choices than anyone else in the group. As more of the other members began to agree with the accomplice, he gained status; that is, he earned idiosyncrasy credits. The accomplice in Hollander's experiment used up his credits in the various groups in one of three ways: by behaving in an obnoxious way from the beginning, by being obnoxious only after he had been accepted as a leader, or through inconsistent behavior. The accomplice had the greatest influence when he became obnoxious well into the trials; this result shows how credits built up early may give a leader latitude in his later actions. In general, a leader who initially conforms creates a positive impression of himself in others and builds up an "account" of idiosyncrasy credits. The credits he builds by conforming early give him increased status and allow him to behave later in idiosyncratic ways without the threat of group penalty. (Remember that groups are more tolerant of deviants who have high status.) After he has built up his account, his credits give him the power to initiate innovative ideas, deviate from accepted behavior, and exert influence on the others. If these actions prove successful in satisfying group objectives, the others will gradually come to perceive him as a leader. However, after a person becomes a leader, group members' expectations of his behavior change; members then expect innovative ideas, assertiveness, and attempted influence of him. If, however, the leader behaves in ways that the group perceives as harmful to it or too deviant or detrimental to group objectives, he will begin to use up the idiosyncrasy credits in his account. A group allows its leaders only so much latitude. For example, college students whose wit makes them leaders may fall from favor if they too often turn their wit against others in their groups.

Bases of Power and Influence

The basis of a leader's influence varies from leader to leader and from group to group. John French and Bertram Raven (1959) have identified five bases

Figure 14.7 Hollander's concept of idiosyncrasy credits in leadership is similar to the notion of a bank account: one must build an account to gain financial power, and indiscriminate spending without replenishing the account will result in loss of that power. When the Russian Rasputin depleted his "account," his fate was far worse. In the early twentieth century, Rasputin accumulated his "credits" with the royal family by supposedly alleviating the young czarevitch's hemophilia. As a result, Empress Alexandra believed that he was a saint, and he gradually obtained virtually total control over political affairs. His actions, both corrupt and unwise, provoked chaos and otherwise paralyzed the government. Although for a time he led a charmed life, his detrimental activities finally incited his opposition to assassinate him.

of influence, or social power; a leader's influence may rest on any one or on several of these. The five bases of power apply not only to the leadership situation but also to any situation in which one individual has influence or power over another. According to French and Raven, a person may have:

1. *Referent power:* Others like, respect, or identify with the person, who is in turn likely to influence them.

2. *Reward power:* People perceive the individual as having the ability to give others rewards, such as favors, approval, or increased status.

3. *Coercive power:* People perceive the person as having the ability to administer or mediate punishments, such as reprimands, threats, and reduction of privileges or status.

4. *Expert power:* The person has special resources of knowledge or skill that others need.

5. *Legitimate power:* Others believe that the person has the right to influence their behavior.

Legitimate, or formally authorized, power is not likely to be a factor in informal group relations, but it is important in many formal groups in

THE JUDGING OF A JURY

By CREATING SIMULATED juries and trials, Fred Strodtbeck, Rita Simon, and Charles Hawkins were able to study some of the dynamics of jury deliberations and especially the effects of sex and social status of the jury members. The results suggested that high-status males tended to be the most important figures in a jury's life—as foremen, as decision makers and as influencers of other jurists. High-status men also tended to feel most satisfied with their participation in the proceedings and were most likely to be chosen by their fellow jurists as persons they would want on a jury panel if members of the other jurists' own families were on trial. Women at all occupational levels were selected only half as often as males for their positive or influential qualities.

Would these findings hold up in real-life courtrooms? What would happen if social psychologists, using this type of data as well as other methodological skills, wanted to influence the outcome of a trial by the people they selected as jurors? Researchers played this type of role in 1971 in an important conspiracy trial. The charge was conspiracy, the prosecutor was the U.S. Government, and the defendants included Father Philip Berrigan, Sister Elizabeth McAlister, and Eqbal Ahmad, a Pakistani sympathizer and friend. A team of psychologists joined the

defense lawyers in trying to prevent a trial that seemed destined for a guilty verdict because of the type of community from which the jurors were to be selected. The jury trial had been set for Harrisburg, Pennsylvania, a strongly conservative community with a judge newly appointed by Richard Nixon.

At first the social psychologists assisted the defense counsel in trying to obtain a change in the site of the trial. After this failed, they served the lawyers by developing data by which to judge the characteristics of prospective jurors in terms of their favorability to the defendants. Survey interviews in the locale indicated that, contrary to much sociological data, being educated or upper-middle class, at least in this part of the country, was a sign of conservatism. An even more powerful predictor of conservatism was religious affiliation. The more strongly attached to the fundamentalist type of religion, the more likely it seemed that a person would find the defendants guilty. This religious factor proved to be even more important than the social psychologists guessed at the time.

The ideal jurist, from the social psychologists' point of view, would be maternal, antiwar in outlook, nonreligious, neither rich nor poor,

which one person is officially designated as the leader or boss. (Chapter 16 examines legitimate leadership, as it applies to work settings and to formal organizations of all types.)

GROUP COHESIVENESS: THE "WE" FEELING

Perhaps the most striking point of the story of the group of privates was the importance of the group to the narrator. Remember his temptation to yield to group pressure so that he could regain the group's support? He even considered making a decision that ran against his fundamental beliefs. Remember his panic and despair when he believed that they were deserting him? He himself considered his reaction to have been most unusual. He even liked bridge!

The group served as a reference group for the private, but that does not entirely explain the degree of its importance to him. These particular soldiers had a strong group spirit; they were loyal, committed, and attracted to one another; they had established very close interpersonal relationships; they were motivated to spend time with one another; and they obviously

and as fair-minded as possible in case none of the other preferred qualities held. When the jury was finally selected, the defense managed to shape the panel quite closely to their desired profile. They had a subgroup of young women whom they believed would seek one another out, develop a common outlook, and dislike the government's chief witness—a former con man who had once proposed to a woman college student, induced her to engage in antiwar demonstrations, and then turned her in to the Federal Bureau of Investigation. The defense had succeeded in including one male Catholic to inhibit the jurors from expressing anti-Catholic sentiments; a black woman, who was assumed to be sympathetic to the civil-rights movement; two other housewives, one with four sons who were conscientious objectors; a fireman; and two Lutheran businessmen. In accordance with the finding reported by Strodtbeck and his colleagues concerning the influence of high-status male jurors, one of the businessmen—an accountant—was elected foreman and held the jury together an extra two days in attempting to reach a solution despite insurmountable problems. The other businessman, who was a retired grocer, became the villain in this courtroom drama.

The jury deliberated more than sixty hours before announcing a deadlock on the conspiracy counts. Post-trial interviews by a psychologist revealed that even before the door had closed on the first session of the deliberation, the grocer had pronounced the defendants guilty by the will of God. As he ranted and raged through the daily sessions, he antagonized all the jurors except the mother of the conscientious objectors. In the end only one charge—that of smuggling letters in and out of a federal prison—was upheld. The jury was hung on every other charge, with all members except the grocer and the angry mother voting "not guilty."

The social psychologists who worked on this case are quite convinced that their efforts contributed heavily to the victory for the defendants. But they also found that even the least likely jurors proved to be more fair-minded and devoted to duty than the social psychologists would have predicted. It is interesting to speculate what might have become of the Berrigan group without the help of this group of social psychologists.

Sources: Adapted from F. Strodtbeck, R. Simon, and C. Hawkins, "Social Status in Jury Deliberations," in I. Steiner and M. Fishbein (eds.), *Current Studies in Social Psychology*, New York: Holt, Rinehart and Winston, 1965, pp. 333–342.

J. Schulman, P. Shaver, R. Colman, B. Emrich, and R. Christie, "Recipe for a Jury," *Psychology Today*, 6 (1973), pp. 37–44.

had great influence over one another. They had the kind of group spirit that made them think of themselves as "we." Social psychologists call this group spirit *cohesiveness.*

Cohesiveness refers to the forces that encourage group members to remain in the group and that prevent them from leaving it (Collins and Raven, 1969). In a highly cohesive group, such as the one the soldiers formed, these forces are quite strong, and members are highly motivated to remain in the group. Equally strong forces operate in many gangs of juveniles and teen-agers, groups of school chums or drinking buddies, athletic teams, work groups, army squadrons, and a legion of other formal and informal groups.

Investigators have used various criteria to identify cohesiveness. Perhaps the most common criterion is the degree of attraction among group members as compared to that among people who are members of less cohesive groups; additional criteria are members' evaluations of the group, their identification with the group, their desire to remain in the group, or some composite of these criteria (Cartwright and Zander, 1968).

Personal Consequences of Cohesiveness

Members of highly cohesive groups usually feel a high degree of liking for one another. As with any individuals who are attracted, members of cohesive groups assume that their liking for one another is reciprocal. Individuals in highly cohesive groups also tend to be more sensitive to one another, although increased sensitivity does not necessarily indicate that their perceptions of one another are any more accurate. Numerous research findings reviewed by Albert and Bernice Lott (1965) indicate that most individuals who like one another also assume that they are more similar than they actually are (see Chapter 6).

With greater liking for one another comes greater satisfaction, both with the group and with general group situations and activities. The general satisfaction expressed by members of highly cohesive groups was demonstrated by Donald Marquis, Harold Guetzkow, and R. W. Heyns (1951),

Figure 14.8 A billboard depicting friendly, cooperative, and happy workers in China. Social-psychology research suggests that this type of propaganda may well strengthen the cohesiveness of the Chinese people.

V BEHAVIOR IN GROUPS

who observed the members of seventy-two business and government conferences at the University of Michigan. They measured cohesiveness as the amount of liking members showed for one another and found that cohesiveness was positively related to the members' satisfaction with their group and with the conference as a whole.

Dorwin Cartwright and Alvin Zander (1968) suggest that membership in cohesive groups has personal consequences for individual group members, such as increasing their self-esteem and feelings of security and reducing their anxieties. This was borne out in a study by Stanley Seashore (1954), who found that highly cohesive work groups reported fewer feelings of being nervous and jittery while working than did work groups with low cohesiveness.

Group cohesiveness also affects the amount and type of interaction among members. People in highly cohesive groups interact more often than do members in less cohesive groups, and the interaction tends to be friendlier, more cooperative, and more generally positive (Shaw, 1971). However, as Lott and Lott point out, frustrated members of cohesive groups appear to express more aggression and hostility toward the source of their frustrations than do people in less cohesive groups. Leonard Berkowitz (1958) suggests that the presence of others who are well liked may lower people's inhibitions about expressing aggression and hostility, which is usually considered socially undesirable behavior.

A general picture of the highly cohesive group contains these elements: its members are motivated to remain within the group, and they like one another, are sensitive to one another, are satisfied with one another, receive security from one another, and interact frequently and freely. From these characteristics, and from what has been learned about group norms, another well-documented characteristic of cohesiveness should not be surprising: A highly cohesive group has more power over its members than does a group with low cohesiveness. This power is reflected in members' greater conformity to group norms and in their greater willingness to yield to group pressure.

Cohesiveness and Conformity

The relationship between cohesiveness and conformity to group norms was demonstrated in a classic study by Leon Festinger, Stanley Schachter, and Kurt Back (1950) of informal groups in a married-student housing complex at the Massachusetts Institute of Technology. The housing complex consisted of many independent units with a group of families per unit (another aspect of the study is described in Chapter 6). Within the total development, there was an older area and a newer one. Festinger and his colleagues investigated the attitudes of the residents toward a controversial tenants' organization. In the older area, they discovered an interesting attitude pattern: homogeneity *within* each housing unit but heterogeneity *between* the units. This pattern was not, however, evident in the newer area. The investigators reasoned that the formation of group norms in the more established units accounted for the pattern. Further analysis revealed that the more cohesive the unit (as measured by members' attraction toward one another), the stronger was the norm—that is, the more the members conformed. Similar relationships between cohesiveness and conformity to group norms have been found in many subsequent studies. John Thibaut and Harold Kelley (1959) have suggested that members are particularly dependent on one another in highly cohesive groups because they are capable of providing many rewards for one another. Furthermore, Thibaut and Kelley maintain that the more individuals believe they can expect rewards from a group (compared with other sources), the more they will allow the group to influence them in return for those rewards.

In the discussion of group norms, it was noted that group tolerance of a deviant member depends on both the status of the deviant and the importance of the norm to the group's functioning. Cohesiveness is another factor that influences a group's tolerance of a deviant member. Highly cohesive groups are less tolerant of deviant members than are groups with low cohesiveness, and they generally put more pressure on their members to conform. Chapter 10 describes an experiment by Stanley Schachter (1951) in which he planted confederates in experimentally created discussion groups and instructed them to take deviant positions. Schachter found that after the deviant had made his position known, group members quickly turned their attention to him, attempting to change his opinion. If the deviant bent to the group's will, the group totally accepted him; if he resisted the pressure, however, the group rejected him. In Schachter's experiment, which in 1954 he repeated in several European countries, the most cohesive groups were the most likely to reject an unyielding deviant.

Because highly cohesive groups have greater power to make their members conform to group norms, they more effectively achieve group goals. And success undoubtedly involves motivational factors. Marvin Shaw (1971) suggests that the positive attitudes of members toward their group make them willing to invest more energy in the group's goals—possibly because less energy is required to deal with interpersonal relationships within the group. The more successful people are at achieving group goals, the more satisfied they are with the group.

Sources of Cohesiveness: The Whys of Togetherness

The causes and effects of cohesiveness are not as easy to distinguish as are the characteristics of a cohesive group and the relationships between its members, because the elements of interaction do not sort into causes and

Figure 14.9   The strong relationship between cohesiveness and conformity is epitomized by this group of Pennsylvania Amish, a tightly knit religious sect living in self-contained communities isolated from modern society. The Amish exhibit a striking degree of conformity in life style, values, beliefs, and dress, and relatively few Amish choose to live otherwise.

effects in the same way that, say, chemicals and heat do in a chemical reaction. Rather, causes and effects influence each other in a spiraling process. An example is the relationship between cohesiveness and interaction that has been demonstrated by Albert and Bernice Lott (1965). Members of highly cohesive groups interact more frequently than do members of less cohesive groups, but interaction itself then becomes one cause of increased attraction. In other words, members of cohesive groups interact more, and through this interaction they become even more cohesive. Say, for example, that you belong to an independent study group that is working on a political-science project. Deep involvement in the project may require many extra hours of work with other group members. During these sessions you may get to know other members better, and your attraction for one another may increase, leading to an even stronger feeling of group cohesiveness.

Because the most common technique of identifying cohesiveness is to measure members' attraction toward one another, the most common approach researchers use to identify the conditions leading to cohesiveness is the study of conditions that lead to attraction toward the group. Chapter 6 deals with some of the antecedents, or causes, of interpersonal attraction.

TURNING SOWS' EARS INTO SILK PURSES

KURT LEWIN, "the father of social psychology," was one of the first to explore the effects of group influences on private behavior. During World War II rationing days, Lewin aimed his research efforts at changing the food preferences of Americans in order to better utilize America's limited food resources. Compelled by evidence of the efficacy of group decision making, Lewin was eager to compare the effects of a lecture with the effects of a group discussion in changing housewives' nutritional habits. His most difficult task may have been to persuade housewives to buy hearts, kidneys, sweetbreads, and brains rather than scarcer and more preferred cuts of meat.

Lewin exposed some women to information about food usage in the form of a lecture and other women to group discussion about the same topics. The same basic arguments about the practical and patriotic virtues of the suggested alternative were injected. Follow-up surveys showed that the participants in the group discussions were more likely to change their food-consumption patterns in the direction of the program's goals.

Lewin was highly intrigued by the consistency of his findings regarding different food practices. He explained the power of groups in terms of (1) the degree of involvement for participants, (2) the complexity of processes that may intervene in the lecture method between beliefs and actions, (3) the social pressure a group can exert on individual members, and (4) the expectation of group members that they would be surveyed in the future about their actions.

Critics of the study point out that although the results are consistent, Lewin did not exercise strict enough experimental controls; for example, he did not always use the same person as lecturer and group leader, and he did not always inform both groups that a follow-up survey would be done. Controls or not, Lewin seems to have been on the right track.

Ironically, the government that has made the most use of the discussion group to reorganize the preferences of its citizens is that of the People's Republic of China.

Source: Adapted from K. Lewin, "Group Decision and Social Change," in T. M. Newcomb and E. L. Hartley (eds.), *Readings in Social Psychology* (New York: Holt, Rinehart and Winston, 1947), pp. 197–211.

The same sources of interpersonal attraction apply to attraction among members of a group, but patterns of attraction are more complex in the group situation.

In their review of the literature, Lott and Lott identify several antecedents of attraction that are specific to the group situation. Cooperation, they believe, is such a factor. Group members who have engaged in a cooperative task together tend to be more attracted to one another than do those who have competed or have worked for different goals. This finding is compatible with the reward explanation of attraction elaborated in Chapter 6; individuals in cooperating groups may be attracted because they see one another as sources of reward.

Also compatible with a reward explanation is evidence that members are more attracted to one another and to the group as a whole when the group is successful in its endeavors. Under some conditions, however, a group's *shared failure* also seems to increase members' attraction toward one another. Lott and Lott suggest that shared failure may actually increase attraction when the group perceives that outside forces or chance events are responsible for the failure. Members may, therefore, be more attracted to one another as a result of a shared sense of injustice.

In a closely related vein, the attraction of group members toward one another also seems to increase with status. A study conducted by Leon Festinger (1953), comparing informal groups in the M.I.T. married-student housing complex with those in a large nonstudent government project, revealed influences of *status*. Residents of the government project were there because of a housing shortage. They resented living there, believed it was undesirable, and perceived their neighbors as being lower-class people. In contrast, people living in the M.I.T. housing were generally satisfied with their living situation. Festinger found many more friendships and informal groups in the married-student housing group than in the government-project groups.

Another group situation, identified by Lott and Lott, that influences members' attraction toward one another is *shared threat;* various studies have found that members' perception of shared threat increases their attraction toward one another. An example was provided by Albert Myers (1962), who created three-man teams. Some of the teams competed against other teams, and many experienced the shared threat of losing to another team. Myers found that members of the competitive teams pulled together more, rated one another as more attractive, and perceived themselves as more accepted by the others than did members of noncompetitive teams. Team members were also asked to indicate their esteem for an absent member by rating him on twenty-four dimensions, such as friendly-unfriendly and cooperative-uncooperative. Myers found that members of competitive teams rated absent members higher than did those in the noncompetitive groups, even though the person's absence caused the group to earn lower scores. Keep in mind that the members of Myers' competitive teams cooperated with one another and competed with other teams; thus, these findings do not contradict those reported earlier about the cohesiveness of cooperative groups. History offers many examples of the power of shared threat. For instance, the cohesiveness of some groups of Jewish people may have arisen from the variety of external threats to their existence throughout the ages.

After reviewing the literature, Lott and Lott have concluded that there is apparently more involved in the relationship between increased attraction and shared threat than Myers' experiment may indicate. Additional research indicates that other factors can reduce the likelihood that a common threat will enhance attraction. For example, if group members perceive the threat as coming from their own incompetence rather than from an external source, if cooperative effort could not reduce the threat anyway, or if they can individually escape either the threat or the group, increased attraction is apparently less likely to result from a common threat.

The group's goals, activities, atmosphere, structure, and individual members' locations within the structure may be additional factors that increase attraction among members.

Intergroup Conflict: We Versus They

Cohesiveness *within* groups has been shown to increase competition *between* groups, and vice versa. From 1949 to 1954, Muzafer Sherif and his colleagues conducted a series of field studies at a boys' summer camp in order to study intergroup relations in conflict situations (Sherif, Harvey, White, Hood, and Sherif, 1961). The subjects were well-adjusted preadolescent boys from white middle-class Protestant families who were unacquainted at the time each experiment began. Unknown to the boys who attended the camp, the experimenters created conditions that would induce cohesiveness within each group and then observed how two groups interacted when brought into competitive rather than cooperative contact.

During the first phase of the experiment, the members of each group interacted in isolation. Each group of boys went hiking and swimming and played baseball separately, and friendships and group spirit soon developed. Each group chose a name and created special symbols, secret words, and in-jokes. By the end of the first phase of each experiment, informal groups had emerged, each with its own unwritten norms and informal leaders. Each group had also developed its own status hierarchy. The groups' structures differed; in some cases it was egalitarian, but in others a

Figure 14.10 Photographs taken during a study of intergroup conflict conducted by Muzafer Sherif and his colleagues at a summer camp for adolescent boys. After a high degree of cohesiveness was created, the researchers introduced intergroup competitions, such as this tug of war (*left*). The competitive atmosphere further increased the cohesiveness within groups but created hostilities between the groups, as reflected in this poster (*inset*), made by one of the teams. Intergroup hostilities gradually lessened when collaboration between groups became necessary to accomplish mutually desired goals. For example, (*right*) members of two previously rivalrous groups pushed a debilitated truck to avoid being stranded on an outing.

steep status hierarchy and clear differentiation between leaders and followers developed. Distinctive group norms also developed. One group developed a norm of toughness, which required the boys to refrain from showing any indication of pain or even from treating cuts and scratches; another developed a norm of being "good," with sanctions against such behavior as swearing and lack of consideration for other members. Many of the groups also developed sanctions for deviant members and those who failed to carry their weight. A common form of punishment for boys in the Bulldogs group was to remove a specified number of stones from the group's swimming hole. These cooperative, satisfying, and successful group experiences led members in all the groups to become highly cohesive, to exhibit strong group loyalties and pride.

In the next phase of the experiment, the experimenters, posing as counselors, brought the groups together under conditions of competitive contact. They arranged a tournament that pitted two groups against each other in tug-of-war, football, baseball, treasure-hunting, and other games.

As it turned out, the high degree of group identification and loyalty fostered in the boys tended to amplify perceived differences between the groups. A usual result was the designation of one's own group as the ingroup and all others as outgroups. This distinction was accompanied by perceptual distortions, in which members perceived their own group as superior and the outgroup as inferior. As soon as the groups in Sherif's experiment came into competitive contact, the participants began to make clear distinctions between "we" and "they." And when the groups challenged one another to competitive sports, each appeared to be confident of its own superiority and chances of victory.

The situation was ripe for intergroup conflict: Each team could achieve its goal only at the expense of the other. In addition, the experimenters arranged things so that competition would be close, and they biased their decisions to slightly favor one of the groups. Good sportsmanship gradually gave way to accusations and name-calling. By the end of the competition, hostilities were so intense that fights and raids broke out. Both interviews and observations revealed that hostile attitudes and negative stereotypes toward the outgroup developed as ingroup cohesiveness increased. Shared threats increased each group's cohesiveness.

The intergroup conflict also affected the groups' internal structures. For example, the leadership of the Eagles group changed when the former leader was reluctant to participate in the intergroup hostilities. Similarly, a large boy who before the tournament had been considered a bully by his comrades became a hero after the hostilities began. Changes in status thus corresponded to changing group norms.

The experimenters planned a party after the tournament to "let bygones be bygones." The experimenters arranged for the losing group to arrive first, however, and its members took the choicest refreshments. When the winning team arrived, they found only picked-over remains. At this point, hostility and conflict reached a peak with threats, food throwing, and general destruction, which in turn intensified conflict and hostility between the groups.

Intense intergroup conflict and ingroup-outgroup distinctions are not unique to adolescent boys engaged in competitive sports. Brawls between ice-hockey teams on the rink, violence between strikers and strikebreakers, gang rivalry, and rivalry between schools and fraternities are familiar examples. An experiment conducted by Robert Blake and Jane Mouton (1961a) demonstrated intergroup conflict among cohesive adult groups engaged in competition, and the results provided additional insights. Blake and Mouton's subjects were two groups of adults engaged in human-relations training programs. Over a ten- to twelve-hour period of group activity, cohesiveness developed, as demonstrated by members' pride in their group and their ratings of group solidarity. The experimenters then gave both groups the same human-relations problem; they had several hours to arrive at a solution. Each group received the other's solution to discuss, analyze, and compare with its own. Representatives of both groups also met to clarify questions. When the groups felt that they had a clear understanding of one another's positions, the individuals took a test of their factual knowledge of both their own and the other group's solutions.

As in Sherif's experiment, the individuals in Blake and Mouton's experiment believed that their own group had the best chance of winning the competition, and they perceived their solution as the best one. During the stage of discussing both solutions, feelings of competitiveness increased, and each group maximized the value of its own solution and minimized the value of the other group's solution. When the judges made a decision, the losing group reacted with hostility and antagonism both to the judges and to the winning team, and members expressed the belief that the decision was unjustified, in view of "the evidence."

Particularly interesting in this experiment were the results of the test that measured each group's understanding of the other's solution. In spite of the belief among members of each group that they clearly understood the other group's position, their factual knowledge of it was relatively poor. Blake and Mouton suggested that identification with one's own group distorted comprehension of the other group's position. The combination of distortion of the other's position and lack of awareness of that distortion makes intergroup negotiations particularly difficult. Imagine the difficulties involved in negotiating an end to a student strike if the students fully believed that the school administration placed repressive political values over educational values and if the administration believed that the students, spurred by foreign revolutionaries, wanted to take over the school. Neither perception is likely to be accurate, but as long as the two groups maintain these beliefs, conflict is likely to continue.

A second experiment conducted by the same investigators (Blake and Mouton, 1961b) illustrates still another difficulty in reducing intergroup conflict between cohesive groups: When one group's position must be accepted at the expense of the other's, loyalty to one's own position supersedes logic. In this experiment, conducted under conditions similar to the first, representatives of both groups discussed both solutions to decide which was superior. Even though impartial judges were able to decide on a clear-cut winner in every case, only two of sixty-two representatives conceded that the solution of the competing group was superior to that of their own group. The results were comparable even when negotiations were secret or when the negotiators expected to remain anonymous.

Reducing Conflict by Sharing Goals

Does a situation necessarily become hopeless when conflict arises between cohesive groups? The Sherif research team found that the free expression of hostility was certainly not effective in reducing hostilities. Name-calling, food throwing, and threats merely served to increase rather than decrease the hostilities. Sherif and his colleagues also attempted to bring the groups into contact under the pleasant circumstances of a movie and a particularly good meal. This, too, was ineffective; in fact, hostilities increased somewhat. In one of their experiments, these researchers introduced a common enemy by inviting an outside group to compete with a team that was composed of members of both camp groups. Although this factor succeeded in reducing hostilities temporarily, strong ingroup preferences persisted.

One method—the creation of *superordinate goals*—reduced conflict between the groups and produced harmony. It has proven effective many times since. Superordinate goals supersede the independent goals of each group and cannot be achieved without mutual cooperation. Sherif and his associates created a series of superordinate goals by contriving several situations. A supposed breakdown in the water supply system meant that unless the boys who had formed cohesive but hostile groups jointly located and fixed the difficulty, they would all have to leave camp. Another time, two groups had to pool their money in order to rent a movie they all wanted to see. One morning two groups took a trip to a lake, and the truck that was to be used for picking up lunch in town would not start. Boys from both groups pushed and pulled until the truck started. As a result of cooperative efforts such as these, intergroup hostilities gradually waned. Group boundaries became less rigid, members of the groups began to intermingle and share their resources, and friendships developed between individuals. At the end of the camp session, members of both groups requested to ride home on the same bus.

INTENSIVE PSYCHOLOGICAL GROUPS

The study of groups has been important to social psychologists for many years. In the past decade, however, people from all walks of life have taken interest in a particular type of small group—the intensive psychological group. Encounter groups, T-groups, sensitivity-training groups, marathons, and human-relations workshops are all types of intensive groups. Distinctions among some of the more common types are represented in Table 14.1. Although the goals of these groups generally involve promoting personal growth, their emphases vary. Some stress sensitivity and social perceptiveness; some focus on authentic experiences, emphasizing openness and confrontation; others attempt to foster creativity; still others focus on motivational or cognitive changes (Gibb, 1972). Groups can consist of total strangers or of individuals who work together in organizational settings such as schools, hospitals, businesses, and rehabilitative centers. Some meet for a short time each week over long periods, some for six to eight hours a day for two- to three-week periods, and others for intensive weekends. Intensive groups use a wide variety of techniques. Many groups are totally unstructured, although some rely heavily on programed experiences, such as role playing, interaction exercises, and training in specific human-relations skills; others explore experiences such as body movement, finger painting, meditation, nudity, and nonverbal encounters. These latter experiences are usually tried in groups focusing on creativity and are intended to reduce inhibitions and fears and to increase spontaneity and communication. There is, however, little documented evidence that such experiences are effective (Gibb, 1972).

In spite of their wide variation, intensive groups share common features. They are usually small enough (between six and twenty members) to allow a great deal of face-to-face interaction; they encourage openness, honesty, self-disclosure, and intense emotional expression; and they focus on the dynamics of the interaction that occur within the group, on each member's behavior in the here-and-now (American Psychiatric Association, 1970).

The group processes already discussed also develop in intensive groups. Norms emerge, patterns of interaction form, and cohesiveness develops. Two distinguishing features of intensive groups are the *intensity* and *short duration* of personal relationships. According to Kurt Back (1972), the most striking features of these groups are the degree to which their members come to care for one another and the importance that they come to have for one another during the group's short lifetime. These short-term but intense relationships become the *medium* through which personal growth potentially develops. For many people, however, the groups become an end in themselves. Many people admittedly join intensive groups in a search for closeness with others, because intimacy is missing in their daily lives. It has been speculated, in fact, that intensive groups are popular because they offer people in our rootless modern society a way to establish meaningful relationships. Carl Rogers (1967), one of the forerunners of the group-encounter movement, suggests that the ability to develop short-term, intense relationships that participants can easily relinquish will become necessary for psychic survival in our highly mobile society.

The short-term intensive relationships that develop in preplanned groups have received bitter criticisms from others. Some psychologists, Ludwig Lefebre (1963), for example, maintain that the group situation creates artificial familiarity. He suggests that the individual within the group does not relate to specific persons, as is generally thought, but to anonymous group members. This type of relating may seem to be a good

Table 14.1 Types of Intensive Psychological Groups

GROUP	EMPHASIS
T-group	Originally tended to emphasize human-relations *skills* but has become much broader in its approach.
Encounter group (or basic encounter group)	Tends to emphasize personal growth and development and improvement in interpersonal communication through direct experiences.
Sensitivity-training group	May resemble either T-group or encounter group.
Task-oriented group	Widely used in industry; focuses on the task of the group in its interpersonal context.
Sensory-awareness group, body-awareness group, body-movement group	Tends to emphasize physical awareness and physical expression through movement, spontaneous dance, and the like.
Creativity workshop	Focuses on creative expression through various art media.
Organizational-development group	Primarily aimed at leadership growth ability.
Team-building group	Used in industry to develop more closely knit and effective working teams.
Gestalt group	Emphasis on a Gestalt therapeutic approach where an expert therapist focuses on one individual at a time but from a diagnostic and therapeutic point of view.
Synanon group or "game"	Developed in the treatment of drug addicts by Synanon; tends to emphasize almost violent attack on the defenses of the participants.

coping device in a society that is heavily influenced by roles, but it may also prevent the participants in an intensive group from discovering their inner selves and perpetuate reliance on their social roles.

Group Processes: The Usual Amidst the Extraordinary

Although there are many different types of intensive groups, leaders of such groups have been impressed by the similarity of events from one group to another. Regardless of the particular focus of the group, its particular composition, or its leader, recognizable sequences seem to emerge. However spontaneous people may feel about their behavior, the phases through which groups progress seem almost preprogramed.

Bruce Tuckman (1965) has identified four sequential stages through which intensive groups seem to progress. In the first stage, members test the situation and wish to be dependent on the facilitator; they realize that the group is largely in their hands and are unsure how to proceed. To many, the situation is unique and frustrating. The second stage is one of conflict; members of the group vie with one another and with the facilitator for control. The group enters the third stage when members establish norms and values and build cohesiveness. Group cohesiveness paves the way for group productivity, which members try to accomplish in the fourth stage.

The fundamental processes that characterize these groups are familiar. A high degree of cohesiveness gradually develops; cohesiveness is facilitated by the nature of the group's task and the focus on openness and self-disclosure. Openness itself facilitates attraction among individuals. In addition, a set of norms emerges that varies from group to group. Robert Luke (1972), in his sample of sensitivity-training groups, found that members consistently developed and highly valued four norms: *acceptance, feedback, awareness* of one's own responses to others and theirs in return, and *spontaneous expression* of feelings and emotions. Luke found that, although all his groups developed these norms and came to value them highly, groups that were guided by active leaders developed them faster than did groups in which leaders used their influence less. Groups with more passive leaders relied more heavily on traditional structure, such as establishing group goals and tasks, in their early phases. The more actively involved leaders apparently provided strong role models and used more initiative in shaping group norms.

Groups differ greatly in the ways in which these highly valued norms are expressed. Members of some groups aggressively confront one another, whereas communication is more gentle and supportive in others. In some

Figure 14.11 Although research has identified developmental stages and norms that characterize most intensive groups, there is wide variation in groups' expressions of them. This sequence of photographs was taken in a group that encouraged confrontation and strong emotional outbursts. Shown are two members aggressively confronting one another. This group would stand in sharp contrast to one characterized by supportiveness and gentle prodding.

V Behavior in Groups

groups, members attempt to deny one another privacy; elsewhere they respect individuals' rights to withhold feelings if they so desire. Other norms also develop, such as that governing how much members talk about their past experiences. The members of some groups more actively try to change one another's behavior and encourage experimentation. In some groups, members become hostile toward the facilitator—an authorized, planted leader—and feel that they can do better on their own. In others, the members actively challenge societal norms governing touching, authority, status, and so on and create norms in contradiction to these.

As the group interacts, a group structure also develops. Informal leaders emerge in any group, particularly if it has a facilitator who is not very active. Some individuals will be more dominant, will be able to keep the group directed toward its objectives of self-exploration and meaningful interaction, and will respond to the personal needs of the other members. Other positions will also develop. One individual may become the gadfly, or aggressive attacker; another the defender; another the group's scapegoat; another the one who always leads the group off its course; and still another the predominantly silent member, who responds only when spoken to. Some members will have more influence than others on the group's direction; some will be more active in confronting one another; and some will be more helpful in suggesting alternatives to those seeking choices.

Apparently, all intensive groups must deal with a series of key issues—issues that are relevant to almost all close relationships. The participants must first *define* the nature of their existence: Who are they? Why are they together? Where are they going? The problem of *leadership* must then be solved: Who is going to exert what kind of control? The problem of *group norms* arises simultaneously: What sorts of standard behavior patterns are the members going to adopt in order to make themselves intelligible and predictable to one another? Then the problem of *attraction* becomes central: To what degree can the participants invest their emotions in one another? These problems confront all of us as we attempt to relate with one another.

Why Join an Intensive Group?

"How," you may ask, "can I personally grow from establishing temporary intensive relationships? What can I possibly learn about myself from a group of strangers?" Imagine a group in which the norms are openness, warmth, and support; feelings are explored and shared; and the interactions of members are in center focus. The participants are encouraged to get in touch with their feelings and to find out how others react to them: "Are my feelings acceptable?" "Will I be accepted in spite of them?" "Do others have such feelings?" Additionally, the individuals can observe themselves and others in interaction and can receive immediate feedback about the ways in which others perceive them and how their behavior affects others. For example, one member might learn that others find her threatening because her behavior seems to reflect an attitude of superiority. She does not actually feel this superiority; it is just her way of keeping "one up" on others so she can avoid being shot down. Another member may realize that his self-centered attitude turns others off. And still another may find that people get impatient when she puts herself down and agrees with others so that they will like her.

The process of giving feedback is helpful. As many individuals report, they did not know that they could become so sensitive to others. Others are surprised to learn that they *can* express anger or hurt or disappointment; these are sometimes new experiences.

Perhaps the most important effect of the intensive-group experience is that it facilitates desired changes in behavior. After an individual has become aware of the impact he has on others and of others' perceptions of him, he can elect to maintain his mode of responding (at least he is now aware of it), or he can attempt to change it. Changing one's behavior is by far the more difficult of these two options. On his own, the person may not be sure how to go about changing his behavior; he may be afraid of making blunders with those individuals with whom he must interact daily; he may never be sure how successful he is in his change. The group situation can provide him with a small-scale society in which he can try out new behaviors. In a sense, it can provide a kind of sheltered workshop in which the individual can receive suggestions about how to implement desired changes, immediate feedback about their effectiveness, and support for his efforts. In this way, the individual may receive some reinforcement for new behavior before he tries it out in the "real world," in which blunders may have serious consequences for him.

The Encounter Group: Sham or Salvation?

Personal reports of participants suggest that the encounter-group experience typically is beneficial and results in significant changes in self-awareness and the ability to relate to others. However, personal reports have built-in biases. Not all participants respond to questionnaires, and those who do are usually the most enthusiastic about the experience. Individuals who have gained little or who have experienced negative consequences are less likely to invest additional time and effort in responding to questionnaires. Participants may also overestimate the effects of the group experience because of the great amount of time, effort, and money they have invested in it. However, some studies—that by Marvin Dunnette and John Campbell (1968), for example—have revealed that people outside the group have perceived changes in participants after their group experiences—changes such as increased sensitivity, consideration, and communication skills. Other studies—for example, Steven Jaffe and Donald Scherl's (1969)—have reported incidents of psychotic breakdown following encounter-group experiences. The individual's previous need for psychiatric assistance is a significant factor, but a group's organizers seldom ask about potential members' psychiatric backgrounds. After reviewing the available literature on the outcomes of group experiences, the American Psychiatric Association (1970) concluded that "no generalization may be made save that, in the hands of some leaders, the group experience can be dangerous for some participants. The more powerful the emotions evoked, the less clinically perspicacious and responsible the leader, the more psychologically troubled the group member, then the greater the risk of adverse outcome."

The competence of the leader is a crucial variable in the success of any group. Unfortunately, with the increasing popularity of the group movement, there are numerous self-styled leaders who lack training in conducting groups, who lack appreciation of people's highly specific individual needs, and who lack the sensitivity, subtlety, and insight to handle difficulties that may arise for particular members. Often amateurs lead groups that emphasize nonverbal experiences and confrontations, because these types of groups seem to require the least skill and sophistication of leaders to stimulate members. But these techniques require a highly skilled and sophisticated leader for the outcome to be a positive learning experience (Birnbaum, 1969), and amateur leadership often magnifies the dangers to the individual.

In addition to competence, *styles* of leaders vary greatly, and research suggests that a leader's style influences the type of experience members will have. Morton Lieberman, Irvin Yalom, and Matthew Miles (1972), for example, compared the outcomes of group experiences that were led by two types of leaders—*energizers* and *providers.* Energizers are strong, authoritarian leaders who impose a great deal of structure. They confront and challenge group members but at the same time are self-revealing and caring. The providers offer information and ideas as well as a great deal of loving and caring but do not impose structure or their own philosophies on the participants. Lieberman and his colleagues measured the participants' estimates of personal gain, self-esteem, and mental health before the group experience, immediately afterward, and six months later. They found that groups led by both types of leaders yielded a large number of individuals who believed that they had learned a great deal from the experience and whose claims were corroborated by either their peers or the leader. In groups led by energizers, members were more likely to have *peak experiences* and were more enthusiastic about their personal growth immediately after the experience. However, after six months their estimates of personal gain had declined significantly. Those in groups led by providers, on the other hand, felt a consistent amount of growth and benefit throughout the six-month follow-up period. Furthermore, in groups led by energizers, the dropout rate was higher, member self-esteem and level of mental health decreased, and participants tended to look less favorably on others.

The compatibility of the individual member with the *techniques* employed by the leader is also an important determinant of the experience's

Figure 14.12 Intensive psychological groups sometimes focus on techniques involving sensory awareness and bodily experience rather than cognitive awareness. Various exercises such as those shown here that have been devised to heighten physical awareness and physical expression often result in intensely positive experiences, if well led, and can provide therapeutic as well as self-actualizing experiences.

effect on that person. All individuals do not benefit similarly from an unstructured verbal group, from a group emphasizing structured exercises, from a group conducted in the nude, or from one encouraging total physical expression. Whereas one method may be beneficial for a particular person with particular needs, the same method may be a waste of time for a second and detrimental to a third. Perhaps unfortunately, the individual is usually left with the responsibility of checking on the competence of the facilitator, the techniques the facilitator uses and their purposes, and of evaluating their potential for his or her own personal growth.

Most people who join encounter groups have few criteria for choosing a competent facilitator and the right kind of group for their needs. Although the interrelation between individual, facilitator, techniques, and other group members is complicated, intensive psychological groups do have the *potential* to foster personal growth in their participants.

Because so much of our lives are spent in the company of others, it is important to understand group processes and structures. Intensive groups, which serve both as social microcosms and as workshops for personal growth, offer only one pathway to understanding group structure and processes. The rest of this unit probes some other aspects of group structures and processes.

SUMMARY

A group is made of more than two persons who are interdependent on one or more dimensions and who perceive the group as having an ongoing existence apart from their membership in it. Almost by definition, we spend much of our daily lives participating in some type of group activity.

We participate in groups both because we are attracted to members of a group and its goals and because it can satisfy our social needs. Affiliation with others can help us to validate our behavior in ambiguous situations and can help us to gain clarity about our world. The presence of others can also serve to reduce our anxiety.

A great deal of uniformity is generally evident among group members; it stems not only from selective membership and similar environmental forces on members but also from the formation of group norms. Group norms—the agreed-upon, acceptable, expected behavior and attitudes for members—can be either implicit or explicit. Norms seem to serve two purposes: they can help members validate beliefs in ambiguous areas, and they can ensure the maintenance of the group. Adherence to group norms brings acceptance from the group, and deviation results in some degree of rejection. An individual may comply to the norms of a membership group only if it is necessary, but he or she will internalize reference-group norms.

Within both formal and informal groups, members develop patterns of relating to one another, which stabilize over the course of interaction. These patterns are the group's structure and can be seen as a combination of the norms the group develops, the personality traits of members, and situational factors.

One position that almost always emerges in a group is that of leader; this person has the most influence over the group. Initial research on leadership investigated the personal characteristics that "make" a leader. Because of a lack of any consistent findings, a structural approach became popular. In this approach, leadership was seen as merely another position in the group that could be filled by any member who could best help the group to achieve its objectives. Unfortunately, this situational approach did not consider the complexity of leadership. Some social psychologists now conceive of leadership as an ongoing *process,* a transaction between leader and followers in a specific situation. It involves a two-way influence relationship in which the leader influences and is influenced.

Cohesiveness is the "we" feeling of a group. Members of highly cohesive groups are more attracted to and sensitive toward one another, are more satisfied with their group membership and activities, feel more generally secure, interact more frequently and freely with one another, are more effective in achieving group goals, have more power over one another, and are less tolerant of deviant members than are members of less cohesive groups. Cohesiveness usually increases conformity in a group, and conformity can make it easier to achieve group goals. Both cohesiveness and attraction between group members can be increased by cooperative activity, success in group endeavors, sharing a high status, and undergoing shared threat. Cohesiveness also has a dark side, however. The members' increasing loyalty to their own group often magnifies the differences between their own and other groups, creating ingroup-outgroup distinctions. Perceptual distortion typically follows, in which the ingroup's achievements are perceived as superior and the outgroup's as inferior. Intergroup conflict is frequently the consequence, particularly under competitive conditions, but conflict can be reduced by the existence of *superordinate goals.*

Intensive groups undergo processes similar to those of other informal groups. They are distinguished, however, by the intensity and short duration of the personal relationships that their members develop. All intensive groups pass through a specific series of stages, develop a variety of specific roles, and deal with a series of key issues. In this framework members potentially achieve their goals of personal growth. The nature and duration of the results of encounter-group experience vary according to the leader's competence, style, and technique. Despite many potential hazards, the intensive psychological group also has a great potential for encouraging personal growth.

SUGGESTED READINGS

Back, Kurt W. *Beyond Words: The Story of Sensitivity Training and the Encounter Movement.* New York: Russell Sage Foundation, 1972. (Excerpted in "The Group Can Comfort But It Can't Cure," *Psychology Today,* 6 (1972), 28–35.)

Birnbaum, Max. "Sense About Sensitivity Training," *Saturday Review,* 52 (1969), 82–83.

Cartwright, Dorwin, and Alvin Zander (eds.). *Group Dynamics: Research & Theory.* 3rd ed. New York: Harper & Row, 1968.

Schachter, Stanley. *The Psychology of Affiliation.* Stanford, Calif.: Stanford University Press, 1959.

Shaw, Marvin. *Group Dynamics: The Psychology of Small Group Behavior.* New York: McGraw-Hill, 1971.

Stoller, Frederick H. "The Long Weekend," *Psychology Today,* 1 (1967), 28–33.

Vertreace, Walter, and Carolyn Simmons. "Attempted Leadership in the Leaderless Group Discussion as a Function of Motivation and Ego Involvement," *Journal of Personality and Social Psychology,* 19 (1971), 285–289.

15

Group Decisions & Conflicts

MODERN SOCIETY IS RUN largely by committees. Governments have thousands of committees, commissions, and panels. The activities of labor groups, management groups, professional societies, and even the smallest social clubs are usually carried out by specialized committees or work groups. We seem to assume that a group of people can work more efficiently on most tasks, yielding better results than can any individual operating alone. Is the assumption always correct?

You have probably faced occasional problems, perhaps assignments for school or personal dilemmas, that you desperately wished you did not have to solve alone. It may have seemed that having someone else to work with would have had many advantages: you could have pooled your knowledge, built on each other's ideas and suggestions, shared the work, and validated your ideas through consensus.

Think, now, of another situation. Your club is planning a dance, and you are on the committee that will make all the arrangements. At the first committee meeting you feel confident that by the end of the meeting your group will be well on the way to organizing a really good event. Everyone on the committee is a good worker, and everyone shares the same goal—having the best possible dance. But somehow, things do not seem to go as smoothly as expected. There are different opinions about the band, the location, and the charging of admission. Everybody wants to get the entertainment and nobody wants to get the refreshments. Eventually you decide that if only you had been given the assignment to handle by yourself, you could have had the whole thing worked out in no time at all.

Are two or more heads really better than one? Or do too many cooks spoil the broth? These questions, which have interested social psycholo-

Figure 15.1 Lost on the Moon.
You can get a feeling for the comparative
merits of group versus individual decision
making by confronting this task first as
an individual and then in a group of four
to seven classmates. You can compare
your solutions with the ideal
solution agreed on by experts at
the National Aeronautics and Space
Administration (NASA), which
appears on page 492.

A Test

*Your spaceship has just crash-landed on the
moon. You were scheduled to rendezvous with
a mother ship 200 miles away on the lighted
surface of the moon, but the rough landing has
ruined your ship and destroyed all the equipment
on board, except for the fifteen items listed below.*

*Your crew's survival depends on reaching the
mother ship, so you must choose the most critical
items available for the 200-mile trip. Your task
is to rank the fifteen items in terms of their
importance for survival. Place number one
by the most important item, number two by the
second most important, and so on through
number fifteen, the least important.*

_____*Box of matches*
_____*Food concentrate*
_____*Fifty feet of nylon rope*
_____*Parachute silk*
_____*Solar-powered portable heating unit*
_____*Two .45-caliber pistols*
_____*One case of dehydrated milk*
_____*Two 100-pound tanks of oxygen*
_____*Stellar map (of the moon's constellation)*
_____*Self-inflating life raft*
_____*Magnetic compass*
_____*Five gallons of water*
_____*Signal flares*
_____*First-aid kit containing injection needles*
_____*Solar-powered FM receiver-transmitter*

gists for more than forty years, become especially important when, for
example, a situation requires the government of a superpower to make a
decision that will have life-or-death consequences for millions of people.
Would the quality of a decision be better if the leader arrived at it alone or if
it emerged from a group of leaders and advisers?

SOLVING PROBLEMS IN GROUPS

By simple probability, several people working independently on a problem
sometimes have a better chance of solving it than does a lone person; the
greater the number of potential solutions, the better the chance that a good
or correct one will be among them. Interaction between group members is
the essential ingredient of a group situation. In the course of making a
collective decision, people affect one another's behavior and decision-
making processes. Consequently, this interaction affects the group's final
decision. Individuals in a group must try to produce their best ideas and
must also reach a collective agreement within the group—either unanimity
(agreement of all) or consensus (agreement of a majority).

What makes for a successful group? Ideally, research focuses not only
on the quality of the decision but also on the quality of interaction between
the individuals who participate in the group. Several factors determine
whether or not a group will be productive:

1. The task—what the group is doing
2. The size—how many members in the group
3. Group composition—who the members are
4. Leadership—who is leading
5. Group structure—how the group members relate to one another

This chapter deals first with these specific points and later with other
phenomena that also have considerable effects on group success:

6. The riskiness of group decisions
7. The effects of conflict

The Task

Several specific kinds of decision-making tasks have been investigated by
psychologists. Sometimes a task involves a problem that has one (or more)
correct and determinable solution; thus, algebra problems and crossword
puzzles are examples of *determinate tasks.* Other tasks may have many
potential solutions, none of which is specifically "correct"—although some
solutions may be more practical or economical than others. Examples of
these *indeterminate tasks* include deciding whether or not an applicant
should be admitted to college or one's manufacturing firm should launch a
new product line. Determinate tasks include the situations that are cus-
tomarily considered as "problem solving," and indeterminate tasks include
those that are usually thought of as "decision making."

These two broad classes of decision-making tasks can have very different effects on group processes. Only recently, psychologists have become
aware of this distinction and have attempted to discover the ways in which
the two types of tasks differ in their effects.

The type of task apparently can affect group performance. In a relatively determinate task, the collective solution may reflect the ability of the
group's most competent member, according to Ernest Hall, Jane Mouton,
and Robert Blake (1963). In an early study, these researchers had subjects

watch the first part of *Twelve Angry Men,* a film about a murder trial and the suspenseful deliberations of a jury trying to reach a verdict. Each subject was then to attempt to predict, individually, what would happen in the rest of the film. Later, the subjects as a group were asked to discuss the film and to make a collective prediction about what would occur in the remainder of the film. Some individual predictions were accurate and some were inaccurate, but the group prediction usually followed the most accurate individual predictions.

Harold Kelley and John Thibaut (1969) have suggested two criteria that would increase the likelihood of a group's decision being as effective as that of the most competent group member. First, the problem should be solvable in relatively few steps, so that the best member can reach a decision in the group setting as well as he or she might have alone. A comparable decision should be possible in spite of any negative effects of the group, such as distraction. Second, it should be easy for the best member to convince the rest of the group that his or her solution is correct. Clearly, then, a determinate task would be more amenable to this solution process than would an indeterminate task.

When a group is faced with a fairly complex task, which requires several partial solutions before a final decision is made, decision making may surpass the performance possible of any individual member—particularly if the solutions to the problem require specialized abilities or knowledge and each group member possesses a different but complementary ability relevant to the task. Then, capabilities can be pooled. Obviously, a group with abilities that are well distributed among its members is likely to perform a complex task better than is any of the individuals operating alone. For example, John Dashiell (1935) compared the reports of individual jury members, made after they had heard the testimony of witnesses to an accident, with the report made by the jury after its group discussion. Although fewer facts revealed about the accident were listed in the group report than in any individual report (because the jury was required to reach a unanimous decision on each point), the overall *accuracy* of

Figure 15.2 A highly complex operation like the NASA Manned Spacecraft Center in Houston, Texas, could not function without the specialized knowledge and abilities, division of labor, many partial solutions, pooled resources, and interaction that groups afford. Because of these group assets, this NASA team can be responsible for tracking spacecraft and making rapid calculations and decisions should anything go wrong with flight plans.

the jury's collective references to testimony was greater than that of any individual report.

Group decisions are not always as good or better than the best judgments of individual members. Complications may arise, for example, when consistency of strategy is required during several stages of a task. According to Kelley and Thibaut (1969), a *multiple-stage task* is a problem that requires a series of steps to its solution, with each step dependent on previous solutions. Because a consistent strategy is needed to solve the problem, group members may interfere with, rather than complement, one another's efforts. As a result, the performance of a group may be lower than the level of the most competent individual member. An example was reported by James Davis and Frank Restle (1963), who also found that groups working through long problems requiring sequential solutions had difficulty in identifying their best members. All members tended to make comments, whether or not the comments were worthwhile.

Group Size

Being a member of a crowd can sometimes be a stimulating, even thrilling, experience. Anyone who has attended a football game, a revival meeting, or a political demonstration or has seen newsreels of the crowds Hitler

Figure 15.3 The ideal solution, suggested by NASA experts, to the Lost on the Moon problem posed on page 490. To arrive at your score, add the absolute differences between each of your rankings and NASA's. The best possible score is 0 and the worst is 112. Twenty-five percent of the experimental groups that have tackled this problem performed better than their best members did individually. When groups received instructions in how to reach a consensus through creative conflict resolution, 75 percent scored better than individuals. The individual and group scores for sixteen instructed groups are shown here.

Items	NASA's Reasoning	NASA's Ranks
Box of matches	No oxygen on moon to sustain flame; virtually worthless	15
Food concentrate	Efficient means of supplying energy requirements	4
Fifty feet of nylon rope	Useful in scaling cliffs, tying injured together	6
Parachute silk	Protection from sun's rays	8
Solar-powered portable heating unit	Not needed unless on dark side	13
Two .45-caliber pistols	Possible means of self-propulsion	11
One case of dehydrated milk	Bulkier duplication of food concentrate	12
Two 100-pound tanks of oxygen	Most pressing survival need	1
Stellar map (of the moon's constellation)	Primary means of navigation	3
Self-inflating life raft	CO_2 bottle in military raft may be used for propulsion	9
Magnetic compass	Magnetic field on moon is not polarized; worthless for navigation	14
Five gallons of water	Replacement for tremendous liquid loss on lighted side	2
Signal flares	Distress signal when mother ship is sighted	10
First-aid kit containing injection needles	Needles for vitamins, medicines, etc. will fit special aperture in NASA space suits	7
Solar-powered FM receiver-transmitter	For communication with mother ship; but FM requires line-of-sight transmission and short ranges	5

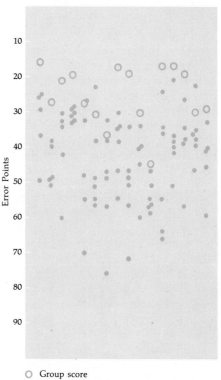

○ Group score
● Individual score

Scoring for individuals:
0–25 = excellent
26–32 = good
33–45 = average
46–55 = fair
56–70 = poor
71–112 = very poor, suggests possible faking or use of earth-bound logic

thrilled knows the power of what Gustave Le Bon (1960) called the "collective mind," whether as an insider or as a dispassionate observer. (Le Bon's and other approaches to collective behavior are the topics of Chapter 17.)

Taking part in the activities of a small group can be equally satisfying in different ways. Quality of decision making can be affected greatly by the size of a group. Research has verified that large groups differ from small groups in several important ways, which are reflected in the interaction and behavior of the individual members.

In a small group, all members usually know one another and communicate directly. To some extent, all members are involved in the decision-making activity of the group. The members of a small group usually feel close to one another and typically try to attain unanimous agreement on decisions. In larger groups, on the other hand, fewer members hold central positions, fewer communicate with all other members, and fewer are involved in decision making. Only a small number of members occupy positions that enable them to communicate with all others in the group, and these few members are usually the only ones who are directly involved in decision making. The large group is likely to be less cohesive and to wield fewer pressures toward uniformity among members. (A thorough discussion of group norms, conformity, and cohesiveness is provided in Chapter 14.) Furthermore, members of larger groups tend to remain strangers and to rely on impersonal means of communication. Much of the communication between members of a large group may take the form of written notices or memos rather than face-to-face discussion. The business organization and the bureaucratic governmental agency are notable for their use of relatively impersonal communication. (This and other facets of organizations are explored in Chapter 16.)

As a result, larger groups often experience (1) lower member satisfaction with the group and their task in it (Porter and Lawler, 1965), (2) more complaints from members, (3) a greater likelihood that the group will break down into subgroups, and (4) increased difficulty in reaching consensus.

The findings cited so far have been based on *descriptive* research (Cartwright and Zander, 1968). What is needed now is more direct experimentation that will provide a better understanding of the effects of group size. Dorwin Cartwright and Alvin Zander have proposed two questions that experimental research may be able to answer: (1) Which group functions are helped and which are hindered by either large or small group size? (2) Why does group size have certain specific effects?

Theoretical answers that are based only partly on experimental work have been suggested by Barry Collins and Harold Guetzkow (1964). Their approach centers on the differences in characteristics of the task with which a group must work. When the task's solution requires that the efforts of members be closely coordinated and that several proposals be integrated into a single answer, group membership should be small (about four or five members). A successful completion of this type of task would not be facilitated by the wide range of alternatives and the necessity of eliminating many bad ideas that a large membership involves, suggest Collins and Guetzkow. Smallness also minimizes the problems of organization within the group and of time wasted through duplication of effort.

For other kinds of tasks, however, Collins and Guetzkow propose that larger groups are more effective. For example, tasks that require a quantitative estimate in which individuals are likely to make random errors (for example, estimating the temperature of a room) or tasks that demand creativity or memory should be performed more effectively with increasing size of the group—up to the point at which duplication of effort and problems of organization begin to reduce effectiveness.

Social Facilitation. The greater the size of the group, the more people there are who potentially can interact with any particular group member. Although a large number of people may interfere with the decision-making process when the task is complex, it has been shown that the mere presence of others can enhance individual performance. The term *social facilitation* is used to refer to the positive effects of the presence of others. The opposite, or negative, effects on performance might be called "social inhibition" or "social interference." Both the positive and negative aspects of the presence of others exert important influences on group decision making.

Psychologists have described two effects of the presence of others: *audience effects* and *co-action effects* (Zajonc, 1966). Audience effects influence an individual's performance when he or she is working alone on a task but can feel the presence of other persons who are watching without actually participating. Audiences influence not only speakers; they also affect, for example, a dancer giving a recital or a pole-vaulter who performs in a stadium. Co-action effects influence an individual's performance when others are present who are also working on the same task, either individually or collectively. Each individual in a group may feel as if he or she is working in the presence of others, even though the others are also absorbed in their respective activities.

Research on audience effects has reported somewhat contradictory findings. Some investigators have found that the presence of an audience has the effect of social facilitation and that it improves the performance of subjects considerably (Bergum and Lehr, 1963; Dashiell, 1930). Other research findings, however, have indicated that the presence of an audience interferes with performance (Husband, 1931; Pessin, 1933).

Research on the effects of co-action has also produced conflicting results. However, many of the investigators have used nonhuman subjects, and the degree to which findings with animals can be generalized to human behavior is difficult to assess. In an early study conducted with human subjects, Floyd Allport (1920) found that people performed better in the presence of others who were working on the same word-association or multiplication task, although social facilitation did not occur when tasks involved judgment or problem solving.

A Little Help From My Friends. One of the most adequate explanations of these conflicting results has been offered by Robert Zajonc (1965), who concluded that whether or not performance will be enhanced by the presence of others depends on the workings of an internal mechanism, arousal, and also on the nature of the task in which the subject is absorbed. Zajonc hypothesized that the presence of other persons increases an individual's general level of arousal. Research has demonstrated that increased arousal tends to increase the individual's tendency to make his or her dominant, or strongest, responses (Spence, 1956). That is, when other persons are present, an individual working on a task will tend to make those responses that are strongest in his or her behavioral repertoire. Zajonc therefore theorizes that the presence of others serves to increase the likelihood of the individual's dominant responses.

A dominant response may be either correct or incorrect. If, for example, you were learning to play the flute, your dominant or most likely

Figure 15.4 An individual's performance is influenced by an audience, but the effect can be either positive or negative. The presence of an audience increases the individual's general level of arousal, which then increases the probability of the response that is dominant in the person's repertoire for that situation. If the response is correct, the performance is improved; if incorrect, it is hampered. How would you expect an audience to affect the performance of The Who rock group, at their practice sessions (*below*) and at a rock festival (*opposite*)?

responses would be wrong, disharmonious notes—or the incorrect responses. Zajonc's research has led him to conclude that a person who is asked to learn new material or to perform a not-yet-mastered task in the presence of others is likely to make more incorrect responses than he or she would if the task were performed in isolation. As a novice flutist, you will probably play more poorly in a recital than you do alone at home. After a task is well learned, however, the correct response becomes the dominant one. Therefore, after you have mastered the flute, the presence of an audience is likely to increase the probability of correct responses, and your performance will be better than it is when you are practicing alone. This explanation can account for the fact that investigators of social facilitation have sometimes found one result, sometimes the other. In both familiar and unfamiliar tasks, the presence of others will raise the subject's arousal level and increase dominant responses. In one case, the dominant responses are correct; in the other, they are incorrect.

In terms of group decision making, it would seem that when the problem area is unfamiliar, people will be likely to make more mistakes when they are working in a group than when they are working alone. As a member of a newly formed committee, you may find yourself making statements that are quite unlike the ideas you would be able to devise while

sitting quietly alone in your room. As your knowledge of the committee's work increases, however, you may find that your best ideas occur during the group's meetings. When a group is working on a familiar kind of task or problem, the fact that the individuals are working in a social environment, in the presence of others, should facilitate and improve the individuals' and therefore the total group's performance.

Group Composition

How do you feel about the groups to which you belong? Does one seem active and interesting, low in key but warm and friendly, whereas others seem dull and impersonal? The group's composition—the people who belong to it—may account for these differences, which are reflected in the ways in which problems are solved. The composition of a group may vary in several ways. And these variations can affect the interaction among group members and the effectiveness of group decision making.

Homogeneity Versus Heterogeneity. A group is composed of the personal characteristics of its members. The composition of a group may be homo-

---

DIFFERENCES THAT IMPROVE DECISIONS

ONE OF THE OUTSTANDING proponents of the superiority of heterogeneous groups has been L. Richard Hoffman. In research he and Norman Maier conducted with a class of University of Michigan students, groups were formed with students who were either similar to (homogeneous) or different from (heterogeneous) one another on personality-test scores. Groups were given diverse types of problems to work on, and the question was whether the heterogeneous or the homogeneous groups would do better. In addition to the quality of group decisions, personal satisfaction with the group was also rated. Problems the groups faced included these:

1. *Mined Road Problem:* The group must formulate a solution to a warfare problem of finding the best way for five men to cross a heavily mined road.

2. *The Painter-Inspector Argument:* Group members play the roles of painter, inspector, foreman, shop steward, and worker who applies primers. In this exercise, the group's task is to try to resolve a conflict between the painter and the inspector. The best solution requires changing the basic organizational structure that precipitated the argument and not just centering on the interpersonal antagonism itself.

3. *Student Assistance Fund:* Each group member plays a needy student applying for a scholarship. The problem requires that

group decisions be reached on which members should and should not receive funds. The investigators found that their experimental sessions became tense as the students pleaded, cringed, or vented their wrath. This problem was designed to test the different depths of antagonism that might be displayed by similar and dissimilar groups.

4. *The Point-Distribution Caper:* This is a clever extension of the preceding problem, which involved only role playing. Toward the last of the group sessions, just following the return of a group examination, each group was given nineteen test points that the members could distribute among themselves as they saw fit. Each member knew the number of points he or she needed to receive each grade. Would the homogeneous groups distribute the points differently from the heterogeneous ones? Would there be bloodshed or tears? This case was used to evaluate fairness in the groups.

The findings indicate that groups with heterogeneous composition were most successful in terms of the quality of their decisions. Two major reasons for this success seem to be: (1) When people of relatively equal status (such as college students) have different perspectives and values, they are able

geneous or heterogeneous with respect to a particular personality trait. If it is homogeneous, all its members possess a specific personality trait to a similar degree; for example, all its members may score high (or all may score low) on the *F* scale, a measure of authoritarianism (see Chapter 7). If, however, some members of the group score high and some score low and some score at intermediate levels, then that group would be heterogeneous with regard to authoritarianism.

The influence of heterogeneity and homogeneity on the productivity and effectiveness of groups has been experimentally investigated, with somewhat contradictory results. Although it may seem logical to assume that you could do a better job when working with others who are like yourself, this assumption does not always prove to be true. It is not possible to conclude that homogeneous groups always perform better—or invariably worse—than do heterogeneous groups.

Barry Collins and Harold Guetzkow (1964) conclude that heterogeneity has two effects. First, it tends to increase interpersonal difficulties within the group. Groups composed of people with different personalities or attitudes experience more conflict, less satisfaction, and less cohesiveness.

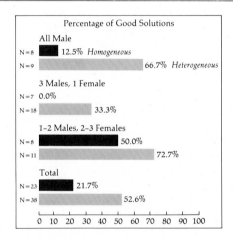

The graph shows the percentage of solutions that were above the median in quality by sex and type of group. Each group contained four people.

Apparently, combining the resources of the two sexes and of different personalities strengthens a group's problem-solving capacities.

There were no differences in the satisfaction members derived from the different groups studied; the most important source of happiness for all members was the feeling of having an impact on a group solution, regardless of the quality of that solution. The members of both types of groups were equally satisfied with their group experiences.

These data suggest that more than token change in representation is needed in *any* decision-making body if novel and sophisticated solutions to society's problems can be expected to emerge—whether the decision-making body be the board of General Motors, the Supreme Court, or the Mafia.

Source: Adapted from L. Hoffman and N. Maier, "Quality and Acceptance of Problem Solutions by Members of Homogeneous and Heterogeneous Groups," *Journal of Abnormal and Social Psychology,* 62 (1961), pp. 401–407.

to bring more novel and integrative solutions to the problems; and (2) group members who differ tend to explore unstated assumptions more than do group members who are basically in agreement.

Furthermore, the beneficial effects of heterogeneity apply to the ratio of male to female members of the group. In forming the groups, the researchers did not take into account whether the subjects were male or female, because a large majority of the students in the class were male. But Hoffman and Maier found that when half or more of the group were women, the quality of decision making was greatly enhanced.

However, heterogeneity also increases the group's potential problem-solving ability. A group composed of people who have dissimilar personalities offers more numerous and more varied alternatives, less random error, fewer constant biases, and a wider basis for criticism of suggested solutions. As a result of these findings, Collins and Guetzkow have concluded that a heterogeneous group will operate more effectively if the task is difficult and if those traits on which members are heterogeneous are relevant to the task. For example, a group composed of both men and women would be able to perform better than would an all-male or all-female group, especially on a task that calls on knowledge of differences between the needs of men and women. Finally, Collins and Guetzkow state that heterogeneous group composition is most helpful in cognitive aspects of task performance and least likely to enhance productivity in the area of interpersonal relations. (A more complete discussion of the effects of group heterogeneity is provided later in this chapter.)

A study by Harry Triandis, Eleanor Hall, and Robert Ewen (1965) tends to support the conclusions of Collins and Guetzkow. These three researchers grouped liberals and conservatives to form heterogeneous groups and placed liberals with liberals and conservatives with conservatives to form homogeneous groups. Half of the heterogeneous and half of the homogeneous groups were given training in resolving interpersonal differences and in increasing interpersonal communication. If the group had been previously trained in interpersonal relations, heterogeneity of group composition enhanced a group's performance on a task involving creativity. The interpersonal difficulties created by heterogeneity apparently had been overcome, and performance-enhancing effects could emerge.

Coalitions: Conflict and Comfort. One of the possible results of heterogeneous group composition is *coalition formation*—the formation of a subgroup that functions within the larger group. A coalition is formed by some members who feel that it would be to their mutual advantage (in relation to the rest of the group) to unite. John Thibaut and Harold Kelley (1954) define a coalition as "two or more persons who act jointly to affect the outcomes of one or more other persons." If a group is heterogeneous with respect to some important personality trait or attitude, members who are similar in this trait or attitude may gravitate toward one another, presumably because they have more in common, like one another better, or have more to talk about. If differences of traits and attitudes are conducive to conflict between members, the likelihood increases that members with similar opinions will form a coalition for mutual advantage against the opposing members. For example, consider a situation in which community leaders have been asked to meet as a group and to reach a decision about initiating a sex-education program in a city's public schools. The members of this group may hold widely divergent opinions and attitudes toward the issue of sex education. If so, it is very likely that those opposed to the teaching of such courses will form a coalition to support one another and to gain strength in their fight against those who are in favor of sex education (who are also likely to form a coalition).

Most of the theory and research on coalition formation has been aimed at predicting when and how coalitions will form. But the effects of coalition formation on group decisions have not yet been revealed. It appears, however, that a group in which many subunits (coalitions) compete for outcomes will be less effective in satisfying the goals of any one subgroup than will be a more cohesive group. Coalition formation implies competition and conflict within the group, and interpersonal discord often has negative effects on group performance.

Leadership Style

Groups must have some kind of leadership. Otherwise, it would be very difficult for group members to coordinate their activities and to produce the necessary or desired outcomes. The group described at the beginning of this chapter—the committee that was planning the dance, for which everyone wanted to hire the musicians and no one wanted to provide the refreshments—was leaderless. With an effective leader, the same group probably would have behaved quite differently. A leader would have organized the discussion of topics in a meaningful way, called for opinions and votes, and made sure that no misunderstandings or contradictions continued after decisions had been reached. As explained in Chapter 14, the leader is the person with the most influence in the group. He or she has the power to make plans and to influence other members to participate and cooperate in reaching the group's goals.

Differences in leadership style create differences in performance. In wielding influence, for example, a leader may have either an authoritarian or a democratic style of leadership (see Chapter 16). An authoritarian leader seeks to be the central and indispensable member of the group; such a leader tries to minimize communication among other members that is not channeled through his or her office. Authoritarian leaders also emphasize obedience. The democratic leader, on the other hand, encourages the involvement of all group members and tries to reduce conflict, to encourage communication, to avoid status differences, and to share responsibility (Krech, Crutchfield, and Ballachey, 1962).

Much research has been done on leadership styles and their varying effects. Marvin Shaw (1964) summarizes some of the results: Authoritarian leadership increases the amount of work a group is able to produce but lowers morale among group members, at least in the United States. Although *quantity* of output may be increased by authoritarian leadership, there is no evidence to suggest how the *quality* of the group's product is affected. However, Shaw did not consider situations or cultures that favor authoritarian leadership patterns. Later research has added evidence that leadership styles are valued according to the circumstances under which a group is operating and that different groups may have different values.

Cecil Gibb (1969) has summarized the circumstances in which either an authoritarian style or a democratic leadership style is more productive. He concludes that democratic leadership is most effective and that it will emerge (1) when none of the group members feels that he or she is more competent to deal with the situation than any other member; (2) when appropriate communication methods are either unknown or not understood; and (3) when all group members feel strongly about maintaining their individual rights. On the other hand, authoritarian leadership will emerge (1) when speed and efficiency in performance outweigh other considerations —for example, in an emergency situation; and (2) when the situation is so novel that individual group members do not feel threatened or criticized if they do not know how to perform, and they thus need direction from the leader.

Many of us have met persons who seemed to be "natural leaders"— people who seem to be so warm, intelligent, and persuasive that we wish they could replace high-ranking leaders who do not have these characteristics. Fred E. Fiedler (1968) has carried out some of the most intensive research on leadership styles, leadership behavior, and group performance. His research program, spanning fifteen years, encompassed more than thirty-five studies and 1,600 groups and organizations ranging from basketball teams to bomber crews.

According to Fiedler, leadership style refers to the personal needs that motivate a leader's behavior in the group. Although the behavior of a leader may change, his or her basic needs remain constant. To classify leadership styles, Fiedler (1964) developed a questionnaire and had leaders describe their feeling toward the co-workers they least preferred. He found that leaders who rated their least-preferred co-workers favorably were *relationship-oriented* individuals who used the task situation to gain prominence in the group. Leaders who rated their least-preferred co-workers unfavorably, on the other hand, were *task-oriented* individuals whose prime motivation was to complete the task, who tended to be controlling and punitive, and whose interpersonal relationships were poor.

Which leadership style works best? Fiedler found that it depends entirely on whether or not the leader has a favorable situation—a situation in which he or she can influence the group. A leader can exert a particularly strong influence in a situation that involves a clearly defined task with the leader in a position of authority. Task-oriented leaders are most effective in situations of either high or low influence, and relationship-oriented leaders perform best in situations of moderate influence (see Figure 15.5). Fiedler's results show that one cannot talk about "good" or "bad" leaders without specifying the type of situation in which a leader with a particular style must operate. In a favorable situation of strong influence, a relationship-oriented leader may find a democratic approach superfluous—perhaps even detrimental. An airline captain, for example, cannot call for a vote from the crew in order to decide on the best landing approach. Fiedler's research shows that types of leaders and types of situations must be matched in order for leadership to be effective. The notion that particular types of people are

Figure 15.5 A summary of Fiedler's research findings regarding leadership effectiveness, compiled in 1968. The success of either a relationship-oriented or task-oriented leadership style depends on (a) the leader's relationship with other members, (b) the degree to which the group's task is structured, and (c) the leader's legitimate power. These three factors in turn determine the favorability of the situation for the leader—that is, the degree to which the leader is in a position to influence the group. Task-oriented leaders tend to be most effective in highly favorable or highly unfavorable situations, whereas relationship-oriented leaders perform best in moderately favorable situations.

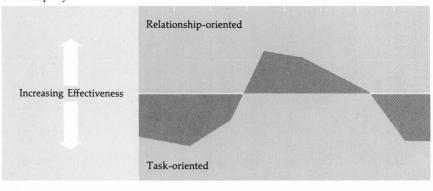

V Behavior in Groups

"natural" leaders who can excel in all situations turns out to be a myth. How, then, can leaders be trained? It is unlikely that training programs can change leadership style because, as previously noted, leadership style reflects personality needs that seem to be relatively permanent. Fiedler suggests, however, that training programs can be developed that will enable individuals to find out in which type of situation they will probably be successful. Effective leadership depends as much on the organization and work environment as it does on personal qualities and attitudes brought to the task.

Group Structure

One does not need the descriptive and analytic skills of the social scientist to realize that a corporation like General Motors is organized differently from a fraternity. Clearly, groups differ in organization. It is often difficult, however, to specify the ways in which organizations differ and to trace the effects of these differences on the behavior of group members. Initially, it might seem that the clearest structural data could be obtained from large and formal organizations (see Chapter 16) in which many persons work at a variety of jobs, hold positions of diverse status, relate to one another in many different ways, and change some of their positions and interactions when task requirements change. Typically, groups with fixed or formal structures specify what the ranks and interactions of the group members should be. For example, the bylaws and job descriptions of corporations specify each person's position, responsibilities, and interactions (who reports to whom). As noted in Chapter 14, however, fixed structures can also occur in informal groups. Set patterns of leadership and task distribution can often be observed among groups or gangs of children, for example; such groups may have a pattern of structure and communication that changes little. Often the same child leads a group of peers for several years. Experimental research has shown similar results with adults, as well (Hare, 1952; Mills, 1953).

Formalized interaction patterns are not, however, the only determinants of what happens in groups; such patterns can, in fact, be misleading. The actual leader in a company may not be the president at all but someone "behind the throne" who may influence what will and what will not be decided by the apparent superior. Thus, as explained further in Chapter 16, studying the organization of a group by ranking all members in terms of status on various official hierarchy dimensions may not be a sufficient means of determining how the group actually operates (Homans, 1950). Describing the function of a person in a specific group (Newcomb, 1950) may help, but that description reveals relatively little about changes in a person's function that result when the group task changes or when the group's environment changes. For example, the working relationships within a subunit of a corporation may suddenly become much more formal when a person from a much higher level in the corporate hierarchy sits in at a group session.

An alternative to exploring the complexities of formal organizations is to create varying group structures in a laboratory setting and then to observe the resulting differences in the behavior of group members. This approach was taken early in the 1950s when investigators began experimenting with groups they organized in various ways (Bavelas, 1950; Leavitt, 1951). For example, groups were created in which communication was restricted to certain patterns. The most commonly created patterns formed chains, hierarchies, stars, or circles, as shown in Figure 15.6. Chains, in which person A communicates with person B, who communicates with C, who communicates with D, are typical in governmental organizations, particularly the military. Hierarchies often occur in business organizations, although they are not necessarily completely formalized. Star patterns indicate that everyone reports to one central person, often an authoritarian leader. Circles are often found in less formal groups.

There are many ways in which a group can organize itself, and its communication channels are greatly affected by its organization. What effects do different communication patterns have on the performance of groups and large organizations? The research of Alex Bavelas (1950) and Harold Leavitt (1951) provided answers to this question. They found that different group structures affected who emerged as a leader, the satisfaction of the group's members, and the group's efficiency in solving problems.

If the group is organized around a central person, as in the star pattern, then that person usually becomes the leader rather quickly, probably because this individual has greater access to information than do the others and is in a position to coordinate the activities of the group. More decentralized groups, represented by the circle pattern, tend to take longer in getting organized and to make more errors.

Any advantages of centralized groups, however, are obtained at the cost of morale: Members of centralized groups, particularly in countries where an egalitarian democratic system is preferred, tend to show low morale. Although the centrally located member in a centralized group is generally satisfied, the members who occupy peripheral positions are typically quite dissatisfied.

As indicated earlier, however, culture and environment greatly affect a person's preference for leadership styles, and they probably also affect the way in which a person evaluates the structure of a group. The nature of the task the group faces is an important variable in determining whether a centralized or a decentralized communication network will be more effective. When the task is a simple one, which primarily requires coordination of information, a centralized network allows workable solutions to be found in less time. On the other hand, when the task is complex, requiring problem-solving ability and manipulation of information, a decentralized

Figure 15.6 Four patterns of group structure: (*top left*) the chain; (*top right*) the star; (*bottom left*) the hierarchy; (*bottom right*) the circle. The type of structure characteristic of a group has consequences for the group's communication patterns and problem-solving efficiency as well as for members' role definitions and satisfaction.

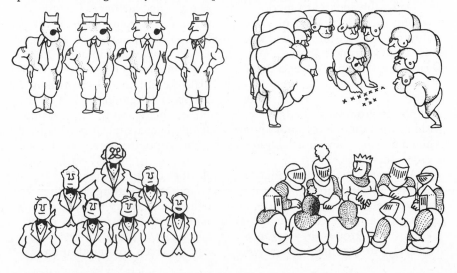

V BEHAVIOR IN GROUPS

network is more effective for correcting errors and finding solutions in less time (Shaw, 1964). Centralized groups may be more susceptible than decentralized ones to communication overload and saturation when tasks are complex, John Gilchrist, Marvin Shaw, and Lawrence Walker (1954) hypothesize. The central person may have to deal with too much information and with too many different channels of communication to work effectively. An additional potential problem produced by a centralized communication system is the authority it places on the central person, who is thus in a position to easily disregard any innovative or creative idea that does not fit into his or her plans.

The group's task, size, composition, leadership, and structure have been examined here in order to identify the ingredients of a successful group. There is yet another aspect of groups that influences decision making in them—the tendency of groups to take risks.

SHIFTS IN DECISION MAKING: LONG SHOTS AND SAFE BETS

Group capacities for collective decision making can be severely impaired by a group's cohesiveness. As explained in Chapter 14, cohesiveness imparts to group members feelings of solidarity, esprit de corps, identification with the group, positive feelings about group tasks, motivation to continue the affiliation, and a desire to abide by the group's norms and decisions. A net result is often a tendency for members to seek agreement for the sake of cohesiveness; as a matter of fact, maintaining the cohesive atmosphere may itself become the primary goal of the group. When this happens, the members of a cohesive group may disregard relevant information at their disposal and embark on whatever course of action will best maintain the supportive atmosphere of the group. And this phenomenon is not limited to groups that are faced with trivial tasks; it has influenced policy-making groups in decisions affecting the lives of millions of people.

Some of the most respected statesmen in American history formed a group that in 1961 unanimously made what has come to be known as one of the worst decisions in recent history. The group was incoming President John F. Kennedy's inner circle of foreign-policy advisers, which included Dean Rusk, Robert McNamara, McGeorge Bundy, Douglas Dillon, and Arthur Schlesinger; and the decision was to go ahead with plans developed under the Eisenhower administration for an invasion of Cuba by CIA-trained Cuban exiles. The invasion was staged at the Bay of Pigs by 1,400 exiles, assisted by the United States Navy and Air Force and the CIA. Three days later, 1,200 of the invaders had been captured and most of the rest had been killed; in addition, ships the invaders were depending on for munitions were sunk by Castro's air force.

Kennedy's inner council had failed to take account of available information about the size and strength of Castro's forces, the deteriorating morale of the invaders, and the likelihood that the invasion would touch off uprisings behind the lines in the Cuban underground; in some cases, these men had even neglected to *seek* relevant information.

Subsequent reflections by President Kennedy, Schlesinger, and McNamara revealed that the deliberations of the advisory group were characterized by selective inattention to available information. Their reports also suggest some of the symptoms by which one can recognize what Yale social psychologist Irving Janis (1971, 1972) terms *groupthink.*

Janis has identified eight major symptoms of groupthink. For one, the high morale and optimism characteristic of highly cohesive groups seems to foster an *illusion of invulnerability,* which sometimes leads them to take risks that their members as individuals would not consider. Kennedy's inner circle was a highly cohesive one; its members prized their membership in the group and felt strongly committed to it. They were highly optimistic about the potential of the new administration and confident in their own wisdom and experience. Janis believes that an illusion of invulnerability also contributed to the negligence of United States Naval officers in preparing for the attack by Japanese military forces on Pearl Harbor, December 7, 1941. He points out that the Naval officers in command at Pearl Harbor before the attack formed a tightly knit group and that until the attack itself this group remained convinced that Pearl Harbor was impregnable and that the Japanese would therefore not attack it. Janis also notes that the excessive optimism leading to an illusion of invulnerability is characteristic of encounter groups, military combat units, athletic teams, and many other types of groups.

A second symptom of groupthink is that of *shared stereotypes,* held by all the members of a group, that lead the group to act unwisely with regard to the objects of its stereotypes. In the case of the Bay of Pigs attack, the stereotype Kennedy's advisers held of the Cubans led them to underestimate the military strength and morale of the Cuban people, with disastrous results. Another example of faulty stereotypes interfering with military decision making is cited by Janis: the decision by President Truman's cohesive circle of advisers to disregard the threats by China's leaders that the Chinese would enter the Korean War if the Allied military forces crossed the 38th parallel and invaded North Korea. According to Janis, Truman's advisers shared a stereotype of "Red China" as a weak country that was completely dependent on Russia for military security; these advisers figured that because the Russian leadership did not want war, the Chinese would not dare to follow through with their threats. This particular stereotype led Truman's advisers to support an invasion of North Korea—a decision that prompted China to enter the war. Because China was far more powerful than Truman's advisers had suspected, its entry into the war almost spelled defeat for the Allied forces.

Another symptom of groupthink is *rationalization*—the tendency of a cohesive group to pool the resources of its individual members in inventing justification for whatever action it decides on. A related symptom is an *illusion of morality*—the tendency to assume that the group's actions are morally justified.

Ironically, the less fearful that members of the cohesive group are of recrimination for their nonconforming opinions, the more they will voluntarily employ *self-censorship.* This symptom belies the fact that maintaining the cohesiveness of the group has become the group's most important goal. When all the members of a cohesive group impose censorship on themselves, a result is the *illusion of unanimity.* For example, although Kennedy's advisers seemed to reach the Bay of Pigs decision unanimously, it has since been revealed that there were silent dissenters; several of the group members harbored private doubts about the decision to proceed with the invasion. Nevertheless, the secret meetings that led up to the Cuban invasion have been described as follows by Arthur Schlesinger, Jr., in his book *A Thousand Days* (1965): "Our meetings were taking place in a curious atmosphere of assumed consensus. Had one senior adviser opposed the adventure, I believe that Kennedy would have canceled it. Not one spoke against it." Apparently, the desire not to risk incurring the disapproval of the other group members overcame any misgivings that the advisers may have had.

Unanimity is often the product of *direct pressure* by group members to suppress the objections of deviants—another symptom by which groupthink can be diagnosed. As a bodyguard can protect one's physical well-being, Janis observes that *mindguards* within the cohesive group protect the group psychologically from information that might disturb the warm glow of group confidence that unanimity can bestow. A mindguard is any group member who finds a way to exclude relevant information from group consideration, to discredit the source of the information, or to relay this information in such a way that it is easily dismissed.

Despite the dangers of groupthink, if members are aware of these dangers, cohesiveness and the commitment it inspires can contribute to the success of many groups. A year and a half after the Bay of Pigs decision, essentially the same group of President Kennedy's advisers were able to handle the 1962 Cuban missile crisis in a much more successful manner. The key to this success may well have been the conscious steps the group took to prevent a recurrence of the earlier fiasco. According to Janis, some effective means of preventing groupthink include the following:

1. Ask each group member to discuss the group's deliberations with trusted associates away from other group members and then to report their reactions. The reactions of outsiders should help counter illusions that might be created within the group.

2. Along the same lines, invite one or two outside experts to each group meeting. This was done during the Cuban missile crisis.

3. Have the leader abstain from stating his or her own position at the outset, so as to prevent group members from adopting it uncritically. During the Cuban missile crisis, for example, President Kennedy deliberately stayed away from the initial meetings of the planning group.

4. Make certain that group members are encouraged to freely express objections and doubts. To attain this goal, the leader should delegate the responsibility of being a critical evaluator to each member and should reinforce free expression by his or her own acceptance of criticism.

5. Assign one or more group members the role of devil's advocate, to challenge the testimony of all those who support the majority decision. Robert Kennedy played this role at the Cuban missile crisis meetings, forcing the group to examine the pros and cons of the proposed action more carefully than it otherwise would have.

6. After a preliminary consensus on the best alternative, hold a special meeting in which all members are encouraged to express their remaining doubts. Such a "second-chance" meeting will help prevent premature consensus based on illusions of invulnerability, morality, or unanimity or other hazards of groupthink.

Underlying all these suggestions is the idea that the best way to prevent groupthink is to be aware of the possibility that it will emerge. If the people in a decision-making group learn to recognize as a warning sign the heady feeling imparted by factors such as invulnerability and convivial unanimity, they will probably be able to keep groupthink from sweeping them off their feet.

In writing of a "collective mind" early in the development of social science, Le Bon was suggesting that a group may think, feel, and behave quite differently from the individuals who compose it. In short, the whole is more—or something other than—the sum of its parts. For example, a group may engage in a lynching although its members never would as individuals. Le Bon believed that a "group mind" sometimes permits the group to act in ways that are not compatible with the thinking of its individual members. Floyd Allport (1924), one of the early social psychologists, disagreed. He suggested that behaviors in which the group engages are parts of each individual member's repertoire and that these parts are not expressed unless a group sanctions them. If the group's action implies that a certain behavior is acceptable, then this activity becomes acceptable to the individuals, even if society in general does not condone it. As explained in Chapters 11 and 12, the responsibility—for example, for the lynching—is diffused among group members so that no individual can view himself or herself as fully responsible for the action.

Risky Shifts

The early "debate" between Le Bon and Allport concerning differences in risk taking between individuals and groups has a modern counterpart, which began with a master's thesis by James A. F. Stoner (1961). Stoner presented his subjects with a set of decision problems called the Choice

Figure 15.7 A group's decisions are often more extreme than the decisions any one individual member would make alone. Here a driver engaged in a game of "chicken" makes a dangerous decision he might not otherwise have made if it were not for the risky attitudes and enthusiasm of his companions. A group member may shift toward riskier decisions or toward greater caution as a result of contact with the group, depending both on his or her original inclinations and on the values of the other group members.

V BEHAVIOR IN GROUPS

Dilemmas Questionnaire (CDQ). For example, subjects were told that Mr. A is an electrical engineer who graduated from college five years ago, is married, has one child, and has been working for a large electronics firm. The company pays him a modest but adequate salary, which will probably not increase much over time. Mr. A is offered a job with a new, small company, which would pay more and would give him a chance to own part of the action. However, it is not certain that the new company will survive competition with other companies in the field. Subjects are then told that they should advise Mr. A whether or not he should take the job with the new company. Specifically, they are given a set of odds, or probabilities, that the new company will prove financially sound: one in ten, three in ten, five in ten, seven in ten, and nine in ten. They are then asked either to pick the lowest acceptable probability that would make it reasonable for Mr. A to take the job or to indicate that they would not advise Mr. A to take the job with the new company at all.

Typically, experimenters have first asked their subjects to respond individually to a series of items of this kind. Then the subjects are brought together in groups and are asked to discuss each of the items. After the discussion the group makes a joint decision. On most items of the CDQ, groups typically derive riskier decisions than the mean (or average) of the decisions of individuals composing the group. This phenomenon has been called the *risky shift* by Stoner (1961) and also by Michael Wallach, Nathan Kogan, and Daryl Bem (1962). Wallach, Kogan, and Bem (1964) attributed the shift toward risk to the *diffusion of responsibility,* suggesting that groups are able to advise (or take) greater risks because none of the members would be fully responsible should things go wrong.

If it is true that groups always take greater risks than individuals, as some of the initial research seemed to suggest, then the diffusion-of-responsibility theory has great importance and many practical implications. For example, one could assume that a team of decision makers, such as the National Security Council, would take greater risks than the president alone. The risky shift was demonstrated in research in Canada, England, France, Germany, Israel, and New Zealand. Some researchers proposed that this theory could be applied to international decision making (Wallach, Kogan, and Bem, 1964). However, the honeymoon between risk-taking theory and empirical applications did not last very long. Problems became apparent rather quickly. First of all, the risky shift did not occur in the responses to two of the CDQ items. One of these items typically yielded no shift at all. The other item tended to produce a shift in the *conservative* direction; rather than becoming more risky, group decisions on this item are typically more cautious than are mean individual decisions.

In item 12 on the CDQ, subjects are told that Mr. M is considering marriage to Miss T, whom he has known for more than a year. Recently Mr. M and Miss T, who view a number of things quite differently, have repeatedly argued. They seek the advice of a marriage counselor and are told that a happy marriage is possible but not certain.

After receiving this information, subjects are given a set of probabilities (one out of ten through nine out of ten) that the marriage will be happy and are asked to advise Mr. M on the lowest probability of happiness that would be acceptable. Typically, subjects are more likely to recommend that Mr. M risk a rotten marriage when they are acting as individuals than when they operate as a group. Why should groups be cautious when marriage is concerned and willing to advise risk taking when job security is at stake?

Diffusion of responsibility suggests that both dilemmas would produce a risky shift. In other words, groups should have been more daring than were individuals in advising both the job change and the marriage to Miss T.

Choice Shifts: Caution Also Rules

Clearly, the term "risky shift" is too restrictive if shifts can occur both in the risky and cautious directions. The two types of shifts can be referred to collectively as *choice shifts.*

Roger Brown (1965) has attempted to explain choice shifts through his *value theory.* He suggests that riskiness in certain situations is a culturally valued characteristic. In these particular situations, people want to be at least as risky as others with whom they compare themselves, and they typically view themselves as more risky than others. When in a group discussion it turns out that they are not more willing to live dangerously than are the others around them, their opinions may become still more daring. In other words, Brown draws two conclusions: (1) that risk is valued on CDQ (and other) problems in which groups shift toward risk, cautiousness being valued in solving problems in which groups shift toward caution, and (2) that people compare themselves with others when the opportunity arises and then shift toward or beyond what they view as the mean of the group (in the valued direction).

The concept of diffusion of responsibility cannot explain the shift toward caution for the marriage problem. But value theory can. Taking risks in one's work situation may be favorably regarded in Western societies but gambling with one's marriage is generally not. Thus, subjects who responded as individuals already valued a particular direction on the risk-caution dimension and thus shifted toward it. When they found that others agreed with them in their preference for risk in the first item or for caution in the twelfth, they felt secure in moving even farther in that direction.

A considerable amount of research has supported value theory as initially proposed by Brown and as later modified by other writers. Excellent reviews of this research have been presented by Dorwin Cartwright (1971) and Dean Pruitt (1971). Additional CDQ-type items have been devised. Some of them produce a risky shift; others, a cautious shift. Additional measures of risk taking have been developed, as have other experimental situations in which risk-taking behavior can be observed. The choice-shift phenomenon can be obtained in a variety of settings and with a variety of measurement techniques. For example, even group responses to attitude scales often differ from the mean responses of the individual members who compose the group.

Another view of the choice shift, advanced by Pruitt (1969, 1971), is his *release theory,* which assumes that people find themselves in conflict when they are asked to make decisions. Being risky is attractive because risk takers are seen as more confident in their ability to cope with a situation. On the other hand, a cautious approach is also attractive, because our society teaches moderation, advising us not to "go out on a limb." Caution seeking, then, would be caused by a fear that the risky alternative will fail. Risk seeking would be produced by an attempt at self-aggrandizement. These dispositions can vie for dominance in each decision that must be made. An interesting product of this conflict between the mutually exclusive desires to be risky and cautious is the *Walter Mitty effect,* which has been demonstrated in the research of Kenneth Higbee (1971) and Dean Pruitt (1969). Mitty, a James Thurber creation who fantasizes about the great risks he takes and the successful adventures he has, really lives a boring life that is characterized by great cautiousness.

With his release theory, Pruitt proposes that the greater riskiness (or caution) of one of the group members releases the other members from the social constraints that force them to be less risky or less cautious than they would like to be. With the group's backing, they can show the "courage of their convictions," because they have found a model to imitate, a model who performs the very actions in which they want to engage. Research data that support other theories of risk taking support release theory as well. In addition, release theory relates the choice-shift phenomenon to other findings of social psychology. For example, many of the subjects in Solomon Asch's (1951) conformity experiment (discussed in Chapter 10) were able to demonstrate the "courage of their convictions" only if at least one other person agreed with them. Further, Ladd Wheeler and Anthony Caggiula (1966) have shown that a subject who was angered by another person would aggress against that person only if a model had previously behaved aggressively. (See Chapter 11 for a discussion of the effects of modeling on aggressive behavior.) Pruitt's theory can therefore be viewed as an integrative interpretation of the choice-shift phenomenon.

A special supplement to the *Journal of Personality and Social Psychology* (December 1971), edited by Pruitt, was concerned with research testing these and various other hypotheses regarding choice shifts. Although the twenty articles published in that issue do not solve all the difficulties encountered by choice-shift theory, they nonetheless help clear up many problems. It was reported in them that both risky and cautious shifts can be reliably obtained. The shift toward risk was demonstrated in the United States, in Canada, and in West Germany. However, research in Uganda showed no similarity to results obtained in Western nations. Ugandans were more cautious to begin with, did not assume that others would be more cautious than they themselves were, and did not show any shifts toward risk. In other words, the rather reliable risky-shift phenomenon appears to be most particularly associated with the value systems of Western cultures.

Initially, the risky-shift phenomenon attracted the attention of social psychologists for two reasons. First, the finding seemed to contradict the commonly held wisdom about the inherent conservatism of group decision making. And second, it seemed to be a reliable and rather general phenomenon. As research on risky shifts proceeded, however, it has become apparent that the effect is by no means universal. Thus, current and future research may well redirect the focus away from the broad question, "Are groups riskier than individuals?" to the more specific question, "Under what conditions are groups riskier than individuals?"

DECISIONS UNDER CONFLICT

We make many of our everyday decisions under some degree of conflict. The outstanding college halfback may have to decide whether he wants to play professional football or to become a dentist. The editor of a college newspaper may have to decide whether she wants to pursue a publishing career or to become a wife and mother. One nation at war with another is aware that by introducing a new weapon it might escalate the war, with serious consequences. All these dilemmas are shaped by existing conflict, but the decisions will probably be influenced by the participants' anticipation of future conflict. In turn, expectations of continued conflict may well become a self-fulfilling prophecy (see Chapter 5), influencing the nature of future conflict. In addition, the nature of conflict can seriously affect decision making itself. Conflict can be interpreted by both sides as a challenge. The response to challenge is generally an escalation of the conflict, and the more serious the conflict becomes and the more problems it presents, the greater will be both the challenge and the response.

There does come a time, however, when a further increase in conflict makes the challenge too great to permit successful coping. After this point has been reached, further increase in conflict will decrease the quality of the response and, when conflict is sufficiently damaging, may force one of the participating individuals or groups to give up entirely.

Conflicts occur between individuals, between individuals and groups, and between groups. Two or more parties may be involved in conflict. Chapter 14 discusses conflict between different groups. Conflict can also occur within groups, among the individual members who are supposedly working toward a common goal.

In many groups, people work together toward common goals; thus, the situation is not one in which they would be expected to compete or to find themselves in conflict with one another. Nonetheless, even though group members want to achieve a shared goal, they do not necessarily cooperate on all aspects of their task, and conflict can emerge for many reasons.

Tasks That Entangle

The characteristics of the particular task a group undertakes are often directly responsible for conflict among decision makers in the same group. Conflict tends to be minor when the task requirements are straightforward, when a single correct solution will resolve the problem, and when the group is able to clearly evaluate whether or not a particular solution will do the job (Kelley and Thibaut, 1969). An example is provided by Frank Restle and James Davis (1962), who gave a group of subjects the task of solving this problem: How can prisoners escape through a window when the rope they have reaches only halfway to the ground? A suggestion by one of the subjects that the rope could be unraveled and the strands tied end to end would be a correct and inarguable solution.

A problem-solving task produces conflict when the group is unable to determine whether or not a particular solution is the desired or correct one, and the conflict necessarily grows as the number of plausible alternative solutions increases. However, if one of the group members expresses more confidence in one of the solutions than do other members, the degree of conflict generated by alternative solutions may be greatly reduced. Marvin Shaw (1961) has demonstrated that solutions proposed by confident group members are likely to be accepted much more frequently and much more quickly than are suggestions offered by less confident persons. If one member is talkative about a solution, others are much more likely to accept it than a suggestion made by a less articulate group member (Riecken, 1958; Thomas and Fink, 1961). And the solution need not even be correct.

Competitive Orientations

What are some of the ways that the personal goals of individual members affect the activities of the group? When personal goals differ within the group, competition may result. Competitiveness in groups is nothing unusual; group members typically compete with one another for influence, social status, and other rewards. The self-oriented motivations of individual members can produce a bottleneck for group goals, as Alexander Mintz (1951) has demonstrated. Appropriately, Mintz used a narrow-necked bottle in his experiment. Every subject in the group was given a string attached to a cone inside the bottle. A pull on the string would extract a cone, but the neck of the bottle was not wide enough to let more than one cone pass through simultaneously. Mintz found that "traffic jams" in the neck of the bottle resulted when members were individually rewarded and punished for the time it took to extract their cones. Subjects who were offered group rewards, on the other hand, got their cones out much more quickly by functioning cooperatively.

Carl Castore (in press) developed a task that represents a similar but much more complex problem. He asked his subjects to sort into rank order an array of phonograph recordings according to the preference of the group. After reaching a group decision about ranking, each member of the group was to receive a phonograph recording—most likely the phonograph recording receiving the highest group rating. The musical preferences of group members often varied widely. If the majority of the group members agreed on a preference, then the solution was simple: The majority ruled. If individual rank orderings were widely discrepant, however, then hard bargaining and coalition formation likely ensued. Castore required unanimous solutions of some of his groups, and in these instances group members had to agree to stand by their groups' solutions. However, when later given an opportunity to modify the group's decision without the group's knowledge, subjects whose preferred recordings had ended up low on the list usually took advantage. The individual goals of members, then, may hamper group decision making as well as the long-run effectiveness of the decisions. Majority rule does not seem to endure for very long if the minority has a chance to overturn secretly the majority decision.

When Differences Are Dangerous

As discussed earlier in this chapter, heterogeneity among the members of a group can produce interpersonal difficulties, which are often conflicting in nature. Status differences, for example, tend to develop in every group, whether a friendship clique, a large corporation, or a commune. Even in groups formed for experimental studies, status differences can have seriously detrimental effects on group behavior. An example is provided by Ralph Exline and Robert Ziller (1959), who assigned different statuses to members of groups that were composed of three women who had to solve two problems. The experimenters varied status by telling the women that they had different problem-solving abilities and by giving some more votes than others. They found that groups in which status levels were diverse experienced more conflict and made incorrect decisions more frequently than did groups in which status levels were similar. Exline and Ziller's study suggests that status discrepancies have negative effects on decision making, especially when they appear to be unjustified.

Differences in attitudes toward the group's goal can also have very detrimental effects. Imagine a jury about to decide on the guilt or innocence of a man who is accused of embezzlement. What if this jury includes members who believe that it is perfectly acceptable to "rip off" society and other members who feel that theft is not only a crime but implies moral turpitude. Lawyers know well that attitudinally based conflict in juries produces ineffective decision making: The jury will stay out longer, holding up the judicial time schedule or become a "hung" jury that is unable to reach any decision at all. To control such attitudinal problems, attorneys for both prosecution and defense tend to carefully question potential jurors.

Personality differences can also interfere with group decision making. Imagine, for example, a group consisting of some individuals who have a high need for achievement and others who are low in that need but are high in fear of failure. The first set of group members may want to take great risks in order to achieve their goals; the second set will continually frustrate these efforts by balking at risks that they fear might lead to failure. Similarly, differences in the ways in which people work at a group task can interfere with decision making. Paul Stager (1967), for example, used an indeterminate decision-making task (one in which no single solution was "correct"). He placed groups of subjects in a simulation (described in Chapter 1) of negotiations between two nations (Streufert, 1970). Stager asked subjects to make decisions about an international conflict. He distinguished between highly complex people (those who tend to think strategically) and less complex persons. Two-person groups composed of complex decision makers made a large number of strategic decisions. When two subjects who were very low in complexity were added, however, the

Figure 15.8 Differences in members' personalities, goals, sex, status, and attitudes can breed conflict within a group and either interfere with or enhance the group's functioning. Legend has it that when the women of ancient Athens once disagreed with their menfolk about the advisability of war, they were able to win the dispute and put a temporary end to war by turning to what may have been the only means of influence at their disposal—the threat of withholding sexual companionship. Nineteenth-century English artist Aubrey Beardsley portrayed the female contingent of the divided Athenian population in this work, "Lysistrata Haranguing the Athenian Women." As explained in the topical insert on pages 496 and 497, groups consisting of both females and males seem to be capable of better decisions than are all-male groups.

complexity of decision making dropped dramatically. Four heads worked far less effectively than the two best heads in this situation.

Heterogeneity does not always handicap a group; as discussed earlier in this chapter, it can also bring rewards. When many alternative solutions are required to solve a problem, increasing the heterogeneity of the group can increase its potential problem-solving ability (Hoffman, Harburg, and Maier, 1962). Heterogeneity of opinions (and attitudes or personalities, as well) can help the group find the correct solution. For example, Robert Ziller (1955) found that when Air Force crews differed widely in their individual estimates of how many dots were on a card, the group's final judgment was nearest the correct number (3,155). On the other hand, Marvin Shaw (1960) says that these results cannot be widely generalized.

Heterogeneity, as it exists in society—in economic levels, political orientations, life styles, and so on—has both advantages and disadvantages. Society, as a large heterogeneous group, is likely to embrace intense conflict, hostility, prejudice, and inferior problem-solving ability. Homogeneity may appear to be ideal, but a society might pay for homogeneity with fewer ideas, inferior ability to solve complex problems, diminished opportunity for individualistic perspectives, and a bland—perhaps boring—similarity among its members. The road to "the ideal society" is thus not easily chosen.

UNDERSTANDING CONFLICT

Conflict occurs among members of a group who have a shared goal toward which all are supposedly working. Conflict occurs among subgroups of larger organizations, such as departments of large corporations. It also occurs between two or more groups, organizations, or nations that directly vie for some valued commodity—the money of consumers or a piece of contested territory, for example.

If human beings can learn to understand the antecedents, the progress, and the consequences of conflict as it develops and terminates, then they might be able to deal with it more effectively. Attempts to understand the causes and development of conflict have generated many models. These models vary in complexity. Simplistic ones assign labels—for example, "good guy" and "bad guy"—to the parties in conflict; more complex models attempt to describe conflict without evaluative labeling.

There are nearly as many conflict models as there are observers of conflict. Three of the most popular are (1) the *aggressor-defender model,* (2) the *conflict-spiral model,* and (3) the *structural-change model.* Each calls attention to certain aspects of social conflict and neglects other aspects.

Aggressor-Defender Models

The most frequently encountered explanation of conflict takes a good part of its substance from the aggressor-defender model. Whether the conflict involves warfare between nations, battles among gangs in urban slums, disagreements among campaigning politicians, or arguments among scientists over the interpretation of data, each party typically describes the other as the villain, the aggressor. The model assumes that the actions and intentions of the parties to the conflict are *asymmetrical,* or quite different from one another. One of the two (which one depends on the bias of the judge) is seen as the originator of the conflict and as actively responsible for its continuation. The observer using an aggressor-defender model believes that the aggressive party views the conflict as a means of gaining some illegitimate advantage; that its motives are consequently "evil"; and that it ought to be deterred from further aggression. The call for "law and order"—an increase in deterrent power—is a predictable outcome of this view. Another example is the view that most nations at war have of each other: The "other" nation is described as the aggressor and villain, whereas one's own nation never does any wrong.

All governments resort to propaganda statements that make ample use of this simplistic model. Politicians frequently use it to "smear" their opponents and enemies. Even scientists are not immune. For example, Seymour Martin Lipset (1970) attributes campus unrest to frustrations and tensions that students experience, to the low status that students have in the university hierarchy, to overcrowding, to youthful idealism, and to the Vietnam war. But, as Dean Pruitt and James Gahagan (1971) have pointed out, Lipset's interpretation dismisses the activities of students as restlessness and may overlook entirely the causes or possible legitimacy of their protest; administrators, on the other hand, are seen as defenders. This view seems to them to exemplify the aggressor-defender model. Law enforcement officials (for example, J. Edgar Hoover) and educational administrators (for example, S. I. Hayakawa and Max Rafferty) have also made statements that reflect an aggressor-defender view of student unrest, but to them student activities are the result of more dangerous motives than simple restlessness. Whether the aggressor-defender model is used to blame the aggressor or to justify the aggressor's actions, the model is based on labels that are usually short-sighted.

The problems inherent in aggressor-defender models are caused primarily by the models' simplicity, which does not cope with the complexities of conflict. First, these models tend to be static; they do not take into account the frequent changes in conflict. For example, after conflict has begun, it is rare that the defender only defends. Much more often the defender counterattacks, either for strategic reasons or because of anger and a conviction that aggression is justified. Pruitt and Gahagan (1971) have pointed out that labeling the other participant as the aggressor might even have the effect of making the supposed defender more aggressive: If the opponent can be labeled as the aggressor, then aggression appears to be legitimate. The supposed defender can now legitimately become aggressive and make believe that he is merely defending himself.

Second, aggressor-defender models typically overgeneralize by assuming unitary characteristics for entire groups and nations. Some Americans, for example, view all Russians and all communists as dangerous and threatening. In fact, however, few groups are so homogeneous in their

Figure 15.9 Stan and Ollie demonstrate the conflict-spiral model, which attributes conflict to a vicious cycle of increasingly severe retaliatory actions by both opponents rather than to aggressiveness by any one party in particular: (*from left to right*) Laurel and Hardy want to unload a Christmas tree; the trouble begins when they try selling it to a stranger; annoyed at their persistence, the stranger makes a retaliatory gesture; in return, Laurel and Hardy "redecorate" the stranger's house; stimulated to further "appropriate" retaliation, the stranger modifies Stan and Ollie's car; and he then angrily returns the unwanted Christmas tree.

V Behavior in Groups

characteristics, particularly groups that are as large as corporations or nations. The so-called "black-top" view of the opposing group's leadership as bad guys and their followers as basically decent but duped is only a small improvement on the oversimplifications of aggressor-defender models.

Conflict-Spiral Models

Conflict tends to lead the participants into an upward spiral of hostilities. One party's action elicits increasingly severe retaliatory actions from the opponent, producing continuously escalating attacks, counterattacks, counter-counterattacks, and so on. The term "conflict spiral" was introduced some time ago (North, Brody, and Holsti, 1964), but the concept is older. The model assumes that neither party by itself can be responsible for the conflict. Rather, conflict develops and is accelerated through the actions and reactions of the opponents. Increasing conflict is the vicious circle that results from each party's view that the other is the aggressor. An observer applying the conflict-spiral model may find that part of the problem results from the opponents' use of aggressor-defender labels.

Where does the conflict originate? Conflict-spiral models suggest no beginning point. Each action of either party can be traced back to a previous and milder action by the other, until one finally arrives at initial actions that were neither intended nor viewed as aggressive. These actions must have started the vicious circle, but the conflict-spiral model does not assign blame to possible first causes; it attends to the dynamic, interactive process of conflict and to its outcome. The model assumes that conflict can end in only one way: through the decrease or cessation of retaliation by one of the parties, which can occur for a number of reasons. For example, one party might be tired of the conflict and might want to quit fighting, or one of the parties may be so weakened by the conflict that it is unable to continue the fight. Conflict can be deescalated as well as escalated. Charles Osgood (1966) proposed that the conflict between the communist and capitalist nations might be deescalated slowly through disarmament; each step in the process would lead to greater trust between opponents until enough international trust were established to make the world safe from nuclear holocaust. When Osgood proposed his ideas, most social scientists and policy makers considered them impractical. At that time, deterrence—with its prospects for more and more sophisticated armaments—was in vogue. Since then, however, the Strategic Arms Limitations Talks (SALT) have produced the faint beginnings of a downward spiral.

Campus unrest has previously been used as an example of conflict. Conflict-spiral models can be used to explain the sequence of events in

some of the conflicts that have occurred on campuses. Such models try to explain the reactions at "choice points" for each party; at each choice point, one of the parties has the choice of either overreacting or underreacting. Typically, both students and administrators have overreacted. Administrators have called police onto campuses when outside help was not actually necessary. Students have occupied and burned buildings when lesser actions could have gained similar—but more favorable—attention. Each of these actions has generally caused the opposing forces to overreact, escalating conflict still further.

Conflict-spiral models appear to account more realistically for international as well as campus conflicts than do aggressor-defender models. The actions and reactions of nations on the brink of war provide many examples of a spiraling pattern. The threats and counterthreats, the mobilizations and countermobilizations that preceded World War I are a good example.

Conflict-spiral models have other advantages over aggressor-defender models. They are more dynamic; they view a conflict at each stage of its development, not statically. Further, they avoid labeling one party the cause of the conflict. Analysis of the behavior of both sides may well reveal similarities in the motives, behavior, and attitudes of both sides. A bilateral understanding of conflict can permit reason rather than moral outrage to control events.

However, spiral models also have some disadvantages. First, they fail to distinguish clearly between the parties in a conflict, which may have real differences. The models usually do not attend to the possibility that one party, at least in the beginning, is intentionally initiating conflict for that party's exclusive benefit. Sometimes, but certainly not always, the cause of conflict may indeed be traceable to one of the parties. Second, conflict-spiral models treat the parties as units, just as aggressor-defender models

Figure 15.10 Structural-change models of conflict stress the changing nature of conflict over time. Although more descriptive than predictive, they are better able to account for the complexities and effects of conflict than are aggressor-defender or conflict-spiral models. Consider the evolution of the civil-rights movement and the apparent impact of early events on subsequent developments.

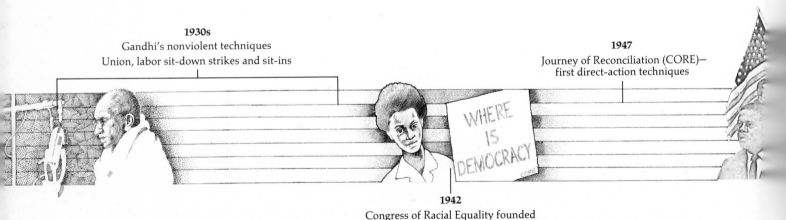

1930s
Gandhi's nonviolent techniques
Union, labor sit-down strikes and sit-ins

1947
Journey of Reconciliation (CORE)—
first direct-action techniques

1942
Congress of Racial Equality founded

do. As noted previously, such a view is often unrealistic because not all group members may have the same attitudes. There are "hawks" as well as "doves" in the United States, which makes it unrealistic to label the United States either a warlike country or a peace-loving one; the same holds for other countries. In addition, group members who are party to conflict not only hold different attitudes but also often change their views over time; even the membership of the groups may change. Such changes produce potentially important differences in group decision making—changes that can strongly affect the direction of the spiral. For example, changes in the attitudes of Americans toward the Vietnam War finally made it expedient for the nation's leaders to end American military involvement in that struggle. Third, there are many occasions when conflicts suddenly die out or are temporarily suspended without any preceding downward spiral. The model cannot account for events such as these. Finally, the model is too simplistic in predicting that a single "underreaction" will start a trend toward deescalation. In reality, an opponent often takes such an action as an indication of the enemy's weakness and then attempts the "final blow" while defenses are lowered.

Structural-Change Models

Structural-change models are important because they suggest that changes occur as effects of the conflict itself. Conflict can modify the views, actions, and goals of the parties in conflict and consequently may modify the composition of the conflicting parties. As a result, present conflict affects future conflict in various ways. Different researchers have emphasized different changes produced by conflict, and several structural-change models have resulted. Ralph White's (1970) theory of international conflict,

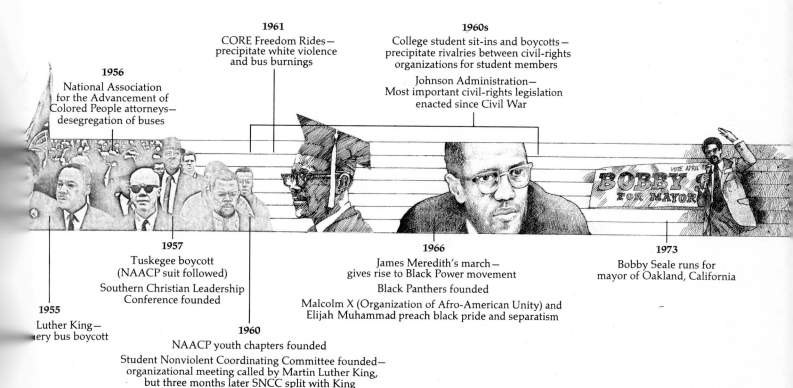

1956
National Association for the Advancement of Colored People attorneys— desegregation of buses

1961
CORE Freedom Rides— precipitate white violence and bus burnings

1960s
College student sit-ins and boycotts— precipitate rivalries between civil-rights organizations for student members

Johnson Administration— Most important civil-rights legislation enacted since Civil War

1955
Luther King— ery bus boycott

1957
Tuskegee boycott (NAACP suit followed)

Southern Christian Leadership Conference founded

1960
NAACP youth chapters founded

Student Nonviolent Coordinating Committee founded— organizational meeting called by Martin Luther King, but three months later SNCC split with King

1966
James Meredith's march— gives rise to Black Power movement

Black Panthers founded

Malcolm X (Organization of Afro-American Unity) and Elijah Muhammad preach black pride and separatism

1973
Bobby Seale runs for mayor of Oakland, California

for example, emphasizes the ways in which conflict alters views about one's adversary. These changed images tend to keep the conflict going. White suggests that when conflict occurs, views of the adversary tend to become simplistic, good-bad evaluations, and when opponents label each other in this way, empathy is reduced and dependence on one's own (military) capacity is increased.

In their explanation of a campus unrest problem, Pruitt and Gahagan (1971) prefer another structural-change theory, that of James Coleman (1957). Coleman views the sequence of emerging conflict in the following way: A precipitating incident makes one of the parties a "defendant" in a controversy. The other party then takes up the fight against the defendant. This second party to the conflict is often composed of people who have long been antagonistic toward members of the first group; these people now see an opportunity to attack, and they find new causes for the fight. The precipitating incident is soon of little importance—it may be forgotten altogether. Both groups now tend to view the other as "bad." The goal of "changing" the opponent now becomes one of "destroying" the opponent. Others who are as yet outside the conflict will come to the defense of one side or the other, and all persons or groups that are potential participants in the conflict will become polarized.

Coleman's model, although not as useful in predicting international conflict, is quite accurate in describing many conflicts in a social community, such as urban conflicts and campus unrest. Other structural-change models may be needed to account for other forms of conflict. The divergence among structural-change models is both an advantage and a disadvantage. The array of models can clearly and precisely account for a wider range of conflicts than can other models of conflict, but they are often not very generalizable from one conflict area to another. Structural-change models are often more descriptive than predictive. More important, they typically lack comparability with one another.

Structural-change models do have certain advantages, accounting for both similarities and differences among the parties in conflict and not viewing the groups in conflict as static. Finally, structural-change models can account for the perpetuation or the cessation of conflict, events that cannot be explained so easily by either of the other two types of models. In comparison, the conflict-spiral view that when one stops overreacting, conflict will decrease seems dangerously optimistic, and this view is not supported by the applications of structural-change models.

THE PSYCHOLOGY OF INTERNATIONAL CONFLICT

During the past two or three decades many social psychologists have become increasingly concerned about the dangers of war, the potential use of nuclear weapons, and the consequent destruction of millions and millions of persons. A social psychology of international conflict is being developed because of this concern. How can people avoid unwanted and irrational warfare, or how can they limit wars to levels that are not generally destructive? If one wants to find meaningful answers, one must first be able to respond positively to a more basic question: Are people able to control their destiny? The conflict-spiral theory implies that if they are not in control of the escalation of conflict, then all efforts to avoid or control war may be useless. Opinions about this issue vary. Some scientists believe in—and cite data to support—the eminently rational nature of human beings. Others are much more pessimistic and, again citing data of their own, attempt to show that the slightest conflict can escalate into total nuclear holocaust. Probably both views are correct and incorrect to some degree. Before considering the data supporting either position, it is important to know about the ways in which these data have been obtained.

Predictions and Solutions

Is international conflict a proper area of study for social psychologists? Or should this field be reserved for political scientists, sociologists, and cultural anthropologists? For that matter, do social psychologists have the research methods necessary for studying conflicts among nations?

Surprisingly, research methods in international conflict originated in social psychology. Until about twenty years ago, political scientists were primarily involved in an armchair approach to conflict that placed major emphasis on the power principle in international relations. Many political scientists still subscribe to that view. Social psychologists—for example, Harold Guetzkow (1959, 1968) and Anatol Rapoport (1957, 1963)—decided to use laboratory experiments with individuals as a basis for predicting international behavior. You might well ask how they were able to generalize from individuals to nations.

The degree to which individual behavior differs from group behavior has been discussed earlier in this chapter. For example, the choice shifts that groups produce among the individual group members have been described: Shifts in risk taking, attitudes, and so forth usually take the direction that the individual holds as more favorable to begin with. Nations are complexly organized conglomerates of groups. Social psychologists typically assume that some aspects of individual psychology will be maintained in modified form in the multigroup organization called a "nation." In other words, the principles of attitude change (Chapter 9), power (Chapter 13), influence (Chapter 10), attribution (Chapter 5), communication (Chapter 3), and social perception (Chapter 5) should have a good amount of impact on the flow of events that occurs when nations are in conflict. In the final analysis, researchers cannot hope to predict the course of international conflict without coordinating knowledge from several fields—from political science, economics, sociology, and social psychology. Social psychologists have used a variety of research tools to understand international behavior. The case study has been used successfully, for example, by Ralph White (1966) to show how psychological processes affected American involvement in Vietnam. Methods of interpersonal bargaining have been used by Martin Deutsch (1965), Anatol Rapoport (1964), and others; and, despite tenuous generalizations, results of such research have profoundly important implications for international policy (see Chapter 13). Simulation research, which is described in Chapter 1, has been creatively applied to studies of international conflict by Harold Guetzkow (1959) and Siegfried Streufert and Howard Fromkin (1969). Guetzkow has also drawn on historical events to formulate a composite model of conflict.

Standard social-psychological research techniques, as well as more specialized techniques, have much to contribute to an understanding of international conflict. What results have been obtained, and what are the conclusions? It may be of value to emphasize in advance that a complete understanding of social-psychological variables in international conflict is not yet available. The present data are scattered; much important work is yet to be done. However, some researchers have already concluded that when a nation's decision makers plan their strategies, they can ensure peaceful international relations by applying the knowledge that social scientists have contributed (Schelling, 1960, 1965). Other researchers have concluded that human beings are irrational and that stress increases their irrationality, and some predict that this world will sooner or later experience nuclear holocaust (Rapoport, 1964). Most researchers and theorists may not share these extreme views.

The social functions and dynamics of communications and of attitudes have been discussed in Chapters 3, 8, and 9. The knowledge gained in standard social-psychological research on these topics can be applied to two areas: within the decision-making groups of a particular nation and between two nations in conflict.

Amitai Etzioni (1964) has noted that effective communications among a nation's decision makers are now of critical importance in protecting the lives of people in that country as well as in others. Etzioni has pointed out that the defense system that has developed in the United States is based on the assumption that all communications among personnel at various positions will reach their destinations and will be understood accurately. Without certainty of high communication capacity, a deterrent system such as that in the United States cannot work effectively. The failure of a few messages to reach their destinations could result in an escalation of conflict. (Whether these messages are to be read by human beings or by computers

The Tenacity of Images:

MIND OVER MATTERS

RUSSIANS, GREEKS, Africans, Poles. . . . The world exists in the mental images people have of other nations, peoples, and places. These images take shape early in human development and seem to be continuous throughout our lives. World events are telescoped for us daily in morning headlines and on television and radio news. As such, they are inputs to our images. For example, during the 1950s and 1960s, many Americans had a relatively stable image of "Communist China," or "Mainland China," as an enemy of the United States. This image has softened considerably since President Nixon took his well-publicized trip to China. Within a seemingly short time, Americans were referring respectfully to China as the "People's Republic of China" and were buying Chinese exports at their stores. Can such long-standing images be reversed by one dramatic incident? How stable are the mental images people have of the invisible reality around them?

Karl Deutsch and Richard Merritt made an extensive study of the impact of world events, both sudden and cumulative, on people's images of

nations. And they found that world events, whether as sudden as a major bombing or cumulative like the Cold War, have only small effects on people's images of other nationalities.

Even in response to the most dramatic events, people's minds apparently continue to function without tremendous restructuring. Consider these examples cited by Deutsch and Merritt from public-opinion surveys conducted internationally:

1. *American agreement with the statement,* "The German people will always want to go to war to make themselves as powerful as possible":

February 1942	41%
June 1943	57%
July 1945	52%
November 1945	45%
May 1946	35%

Only a minority of Americans were willing to attribute great warlike character to Germans, even during one of the greatest German offensives of World War II, in December 1944.

2. *American agreement with the statement,* "The Japanese people will always want to

is quite irrelevant.) Human errors are always possible, particularly under the kind of stress that people feel during enemy attacks. A number of novels and motion pictures have portrayed situations in which a technical failure or one man's decision to escalate a conflict has resulted in total nuclear war.

Certainly, sophisticated control systems avoid many errors in the use of weapons in the United States and other nations. But the question remains: Will these controls work if massive communication disruption were to occur, creating stress for individual decision makers that clouds their judgment? Research has shown that people do not easily cope with stressful situations in which they must consider too much information in too limited a time (Streufert, 1970). One or more of these conditions is likely to occur in the event of serious international conflict, and one condition is enough to reduce the capacity to make rational strategic decisions in stressful situations.

This lack of rational strategic thinking under stress is precisely what Rapoport (1964) has suggested is an outcome of international conflict. When communications must cross national boundaries, problems are even greater. International conflict carries all the dangers to information processing that can occur during intranational conflicts: Important information may be lost, too large an information load may impair decision making, and so on. In addition, the problems in judgment caused by prejudices are often

---

go to war to make themselves as powerful as possible":

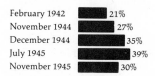

February 1942 — 21%
November 1944 — 27%
December 1944 — 35%
July 1945 — 39%
November 1945 — 30%

Immediately following the attack on Pearl Harbor, the percentage of Americans interviewed who believed that the Japanese people had strong warlike inclinations remained a minority, although Americans were more likely to impute aggressive characteristics to the Japanese than to the Germans.

3. Proportions of Germans who expressed a "willingness to surrender" near the end of the war:

Citizens of heavily bombed cities—58 percent

Citizens of umbombed cities—51 percent

Destruction of civilian areas by the United States and Allied Air Forces had few of the intended morale-reducing effects on the enemy population. The bombs had not destroyed some important images the Germans had.

In accounting for the apparent unwillingness of people to change their basic images, Deutsch and Merritt note that social pressures can be more compelling than are enemy bullets or bombs; for example, one can well imagine that toward the end of World War II the average German felt constrained by social pressure from speaking in favor of surrender to the enemy. Although images can change, change is most likely to occur after similar events repeatedly provoke small changes that accumulate from generation to generation.

Deutsch and Merritt conclude: "The greater openness of adolescents and young adults to new images and impressions—not only in the negative sense of being less burdened with old images and hardened psychic structures, but also in the positive sense of greater sensitivity and ability to learn—is thus a major resource for the long-run learning process of their societies."

Source: Adapted from K. Deutsch and R. Merritt, "Effects of Events on National and International Images," in H. Kelman (ed.), *International Behavior* (New York: Holt, Rinehart and Winston, 1965), pp. 132–187.

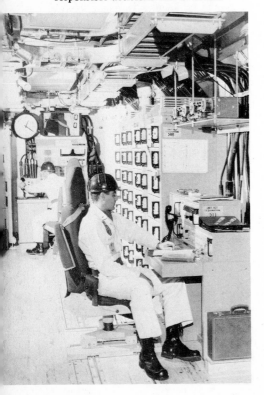

Figure 15.11 An Air Force Minuteman missile launch-control center underground in Wyoming. The master control panel displays the operational status of each missile. A complex system of checks minimizes the possibility of an inadvertent launch. But missile launches are ordered from thousands of miles away, and if the communication link fails, there is no guarantee that responsible decisions will be made.

intensified when the conflict involves different national interests or cultural perspectives. Decision makers no doubt are under pressure to conform to the views of their national constituencies. And to worsen matters further, linguistic misunderstandings may abound in communication between nations, as discussed in Chapter 3. Some of these problems are created by changes in perceptions that are produced by conflict itself. For example, some of these changes may make thinkable the unthinkable: After nuclear war has been considered, it seems more acceptable (Rapoport, 1964). Other problems, however, are present long before actual conflict occurs. As explained in Chapter 1, Urie Bronfenbrenner (1961) had the opportunity during a trip to the Soviet Union in the early 1960s to experience first hand the views that Russians had of Americans and of the United States and to compare these views with American opinions about Russia and the Russians. After returning to the United States, Bronfenbrenner reported that the views that Russians have about Americans are surprisingly similar to American views about the Soviets. For example, the citizens of both nations view the other as the aggressor. Both view the leadership of the other nation as bad. And both populations are able to cite an impressive list of events that they believe support their views. As Bronfenbrenner concluded, international conflict may cause a *mirror-image effect,* in which the antagonists come to closely resemble one another.

Bronfenbrenner is not the only researcher who has spoken of international mirror images. For example, Ralph White (1966) and others have made similar observations. Do mirror images form during years of experience, or can people be made to believe that they are "good" and the opponent is "bad" without much effort? If the latter is true, as suggested in Chapter 7, the danger exists that any demagogue might quickly change the public's attitudes to suit almost any purpose.

To find out how easily people fall into mirror-image thinking, Siegfried Streufert and Sandra Sandler (1971) simulated a war between two hypothetical nations and assigned college sophomores to be decision makers for these nations. (This study is described in detail in Chapter 1.) They found that after only two hours of indoctrination, the participants established mirror-image views of themselves and of their opponents. Other findings are equally disconcerting. In a simulation of a major international confrontation resembling World War I, Michael Driver (1965) found that the views that representatives of various "nations" had of each other tended to become simplified as actual conflict was threatened or initiated. Before the war began, decision makers viewed other nations in at least two ways: how strong they were and who their allies were. After conflict was underway, they were concerned only with alliances. Research by political scientists who have studied the content of communications among nations preceding World War I confirms Driver's simulation findings. The findings are also reminiscent of White's observation, which was discussed in the section on conflict models: Decision makers tend to overestimate their own military strength after conflict has been initiated. Research by Siegfried Streufert and Sandra Sandler (1973), again using a simulation technique, suggests that this is particularly true of decision makers in Western nations.

Strategies for Decreasing Conflict

Conflict-spiral models suggest that nothing more than an underreaction to aggression is needed to decrease conflict between two parties. Studies of actual world events and laboratory research do not bear out this proposi-

V Behavior in Groups

tion, however. It holds true more often when conflict is beginning than after "structural change" has occurred—that is, after the perceptions of opponents have crystallized into mirror images and injury has been experienced by both nations.

An alternative is to establish a favorable attitude between nations *before* conflict develops. Past preventative strategies have not always worked, however. For example, preventing conflict has been one of the purposes of foreign aid. Strangely enough, the expected gratitude and friendliness of receiver nations toward donor nations has not typically developed as a result of foreign-aid programs.

Recipients of aid often become resentful, if not directly hostile. Kenneth Gergen, Mary Gergen, and Stanley Morse have studied this phenomenon both in the field (by interviewing aid personnel in various nations) as well as in the laboratory and with opinion interviews. Using these various methods, they have found remarkable cross-cultural similarities in the factors that cause people to react negatively to aid (see also Chapter 12). Aid apparently has negative impact when the donor has selfish intent, does not truly care for the recipient, or seems to be aggressive, assertive, or unfair to others (Gergen and Gergen, 1971). Opinion surveys from many nations show that these same factors affect reactions to aid in the recipient populations at large (Gergen and Gergen, 1973). Experimental evidence (Gergen and Morse, 1971) indicates that after aid comes to be expected, it does very little to create positive feelings in recipients. Thus, ongoing aid programs do little to increase international good will. In addition, when an aid program is terminated, or expected aid is not received, the recipient may become extremely hostile (Gergen and Morse, 1971; Morse, 1972). It appears, then, that people come to feel that they deserve the rewards they receive and that it is unfair of the donor to take them away. Responses to foreign aid thus appear far less dependent on economic matters than on attitudinal and perceptual processes.

It is not yet possible to draw firm conclusions about the social psychology of international conflict. Although much useful knowledge has accumulated, "laws" of international conflict cannot yet be formulated. The present state of knowledge makes it clear, however, that it is important to act as early as possible in reducing conflict. After conflict has led to direct aggression—after attitudes have hardened and strategic decision making

Figure 15.12 As Vice-President, Richard Nixon demonstrated during his 1958 tour of South America that foreign aid can produce resentment and hostility in recipient nations. His presence in various South American nations that had received aid from the United States continually provoked outbursts from jeering, rock-throwing crowds, as evidenced by the car Nixon rode in *(below)*.

has suffered—it is extremely difficult to alter the course of events. Unfortunately, the means used to influence relations among nations do not always have the desired results; aid, for example, may cause hostility. Detailed research in the future should reveal (1) the most dangerous signs of developing conflict, (2) specific actions that might head off spiraling and structural change in international conflict, and (3) specific actions that would serve to protect nations against the development of conflict. In the field of international conflict, more extensive research and theory are needed—work that in the long run might save the people of the world from the destructive potential of modern weaponry.

Governments are among the most powerful formal organizations on earth. Other powerful organizations include business establishments and schools. The effects that these institutions have on each of us are profound. The effects of these formal institutional structures and processes on group performance and individual satisfaction are explored in Chapter 16.

SUMMARY

Many decisions at all levels of society are made by groups. Groups can often function more effectively than individuals working alone, especially when the chances of a good or correct solution to a problem can be improved by increasing the cognitive or perceptual resources available.

Two types of tasks that may demand different group processes are problem solving, or *determinate* tasks, and decision making, or *indeterminate* tasks. These types of tasks are of value in different situations.

The size of the group also influences the group's ability to solve problems. Small groups tend to be more cohesive and to arrive at unanimous decisions more often than do large groups, which are usually characterized by more formal relationships among group members. In addition, small groups tend to do better with indeterminate tasks, whereas large groups tend to do better with quantitative problems, creation of ideas, and tasks that require remembering. The positive effects on task performance of having an audience present is called *social facilitation* by social psychologists. If present, an audience may also influence the ways in which problems are solved.

The composition of the group can be important. *Homogeneity*, or similarity, of group members can make it easier to arrive at group decisions, whereas *heterogeneity*, or dissimilarity, can enlarge the cognitive resources of groups. When competing subgroups are formed—*coalition formation*—the group tends to become less effective in performing its tasks.

A group's effectiveness can be influenced by the style of the leader. An authoritarian leader helps most in increasing the quantity of output, but group morale suffers in the process. Evidence also suggests that there may be no "natural leaders" who are free of the demands of the situations in which they operate.

Group structures differ in the degrees of formality displayed between members and take many forms. Differences in group structure affect who will likely emerge as a leader and how effective he or she will be, how satisfied members will be, and how efficient the group will be in solving problems.

Sometimes a group's solution is different from any that would arise from any one of the individual members. One such phenomenon is *groupthink.* When groups arrive at solutions that are riskier than the average member's individual solutions, the result is the *risky shift.* In contrast, solutions may also become more cautious when *choice shifts* occur.

In many cases, group decisions are made in an atmosphere of conflict, whether conflict within or between groups. Conflicts within groups can develop from task characteristics; problems with ambiguous solutions produce more conflict than do simple, straightforward problems, although the confidence of one member in a particular solution sometimes reduces conflict by rallying the group to one of the alternatives. Conflict may result if group members are too competitive and if they differ too much in status, attitudes toward group goals, initial attitude sets, or personality.

Conflict models are used by social psychologists to describe the antecedents, progress, and consequences of conflict. (1) According to an *aggressor-defender model,* one party to a conflict is responsible for an outbreak of hostilities. (2) According to a *conflict-spiral model,* conflict is an interactive process in which one action prompts the opponent to escalate, arousing the first party to still greater fury. And (3) according to a *structural-change model,* conflict is a dynamic process that continually changes the attitudes of the parties, affecting the nature of future conflict.

Social-psychological research has much to contribute to an understanding of international conflict. For example, among the existing areas of investigation are communications, because they often break down under stress, and the attitudes of opponents toward one another that change as conflict escalates. Research suggests that the most effective means of minimizing conflict is to establish positive attitudes between groups before conflict has a chance to begin. If applied, the use of this knowledge could have important international consequences.

In the future, researchers will continue to search out answers to the questions of why conflict develops, what the signs are, what can be done to end it, and what can be done to prevent it.

SUGGESTED READINGS

Bronfenbrenner, Urie. "The Mirror Image in Soviet-American Relations: A Social Psychologist's Report," *Journal of Social Issues,* 17 (1961), 45–56.

Davis, James H. *Group Performance.* Reading, Mass.: Addison-Wesley, 1969.

Fiedler, Fred. "Style or Circumstance: The Leadership Enigma," *Psychology Today,* 2 (1969), 38–43.

Hollander, Edwin P. *Leaders, Groups, and Influence.* New York: Oxford University Press, 1964.

Janis, Irving L. *Victims of Groupthink.* Boston: Houghton Mifflin, 1972.

Kelman, Herbert C. (ed.). *International Behavior: A Social-Psychological Analysis.* New York: Holt, Rinehart and Winston, 1965.

16

The Psychology of Organizations

Ours is an almost totally institutionalized environment. Take a look around you. If you are a college student, numerous organizations affect your daily life as well as the skills, aspirations, and attitudes that will determine to a large extent how you will spend the rest of your life. Your classes affect your "career orientation" and are the basis on which your skills will be judged and certified. Your department, if effective, steers you into a career that is marketable. The administration of your college is responsible for recording and charting your progress through college. In addition to the groups you encounter on campus, you depend on organizations whenever you shop, go to the bank, attend church, or mail a letter. Your family and the state and country you live in are organizations—organizations that have profound effects on your life, even when you are alone. Your contact with organizations may not always be voluntary. It is possible that when you pay your taxes on April 15, you do not do so cheerfully. And when a policeman pulls you over to give you a traffic ticket, your contact with the organization of law enforcement is not voluntary.

In theory, the social psychology of organizations encompasses any formal collection of people who have defined relationships, such as authority hierarchies and task differentiations, and who share the purpose of achieving a common goal. In practice, however, research in this field has concentrated on the few groups that are run systematically and formally as organizations. Work organizations—businesses, offices, and factories—have been particularly eager to benefit from analyses of their efficiency. Because commercial enterprises have financed much of the research conducted by organizational psychologists, the study of organizational behavior is commonly thought of as dealing with work organizations in their present forms. On many campuses, the study of organizations is the province of the business school or department. However, most of the theories and practices of organizational psychologists have wide applicability outside business organizations; examples of these applications are presented throughout this chapter.

The *formal organizations* in which we are enmeshed throughout our lives often have even greater influence on us than do informal groups, which are discussed in Chapter 14. Many formal organizations embody institutionalized forms that have been around for centuries; they pervade not only our individual lives but also certain cultural attitudes toward work, fulfillment, and one another. In fact, organizations depend on a compatible cultural orientation for survival. The organizations that dominate contemporary society—whether corporations, churches, government agencies, or schools—require people who are willing to produce and consume their goods and services.

In this chapter, the focus is on the impact of various organizational structures, procedures, and products on individuals as well as the ways in which individuals can influence the organizations in which they participate. In particular, an organization's goals, the way in which it is managed, and the ways in which it is changed by its members are all factors that contribute to its distinctive character. After reviewing the theories and research that have been generated by mainstream organizational psychology, some possible answers to a question rarely asked of the consultants hired by business organizations will be examined: Should the form of existing organizations be reshaped altogether?

GOALS IN COMMERCIAL ORGANIZATIONS

The need to set and monitor goals characterizes all complex organizations. And these goals affect the lives of all members of an organization. Goals affect individual members' expectations about what rewards will come their way; they also affect the standards by which the individual's performance will be evaluated.

The actions taken by an organization are not always compatible with the goals the organization expresses to its public. Discrepancies of this sort are probably most noticeable in noncommercial organizations, in which stated goals serve to legitimize the organization to society. For example, although the stated goal of prisons is rehabilitation, Donald Cressey noted in 1959 that the real goal is confinement and perhaps even retribution. And although the stated goal of schools is education, educators and students alike often complain that many schools in the United States serve to strip people of imagination and initiative and to groom them for lives of subservient labor and competitive consumption.

An organization's goals may even be unclear to many of the group's members, because leaders may deliberately distort their organizations' goals to other members. For example, religious leaders have often distorted the original precepts of the religious organizations they manage in order to justify participation in wars, crusades, and other dubious proselytising endeavors.

Strangely enough, one problem an organization can face is the complete fulfillment of its goals. In fact, goals are not intended to be completely accomplished; a total triumph removes the purpose for an organization's existence. Such a crisis seldom occurs, but when it does, the organization must either disband or adopt new goals. When the March of Dimes succeeded in its original aim—the prevention of infantile paralysis—it undertook a new cause: the battle against birth defects (Marlow, 1971).

Business organizations usually seem to have concrete and clear-cut goals. One need only examine the record of profits and losses to determine whether or not a business is performing at a satisfactory level. The business manager himself would typically describe the purpose of his organization as being "to maximize the return to the stockholder."

Even when the goals that direct an organization's operations are self-evident, however, they seldom remain static. On the contrary, goals are frequently expanded or otherwise modified. Among the forces that can transform goals are societal, economic, or technological changes; repeated failure to achieve stated goals; and the attitudes and expectations of the organization's members.

The history of profit-seeking organizations affords many examples of goals that have been expanded. For example, changes at all hierarchical levels in members' attitudes regarding worker satisfaction and its importance relative to productivity and efficiency have brought striking changes in organizational goals and processes. A series of cultural shifts in values and in work-force composition have produced workers who today are less exclusively concerned with pay than were workers of a century or even a generation ago. A recent survey of more than 1,500 workers conducted by the University of Michigan Survey Research Center (1970) revealed that "good pay" is deemed less important than "interesting work," "enough help and equipment to get the job done," "enough information," and "enough authority" to do the job.

Life is not as simple as it once was for businessmen. With Ralph Nader breathing down the businessman's neck, with groups like the Council on Economic Priorities releasing increasingly well-heeded reports about the "social performance" of industries, and with even the government cracking down, new concepts of *social accounting* are developing. As a result, the criteria by which business performance is evaluated have been expanding. Organizations like the Bank of America are creating departments to assess the social impact of any new project or organizational thrust (although

Figure 16.1 The consuming position organizations have come to occupy in our personal lives is portrayed in Franz Kafka's story *Metamorphosis.* Even in the weird situation in which Gregor Samsa finds himself, he is still concerned about doing his job.

Gregor Samsa awakes one morning to find himself changed into a man-size cockroach. When the chief clerk comes from his office to ask why Gregor is late, Gregor opens the door with his mouth and replies:

Well. . . I'll put my clothes on at once, pack up my samples and start off. Will you only let me go? You see, sir, I'm not obstinate, and I'm willing to work; traveling is a hard life, but I couldn't live without it. . . . One can be temporarily incapacitated, but that's just the moment for remembering former services and bearing in mind that later on, when the incapacity has been got over, one will certainly work with all the more industry and concentration. I'm loyally bound to serve the chief, you know that very well. Besides, I have to provide for my parents and my sister.

these efforts are often a matter of window dressing and of public relations).

Perhaps the social concern that most preoccupies business itself is worker morale. Because business managers believe that worker morale strongly affects productivity and therefore the primary economic goal of their organizations—to maximize the return on investments—they have taken the initiative in sponsoring studies of the relationships between workers' expectations, workers' satisfaction, and productivity.

Scientific Management: The Early Days

To obtain some appreciation of the ways in which an organization's goals can expand and change—even within the most traditional business organizations—some of the ways in which organizational goals have already changed will be examined. The first systematic attention paid by business managers to their workers was frankly manipulative, although at that time nobody except socialists seemed to question managerial motives (Copley, 1923). The intentions of early organizational psychologists were not malevolent, however; to the contrary, these pioneers believed that increased rationality and efficiency would improve the work setting for everyone.

The earliest studies of worker motivation and performance were made by Frederick W. Taylor (1911), who prescribed *scientific management* to maximize efficiency, discipline, and standardization of jobs. Taylor reasoned that if work were defined precisely, if workers knew what they had to do, and if rewards and punishments were arranged to encourage a high rate of performance, then the largest possible output would be produced and everyone would profit. Among the techniques developed by scientific-management proponents were *time-and-motion studies,* which revealed the quickest, smoothest series of physical movements by which any given task

Figure 16.2 During the days of scientific management, organizations were admittedly unconcerned about their employees, except as productivity was directly affected. Although today management espouses a human-relations philosophy and has made conscious efforts to improve employees' satisfaction and working conditions, the overriding concern is still with production. Thus some observers question how basic the changes have been. Are working conditions and management philosophy really so different now, or has change been merely a face lifting?

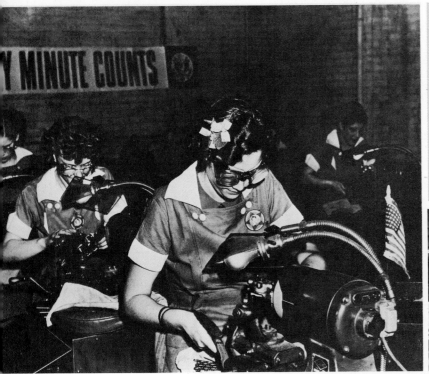

could be performed, and *piecework incentive systems,* intended to make it clear that the more a worker produced, the more he or she would be paid.

The scientific-management approach proved inadequate, because it did not account for the social needs of the worker. Before the next major step could be taken by organizational psychologists, an awareness of the worker as a complete human being had to emerge. The first evidence of the multidimensional nature of workers' needs appeared unexpectedly during the now-famous studies of workers at the Hawthorne Plant of the Western Electric Company, which spanned the decade beginning in 1924. This research, reported by Fritz Roethlisberger and William Dickson in 1939, began modestly as an attempt to determine the effect of lighting on worker productivity (in this case, women assembling small telephone relays), which gives a clue as to the preoccupations of organizational researchers at the time. The investigators were mystified by their finding that the productivity of a control group, which did not experience a change in lighting, increased about as much as did the productivity of the experimental (improved-lighting) group. Then the experimenters tested another group to determine the effects of a *decrement* in lighting, and this group, too, responded with an increase in productivity!

The apparent paradox was not resolved until after Elton Mayo had joined the Hawthorne team in 1927. This time the researchers studied the women to determine whether or not more frequent rest periods and a shorter work week would increase productivity. Again, productivity increased consistently in all conditions.

The experimenters finally realized that their subjects had probably been responding to the unusual interest shown in them during the experiment rather than to the specific changes in the environment. All the women had been gathered into small groups under the supervision of the experimenters and their assistants. The supervisory styles of the research team differed considerably from those of factory supervisors. These new supervisors were more lenient and more solicitous, and they engaged in friendly interchanges with the workers. When the women objected to certain of the experimental manipulations, to their amazement the new supervisors quickly discontinued the offensive conditions. In short, this situation offered unprecedented intimacy and support from peers as well as individual recognition from supervisors (Roethlisberger and Dickson, 1939). The *Hawthorne effect* is now a popular term, used by organizational psychologists to refer to any instance of improvement in performance that is a by-product of attention.

The Human-Relations Approach

The message to management was that workers could be motivated just by paying attention to them as human beings. Contrary to the scientific-management school's way of thinking, job specialization and isolation cannot guarantee better performance. Hawthorne had shown that the effects of scientific management could be detrimental and that a policy of neglecting the social side of work could cause men and women to become dissatisfied and recalcitrant and to work less efficiently.

Another social variable identified in the work structure during the Hawthorne studies is that of the *informal organization,* in contrast to the formal structure that Taylor and his colleagues had recognized. In this uncharted region, group standards developed out of stable social relationships and informal sanctions such as group pressure (see Chapter 14). These unofficial standards could either reinforce or undercut the standards explicitly set down by the organization. For example, Stanley Seashore (1954) reported that very cohesive work groups produced at above-average rates when they accepted their company's goals and at substandard rates when they did not accept company goals. Less cohesive work groups, on the other hand, performed near the average no matter what their attitudes toward management. In other words, the more cohesive the work group, the more effective it can be in either facilitating or impeding the success of the larger organization.

Out of the Hawthorne research developed the *human-relations* school of industrial psychology, which remains popular with businessmen and with most organizational psychologists. The human-relations approach attempts to increase productivity by increasing the worker's satisfaction. The techniques that typically have been employed involve greater awareness by supervisors of workers' feelings. More recently, some degree of effort has been made to permit the work group to set its own goals, to participate in decision making, or to set its own pace.

The continuing emphasis on productivity, however, explains why moral objections have been raised against the human-relations approach and against organizational psychology in general: Why, indeed, should a person's satisfaction be measured in terms of organizational efficiency? As some observers have pointed out (for example, Loren Baritz, 1960), organizational researchers have always been hired by the companies and firms that employ the workers, and therefore the researchers are not likely to make recommendations that, although they might benefit the employee, would not serve company goals. Most human-relations theorists during the past half-century have assumed that a satisfied worker is a productive worker, that a happy conjunction of individual and organizational aims is indeed possible as well as desirable.

Productivity and Satisfaction

Because they have looked at human satisfaction almost exclusively insofar as it is instrumental to productivity, human-relations theorists have largely neglected to study the effects of productivity on workers' satisfaction. In addition, these researchers have shown little curiosity regarding what conditions (beyond those that ensure a given level of performance) make for a contented organization member.

During the past decade, several organizational psychologists have been developing a broader notion of what constitutes an effective organization. For example, Rensis Likert (1967) uses the term "human organization" in reference to human resources that are often overlooked by the organization's formal accounting system. From this perspective, efforts to enhance the quality of employees' work lives will nearly always show up in some deeper, more solid, and more flexible social structure underlying the formal organizational structure. Consequently, it is possible for managers to fit a concern for individual mental health into an enlarged view of organizational health (Argyris, 1972). Nevertheless, there remains a strong tendency, even among organizational psychologists of this expanded outlook, to want to show that a consciousness of human relations contributes to successful economic coping by the profit-seeking organization.

Despite the hope among human-relations proponents that a happy worker will be a productive worker, evidence of a clear relationship between satisfaction and performance has not emerged. Victor Vroom (1964) reviewed twenty studies of satisfaction and performance and found a negligible correlation between the two variables. One problem with comparing these twenty studies is that different measures of performance were used. In some studies, performance was defined as the amount produced or as voluntary and innovative behavior in the service of the organization; in other studies, rates of turnover and absenteeism were used as indications of *non*performance. Clearly, different kinds of jobs demand different forms of productivity and give different qualities of satisfaction. In general, skilled jobs demand more involvement and provide greater enjoyment (Hull and Kolstad, 1942; Morse, 1953).

Different Jobs, Different Satisfactions. Several organizational psychologists have attempted to build a theoretical structure that weaves together many of the factors discussed thus far. The most ambitious effort was made by Daniel Katz and Robert Kahn in a classic work, *The Social Psychology of Organizations* (1966). A modified and condensed model of the original work accounts for four dimensions of the work situation: the *job requirements;* the *psychological mechanism* by which the worker becomes motivated; the *organizational policy,* or input from management; and the *productivity measure* by which the worker's performance is judged. Katz and Kahn believe that different jobs make possible different fulfillments and that worker productivity will be maximized when management researches the possibilities for satisfaction and then does its best to fulfill them.

The influence of models as complex as Katz and Kahn's could lead to an expansion of the manager's conception of his responsibility to his workers; they suggest that processes like productivity and satisfaction cannot be reduced to single dimensions.

Some jobs require only a minimal level of involvement from an employee. Not much more may be required of a guard than his physical presence at the right place at the right time. And some workers need only keep alert enough to notice when their machines need to be fed, emptied, or repaired and to remember to turn the machines on and off. In comparison, positions that involve more intricate decisions—as those of foremen, craftsmen, and salesmen—require greater attention to broad detail, greater awareness of company aims, and higher motivation to act in the

Figure 16.3 A society as thoroughly permeated by organizations as ours must contend with the issue of balancing productivity and satisfaction. To what extent does a society's efficiency take precedence over the satisfaction of its members? The film *Metropolis* (*left*) portrays an industrialized state that usurps the rights of individuals and operates at their expense. According to philosopher and architect Paolo Soleri, however, productivity and satisfaction need not be incompatible. He has conceptualized and is presently constructing in Arizona an experimental community (*right*) based on the dual principles of preserving the ecology of an area and enriching the human environment. Built on ten acres of desert land, Soleri's prototype urban environment will be surrounded by parks, farmlands, and wilderness. The city itself will be so compact that none of the 3,000 inhabitants will have more than a fifteen- or twenty-minute walk from their homes to the areas set aside for work, school, and entertainment. The design offers the vitality of city life without the problems of urban sprawl, transportation, and pollution that presently plague cities.

best interests of the company. Positions of still greater responsibility, like that of scientist and high-level manager, require that the workers who fill them identify sufficiently with their work or with their organizations to be motivated to develop new solutions for novel and undefined conditions.

The type of behaviors desired for any one of these three types of jobs determines the psychological mechanism that will be effective in motivating those behaviors. Menial or mechanical work requires no more from the worker than simple, legalistic *compliance,* or acceptance of organizational prescriptions. Skilled and supervisory roles demand *instrumental involvement* in the work activity, which the worker views as a means of obtaining a personal reward, such as praise, a raise, or a promotion. And *internalization of professional values* is necessary to motivate managerial and creative work, whether the internalization is prompted by the satisfactions of achievement and expression or by identification with the goals of the organization.

The organization can make salient the conditions that facilitate each of these psychological mechanisms by setting up and publicizing policies that cater to the desired mechanism. For example, when compliance is sought, regulations should be set forth clearly, consistently, and fairly, so that workers can agree and rely on the standards they work by; furthermore, these regulations should be evenly enforced. In encouraging instrumentally motivated behavior, the organization must yoke rewards directly to the desired behaviors, so that better performance clearly leads to greater rewards. The type and size of rewards workers consider appropriate for a given level of performance, however, depend on the individual workers' frames of reference (see Chapter 9)—the people to whom they compare themselves and the distance they see themselves as having come from their earlier stations in life. To use internalized values as motivators, the organization must either provide jobs that workers regard as meaningful and inherently rewarding, or it must ensure that employees agree with company aims, as occurs in voluntary organizations and when workers believe their personal earnings will vary directly with their company's profits.

Whichever of the three types of psychological mechanisms is activated, the characteristic mode of productivity that results will be different from that generated by the other two mechanisms. If workers are being asked only to comply, then productivity can be expected to be minimally but reliably acceptable. When they see their work as leading to the rewards they seek, then absenteeism may be reduced and their efficiency increased. And if internal motivators can be employed, workers will not only be absent less and produce more; in addition, they can probably be counted on to extend themselves beyond the stated requirements of their jobs and the specified behaviors they have been taught in order to fill their positions.

The relationships between these four interrelated variables are summarized in Table 16.1. If a job requires fairly low levels of competence and self-regulation, then all that workers need is an understanding of what to do and simple rewards and punishments commensurate with their performance. A more skilled task that demands an efficient and high-quality performance might effectively feature contingency rewards, like piece-rates or quality bonuses or commissions. But when a job demands high productivity and creativity, workers must be able to find self-expression in their work. This distribution of rewards is not an indication that persons engaged in menial activities have fewer or weaker needs than do more skilled workers; rather, it is undertaken by managers as an efficiency measure. Incentives for instrumental involvement are more costly to most profit-making enterprises than are the incentives for compliance, and neither of these types of incentives represent as large an investment as do the incentives for creative, productive involvement.

Deepening Satisfactions at Work. There is reason to believe that the more an activity engages a person's potentialities, the deeper the satisfaction it produces. The late Abraham Maslow (1954) spoke of a *need hierarchy* by which all individuals are first compelled to satisfy basic needs, such as hunger and thirst, physical security, and protection from the elements. When these deficiency needs have been met, the individual will seek satisfactions for *metaneeds,* or growth needs, that are less urgent and more rarefied. If the individual's progress up this hierarchy is unimpeded, Maslow believed, he or she approaches a state of *self-actualization* in which the deepest personal impulses are fulfilled in life activities. Both basic needs and metaneeds are innate in human beings, and even if all basic needs have been fulfilled, the individual may become psychologically sick if the growth needs are ignored. Some of the symptoms of this psychological sickness—alienation, apathy, and cynicism—appear with unusually high frequency among assembly-line workers and others who perform menial, fractionalized services. Clearly, work can be an important part of a person's actualization. And, as a rule, the more skilled the job, the greater the possibilities for contentment. Even when workers continue to do the same kind of work, satisfaction can be increased by expanding the range of each worker's operations (Trist, Higgin, Murray, and Pollack, 1963; Walker and Guest, 1952). In a classic demonstration of the successful use of *job enlargement,* Eric Trist and his colleagues at the Tavistock Institute in London were able to increase the satisfaction of British coal miners by extending the cycle of their activities in the mining process. These workers had become dissatisfied when conveyor systems were introduced into the mine shafts. The mine's management figured this innovation would make it more efficient to divide the mining cycle, which previously had been performed in its entirety by all the miners, into three separate functions, performed by different individuals. The impact on the individual worker of the new method was considerable. His relationship with his fellow workers grew strained and competitive, because he depended on them but could not communicate with them. He no longer identified with the entire mining process, and his

Table 16.1   Dimensions of Job Satisfaction

JOB REQUIREMENTS	PSYCHOLOGICAL MECHANISM	ORGANIZATIONAL POLICY	PRODUCTIVITY MEASURE
Menial, mechanical	Compliance	Clear rule setting, equitable enforcement	Reaching acceptable productivity baselines
Skilled, supervisory, synthesizing (for example, salesman)	Instrumental involvement	Contingency reward allocation	Efficiency, quality
Managerial	Internalization of professional values	Gaining value alignment through recruiting, goal-setting	Innovativeness, low absenteeism, high productivity
Intellectual, creative	Internalization of professional values	Devising involving jobs	Creativity, low absenteeism, high productivity

Source: Adapted from D. Katz and R. Kahn, *The Social Psychology of Organizations* (New York: Wiley, 1966), pp. 336–389.

production dropped off. In short, this was a classic case in which a technical advance (accompanied by efficiency measures that regarded men as machine-substitutes) failed to bring about an expected increase in production because enthusiastic managers ignored the satisfactions workers derived from their jobs.

Not all the shafts had been totally reorganized along the lines of the new system, however; some of them took on a composite form, retaining aspects of the old system. All the miners in a composite system rotated among the three tasks, and they themselves, within six-man teams, made the job assignments. The composite method alleviated the problems of the new, fractionalizing system, because each worker still felt a part of the overall process and worked as a member of a group. As a result, miners in composite arrangements were more satisfied and more productive than were workers in the new, fragmented system. Absenteeism was two-thirds what it was under the fragmented method, uninterrupted extraction runs were more than five times as long, and more tonnage of coal was removed. In other words, whether productivity was measured in terms of reliability or efficiency, the composite approach proved superior.

Workers in a setting such as an automobile assembly line have few opportunities for pride in a product, for they exercise little control, feel little involvement, and rarely have the satisfaction of seeing the results of their labors. Assembly workers may even have to ask their foreman for permission to go to the lavatory. But even on the assembly line, efforts are being made both by management and by labor to increase worker satisfaction. Labor unions such as the United Auto Workers (UAW) are actively bargaining for improved conditions, although these efforts still revolve less around job enrichment than they do around escape from the job through shorter work weeks, early retirement, and the right to reject overtime assignments. The managements of a few automobile factories—most notably Volvo and Saab in Sweden—have broken up their assembly lines into work teams that

Figure 16.4 Although many work conditions can be improved, and although some organizations make improvements, many other jobs are still tedious and less than stimulating. Old-time miners (*left*) did not have the modern equipment that their contemporary counterparts have (*center*), but the present-day miner (*right*) is probably just as exhausted and uninspired after a long day's labor as his predecessors were. In fact, because fragmented production-line procedures often follow technological improvements, alienation from the products of his labors and loneliness may be added to the contemporary miner's miseries.

perform several tasks rather than one repetitive task. And in Japan, factories are evolving a decision-making process based on consensus: policies are reviewed by workers at all hierarchical levels before decisions are made.

Clearly, the way in which the work is organized is one of the most important determinants of worker satisfaction. Studies like that by Trist and his associates indicate that conditions are conducive to satisfaction when the job is enlarged beyond a single, repetitive task and when employees can work cooperatively with others and organize their own work. Other factors that can contribute to job satisfaction range from prohibiting conspicuous executive privileges, such as reserved parking and thicker carpets, to providing workers with opportunities for initiative and for an influence in company policy. Arnold Tannenbaum (1968) found that productivity was greatest in organizations in which low-level members felt they exerted an influence on the conduct of the organization. Furthermore, Tannenbaum found that this feeling of power increased the effectiveness of members in noncommercial organizations, like labor unions and local chapters of the League of Women Voters, as well as in commercial enterprises.

Whether measured by management or worker goals, by profits or satisfaction, the effectiveness of organizations of all types seems to be intimately linked to the psychological and social effects of those organizations on their individual members. An organization's structure, its leadership, and the control system by which it tries to ensure that goals are accomplished are all important threads in the social-psychological fabric of that organization. These factors are discussed in the following section.

MANAGING THE ORGANIZATION

Management is the skeleton on which the organization hangs. Management consists of the people and devices that give an organization its form and direct its activities. Whether the organization is a commercial enterprise or a university, a hospital or a club, a nation or a family, it must be

Figure 16.5 Some organizations are attempting to increase worker involvement and satisfaction even on the assembly line. (*Left*) Saab, for example, is utilizing the job-enlargement principle and replacing many assembly lines with work teams. (*Right*) this assembly-line worker, whose job consists exclusively of installing automobile side windows, is well aware that such attempts in large-scale industry are rare and slow to occur.

managed. Among the factors that can affect management's progress in accomplishing goals are the organization's structure as well as the leadership style, atmosphere, and methods management uses to motivate and control the other members of the organization.

Structure: Up and Down the Organization

The most basic concern of a manager, after organizational goals have been established, is the shape, or structure, the organization should assume. The manager must determine the external boundaries of the organization, including its size and the scope of operations it will undertake. The organization's internal structure must also be determined—how the work will get done, what roles individual members will fill, and the relationships between people filling those roles.

Mechanical Versus Organic Models. Organizations as we know them are almost always based on a *mechanical model* in which the structure, systems of control, and the roles of their members are precisely defined. For example, both commercial enterprises and universities typically exhibit the highly defined structures characteristic of a mechanical model. Workers are expected to heed the instructions of their bosses, to meet certain standards of productivity, and to resist challenging the authority of their superiors. This subordination can minimize workers' satisfactions with their jobs and also sap the organization of some of its innovative and productive potential. In much the same way, the docile subordination of the student role may interfere with education—a possibility explored later in this chapter.

Role expectations are not often totally arbitrary. A role originally evolves because its designers consider it a viable approach to accomplishing the organization's goals. And such role expectations persist because they come to be valued by members at all hierarchical levels as a means by which everyone knows what to do and how what one is doing relates to what others are doing. In other words, role expectations can be a valuable means of guaranteeing that individual efforts are coordinated. This *mutual compatibility of expectations* is precisely what makes a group of people act as an organization rather than as a random collection of independently functioning individuals.

Although necessary for an organization to be effective, mutual compatibility of expectations does not *create* the organization. Rather, the way must be paved for compatibility of expectations by those individuals who originally define the expectations and encourage their acceptance. The promise of fulfillment of these expectations is what attracts the body of an organization's members. For many members, the organization precedes their expectations. For example, the lowest social strata of American blacks —outcasts among both whites and blacks—accepted their status until Elijah Muhammad and Malcolm X gave them a definition of their innate humanity and offered them dignity in the Black Muslim organization.

Even in highly structured organizations, not all roles are determined in all their aspects by formal prescriptions. There is always a gray area in which organizational members do not know the limitations of their roles—what exactly is expected of them, how far deviations will be tolerated, and what sanctions will be applied. As long as these limits remain untested, members will tend to fall back on tacitly accepted, often irrational, and usually conservative conceptions of their roles. But if an individual dares to explore the limits of the standard role, he or she may succeed in broadening its definition for everyone concerned. For example, an employee may come in late every morning and make up for this tardiness by working during the scheduled coffee break. If this behavior is not immediately declared out-of-bounds by a superior, then this employee will have succeeded in making more flexible a job definition that everyone else had interpreted rigidly. This sort of personal influence probably is strongest in changing role expectations that are not work-related, as in the example just cited or as in the case of an employee dressed in patched blue jeans who by his example causes his co-workers to loosen their neckties a bit.

There is an alternative to the mechanical model of management. In the classroom situation, for example, the class members usually assume from the beginning of the school term that one person among them (the instructor) will deliver lectures and have the coercive power of grades over the others. The rest of the class typically assumes the role, which is set forth by the educational institution, of listening to the lectures, studying, and heeding the instructions of the teacher. But if instead the class members assumed only that everyone would contribute what he or she could and that each member would teach or learn when it suited the occasion, then the class would be proceeding according to an *organic model* of cooperative action. The organization of the class would be internally defined, and class members (students and instructor alike) would be responding to intrinsic rewards rather than coercion. The structure of an organization and the roles of its members are not predetermined and precisely defined in the organic model but develop informally during the course of the organization's functioning. Additionally, the organization that follows an organic model does not have any formal system of control.

To many people, the organic model seems far more preferable than the mechanical model; perhaps it even seems ideal. But it is also a difficult model to put into practice. Consider marriage as a popular attempt to achieve this ideal and how infrequently it works (less than fifty percent of the time, Vance Packard reported in 1972). In desperation, people are increasingly defining in explicit terms before marriage what it is they want—and do not want—from the institution and from an intimate relationship. If an organization of two has difficulty maintaining an atmosphere of trust and cooperation, then the obstacles are obviously far greater at General Motors or at a university, where only a fraction of the membership is known by any one individual. (The difficulties involved in developing cooperation even in groups of only two persons are discussed in Chapter 13.)

Although totally organic institutions are rare among large organizations, they are not unheard of. Business students often have difficulty understanding how things work at the Marshall Company—an old papermill in the northeastern section of the United States (Dalton and Lawrence, 1971). If a worker is not performing well there, his supervisor will not transfer, demote, or fire him. Rather, the supervisor will wait for the work group as a whole to become aware of the problem, to reach a consensus about what should be done, and to suggest a remedy. What makes this organic form of decision making possible is a longstanding, informal system of social control that is rooted in the cohesive, small-town environment in which Marshall Company is set. When something is going wrong in the production process and one of the men is at fault, everyone—*including the man who is falling short of the standard*—is soon aware of the problem. The men generally acknowledge when personnel adjustments must be made, so that these adjustments seem to happen by consensus. Consensus is possible because all the information relevant to a decision is equally available to all the workers. Furthermore, each man is not likely to want to be promoted beyond the level of responsibility he is capable of discharging, because such a promotion would place him in a rather dangerous position socially. dangerous position.

Process Versus Product. Assuming a mechanical model, there are many ways to slice the work sequence in a complex organization. The experience of the coal miners studied by Trist and his colleagues indicated that specialized jobs tend to fragment the flow of work and to alienate the individual member from the overall production cycle. This fragmentation of work is characteristic of a *process organization,* so named because members specialize in separate functions, or processes, and never see a project through all its stages of production. This division of labor is attractive to managers because it encourages individuals to become proficient at specialized tasks, makes possible uniform work standards, and permits efficient assignment of tasks as they arise in different projects. The increasing task specialization in most large organizations has also had its effects on campuses, so that educational critics complain that many courses of study leave the student with too narrow a perspective and thereby defeat a fundamental purpose of education—to widen the student's vision.

An alternative is *product organization,* in which an individual or group is responsible for the entire cycle of a product, from start to finish. Although this arrangement seems more conducive to high morale than is process organization, it is not always easy to engage everyone in a product cycle. For example, it might prove difficult to instill in a night-shift maintenance worker a feeling of investment in the performance of the regular shift's production crew. Similarly, it might not be a simple matter for a graduate student to spark product consciousness in the person she is paying to type her doctoral dissertation. Bonuses and job enlargement are among the specific methods by which a manager can get those he manages to become involved in the organization's operations.

Some managers have elected to combine elements both of process specialization and of a product orientation. In the resulting *project organization,* or *matrix organization,* illustrated in Figure 16.6, a person whose primary organizational identity lies with a process subgroup is assigned to a succession of temporary project groups and performs more or less the same function in each one. This arrangement allows everyone a sense of participation in the overall project without compromising the competence that specialization can foster. On the other hand, the individual may receive conflicting messages from process and project groups. Or, he or she may depend for rewards on a process supervisor who only hears of the individual's performance from a project director, rather than witnessing it directly. Despite such problems, this form of organization is becoming increasingly popular in contemporary organizations.

The Leader Creates the Climate

The *effectiveness* of various types of leadership style has already been discussed (see Chapter 14). Leadership style also influences the atmosphere pervading an organization. Research on the effects of different leadership styles on a group's atmosphere or climate supports many of our common biases. Kurt Lewin, Ronald Lippitt, and Ralph White contributed the classic study of the effects of leadership styles on group atmosphere (Lewin, Lippitt, and White, 1939; Lippitt, 1940; Lippitt and White, 1943). These researchers wanted to learn the effects of three leadership styles, in particular, on groups of adolescent male subjects. A group under autocratic, or authoritarian, leadership was totally dominated by the adult who led the group; he decided everything—policies, assignments, procedures—without even informing the boys what would come next. In contrast, boys who experienced a *democratic* style of leadership established their own policies and consulted the leader for technical advice; they also selected their work partners and distributed the tasks among themselves. Finally, a *laissez-faire* style of leadership allowed the boys complete freedom; the leader presented the work materials but did not direct or regulate the activity.

Distinct atmospheres developed in the groups, along with corresponding differences in effectiveness and contentment. The least work, and of the poorest quality, was produced in the laissez-faire atmosphere; this group was disorganized, and its members frequently became discouraged and even hostile. More work was accomplished under autocratic leadership, but there were indications of a psychic cost; the autocratic setting seemed to generate hostility, which was manifested as aggression toward scapegoats and was expressed less overtly as a dislike of authoritarian leaders. Paradoxically, boys also were the most dependent on their leader under autocracy, and this dependence, combined with their resentment, made them most likely to stop working when the leader was not present. Satisfaction was greatest in the democratic atmosphere because there was less tension than in the autocratic setting and a greater feeling of accomplishment than under nondirective, laissez-faire leadership—although productivity was about equal under democratic and autocratic conditions. In addition, more group-minded and friendly comments were volunteered under democratic leadership than in either autocratic or laissez-faire settings. And the boys' interest in their work seemed more genuine, as indicated by the fact that they kept on working even when the leader left the room. More recent work conducted by Fred E. Fiedler in 1968 (discussed

Figure 16.6 Work within an organization can be organized in a variety of ways. Process organization (*top*) requires specialization and work fragmentation; product organization (*bottom left*) allows involvement in the entire cycle of production; and project organization (*bottom right*) combines the two to attain both the high morale that is characteristic of the product approach and the efficiency that is characteristic of the process approach.

in Chapter 15) suggests that the type of task involved and the relations within the group may be factors influencing the effectiveness of a leader's style in a given situation.

In some organizations under laissez-faire leadership, notably in a few educational and communal experiments, there has been a reaction against even the mild task direction of the democratic atmosphere as Lewin conceived it. Lewin and his co-workers would today probably warn that, without direction, people are unable to achieve their goals or to perform satisfying work and will consequently become frustrated and unhappy. On the other hand, any kind of task direction by an authority figure—as opposed to availability of a resource person—may hamper initiative and spontaneous activity, as noted in the final section of this chapter.

The issues raised by the early group-climate studies were not explored systematically in formal organizations until the 1960s, when interest in *organizational climate* grew rapidly. To assess the climates in various organizations, George Litwin and Robert Stringer (1968) developed a questionnaire that focused on six variables: the *structure* of the group, the individual's *responsibility* within the group, the *risk* involved in a member's tasks, the *rewards* offered the member for successful completion of tasks, the degree of *warmth and support* available to the individual from the group, and the amount of *conflict* the group could handle. Litwin (1968) wanted to know the impact of different leadership styles on organizational climate and, in particular, on individual personality and motivation. He organized his subjects into simulated business firms and into each firm introduced one of three leadership styles that correspond roughly to Lewin's autocratic, laissez-faire, and democratic styles. These three styles, as Litwin defined them, emphasized (1) formal organization and structures, with deference to rules and authority; (2) informal association, maximizing friendliness and personal comfort; or (3) productivity, featuring openness to innovation and rewards for good work.

Litwin's work revealed that the self-acceptance, responsibility, and communality of adult members of simulated business firms are influenced by leader-induced climate in much the same ways as were adolescent subjects three decades earlier. Subjects in the most structured group became less at ease with themselves and with others and those in the least structured group showed little change in these respects. But subjects in the productivity group, like the boys Lewin's team studied under democratic leadership, became better able to handle themselves, their work, and their interpersonal situations. These results, obtained in a laboratory context, were replicated by Herbert H. Meyer (1968) in field studies at General Electric plants. Meyer concluded that leadership and resulting climate in industrial settings must change to meet the needs of today's employee, who is educated and is the product of tolerant parents and better schools.

An element of organizational climate over which a leader has no control is the influence of the prevailing *cultural climate* in which the organization is set. The bulk of research on organizations in different cultures indicates that to be effective, leadership must take into account the standards and customs of the particular larger society. For example, Mason Haire, Edwin Ghiselli, and Lyman Porter (1963, 1966) found that Japan, Great Britain, and the United States were the only nations among advanced economic powers that harbored a widespread belief in the individual's capacity for leadership and initiative. In contrast, people in continental European countries had a much lower opinion of the adaptive powers of most individuals; this belief may be sufficiently low to make unfeasible, say, an application of human-relations principles in continental European organizations. Further obstacles to modern management techniques, at least as we know them in the United States, are encountered in nonadvanced economies, especially where production has been largely limited to agricultural output or to one or two crops or products and where educational standards and perhaps interpersonal trust are low (Williams, Whyte, and Green, 1966).

Control Systems

In directing an organization to its desired goals, managers rely on control mechanisms that are woven into the structural fabric of an organization. These mechanisms make up a control system that must serve two functions: it must focus on the system as a whole in order to keep the organization on course, and it must also focus on the individual in order to create and maintain compatible expectations. Like a radar-directed craft, the control system must include a mechanism that picks up deviations from the plotted flow of events. Most control systems work by initially establishing a criterion and evaluating actual subsequent outcomes against this criterion. If the two are discrepant a critical assessment is made, which is followed by an attempt to pinpoint and eliminate the cause of the discrepancy. Admission procedures and a grading system usually serve universities as means of weeding out students who do not meet certain predetermined requirements.

Control Mechanisms. From the viewpoint of individual members, the control process begins long before they enter an organization. In many ways, the long process of socialization prepares them for the control mechanisms they will respond to and the roles they will assume in specific

Figure 16.7 An autocratic leader rules his group with an iron hand, determines group policies and member functions, and gives other members little voice in their own fate. Such a style is represented by the character Fagin in *Oliver Twist,* who taught and forced his band of orphans to steal and who beat them if they failed in their daily assignments.

organizations throughout their lives (see Chapter 2). What will be expected of them as members of the organization is specified in job descriptions. And after the individual members enter the organization, they are indoctrinated in the specific norms of the organization. They are motivated to maintain their organizational roles by a number of specific devices usually referred to as *control mechanisms,* or *operating mechanisms.* Specifically, these devices are used to evaluate members' performances and to reward or punish the individuals accordingly.

Evaluation itself is a source of motivation for individuals. To be effective, evaluation must carry a clear message to the persons being evaluated; when students do not understand why they have received lower grades for class assignments than they expected, they will be no better equipped to deal with the next writing assignment and may, in fact, be even less equipped because their diminished faith in their own competence may have them on the defensive.

If an individual's performance is substandard, the organization or its leadership may try to improve his work, criticize him, severely reprimand him, demote him, or terminate his affiliation with the organization.

To know how an organization's reward system operates tells much about that organization's true goals. These true goals are not always apparent, nor are they the goals an organization always professes to the public. A profusion of intentions—both malevolent and benign—have been cloaked from public awareness with invocations of education, public service, and charity. For example, state universities have been established for the benefit of all who seek a higher education. Yet the way many senior faculty members distribute their time among undergraduates, graduate students, and research clearly indicates that many universities consider

OPS CAPTURES THE HEW MONSTER

IN ITALY, AN EMERGENCY committee to oversee housing reconstruction after the devastating Sicilian earthquake was recently disbanded. During the ten years of its existence, the committee had managed to spend more than 80 million lire (the equivalent of $131,200 at July 1973 exchange rates) without building one house. This type of organizational failure is not unique to Italy. In many countries, nonprofit organizations as well as businesses tend to grow like Topsy, without built-in controls that regulate and evaluate the policies and programs they spawn. In the United States, the Department of Health, Education, and Welfare (HEW) is a monster agency among the bureaucracies in Washington, D. C., both in size and administrative complexity. In order to bring business techniques of management to HEW, Fred Malek was hired to create a control system for

them. Malek labeled his creation Operational Planning System (OPS).

OPS is a system for granting funds to different programs and then testing their effectiveness so that they can be redesigned and funds can be allocated accordingly on an informed basis. The chief task of OPS is to assess how well ongoing programs are meeting the objectives that have been set for them by top-level management. In order to establish criteria for this assessment, OPS has introduced Management by Objectives (MBO), a process geared to making individuals accountable for their performance and at the same time ensuring that performance goals are flexible and reasonable.

MBO centers on a negotiation between an individual and his or her immediate supervisor. Together they agree on a statement of what will be

graduate students and research to be more deserving of their rewards than are undergraduates.

There are many types of rewards that a leader can use to increase the likelihood that desired performances will be repeated. Some of these rewards are economic and others are social. Some have to do with raises, bonuses, and fringe benefits; others, with praise, status, and promotions. Early organizational psychologists considered pay the only factor relevant to worker satisfaction, but the Hawthorne studies revealed that social satisfactions such as recognition and group support are possible even in a commercial setting. There is evidence, in fact, that pay is rated less important by workers than are intrinsic aspects of the work activity and opportunities for control, authority, and promotion (Herzberg, Mausnes, Peterson, and Capwell, 1957; Schwartz, Jenusaitis, and Stark, 1963). Findings such as these have been criticized, however, on the grounds that the self-reports on which they are based may tempt respondents to play down their materialistic interests.

A distinct separation between social and economic rewards may not be realistic. For example, a raise can indicate appreciation by management, can bestow status, can enhance self-esteem, and so on. Basketball superstar Bill Russell once asked that a few dollars be added to his six-figure annual salary so that he would be paid more than his friend Wilt Chamberlain. Both social and economic rewards qualify as recognition and, therefore, probably interact and overlap in their effects on behavior when they are used at the same time.

Dysfunctionality. The purpose of rewards and punishments is to ensure that members behave in ways that will help the organization accomplish its

expected from that individual, and the projected accomplishments are subdivided into manageable and measurable steps. Defining objectives precisely helps to reduce ambiguity during feedback sessions and in the evaluation process at the end of the accounting period.

OPS has helped HEW managers to think of their programs in terms of measurable, achievable, directed, results-oriented objectives. With OPS personnel acting as consultants throughout the organization, this planning-checking-evaluating process goes on at all levels of the department. This type of process makes it possible for organizational members at all levels to have a coherent picture of what is being accomplished on both a large and a small scale. This is much the same way that order is brought to the potential chaos of a large bureaucracy in private business, but the evaluative

criteria are different. Large-scale criteria applied to HEW include the effectiveness of the Food and Drug Administration in its surveillance of the 100,000–200,000 drugs sold over the counter in the United States as well as the benefits to underprivileged preschoolers of the Head Start program. These criteria demonstrate that control systems can be used to serve humane ends. Hopefully, a result of the management system now in operation at HEW will be that the taxpayers will get a better accounting of the billions of dollars that are spent by that agency.

Source: Adapted from T. Riesing and S. Peele, "United States Department of Health, Education, and Welfare," Case Number 4–172–2847, Harvard School of Business Administration, 1971.

goals. Even when they are effective, however, rewards and punishments do not always do what they are intended to do.

A dysfunctional control system is one that motivates people to work at cross-purposes with the intended goals of the organization. Such a control system is badly designed, because it is based on insufficient recognition of its impact on system members. An aware leader will detect these flaws and eliminate them. In a healthy organization, therefore, influence in developing and modifying a control system flows both ways between the agents of control and the people and activities governed by the control measures. Like all elements of an organization, a control system must be adaptable; that is, it must be capable of being adjusted in response to feedback.

Consider some ways in which controls can dysfunction in a business setting. Suppose that a control system assigned bonuses to departments on the basis of profits, but the only means of making a profit was to cut costs. This system of control might then produce an irresistible temptation for departments to cut costs to an extent that, in the long run, would prove detrimental to the departments and to the organization. Or, if the managers of a department decided to fire some nonessential personnel because profits were down, the extra costs of regearing and the resulting deterioration in morale might render these moves ridiculously costly. Or, bonuses for individual productivity may discourage cooperation that would yield greater benefits for both management and workers. On the other hand, although group bonuses might encourage cooperative effort, they may permit individuals to shirk their responsibilities.

Dysfunctions are in no way limited to control systems in business. For example, some critics of drug laws in the United States argue that the ultimate impact of making heroin illegal (a policy intended to safeguard the public) has been to turn addicts into thieves and to funnel the money they steal into the coffers of organized crime. And critics of American universi-

TRUSTING THOSE YOU CAN'T SEE

MOST TEACHERS, supervisors, and coaches know that there are two basic kinds of people: those you have got to keep after every minute and those you can trust to stay at it. Persons in the first group goof off the moment your back is turned, whereas the others will work doggedly without supervision.

Social psychologist Lloyd Strickland was interested in the ways in which people judge one another as being trustworthy or as being laggards. His subjects, forty male undergraduates, were told that they would supervise the work of two assistants, aliases A and B. If the two successfully performed a series of mathematical computations during the work sessions, the supervisor could win $10, but it was also necessary for A and B to work as hard during the second half of the sessions as they had during the first in

order for the subject to win. The first half included ten work and rest sessions. During this period the supervisor was allowed to monitor A's work during each session by means of a summary sheet brought to the supervisor by the experimenter. Assistant B was monitored only twice, after the fifth session and after the tenth. At the end of the first half of the sessions, both A and B appeared to have averaged the same amount of work. The subject was asked to rate their work as well as his feelings of trust for each.

During the second series of work sessions, the experimenter told the supervisor that he was free to monitor the workers as he chose but that he would also need to correct the workers' computations in order to win the $10. The workers could be fined 10 percent of their pay if the supervisor was

ties object that these institutions often subvert basic educational goals, such as academic freedom and flexibility, by using control mechanisms that encourage academic conformity and channel faculty attention away from students to research. Consider the position of a student who feels under pressure from the control device of grades to present correct answers in class. Anxious to please the instructor, he attempts to anticipate the response the instructor has in mind, rather than thinking a problem through. He may be rewarded with good grades, but the system is not motivating him to learn, as it ideally aims to do.

In all these cases, people are swept along by the currents that a control system inadvertently creates, but they are not swept in the direction of the organization's professed goals.

BUREAUCRACIES, FORMALITIES, AND RITUALS

Implicit in the preceding discussions of organizational goals and structures is the concept of *bureaucracy*—a term that refers both to the advantages of formal organization and to the often disadvantageous aspects of rigid, rule-bound, and inefficient organizational forms. Bureaucracies develop when needs emerge for specialization and for administrative machinery that will plan, oversee, and coordinate the highly diversified activities of a large organization—either public or private (Blau and Scott, 1962).

The man who was first to comment extensively on the prevalence of bureaucratic forms in modern society—German sociologist Max Weber (1947), who lived from 1864 to 1920—lauded bureaucratic forms as the most "efficient and rational known means of carrying out imperative control over human beings." Among the efficient characteristics of bureaucracies that he applauded were recruitment and promotion on the basis of technical competence as judged by impersonal, formalized rules rather than on the basis

---

displeased with their performance. The supervisor was thus under some pressure not to monitor both A and B on every trial, because then it would be impossible for him to finish his work in the time allotted. He had to choose, therefore, to trust one of his workers or to trust them both to some degree.

Which worker, A or B, was likely to be trusted more? Strickland found that supervisors tended to continue monitoring A significantly more than they did B. Furthermore, the relatively isolated B was thought to be more trustworthy and dependable than was A, as shown in the table. Judges rated the supervisors' explanations for A and B's efforts. In general, the supervisors attributed A's output to compliance with the supervisor, who frequently had A under surveillance; B's work, on the other hand, was attributed to B's self-motivated desire to do well. The supervisor had "learned" enough about his workers through his selective surveillance to conclude that they produced for different motives. However, both workers had the same output. It appears, then, that the simple opportunity for a supervisor to check up on a worker can lead to that worker's downfall. In contrast, through circumstances that may be equally beyond a worker's control, the unwatched worker is likely to emerge the hero.

Judgments of Supervisors*

RATING OF WORKER	A	B	EQUAL
Most trustworthy worker	1	24	15
Most dependable worker	1	35	4

*Total of 40

Source: Adapted from L. Strickland, "Surveillance and Trust," *Journal of Personality*, 26 (1958), pp. 200–215.

of individualistic concerns; explicit role specifications; role diversification; hierarchy of authority; disciplined and impersonal performance; and career orientation.

The status of bureaucratic structures as totally advantageous in their effects has been challenged by writers since Weber's time. Critics of Weber have pointed out that he did not recognize the existence and importance of informal structures, which are discussed earlier in this chapter; that some of the bureaucratic features he described conflict with others or are dysfunctional for the attainment of goals; and that he appeared to confuse authority based on occupancy of a position with that based on the personal ability of the worker (Blau, 1956; Blau and Scott, 1962; Parsons, 1947).

Even before Weber's time, Karl Marx was writing that as workers progressively lost control over their work situation, they became alienated from the work process, from the product of their labors, and from one another. Marx believed that workers occupy a position as "wage slaves" in society and that the worker is thereby psychologically degraded to a mere "appendage of the machine." Hans Gerth and C. Wright Mills (1946) have suggested that Marx's emphasis on the worker's alienation from the means of production is only one aspect of a pervasive modern trend: the separation of individuals from control over the conditions of their own lives. Thus, the modern soldier is separated from control of the means of violence, the scientist from control of the means of inquiry, and the civil servant from control of the means of administration.

Another sociologist, Robert K. Merton (1968), observes that "formality facilitates the interaction of the occupants of offices despite their (possibly hostile) private attitudes toward one another." Merton has suggested that a structural pattern that produces effectiveness in some circumstances may prove ineffective in others. He believes that the formal definition of positions, the proliferation of rules and regulations, and the reward systems of formal organizations all encourage organizational members to be timid, conservative, and to follow a narrow technical approach. According to Merton, these aspects of formal organizations encourage *ritualism*. The long-term effects of ritualism on an organization can be to make it inflexible, inefficient, and dehumanizing. Ritualism may be thought of as a particular manifestation of a more general social phenomenon—that of *goal displacement*—in which conformity to rules becomes an end in itself rather than a means toward accomplishing the organization's objectives or the individual member's personal objectives.

The Chinese have perhaps conducted the most extensive and continuous effort to guard against the distorting effects of bureaucracy on organizational goals. During the past two decades, the Chinese leadership has tried to protect China from the tendency of people in bureaucratic positions to lose sight of the needs and problems of working men and women. Consequently, they have followed a policy of assigning Chinese bureaucrats to work in factories or communal farms for a short period of time each year. Efforts in Western countries to curb the dysfunctional influences of bureaucracies have typically been far less systematic.

In the following section, some of the ways by which organizations—low-ranking members as well as management—can correct their internal dysfunctions and other sources of strain that impede their progress in accomplishing their goals will be explored. Keep in mind, however, that these means of change are sometimes very superficial; they may depend on the idiosyncrasies of a few members, or they may amount to tinkering with

Figure 16.8 Excessive rationality can result in irrationality, as demonstrated by the "red tape" and other inefficient practices that almost always evolve in bureaucracies.

Mail For 20-Mile Trip Would Travel 2,309 Miles.

WASHINGTON, Sept. 26 (UPI)— A package mailed from Modena, Utah to Panaca, Nev., a distance of 20 miles, will have to cover a 2,309-mile route before delivery under the United States Postal Service's new bulk mail system, Representative Robert N. C. Nix charged today.

The extreme example was one of 52 instances the Pennsylvania Democrat cited to show added travel for parcels that will result in some sections of the nation when the new system becomes operational in 1976.

Similarly, a package mailed from Chapel Hill, N.C., to Carrboro, N.C., a distance of one mile, will "under the new postal organization, with its businesslike methods, travel 160 miles to arrive at the same destination a mile away," Mr. Nix said.

Mr. Nix, chairman of the House Postal Facilities and Mail Subcommittee, made the charges in prepared remarks as his panel renewed hearings on the Postal Service's construction program.

The system calls for construction of 21 large sorting centers and 12 auxiliary centers around the country where all parcels will be shipped for sorting by machine before being sent out for delivery.

In the Modena example, a truck now delivers such a package the 20 miles to Panaca. Under the new bulk system, Mr. Nix said, the package would go from Modena to Salt Lake City, then to Denver, then to Los Angeles, then to Las Vegas and finally to Panaca, a distance of 2,309 miles.

organizational machinery by paid consultants whose prescriptions are subject to approval by the managers who hire them. After discussing the ways in which an organization can improve its performance, an aspect of organizations will be examined that consultants never question, at least in their official roles: the goals for which the organizations exist. At this chapter's conclusion, the discussion will turn to some of the ways in which these goals themselves may be altered, requiring nothing short of a transformation of our cultural priorities.

THE ORGANIZATION CHANGES ITSELF

No organization is exempt from the need for change, whether particular needs arise from dysfunctions within the organization itself or from shifts in cultural attitudes that affect the expectations of the organization's members and of the public it strives to please. There are several means by which an organization can respond to a need for change. Change can occur informally or formally, through individual influences or group consensus, and can be initiated by rank-and-file members or by top management. But whatever the source of influence, change from within nearly always proceeds at the metaphorical pace of a snail. For example, prison riots have prompted gradual reform in some prisons, and the Roman Catholic Church has updated some of its teachings and rituals in response to societal change and to dissension among members. And the dissatisfaction of many contemporary psychologists with the debilitating effects of mental institutions is producing a trend toward day and night hospitals, outpatient clinics,

Figure 16.9 People who hold bureaucratic positions for extended periods often lose sight of the needs and problems of the men and women whose lives they affect by their decisions as bureaucrats. To combat this tendency toward a "bureaucratic mentality," Chinese bureaucrats spend a short period of time each year working in factories and on communal farms. Chen Yung-Kuei (in front), Vice-Chairman of the Shansi Provincial Revolutionary Committee and Secretary of the party branch of the Tachai brigade, is shown here joining commune members in building terraced fields as part of a mass campaign to develop irrigation and water-control facilities.

halfway houses, and various other arrangements that permit compromises between total institutionalization and community life. But these changes are all gradual and well within the parameters laid down by each organization's traditional goals. Most organizations are simply resistant to changes not deemed imperative for survival and success at predetermined goals. The final section of this chapter will show that some critics are questioning more than the particular policies and goals of particular organizations; they are calling for an overhaul of the total form of organizations as we know them.

Influences of Individual Members

How are organizational structures and goals changed? Individuals are the agents of change, whether they are driven to change the organization by their personal dispositions, organizational requirements, or societal pressures. Some of the means of change that individual members may have at their disposal will be discussed now. The reader must use his or her imagination to see the range of ends to which these means can be applied.

David Mechanic (1963) has observed that even relatively low-ranking individuals can wield considerable informal influence in most organizations. This informal power is often obtained by gaining control of the access to information, to individuals who exert formal influence, or to organizational resources. For example, the secretary of a high-ranking member often has access to a great deal of high-level information and also has control over scheduling and over who has access to the boss. Or a person may have informal contacts in other parts of the organization that allow that individual to "get things done fast" by avoiding red tape. Even low-status persons with informal contacts often have many high-ranking members dependent on their assistance—a position that can bestow a great deal of bargaining power on the low-ranking individual.

To the extent a person is assigned responsibilities, he or she is also indirectly granted a degree of power. For example, Thomas J. Scheff (1966) reported a case in which attendants in a mental hospital frustrated the

Figure 16.10 Low-ranking members of organizations often subtly wield a large degree of power because they control access to resources that others need. The executive secretary, for example, who decides which transactions should come to the boss's attention, may obtain the upper hand with individuals who have higher formal status than the secretary.

attempts of the hospital's administration to institute reforms. The attendants had assumed some of the responsibilities officially assigned to ward physicians, but they expected in return a greater voice in hospital policy regarding patients. When the reforms were introduced, the physicians did not honor their part of this tacit bargain, and the attendants retaliated by refusing to carry out the duties they had informally assumed. A position that commonly carries responsibilities voluntarily relinquished by higher-ups is that of the school secretary, who frequently chooses substitute teachers, makes major decisions about supplies and scheduling, screens complaints, and deals with parent groups.

Mechanic found still other factors that influence the degree of power that individuals can attain within an organization. Individuals with expertise that is lacking in higher-ups have a great deal of potential power, which can be exerted by withholding information and otherwise influencing the organization's policies and procedures. People have been known to conduct successful *work-to-rule* protests, by rigidly adhering to organizational rules that are usually disregarded for the sake of efficiency—such as bypassing unnecessary links in the chain of command, and the like. Personal attractiveness—physical, social, or professional—can also be a source of power, and highly attractive individuals often have access to an inordinate number of influential members of an organization.

Individuals within an organization may have power to change some aspects of the organization, but such change is usually rather limited in scope. On the other hand, an organization's leaders are in a position to implement changes that are much more sweeping, although managers rarely exercise this power to any profound extent.

Organizational Development: The View From the Top

The recipes for change that business and government managers follow affect only an organization's efficiency in accomplishing its fundamental goals; these programs do not affect the goals themselves. For example, a more sophisticated accounting system does not help the manager rearrange his priorities to increase the value of a product to humanity, or even to his organization. On the other hand, whatever deficiencies characterize the product are not by-products of the accounting techniques; the deficiencies derive, rather, from the inadequacies of experience, vision, judgment, courage, and power that beset the organization's managers.

The highly rationalized accounting procedures (by which the effectiveness of investments is evaluated) and more responsive managerial modes that produced what many observers refer to as a management revolution during the 1950s has served many purposes. For example, it has helped businessmen maximize their "return on investments"; it has served the interests of weapons management and law enforcement; and it has helped government officials dispense various goods and services to the citizenry. But no accounting procedure yet devised can tell the Secretary of Defense when further stockpiling of weapons will result only in overkill capacity, nor will it help our government's managers decide whether to spend more tax dollars on bombs or on schools.

Organizational consulting has become a major social force in recent years, at least within the universe of business, government, and research groups. Consultants are employed to conduct what they call *organizational-development* programs. Organizational development is the organization's answer to cultural changes that have rendered the nineteenth-century bureaucracy unsuited to today's conditions. The bureaucratic structure—rigid, impersonal, unimaginative, slow to adapt—has no place in an era when communication and change are rapid and when many organizations' activities are not largely routine.

Almost all existing organizations started out with bureaucratic hierarchies. Most have long since begun to respond with innovations and modifications, but these moves as often as not have been piecemeal, symptomatic responses to particular emergencies. The goal of organizational development is to resolve the dysfunction created by historical accidents and to set the whole organization on a planned course of development that is based on a full assessment of its present situation and on up-to-date principles of management.

Organizational consultants usually espouse a human-relations philosophy and thus commonly seek to create organic rather than mechanical systems where possible. An organic system, you may remember from a discussion earlier in this chapter, emphasizes interdependence, shared responsibility and control, and intergroup communication. One technique that has enjoyed recent popularity as a means of improving human-relations skills is the sensitivity-training group (discussed in Chapter 14). Usually these groups are limited to managers and supervisors, but recently entire units within an organization have participated in common groups. Different consultants have come up with differing procedures for attaining similar goals. Two of the most popular approaches that organizational consultants have devised are the Blake-Mouton Managerial Grid and the Lawrence-Lorsch model of contingency management.

The Blake-Mouton Managerial Grid. Robert Blake and Jane Mouton (1969) have devised one of the most popular programs for organizational development in use today. Unlike most consulting strategies, which require the active presence of their authors as change agents at the site of the client organization, the Blake-Mouton program has been developed for use by the organization itself. Its unique feature is the Grid, a simple rectangular coordinate graph, illustrated in Figure 16.11, that helps managers understand themselves as well as the workings of their organization by mapping its "concern for production" against its "concern for people."

Each point on the Grid represents a style of management. The horizontal coordinate is the strength of the production values in that style, the vertical coordinate the strength of its human values. The *9,9* style—high in both concerns—is the completely committed managerial style that Blake and Mouton's clients generally select as "best." The *1,9* style emphasizes human relations at the expense of output, and the *9,1* style does just the reverse; the *5,5* style is a moderate, compromising style; and the *1,1* style embodies inertia. Blake and Mouton have asserted that every aspect of an organization can be interpreted with the Grid. The personalities of managers, the personal goals of organization members, the degree of conformity or creativity that the organization encourages, and so on can all be charted in terms of products versus people.

Consider the different supervisory styles that would be practiced by managers on various points of the Grid. A *1,9* manager, in his desire to keep everyone happy, may sacrifice productivity for warmth. In contrast, a *9,1* manager would simply order people to do whatever he thought best for achieving the goals of the organization. The *5,5* manager would compromise between these two alternatives without really producing *or* resolving conflict. The *1,1* manager would simply do as little as possible. And the *9,9* manager would solicit all possible outlooks and attitudes from those under him, so that he would have access to the widest range of alternatives from which to choose.

Blake and Mouton use political analogies to dramatize the differences between their styles. The *9,1* style, they believe, occurs with revolutionary change, which is forced and abrupt. The *5,5* style, on the other hand, is associated with evolutionary progress within a framework of respect for the status quo, because developmental needs tend to be compromised. With the *9,9* style, development is planned and deliberately conducted. And here is the core of Blake and Mouton's value system, for they regard as undesirable both revolutionary upheaval, which they believe is arbitrary and inhumane, and evolutionary change, which they believe embodies too great an acceptance of unrecognized organizational or cultural assumptions. The *9,9* style alone is capable of contrasting what *should be* with what *is* and of thereby indicating the optimum strategy.

The Grid approach to organizational change operates in the following way. First, the consultants instruct a company's (or a government agency's) key managers during "laboratory-seminar" sessions in Managerial Grid concepts. Each manager reviews his own style in terms of the Grid and works with other managers in teams on a series of problems involving hypothetical, competitive group efforts. After they have been trained, these key personnel return to their work groups and conduct on-the-job extensions of the laboratory. Each work group or department analyzes its own situation and the directions in which it can best move. In the third stage of the Grid's application, Grid concepts are applied to intergroup networks. Tensions that exist between departments are brought out into the open in an effort to handle them in a *9,9* fashion. Eventually, problems that affect all members receive company-wide attention in phases four to six.

Blake and Mouton have achieved wide recognition with their methods. Yet there have been few systematic attempts to assess an organization's

Figure 16.11 The Managerial Grid. According to Blake and Mouton (1969), all aspects of an organization's functioning can be better understood by plotting the organization's concern for production against its concern for people. Each point on this grid represents a management style; the *9,9* style (high on both concerns) represents the ideal.

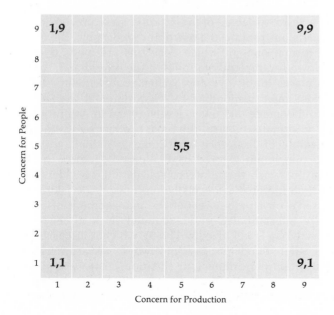

9,9 Management A completely committed managerial style yields optimum results—efficiency in operations *and* satisfying relationships among members; interdependence through a common stake in organizational goals leads to relationships based on trust and respect.

1,9 Management Attention to the needs of people for satisfying relationships leads to a friendly organizational atmosphere and a comfortable work tempo, but human needs are satisfied at the expense of output.

9,1 Management Efficiency and output are emphasized at the expense of human needs.

5,5 Management An adequate organizational performance is possible through compromising between output needs and the need to maintain the morale of members at a satisfactory level.

1,1 Management Exerting minimum effort to get the required work done accomplishes no more than sustain the organizational membership; it is the least successful style in terms of either human or production needs.

development after Grid consultants have worked with it, leaving the possibility that improvements are only apparent. A study by Louis Barnes, Larry Greiner, Robert Blake, and Jane Mouton (1964) did reveal that the Grid enhanced performance in a large organization (a prominent petrochemical company, which is not named in the study) and produced significant behavioral and attitudinal changes. But the study could hardly be called a conclusive one; there were no controls, such as requiring some departments to hold meetings without Grid techniques; thus, it cannot be established that the Grid, rather than interpersonal contact or introspection or attention, caused the changes in attitudes, behavior, and productivity.

Of the better-known approaches to organizational development, Blake and Mouton's puts the most stress on systematic analysis, thorough overhaul, full commitment on the part of all organization members, and a forceful style of leadership.

Contingency Management. Implicit in the Grid is the idea that effective management must adapt to diverse situations, or contingencies. This is the essence of the approach to organizational development devised by Paul Lawrence and Jay Lorsch (1967), who have asserted that leadership must be flexible enough to embrace the different styles appropriate to a variety of conditions, or contingencies. Based on comparative studies of many business organizations, Lawrence and Lorsch conclude that when an organization faces environmental conditions that are either very predictable or very unstable, the most effective managers attend primarily to the task needs, rather than the social needs, of their workers. In other words, when workers need either a very high degree of direction or very little management beyond a few basic instructions, they respond best to a forceful, task-competent leader who will motivate them and provide them with the information needed to perform their tasks. On the other hand, workers who face a moderately challenging situation respond best to a more socially oriented leader who can both direct the technical aspects of work and deal with the personal needs of subordinates.

Lawrence and Lorsch strive for the best "fit," not only between environmental circumstances and managerial orientation but also between these two factors and a third variable: organizational structure. When a stable situation makes decisions routine and outcomes predictable, the most efficient structure is a formal one, in which decisions are made by top managers and passed down for implementation. On the other hand, when an unfamiliar situation places innovative approaches at a premium, structural informality facilitates rapid responding to environmental change by permitting decisions to be made at lower levels of an organizational hierarchy. In fact, this informal structure, the most productive of innovations and the most flexible of Lawrence and Lorsch's models, closely parallels the style of management favored by Blake and Mouton for its flexibility—the *9,9* style, in which the manager solicits and considers the viewpoints of persons at all hierarchical levels before making decisions.

Lawrence and Lorsch's observations about the management of business organizations were substantiated and expanded in a fifteen-year research program conducted by Fred E. Fiedler (1968), which is discussed in detail in Chapter 15. Fiedler found that task-motivated, task-controlling leaders elicited the best group performance in situations that were either very favorable or very unfavorable in terms of task difficulty and leader-group relations. On the other hand, interpersonally motivated leaders in

Fiedler's study were most effective in situations that were only moderately favorable. Fiedler's results can easily be understood by translating his findings into commonsense terms. When a situation is particularly difficult to deal with, then a forceful, task-competent leader is able to direct a group and keep it moving in the completion of its hard-to-cope-with job. When the situation is so simple as to require little management besides some instructions about the nature of the work to be done, a similarly task-oriented leader can do well. But when the work situation is of moderate challenge, then a leader who can both direct the technical aspects of work and deal with the personal needs of subordinates is most likely to handle the group and its task successfully.

The notion of contingency pervades all of Lawrence and Lorsch's organizational prescriptions. They describe organizational phenomena in terms of *interfaces,* or transaction patterns, between interacting systems (for example, the organization and the environment, one subgroup and another within the organization, the individual and the organization). They recognize that different parts of an organization require different qualities in order to deal with different conditions. Thus, they have introduced the concept of *differentiation* to indicate the degree to which the different parts of an organization vary, both in the uncertainty or certainty (unpredictability or predictability) characteristic of their particular environments and in the managerial orientations and formal structures that characterize those different parts. Not surprisingly, Lawrence and Lorsch report that successful firms operating in a highly differentiated environment are characterized by higher internal differentiation than are less successful firms—another instance of proper "fit."

Although differentiation must develop in order for the organization to adapt to variations in the environment, a successful organization also requires differentiated work groups to contribute to unified goals and policies. Thus, a process of *integration* is also necessary in coping with a highly differentiated environment. Integration is defined as the tendency to collaborate in order to achieve unity of effort—a tendency that is necessitated by the environment.

Much of Lawrence and Lorsch's research has been concerned with exploring the complex relationship between these two key variables of differentiation and integration. In each industry they have studied, the more successful firms have achieved better differentiation *and* integration, when and where required to do so by the environment, than have the less successful firms. This is true even though integration not only does not necessarily coexist with differentiation but, in fact, is harder to achieve where differentiation is great.

Bear in mind that differentiation and integration are not limited to business enterprises. For example, in a university, faculty typically tend to the dissemination of knowledge while certain branches of the administration try to keep organizational machinery well-oiled and finances sound. Professors usually favor an informal structure with a rather long-range time orientation (in order to conduct research and to write). The administration characteristically has a more narrow understanding of pacing and scheduling (that is, the school year). Thus, it is probable that discrepancies in priorities will arise between these differentiated parts of the organization. Managers in different parts of an organization such as a university may therefore need to tailor their leadership styles to the needs and expectations of those they deal with. The cool, executive style of a college dean may be highly ineffective in dealing with a group of, for example, radical faculty sociologists—which cannot be ignored by the university administration.

Lawrence and Lorsch's model of organizational adaptation to the environment points to a different set of predictions about organizational effectiveness than does Blake and Mouton's model.

To date, Lawrence and Lorsch have provided better empirical support for their hypotheses than have Blake and Mouton, although their observations have been limited to the range of managerial styles actually found in organizations. Blake and Mouton's 9,9 organizational style, like their ideal "dynamic corporation," rarely exists in reality, and where it does exist it may well turn out to be more effective than any of the variations Lawrence and Lorsch have observed. The question awaits further experimentation and perhaps further theoretical clarification as well.

However, the ways in which organizations choose to change themselves are not shaped by research findings alone. In fact, it is possible that these models of organizational development are themselves culturally determined by the existing economic and political system under which the organizations they mirror function. For example, Blake and Mouton speak of corporate development in enthusiastic accents:

The failure of society to comprehend and to communicate clearly to its youth the free enterprise theory of competition continues to be the major long-term problem that must be dealt with in the corporation itself. . . .What other institutions have furthered the well-being of societies as much as the corporation? What others are able to provide the kind of meaningful experiences a corporation provides to the individuals who work within them? (1969, page 13)

Statements such as these may well make pleasant reading for the authors' corporate clients, but they also clearly reflect the values and interests represented in "the free-enterprise theory of competition," as Blake and Mouton identified it. However, this free-enterprise theory is not particularly useful in a place and age characterized by monopolization of markets, diminishing resources, and workers' high expectations. Catering to executive sentimentality regarding the virtues of free enterprise may diminish the corporate manager's ability to satisfy the needs of the organization's environment and the needs of the individuals who *are* the organization.

Although the research commissioned by business and government establishments has identified some of the strains that besiege many existing organizations, such studies tell us very little about the shape of things to come. The consultants who typically conduct the research, as illustrated by the solicitous tone of Blake and Mouton's writings, scrupulously avoid any evidence that contemporary goals and procedures are fundamentally inadequate. Their contribution very often is to oil the machinery while ignoring the fact that the machinery often continues to manufacture and satisfy artificial needs. In doing so, they often diminish the member's involvement with the product. Clues as to how existing organizations are lacking and a glimpse of possible organizations of the future exist at the fringes of academic respectability, where empirical reassurance may be hard to come by.

OVERCOMING INSTITUTIONALIZATION

The trend toward almost total institutionalization in our society is leaving unanswered numerous questions in the area of individual self-realization. It should be apparent that future research in organizational behavior will be increasingly concerned with modifying organizational structures so as to allow the individual more independence of action and more control over his or her destiny. Although current research reveals much about the strains on present organizations—for example, by documenting worker dissatisfaction and some of its causes (Kahn, Wolfe, Quinn, Snoek, Diedrich, and Rosenthal, 1964)—such studies can go only so far in pointing out the directions in which organizations will change in the future. Most of today's empirical research is necessarily based on existing organizational forms. Clues to the organizational forms (and *non*organizational forms) of the future may come from those thinkers who have a more comprehensive (if sometimes more controversial) vision of the desirable and undesirable alternatives to be faced—those who are actively involved in criticizing and reshaping our institutions.

Among these thinkers, Ivan Illich is especially perceptive. According to Illich (1971), the power that schools exert over our myths, our expectations, our opportunities, and our values provides full support for present-day commercial institutions. Illich distinguishes between education and schooling: he feels that public schools usually deny students education in order to dispense schooling. Schooling, believes Illich, prepares most of us for lives of production and consumption—for the satisfaction of artificial needs. Further, opportunities and positions of influence are denied to individuals who do not conform to the arbitrary regulations often imposed in schools. Schooling perpetuates the world view that scarcity is inevitable and that the road to individual fulfillment demands that its traveler compete and consume. Illich compares the artificiality of many of our needs with the "cargo cult" in which natives of the South Pacific became fixated on certain aspects of Western materialism:

School combines the expectations of the consumer expressed in its claims with the beliefs of the producer expressed in its ritual. It is a liturgical expression of a world-wide "cargo cult," reminiscent of the cults which swept Melanesia in the forties, which injected cultists with the belief that if they but put on a black tie over their naked torsos, Jesus would arrive in a steamer bearing an icebox, a pair of trousers, and a sewing machine for each believer. (page 45)

Although Illich is best known for his critiques in the educational field, his work is useful to anyone concerned with the psychology of organizations, because his ideas extend across the board to all organizations and he casts educational institutions specifically in organizational terms. Illich's observations and projections are best understood as structural diagnoses of institutions and institutional styles as these affect individual well-being.

Manipulative and Convivial Institutions

In setting up his spectrum of institutional styles, Illich distinguishes between manipulative and convivial institutions. Whether it is a school, an army, a prison, a mental hospital, or a corporation producing a heavily advertised commercial product, a *manipulative institution* yields products and services for which it must first create artificial needs. These artificial needs may be created either through advertising or by legal force, which includes prison sentences, commitments to mental hospitals, and conscription. Furthermore, manipulative institutions require costly bureaucracies or promotional machinery to enforce "unwilling consumption or participation." Manipulative institutions maintain the myth of their own irreplaceability and encourage or compel overuse of their products or services. In doing so, they serve the economic interests surrounding the

EDWARD WILLIAM CARTER

Business Affiliations
President
Broadway-Hale Stores, Inc.
Director
American Telephone and Telegraph Company
Del Monte Corporation
Pacific Mutual Life Insurance Company
Southern California Edison Company
United California Bank
Western Bancorporation

Cultural Associations
Director
Music Center Opera Association
San Francisco Opera Association
Southern California Symphony—Hollywood Bowl Association
Trustee
Los Angeles County Museum of Art
Member
Business Committee for the Arts

Educational and Other Affiliations
Regent
University of California
Trustee
The Brookings Institution
Committee for Economic Development
Occidental College
Director
Council for Financial Aid to Education
Stanford Research Institute
Member
Overseers Visiting Committee, Harvard Business School
Visiting Committee, UCLA Business School
Advisory Committee, Stanford Business School
National Industrial Conference Board
National Commission on Productivity

Charitable Activities
Director
The James Irvine Foundation
Santa Anita Foundation

Honors
Member
President Nixon's National Commission on Productivity

Figure 16.12 A broad array of contemporary organizations are influenced by relatively few of society's members. For example, the Board of Regents of the University of California, which makes the highest-level policy decisions for the largest university system in the United States, is composed of members who often have strong ties to business and other organizations. Edward William Carter is one such person.

product or the political, professional, and bureaucratic interests surrounding the service.

Illich contrasts manipulative institutions with *convivial institutions*, which provide "facilitative networks" that people use naturally in the course of getting around in life and communicating with one another. Convivial institutions do not have to advertise, because they exist to help people do the things they would want to do even if they were not subjected to advertising. Therefore, they need maintain no greater bureaucracy or public-pleasing machinery than is necessary to prepare, maintain, and operate the facility. Examples are those organizations necessary to provide water, parks, and transportation systems. Figure 16.13 shows how institutions would range in Illich's perspective from some of the most manipulative to some of the most convivial.

The Effects of Schools on Society

There is probably no institution that has had a greater impact on contemporary society than the school has had. Most people spend a greater proportion of their lives in schools than they do in any other institution.

Schools are the cornerstone of a society that is dominated by institutions because they set the pattern for the individual's later involvements with other institutions. "Once we have learned to need school," Illich believes, "all our activities tend to take the shape of client relationships to other specialized institutions." The key psychological effect of these client relationships is "the transfer of responsibility from self to institution." By this process the individual becomes persuaded that the intake of external products, whether institutional learning or sleeping pills, constitutes the satisfaction of needs that are basic and internal. As students, most of us consume what we are told is education. We "take" courses and feel we have learned the "material" when we complete a course. We feel satisfied if our expenditures of time and effort and money bring us the product—a degree—and dissatisfied if we do not get this reward.

The pattern of consumption learned in school can be extended to nearly all our organizational involvements. The psychological derivatives of these patterns of consumption are translations of needs into institutional fulfillments, of abilities into institutional tools, and of the human being into an institutional role. The individual finds it increasingly difficult to locate his or her worth, or the worth of others, outside of organizational contexts and to experience the world independently. In addition, actions and accomplishments may seem to have meaning only in an organizational context or when certified by institutions. One does not become a plumber, doctor, housewife, businessman, teacher, or architect on the basis of indicated ability to satisfy real needs in a community. All these functions are delegated, rather, on the basis of institutional certification. And qualification-through-certification dominates more and more professions from haircutting to philosophy. As an alternative to measuring people against the yardsticks of academic performance and prestige of alma mater, Illich proposes performance criteria that could be used to judge the competence of professionals here and now.

Should We Deschool Society?

Illich believes we can restore the capabilities lost through institutionalization by fundamentally changing the character of our institutions. "We need a set of criteria which will permit us to recognize those institutions which

Since education is not a means to living, but is identical with the operation of living a life which is fruitful and inherently significant, the only ultimate value which can be set up is just the process of living itself. And this is not an end to which studies and activities are subordinate means; it is the whole of which they are ingredients.
—JOHN DEWEY

support personal growth." Those institutions would be convivial rather than manipulative. And for these criteria to be accepted, we certainly need education, but not education as now administered in public schools. "Most learning is not the result of instruction. It is rather the result of unhampered participation in a meaningful setting." This belief makes good intuitive sense, and it is supported by Paulo Friere's (1970) finding that illiterate Brazilian adults can begin to read in forty hours if the first words they learn describe their economic or political situations. On the other hand, the reward systems used in North American schools—the grading system, for example—may have stultifying effects. Mark Lepper, David Greene, and Richard Nisbett (in press) found that children return to an activity more readily if they have learned it by performing it for its own sake rather than for an extrinsic reward; in other words, when an already attractive activity is rewarded by an authority figure, the activity becomes less attractive.

According to Illich, deschooling is "at the root of any movement for human liberation." Illich's program for "deschooling society," to quote the title of the book (1971) in which he outlines this program, is designed to free the individual to develop his or her own independent points of contact with the world. Such a program must demystify the institutional processes that presently stand between the individual and any direct experience. In this scheme, education is conceived as a lifelong process. Illich would give everyone initiative and accountability for his or her own education. At birth, an individual would receive an educational grant for a share of society's educational resources, to be claimed whenever and in whatever form the individual chose.

Following a convivial or facilitative model, educational facilities would not dispense learning to passive classroom consumers but would put people in contact with the educational resources they wished to make use of. Directories would be published listing teachers of various skills and

Figure 16.13 The spectrum of institutional styles, as conceived by Illich, ranges from the convivial (those satisfying real public needs and used naturally in the course of living and communicating) to the manipulative (those satisfying artificial needs that are created by the institutions themselves, often through advertising).

Convivial	Intermediate	Manipulative

True public utilities
  Sidewalk and sewage systems
  All-purpose roads
  Public transportation systems
  Telephone systems
  Postal systems
Small businesses that acquire a clientele more from location and quality of service than from advertising
	Businesses that exist primarily to serve basic human needs
	  Hotels
	  Cafeterias
	Producers of staples and perishable goods
		Educational, military, punitive, and therapeutic institutions
		Producers of consumer goods
		  Automobile manufacturers
		  Superhighway systems

humanistic educators-at-large. Computers would match people interested in exploring the same subjects. And the notion of an education would be expanded to encompass all the major institutions of society. Learning would take place in many institutions—factories, laboratories, businesses, and governing bodies rather than in buildings set aside for education. An educational mode such as this would tend to make the workings of these institutions more visible and less mysterious, to familiarize people with their operations, and to prepare people to deal confidently with them.

Ideally, nonacademic institutions, including economic organizations, would also follow Illich's facilitative model. All enterprises would be organized around the needs, wishes, and skills of people who collaborated because together they could fulfill their human needs as alone they could not. An awareness of the advantages of a convivial mode of organization has already spawned many forms of cooperative enterprises, including stores, farms, establishments to produce and distribute goods, medical clinics, counseling centers, living arrangements, and even a few credit unions. However, existing convivial organizations are still limited primarily to satisfying needs for food and shelter. A transformation from manipulative to convivial institutions, if it is occurring at all, is currently at an elementary stage.

Some organizational psychologists, as well as leaders of existing organizations, discount perspectives such as Illich's as offensively irrelevant, because such views challenge established assumptions. Others will probably welcome Illich's contribution as corrective of the moral imbalance that they sense exists in the field of organizational psychology. Yet when even the human-relations orientation (as adapted by the business world) views personal satisfaction as supportive of organizational effectiveness, there is something quite compelling about a perspective that defines organizational effectiveness in terms of how completely it serves to fulfill human needs.

A danger that confronts any movement toward more cooperative and humane attitudes and forms of organization is that established institutions will adopt only those aspects of the movement that are least threatening to their own means and ends. The business world has, by and large, heeded only those wisdoms of the human-relations movement that increase profits. In fact, the business world as it exists may be inclined to follow only the least potent prescriptions of any blueprint for radical change.

SUMMARY

Organizational psychologists study the ways in which individuals relate within organizations. An organization is defined as a collection of people who come together for the purpose of performing some task or attaining some goal they see themselves as sharing. As a consequence of this shared purpose, individual members usually have defined relationships to one another, and the pattern of these relationships gives organizational psychology its special province within the field of social psychology. Organizations range from the informal—such as a family, team, or circle of friends—to the very formal—governmental, commercial, religious, educational, and other institutions, but most research in organizational psychology goes on at the latter end of the continuum. It is, therefore, the formal end of the continuum that has given focus to the study of organizations.

To take form and to persist, organizations must have goals. An organization's real goals are not always the same goals as are publicly avowed by the group's leaders; real goals may be unknown even to most of the organization's members. For example, in business organizations, the goals traditionally stressed have been those of profit and, insofar as required to maximize profits, productivity and worker morale. From the early-twentieth-century scientific-management approach, which ignored morale in favor of efficiency, discipline, and standardization of jobs, organizational theory and practice have evolved into the human-relations approach, which emphasizes the human and social aspects of the work situation. Largely because business managers are interested in those aspects of the work environment that affect productivity, human-relations research has centered on the effects of different work satisfactions on productivity, but no clear relationship between the two variables has emerged. To uncover a relationship between worker satisfaction and productivity may necessitate matching job requirements and management methods to different psychological rewards and productivity measures. In practice, efforts to increase worker satisfaction have featured job enlargement, whereby a worker is allowed to participate in a whole production cycle rather than be limited to a single, repetitive task. In addition, greater autonomy, responsibility, and participation in decision making have all been effective in enhancing both satisfaction and productivity.

To accomplish their goals, all organizations require management. Managers must make decisions governing the basic external and internal structures of their organizations. Internal structure determines the roles that members are expected to fill. A manager's style of leadership, which determines the climate of the organization, is also an important determinant of the degree to which the organization is effective. For example, the climate created by *democratic leadership* apparently is more conducive to both individual satisfaction and group performance than are the climates created by *autocratic* or *laissez-faire* styles.

Prevalent features of formal organizations are their *bureaucratic* structures and procedures. Although bureaucratic forms can bestow some advantages on organizations in terms of rationality, impersonality, discipline, and career orientation, they also are often accompanied by disadvantages, including excessive formality, alienation, rigidity of rules, inefficiency, and goal displacement.

Organizations can be changed from the inside by either relatively low-ranking members or by management, but the two contingents usually exert very different influences. A low-ranking individual may exert an influence because he or she has access to important resources, information, or people or assumes the responsibilities that higher-ups neglect. The effects of these types of influence are, however, often limited by the particular assets or weaknesses of individual members. In contrast, managers can exert much more profound influences on the policies of their organizations, although these high-ranking members rarely put this power to very startling uses.

The need felt by managers to rationalize their organizations' relationships to a changing cultural and economic environment has created a demand for organizational-development programs, usually conducted by consultants schooled in the human-relations approach to management. An organizational-development program provides a manager with a formula for planned organizational change and thereby enables the business or government agency to make a transition from the outmoded bureaucratic model to a more flexible, organic design. Although organizational development is largely a matter of application rather than of theory, the concerns it raises have stimulated a respectable body of research data. But the interpretations are split as to whether there is one optimal managerial style, such as a combination of intensely *task-oriented* and intensely *social-oriented,* as Robert Blake and Jane Mouton claim, or whether the best policy is one of *contingency management,* espoused by Paul Lawrence and Jay Lorsch, by which managers adapt to particular conditions by varying their task and social orientations.

Farther out on the frontiers of organizational change are those thinkers who repudiate current organizational forms. One such thinker is Ivan Illich, who describes the psychologically debilitating effects of contemporary institutional schooling as both illustrations and causes of institutional dependence. Illich's suggestions for convivial rather than manipulative educational arrangements that would enable people to connect the learning process with their actual experiences and competencies can be taken as a model for radical change in other organizations as well.

SUGGESTED READINGS

Bennis, Warren G. *Changing Organizations.* New York: McGraw-Hill, 1966.

———, Kenneth D. Benne, and Robert Chin (eds.). *The Planning of Change,* 2nd ed. New York: Holt, Rinehart and Winston, 1969.

Illich, Ivan. *Deschooling Society.* New York: Harper & Row, 1971.

Kahn, Robert L., Donald M. Wolfe, Robert P. Quinn, J. Diedrich Snoek, and Robert A. Rosenthal. *Organizational Stress.* New York: Wiley, 1964.

Katz, Daniel, and Robert L. Kahn. *The Social Psychology of Organizations.* New York: Wiley, 1966.

March, James G., and Herbert A. Simon. *Organizations.* New York: Wiley, 1958.

McGregor, Douglas. *The Human Side of Enterprise.* New York: McGraw-Hill, 1960.

Schein, Edgar H. *Organizational Psychology,* 2nd ed. Englewood Cliffs, N. J.: Prentice-Hall, 1970.

Tannenbaum, Arnold S. *The Social Psychology of the Work Organization.* London: Tavistock Publications, 1966.

Weick, Carl. *The Social Psychology of Organizing.* Reading, Mass.: Addison-Wesley, 1969.

17

Collective Behavior

After the Homecoming football game, which their school lost in the last five minutes of play, Ken and Jill made their way to the stadium parking lot. They were unable to reach their car because the lot was filled with a crowd of strangers who were shouting and throwing rocks. By the time the police finally arrived, Ken had helped turn over a car and Jill had broken a car window. Yet, when a policeman asked them what had caused the riot and why they had participated in it, they didn't know the answer.

WHAT CAUSES A PEACEFUL CROWD to turn into a violent mob? What kind of people participate? For several reasons, these and other issues of collective behavior are ignored in most social-psychology textbooks. First, the trend toward laboratory studies, in which social phenomena are studied under rigidly controlled conditions, has profoundly influenced social psychology since the 1950s. The amorphous, large-scale phenomena embraced by the term "collective behavior"—crowds, panics, social movements, for example—simply do not lend themselves to laboratory study. Another reason for the relative neglect of this field is that collective behavior is a complex topic that requires analysis of both psychological and sociological variables. Most social psychologists have received training in only one of these academic disciplines.

Perhaps an even more important reason that collective behavior is seldom covered in social psychology textbooks is that only rarely are studies in this area politically neutral. The social psychologist who collects and analyzes information about the kinds of people who become involved in political movements, for example, draws conclusions that have obvious political implications. Suppose that an investigator were to conclude that blacks participating in ghetto riots had legitimate grievances. This conclusion would certainly suggest that their grievances should be subjected to scrutiny and that the causes should perhaps be eliminated. Should the investigator decide, however, that most rioters are criminal or mentally ill, the implication would be that more prisons and mental hospitals should be built and that more police are needed in ghetto areas. The political pressures to which investigators of riots may be subjected and the political implications of reaching various conclusions about the causes of riots emerge in Anthony Platt's book *The Politics of Riot Commissions* (1971).

As you read this chapter, keep in mind that social scientists, like all other scientists, are products of their times; they reflect the norms and biases inherent in both the intellectual community and in the wider society.

A DEFINITION OF COLLECTIVE BEHAVIOR

What do social and political movements, riots, crowds, panics, lynch mobs, and revolutions have in common? And how do the behaviors of individuals within these groups differ from those of people milling around a park on Sunday, spectators watching a wrestling match, or participants at a political convention? These events, like most human activity, cover a broad range of complex motives, interactions, and behaviors.

Two Dimensions: Organization and Deviance

All of the events mentioned so far can be placed along a continuum. One end of the continuum represents a group of people who are standing around, not interacting with one another and not organized in any particular way—an *aggregate,* rather than a group (see Chapter 14). The other end represents a group of people who are organized, with every person having a clearly defined role in relation to every other person—an *organization* (see Chapter 16).

Collective behavior falls between the two end points of this continuum. It is a social activity in which the participants have at least a moderate level of interaction with one another but in which the interaction is not as highly patterned as in a social organization. In collective behavior, in other words, most people are simply participants.

There is another dimension to collective behavior, with normatively sanctioned behavior at one end of the continuum and nonnormative behavior at the other end. *Normative* social behavior includes activities that most members of society, the government, and the press would view as acceptable and legitimate. *Nonnormative,* or deviant, behavior includes activities that most people would consider unacceptable and would probably describe as "immoral" or "irrational." Collective behavior is generally not normatively sanctioned.

Considering the two dimensions simultaneously, collective behavior can be defined as the nonnormative, diffusely organized behavior of a large number of interacting individuals. In Figure 17.1, the level of social organization increases gradually from bottom to top. At the extreme represented at the bottom, members of a group (actually an aggregate) do not interact; at the other end, they are rigidly organized into specific roles. The figure is also divided vertically, with normatively acceptable behavior on the left and normatively unacceptable behavior on the right. Whereas the organizational dimension is a continuum, the normative dimension is divided sharply—because most people seem to be rigid rather than flexible in distinguishing acceptable from unacceptable behavior.

In Figure 17.1, collective behavior appears in the shaded area. When Ken and Jill were spectators cheering at a football game, their behavior was normatively sanctioned and could not be considered collective behavior. When they joined the rioting crowd, however, their behavior changed to activity that is not sanctioned: it became collective behavior. Participants at a rally protesting unfair treatment of American Indians—an activity that is similarly unsanctioned—are also engaging in collective behavior. Although spectators at the football game and the participants at the pro-Indian rally may be cheering with equal enthusiasm, the spectators at the game are not involved in collective behavior, and the Indian partisans are. However, should the football game become a riot both groups will be on the right-hand, nonnormative side of Figure 17.1 and both will therefore be involved in collective behavior.

Consider the organizational dimension now. The pacifists represented at the bottom of the chart are isolated from one another in separate jail cells and thus cannot join together in collective behavior—even though they might consider themselves to be part of a common group. However, if these individuals were attending the same protest rally before being jailed, they were engaging in collective behavior—they were members of an interacting group of people who were engaged in nonnormative activity. If their protest movement becomes so highly organized that it acquires various officers—a leader, a march organizer, a public-relations representative, and so on—its activities will no longer be regarded as collective behavior.

The Russian Revolution is a good example of how a movement might shift from one category to another. It "began" with isolated revolutionaries meeting in small groups inside Russia and in Zurich and Berlin; this was not collective behavior but aggregates of revolutionaries. After Lenin organized these aggregates into highly structured conspiratorial groups, their actions were too well organized to qualify as collective behavior (although their behavior was still nonnormative). The revolutionary movement did not become collective behavior until fighting broke out and the masses took to the streets to overthrow the Czar's government. Then, as the Communist Party gained and consolidated its power, the movement again left

	Normative Activity	Nonnormative Activity
Highly Organized Structure	C.O.R.E. (Congress of Racial Equality) The Communist Party of the U.S.S.R.	The Communist Party of the U.S. N.O.W. (National Organization of Women)
Increasing Organization	A Fourth of July parade A strike A crowd cheering at a football game	The Gay Liberation Movement The Russian Revolution An antiwar rally A riot at a soccer match A panic A lynch mob
No Interaction	A crowd at a political rally An aggregate	Individual homosexuals Pacifists in jail

Figure 17.1 Both diffuse organization and nonnormative activity are necessary ingredients in collective behavior. Examples of behavior meeting both criteria fall in the shaded area.

the realm of collective behavior, because its activities had become socially sanctioned.

It may well be the case that a movement attains legitimacy (and thus leaves the realm of collective behavior) as it becomes more highly organized. The Congress of Racial Equality (CORE) provides an example. Where would you place the present activities of CORE in Figure 17.1? When CORE organized scattered sit-ins in the South early in the 1960s, it was engaging in collective behavior. Later, it established a large national office with various officials and became highly organized. At the same time, its activities became more legitimate, as Figure 17.1 shows.

Components of Collective Behavior

The examples of collective behavior that have been considered so far in this chapter obviously differ greatly—yet there are some common characteristics. Social scientists, in studying such behavior, have observed at least two components that can be used descriptively: (1) the participants' goals and (2) the actions they take to accomplish these goals.

Goals: Escape and Change. In many cases, the individuals who participate in a display of collective behavior have no common goal. Bob and Alice may both take part in a campus riot—Bob to let off steam and Alice to show how brave she is by attacking symbols of authority. It is more usual, however, for most of the participants in collective behavior to share a goal. Two basic types of goals predominate—*escape goals* and *change goals.* People who are trying to escape from a threatening situation, such as a burning building or a sinking ship, have escape goals. When people become fearful that the means of escape are limited and thus begin to rush aggressively toward exits, an escape situation can turn into a *panic.*

Change goals characterize political and social movements, which may seek either profound or limited changes. The gay-liberation and women's-liberation movements, for example, seek to bring about fundamental changes in the status of homosexuals and women within American society. Movements with more limited change goals may occur on university campuses, as when student activists seek to obtain more decision-making power or attempt to reinstate professors who have been fired because of nonconforming activities.

Many kinds of collective behavior involve change goals of one sort or another, but it is useful to distinguish between political and social change. Therefore, the term *political event* is applied to an instance of collective behavior involving participants who are attempting to bring about political change that would alter the way in which power is distributed or exercised within a social system. Political events may occur at a university, at a summer camp, or at a national level. A *political movement* involves collective behavior that occurs during a series of coordinated political events, which usually extend over a considerable period of time. A third form of collective behavior occurs in a *social movement*—a series of coordinated events intended to bring about social rather than political change. Although there is no neat line of demarcation between the two general types of change, social change primarily affects cultural values and political change transforms power relations. If an attempt at social change is successful, however, the movement will almost certainly affect political structures, just as political change will probably affect social structures.

The following examples may help to clarify the distinction between political and social movements: When a revolution that is the outgrowth of a political movement succeeds, one ruling group replaces another—as when peasants and workers ousted the middle class and military elite from power in China and when peasant revolutionaries brought about the breaking up of large land holdings in Mexico. In contrast, the women's-liberation movement is intended to bring changes that have primarily social and cultural, rather than political, ramifications. Although this movement proposes changes in power relationships, its main thrust remains social.

Actions: Peace or Damage?   The actions that accompany collective behavior may be categorized as either violent or nonviolent, as either damaging or nondamaging to life, property, and the physical environment. Collective behavior may be analyzed in terms of both goals and actions. In such an analysis, it may be concluded that the mob of people who throw rocks at the stadium is made up of interacting individuals with no common goal who are taking violent action. A rally called to show support for Indian rights, however, may be composed of individuals with a political-change goal who are engaging in nonviolent action.

The definition of collective behavior as group behavior that is non-normative and not tightly organized allows analysis from two different perspectives. First, consider an existing interacting group that engages in normatively sanctioned behavior: Under what conditions will the nature of the group's behavior change from being acceptable (normative) to unacceptable (nonnormative)? Second, consider a collection of isolated individuals who are already engaged in behavior that is not considered acceptable but who are not in contact with one another: How do they come together to engage in collective behavior?

The first question is pertinent to riots and panics—events that usually occur among already existing groups. The spectators at the football game were already organized and interacting before they began to riot. What caused them to switch to nonnormative collective behavior? The second question applies especially to political and social movements, which usual-

Figure 17.2   One useful way to distinguish between the many forms that collective behavior can take is an analysis of participants' goals and the nature—violent or nonviolent—of their activities in trying to accomplish these goals. Escape goals characterize panics, as (*upper center*) when people flocked to banks to withdraw their savings during the Depression and (*lower center*) when people flee from a fire or other danger. Goals of changing the status quo are characteristic of political and social movements; a nonviolent example (*upper right*) is the antiwar movement, and a violent example (*lower right*) is the Cuban Revolution. Some instances of collective behavior are not characterized by apparent common goals; a violent example (*lower left*) is a riot at a football game, and an example that was remarkable for its lack of violence (*upper left*) was the events sparked by the concert near Woodstock, New York, where an estimated 500,000 people lived together peacefully for several days despite overcrowded conditions, bad weather, and shortages of food, water, and other facilities. People may be drawn to any large concert of the Woodstock variety for reasons as varied as listening to music, being with friends, meeting others, taking drugs, and being seen.

	Goal		
	No Goal	To Escape	To Change Something
Nonviolent			
Violent			

(Action)

ly involve isolated individuals with nonnormative political beliefs or radical lifestyles who move toward greater interaction with one another and more coordinated political efforts. For example, many women felt that females were subject to discrimination and were restricted to subservient roles long before any social movement was concerned with this problem. What transformed this aggregate into a movement?

Smelser's Theory of Collective Behavior

Although many social scientists have investigated the causes of collective behavior, most of them have concentrated on a rather limited set of collective incidents and have produced different definitions of the field (Blumer, 1964; Brown, 1954, 1965; Lang and Lang, 1961; Milgram and Toch, 1969). Neil Smelser has taken the most broad and systematic approach in his *Theory of Collective Behavior* (1963).

Smelser's theory is complex, and it draws on concepts from many academic fields—the concept of value-added determinants from economics; the notion of breaking down complex forms of social behavior into components from sociology (Parsons, 1951).

Six Steps to Social Explosion. Smelser asserts that six factors determine whether or not collective behavior occurs: (1) structural conduciveness, (2) structural strain, (3) the growth and spread of a belief, (4) a precipitating event that sets off the collective behavior, (5) the mobilization of participants for collective action, and (6) mechanisms of social control that, when operating properly, work against the emergence of collective behavior. These determinants must follow one another in the order in which they are presented here. Each determinant is shaped by those that precede and, in turn, helps to shape the determinants that follow. Smelser characterizes this process as "value-added."

To understand the value-added approach, consider the manufacturing process that produced the textbook you are reading. In the beginning, there was a tree—which could have been made into a box or a book or a baseball bat. After it was converted into paper, its possible uses were narrowed; it could still be made into a box or a book, but not into a baseball bat. After the material was made into book paper, its possible uses were limited still further. It might have turned into a cookbook or a Bible or a textbook—but it could no longer be made into a box. Each step in the process added a specific "value" to the tree, and at the same time, it subtracted from the previous potentialities.

It is helpful to keep this value-added approach in mind as you consider each of Smelser's six determinants. To simplify the discussion, each determinant will be considered here as it applies to a specific political situation—the plight of the black people who constitute the majority of the population of the Republic of South Africa.

The prerequisite for all the other factors is *structural conduciveness,* or the social conditions that make collective behavior possible. In South Africa, racial segregation is rigidly enforced by the whites who are in power. At the same time, members of both black and white segments of the population, because they are segregated, can communicate within their own groups and can organize in various ways. Thus, each group has the potential for engaging in collective behavior.

When various parts of the social system are in conflict, *structural strain* occurs. Smelser believes that collective behavior represents an attempt to

Figure 17.3 *(Opposite)* according to Smelser's theory (1963), collective behavior occurs when the need for social change is felt but no institutional means are available for attaining the needed changes. The approach is a value-added one, in which all of the six determinants must occur and in which each is a prerequisite for the next. The segregation of South African blacks in ghettos and the possibilities for revolution there are presented in the photographs on the opposite page and on page 572. *(Upper left)* the living conditions of South African blacks provide glaring evidence of Smelser's first determinant, structural conduciveness, which consists of broad social conditions that set the stage for the occurrence of future collective behavior. *(Upper right)* in South Africa, the requirement that all blacks carry passbooks and the subjection of blacks to other harassments serve the purpose of the second determinant, structural strain, which refers to conflict in the social system that might be reduced by collective behavior. *(Bottom)* South African blacks demonstrate their opposition to the government's policies—proof that they have a generalized belief, Smelser's third determinant.

V BEHAVIOR IN GROUPS

reduce or eliminate the strain. In South Africa, whites monopolize the political power. Blacks are demanding a larger voice in decision making, but there is no normatively sanctioned way for them to change the situation, because they cannot vote. Thus, structural strain is built into the very fabric of South African society.

Although structural conduciveness and structural strain are necessary for collective behavior, they are not by themselves sufficient to produce it. The crux of Smelser's analysis is that a *generalized belief* must arise among the victims of structural strain. This belief must include a diagnosis of the forces causing the strain and—more important—a program of action for correcting the situation. Therefore, collective political action cannot occur in South Africa just because blacks feel oppressed; they must also have a

specific notion of what is causing their oppression, and they must propose a concrete program of action designed to eliminate it. Such a program could involve either a nonviolent march on the Parliament or violent guerrilla activity against the government, for example.

The three preceding determinants set the stage for collective behavior—but for the curtain to go up, a *precipitating event* must occur. There is no way to predict the exact kind of event that will trigger collective behavior, but one that might have served such a purpose occurred in South Africa on March 21, 1960. At Sharpeville, about forty miles from Johannesburg, black Africans staged an event as part of their nonviolent campaign against the "pass laws" requiring them to carry identification with them at all times. Blacks presented themselves at the police station and asked to be arrested for not having the mandatory passes. Police, who later claimed that the demonstrators had stormed the station, reacted by firing on the blacks, killing 67 and wounding 186. Although this occurrence caused a world-wide outcry against South African apartheid, it failed to trigger more intense protest activity within the country. Why did the event fail to precipitate collective behavior? According to Smelser's theory, it may have failed because the fifth necessary factor was lacking—mobilization.

In order for the four factors to result in collective behavior, there must also be an opportunity for the *mobilization of participants for collective action*. Mobilization usually requires a leader who can galvanize people into action, a duplicating machine for producing meeting announcements and propaganda, a network for distributing this literature, and so forth. Most of the forceful black leaders of South Africa were in jail and the government forbade blacks to hold political meetings. These conditions impeded the mobilization that is a necessary component of collective behavior, although four determinants were present.

In the Smelser model, the sixth determinant includes the *mechanisms*

Figure 17.4 Given the three conditions portrayed on the preceding page, a precipitating event must occur in South Africa to spark collective behavior. (*Left*) a mass burning of passbooks triggered the Sharpeville incident, which ended when police opened fire on protesting blacks. (*Upper right*) the result could have provided the precipitating event for revolution. (*Bottom right*) although mobilization, Smelser's fifth determinant, did occur to some degree, and although many marched in protest of the Sharpeville incident, the leaders had been jailed, and the government effectively squelched the protests. Thus, the failure of Smelser's sixth determinant, weak social controls, to emerge in South Africa has so far prevented revolution from occurring there.

V Behavior in Groups

of social control that, when operating properly, work against the emergence of collective behavior. These mechanisms are used by those in authority to prevent collective behavior. How strong are the police? Will they be present at the right place and time? In the Sharpeville incident, the South African government immediately mobilized the armed forces, declared a state of emergency, and arrested numerous black leaders. The major black political organizations were outlawed. Finally, police raided the largest black townships. Within two months, authorities had established emergency rule—nearly 20,000 blacks were arrested or held in detention. The South African mechanisms of social control thus proved in this instance to be in very good working order, providing the authorities with an effective block to the development of collective behavior.

Components of Social Action. Many different types of collective behavior can occur within the pattern of Smelser's six determinants. Therefore, still another set of relevant variables—the components of social action—have been incorporated into the model. Each of these four components describes a fundamental feature of society: (1) values, (2) norms, (3) organizational specifications, and (4) situational facilities. The components are presented in descending order of abstractness and scope in Figure 17.5.

Very general expressions of those qualities that a society considers good or desirable are *values.* In the United States, for example, "democracy," "freedom," and "affluence" are important values. *Norms,* which are more specific than values, indicate how people may go about realizing their values. Those who are interested in protecting "democracy," for example, may support norms requiring that elections be held, that the headquarters of political parties not be "bugged" or raided, that ballot boxes not be stuffed, and that candidates not spread false information about their opponents. *Organizational specifications,* even more specific than values and norms, are the beliefs that a society holds about how it should be organized in order for its members to adhere to established norms and values. For example, a democracy may have specifications indicating who may vote in elections or run for office, how various nonelective governmental positions are to be filled, and so on. The final and most specific components of social action are *situational facilities*—the physical means, provided by the system, by which people fulfill their society's organizational specifications. In a democratic political system, these facilities might include voting booths and political advertising in the mass media.

These components have been presented here from most to least inclusive. This hierarchical order is crucial to Smelser's analysis. He suggests that any change in one element will be reflected in those components below it (those that are more specific). If, for example, the value "democracy" is replaced by the value "dictatorship of the proletariat," then there must also be a change in the norms concerning elections, in the organizational specifications about how the government is to be set up, and in the facilities needed by the government.

Structural strain may occur at any of the four levels, and the characteristics of the level will influence the form that collective behavior may take. In a panic, for example, people act on the basis of their belief about the situational facilities—perhaps the belief that there are not enough escape exits for everyone to emerge safely. In a social or political movement, participants act on the basis of a shared belief about norms, proposing changes in the ways that the society may achieve its basic goals. Thus, the

Figure 17.5 Smelser's components of social action. Although Smelser's six steps to collective behavior help to specify whether or not collective behavior will occur, these four components help to specify the form that it will take if it does occur. Each of the four components represents a fundamental level of society, shown in descending order from the most general to the most specific. The six factors leading to collective behavior may occur at any of these four levels. According to the theory, changes in one component will bring about changes in all more specific components.

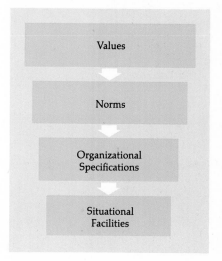

movement for black civil rights does not necessarily represent a desire to change basic American values; its aim may be to bring about a less conflicting relationship between American values and the norms that do not allow blacks to fully share those values.

Although strain may first become apparent on any level, Smelser believes that participants in collective behavior do not direct their attention to this initial level. Instead, they may quickly shift attention to a higher level. The women's-liberation movement provides an example. Initially, many women were outraged by the fact that they are usually paid less than are men who do the same work. This situation represented a strain at the level of situational facilities, a discrepancy in the physical means by which workers are rewarded in a society that values work. Activists in the movement soon shifted their attention upward to the component of organizational specifications, asserting that inequality of pay was merely one symptom of the subservient roles to which American society relegates its female members. Some women's groups focus on a still higher component, charging that the norms of society must change before organizational specifications and facilities can change, that Americans must permit women to work or live as they like. In this and other cases, people tend to reduce strain at one level by shifting focus to a more abstract level.

Evaluation of Smelser's Theory

The theory of collective behavior devised by Smelser is an insightful, well-organized attempt to explain when and why collective behavior occurs. In the predictive sense, however, it is not a theory but a series of categories into which pieces of information about collective behavior can be fitted after an event has occurred. Although such analysis is helpful, it does not allow social scientists to predict when the six elements will combine in a manner that will result in collective behavior, to predict when a precipitating event is likely to occur, to predict whether or not it will be possible to mobilize participants for action, and so on.

In addition, the idea that people focus attention on a higher-level component than the one in which strain is first apparent seems to have limited application. In many instances of collective behavior, there does not seem to be a jump from a lower to a higher-order component. When labor unions first began organizing strikes in American factories, for example, they did not focus on achieving political power or on changing the role of factory workers but solely on the concrete issues: higher pay and better working conditions. There are also instances of collective behavior in which attention has been shifted from a higher to a lower component. The first aim of the socialist movement in Europe was to replace capitalist society with socialism. However, as the movement progressed and as socialists became members of legislative bodies in various countries, many parties abandoned their original "value" goals and started to work instead for lower-level changes, such as free medical care and social security. The Russian revolutionary leader Lenin foresaw these shifts in emphasis and warned against them.

The importance of the role of generalized beliefs may also be questioned. They are undoubtedly important in political movements, social movements, and panics—but what role do they play in riots and mob actions? In a riot, for example, participants might simply be imitating others without having a particular goal in mind. Or a riot participant may have a specific individual goal, such as obtaining a television set without paying for it, that is not shared by all other participants.

Social psychologists can be expected to contribute to the refinement of the Smelser theory, which emphasizes sociology, Smelser's major field of research. Accordingly, the theory largely neglects psychological variables. The social psychologist recognizes that collective behavior requires structural conduciveness and structural strain, but these two factors are present in a wide range of situations. Hence, the psychologist raises several crucial questions, which are based on the knowledge accumulated by psychologists. Under what conditions is a given structural strain likely to be perceived as a strain? What kinds of people are likely to perceive the strain and act on this perception? Similar questions may be directed at another determinant, the mobilization of participants for action, which is analyzed rather imprecisely by Smelser. Given a nucleus of people engaged in collective behavior, under what specific conditions are other people likely to join? Why? It requires more than just a leader and a duplicating machine, after all, to stage an antiwar demonstration or to close down a university. In summary, Smelser's formulation contains some important insights into collective behavior, but there are many missing pieces to the puzzle.

COLLECTIVE RESPONSES TO STRAIN

Collective behavior occurs at specific times and places, and the historical and cultural elements that influence such behavior cannot be ignored. Thus, it is unsafe to assume that because student activists in the United States, Germany, and France usually espouse a left-wing ideology, students in other time periods and in other countries will follow a similar pattern of response. Indeed, two books edited by Seymour Martin Lipset present examples that directly refute that assumption (Lipset, 1967; Lipset and Altback, 1969). Even in investigating behavior in a specific country during a limited time period, it must be kept in mind that different individuals may be attracted to the same political or social movement for very different reasons or that they may be attracted to seemingly different movements for similar reasons. Still, there seem to be some general psychological and cultural conditions that facilitate collective responses to strain.

Relative Deprivation: Is Poverty a Powderkeg?

It might be assumed that the greater the structural strain in a society, the more likely it is that collective action designed to reduce the strain will occur. This assumption is the basis of Marxist theory. According to Karl Marx (1968), the "workers of the world" will "throw off their chains" when life for them becomes intolerably bad. But this notion is too simple. Individuals cannot respond to the strain without first experiencing it as aversive and unjust. How do people actually *evaluate* their objective circumstances? John Thibaut and Harold Kelley (1959) propose that this evaluation is relative. Individuals compare their objective situations with their *expectations* and with the *outcomes* they believe others in their immediate environments are experiencing. It is this level of *relative,* not absolute, deprivation that makes a given objective situation unbearable and that may generate collective behavior. Studies of both left- and right-wing political movements seem to support this theory. James Davies (1962) examined income statistics for several countries, including France and Russia, during the years immediately before the outbreak of revolutionary activity. He found that each revolution followed a sudden economic depression that had been preceded by a long period of economic prosperity. Revolution erupted only after rising expectations were suddenly disappointed (see the topical insert below). In studying the black civil-rights movement in America, Thomas Pettigrew (1967) observed that civil-rights activities became cohesive and forceful during the 1960s, a period when income and opportunities for blacks were increasing rapidly but at a much slower rate than black expectations (which were based largely on government promises). A study by Nathan Caplan and Jeffery Paige (1968) of the 1967 riots in the black ghettos of Detroit and Newark clearly indicates that the experience of relative deprivation was a causative factor. These authors, who interviewed representative samples of both rioters and nonrioters, found that rioters had higher occupational aspirations and more education than did nonrioters. More important, the rioters were more likely than nonrioters to believe that the income gap between relatively rich and relatively poor blacks was increasing rather than remaining stable or decreasing. Interestingly, rioters and nonrioters did not differ in their perceptions of white as opposed to black incomes; whites were apparently an irrelevant "reference group" to these ghetto residents.

The concept of relative deprivation may also help to explain support for such right-wing movements as that associated with the late Senator Joseph McCarthy. Martin Trow (1958) found, for instance, that McCarthy's supporters were drawn from groups such as shopkeepers and retired army officers, who had once occupied influential roles in American society but had been replaced by "technocrats" and large corporations. Although these

---

The Causes of Revolution:
NO TEA
& NO SYMPATHY

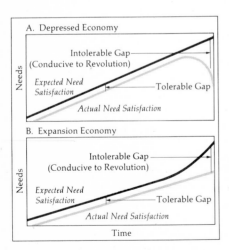

ONE OF THE MOST provocative aspects of revolutions is why they occur when they do. Intellectuals have often noted that revolutions do not necessarily occur when people are under the heaviest yoke of oppression and scarcity. Rather, as de Tocqueville said, "Evils which are patiently endured when they seem inevitable become intolerable when once the idea of escape from them is suggested." The idea emerges that lightening the burden produces a hopeful state of mind, and with the birth of optimism frequently comes the crushing blow of disillusionment and frustration.

James C. Davies has attempted to clarify these ideas of political upheaval based on the dynamics of unfulfilled expectations. Although still underway, Davies' investigation seems to have revealed certain indicators of revolt. The figures shown here represent the psychic forces that Davies feels operate to produce strife. Example A shows what might occur in a depressed economy, and B, when a moderate

improvement leads eventually to dissatisfaction.

In both cases, an intolerable gap occurs between what people expect and what they are actually obtaining. As a result, this theory would predict that developmental foreign aid that improved a country's productivity could become, intentionally or not, an instrument of revolution. If rebellion is fostered by unattainable expectations, then this pattern has interesting implications for the world's tyrants as well as for the tyrannized. It would be a foolish dictator who falsely raised the hopes of miserable but docile followers.

Source: Adapted from J. Davies, "Toward a Theory of Revolution," *American Sociological Review,* 27 (1962), pp. 5–19.

shopkeepers and military officers were not experiencing much absolute deprivation, their relative deprivation was apparently great.

Attitudes and Action Potential

Even if a group of persons experiences relative deprivation in a situation of structural conduciveness, most of its members will not attempt to improve the situation. Thus, several other cultural and psychological factors—principally attitudes and beliefs—may also be crucial in the emergence of collective action.

Cultural Differences.   Societies, and subgroups within societies, may differ in their conceptions of what kinds of action can be taken in order to change the environment. The most clear-cut example of this difference comes from a comparison of Eastern and Western philosophies of life. In the East, Taoism and Hinduism teach that the highest "good" is a resigned acceptance of the status quo; if life is unpleasant, the solution is not to change it but to look inward for individual salvation. Western philosophy has a much more active orientation toward the environment. In this dimension, Eastern societies are passive, and Western societies are active. It is quite likely, therefore, that Easterners and Westerners faced with the same objective circumstances will respond quite differently. Even within Western culture, there are important differences along this dimension. Gabriel Almond and Sidney Verba (1963) obtained data on the political attitudes of persons living in five Western democracies—Italy, the United States, Mexico, Germany, and Great Britain—and found marked differences in the degree to which citizens of these countries believed that they should take an active role in political processes. In Italy, for example, only 10 percent of the respondents felt that an "ordinary man" should be active in his community. In the United States, this figure was 51 percent and in Germany, 22 percent.

Who to Blame?   Another important dimension, which is relevant to collective action in the political sphere, is the extent to which individuals in subordinate positions tend to blame either themselves or "the system" for their low status. In the United States, a popular national symbol is "Horatio Alger," the pen name of an author whose rags-to-riches novels told how any poor boy could succeed in this country through hard work. (The fact that the poor boy usually got his start by marrying his rich boss's daughter is conveniently ignored.) Persons who accept the view that hard work always brings success, who work hard, and who nevertheless fail to achieve tend to blame themselves for their failure. Other people, however, tend to blame the system—which, in reality, may often be at fault. One study indicates, not surprisingly, that black college students who felt the system was responsible if blacks failed to achieve in American society were much more likely to support collective political action than were those who thought that nonachievers had only themselves to blame (Gurin, Gurin, Lao, and Beattie, 1969). Several psychoanalysts, including Abraham Kardiner and Lionel Ovesey (1951) and Frantz Fanon (1967), have additionally pointed out that self-blame will not only inhibit political action but may also cause irreparable psychic damage to members of minority groups. To counteract this situation, the main thrust of the black-power movement has been to convince blacks that they should be proud of their race, that the system is to blame for their subordination within American society, that sociological factors rather than inherent racial weaknesses are the hub of the black problem, and that blacks should take collective action to change the structure of American society. Such action would serve to reduce the structural strain that victimizes blacks.

Internal Versus External Control.   Blaming the system (especially when it really is at fault) is not enough to cause people to seek to change it. Individuals must believe that they can improve their lot—even in a hostile environment. Julian Rotter (1966), whose personality typology is discussed in Chapter 4, has observed that people differ widely in how they interpret the relationship between their individual actions and their successes and failures. Some individuals see little connection between the two and attribute rewards and punishments (successes and failures) to external forces—to luck, to the actions of powerful people, to fate. Such people are said to be high in *external control.* Conversely, other individuals believe that their successes and failures are the direct consequences of their own behaviors, that they in effect determine their own outcomes. These individuals are high in what Rotter calls *internal control.* Numerous studies support the idea that this distinction is useful in predicting how an individual is likely to respond to a wide range of situations. Not only are individuals who are high in internal control much more likely to participate in political action (Gore and Rotter, 1963) but they also have higher occupational and educational aspirations, persist longer in trying to solve difficult tasks, do better in school, and try more often to influence the opinions of others. The internal-external control dimension may be viewed as the psychological counterpart of the activity-passivity dimension, applied earlier to the different degrees to which Western and Eastern societies view collective political action as "legitimate." If the recent findings about black activists (described in Chapter 7) are any indication, the individuals who blame the system *and* who have a high sense of personal control over their own lives are prime candidates for becoming political activists.

Political Altruism

So far, this discussion has considered some of the important variables that seem to determine whether persons on the losing end of structural strain will rebel against it. People who are not in this position but who act to ease the strain should also be considered. Why was Jane Fonda active in the antiwar movement? Why have middle-class white housewives traveled to Alabama to participate in "freedom rides" against segregation? In neither case have the individuals experienced personal deprivation, although they publicly expressed their concern for the relative deprivation experienced by the Vietnamese peasants or Southern blacks on whose behalf they acted. Such persons can be called "political altruists"—although "altruism" is given a somewhat different meaning in Chapter 12 in a discussion of the conditions under which an individual is likely to selflessly help another individual. Here, the focus is on individuals who act on behalf of "others" in general, who may love "mankind" but may not necessarily display concern for individual men and women. The similarities between these two types of altruism are at best obscure.

In determining the conditions that may produce political altruists, it is helpful to think about why college campuses are often politically active. There seem to be three basic reasons. First, college students often think differently from other people, because they are in an environment that encourages them to apply *ideological concepts* such as "justice," "truth," and "equality" to the world surrounding them. This type of philosophical stance, which may be a prerequisite to taking action on behalf of others, is not often the stance of people who are faced with the task of earning a daily living in an imperfect world. Second, college students are a *marginal group* within society. While in school, they have little investment in the status quo; therefore they have the necessary freedom and impartiality to be altruistic. Finally, most college students have relatively *high socioeconomic status,* which also gives them freedom and detachment. Operating from a secure economic base, they need not worry much about themselves, and they can be more concerned with others who are in less fortunate positions.

If it is true that ideology, marginality, and socioeconomic security are key variables in accounting for student activism, then students who are high on each of these dimensions should prove to be more active politically than those who are low on these counts. Numerous studies of student activism suggest that the assumption is valid.

Researchers have examined the relationship between the degree of protest activity at specific colleges and characteristics of the institutions, such as their size and whether they were public or private (Bayer and Astin, 1969; Peterson, 1967, 1968). The greatest amount of activity occurred at the most selective institutions, like Harvard and Vassar, rather than at small community colleges. The selective schools attract the most intellectually oriented and affluent students. Several studies, including that of William Watts and David Whittaker (1966), have compared participants and nonparticipants in the free-speech movement at Berkeley, making similar observations within a single university. Activists in the free-speech movement tended to obtain higher scores than nonactivists on personality scales measuring theoretical and intellectual orientation, to have higher grades, and to have higher academic aspirations. The politically involved students,

Figure 17.6 Political altruists, like Joan Baez, are those on the winning side of society who are concerned with actively reducing the strain of those who are not. There is suggestive evidence that ideology, marginality, and socioeconomic security are related to political altruism, but the relationship between political altruism and altruistic behavior toward particular individuals in need (discussed in Chapter 12) is not known.

in short, were not academic "dropouts" as some writers have claimed; they were the most intellectually gifted students at Berkeley.

It has also been asserted that political altruists are people who dislike their country. Stanley Morse and Stanton Peele (1971) administered questionnaires to several hundred persons—both students and nonstudents—who traveled by bus and train from Chicago to an antiwar rally in Washington and obtained data relevant to this point. Respondents were asked to indicate how positive they felt toward a variety of United States national symbols. Although most respondents had relatively neutral feelings toward traditional national symbols such as the flag and the national anthem, they had extremely positive feelings toward symbols reflecting the basic principles on which they believed the country was founded—the Bill of Rights and the Constitution. The Morse and Peele data indicate that the activists were motivated not by a dislike for their country but by the perception that the United States had deviated from its basic commitment to such concepts as "democracy" and "fair play."

Data on the socioeconomic backgrounds of activists are more plentiful and consistent than are data on their ideologies. Numerous studies show that the socioeconomic backgrounds of campus activists are higher than are those of nonactivists (Sampson, 1967). At a University of Chicago dormitory, Richard Flacks (1967) found that of twenty-four residents whose family incomes were above $15,000, half took part in a sit-in, whereas of twenty-three whose family incomes were below $15,000, only two participated.

Marginality is another factor that repeatedly emerges from studies of campus activists. For example, Jews participate more heavily in protest activities than do non-Jews, even when family-income levels are constant. And, of course, this is not a recent phenomenon. Jews played a disproportionately important role in the Russian revolutions and in left-wing politics in Central Europe between 1815 and 1848 (Altbach, 1969), to name only a few instances. There may be several reasons for this heavy Jewish involvement in leftist causes; one significant factor is that Jews are a marginal group. Gerhard Lenski (1961) notes that, as a group, American Jews are affluent, but their marginality permits them to examine society critically.

Personality factors may also affect political altruism, a point that will be discussed in a later section of this chapter.

JOINING THE MASS MOVEMENT

So far, the conditions under which isolated individuals may band together to act politically have been outlined. But what about new recruits to an ongoing movement? What conditions may draw them into a movement?

Recruitment: Filling the Ranks

In order to recruit new members, a movement must be *visible*. Potential recruits must be able to identify members of a movement and must be able to interact with them if they so choose. The previously mentioned studies that were devised by Bayer and Astin and by Peterson revealed that the most important institutional characteristic associated with campus protest activity was the size of the school. Although 22 percent of all United States colleges and universities reported protest activity in 1968 and 1969, activity at schools with enrollments of less than 1,000 was negligible. Similarly, the Russian revolution broke out in St. Petersburg (Leningrad), not

Figure 17.7 Visibility is a necessary characteristic of political and social movements if they are to recruit new members. Whereas such movements in our society rely heavily on television, radio, and newspapers to reach the population, means such as billboards (*below*), posters, and the dropping of leaflets (*opposite*) from aircraft are used in less technologically advanced societies and in remote areas.

V BEHAVIOR IN GROUPS

Novosibirsk, and the French revolution began in Paris, not Lyons.

This situation may be changing, however, because of the mass media. In the United States, for example, television has brought coverage of collective behavior to the attention of people in localities far removed from the site of the activity. Television therefore increases the probability that sympathizers in isolated areas will become involved in collective action. The women's-liberation movement is more widespread today than was the earlier women's-suffrage movement, which had to recruit members at a time when communication was much more limited.

Familiarity, in social movements, seems to breed respect or acceptance. A movement may gain new recruits simply by enduring. The significance of a movement's duration can be inferred from experiments involving repeated exposure to a stimulus. A series of studies by Robert Zajonc (1968) demonstrated that subjects who are exposed to a previously neutral stimulus like it more as they are more frequently subjected to it (see Chapter 6). The more someone is subjected to the activities of a group, the more likely it is that he or she will feel favorably toward the group and join it.

Another important factor is who belongs to the movement. Research on imitation, including that by Albert Bandura and Richard Walters (1963), indicates that most imitation occurs when models are liked, when they are perceived to be powerful, or when they have high prestige. Perhaps this is why many campus movements attempt, intentionally or not, to place respected professors and graduate students in visible positions within their organizations. Making prestigious models visible may also facilitate attitude change. Carl Hovland, Irving Janis, and Harold Kelley (1953) note that most attitude change is likely to occur if the "communicator" is of high status, is admired, or is seen as an expert (see Chapter 9).

Personality Needs and Motivation

Personality needs also play a role in pulling individuals into a political group, particularly a mass movement. The relationship between personality and political involvement has been investigated by many researchers whose concern goes beyond the bounds of theory. Political events have been major catalysts. During and after World War II, for example, many psychologists joined the ranks of the journalists, philosophers, and historians who attempted to explain the appeal of Nazism. Because these writers viewed Nazism as categorically evil, they inevitably portrayed the personality of a typical Nazi, too, as evil. Suspending criteria of good and evil is difficult when one is morally outraged. Psychologists who use moralistic models, for example, cannot objectively study personality as a variable. Nazism, however, was not a unique instance of collective behavior—nor were Nazis the only personalities whose actions have been explained on the basis of moral rather than scientific criteria. (Later on, when Communism entered the American pantheon of categorical evils, many writers also portrayed American Communists as evil personalities.)

Social scientists began trying to supply a link, suggesting that individuals who join mass movements—whether on the political right or the left—must have similar personalities and must derive similar satisfactions from immersing themselves in movements with powerful ideologies, movements that promise to construct a new world order.

Some of the most influential works in this area have been provided by Theodor Adorno, Else Frenkel-Brunswik, Daniel J. Levinson, and R. Nevitt

Sanford (1950); Erich Fromm (1941); and Eric Hoffer (1951). These authors, with the exception of Hoffer, in trying to explain the appeal of Nazism and fascism, draw a clear distinction between supporters of right-wing and left-wing movements. Hoffer, a longshoreman turned social philosopher, does not make this distinction: "When people are ripe for a mass movement," he says, "they are usually ripe for any effective movement, and not solely for one with a particular doctrine or program."

These three works indicate that the moral model is still in use, insofar as all six authors reach remarkably similar conclusions about why people join whichever mass movements the writer happens to dislike (Nazism and fascism for Adorno and his colleagues and Fromm; Communism, fascism, and even Christianity for Hoffer). These observers claim that followers of

DIFFERENT DRUMMERS, SAME SONG

THE MEMBERSHIP of mass movements—members' personal characteristics, motivations, and loyalties—have often been a source of heated controversy among intellectuals. The irrationality of the crowd was a central focus of classic authors such as Sigmund Freud and Gustave Le Bon, although the positive qualities of members of mass movements have been emphasized by current writers, such as Kenneth Keniston.

One social critic, Eric Hoffer, who raised himself by his bootstraps in the traditional American-dream style from longshoreman to late-night TV guest is inclined toward the former position. He says this about mass movements and their appeal to certain persons:

A rising mass movement attracts and holds a following . . . by the refuge it offers from the anxieties, barrenness and meaninglessness of an individual existence. It cures the poignantly frustrated not by conferring on them an absolute truth or by remedying the difficulties and abuses which made their lives miserable, but by freeing them from their ineffectual selves—and it does this by enfolding and absorbing them into a closely knit and exultant corporate whole. (1966, page 44)

An effective mass movement cultivates the idea of sin. It depicts the autonomous self not only as barren and helpless but also as vile. To confess and repent is to slough off one's individual distinctness and separateness, and salvation is found by losing oneself in the holy oneness of the congregation. (pages 55–56)

The vigor of a mass movement stems from the propensity of its followers for united action and self-sacrifice. . . . Both . . . require self-diminution. . . . To ripen a person for self-sacrifice he must be stripped of his individual identity and distinctness. He must cease to be George, Hans, Ivan, or Tadao . . . . The fully assimilated individual does not see himself and others as human beings. When asked who he is, his automatic response is that he is a German, a Russian, a Japanese, a Christian, a Moslem, a member of a certain tribe or family. He has no purpose, worth and destiny apart from his collective body; and as long as that body lives he cannot really die. (pages 57–60)

The impression that mass movements, and revolutions in particular, are born of the resolve of the masses to overthrow a corrupt and oppressive tyranny and win for themselves freedom of action, speech and conscience has its origin in the din of words let loose by the intellectual originators of the movement in their skirmishes with the prevailing order. . . . They take it for granted that the masses who respond to their call and range themselves behind them crave the same things. However the freedom the masses crave is not freedom of self-expression and self-realization, but freedom from the intolerable burden of an autonomous existence. (page 129)

Hoffer is surely a dour spectator on the sidelines of mass movements. From his perspective, neither the insecure common man nor the rhetorically overblown intellect understands or deserves the power and prerogatives that mass movements gain. Of what value is Hoffer's perspective? How can he help explain the rise and fall of student activism in recent years? Whether or not Hoffer's rhetoric withstands the scrutiny of empirical tests remains to be seen.

Source: Adapted from E. Hoffer, *The True Believer* (New York: Harper & Row, 1966).

such movements are attempting to bring meaning to their empty lives by submerging their weak egos in a large collectivity whose power may be extended to them. According to Fromm, such individuals are unable to accept the freedom and responsibility to organize their own lives, so they allow others to do this for them. Adorno and his co-workers use the term *authoritarian* to describe these people.

Authoritarianism and Radical Movements. According to Adorno and his colleagues, authoritarians feel most secure in situations where those above them in a status hierarchy issue clear commands that must be obeyed without question and in situations where they in turn can demand the unquestioned obedience of those beneath them. It is also alleged that authoritarian individuals see everything in very clear-cut, black-and-white terms. There are only good guys and bad buys—and "we" are the good guys. This personality trait, according to Hoffer, explains why many ex-Communists do not become inconspicuous citizens but instead turn into fervent anti-Communists, as firmly committed to the belief that Communism is an unspeakable evil as they had previously been committed to the notion that it would save mankind. Hoffer bases his conclusions on impressionistic observations and historical analyses. Fromm goes further and adds in-depth psychological case studies. Adorno and his co-workers developed a test, the *F* scale, to measure authoritarianism.

In numerous studies, application of the *F* scale has indicated that supporters of right-wing movements and individuals with conservative political beliefs have significantly higher authoritarianism scores than do left-wingers and liberals. Does the concept of authoritarianism then explain the appeal of right-wing, but not left-wing, mass movements?

Adorno's work has been criticized on a number of serious methodological counts by Herbert Hyman and Paul Sheatsley (1954) and others (see Chapter 7). Milton Rokeach (1960), for example, suggests that the attitude statements on the *F* scale tap only right-wing authoritarianism. An item such as, "A person who has bad manners, habits, and breeding can hardly expect to get along with decent people," may reflect a sort of authoritarianism, but it also suggests a right-wing political bias—conservative people are more likely to associate decency with manners and etiquette than are radicals. Rokeach developed a new measure of authoritarianism, the dogmatism scale. The items on this test are free of explicit political content, yet they still measure the extent to which a person is rigid in his thinking, intolerant, and sympathetic to authoritarian ideas (see samples at right). In 1954 Rokeach administered his new test to British college students who identified themselves as supporters of the Conservative, Liberal, Labour, or Communist parties (Rokeach, 1960). When these students were tested with the *F* scale, Communists obtained the lowest mean score on authoritarianism and Conservatives, the highest. But on the new dogmatism scale, Communists and Conservatives both scored higher than supporters of middle-of-the-road parties. Rokeach concluded that authoritarian (dogmatic) individuals are ripe for extremist politics of either the right or the left.

Activists and Dissenters. During the past decade, several social scientists have investigated the personalities and home backgrounds of individuals involved in campus and civil-rights demonstrations. These activities are relatively unstructured, and they do not offer a political ideology so much as a catalog of specific evils that they would like to correct. Jeanne Block,

Items From Rokeach's Dogmatism Scale:

It is when a person devotes himself to an ideal or cause that he becomes important.

It is sometimes necessary to resort to force to advance an ideal one strongly believes in.

It's all too true that most people just won't practice what they preach.

If given the chance I would do some things that would be of great benefit to the world.

Norma Haans, and M. Brewster Smith (1968) investigated more than 1,000 students at the University of California at Berkeley, first dividing them into five subgroups according to participation or nonparticipation in both social-service and protest activities. One group—called the *dissenters*—scored high on a scale measuring involvement in protest activities and low on a scale assessing social-service participation; the second group—called the *activists*—scored high on both scales. Then these students were asked to write descriptions of the values and the child-rearing practices of their parents. Most of the dissenters said that their parents were very permissive and indulgent, but at the same time they placed great stress on achievement and competition. The apparent result was an unsatisfying parental relationship, characterized by conflict and inconsistency. Parents of most of the activists were also permissive, but they encouraged self-expression and independence. Thus, the conflict between indulgence and the demand for achievement was absent in the home backgrounds of the activists. The activists scored high on both political and social activism, while the dissenters were politically oriented but not interested in social-service activities, which require helping people on a one-to-one basis. Dissenters could be considered "political altruists," without necessarily being "altruistic" in the sense the term is used in Chapter 12.

Kenneth Keniston, in his book *Young Radicals* (1968), portrays his subjects as political altruists who are psychologically secure and who seek social justice. But he also mentions that left-wing radicals are not willing to make the type of commitment—to a career and to a stable role within the existing society—that adulthood demands. As noted earlier, marginal groups are predisposed to political altruism. Keniston's portrait of marginality fits not only certain groups, such as Jews and college students, but also has a psychological equivalent. Do activists, who are motivated to participate in social-service as well as protest activities, show less psychological "marginality" than dissenters? And what about authoritarianism? If dissenters are viewed as more ideological in their orientation, they are found to be somewhat like the student radicals in Rokeach's study, who, regardless of their political ideologies—Conservative or Communist—scored high on authoritarianism (dogmatism). The dissenters seem to have different motivations from those of activists: they appear to have authoritarian ego needs, and their limited participation suggests limited altruism.

Altruism and Commitment. The combination of certain conditions—an ideological climate, socioeconomic security, and marginality—facilitates political altruism because it makes people more likely to respond on behalf of others who are experiencing the strain of relative deprivation. But personality factors, too, may influence the expression of commitment in the political altruist.

David Rosenhan (1970) discovered an interesting distinction between fully committed political altruists and those who were only partially committed. The fully committed political altruists had been involved consistently in civil-rights activities for at least a year, but the partially committed individuals had participated in only one or two "freedom rides." In-depth interviews revealed that the fully committed individuals had positive feelings toward their parents, and they felt that relationships with their parents were characterized by warmth and respect. In sharp contrast, the partially committed individuals described their parents negatively or ambivalently. More striking, according to Rosenhan, was what he called the "cognitive substance" of the relationship. Parents of both the fully committed and the partially committed were concerned with moral questions. The parents of partially committed political altruists usually had ambivalent and inconsistent attitudes about morality. Most parents of fully committed political altruists, however, had actually engaged in extended altruistic activity at some time during their children's formative years; they therefore served as altruistic models for their children. Rosenhan suggests that the altruistic behavior of the fully committed group is greatly influenced by close identification with altruistic models whose values are already affirmed and that behavior of the partially committed group reflects an ongoing search for values.

Social-Psychological Needs.   Larry Kerpelman (1970) offers additional data on personality factors. In conducting a careful study of 229 students in three American colleges, he grouped the participants by ideology (right-wing, left-wing, and liberal) and by degree of activism (activist right-wing, nonactivist right-wing, activist left-wing, and so on). He found only a few personality differences among members of the six different groups. To assess authoritarianism, Kerpelman devised a personality test that differs from both Adorno's *F* scale and Rokeach's dogmatism scale. His results support Adorno's claims about personality and political persuasion—people with right-wing beliefs, whether activists or nonactivists, scored highest in authoritarianism, and left-wing activists scored lowest. Kerpelman also found that activists showed more independence, needed less support and nurturing, and placed more value on leadership. It follows that they were also more socially ascendant, assertive, and autonomous—and more sociable. Kerpelman discovered no differences between activists and nonactivists on measures of emotional stability, responsibility, and restraint. The correlation between sociability and activism may be Kerpelman's most significant finding: it suggests that people may be drawn to collective activities because they promise a good deal of social interaction. If such activities also offer leadership possibilities, they will be still more attractive to the activist personality.

In conclusion, it is difficult to specify the personality needs and the traits that predispose an individual toward collective behavior. Studies suggest that authoritarian people are drawn to radical movements, probably most often to right-wing radical activities. However, methodologies that show correlations between authoritarianism and political ideologies have to be rigorously examined for biases. Studies distinguishing activists from dissenters suggest that the activists—people who are engaged in both protest and social-service activities—are motivated by social as well as political altruism and that they have already found meaning in their lives. Neither of these qualities appears in the authoritarian personality. Certainly there are other personality factors, such as the needs for interaction and leadership, that might lead individuals to participate in collective action.

WHY COLLECTIVE OUTBURSTS?

Earlier in this chapter, two questions were asked about collective behavior, and possible answers have been supplied to one of these: Why and when do certain people decide to join together to engage in collective behavior? Cultural factors and personal attitudes that may promote collective responses to strain were discussed, as were variables that influence successful mobilization of recruits; the effects of personality needs and traits on an individual's attraction to political movements were also considered.

The other question remains to be investigated: How does a group of individuals engaged in normative group activity turn into one displaying nonnormative collective behavior?

The Collective Mind

Phenomena such as mobs and panics conjure up a specter of ordinary social life gone berserk. When caught in the grip of "mob psychology," the meek and well-socialized individual is supposedly transformed into an entirely different being. Writers have painted this metamorphosis in vivid terms.

Gustave Le Bon's book *The Crowd* (1960) is now a classic and was first published in France in 1895. According to Le Bon, "under certain given circumstances . . . an agglomeration of men presents new characteristics very different from those of the individuals composing it." Le Bon described some of these characteristics as:

> . . . impulsiveness, irritability, incapacity to reason, the absence of judgment and of the critical spirit, the exaggeration of the sentiments, and others besides—which are almost always observed in beings belonging to inferior forms of evolution—in women, savages, and children, for instance. (page 36)

Le Bon, a French aristocrat, felt threatened by the "era of crowds" unleashed by the French revolution. Three chapters in his book, for instance, depict "criminal juries," "electoral crowds," and "parliamentary assemblies" in equally bleak terms. In addition, Le Bon's views of human behavior were based on cultural myths rather than scientific research, as shown by his reference to women, savages, and children. Although his book has become a classic, it must be interpreted in the light of its time.

Other writers since Le Bon's time have invoked less colorful terms while agreeing with Le Bon in broad outline. Stanley Milgram and Hans

Figure 17.8 Gustave Le Bon's nineteenth-century theory of crowd behavior suggests that individuals in a crowd may undergo a radical transformation—personal identities and consciences are relinquished to a collective mind that is both irrational and violent. The result is a collective display of feelings, thoughts, and actions that are usually alien to any of the individual participants.

Toch (1969), who recently reviewed published works on collective behavior, believe that mobs and other types of unruly crowds are characterized by three essential features. First, they show *uniformity of behavior:* Personal idiosyncrasies seem to be submerged into what Le Bon called a "collective mind." Second, crowds of this sort often engage in *violent acts,* which the participants as individuals would neither engage in nor condone. And, finally, there is a *heightened emotionality* that causes people to overreact to a situation—to respond in extreme and uncritical ways to beliefs and instructions that are often contradictory.

What forces eradicate idiosyncrasies in personality and destroy social restraints? Le Bon cited two basic mechanisms. First, individuals immersed in a crowd lose their unique personalities and their sense of responsibility because they have become anonymous. The *anonymity* of a crowd, furthermore, gives people a feeling of invincibility; they have become part of a collectivity whose will and actions are stronger than their own. Second, Le Bon (a physician) believed that *contagion* is a factor, with one person's feelings and actions spreading to others like an infectious disease.

The Psychoanalytic Model

Sigmund Freud (1922) agreed that Le Bon had described an important social phenomenon but felt that he had not adequately explained the underlying psychological dynamics. Freud's approach to collective behavior is exceedingly complex and cannot be discussed here in detail, but concepts that are basic to his views can be summarized. Freud believed that all individuals possess certain "libidinal forces"—instinctive drives or desires, such as the sex drive, and that these forces lead to processes he called *repression* and *sublimation.* A particular libidinal force may be so effectively controlled by the environment that it is *repressed* in the individual's subconscious. Although the environment may initiate this repression, the individual himself must use his own limited supply of psychic energy to keep the desires repressed—and this effort leaves little energy available for other endeavors. Repression is never completely successful. Specific desires may be controlled, but they will become manifest in other ways: they will be *sublimated* in disguised forms.

Another set of concepts central to Freud's scheme are the *id* and *superego.* The id is man's basic instinctive nature, which is composed of the libidinal forces that are the source of all psychic energy. We are born with ids. The superego, in contrast, is a product of our interactions with the environment. In the superego are stored all the rules we have learned for how we should and should not behave, what we can and cannot do. The superego helps to keep the id's forces in check.

In Freud's analysis of collective behavior, the leader plays a key role; social-psychological variables are not emphasized. Freud believed that libidinal forces tie group members to the leader, because everyone wants to be loved by the leader. The leader, however, cannot love all group members totally or equally; he therefore becomes a source of frustration as well as an object of love. How can this frustration be resolved? Freud stated that people resolve this conflict in the same way a son resolves his "Oedipal conflict" toward his father (a process described in Chapter 2).

In Freud's view, each crowd member can resolve the conflict produced by ambivalent feelings toward the leader by identifying with him, just as a son resolves the competition for his mother's affection by identifying with his father. In doing this, the crowd member renounces his own superego, replacing its dictates with the leader's commands. As a consequence, crowd members may revert to a childlike state of hypnotic dependence on the leader, unquestioningly following his orders. With the individual's superego thus relaxed, his libidinal drives may be expressed without interference. This relaxation of the superego may be used by a clever leader.

Freud also believed that crowd members have very strong psychic ties with one another. Because all identify with the same leader, they identify strongly with each other. This process of identification requires a good deal of psychic energy. When not part of a crowd, the individual expends most of this energy on himself in order to preserve his own unique identity. The effort to preserve one's identity results in an aversion to the peculiarities of others. However, members of the crowd have an insufficient supply of energy left for such isolationism and individuality. As a result, other crowd members are not only tolerated but loved, and a high degree of behavioral uniformity becomes possible.

The Emergent-Norm Model

Freud's analysis of violent crowds is an outgrowth of his work on individual personality dynamics. In contrast, the *emergent-norm theory* attempts to extrapolate the findings of small-group research (see Chapter 14) to the study of collective behavior. Investigators have suggested that crowds often evolve norms that create a certain amount of uniformity in the behavior of participants (Turner, 1964; Turner and Killian, 1957). However, the amount of uniformity that crowds seem to show is somewhat illusory. What may actually happen in a crowd is that a few highly visible participants, behaving in a violent way, may establish a norm of conduct to be followed by others in the group. According to this view, because all members of the crowd are faced with an ambiguous social situation and are wondering how to respond, the norm may readily take hold. Even those who do not subscribe to the norm by imitating the behavior of highly active participants may

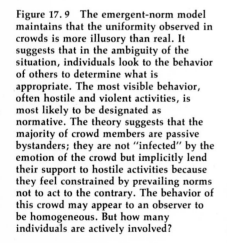

Figure 17.9 The emergent-norm model maintains that the uniformity observed in crowds is more illusory than real. It suggests that in the ambiguity of the situation, individuals look to the behavior of others to determine what is appropriate. The most visible behavior, often hostile and violent activities, is most likely to be designated as normative. The theory suggests that the majority of crowd members are passive bystanders; they are not "infected" by the emotion of the crowd but implicitly lend their support to hostile activities because they feel constrained by prevailing norms not to act to the contrary. The behavior of this crowd may appear to an observer to be homogeneous. But how many individuals are actively involved?

perceive a norm that sanctions violent acts. They will consequently refrain from violating this norm. This state of affairs in itself creates uniformity. Outside observers who are impressed with a crowd's homogeneity may be misled by this surface uniformity; they may fail to recognize that there probably are a large number of crowd members who, Ralph Turner and Lewis Killian (1957) claim, are largely passive bystanders.

Ralph Turner (1964) attempts to spell out this emergent-norm process in some detail. He states that situations frequently arise in which old norms of behavior are no longer appropriate and people do not know how to act. How, he asks, should students react when a teacher is late for class? What should people do when they see an automobile accident? Turner studied these and similar situations—which really do not seem to be instances of collective behavior as the term has been defined. He observed that individuals readily joined together into small groups, even though they may never have met before, and that they responded to situations as group members rather than as individuals. Frequently, one group member took the lead and others followed. A norm had arisen, according to Turner, through the process of registering approval and disapproval for various suggested actions. Three types of "cues" were sought in this process. Individuals first tried to determine what *rule of action* applied to the situation and how they should or should not respond. They also attempted to *define* or explain the situation so that everyone would adequately understand what was happening. Finally, they looked for a *potential leader* by quickly appraising each candidate for leadership and evaluating his or her credentials.

Evaluating the Models

To understand the mechanisms that transform a group engaging in normative behavior into a mob, the social-psychological forces operating within crowds and the types of impact these forces might have under different conditions must be considered. For example, if anonymity is important, under what conditions will it facilitate or hinder violence? Does anonymity influence uniformity in crowd behavior? Le Bon assumes that anonymity helps to "release" primitive forces within people. In contrast, Turner and Killian claim that it is not anonymity that produces behavioral uniformity, but its opposite—the fact that group members who do not behave as they "should" can be singled out for negative sanctions.

Freud's theory is the most complex and is extremely difficult to test. In addition, it is very imprecise and undifferentiated. The only necessary ingredients in Freud's formulation are a leader and one or more potential followers. Not only are there many instances of leaderless collective behavior—a riot at a football game is an example—but crowds that have a leader are likely to have chosen him suddenly. It is difficult to believe, therefore, that much libidinal energy will flow in his direction. Freud's analysis is probably most pertinent to mass movements in which there is a person who remains leader for an extended period of time.

Le Bon advances a number of hypotheses that may help account for aggressive crowd behavior, but he never defines the "certain given circumstances" that will lead crowds to become violent. Le Bon's analysis (and Freud's as well) is based on the notion that crowds somehow release forces within people that are usually kept repressed. Can seemingly irrational crowd behavior be explained only in terms of such forces? It may be more useful to assume that human behavior is not very consistent in general, that a given individual who plays a meek and subservient role at work may beat his wife. From this viewpoint—that behavior, in or out of crowds, is highly susceptible to situational influences—the question might be restated: What is it about being in a crowd that may induce individuals to engage in behavior patterns that they normally do not display?

Although emergent-norm theory dispenses with the primitive forces stressed by Freud and Le Bon, it too leaves many questions unanswered. For instance, norms do not always emerge clearly within crowds. Even when they do, what factors determine the specific forms that the norms will take? It seems plausible that a constructive norm might emerge as often as a destructive one. According to Turner and Killian's theory, the behaviors shown by visible members of the crowd will determine the norm. However, it is probable that many different types of behavior will surface in a crowd. Unless one behavior pattern is particularly dominant to start with, there is still the problem of determining how one particular model is singled out for the group norm. Finally, Turner and Killian's approach stresses the cognitions of crowd members, rather than their emotions, although many observers consider one of the most significant features of crowd behavior to be heightened emotionality.

SOCIAL PSYCHOLOGY OF THE CROWD

The problem of crowd behavior can also be approached, on a less theoretical level, by considering some of the forces that might account for the violence, uniformity, and heightened emotionality that many crowds display.

Crowding: From Push to Shove

Crowds are composed of individuals packed densely together. Within a social-psychological perspective, crowding means that the sheer amount of stimulation to which each individual is exposed may be overwhelming. A person may therefore not know which stimuli to tune out and which to respond to. In such an ambiguous social situation, the individual is forced to look to others for cues and may readily adopt the most simple behavioral prescription—a slogan or a violent act, for example.

Crowding may also have another effect. As Edward Hall (1966) and Robert Sommer (1966) note, individuals attempt to maintain a certain psychological or physical distance between themselves and others—to guard "interpersonal space" (see Chapter 6). In a crowd this barrier might well collapse, resulting in increased tension, competitiveness, and possibly violence—the essential ingredients for an explosive situation.

There is little direct evidence to support these contentions, although some studies are suggestive. John Calhoun (1962) reports that when Norway rats are given sufficient food, water, and nesting material but are crowded together to an abnormal extent, they show increased infant mortality, cannibalism, and aggression. Perhaps most significant, crowding in rats seems to produce confused behavior—male rats attempt to mount other male rats, for example. Even with humans, a positive correlation has been found between population density in urban areas and levels of infant mortality, crime, and other forms of individual and societal breakdown (Windsborough, 1965). Jonathan Freedman (1970) conducted an experiment in which men spent long periods in a crowded or uncrowded room. Crowding increased competitiveness and other negative interpersonal effects. Although it is dangerous to generalize from a few studies to actual situations, crowding seems to generate behaviors similar to those Le Bon described—uniformity, violence, and emotionality.

Contagion: Causes Are Catching

A concept that is frequently used to account for collective behavior is *contagion,* the process by which feelings and responses spread from one crowd participant to another. This mechanism has been used to account not only for uniformity within a crowd but also for heightened emotionality. Floyd Allport (1924) introduced the notion of *circular reaction* to describe the interactive process that occurs when one person's behavior serves as a model for another's—and the model, observing the other's imitation, becomes stimulated to even higher levels of activity and excitement. Among persons engaged in the same type of behavior, circular reactions can stimulate higher and higher intensity.

Considering the popularity of the contagion concept, it is surprising that few social psychologists have attempted to explain why and when it occurs. The most comprehensive approach has been taken by Ladd Wheeler (1970); his conclusions are based only on experiments done with small groups, but what he says is quite useful to an understanding of crowds. Wheeler believes that contagion will occur when (1) an observer is motivated to behave in a certain way; (2) he knows how to behave in this way but is not doing so; and (3) he sees someone else perform this behavior. It is interesting to note the similarity between Wheeler's model and those of Freud and Le Bon. All three models assume that restraints govern a person's behavior but that these restraints may be removed when a person observes others behaving in a tabooed way. The reason for the assumption that restraints exist is unclear. It may be the case that individuals learn nonnormative behavior for the first time when they see others displaying it. If this view is correct, there is no need to posit unobservable psychic forces. In any case, Wheeler has shown in a number of experiments that contagion will not occur when the model is punished for his behavior; if he gets away with it, however, observers will probably follow his lead.

Research by Alan Kerckhoff and Kurt Back (1968) indicates that emotional reactions can very easily be spread through contagion. They investigated a small Southern textile factory employing 200 women, about one-fourth of whom reported having been bitten by a mysterious bug and experiencing nervousness, nausea, weakness, and numbness as a consequence. No one found the bug, but Kerckhoff and Back found an interesting pattern: Social interaction in the factory had determined the bug's biting pattern. The imaginary bug first bit social isolates, people who had few friends in the factory. Social restraints preventing bizarre behaviors such as nervousness and fainting seemed not to affect the isolates, and soon their few friends also experienced the symptoms. After this point, the symptoms spread rapidly among friends. If one member of a friendship group reported being bitten, the others soon succumbed. The investigators noted that women who experienced the most strain in the factory—by working overtime, by being responsible for more than half their family's income, and so on—were more likely to be bitten than were others.

What implications about crowd behavior can be drawn from this study of contagion? Applying Kerckhoff and Back's finding about women who experienced the most strain, it might be assumed that when tensions in a

Figure 17.10 Reactions of a crowd to the behavior of a model can lead to the crowd's increasing excitement—a factor in crowd psychology known as contagion. Here, the citizens of Rome are spurred by Antony's revelation of the manner of Caesar's death to advocate violent acts that they might not have individually considered.

ANTONY:... *Kind souls, what weep you*
   when you but behold Our Caesar's
   vesture wounded? Look you here,
   Here is himself, marred, as you see,
   with traitors.
(Antony plucks off the mantle)
FIRST PLEBEIAN: *O piteous spectacle!*
SECOND PLEBEIAN: *O noble Caesar!*
THIRD PLEBEIAN: *O woeful day!*
FOURTH PLEBEIAN: *O traitors! villains!*
FIRST PLEBEIAN: *O most bloody sight!*
SECOND PLEBEIAN: *We will be revenged.*
ALL: *Revenge! About! Seek! Burn!*
   Fire! Kill! Slay! Let not
   a traitor live.
—*William Shakespeare,* Julius Caesar

crowd run high (when structural strain is great), crowd members will be more likely to believe and respond to outlandish stories. The finding that beliefs and behavioral responses are more likely to spread among friends may also apply to the transmission of beliefs and responses in crowds. Further, it is probable that this transmission will be most rapid when members of the crowd identify strongly with each other—either because they know one another or because they perceive themselves to be in the same situation—particularly if the situation is ambiguous or fear-provoking. Contagion of beliefs and responses will be greater, then, when people at an antiwar demonstration believe that all participants oppose the war.

Wheeler's findings that models are imitated only when their behavior is not punished and that imitation occurs when people are motivated to

THE CALCULUS OF MAGNETISM

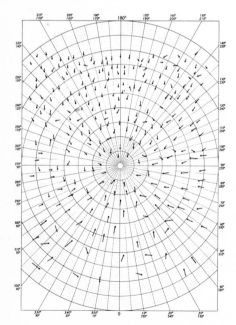

JUST AS METAL FILINGS point toward a magnetic pole in their vicinity, followers are attracted by charismatic leaders. Analysts of public behavior have described the relationship between a speaker and a crowd in terms of polarization, or magnetization. Here, too, the magnetism of the speaker is understood in terms of "file" behavior. The attention that the central figure can elicit from the audience is considered crucial to his or her capacity to influence them.

Although at first glance a speaker may seem to have his or her listeners spellbound, closer examination of the audience may reveal a couple that is romantically absorbed in one another, a woman trying to locate something in a large purse, someone trying to suppress a cough, people cleaning their fingernails or doodling, a man trying to restrain two active children, a nature lover examining a leaf, a photographer, a maintenance man going about his job, as well as other people who are not engaged by the speaker.

In order to better understand the behavior of some crowds, in regard to the magnetism of a speaker, Stanley Milgram and Hans Toch developed a formula for estimating a crowd's attentiveness. The numerator represents the number of people in the crowd who are actually looking at the speaker, and the denominator is the total number in attendance:

$$\frac{\text{sum of polarization values for crowd}}{\text{size of crowd}}$$

In order to apply this formula in evaluating the polarization of a crowd,

Milgram envisions the possibility of an aerial-view photograph being taken with a telescopic lens. An aerial photograph would supply a sample of crowd attentiveness. The information yielded by this photo could then be translated into a diagram such as the accompanying diagram of polarity in a crowd listening to Nelson Rockefeller speak at the Berkeley campus of the University of California. The arrows are drawn according to the eye position of each spectator.

Interestingly, just as in laws of physics regarding magnetism, the objects closest to the magnetic source are most polarized, and those further away are less so. The crowd numbers 266, and those looking at Rockefeller total 148. Thus, $^{148}/_{266} = .56$. In other words, the polarization ratio is .56. The density of the crowd also increases as the distance to the speaker decreases.

This type of research offers more standardized, accurate, and comparable statistics concerning the strength of a speaker's influence on a crowd's attentiveness. Imaginative use of this device might aid political parties in selecting candidates, might help police and other civil authorities handle crowds, and might aid media personnel in describing more accurately the activities of a crowd.

Source: Adapted from S. Milgram and H. Toch, "Collective Behavior: Crowds and Social Movements," in G. Lindzey and E. Aronson (eds.), *The Handbook of Social Psychology,* Vol. 4 (Reading, Mass.: Addison-Wesley, 1969), pp. 507–610.

perform the model's behavior are also applicable to contagion in a crowd. The behavior of the initial model will spread rapidly if the behavior seems successful, particularly if individuals are predisposed to that behavior. How might these findings apply to the eruption of nonnormative behavior, such as violence? It can be assumed that crowds of ardent sports fans or other potentially violent individuals would be much more likely to switch from normative to nonnormative behavior than would a crowd composed of individuals who are pacifists.

Anonymity: Nobody Knows My Name

Another concept that is frequently applied in accounting for nonnormative behavior in crowds is *anonymity.* It is difficult to identify the individuals who make up a crowd and these individuals may lose consciousness of their own unique identities and personalities. In the terminology of experimental social psychology, anonymity is called *deindividuation* (see Chapter 11). A wide range of studies clearly indicate that deindividuation alone can reduce restraints against nonnormative behavior.

Leon Festinger, Albert Pepitone, and Theodore Newcomb (1952) encouraged subjects participating in a group discussion to make hostile statements about their parents. Sometimes the discussion took place under conditions of deindividuation, in a semidark room with participants wearing shapeless gray coats over their clothes. Under these conditions, people made many more hostile remarks than they did in ordinary situations where they were identifiable. Philip Zimbardo (1969), in a similar experiment described in Chapter 11, had subjects in the deindividuation group wear hoods over their heads, forbade them to use each other's names, and put them in a dark room. Subjects in Zimbardo's *identifiability* group were given large name tags, placed in a well-lit room, and were greeted individually by experimenters when they arrived for the session. The experimenters instructed subjects in both groups to administer shocks to a "target person" whom they were observing. Subjects in the deindividuation condition gave shocks of greater duration than did those in the identifiability condition. And Zimbardo (1970) has not restricted his investigations of deindividuation to the laboratory; he also conducted a comparative study that was based on the supposition that anonymity is higher in large cities than in small ones. Zimbardo abandoned a car on a street corner in New York City, and he abandoned another car on a street in Palo Alto, California. Within twenty-five hours the car left in New York had been stripped of its battery, radiator, air cleaner, radio antenna, windshield wipers, side chrome, and all four hubcaps. And all the looters were well-dressed, clean-cut, and white. The car left in California remained completely unharmed during its seven days on the street.

Although none of this research is conclusive, it seems apparent that anonymity—the state of not being identifiable—can lead to violent behavior and that the threat of being singled out for punishment can keep such behavior in check. This proposition seems to clash with emergent-norm theory, which states just the opposite: that powerful crowd norms arise precisely because crowd members *can* identify each other, or, at least, can monitor each other's behavior. This apparent contradiction can be resolved if it is assumed that anonymity within the crowd gives individual members the feeling that outside authorities—not others in the crowd—will be unable to single them out for punishment. Other crowd members do not punish nonnormative behavior but reinforce it, so identifiability *within* the crowd is not threatening to the individual. It is even conceivable that if members of a crowd were completely anonymous both to fellow crowd members and to outside observers, the nonnormative behavior might be random and uncoordinated rather than collective.

One possible reason why anonymity generates nonnormative behavior, then, is that individual crowd members perceive that they are safe from possible negative sanctions from the outside but are identifiable within the crowd, which reinforces the very behaviors that outsiders might punish. Another explanation goes in an entirely different direction; it is conceivable that participants merged in a large crowd feel that they are not responsible for their own actions. Others are to blame, no matter what the individual may be doing.

Research on the *diffusion of responsibility* bears on this point. Bibb Latané and John Darley (1970) had experimental subjects witness or hear an emergency situation and gave them the opportunity to come to the victim's aid (described in Chapter 12). Individuals readily helped if they thought no one else was present at the scene. People who believed there were other bystanders were less likely to help. As the number of perceived bystanders increased, helping dramatically decreased—apparently because subjects came to feel that helping was the responsibility of others and that others would act to help the victim. These findings on diffusion of responsibility suggest that the larger the crowd, the more likely it is that any given individual will not feel responsible for whatever is going on.

These two lines of research can be tied together with a hypothesis: Given a crowd in which (1) there are visible models of violent behavior and (2) individuals are looking to each other for cues, it is safe to predict that (3) the people most likely to show nonnormative aggressive behavior will be those crowd members who feel most anonymous, who most subscribe to the view that "others" are responsible, and who perhaps rank highest on measures of external control.

Rumors Are Flying

The social-psychological mechanisms mentioned so far help to explain a crowd's heightened emotionality, uniformity, and violence. In a situation of great strain and fear, however, a trigger (precipitating event) is still necessary to activate these various mechanisms. Here, Smelser's concept of a generalized belief has application. It is likely that a strong belief must spread among at least some crowd members if group behavior is to become nonnormative. This belief will work more effectively to trigger collective behavior if it is simple and readily assimilated and if it suggests a course of

Figure 17.11 In 1964, a referee's decision resulted in Peru's loss of an Olympic soccer elimination match and triggered a riot in which more than 250 persons were killed. A single argument about the decision (*left*) led to (*center*) the crowd storming the field and (*right*) trampling and maiming one another. Crowding, contagion, and anonymity could each have been factors contributing to the explosive results of the referee's call.

action that might make more acceptable the situation in which crowd members find themselves. Suppose that the home team has just lost the World Series—in the ninth inning of the seventh final game—after having come from behind to tie the series at three games per team. At this point, people in the stands may pass along the word that an umpire who called a possible winning home run a "foul" is married to the daughter of the rich man who owns the opposing team.

This type of belief is called a *rumor,* because it has two essential features: (1) it is transmitted from one person to another through informal rather than formal channels of communication—by word of mouth, rather than through the press, for example—and (2) it cannot be easily verified. Gordon Allport and Leo Postman's (1947) classic statement suggests that rumors are made and circulated under two conditions: when (1) people attach a high level of interest and importance to an event and (2) the actual facts are ambiguous. Rumors also change as they pass from one person to another. First, the original message or claim gets *leveled;* it becomes shorter, more concise, and more easily grasped. Second, the message gets *sharpened;* certain pieces of information are highlighted, and others are played down. How items become leveled and sharpened depends on each individual's personality needs and probably on the demands of the particular situation. For example, a rumor about a black man stabbing a white woman might be distorted by a prejudiced individual into a story about a rape-murder; if this rumor circulated in a lynch mob, it might be transformed into a case of gang rape and murder premeditated by a black liberation organization. Allport and Postman use the term *assimilation* to describe how information changes when rumors circulate. Various processes were demonstrated in a study in which one person described a still picture to another person, and so on down the line. One of the findings of the experiment showed that, in the process of leveling, 70 percent of the details of the picture were lost during five or six transmissions.

Are such studies pertinent to what goes on in the far more complex and unstructured situations of collective behavior? Studies have been conducted in field settings, some of which also show leveling and sharpening. Melvin DeFleur (1962), for instance, gave 17 percent of the housewives in a small community a pound of coffee each, together with a simple slogan about the coffee, and promised them another pound if they remembered the slogan three days later. At the same time, thirty thousand leaflets were dropped in the community promising a pound of coffee to all people who could discover the slogan. In support of Allport and Postman's contentions, the six-word slogan became shorter as it passed from the housewives who knew the slogan to others who received leaflets and also wanted the coffee.

DeFleur's study, like that of Allport and Postman, used very simple original messages and revealed the way they were transmitted in contexts that elicited little emotional investment from the participants. In a situation involving collective behavior, there is usually a high level of emotionality and probably many contrary rumors circulating at the same time. In such a context, distorted amplification of portions of the original message may occur. This is what Warren Peterson and Noel Gist (1951) found in their study of rumors that circulated in a Midwestern city following the reported rape-murder of a fifteen-year-old girl. Imaginative new themes were constantly added to and subtracted from the original report as the rumor made the rounds. Although it may not be clear precisely what happens to rumors as they circulate within a crowd, one thing is clear: they are distorted, either through subtraction or addition of content. The World Series game would be an ideal breeding ground for rumors. A rumor circulating in such a context of high emotionality might become progressively more concise and outlandishly distorted. It would in the process be transformed into an effective mechanism for triggering collective action.

SUMMARY

Collective behavior is difficult to study, because it involves the norms and biases of a particular culture. Nevertheless, collective behavior has been defined as *nonnormative, diffusely organized behavior of a large number of interacting people.*

Neil Smelser has proposed the most comprehensive theory to explain collective behavior. He posits six main determinants: structural conduciveness, structural strain, the growth and spread of a "generalized" belief, the mobilization of participants for action, a precipitating event, and inadequate mechanisms of social control. These six factors combine in a "value-added" way so that the form of the first determinant limits the way the second can develop, and so on. The components of social action are (in order of decreasing abstractness and inclusiveness) values, norms, organizational specifications, and situational facilities. Strain may occur at any of these levels, but people responding to the strain often try to change a higher-level component. Although Smelser's theory explains much collective behavior, it is not yet useful as a predictive device, and it tends to ignore individual motivations and reactions.

The same conditions do not always generate the same kind of response from people. For example, the concept of *relative deprivation* suggests that individuals who feel that their rewards are not equal to the situation's potential reward will be most likely to react to strain. Other factors that may affect change are differences in attitudes toward striving for change, the tendency for individuals to blame themselves or the system, and a person's belief in external or internal control over outside events.

Those who do not directly experience structural strain but act on behalf of those who do—*altruists*—are likely to be young people who think in ideological and idealistic terms, who come from relatively high socioeconomic backgrounds, and who are *marginal* members of their society without substantial interest in the status quo.

When a movement wishes to recruit new members, it must expose others to its activities—become *visible*—and it must draw others to the respected and influential members who also participate.

In the midst of much moral judgment, social psychologists are trying to define the type of person who will or will not join a mass movement. Personality scales are used to measure the extent to which an individual is closed-minded, rigid in his thinking, intolerant, and sympathetic to authoritarian ideas. Another personality variable is the degree to which an individual will involve himself in social-service or protest activities. Altruism, a third personality variable, may have been learned from altruistic models at some time in the individual's past.

Mobs and other violent crowds have three major features: individuals in the crowd show *uniformity of behavior;* they often engage in *violent acts* that they would not perform on their own; and *heightened emotionality* leads them to overreact. One explanation (represented by Sigmund Freud and Gustave Le Bon) suggests that being in a crowd releases repressed, unconscious, unsocialized forces in crowd members. Another position, *emergent-norm theory,* suggests that crowd members simply adopt new norms of behavior that are enforced by social pressures operating within the crowd.

Mob behavior can also be explained in terms of other factors that may, in part or whole, produce collective action. Crowding by itself generates a good deal of tension and emotionality and may also lead to violence. The uniformity, violence, and emotionality of a crowd may spread through *contagion. Anonymity,* or *deindividuation,* leads the individual crowd member to believe that he is safe from outside negative sanctions but identifiable within the crowd and thereby reinforces the behaviors that outsiders might punish. Crowd behavior may also be facilitated by *diffusion of responsibility,* which leads individual members to feel that others, and not they, are responsible for the acts of the crowd.

The social-psychological mechanisms mentioned may explain a crowd's uniformity, violence, and heightened emotionality, but the trigger of an event is likely to be a generalized belief or *rumor,* which is transmitted from one person to another informally rather than formally and is not easily verified. In a rumor, the basic information is both *leveled* and *sharpened.* Rumors can easily goad crowd members into action.

SUGGESTED READINGS

Brinton, Crane. *The Anatomy of Revolution.* New York: Vintage Books, 1965.

Caplan, Nathan, and Jeffery Paige. "A Study of Ghetto Rioters," *Scientific American,* 219 (1968), 15–21.

Keniston, Kenneth. *Young Radicals: Notes on Committed Youth.* New York: Harcourt Brace Jovanovich, 1968.

Le Bon, Gustave. *The Crowd.* New York: Viking, 1960.

Milgram, Stanley, and Hans Toch. "Collective Behavior: Crowds and Social Movements," in G. Lindzey and E. Aronson (eds.), *The Handbook of Social Psychology,* Vol. 4, 2nd ed. Reading, Mass.: Addison-Wesley, 1969, pp.507–610.

Smelser, Neil. *Theory of Collective Behavior.* New York: Free Press, 1963.

CONTRIBUTING CONSULTANTS

William Barton received a B.A. and M.A. in psychology from Swarthmore College and is seeking further graduate training in clinical psychology. His main areas of research interest are small-group processes, the relationship

of Piagetian cognitive development to linguistic development, and adaptation in processes of visual perception. In addition to pursuing his goals in the field of psychology, he has ambitions in the areas of musical performance and composition. Mr. Barton contributed to the following chapter: Exchange & Strategy in Social Life.

Lola Bogyo received a B.A. in psychology from Swarthmore College in 1973, where she , worked as a research assistant investigating R. L. Soloman's "opponent-process" theory of motivation. She is primarily

interested in experimental psychopathology and plans to continue doctoral training in clinical psychology. Ms. Bogyo contributed to the chapter on Perceiving Others.

Genevieve Clapp received her Ph.D. in social psychology from the University of Iowa. Since that time she has taught graduate and undergraduate courses in psychology and sociology at California State University at Los Angeles, Arizona State University, and Grossmont College. She also

has held the position of associate publisher of social sciences at CRM Books. She is currently involved in consulting and served as a unit adviser for several chapters in this book. She is particularly responsible for the following chapters: Interpersonal Attraction and Informal Groups.

Alice Hendrickson Eagly did her undergraduate work in social relations at Radcliffe College and received her Ph.D. in social psychology at the University of Michigan in 1965. She has been a Fulbright Fellow at the University of Oslo, has taught at Michigan State University, and was a visiting faculty member at the University of Illinois in Champaign-Urbana. Dr. Eagly is currently an associate professor of psychology at the University of Massachusetts. Most of her research has concerned attitude change and

social influence. Within this area she maintains a strong interest in individual differences; has researched the effects of self-esteem, intelligence, and cognitive structure on response to persuasive communications; and has researched sex roles in their relationship to both attitude change and family planning. Professor Eagly is responsible for the chapter on Personalities: Pegs, Round & Square.

Sheldon Feldman received his Ph.D. from Yale University. He has previously taught at the Annenberg School of Communications at the University of Pennsylvania. He is currently assistant professor of psychology at Swarthmore College. He contributed to the chapter on Language & Communication.

Kenneth J. Gergen received his undergraduate degree at Yale University and his Ph.D. at Duke University. After teaching at Harvard, he took over the post of chairman of the psychology department at Swarthmore College, where he now teaches courses in social psychology, personality, and

group dynamics. Through fellowship awards, he has also held research appointments in Stockholm, Rome, and Kyoto. His research has included such diverse topics as self-conception, social perception, reactions to help, aesthetics, and various social issues. He has authored or edited five books, including *The Self in Social Interaction, The Study of Policy Formation, The Psychology of Behavior Exchange, Personality and Social Behavior*, and *The Concept of Self*. Professor Gergen served as the principal academic adviser on this book and is responsible for the following chapters: Perceiving Others and Exchange & Strategy in Social Life.

Mary McCanney Gergen earned her undergraduate and graduate degrees at the University of Minnesota. After teaching in the Minneapolis public schools, she was employed as a researcher at Harvard University. She is presently a research associate at Swarthmore College, where she also teaches group dynamics. Her published papers have emphasized broad concerns of contemporary society such as the radical

movement, marijuana use, foreign aid, women's liberation, and anonymity. With Kenneth J. Gergen she is currently writing *The Psychology of Social Issues.* Ms. Gergen contributed to the chapters on Perceiving Others and Exchange & Strategy in Social Life, and she is responsible for most of the topical inserts throughout the book.

James M. Jones is assistant professor of social psychology at Harvard University. After completing his undergraduate studies at Oberlin College, he received an M.A. from Temple University in 1967 and a Ph.D. from Yale University in 1970. His doctoral thesis was an experimental and theoretical analysis of cognitive factors in humor appreciation, and his current research focuses on personality dimensions of sense of humor and athletic performance. He is the author of *Prejudice and Racism.* Professor Jones is responsible for the Social Attitudes and Attitude Change chapters.

Louise H. Kidder received a B.A. from Oberlin College in 1964, after which she spent two years teaching in India. She was awarded a Ph.D. in social psychology from Northwestern University in 1971, where her graduate studies involved another year in India studying the acculturation of Westerners in that country. She is currently an assistant professor of psychology at Temple University. Her research interests have included social-psychological studies of hypnosis and yoga, studies of intergroup relations, as well as the application of quasi-experimental designs to studies of social problems. She is co-author of a forthcoming book, *Intergroup Relations: Conflict and Consciousness,*

and author of other articles on attitude change and measurement. Her nonacademic interests are in the areas of organic farming and communitarian living, and she resides in an intentional community outside Philadelphia. Professor Kidder is responsible for the chapter on Prejudice.

Robert M. Liebert is professor of psychology at the State University of New York at Stony Brook. He has previously taught at Vanderbilt University and Antioch College and has been senior investigator at the Fels Research Institute in Ohio. A graduate of Tulane University, he did his doctoral work in

child clinical psychology at Stanford University. In addition to numerous journal articles, he has published three books: *Personality* (with Michael D. Spiegler), *Human Social Behavior* (with Robert A. Baron), and *Science and Behavior: An Introduction to Methods of Research* (with John M. Neale). He is also consulting editor for the *Journal of Abnormal Psychology.* His main research interest is the role of observational learning in children's personality development and social behavior. Professor Liebert contributed, along with Ms. Poulos, to the chapters on Socialization: The Humanizing Processes and Aggression.

Harvey London, currently associate professor of psychology at Long Island University, received an A.B. in philosophy from Princeton University in 1959 and a Ph.D. in social psychology from Columbia University in 1964. He spent the following academic year as a Russell

Sage Foundation Resident in Social Science and Law at Harvard Law School. From 1965 to 1972 he was assistant professor of psychology at Brandeis University. While the bulk of his research has been on persuasion, he has also investigated boredom and psychological time. Professor London contributed to the chapter on Social Influence: Advice & Consent.

Bert Moore is assistant professor of psychology at Wellesley College. He received an M.A. in clinical psychology from the University of Illinois and a Ph.D. degree in personality and social psychology at Stanford University. His interests include prosocial behavior and cognitive strategies in self-control. Professor Moore, along with Professor Underwood, is responsible for the Prosocial Behavior chapter.

Stanley J. Morse received a B.A. in sociology from Antioch College and a Ph.D. from the University of Michigan in 1971. He has spent a year at the National Institute of Psychology in Rome, Italy, and one at the University of Cape Town, South Africa, and has taught at New York University. He is currently on a Fulbright Fellowship at the Catholic University of Sao Paulo, Brazil. The author of several journal articles, he will soon publish (with Stanton Peele) results of studies of determinants of political attitudes and voting behavior among whites and

nonwhites in South Africa and a collection of readings, *Contemporary South Africa: Social Psychological Perspectives* (edited with C. Orpen). His major research interests are in interpersonal attraction, equity theory, reactions to help from others, and political social psychology. He is also involved in a large-scale study of the landlord and tenants courts in New York City and is working on two books, *Psychology of Politics* and a text in social psychology. Professor Morse is responsible for the chapter on Collective Behavior.

Richard E. Nisbett did his undergraduate work in psychology at Tufts University and continued graduate studies in social psychology at Columbia University, where he received a Ph.D. in 1966. He taught at Yale University for five years prior to joining the faculty of the University of Michigan, where he is currently associate professor of psychology. He has received

the National Science Foundation Fellowship honor for research and writing and the Morse Junior Faculty Fellowship award from Yale University for research and writing. In addition, he has served as editorial consultant for the *Journal of Personality and Social Psychology* and is the author of numerous papers focusing primarily on obesity and eating behavior. Professor Nisbett served as a unit adviser for several chapters in this book.

Stanton Peele is assistant professor of organizational behavior at the Graduate School of Business Administration, Harvard University. He received a Ph.D. in social psychology from the University of Michigan and has worked as an organizational consultant with the National Institute for Personnel Research in Johannesburg, South Africa. He is also a consultant with the Massachusetts Department of Corrections. His major academic and political interest is in helping people achieve control over their lives in an institutionalized environment. This has led him to investigate the feelings and actions of both guards and prisoners at Walpole State Prison, Massachusetts, and to look toward the further application of his ideas to police work and police administration. The major expression of his outlook is in his forthcoming book, *Love and Addiction*. Professor Peele is responsible for the chapter on The Psychology of Organizations.

Rita W. Poulos earned both a B.A. and Ph.D. in psychology at the State University of New York at Stony Brook, where she is now actively engaged in research and teaching a special course in behavior modification. Her primary interest is in observational learning in children, particularly with regard to

prosocial behavior. She has published professional journal articles on children's sharing, the use of rewards in behavior modification, and language-training programs for the retarded. A co-author of *Developmental Psychology* (with Robert M. Liebert and Gloria D. Strauss) and Special Coordinating Consultant for *Educational Psychology: A Contemporary View* (CRM, 1973), her present efforts are directed largely toward investigating the influence of television on social learning. Ms. Poulos, along with Professor Liebert, contributed to the chapter on Socialization: The Humanizing Processes and to the chapter on Aggression.

David L. Rosenhan is professor of psychology and law at Stanford University. He has taught at several schools, including Swarthmore College and Princeton University, and has been research psychologist at the Educational Testing Service in Princeton. An undergraduate of Yeshiva College, he received an M.A. and did his doctoral work in psychology at Columbia University. In addition to publishing many journal

psychologist working in public elementary schools, he has been active in applying psychological principles to the classroom situation. Mr. Siegler contributed to the chapter on Aggression.

articles, he has edited (with Perry London) two books: *Foundations of Abnormal Psychology* and *Theory and Research in Abnormal Psychology.* He is also consulting editor of *Developmental Psychology* and the *Journal of Personality and Social Psychology* and is associate editor of the *International Journal of Clinical and Experimental Hypnosis.* He is interested in the social psychology of institutions and the study of moral and altruistic behavior. Professor Rosenhan was a unit adviser for several chapters in this book.

Robert S. Siegler is currently finishing his Ph.D. work at the State University of New York at Stony Brook. He earned his B.A. in psychology at the University of Illinois, where he participated in the development of a language-instruction program for the mentally retarded. He has published several articles on the learning of Piagetian conservation tasks by young children. As a clinical

Siegfried Streufert received a B.A. in sociology and social science in 1958 and an M.A. from Southern Methodist in 1960. He obtained a Ph.D. from Princeton University in 1962. Currently professor of psychological sciences at Purdue University and visiting professor at the University of Mannheim in West Germany, he is known for his contributions to complexity theory, congruity theory, decision-making research, and the development of the experimental-simulation research method. His interests range from research on human information processing and decision making to applications of experimental research techniques to solving problems of society. Professor Streufert, along with Professor Susan Streufert, is responsible for the following chapters: A Science of Social Behavior and Group Decisions & Conflicts.

Susan C. Streufert received an A.B. in psychology from Douglass College and an M.A. and Ph.D. in social psychology from Purdue University. She is currently working as a research associate and visiting assistant professor at Purdue University and the University of Mannheim in West Germany. She has published

extensively in experimental and social psychology, and her interests include complexity theory, complex decision making, negotiation processes, and communication. Professor Streufert, along with Professor Siegfried Streufert, is responsible for the following chapters: A Science of Social Behavior and Group Decisions & Conflicts.

Dalmas A. Taylor is professor of psychology at the University of Maryland and was former chairman of the psychology department at Federal City College in Washington, D.C. Completing his undergraduate study at Western Reserve University, he received an M.A. in psychology from Howard University and a Ph.D. from the University of Delaware. An experimental social psychologist, his major interests are in the areas of interpersonal attraction, person perception, and small groups. Professor Taylor contributed to the chapter on Aggression.

Bill Underwood is assistant professor of psychology at Boston College. He received an M.A. in mathematics from the University of Texas and a Ph.D. in personality and social

psychology from Stanford University in 1973. His interests include prosocial behavior, affect, and self-control. Professor Underwood, along with Professor Moore, is responsible for the chapter on Prosocial Behavior.

REVIEWERS

Philip Gallo, Ph.D.,
San Diego State University
David Kanouse, Ph.D.
University of California
at Los Angeles
Clara Mayo, Ph.D.,
Boston University
Dorothy Nevill, Ph.D.,
University of Florida
Robert Schell, Ph.D.,
San Diego Center for Research,
Education, Applied Training,
and Evaluation
David Shaffer, Ph.D.,
Kent State University
John Sheposh, Ph.D.,
San Diego State University
Harry Triandis, Ph.D.,
University of Illinois

SEMINAR CONSULTANTS

Genevieve Clapp, Ph.D.,
private consultant, San Diego
Philip Gallo, Ph.D.,
San Diego State University
Norman Goodman, Ph.D.,
State University of New York
at Stony Brook
Robert Kleck, Ph.D.,
Dartmouth College
Robert Liebert, Ph.D.,
State University of New York
at Stony Brook
William Morris, Ph.D.,
Dartmouth College

BIBLIOGRAPHY

1

Allport, G. *Personality: A Psychological Interpretation.* New York: Holt, Rinehart and Winston, 1937.

Aronson, E., and J. M. Carlsmith. "Experimentation in Social Psychology," in G. Lindzey and E. Aronson (eds.), *The Handbook of Social Psychology*, Vol. 2, 2nd ed. Reading, Mass.: Addison-Wesley, 1969, pp. 1–79.

———, and J. Mills. "The Effect of Severity of Initiation on Liking for a Group," *Journal of Abnormal and Social Psychology*, 59 (1959), 177–181.

Berkowitz, L. "The 'Weapons Effect': Demand Characteristics and the Myth of the Competent Subject," *Journal of Personality and Social Psychology*, 20 (1971), 332–338.

Bronfenbrenner, U. "The Mirror Image in Soviet-American Relations: A Social Psychologist's Report," *Journal of Social Issues*, 17 (1961), 45–56.

Brown, R. *Social Psychology.* New York: Free Press, 1965.

Byrne, D. *The Attraction Paradigm.* New York: Academic Press, 1971.

———, G. D. Baskett, and L. Hodges. "Behavioral Indicators of Interpersonal Attraction," *Journal of Applied Social Psychology*, 1 (1971), 137–149.

Drabek, T. E., and J. S. Stephenson. "When Disaster Strikes," *Journal of Applied Social Psychology*, 1 (1971), 187–203.

Fromkin, H., R. Baron, and T. Brock. "An Experimental Study of Aggression Under Naturalistic Conditions: Mediating Effects of Symbolic Modeling and Degree of Prior Provocation" (unpublished manuscript, Purdue University, 1973).

———, and S. Streufert. "Laboratory Experimentation," in M. Dunnette (ed.), *Handbook of Organizational and Industrial Psychology.* Chicago: Rand McNally, (in press).

Gergen, K. J. "Social Psychology as History," *Journal of Personality and Social Psychology*, 26 (1973), 309–320.

Gergen, M. K., K. J. Gergen, and S. J. Morse. "Correlates of Marijuana Use Among College Students," *Journal of Applied Social Psychology*, 2 (1972), 1–16.

Guetzkow, H. "A Decade of Life With the Inter-Nation Simulation," in R. G. Stogdill (ed.), *The Process of Model-Building in the Behavioral Sciences.* Columbus: Ohio State University Press, 1970.

Haney, C., C. Banks, and P. Zimbardo. "Interpersonal Dynamics in a Simulated Prison," *International Journal of Crime and Penology*, 1 (1973), 69–97.

Latané, B., E. Schneider, P. Waring, and R. Zweigenhaft. "The Specificity of Social Attraction in Rats," *Psychonomic Science*, 23 (1971), 28–29.

Milgram, S. "Behavioral Study of Obedience," *Journal of Abnormal and Social Psychology*, 67 (1963), 371–378.

Newcomb, T. M. "An Approach to the Study of Communicative Acts," *Psychological Review*, 60 (1953), 393–404.

Nisbett, R. "Determinants of Food Intake in Obesity," *Science*, 159 (1968), 1254–1255.

Orne, M. T. "The Nature of Hypnosis: Artifact and Essence," *Journal of Abnormal and Social Psychology*, 58 (1959), 277–299.

———. "On the Social Psychology of the Psychological Experiment: With Particular Reference to Demand Characteristics," *American Psychologist*, 17 (1962), 776–783.

Piliavin, I., J. Rodin, and J. Piliavin. "Good Samaritanism: An Underground Phenomenon?" *Journal of Personality and Social Psychology*, 14 (1969), 289–299.

Rosenthal, R. *Experimenter Effects in Behavioral Research.* New York: Appleton-Century-Crofts, 1966.

Schachter, S. "Obesity and Eating," *Science*, 16 (1968), 751–756.

Streufert, S., S. C. Kliger, C. H. Castore, and M. J. Driver. "Tactical and Negotiations Game for Analysis of Decision Integration Across Decision Areas," *Psychological Reports*, 20 (1967), 155–157.

———, and S. I. Sandler. "A Laboratory Test of the Mirror Image Hypothesis," *Journal of Applied Social Psychology*, 1 (1971), 378–397.

2

Aberle, D. F., and K. D. Naegele. "Middle-class Fathers' Occupational Role and Attitudes Toward Children," *American Journal of Orthopsychiatry*, 22 (1952), 366–378.

Ainsworth, M. D. "The Development of Infant-Mother Interaction Among the Ganda," in B. M. Foss (ed.), *Determinants of Infant Behavior*, Vol. 2. New York: Wiley, 1961, pp. 67–112.

———, and B. A. Wittig. "Attachment and Exploratory Behavior of One-Year-Olds in a Strange Situation," in B. M. Foss (ed.), *Determinants of Infant Behavior IV.* London: Methuen, 1969, pp. 111–136.

Allport, G. W. *Pattern and Growth in Personality.* New York: Holt, Rinehart and Winston, 1961.

Aronfreed, J. *Conduct and Conscience.* New York: Academic Press, 1968.

———, and A. Reber. "Internalized Behavior Suppression and the Timing of Social Punishment," *Journal of Personality and Social Psychology*, 1 (1965), 3–16.

Baker, B. L. "Symptom Treatment and Symptom Substitution in Enuresis," *Journal of Abnormal Psychology*, 74 (1969), 42–49.

Bandura, A. "Influence of Models' Reinforcement Contingencies on the Acquisition of Imitative Responses," *Journal of Personality and Social Psychology*, 1 (1965), 589–595.

———. "Social-Learning Theory of Identificatory Processes," in D. A. Goslin (ed.), *Handbook of Socialization Theory and Research.* Chicago: Rand McNally, 1969, pp. 213–262.

———, and F. J. McDonald. "The Influence of Social Reinforcement and the Behavior of Models in Shaping Children's Moral Judgments," *Journal of Abnormal and Social Psychology*, 67 (1963), 274–281.

Boehm, L. "The Development of Independence: A Comparative Study," *Child Development,* 28 (1957), 85–92.

Bowlby, J. "Separation Anxiety: A Critical Review of the Literature," *Journal of Child Psychology and Psychiatry,* 1 (1961), 251–269.

Brim, O. G. "Family Structure and Sex Role Learning by Children: A Further Analysis of Helen Koch's Data," *Sociometry,* 21 (1958), 1–16.

Brown, D. G. "Masculinity-Femininity Development in Children," *Journal of Consulting Psychology,* 21 (1957), 197–202.

D'Andrade, R. G. "Sex Differences and Cultural Institutions," in E. E. Maccoby (ed.), *The Development of Sex Differences.* Stanford, Calif.: Stanford University Press, 1966, pp. 174–204.

Davis, K. "Extreme Social Isolation of a Child," *American Journal of Sociology,* 45 (1940), 554–564.

———. "Final Note on a Case of Extreme Isolation," *American Journal of Sociology,* 50 (1947), 432–437.

———. *Human Society.* New York: Macmillan, 1949.

Dekker, E. and J. Groen. "Reproducible Psychogenic Attacks of Asthma: A Laboratory Study," *Journal of Psychosomatic Research,* 1 (1956), 58–67.

Freud, S. *A General Introduction to Psychoanalysis.* Garden City, N. Y.: Doubleday, 1938.

Gallup, G. *Gallup Poll.* Princeton: Audience Research, Inc., June, 1955.

Grusec, J. E., and D. B. Brinker. "Reinforcement for Imitation as a Social Learning Determinant With Implications for Sex-Role Development," *Journal of Personality and Social Psychology,* 21 (1971), 149–158.

Harlow, H., and M. Harlow. "The Young Monkeys," in P. Kramer (ed.), *Readings in Developmental Psychology Today.* Del Mar, Calif.: CRM Books, 1970.

———, and R. R. Zimmerman. "Affectional Responses in the Infant Monkey," *Science,* 130 (1959), 431–432.

Hartshorne, H., and M. A. May. *Studies in the Nature of Character, Vol. I : Studies in Deceit.* New York: Macmillan, 1928.

———, ———, and F. K. Shuttleworth. *Studies in the Nature of Character, Vol. III : Studies in the Organization of Character.* New York: Macmillan, 1930.

Hartup, W. W. "Dependence and Independence," in H. W. Stevenson (ed.), *Child Psychology: The Sixty-Second Yearbook of the National Society For the Study of Education.* Chicago: University of Chicago Press, 1963, pp. 333–363.

Hess, R. D., and J. V. Torney. *The Development of Political Attitudes in Children.* Chicago: Aldine, 1960.

Hill, J. H., and R. M. Liebert. "Effects of Consistent or Deviant Modeling Cues on the Adoption of a Self-imposed Standard," *Psychonomic Science,* 13 (1968), 243–244.

Hraba, J., and G. Grant. "Black is Beautiful: A Reexamination of Racial Preference and Identification," *Journal of Personality and Social Psychology,* 16 (1970), 398–402.

Joncich, G. M. *Psychology and the Science of Education.* New York: Columbia University Press, 1962.

Kohlberg, L. "Stage and Sequence: The Cognitive-Developmental Approach to Socialization," in D. A. Goslin (ed.), *Handbook of Socialization Theory and Research.* Chicago: Rand McNally, 1969, pp. 347–479.

Lipsitt, L. P. "The Concepts of Development and Learning in Child Behavior," in D. B. Lindsley and A. A. Lumsdaine (eds.), *Brain Function: Brain Function and Learning,* Vol. 4. Los Angeles: University of California Press, 1967.

Lundin, R. W. *Personality.* New York: Macmillan, 1961.

Maccoby, E. E. "Sex Differences in Intellectual Functioning," in E. E. Maccoby (ed.), *The Development of Sex Differences.* Stanford, Calif.: Stanford University Press, 1966, pp. 25–55.

———, and J. C. Masters. "Attachment and Dependency," in P. H. Mussen (ed.), *Carmichael's Manual of Child Psychology,* Vol. 2, 3rd ed. New York: Wiley, 1970.

McCandless, B. R. *Children: Behavior and Development.* New York: Holt, Rinehart and Winston, 1967.

McMains, M. J., and R. M. Liebert. "The Influence of Discrepancies Between Successively Modeled Self-reward Criteria on the Adoption of a Self-imposed Standard," *Journal of Personality and Social Psychology,* 8 (1968), 166–171.

Minuchin, P. "Sex-Role Concepts and Sex-Typing in Childhood as a Function of School and Home Environments," *Child Development,* 36 (1965), 1033–1048.

Mischel, W., and R. M. Liebert. "Effects of Discrepancies Between Deserved and Imposed Reward Criteria on Their Acquisition and Transmission," *Journal of Personality and Social Psychology,* 3 (1966), 45–53.

———, and H. Mischel. "The Nature and Development of Psychological Sex Differences," in G. S. Lesser (ed.), *Psychology and Educational Practice.* Glenview, Ill.: Scott, Foresman, 1971, pp. 357–379.

Montagu, M. F. A. *The Natural Superiority of Women,* Rev. ed. New York: Macmillan, 1968.

Mussen, P. H. "Early Sex-Role Development," in D. A. Goslin (ed.), *Handbook of Socialization Theory and Research.* Chicago: Rand McNally, 1969, pp. 707–731.

———, J. J. Conger, and J. Kagan. *Child Development and Personality.* New York: Harper & Row, 1969.

———, and A. Parker. "Mother Nurturance and Girls' Incidental Imitative Learning," *Journal of Personality and Social Psychology,* 2 (1965), 94–97.

Nunnally, J. C., A. J. Duchnowski, and R. K. Parker. "Association of Neutral Objects with Rewards: Effect on Verbal Evaluation, Reward Expectancy, and Selective Attention," *Journal of Personality and Social Psychology,* 1 (1965), 270–274.

Parke, R. D. "Nurturance, Nurturance Withdrawal, and Resistance to Deviation," *Child Development,* 38 (1967), 1101–1110.

———. "Effectiveness of Punishment as an Interaction of Intensity, Timing, Agent Nurturance and Cognitive Structuring," *Child Development,* 40 (1969), 213–235.

———. "The Role of Punishment in the Socialization Process," in R. A. Hoppe, G. A. Milton, and E. C. Simmel (eds.), *Early Experiences and the Processes of Socialization.* New York: Academic Press, 1970, pp. 81–108.

Pavlov, I. P. *Conditioned Reflexes.* New York: Dover, 1960. (Originally, Oxford University Press, 1927.)

Piaget, J. *The Origins of Intelligence in Children.* New York: International Universities Press, 1956.

———, and B. Inhelder. *The Psychology of the Child.* New York: Basic Books, 1969.

Rheingold, H. L., and C. O. Eckerman. "The Infant Separates Himself From His Mother," *Science,* 168 (1970), 78–83.

Rogers, C. *Freedom to Learn.* Columbus, Ohio: Merrill, 1969.

Roper, E. "Fortune Survey: Women in America, Part I," *Fortune,* 36 (1946), 5–14.

Rosenberg, B. G., and B. Sutton-Smith. "Ordinal Position and Sex-Role Identification," *Genetic Psychology Monographs,* 70 (1964), 297–328.

———, and ———. "Family Interaction Effects on Masculinity-Femininity," *Journal of Personality and Social Psychology,* 8 (1968), 117–120.

Rosenberg, M., and R. G. Simmons. *Black and White Self-esteem: The Urban School Child.* Washington, D. C.: American Sociological Association, 1971.

Rosenhan, D., F. Frederick, and A. Burrowes. "Preaching and Practicing: Effects of Channel Discrepency on Norm Internalization," *Child Development,* 39 (1968), 291–301.

Schaffer, H. R., and P. E. Emerson. "The Development of Social Attachments in Infancy," *Monographs of the Society for Research in Child Development,* 29 (1964), 251–282.

Sears, R. R., E. E. Maccoby, and H. Levin. *Patterns of Child Rearing.* New York: Harper & Row, 1957.

Skinner, B. F. *Beyond Freedom and Dignity.* New York: Vintage Books, 1971.

———. *Walden Two.* London: Macmillan, 1948.

Solomon, R. L. "Punishment," *American Psychologist,* 19 (1964), 239–253.

Staats, A. W., and C. K. Staats. "Attitudes Established by Classical Conditioning," *Journal of Abnormal and Social Psychology,* 57 (1958), 37–40.

Terman, L. M. *Psychological Factors in Marital Happiness.* New York: McGraw-Hill, 1938.

Thorndike, E. L. *The Elements of Psychology.* New York: Seiler, 1907.

Ward, S. H., and J. Braun. "Self-esteem and Racial Preference in Black Children," *American Journal of Orthopsychiatry,* 42 (1972), 644–647.

Watson, J. B. *Behaviorism,* rev. ed. Chicago: University of Chicago Press, 1962.

———, and R. Rayner. "Conditioned Emotional Reactions," *Journal of Experimental Psychology,* 3 (1920), 1–14.

Whiting, J. W. "Fourth Presentation," in J. W. Tanner and B. Inhelder (eds.), *Discussions on Child Development: II.* London: Tavistock Publications, 1954, pp. 185–212.

Zigler, E., and I. L. Child. "Socialization," in G. Lindzey and E. Aronson (eds.), *The Handbook of Social Psychology,* Vol. 3, 2nd ed. Reading, Mass.: Addison-Wesley, 1969, pp. 450–489.

3

Atkinson, K., B. MacWhinney, and C. Stoel. "An Experiment on Recognition of Babbling," *Children's Language Structure,* No. 15. Berkeley, Calif.: Language Behavior Research Laboratory, April 1969.

Bateson, G., D. O. Jackson, J. Haley, and J. Weakland. "Toward a Theory of Schizophrenia," *Behavioral Science,* 1 (1956), 251–264.

Bernstein, B. "A Sociolinguistic Approach to Socialization: With Some Reference to Educability," in F. Williams (ed.), *Language and Poverty: Perspectives on a Theme.* Chicago: Markham, 1970, pp. 25–61.

Bronowski, J., and U. Bellugi. "Language, Name, and Concept," *Science,* 168 (1970), 669–673.

Brown, R. "Linguistic Determinism and the Part of Speech," *Journal of Abnormal and Social Psychology,* 55 (1957), 1–5.

———. *Words and Things.* New York: Free Press, 1958.

———, and M. Ford. "Address in American English," *Journal of Abnormal and Social Psychology,* 62 (1961), 375–385.

———, and C. Fraser. "The Acquisition of Syntax," in C. N. Cofer and B. S. Musgrave (eds.), *Verbal Behavior and Learning: Problems and Processes.* New York: McGraw-Hill, 1963, pp. 158–197.

———, and A. Gilman. "The Pronouns of Power and Solidarity," in T. A. Sebeok (ed.), *Style in Language.* Cambridge, Mass.: MIT Press, 1960, pp. 253–275.

———, and A. E. Horowitz, in R. Brown. *Words and Things.* New York: Free Press, 1958, pp. 125–127.

———, and E. Lenneberg. "A Study in Language and Cognition," *Journal of Abnormal and Social Psychology,* 49 (1954), 454–462.

Carroll, J., and J. Casagrande. "The Function of Language Classifications in Behavior," in E. E. Maccoby, T. M. Newcomb, and E. L. Hartley (eds.), *Readings in Social Psychology,* 3rd ed. New York: Holt, Rinehart and Winston, 1958, pp. 18–31.

Chomsky, N. *Syntactic Structures.* The Hague: Mouton, 1957.

———. *Aspects of the Theory of Syntax.* Cambridge, Mass.: MIT Press, 1965.

Cuceloglu, D. "A Cross-Cultural Study of Communication via Facial Expressions" (unpublished doctoral dissertation, University of Illinois, 1967).

Ekman, P. "Universal Facial Expressions of Emotion," *California Mental Health Research Digest,* 8 (1970), 151–158.

———, and W. Friesen. "Nonverbal Leakage and Clues to Deception," *Psychiatry,* 32 (1969a), 88–106.

———, and ———. "The Repertoire of Nonverbal Behavior: Categories, Origins, Usage, and Coding," *Semiotica,* 1 (1969b), 49–98.

———, ———, and P. Ellsworth. *Emotion in the Human Face: Guidelines for Research and an Integration of Findings.* New York: Pergamon, 1972.

Exline, R. V., and A. Yellin. "Eye Contact as a Sign Between Man and Monkey," *Proceedings of the 19th International Congress of Psychology,* (1969), 199.

Ferguson, C. A. "Baby Talk in Six Languages," in J. J. Gumperz and D. Hymes (eds.), "The Ethnography of Communication," *American Anthropologist,* 66 (1964), 103–114.

Flavell, J. H. "The Development of Two Related Forms of Social Cognition: Role-Taking and Verbal Communication," in A. H. Kidd and J. L. Rivoire (eds.), *Perceptual Development in Children.* New York: International Universities Press, 1966, pp. 246–272.

Gardner, R. A., and B. T. Gardner. "Teaching Sign Language to a Chimpanzee," *Science,* 165 (1969), 664–672.

Glucksberg, S., R. M. Krauss, and R. Weisberg. "Referential Communication in Nursery School Children: Method and Some Preliminary Findings," *Journal of Experimental Child Psychology,* 3 (1966), 333–342.

Greenspoon, J. "The Reinforcing Effect of Two Spoken Sounds on the Frequency of Two Responses," *American Journal of Psychology,* 68 (1955), 409–416.

Hayakawa, S. I. *Language in Action.* New York: Harcourt, Brace & World, 1941.

Hess, R., and V. Shipmen. "Early Experience and the Socialization of Cognitive Modes in Children," *Child Development,* 36 (1965), 869–886.

Hockett, C. F. "The Origin of Speech," *Scientific American,* 203 (1960), 89–96.

Howes, D., and C. E. Osgood. "On the Combination of Associative Probabilities in Linguistic Contexts," *American Journal of Psychology,* 67 (1954), 241–258.

Jensen, A. "Social Class and Verbal Learning," in M. Deutsch, I. Katz, and A. R. Jensen (eds.), *Social Class, Race, and Psychological Development.* New York: Holt, Rinehart and Winston, 1968, pp. 115–174.

Kendon, A. "Some Functions of Gaze-Direction in Social Interaction," *Acta Psychologica,* 26 (1967), 22–63.

Kohlberg, L. "From Is to Ought: How to Commit the Naturalistic Fallacy and Get Away With It in the Study of Moral Development," in T. Mischel (ed.), *Cognitive Development and Epistemology.* New York: Academic Press, 1971, pp. 151–235.

Korzybski, A. *Science and Sanity: An Introduction to Non-Aristotelian Systems and General Semantics,* 1st ed. Lancaster, Penn.: Science Press, 1933.

Krauss, R. M., and S. Glucksberg. "The Development of Communication: Competence as a Function of Age," *Child Development,* 40 (1969), 255–266.

Labov, W. "The Logic of Nonstandard English," in F. Williams (ed.), *Language and Poverty: Perspectives on a Theme.* Chicago: Markham, 1970, pp. 153–189.

Ledvinka, J. "Race of Interviewer and the Language Elaboration of Black Interviewees," *Journal of Social Issues,* 27 (1971), 185–197.

Lenneberg, E. *Biological Foundations of Language.* New York: Wiley, 1967.

———, and J. M. Roberts. "The Language of Experience," *Memoir of the International Journal of American Linguistics,* 22 (1956), Whole No. 13.

Lovaas, O. I., J. P. Berberich, B. F. Perloff, and B. Schaeffer. "Acquisition of Imitative Speech by Schizophrenic Children," *Science,* 151 (1966), 705–709.

McLuhan, M. *The Gutenberg Galaxy: The Making of Typographic Man.* Toronto: University of Toronto Press, 1962.

————. *Understanding Media: The Extensions of Man.* New York: McGraw-Hill, 1964.

McNeill, D. "Developmental Psycholinguistics," in F. Smith and G. A. Miller (eds.), *The Genesis of Language: A Psycholinguistic Approach.* Cambridge, Mass.: MIT Press, 1966, pp. 15–84.

Miller, G. A., and N. Chomsky. "Finitary Models of Language Users," in R. D. Luce, R. R. Bush, and E. Galanter (eds.), *Handbook of Mathematical Psychology,* Vol. 2. New York: Wiley, 1963, pp. 419–491.

————, **and J. A. Selfridge.** "Verbal Context and the Recall of Meaningful Material," *American Journal of Psychology,* 63 (1950), 176–185.

Miller, W., and S. Ervin. "The Development of Grammar in Child Language," in U. Bellugi and R. Rrown (eds.), "The Acquisition of Language," *Monographs of the Society for Research in Child Development,* No. 92, 29 (1964).

Osgood, C. E. "Interpersonal Verbs and Interpersonal Behavior," in J. L. Cowan (ed.), *Studies in Thought and Language.* Tuscon: University of Arizona Press, 1970, pp. 133–228.

————, **G. J. Suci, and P. Tannenbaum.** *The Measurement of Meaning.* Urbana: University of Illinois Press, 1957.

————, **Y. Tamaka, and T. Oyama.** "A Cross-culture and Cross-concept Study of the Generality of Semantic Spaces," *Journal of Verbal Learning and Verbal Behavior,* 2 (1963), 392–405.

Piaget, J. *The Language and Thought of the Child.* New York: Harcourt, Brace & World, 1926.

————. *Judgment and Reasoning in the Child.* New York: Harcourt, Brace & World, 1928.

Premack, D. "The Education of S*A*R*A*H: A Chimp Learns the Language," *Psychology Today,* 4 (1970), 54–58.

Robinson, W. P. "The Elaborated Code in Working Class Language," *Language and Speech,* 8 (1965), 243–252.

————, **and S. J. Rackstraw.** "Variations in Mothers' Answers to Children's Questions, as a Function of Social Class, Verbal Intelligence Test Scores and Sex," *Sociology,* 1 (1967), 259–276.

Rubin, Z. "Measurement of Romantic Love," *Journal of Personality and Social Psychology,* 16 (1970), 265–273.

Ruesch, J., and W. Kees. *Nonverbal Communication.* Berkeley, Calif.: University of California Press, 1956.

Sapir, E. *Language: An Introduction to the Study of Speech.* New York: Harcourt, Brace & World, 1949.

Shipley, E. F., C. S. Smith, and L. R. Gleitman. "A Study in the Acquisition of Language: Free Responses to Commands," *Language,* 45 (1969), 322–342.

Slobin, D. I. "Children and Language: They Learn the Same Way All Around the World," *Psychology Today,* 6 (1972), 71–74, 82.

Snow, C. E. "Mothers' Speech to Children Learning Language," *Child Development,* 43 (1972), 549–565.

Whorf, B. L. *Language, Thought, and Reality.* New York: Wiley, 1956.

4

Atkinson, J. W., and N. T. Feather (eds.). *A Theory of Achievement Motivation.* New York: Wiley, 1966.

Berscheid, E., and E. Walster. *Interpersonal Attraction.* Reading, Mass.: Addison-Wesley, 1969.

Coleman, J. S., E. Q. Campbell, C. J. Hobson, J. McPartland, A. M. Mood, F. D. Weinfeld, and R. L. York. *Equality of Educational Opportunity* (report from Office of Education). Washington, D. C.: US Government Printing Office, 1966.

Cooley, C. H. *Human Nature and the Social Order.* Boston: Scribner, 1902.

Crowne, D. P., and D. Marlowe. *The Approval Motive: Studies in Evaluative Dependence.* New York: Wiley, 1964.

Dittes, J. E. "Attractiveness of Group as Function of Self-esteem and Acceptance by Group," *Journal of Abnormal and Social Psychology,* 59 (1959), 77–82.

Eagly, A. H. "Sex Differences in the Relationship Between Self-esteem and Susceptibility to Social Influence," *Journal of Personality,* 37 (1959), 581–591.

Edwards, A. L. "The Relationship Between the Judged Desirability of a Trait and the Probability that the Trait Will Be Endorsed," *Journal of Applied Psychology,* 37 (1953), 90–93.

Festinger, L. "A Theory of Social Comparison Processes," *Human Relations,* 7 (1954), 117–140.

Fiedler, F. E. *A Theory of Leadership Effectiveness.* New York: McGraw-Hill, 1967.

Gergen, K. J. "Personal Consistency and the Presentation of Self," in C. Gordon and K. J. Gergen (eds.), *The Self in Social Interaction,* Vol. 1. New York: Wiley, 1968, pp. 299–308.

Graen, G., K. Alvares, J. B. Orris, and J. A. Martella. "Contingency Model of Leadership Effectiveness: Antecedent and Evidential Results," *Psychological Bulletin,* 74 (1970), 285–296.

Gurin, P., G. Gurin, R. C. Lao, and M. Beattie. "Internal-External Control in the Motivational Dynamics of Negro Youth," *Journal of Social Issues,* 25 (1969), 29–53.

Hartshorne, H., and M. A. May. *Studies in the Nature of Character, Vol. I: Studies in Deceit.* New York: Macmillan, 1928.

Horner, M. S. "Fail: Bright Women," *Psychology Today,* 3 (1969), 36–38.

————. "Toward an Understanding of Achievement-Related Conflicts in Women," *Journal of Social Issues,* 28 (1972), 157–175.

Hovland, C. I., and I. L. Janis (eds.). *Personality and Persuasibility.* New Haven, Conn.: Yale University Press, 1959.

Janis, I. L., and P. B. Field. "Sex Differences and Personality Factors Related to Persuasibility," in C. I. Hovland and I. L. Janis (eds.), *Personality and Persuasibility.* New Haven, Conn.: Yale University Press, 1959, pp. 55–68.

Lefcourt, H. M. "Recent Developments in the Study of Locus of Control," in B. Maher (ed.), *Progress in Experimental Personality Research,* Vol. 6. New York: Academic Press, 1972, pp. 1–39.

————, **and G. W. Ladwig.** "The Effect of Reference Group Upon Negroes Task Persistence in a Biracial Competitive Game," *Journal of Personality and Social Psychology,* 1 (1965), 668–671.

Leventhal, H., and S. I. Perloe. "A Relationship Between Self-esteem and Persuasibility," *Journal of Abnormal and Social Psychology,* 64 (1962), 385–388.

McClelland, D. C. *The Achieving Society.* Princeton, N. J.: Van Nostrand, 1961.

McGuire, W. J. "Personality and Susceptibility to Social Influence," in E. F. Borgatta and W. W. Lambert (eds.), *Handbook of Personality Theory and Research.* Chicago: Rand McNally, 1968, pp. 1130–1187.

Mead, G. H. *Mind, Self, and Society from the Standpoint of a Social Behaviorist.* Chicago: University of Chicago Press, 1934.

Miller, N., A. N. Doob, D. C. Butler, and D. Marlowe. "The Tendency to Agree: Situational Determinants and Social Desirability," *Journal of Experimental Research in Personality,* 1 (1965), 78–83.

Mischel, W. *Personality and Assessment.* New York: Wiley, 1968.

Morse, S., and K. J. Gergen. "Social Comparison, Self-Consistency, and the Concept of Self," *Journal of Personality and Social Psychology,* 16 (1970), 149–156.

Nisbett, R. E., and A. Gordon. "Self-esteem and Susceptibility to Social Influence," *Journal of Personality and Social Psychology,* 5 (1967), 268–276.

Platt, E. S. "Internal-External Control and Changes in Expected Utility as Predictors of the Change in Cigarette Smoking Following Role Playing" (paper presented at the meeting of the Eastern Psychological Association, Philadelphia, April 1969).

Rogers, C. R. *Client-Centered Therapy: Its Current Practice, Implications, and Theory.* Boston: Houghton, 1951.

Rotter, J. B. "Level of Aspiration as a Method of Studying Personality. III. Group Validity Studies," *Character and Personality,* 11 (1943), 254–274.

————. *Social Learning and Clinical Psychology.* Englewood Cliffs, N. J.: Prentice-Hall, 1954.

————. "Generalized Expectancies for Internal Versus External Control of Reinforcement," *Psychological Monographs,* 80 (1966), Whole No. 609.

Sherman, S. J. "Internal-External Control and Its Relationship to Attitude Change Under Different Social Influence Techniques," *Journal of Personality and Social Psychology,* 26 (1973), 23–29.

Videbeck, R. "Self-Conception and the Reactions of Others," *Sociometry,* 23 (1960), 351–359.

Walster, E. "The Effect of Self-esteem on Romantic Liking," *Journal of Experimental Social Psychology,* 1 (1965), 184–197.

5

Anderson, N. H. "Likeableness Ratings of 555 Personality Trait Words," *Journal of Personality and Social Psychology,* 9 (1968), 272–279.

————, and S. Hubert. "Effects of Concomitant Verbal Recall on Order Effects in Personality Impression Formation," *Journal of Verbal Learning and Verbal Behavior,* 2 (1963), 379–391.

Asch, S. E. "Forming Impressions on Personality," *Journal of Abnormal and Social Psychology,* 41 (1946), 258–290.

Bem, D. J. "Self-perception: An Alternative Interpretation of Cognitive Dissonance Phenomena," *Psychological Review,* 74 (1967), 183–200.

Brown, R. *Words and Things.* New York: Free Press, 1958.

Bruner, J. S., and C. Goodman. "Value and Need as Organizing Factors in Perception," *Journal of Abnormal and Social Psychology,* 42 (1947), 33–44.

Eriksen, C. W., and C. T. Browne. "An Experimental and Theoretical Analysis of Perceptual Defense," *Journal of Abnormal and Social Psychology,* 52 (1956), 224–230.

Festinger, L. *A Theory of Cognitive Dissonance.* Evanston, Ill.: Row, Peterson, 1957.

Gollin, E. S. "Forming Impressions of Personality," *Journal of Personality,* 23 (1954), 65–76.

Hastorf, A. H., D. J. Schneider, and J. Polefka. *Person Perception.* Reading, Mass.: Addison-Wesley, 1970.

Heider, F. *The Psychology of Interpersonal Relations.* New York: Wiley, 1958.

Johnson, T. J., R. Feigenbaum, and M. Weibey. "Some Determinants and Consequences of the Teachers Perception of Causation," *Journal of Educational Psychology,* 55 (1964), 237–246.

Jones, E. E., and K. E. Davis. "From Acts to Dispositions: The Attribution Process in Person Perception," in L. Berkowitz (ed.), *Advances in Experimental Social Psychology,* Vol. 2. New York: Academic Press, 1965, pp. 219–266.

————, and R. Nisbett. *The Actor and the Observer: Divergent Perceptions of the Causes of Behavior.* New York: General Learning Press, 1971.

————, L. Rock, K. G. Shaver, G. R. Goethals, and L. M. Ward. "Pattern Performance and Ability Attribution: An Unexpected Primacy Effect," *Journal of Personality and Social Psychology,* 10 (1968), 317–341.

Kanouse, D. E., and L. R. Hanson, Jr. *Negativity in Evaluations.* New York: General Learning Press, 1972.

Kelley, H. H. *Causal Schemata and the Attribution Process.* New York: General Learning Press, 1972.

Lanzetta, J. T., and T. E. Hannah. "Reinforcing Behavior of 'Naive' Trainers," *Journal of Personality and Social Psychology,* 11 (1969), 245–252.

Luchins, A. S. "Primacy-Recency in Impression Formation," in C. Hovland (ed.), *The Order of Presentation in Persuasion.* New Haven, Conn.: Yale University Press, 1957, pp. 62–75.

Merton, R. K. *Social Theory and Social Structure.* New York: Free Press, 1957.

Michotte, A. *Perception of Causality.* New York: Basic Books, 1963.

Nisbett, R. E., G. C. Caputo, P. Legant, and J. Maresek. "Behavior as Viewed by the Actor and as Viewed by the Observed," *Journal of Personality and Social Psychology,* (in press).

————, and S. Schachter. "Cognitive Manipulation of Pain," *Journal of Experimental Social Psychology,* 2 (1966), 227–236.

Osgood, C., G. J. Suci, and P. H. Tannenbaum. *The Measurement of Meaning.* Urbana: University of Illinois Press, 1957.

Pepitone, A. "The Determinants of Distortion in Social Perception," in H. Proshansky and B. Seidenberg (eds.), *Basic Studies in Social Psychology.* New York: Holt, Rinehart and Winston, 1965, pp. 71–80.

Rosen, A. C. "Change in Perceptual Threshold As a Protective Function of the Organism," *Journal of Personality,* 23 (1954), 182–195.

Rosenthal, R. "On the Social Psychology of the Self-fulfilling Prophecy: Further Evidence for Pygmalion Effects and their Mediating Mechanism," *Psychology Today,* (in press).

————, and L. Jacobson. *Pygmalion in the Classroom.* New York: Holt, Rinehart and Winston, 1968.

Schachter, S., and J. E. Singer. "Cognitive, Social, and Physiological Determinants of Emotional State," *Psychological Review,* 69 (1962), 379–399.

————, and L. Wheeler. "Epinephrine, Chlorpromazine, and Amusement," *Journal of Abnormal and Social Psychology,* 65 (1962), 121–128.

Schneider, D. J. "Implicit Personality Theory: A Review," *Psychological Bulletin,* (in press).

Steiner, I. D., and W. L. Field. "Role Assignment and Interpersonal Influence," *Journal of Abnormal and Social Psychology,* 61 (1960), 239–245.

Stewart, R. "Effect of Continuous Responding on the Order Effect in Personality Impression Formation," *Journal of Personality and Social Psychology,* 1 (1965), 161–165.

Streufert, S., and S. Streufert. "Effects of Conceptual Structure, Failure, and Success on Attribution of Causality and Interpersonal Attitudes," *Journal of Personality and Social Psychology,* 11 (1969), 138–147.

Thibaut, J. W., and H. W. Riecken. "Some Determinants and Consequences of the Perception of Social Causality," *Journal of Personality,* 24 (1955), 113–133.

Thorndike, E. L. "A Constant Error in Psychological Ratings," *Journal of Applied Psychology,* 4 (1920), 25–29.

Valins, S. "Cognitive Effects of False Heart-Rate Feedback," *Journal of Personality and Social Psychology,* 4 (1966), 400–408.

Wishner, J. "Reanalysis of Impressions of Personality," *Psychological Review,* 67 (1960), 96–112.

#

Aronson, E. "Some Antecedents of Interpersonal Attraction," in W. J. Arnold and D. Levine (eds.), *Nebraska Symposium on Motivation, 1969,* Vol. 17. Lincoln: University of Nebraska Press, 1970, pp. 143–173.

————, and D. Linder. "Gain and Loss of Esteem as Determinants of Interpersonal Attractiveness," *Journal of Experimental Social Psychology,* 1 (1965), 156–172.

Berscheid, E., K. Dion, E. Walster, and G. W. Walster. "Physical Attractiveness and Dating Choice: A Test of the Matching Hypothesis," *Journal of Experimental Social Psychology,* 7 (1971), 173–189.

Bossard, J. "Residential Propinquity as a Factor in Marriage Selection," *American Journal of Sociology,* 38 (1932), 219–224.

Byrne, D. "Interpersonal Attraction and Attitude Similarity," *Journal of Abnormal and Social Psychology,* 62 (1961), 713–715.

———. *The Attraction Paradigm.* New York: Academic Press, 1971.

———, W. Griffitt, and D. Stephaniak. "Attraction and Similarity of Personality Characteristics," *Journal of Personality and Social Psychology,* 5 (1967), 82–90.

Carnegie, D. *How To Win Friends and Influence People.* New York: Simon and Schuster, 1936.

Darley, J. M., and E. Berscheid. "Increased Liking as a Result of the Anticipation of Personal Contact," *Human Relations,* 20 (1967), 29–40.

Dickoff, H. "Reactions to Evaluations by Another Person as a Function of Self-evaluation and the Interaction Context," *Dissertation Abstracts,* 24 (1963), 2166.

Dion, K. "Physical Attractiveness and Evaluation of Children's Transgressions," *Journal of Personality and Social Psychology,* 24 (1972), 207–213.

Dittes, J. E. "Attractiveness of Group as a Function of Self-esteem and Acceptance by Group," *Journal of Abnormal and Social Psychology,* 59 (1959), 77–82.

———, and H. H. Kelley. "Effects of Different Conditions of Acceptance on Conformity to Group Norms," *Journal of Abnormal and Social Psychology,* 53 (1956), 100–107.

Festinger, L. "A Theory of Social Comparison Processes," *Human Relations,* 7 (1954), 117–140.

———, S. Schachter, and K. Back. *Social Pressures in Informal Groups: A Study of Human Factors in Housing.* Stanford, Calif.: Stanford University Press, 1950.

Floyd, J. M. K. "Effects of Amount of Reward and Friendship Status of the Other on the Frequency of Sharing in Children" (unpublished doctoral dissertation, University of Minnesota, 1964).

Freedman, J. L., J. M. Carlsmith, and D. O. Sears. *Social Psychology.* Englewood Cliffs, N. J.: Prentice-Hall, 1970.

———, ———, and S. Suomi. "The Effect of Familiarity on Liking" (unpublished paper, Stanford University, 1967).

Gergen, K. J., and M. K. Gergen. "Encounter: Research Catalyst for General Theories of Social Behavior" (paper presented at American Association for the Advancement of Science meeting, 1971).

Griffitt, W. "Environmental Effects on Interpersonal Affective Behavior: Ambient Effective Temperature and Attraction," *Journal of Personality and Social Psychology,* 15 (1970), 240–244.

———, and R. Veitch. "Hot and Crowded: Influences of Population Density and Temperature on Interpersonal Affective Behavior," *Journal of Personality and Social Psychology,* 17 (1971), 92–98.

Hall, E. T. *The Hidden Dimension.* New York: Doubleday, 1966.

Harvey, O. J. "Personality Factors in Resolution of Conceptual Incongruities," *Sociometry,* 25 (1962), 336–352.

Heider, F. *The Psychology of Interpersonal Relationships.* New York: Wiley, 1958.

Heron, W. "The Pathology of Boredom," *Scientific American,* 196 (1957), 52–56.

Homans, G. C. *Social Behavior: Its Elementary Forms.* New York: Harcourt, Brace & World, 1961.

Howard, A. (ed.). *Polynesia: Readings on a Culture Area.* San Francisco: Chandler, 1972.

Jacobs, L., E. Berscheid, and E. Walster. "Self-esteem and Attraction," *Journal of Personality and Social Psychology,* 17 (1971), 84–91.

James, G., and A. J. Lott. "Reward Frequency and the Formation of Positive Attitudes Toward Group Members," *Journal of Social Psychology,* 62 (1964), 111–115.

Jones, E. E. *Ingratiation.* New York: Appleton-Century-Crofts, 1964.

———, L. Bell, and E. Aronson. "The Reciprocation of Attraction from Similar and Dissimilar Others: A Study in Person Perception and Evaluation," in C. C. McClintock (ed.), *Experimental Social Psychology.* New York: Holt, Rinehart and Winston, 1970, pp. 142–176.

Katz, A. M., and R. Hill. "Residential Propinquity and Marital Selection: A Review of Theory, Method and Fact," *Marriage and Family Living,* 20 (1958), 27–35.

Kerckhoff, A. C., and K. E. Davis. "Value Consensus and Need Complementarity in Mate Selection," *American Sociological Review,* 27 (1962), 295–303.

Lerner, M. J., and C. H. Simmons. "Observer's Reaction to the Innocent Victim: Compassion or Rejection?" *Journal of Personality and Social Psychology,* 4 (1966), 203–210.

Levinger, G. "Note on Need Complementarity in Marriage," *Psychological Bulletin,* 61 (1964), 153–157.

———, and J. Breedlove. "Interpersonal Attraction and Agreement: A Study of Marriage Partners," *Journal of Personality and Social Psychology,* 3 (1966), 367–372.

———, D. J. Senn, and B. W. Jorgensen. "Progress Toward Permanence in Courtship: A Test of the Kerckhoff-Davis Hypothesis," *Sociometry,* 33 (1970), 427–443.

———, and J. D. Snoek. *Attraction in Relationships: A New Look at Interpersonal Attraction.* Morristown, N. J.: General Learning Press, 1972.

Levy, R. I. "Personality Studies in Polynesia and Micronesia: Stability and Change Monograph," No. 8. Honolulu: Social Science Research Institute, University of Hawaii, 1970.

Lipetz, M. E., I. H. Cohen, J. Dworin, and L. Rogers. "Need Complementarity, Marital Stability and Marital Satisfaction," in D. Marlowe and K. Gergen (eds.), *Personality and Social Behavior.* Reading, Mass.: Addison-Wesley, 1970, pp. 201–212.

Little, K. B. "Personal Space," *Journal of Experimental Social Psychology,* 1 (1965), 237–247.

Marlowe, D., and K. Gergen (eds.). *Personality and Social Behavior.* Reading, Mass.: Addison-Wesley, 1970.

Mead, M. *Male and Female.* New York: William Morrow, 1949.

Mettee, D. R., and P. C. Wilkins. "When Similarity 'Hurts': Effects of Perceived Ability and a Humorous Blunder on Interpersonal Attraction," *Journal of Personality and Social Psychology,* 22 (1972), 246–258.

Morse, S. J. "Help, Likeability and Social Influence," *Journal of Applied Social Psychology,* 2 (1972), 34–46.

Murstein, B. I. (ed.). *Theories of Attraction and Love.* New York: Springer, 1971.

———. "Physical Attractiveness and Marital Choice," *Journal of Personality and Social Psychology,* 22 (1972), 8–12.

Newcomb, T. M. "The Prediction of Interpersonal Attraction," *American Psychologist,* 11 (1956), 575–586.

———. *The Acquaintance Process.* New York: Holt, Rinehart and Winston, 1961.

Priest, R. F., and J. Sawyer. "Proximity and Peership: Basis of Balance in Interpersonal Attraction," *American Journal of Sociology,* 72 (1967), 633–649.

Rubin, Z. "Measurement of Romantic Love," *Journal of Personality and Social Psychology,* 16 (1970), 265–273.

Senn, D. J. "Attraction as a Function of Similarity-Dissimilarity in Task Performance," *Journal of Personality and Social Psychology,* 18 (1971), 120–123.

Taylor, S. E., and D. R. Mettee. "When Similarity Breeds Contempt," *Journal of Personality and Social Psychology,* 20 (1971), 75–81.

Thibaut, J. W., and H. H. Kelley. *The Social Psychology of Groups.* New York: Wiley, 1959.

Tognoli, J., and R. Keisner. "Gain and Loss of Esteem as Determinants of Interpersonal Attraction: A Replication and Extension," *Journal of Personality and Social Psychology,* 23 (1972), 201–204.

Walster, E., V. Aronson, D. Abrams, and L. Rattman. "Importance of Physical Attractiveness in Dating Behavior," *Journal of Personality and Social Psychology*, 4 (1966), 508–516.

Winch, R. F. *Mate Selection: A Study of Complementary Needs.* New York: Harper & Row, 1958.

Zajonc, R. B. "Attitudinal Effects of Mere Exposure," *Journal of Personality and Social Psychology*, No. 9 (1968), 1–27.

Ziller, R. C., and R. Behringer. "Assimilation of the Knowledgeable Newcomer Under Conditions of Group Success and Failure," *Journal of Abnormal and Social Psychology*, 60 (1960), 288–291.

7

Adorno, T. W., E. Frenkel-Brunswik, D. J. Levinson, and R. N. Sanford. *The Authoritarian Personality.* New York: Harper & Row, 1950.

Allport, G. W. *The Nature of Prejudice.* New York: Anchor, 1958.

Barth, E. A. T., and D. L. Noel. "Conceptual Frameworks for the Analysis of Race Relations: An Evaluation," *Social Forces*, 50 (1972), 333–348.

Bayton, J. A. "The Racial Stereotypes of Negro College Students," *Journal of Abnormal and Social Psychology*, 36 (1941), 97–102.

——, L. McAlister, and J. Hamer. "Race-Class Stereotypes," *Journal of Negro Education*, 25 (1956), 75–78.

Bem, S. L., and D. J. Bem. "Case Study of a Nonconscious Ideology: Training the Woman to Know Her Place," in D. J. Bem, *Beliefs, Attitudes and Human Affairs.* Belmont, Calif.: Brooks-Cole, 1970, pp. 89–99.

Berscheid, E., and E. H. Walster. *Interpersonal Attraction.* Reading, Mass.: Addison-Wesley, 1969.

Bettelheim, B., and M. Janowitz. *Dynamics of Prejudice: A Psychological and Sociological Study of Veterans.* New York: Harper & Row, 1950.

Brown, R. *Social Psychology.* New York: Free Press, 1965.

Byrne, D., and T. S. Wong. "Racial Prejudice, Interpersonal Attraction, and Assumed Dissimilarity of Attitudes," *Journal of Abnormal and Social Psychology*, 65 (1962), 246–253.

Campbell, A., and H. Schuman. *Racial Attitudes in Fifteen American Cities.* Ann Arbor, Mich.: Institute for Social Research, 1969.

Campbell, D. T. "Conformity in Psychology's Theories of Acquired Behavioral Dispositions," in I. A. Berg and B. M. Bass (eds.), *Conformity and Deviation.* New York: Harper & Brothers, 1961.

——. "Stereotypes and the Perception of Group Differences," *American Psychologist*, 22 (1967), 817–829.

——, N. Miller, J. Lubetsky, and E. J. O'Connell. "Varieties of Projection in Trait Attribution," *Psychological Monographs*, No. 592, 78 (1964).

Campbell, E. Q. "Some Social Psychological Correlates of Direction in Attitude Change," *Social Forces*, 36 (1958), 335–340.

Christie, R., and M. Johoda (eds.). *Studies in the Scope and Method of "The Authoritarian Personality."* New York: Free Press, 1954.

Clark, K. B., and M. Clark. "Racial Identification and Preference in Negro Children," in E. E. Maccoby, T. M. Newcomb and E. L. Hartley (eds.), *Readings in Social Psychology.* Rev. ed. New York: Holt, Rinehart and Winston, 1958, pp. 602–611.

Clore, G. L., and K. M. Jeffery. "Emotional Role Playing, Attitude Change, and Attraction Toward a Disabled Person," *Journal of Personality and Social Psychology*, 23 (1972), 105–111.

Cox, O. C. *Caste, Class and Race.* New York: Doubleday, 1948.

Dollard, J. L., L. W. Doob, N. E. Miller, O. H. Mowrer, and R. R. Sears. *Frustration and Aggression.* New Haven, Conn.: Yale University Press, 1939.

Elkins, S. M. *Slavery: A Problem in American Institutional and Intellectual Life.* 2nd ed. Chicago: University of Chicago Press, 1968.

Forward, J. R., and J. R. Williams. "Internal-External Control and Black Militancy," *Journal of Social Issues*, 26 (1970), 75–92.

Garcia, A. B., and B. J. Zimmerman. "The Effect of Examiner Ethnicity and Language on the Performance of Bilingual Mexican-American First Graders," *Journal of Social Psychology*, 87 (1972), 3–12.

Glass, D. C. "Changes in Liking as a Means of Reducing Cognitive Discrepancies Between Self-esteem and Aggression," *Journal of Personality*, 32 (1964), 531–549.

Goffman, E. *Stigma: Notes on the Management of Spoiled Identity.* Englewood Cliffs, N. J.: Prentice-Hall, 1963.

Goldberg, P. "Are Women Prejudiced Against Women?", *Trans-action*, 5 (1968), 28–30.

Goldstein, M., and E. E. Davis. "Race and Belief: A Further Analysis of the Social Determinants of Behavioral Intentions," *Journal of Personality and Social Psychology*, 22 (1972), 346–355.

Gurin, P., G. Gurin, R. Lao, and M. Beattie. "Internal-External Control in the Motivational Dynamics of Negro Youth," *Journal of Social Issues*, 25 (1969), 29–53.

Harding, J., and R. Hogrefe. "Attitudes of White Department Store Employees Toward Negro Co-workers," *Journal of Social Issues*, 8 (1952), 18–28.

——, H. Proshansky, B. Kutner, and I. Chein. "Prejudice and Ethnic Relations," in G. Lindzey and E. Aronson (eds.), *The Handbook of Social Psychology*, Vol. 5. Reading, Mass.: Addison-Wesley, 1969, pp. 1–76.

Horner, M. S. "Femininity and Successful Achievement: A Basic Inconsistency," in M. H. Garskoff (ed.), *Roles Women Play.* Belmont, Calif.: Brooks-Cole, 1971, pp. 97–122.

Horowitz, E. L. "The Development of Attitude Toward the Negro," *Archives of Psychology*, No. 194, 28 (1936).

——, and R. Horowitz. "Development of Social Attitudes in Children," *Sociometry*, 1 (1938), 301–338.

Hraba, J., and G. Grant. "Black is Beautiful: A Reexamination of Racial Preference and Identification," *Journal of Personality and Social Psychology*, 16 (1970), 398–402.

Hughes, E. C. "Good People and Dirty Work," in R. Perrucci and M. Polisuk (eds.), *The Triple Revolution: Social Problems in Depth.* Boston: Little, Brown, 1968, pp. 596–607.

Jensen, A. R. "How Much Can We Boost I. Q. and Scholastic Achievement?" *Harvard Educational Review*, 39 (1969), 1–123.

Jones, E. E., K. E. Davis, and K. J. Gergen. "Some Determinants of Reactions to Being Approved or Disapproved as a Person," *Psychological Monographs*, No. 2, 76 (1962).

Jones, J. M. *Prejudice and Racism.* Reading, Mass.: Addison-Wesley, 1972.

Kagan, J. S. "Inadequate Evidence and Illogical Conclusions," *Harvard Educational Review*, 39 (1969), 274–277.

Karlins, M., T. L. Coffman, and G. Walters. "On the Fading of Social Stereotypes: Studies in Three Generations of College Students," *Journal of Personality and Social Psychology*, 13 (1969), 1–16.

Katz, D., and K. W. Braly. "Racial Stereotypes of 100 College Students," *Journal of Abnormal and Social Psychology*, 28 (1933), 280–290.

Kerner, O. (chairman). *Report of the National Advisory Commission on Civil Disorders.* New York Times editors. New York: Dutton, 1968.

Kipnis, D. "The Powerholder" (paper presented at the Albany Symposium on Power and Influence, October 1972).

Koslin, S. C., B. L. Koslin, J. Cardwell, and R. Pargament. "Quasi-Disguised and Structural Measure of School Children's Racial Preferences," *Proceedings of the 77th Annual Convention of the American Psychological Association*, 4 (1969), 661–662.

Kramer, B. M. "Residential Contact As a Determinant of Attitudes Toward Negroes" (unpublished doctoral dissertation, Harvard, 1950).

LaPiere, R. T. "Type-Rationalizations of Group Antipathy," *Social Forces,* 15 (1936), 232–237.

Lerner, M. J. "The Effect of Responsibility and Choice On a Partner's Attractiveness Following Failure," *Journal of Personality,* 33 (1965), 178–187.

Martin, W. T., and D. L. Poston, Jr. "The Occupational Composition of White Females: Sexism, Racism and Occupational Differentiation," *Social Forces,* 50 (1972), 349–355.

Merton, R. K. *Social Theory and Social Structure.* New York: Free Press, 1957.

Muhr, M., and K. Bogard. "Sex, Self-perception and the Perception of Others" (paper presented at the Eastern Psychological Association, Boston, April 1972).

Noel, D. L. "Group Identification Among Negroes: An Empirical Analysis," *Journal of Social Issues,* 20 (1964), 71–84.

Orpen, C., and L. Van der Schyff. "Prejudice and Personality in White South Africa: A 'Differential Learning' Alternative to the Authoritarian Personality," *Journal of Social Psychology,* 87 (1972), 313.

Park, R. E. *Race and Culture.* New York: Free Press, 1950.

Peabody, D. "Group Judgments in the Philippines: Evaluative and Descriptive Aspects," *Journal of Personality and Social Psychology,* 10 (1968), 290–300.

Rokeach, M. (ed.). *The Open and Closed Mind.* New York: Basic Books, 1960.

———. "Belief Versus Race as Determinants of Social Distance: Comment on Triandis' Paper," *Journal of Abnormal and Social Psychology,* 62 (1961), 187–188.

———, and L. Mezei. "Race and Shared Belief as Factors in Social Choice," *Science,* 151 (1966), 167–172.

———, and S. Parker. "Values as Social Indicators of Poverty and Race Relations in America," *The Annals of the American Academy of Political and Social Science,* 388 (1970), 97–111.

———, P. W. Smith, and R. I. Evans. "Two Kinds of Prejudice or One?" in M. Rokeach (ed.), *The Open and Closed Mind.* New York: Basic Books, 1960, pp. 132–168.

Rose, A. "Anti-Semitism's Root in City-Hatred," *Commentary,* 6 (1948), 374–378.

Rosenberg, M., and R. G. Simmons. *Black and White Self-esteem: The Urban School Child.* Washington, D. C.: American Sociological Association, 1971.

Rosenthal, R. *Experimenter Effects in Behavioral Research.* New York: Appleton-Century-Crofts, 1966.

———, and L. Jacobson. *Pygmalion in the Classroom: Teacher Expectations and Pupils' Intellectual Development.* New York: Holt, Rinehart and Winston, 1968.

Rubovitz, P., and M. L. Maehr. "Pygmalion Black and White," *Journal of Personality and Social Psychology,* 25 (1973), 210–218.

Sapir, R. "A Shelter," *Megamot,* 3 (1951), 8–36.

Sherif, M., and C. Hovland. *Social Judgment; Assimilation and Contrast Effects in Communication and Attitude Change.* New Haven, Conn.: Yale University Press, 1961.

Sigall, H., and R. Page. "Current Stereotypes: A Little Fading, A Little Faking," *Journal of Personality and Social Psychology,* 18 (1971), 247–255.

Singer, D. "The Impact of Interracial Classroom Exposure on the Social Attitudes of Fifth Grade Children" (unpublished study cited in Harding, Proshansky, Kutner and Chein, "Prejudice and Ethnic Relations," in G. Lindzey and E. Aronson (eds.), *The Handbook of Social Psychology,* Vol. 5. Reading, Mass.: Addison-Wesley, 1954, p. 49).

Skolnick, J. H. (director). *Report of the Task Force on Violent Aspects of Protest and Confrontation of the National Commission on the Causes and Prevention of Violence.* New York: Simon and Schuster, 1969, pp. 218–224.

Stein, D. H., J. A. Hardyck, and M. B. Smith. "Race and Belief: An Open and Shut Case," *Journal of Personality and Social Psychology,* 1 (1965), 281–289.

Triandis, H. C. "A Note on Rokeach's Theory of Prejudice," *Journal of Abnormal and Social Psychology,* 62 (1961), 184–186.

———, and E. E. Davis. "Race and Belief as Determinants of Behavioral Intentions," *Journal of Personality and Social Psychology,* 2 (1965), 715–725.

Ward, S. H., and J. Braun. "Self-esteem and Racial Preference in Black Children," *American Journal of Orthopsychiatry,* 42 (1972), 644–647.

Watson, P. "I. Q.: The Racial Gap," *Psychology Today,* 6 (1972), 48–52.

Weber, S. J., T. D. Cook, and D. T. Campbell. "The Effect of School Integration on the Academic Self-Concept of Students," (paper presented at the 43rd Meeting of the Midwestern Psychological Association, Detroit, Mich., 1971).

8

Abelson, R. P. "Are Attitudes Necessary?" in B. T. King and E. McGinnis (eds.), *Attitudes, Conflict and Social Change.* New York: Academic Press, 1972, pp. 19–32.

———. "Psychological Implication," in R. P. Abelson, *et al.* (eds.), *Theories of Cognitive Consistency: A Source Book.* Chicago: Rand McNally, 1968, pp. 112–139.

Allport, G. "Attitudes," in C. M. Murchison (ed.), *Handbook of Social Psychology.* Worcester, Mass.: Clark University Press, 1935, pp. 798–844.

———, and L. Postman. *The Psychology of Rumor.* New York: Holt, Rinehart and Winston, 1947.

Anderson, L. R., and M. Fishbein. "Prediction of Attitudes From Number, Strength, and Evaluative Aspects of Beliefs About the Attitude Object," *Journal of Personality and Social Psychology,* 3 (1965), 437–443.

Aronson, E., and J. M. Carlsmith. "Experimentation in Social Psychology," in G. Lindzey and E. Aronson (eds.), *The Handbook of Social Psychology,* Vol. 2, 2nd ed. Reading, Mass.: Addison-Wesley, 1968, pp. 1–79.

Bem, D. J. (ed.). *Beliefs, Attitudes and Human Affairs.* Belmont, Calif.: Brooks-Cole, 1970.

Berlyne, D. E. "Arousal and Reinforcement," *Nebraska Symposium on Motivation,* Vol. 15. Lincoln: University of Nebraska Press, 1967, pp. 1–10.

Bogardus, E. S. *Immigration and Race Attitudes.* Boston: D. C. Heath, 1928.

Brehm, J. W. *A Theory of Psychological Reactance.* New York: Academic Press, 1966.

———, and A. Cole. "Effect of a Favor Which Reduces Freedom," *Journal of Personality and Social Psychology,* 3 (1966), 420–426.

Campbell, D. "Social Attitudes and Other Acquired Behavioral Dispositions," in S. Koch (ed.), *Psychology: A Study of a Science,* 2nd ed. New York: McGraw-Hill, 1963, pp. 94–172.

Cartwright, D., and F. Harary. "Structural Balance: A Generalization from Heider's Theory," *Psychological Review,* 63 (1956), 277–293.

DeFleur, M. L., and F. R. Westie. "Verbal Attitudes and Overt Acts: An Experiment on the Salience of Attitudes," *American Sociological Review,* 23 (1958), 667–673.

Deutsch, M., and M. Collins. *Interracial Housing.* Minneapolis: University of Minnesota Press, 1951.

Festinger, L. *A Theory of Cognitive Dissonance.* Stanford, Calif.: Stanford University Press, 1957.

Fishbein, M., and R. Hunter. "Summation Versus Balance in Attitude Organization and Change," *Journal of Abnormal and Social Psychology,* 65 (1964), 505–510.

Guttman, L. "A Basis for Scaling Quantitative Data," *American Sociological Review,* 9 (1944), 139–150.

———. "The Third Component of Scalable Attitudes," *International Journal of Opinion and Attitude Research,* 4 (1950), 285–287.

Heider, F. *The Psychology of Interpersonal Relations.* New York: Wiley, 1958.

James, W. *The Principles of Psychology.* New York: Dover, 1890.

Janis, I., D. Kaye, and P. Kirschner. "Facilitating Effects of 'Eating-While-Reading' on Responsiveness to Persuasive Communications," *Journal of Personality and Social Psychology,* 1 (1965), 181–186.

Jones, J. M. "Psychological Contours of Black Athletic Performance and Expression" (paper presented at the Physical Education Symposium on Race and Sport, Slippery Rock State College, Slippery Rock, Pennsylvania, June 21, 1972).

Katz, D., and E. Stotland. "A Preliminary Statement to a Theory of Attitude Structure and Change," in S. Koch (ed.), *Psychology: A Study of a Science.* New York: McGraw-Hill, 1959, pp. 423–475.

LaPiere, R. T. "Attitudes Versus Actions," *Social Forces,* 13 (1934), 230–237.

Lecky, P. *Self-Consistency: A Theory of Personality.* Garden City, N. Y.: Doubleday, 1951.

Likert, R. "A Technique for the Measurement of Attitudes," *Archives of Psychology,* 140 (1932), 44–53.

Milgram, S. "The Experience of Living in Cities," *Science,* 167 (1970), 1461–1468.

Osgood, C. E., P. H. Tannenbaum, and G. J. Suci. *The Measurement of Meaning.* Urbana: University of Illinois Press, 1957.

Razran, G. "The Observable and Inferable Conscious in Current Soviet Psychophysiology: Interoceptive Conditioning, Semantic Conditioning, and the Orienting Reflex," *Psychological Review,* 68 (1961), 81–147.

Robinson, J. P., and P. R. Shaver. *Measures of Social Psychological Attitudes (Appendix B to Measures of Political Attitudes).* Ann Arbor: Survey Research Center, Institute for Social Research 1969.

Rosenberg, M. J. "Cognitive Structure and Attitudinal Affect," *Journal of Abnormal and Social Psychology,* 53 (1956), 367–372.

———, and R. P. Abelson. "An Analysis of Cognitive Balancing," in C. I. Hovland and I. L. Janis (eds.), *Attitude Organization and Change.* New Haven, Conn.: Yale University Press, 1960, pp. 112–163.

Schachter, S., and H. Burdick. "A Field Experiment in Rumor Transmission and Distortion," *Journal of Abnormal and Social Psychology,* 50 (1955), 363–372.

Sherif, M. *In Common Predicament: Social Psychology of Intergroup Conflict and Cooperation.* Boston: Houghton Mifflin, 1966.

Thurstone, L. L. "Attitudes Can Be Measured," *American Journal of Sociology,* 33 (1928), 529–554.

Webb, E. J., D. T. Campbell, R. D. Schwartz, and L. Sechrest. *Unobtrusive Measures: Nonreactive Research in the Social Sciences.* Chicago: Rand McNally, 1966.

White, R. W. "Motivation Reconsidered: The Concept of Competence," *Psychological Review,* 66 (1959), 297–333.

Zajonc, R. B. "Attitudinal Effects of Mere Exposure," *Journal of Personality and Social Psychology, Monograph Supplement,* 9 (1968), 1–27.

Zanna, M., C. A. Kiesler, and P. A. Pilkonis. "Positive and Negative Attitudinal Affect Established by Classical Conditioning," *Journal of Personality and Social Psychology,* 14 (1970), 321–328.

Abelson, R. P. "Modes of Resolution of Belief Dilemmas," *Journal of Conflict Resolution,* 3 (1959), 343–353.

Aronson, E. "The Theory of Cognitive Dissonance: A Current Perspective," in L. Berkowitz (ed.), *Advances in Experimental Social Psychology.* Vol. 4. New York: Academic Press, 1969, pp. 1–34.

———, and J. M. Carlsmith. "Effect of Severity of Threat on the Devaluation of Forbidden Behavior," *Journal of Abnormal and Social Psychology,* 66 (1963), 584–588.

———, and J. Mills. "The Effect of Severity of Initiation on Liking for a Group," *Journal of Abnormal and Social Psychology,* 59 (1959), 177–181.

Bem, D. "An Experimental Analysis of Self-persuasion," *Journal of Experimental Social Psychology,* 1 (1965), 199–218.

———. "Self-perception: An Alternative Interpretation of Cognitive Dissonance Phenomena," *Psychological Review,* 74 (1967), 183–200.

———, and H. K. McConnell. "Testing the Self-perception Explanation of Dissonance Phenomena: On the Salience of Premanipulation Attitudes," *Journal of Personality and Social Psychology,* 14 (1970), 23–31.

Brehm, J. "Postdecision Changes in the Desirability of Alternatives," *Journal of Abnormal and Social Psychology,* 53 (1956), 384–389.

———, and A. R. Cohen. *Explorations in Cognitive Dissonance.* New York: Wiley, 1962.

———, and A. Cole. "Effect of a Favor Which Reduces Freedom," *Journal of Personality and Social Psychology,* 3 (1966), 420–426.

Cohen, A. R. "A Dissonance Analysis of the Boomerang Effect," *Journal of Personality,* 30 (1962), 75–88.

Davis, K., and E. E. Jones. "Changes in Interpersonal Perception as a Means of Reducing Cognitive Dissonance," *Journal of Abnormal and Social Psychology,* 61 (1960), 402–410.

Elms, A. C., and I. Janis. "Counter-Norm Attitudes Induced by Consonant Versus Dissonant Conditions of Role-Playing," *Journal of Experimental Research in Personality,* 1 (1965), 50–60.

Festinger, L. *A Theory of Cognitive Dissonance.* Stanford, Calif.: Stanford University Press, 1957.

———, and J. M. Carlsmith. "Cognitive Consequences of Forced Compliance," *Journal of Abnormal and Social Psychology,* 58 (1959), 203–210.

Gergen, K., and R. Bauer. "The Interactive Effects of Self-esteem and Task Difficulty on Social Conformity," *Journal of Personality and Social Psychology,* 6 (1967), 16–22.

———, and D. Marlowe (eds.). *Personality and Social Behavior.* Reading, Mass.: Addison-Wesley, 1969.

Hovland, C. I. *The Order of Presentation in Persuasion.* New Haven, Conn.: Yale University Press, 1957.

———, O. J. Harvey, and M. Sherif. "Assimilation and Contrast Effects in Reactions to Communication and Attitude Change," *Journal of Abnormal and Social Psychology,* 55 (1957), 244–252

———, and I. L. Janis (eds.). *Personality and Persuasibility.* New Haven, Conn.: Yale University Press, 1959.

———, ———, and H. H. Kelley. *Communication and Persuasion.* New Haven, Conn.: Yale University Press, 1953.

———, A. Lumsdaine, and F. Sheffield. *Experiments on Mass Communication.* Princeton, N. J.: Princeton University Press, 1949.

———, and W. Mandell. "An Experimental Comparison of Conclusion-Drawing by the Communicator and by the Audience," *Journal of Abnormal and Social Psychology,* 47 (1952), 581–588.

———, and W. Weiss. "The Influence of Source Credibility on Communication Effectiveness," *Public Opinion Quarterly,* 15 (1951), 635–650.

Janis, I. L. "Effects of Fear Arousal on Attitude Change: Recent Developments in Theory and Experimental Research," in L. Berkowitz (ed.), *Advances in Experimental Social Psychology,* Vol. 3. New York: Academic Press, 1967, pp. 167–222.

———, and S. Feshbach. "Effects of Fear-Arousing Communications," *Journal of Abnormal and Social Psychology,* 48 (1953), 78–92.

———, and J. B. Gilmore. "The Influence of Incentive Conditions on the Success of Role-Playing in Modifying Attitudes," *Journal of Personality and Social Psychology,* 1 (1965), 17–27.

————, and **B. T. King.** "The Influence of Role-Playing on Opinion Change," *Journal of Abnormal and Social Psychology,* 49 (1954), 211–218.

————, and ————. "Comparison of the Effectiveness of Improvised Versus Non-Improvised Role-Playing In Producing Opinion Changes," *Human Relations,* 9 (1956), 177–186.

————, and **L. Mann.** "Effectiveness of Emotional Role-Playing in Modifying Smoking Habits and Attitudes," *Journal of Experimental Research in Personality,* 1 (1965), 84–90.

————, and ————. "A Follow-up Study on the Long-term Effects of Emotional Role-Playing," *Journal of Personality and Social Psychology,* 8 (1968), 339–342.

Jones, R. A., D. E. Linder, C. A. Kiesler, M. P. Zanna, and J. W. Brehm. "Internal States or External Stimuli: Observers' Attitude Judgements and the Dissonance Theory—Self-persuasion Controversy," *Journal of Experimental Social Psychology,* 4 (1968), 247–269.

Leventhal, H. "Fear—For Your Health," in *Readings in Psychology Today,* 2nd ed. Del Mar, Calif.: CRM Books, 1972, pp. 627–631.

McGuire, W. J. "Order of Presentation as a Factor in Conditioning Persuasiveness," in C. I. Hovland (ed.), *The Order of Presentation in Persuasion.* New Haven, Conn.: Yale University Press, 1957, pp. 98–114.

Miller, N., and D. Campbell. "Recency and Primacy in Persuasion as a Function of the Timing of Speeches and Measurements," *Journal of Abnormal and Social Psychology,* 59 (1959), 1–9.

Nel, E., R. Helmreich, and E. Aronson. "Opinion Change in the Advocate as a Function of the Persuasibility of His Audience: A Clarification of the Meaning of Dissonance," *Journal of Personality and Social Psychology,* 12 (1969), 117–124.

Osgood, C. E., and P. H. Tannenbaum. "The Principle of Congruity in the Prediction of Attitude Change," *Psychological Review,* 62 (1955), 42–55.

Piliavin, J. A., I. M. Piliavin, E. P. Loewenton, C. McCauley, and P. Hammond. "On Observers' Reproductions of Dissonance Effects: The Right Answers for the Wrong Reasons?" *Journal of Personality and Social Psychology,* 13 (1969), 98–106.

Sherif, M., and C. Hovland. *Social Judgement.* New Haven, Conn.: Yale University Press, 1961.

Skinner, B. F. *Beyond Freedom and Dignity.* New York: Knopf, 1971.

Wilkins, W. "Desensitization: Social and Cognitive Factors Underlying the Effectiveness of Wolpe's Procedure," *Psychological Bulletin,* 76 (1971), 311–317.

10

Asch, S. "Studies of Independence and Conformity: A Minority of One Against a Unanimous Majority," *Psychological Monographs,* 70(1956), Whole No. 416.

Brehm, J. W. *A Theory of Psychological Reactance.* New York: Academic Press, 1966.

Carlsmith, J. M., and A. E. Gross. "Some Effects of Guilt on Compliance," *Journal of Personality and Social Psychology,* 11 (1969), 232–239.

Carnegie, D. *How to Win Friends and Influence People.* New York: Simon and Schuster, 1936.

Crutchfield, R. S. "Conformity and Character," *American Psychologist,* 10 (1955), 191–198.

Elms, A. C., and S. Milgram. "Personality Characteristics Associated with Obedience and Defiance Toward Authoritative Command," *Journal of Experimental Research in Personality,* 1 (1966), 282–289.

Festinger, L. "A Theory of Social Comparison Processes," *Human Relations,* 7 (1954), 117–140.

Freedman, J. L., and A. N. Doob. *Deviancy.* New York: Academic Press, 1968.

————, and **S. C. Fraser.** "Compliance Without Pressure: The Foot-in-the-Door Technique," *Journal of Personality and Social Psychology,* 4 (1966), 195–202.

Kant, H., and M. Goldstein. "Pornography," *Psychology Today,* 4 (1970), 58–61.

Kelman, H. C. "Processes of Opinion Change," *Public Opinion Quarterly,* 25 (1961), 57–78.

London, H. *Psychology of the Persuader.* Morristown, N. J.: General Learning Press, 1973.

————, **D. McSeveney, and R. Tropper.** "Confidence, Overconfidence, and Persuasion," *Human Relations,* 24 (1971), 359–369.

————, **P. Meldman, and A. V. Lanckton.** "The Jury Method: How the Persuader Persuades," *Public Opinion Quarterly,* 34 (1971), 171–183.

McGuire, W. J. "Inducing Resistance Persuasion: Some Contemporary Approaches," in L. Berkowitz (ed.), *Advances in Experimental Social Psychology.* New York: Academic Press, 1964, pp. 192–227.

Milgram, S. "Nationality and Conformity," *Scientific American,* 205 (1961), 45–51.

————. "Behavioral Study of Obedience," *Journal of Abnormal and Social Psychology,* 67 (1963), 371–378.

————. "Some Conditions of Obedience and Disobedience to Authority," *Human Relations,* 18 (1965), 57–75.

Miller, A. *Death of a Salesman.* New York: Viking Press, 1949.

Schachter, S. "Deviation, Rejection, and Communication," *Journal of Abnormal and Social Psychology,* 46 (1951), 190–207.

Sherif, M. "A Study of Some Social Factors in Perception," *Archives of Psychology,* No. 187 (1935).

Tuddenham, R. D., and P. MacBride. "The Yielding Experiment from the Subject's Point of View," *Journal of Personality,* 27 (1959), 259–271.

11

Ardrey, R. *The Territorial Imperative.* New York: Atheneum, 1966.

Azrin, N. H., R. R. Hutchinson, and R. D. Sallery. "Pain Aggression Toward Inanimate Objects," *Journal of the Experimental Analysis of Behavior,* 7 (1964), 223–228.

Bandura, A. "Influence of Model's Reinforcement Contingencies on the Acquisition of Imitative Responses," *Journal of Personality and Social Psychology,* 1 (1965), 589–595.

————, **D. Ross, and S. A. Ross.** "Imitation of Film-Mediated Aggressive Models," *Journal of Abnormal and Social Psychology,* 66 (1963a), 3–11.

————, ————, and ————. "Vicarious Reinforcement and Imitative Learning," *Journal of Abnormal and Social Psychology,* 67 (1963b), 601–607.

Barker, R. G., T. Dembo, and K. Lewin. "Frustration and Regression: An Experiment with Young Children," *University of Iowa Studies in Child Welfare,* 18 (1941), 1–314.

Baron, R. A. "Aggression as a Function of Audience Presence and Prior Anger Arousal," *Journal of Experimental Social Psychology,* 7 (1971a), 515–523.

————. "Aggression as a Function of Magnitude of Victim's Pain Cues, Level of Prior Anger Arousal, and Aggressor-Victim Similarity," *Journal of Personality and Social Psychology,* 18 (1971b), 48–54.

————. "Reducing the Influence of an Aggressive Model: The Restraining Effects of Peer Censure," *Journal of Experimental Social Psychology,* 8 (1972), 266–275.

————, and **C. R. Kepner.** "Model's Behavior and Attraction Toward the Model as Determinants of Adult Aggressive Behavior," *Journal of Personality and Social Psychology,* 14 (1970), 335–344.

Bettelheim, B. "Individual and Mass Behavior in Extreme Situations," *Journal of Abnormal and Social Psychology,* 38 (1943), 417–452.

Brown, P., and R. Elliott. "Control of Aggression in a Nursery School Class," *Journal of Experimental Child Psychology, 2* (1965), 103–107.

DeCharms, R., and E. J. Wilkins. "Some Effects of Verbal Expression of Hostility," *Journal of Abnormal and Social Psychology,* 66 (1963), 462–470.

Deur, J. D., and R. D. Parke. "Effects of Inconsistent Punishment on Aggression in Children," *Developmental Psychology, 2* (1970), 403–411.

Dollard, J., L. W. Doob, N. E. Miller, O. H. Mowrer, and R. R. Sears. *Frustration and Aggression.* New Haven, Conn.: Yale University Press, 1939.

Eisenhower, M. S. (chairman). *National Commission on the Causes and Prevention of Violence.* Washington, D. C.: US Government Printing Office, 1969.

Estes, W. K. "An Experimental Study of Punishment," *Psychological Monographs, 57* (1944), Whole No. 263.

Feshbach, S. "The Drive-Reducing Function of Fantasy Behavior," *Journal of Abnormal and Social Psychology,* 50 (1955), 3–11.

Festinger, L., A. Pepitone, and T. Newcomb. "Some Consequences of De-Individuation in a Group," *Journal of Abnormal and Social Psychology,* 47 (1952), 382–389.

Geen, R. G. "Effects of Frustration, Attack and Prior Training in Aggressiveness Upon Aggressive Behavior," *Journal of Personality and Social Psychology,* 9 (1968), 316–321.

Gentry, W. D. "Effects of Frustration, Attack, and Prior Aggressive Training on Overt Aggression and Vascular Processes," *Journal of Personality and Social Psychology,* 16 (1970), 718–725.

Gerbner, G. "Violence in Television Drama: Trends and Symbolic Functions," in G. A. Comstock and E. A. Rubenstein (eds.), *Television and Social Behavior, Vol. 1: Media Content and Control.* Washington, D. C.: US Government Printing Office, 1972, pp. 28–187.

Greenwell, J., and H. A. Dengerink. "The Role of Perceived Versus Actual Attack in Human Physical Aggression," *Journal of Personality and Social Psychology,* 26 (1973), 66–71.

Haney, C., C. Banks, and P. G. Zimbardo. "Interpersonal Dynamics in a Simulated Prison," *International Journal of Crime and Penology,* 1 (1973), 69–97.

Hovland, C. I., and R. R. Sears. "Minor Studies in Aggression, VI : Correlation of Lynchings With Economic Indices," *Journal of Psychology,* 9 (1940), 301–310.

Kerner, O. (chairman). *Report of the National Advisory Commission on Civil Disorders.* New York Times editors. New York: Dutton, 1968.

Klapper, J. T. "The Impact of Viewing 'Aggression': Studies and Problems of Extrapolation," in C. N. Larsen (ed.), *Violence and the Mass Media.* New York: Harper & Row, 1968, pp. 131–139.

Lorenz, K. *On Aggression.* New York: Harcourt, Brace & World, 1966.

Mallick, S. K., and B. R. McCandless. "A Study of Catharsis of Aggression," *Journal of Personality and Social Psychology, 4* (1966), 591–596.

Milgram, S. "Behavioral Study of Obedience," *Journal of Abnormal and Social Psychology,* 67 (1963), 371–378.

———. "Liberating Effects of Group Pressure," *Journal of Personality and Social Psychology,* 1 (1965), 127–134.

Miller, N. E. "The Frustration-Aggression Hypothesis," *Psychological Review,* 48 (1941), 337–342.

———. "Theory and Experiment Relating Psychoanalytic Displacement to Stimulus-Response Generalization," *Journal of Abnormal and Social Psychology,* 43 (1948), 155–178.

———, and R. Bugelski. "The Influence of Frustrations Imposed by the In-Group on Attitude Expressed Toward Out-Groups," *Journal of Psychology,* 25 (1948), 437–442.

Montagu, M. F. A. *Man and Aggression.* Fairlawn, N. J.: Oxford University Press, 1968.

O'Kelly, L., and L. Steckle. "A Note on Long Enduring Emotional Responses in the Rat," *Journal of Psychology,* 8 (1939), 125–131.

Patterson, G. R., R. A. Littman, and W. Bricker. "Assertive Behavior in Children: A Step Toward a Theory of Aggression," *Monographs of the Society For Research in Child Development,* 32 (1967), 1–43.

Pisano, R., and S. P. Taylor. "Reduction of Physical Aggression: The Effects of Four Strategies," *Journal of Personality and Social Psychology,* 19 (1971), 237–242.

Rosenbaum, D. E. "Protest Leader Condemns Daley," *New York Times,* December 3, 1968, p. 28.

Smith, D. E., M. B. King, and B. G. Hoebel. "Lateral Hypothalamic Control of Killing: Evidence For a Cholinoceptive Mechanism," *Science,* 167 (1970), 900–901.

Stein, A. H., L. K. Friederich, and F. Vondracek. "Television Content and Young Children's Behavior," in G. A. Comstock and E. A. Rubenstein (eds.), *Television and Social Behavior, Vol. 2 : Television and Social Learning.* Washington, D. C.: US Government Printing Office, 1972, pp. 202–317.

Steuer, F. B., J. M. Applefield, and R. Smith. "Televised Aggression and the Interpersonal Aggression of Preschool Children," *Journal of Experimental Child Psychology,* 11 (1971), 442–447.

Tilker, H. A. "Socially Responsible Behavior as a Function of Observer Responsibility and Victim Feedback," *Journal of Personality and Social Psychology,* 14 (1970), 95–100.

Walters, R. H., and M. A. Brown. "Studies of Reinforcement of Aggression, Part III : Transfer of Responses to an Interpersonal Situation," *Child Development,* 34 (1963), 563–572.

———, and E. L. Thomas. "Enhancement of Punitiveness by Visual and Audiovisual Displays," *Canadian Journal of Psychology,* 17 (1963), 244–255.

Wheeler, L., and S. Smith. "Censure of the Model in the Contagion of Aggression," *Journal of Personality and Social Psychology,* 6 (1967), 93–98.

Zillman, D. "Excitation Transfer in Communication-Mediated Aggressive Behavior," *Journal of Experimental Social Psychology,* 7 (1971), 419–434.

Zimbardo, P. G. "The Human Choice: Individuation, Reason and Order Versus Deindividuation, Impulse, and Chaos," in W. J. Arnold and D. Levine (eds.), *Nebraska Symposium on Motivation, 1969.* Lincoln: University of Nebraska Press, 1970, pp. 237–307.

12

Allen, H. "Bystander Intervention and Helping on the Subway," in L. Bickman and T. Henchy (eds.), *Beyond the Laboratory: Field Research in Social Psychology.* New York: McGraw-Hill, 1972, pp. 22–33.

Berkowitz, L., and W. H. Connor. "Success, Failure and Social Responsibility," *Journal of Personality and Social Psychology, 4* (1966), 664–669.

———, and L. R. Daniels. "Responsibility and Dependency," *Journal of Abnormal and Social Psychology,* 66 (1963), 429–436.

Berscheid, E., and E. Walster. *Interpersonal Attraction.* Reading, Mass.: Addison-Wesley, 1969.

Bickman, L. "The Effect of Another Bystander's Ability to Help on Bystander Intervention in an Emergency," *Journal of Experimental Social Psychology,* 7 (1971), 367–379.

Bramel, D. "Interpersonal Attraction, Hostility, and Perception," in J. Mills (ed.), *Experimental Social Psychology.* New York: Macmillan, 1969, pp. 1–120.

Brehm, J., and A. Cole. "Effect of a Favor Which Reduces Freedom," *Journal of Personality and Social Psychology,* 3 (1966), 420–426.

Bryan, J., and M. Test. "Models and Helping: Naturalistic Studies in Aiding Behavior," *Journal of Personality and Social Psychology,* 6 (1967), 400–407.

———, and N. Walbek. "Preaching and Practicing Generosity: Children's Actions and Reactions," *Child Development,* 41 (1970), 329–353.

Darley, J. "Diffusion of Responsibility and Helping Behavior" (paper presented at the 78th Annual Meeting of the American Psychological Association, September 1970).

———, and B. Latané. "Bystander Intervention in Emergencies: Diffusion of Responsibility," *Journal of Personality and Social Psychology,* 8 (1968), 377–383.

Feldman, R. E. "Response to Compatriot and Foreigner Who Seek Assistance," *Journal of Personality and Social Psychology,* 10 (1968), 202–214.

Fisher, R. "The Effects of Guilt and Shame on Public and Private Helping," *Dissertation Abstracts,* 31 (1971), 6897–6898.

Floyd, J. "Effects of Amount of Reward and Friendship Status of the Other on the Frequency of Sharing in Children," *Dissertation Abstracts,* 25 (1964), 5396–5397.

Freedman, J., and S. Fraser. "Compliance Without Pressure: The Foot-in-the-Door Technique," *Journal of Personality and Social Psychology,* 4 (1966), 195–202.

———, S. Wallington, and E. Bless. "Compliance Without Pressure: The Effect of Guilt," *Journal of Personality and Social Psychology,* 7 (1967), 117–124.

Gergen, K. J., and M. M. Gergen. "International Assistance From a Psychological Perspective," *Yearbook of World Affairs,* Vol. 25. London: Institute of World Affairs, 1971, pp. 87–103.

Goranson, R., and L. Berkowitz. "Reciprocity and Responsibility Reactions to Prior Help," *Journal of Personality and Social Psychology,* 3 (1966), 227–232.

Gouldner, A. "The Norm of Reciprocity," *American Sociological Review,* 25 (1960), 161–178.

Grusec, J. E., and S. L. Skubiski. "Model Nurturance, Demand Characteristics of the Modeling Experiment, and Altruism," *Journal of Personality and Social Psychology,* 14(1970), 352–359.

Harris, M. "Some Determinants of Sharing in Children," *Dissertation Abstracts,* 29 (1968), 2633.

Hartup, W. W., and B. Coates. "Imitation of a Peer as a Function of Reinforcement From the Peer Group and the Rewardingness of the Model," *Child Development,* 38 (1967), 1003–1016.

Hebb, D. O. "Comment on Altruism: The Comparative Evidence," *Psychological Bulletin,* 76 (1971), 409–410.

Heider, F. *The Psychology of Interpersonal Relations.* New York: Wiley, 1958.

Hornstein, H. A., E. Fisch, and M. Holmes. "Influence of a Model's Feeling About His Behavior and His Relevance as a Comparison Other on Observers' Helping Behavior," *Journal of Personality and Social Psychology,* 10 (1968), 222–226.

Isen, A. M. "Success, Failure, Attention, and Reaction to Others," *Journal of Personality and Social Psychology,* 15 (1970), 294–301.

———, and P. F. Levin. "Effects of Feeling Good on Helping: Cookies and Kindness," *Journal of Personality and Social Psychology,* 21 (1972), 384–388.

Kanfer, F., and J. Philips. *Learning Foundations of Behavior Therapy.* New York: Wiley, 1970.

Kazdin, A. E., and J. H. Bryan. "Competence and Volunteering," *Journal of Experimental Social Psychology,* 7 (1971), 87–97.

Kimble, G., and L. C. Perlmuter. "The Problem of Volition," *Psychological Review,* 77 (1970), 361–384.

Konecni, V. J. "Some Effects of Guilt on Compliance: A Field Replication," *Journal of Personality and Social Psychology,* 23 (1972), 30–32.

Korte, C. "Effects of Individual Responsibility and Group Communication on Help-Giving in an Emergency," *Human Relations,* 24 (1971), 149–159.

Krebs, D. L. "Altruism—An Examination of the Concept and a Review of the Literature," *Psychological Bulletin,* 73 (1970), 258–302.

Latané, B., and J. M. Darley. "Group Inhibition of Bystander Intervention in Emergencies," *Journal of Personality and Social Psychology,* 10 (1968), 215–221.

———, and J. Rodin. "A Lady in Distress: Inhibiting Effects of Friends and Strangers on Bystander Intervention," *Journal of Experimental Social Psychology,* 5 (1969), 189–202.

Lerner, M. J. "The Desire for Justice and Reactions to Victims," in J. Macaulay and L. Berkowitz (eds.), *Altruism and Helping Behavior.* New York: Academic Press, 1970, pp. 205–230.

———, and C. H. Simmons. "Observer's Reactions to the 'Innocent Victim': Compassion or Rejection?" *Journal of Personality and Social Psychology,* 4 (1966), 203–210.

Midlarsky, E. "Some Antecedents of Aiding Under Stress," *Proceedings of the 76th Annual Convention of the American Psychological Association,* 3 (1968), 385–386.

———. "Aiding Under Stress: The Effects of Competence, Dependency, Visibility and Fatalism," *Journal of Personality,* 39 (1971), 132–149.

Midlarsky, M., and E. Midlarsky. "Additive and Interactive Status Effects on Altruistic Behavior," *Proceedings of the 80th Annual Convention of the American Psychological Association,* 7 (1972), 213–214.

Mills, J., and R. Egger. "Effect on Derogation of a Victim of Choosing to Reduce His Distress," *Journal of Personality and Social Psychology,* 23 (1972), 405–408.

Moore, B. S., B. Underwood, and D. Rosenhan. "Affect and Self-gratification," *Developmental Psychology,* 8 (1973), 209–214.

Morse, S. "Expectations and Task Reward Structure as Factors Affecting Reactions to Aid Receipt and Denial," *Dissertation Abstracts International,* 32 (1972), 4109.

Muir, D., and E. Weinstein. "The Social Debt: An Investigation of Lower-class and Middle-class Norms of Social Obligation," *American Sociological Review,* 27 (1962), 532–539.

Parsons, T. *The Social System.* New York: Free Press, 1951.

Presbie, R. J., and P. F. Coiteux. "Learning to be Generous or Stingy: Imitation of Sharing Behavior as a Function of Model Generosity and Vicarious Reinforcement," *Child Development,* 42 (1971), 1033–1038.

Pruitt, D. G. "Reciprocity and Credit Building in a Laboratory Dyad," *Journal of Personality and Social Psychology,* 8 (1968), 143–147.

Rawlings, E. I. "Witnessing Harm to Other: A Reassessment of the Role of Guilt in Altruistic Behavior," *Journal of Personality and Social Psychology,* 10 (1968), 377–380.

Rettig, S. "An Exploratory Study of Altruism," *Dissertation Abstracts,* 16 (1956), 2229–2230.

Rosenbaum, M., and R. Blake. "Volunteering as a Function of Field Structure," *Journal of Abnormal and Social Psychology,* 50 (1955), 193–196.

Rosenhan, D. L. "The Natural Socialization of Altruistic Autonomy," in J. Macaulay and L. Berkowitz (eds.), *Altruism and Helping Behavior.* New York: Academic Press, 1970, pp. 251–268.

Ross, A. S. "The Effect of Observing a Helpful Model on Helping Behavior," *Journal of Social Psychology,* 81 (1970), 131–132.

Sawyer, J. "The Altruism Scale: A Measure of Cooperative, Individualistic, and Competitive Interpersonal Orientation," *American Journal of Sociology,* 71 (1966), 407–416.

Schopler, J. "An Investigation of Sex Differences on the Influence of Dependence," *Sociometry,* 30 (1967), 50–67.

———, and N. Bateson. "The Power of Dependence," *Journal of Personality and Social Psychology,* 2 (1965), 247–254.

———, and M. Matthews. "The Influence of the Perceived Causal Locus of Partner's Dependence on the Use of Interpersonal Power," *Journal of Personality and Social Psychology,* 2 (1965), 609–612.

———, and V. Thompson. "The Role of Attribution Processes in Mediating Amount of Reciprocity For a Favor," *Journal of Personality and Social Psychology,* 10 (1968), 243–250.

Schwartz, S. H., and G. Clausen. "Responsibility, Norms, and Helping in an Emergency," *Journal of Personality and Social Psychology,* 16 (1970), 299–310.

Staub, E. "A Child in Distress: The Influence of Age and Number of Witnesses on Children's Attempts to Help," *Journal of Personality and Social Psychology,* 14 (1970), 130–140.

——, and L. Sherk. "Need For Approval, Children's Sharing Behavior, and Reciprocity in Sharing," *Child Development,* 41 (1970), 243–253.

Teger, A. "Defining the Socially Responsible Response" (paper presented at the 78th Annual Meeting of the American Psychological Association, 1970).

Tesser, A., R. Gatewood, and M. Driver. "Some Determinants of Gratitude," *Journal of Personality and Social Psychology,* 19 (1968), 233–236.

Trivers, R. L. "The Evolution of Reciprocal Altruism," *The Quarterly Review of Biology,* 46 (1971), 35–57.

Wagner, C., and L. Wheeler. "Model, Need, and Cost Effects in Helping Behavior," *Journal of Personality and Social Psychology,* 12 (1969), 111–116.

Wilke, H., and J. T. Lanzetta. "The Obligation to Help: The Effects of Amount of Prior Help on Subsequent Helping Behavior," *Journal of Experimental Social Psychology,* 6 (1970), 488–493.

Wright, B. A. "Altruism in Children and the Perceived Conduct of Others," *Journal of Abnormal and Social Psychology,* 37 (1942), 218–233.

Zimbardo, P. "The Human Choice: Individuation, Reason and Order Versus Deindividuation, Impulse and Chaos," in W. J. Arnold and D. Levine (eds.), *Nebraska Symposium on Motivation.* Lincoln: University of Nebraska Press, 1969, pp. 237–307.

13

Adams, J. S. "Inequity in Social Exchange," in L. Berkowitz (ed.), *Advances in Experimental Social Psychology,* Vol. II. New York: Academic Press, pp. 267–299.

——, and P. B. Jacobson. "Effects of Wage Inequities on Work Quality," *Journal of Abnormal and Social Psychology,* 69 (1964), 19–25.

Berlyne, D. E. *Conflict, Arousal, and Curiosity.* New York: McGraw-Hill, 1960.

Bixenstine, V. E., H. M. Potash, and K. V. Wilson. "Effects of Level of Cooperative Choice by the Other Player on Choices in a Prisoner's Dilemma Game, Part I," *Journal of Abnormal and Social Psychology,* 66 (1963), 308–313.

——, and K. V. Wilson. "Effect of Level of Cooperative Choice by the Other Player in a Prisoner's Dilemma Game, Part II," *Journal of Abnormal and Social Psychology,* 67 (1963), 139–148.

Brown, B. R. "The Effects of Need to Maintain Face on Interpersonal Bargaining," *Journal of Experimental Social Psychology,* 4 (1968), 107–122.

Christie, R., and F. L. Geis (eds.). *Studies in Machiavellianism.* New York: Academic Press, 1970.

Clark, J. V. "A Preliminary Investigation of Some Unconscious Assumptions Affecting Labor Efficiency in Eight Supermarkets" (unpublished doctoral dissertation, Graduate School of Business Administration, Harvard University, 1958).

Cooper, J., and E. E. Jones. "Opinion Divergence as a Strategy to Avoid Being Miscast," *Journal of Personality and Social Psychology,* 13 (1969), 23–40.

Crowne, D. P., and B. R. Strickland. "The Conditioning of Verbal Behavior as a Function of the Need for Social Approval," *Journal of Abnormal and Social Psychology,* 63 (1961), 395–401.

Deutsch, M. "The Effect of Motivational Orientation Upon Trust and Suspicion," *Human Relations,* 13 (1960), 123–139.

——, and R. M. Krauss. "The Effect of Threat Upon Interpersonal Bargaining," *Journal of Abnormal and Social Psychology,* 61 (1960), 181–189.

Exline, R. V., J. Thibaut, C. Hickey, and P. Gumpert. "Visual Interaction in Relation to Machiavellianism and An Unethical Act," in R. Christie and F. Geis (eds.), *Studies in Machiavellianism.* New York: Academic Press, 1970, pp. 53–75.

Fromm, E. "Selfishness and Self-love," in C. Gordon and K. Gergen (eds.), *The Self in Social Interaction.* New York: Wiley, 1968, pp. 327–337.

Gallo, P. S. "Effects of Increased Incentives Upon the Use of Threat in Bargaining," *Journal of Personality and Social Psychology,* 4 (1966), 14–20.

Garfinkle, H. *Studies in Ethnomethodology.* Englewood Cliffs, N.J.: Prentice-Hall, 1967.

Geis, F., R. Christie, and C. Nelson. "In Search of the Machiavel," in R. Christie and F. Geis (eds.), *Studies in Machiavellianism.* New York: Academic Press, 1970, pp. 76–95.

Gergen, K. J. "Personal Consistency and the Presentation of Self," in C. Gordon and K. J. Gergen (eds.), *The Self in Social Interaction.* New York: Wiley, 1968, pp. 299–308.

——. "Multiple Identity: The Healthy, Happy Human Being Wears Many Masks," *Psychology Today,* 5 (1972), 31, 64, 66.

——, and M. G. Taylor. "Social Expectancy and Self-Presentation in a Status Hierarchy," *Journal of Experimental Social Psychology,* 5 (1969), 79–92.

——, and B. Wishnov. "Other's Self Evaluations and Interaction Anticipation as Determinants of Self-Presentation," *Journal of Personality and Social Psychology,* 2 (1965), 348–358.

Goffman, E. "On Face-Work: An Analysis of Ritual Elements in Social Interaction," *Psychiatry,* 18 (1955), 213–231.

——. *The Presentation of Self in Everyday Life.* New York: Doubleday, 1959.

——. *Asylums.* New York: Doubleday, 1961.

Gouldner, A. "The Norm of Reciprocity. A Preliminary Statement," *American Sociological Review,* 25 (1960), 161–179.

Jones, E. E. *Ingratiation.* New York: Appleton-Century-Crofts, 1964.

——, K. J. Gergen, and K. Davis. "Some Reactions to Being Approved or Disapproved as a Person," *Psychological Monographs,* No. 521, 76 (1962).

——, P. Gumpert, and J. Thibaut. "Some Conditions Affecting the Use of Ingratiation to Influence Performance Evaluation," *Journal of Personality and Social Psychology,* 1 (1965), 613–625.

Kelley, H. H. "Interpersonal Accommodation," *American Psychologist,* 23 (1968), 399–410.

Kipnis, D. "Does Power Corrupt?" *Journal of Personality and Social Psychology,* 24 (1972), 33–41.

Lane, I., and L. A. Messé. "Equity and the Distribution of Rewards," *Journal of Personality and Social Psychology,* 20 (1971), 1–17.

Lawler, E. E. "Effects of Hourly Overpayment on Productivity and Work Quality," *Journal of Personality and Social Psychology,* 10 (1968), 306–313.

Marlowe, D., K. J. Gergen, and A. Doob. "Opponents' Personality, Expectation of Social Interaction, and Interpersonal Bargaining," *Journal of Personality and Social Psychology,* 3 (1966), 206–213.

Matarazzo, J. D., G. Saslow, A. Wiens, M. Weitman, and B. V. Allen. "Interviewer Head-Nodding and Interviewer Speech Deviations," *Psychotherapy,* 1 (1964), 54–63.

Minas, J. S., A. Scodel, D. Marlowe, and H. Rawson. "Some Descriptive Aspects of Two-Person Non-Zero-Sum Games," *Journal of Conflict Resolution,* 4 (1960), 193–197.

Modigliani, A. "Embarrassment, Face-Work, and Eye-Contact: Testing a Theory of Embarrassment," *Journal of Personality and Social Psychology,* 17 (1971), 15–24.

Rapoport, A., and C. Orwant. "Experimental Games: A Review," *Behavioral Science,* 7 (1972), 1–38.

Riesman, D. *The Lonely Crowd.* New Haven, Conn.: Yale University Press, 1950.

Rogers, C. *On Becoming a Person*. Boston: Houghton Mifflin, 1961.

Rubin, Z., and J. C. Moore. "Assessment of Subjects Suspicions," *Journal of Personality and Social Psychology*, 17 (1971), 163–170.

Schneider, D., and A. Eustis. "Effects of Ingratiation Motivation, Target Positiveness, and Revealingness on Self-Presentation," *Journal of Personality and Social Psychology*, 22 (1972), 149–155.

Sidowski, J. "Reward and Punishment in a Minimal Social Situation," *Journal of Experimental Social Psychology*, 54 (1957), 318–326.

———, L. B. Wyckoff, and L. Tabory. "The Influence of Reinforcement and Punishment in a Minimal Social Situation," *Journal of Abnormal and Social Psychology*, 52 (1956), 115–119.

Simmons, J. *Deviants*. Berkeley, Calif.: Glendessary Press, 1969.

Smith, W. P., and W. A. Leginski. "Magnitude and Precision of Punitive Power in Bargaining Strategy," *Journal of Experimental Social Psychology*, 6 (1970), 57–76.

Thibaut, J. W., and H. H. Kelley. *The Social Psychology of Groups*. New York: Wiley, 1959.

Umeoka, Y., and H. Shnotsuka. "Game Behavior in an Incomplete Information Situation (II): Structural Analysis of Two-Person Non-Zero-Sum Games." (paper presented at the 29th Japanese Psychological Association Convention, 1965a).

———, and ———. "Game Behavior in an Incomplete Information Situation (III): Experiments on Two-person Non-zero-sum Games" (paper presented at the 29th Japanese Psychological Association Convention, 1965b).

Verplanck, W. "The Control of the Content of Conversation: Reinforcement of Statements of Opinion," *Journal of Abnormal and Social Psychology*, 51 (1955), 668–676.

Von Neumann, J., and O. Morgenstern. *Theory of Games and Economic Behavior*. Princeton, N. J.: Princeton University Press, 1944.

Walster, E. "The Effect of Self-esteem on Romantic Liking," *Journal of Experimental Social Psychology*, 1 (1965), 184–197.

Weinstein, A. "Altercasting and Interpersonal Relations," in P. Secord and C. Backman (eds.), *Readings in Social Psychology*. New York: Prentice-Hall, 1967.

14

American Psychiatric Association. *Task Force Report: Encounter Groups and Psychiatry*. Washington, D. C.: American Psychiatric Association, 1970.

Aronoff, J., and L. A. Messé. "Motivational Determinants of Small-Group Structure," *Journal of Personality and Social Psychology*, 17 (1971), 319–324.

Asimov, I., in *Psychology Today: An Introduction*, 2nd ed. Del Mar, Calif.: CRM Books, 1972, p. 471.

Back, K. W. *Beyond Words: The Story of Sensitivity Training and the Encounter Movement*. New York: Russell Sage Foundation, 1972.

Bales, R. F. "The Equilibrium Problem in Small Groups," in T. Parsons, R. F. Bales, and E. A. Shils (eds.), *Working Papers in Theory of Action*. New York: Free Press, 1953, pp. 111–161.

Bavelas, A., A. H. Hastorf, A. E. Gross, and W. R. Kite. "Experiments on the Alteration of Group Structure," *Journal of Experimental Social Psychology*, 1 (1965), 55–70.

Berkowitz, L. "The Expression and Reduction of Hostility," *Psychological Bulletin*, 55 (1958), 257–283.

Birnbaum, M. "Sense About Sensitivity Training," *Saturday Review*, 52 (1969), 82–83.

Blake, R. R., and J. S. Mouton. "Comprehension of Own and of Outgroup Positions Under Intergroup Competition," *The Journal of Conflict Resolution*, 5 (1961a), 304–310.

———, and ———. "Loyalty of Representatives to Ingroup Positions During Intergroup Competition," *Sociometry*, 24 (1961b), 177–183.

Cartwright, D., and A. Zander. *Group Dynamics*, 3rd ed. New York: Harper & Row, 1968.

Collins, B. E., and B. H. Raven. "Group Structure: Attraction, Coalitions, Communication, and Power," in G. Lindzey and E. Aronson (eds.), *The Handbook of Social Psychology*, Vol. 4, 2nd ed. Reading, Mass.: Addison-Wesley, 1969, pp. 102–204.

Dunnette, M. D., and J. P. Campbell. "Effectiveness of T-Group Experiences in Managerial Training and Development," *Psychological Bulletin*, 70 (1968), 73–104.

Festinger, L. "Informal Social Communication," *Psychological Review*, 57 (1950), 271–282.

———. "Group Attraction and Membership," in D. Cartwright and A. Zander (eds.), *Group Dynamics: Research and Theory*. Evanston, Ill.: Row, Peterson, 1953, pp. 92–101.

———, S. Schachter, and K. Back. *Social Pressures in Informal Groups*. New York: Harper & Row, 1950.

French, J. R., Jr., and B. Raven. "The Bases of Social Power," in D. Cartwright (ed.), *Studies of Social Power*. Ann Arbor, Mich.: Institute for Social Research, 1959, pp. 150–167.

Gerard, H. B., and J. M. Rabbie. "Fears and Social Comparisons," *Journal of Abnormal and Social Psychology*, 62 (1961), 586–592.

Gibb, J. R. "Meaning of the Small Group Experience," in L. N. Solomon and B. Berzon (eds.), *New Perspectives on Encounter Groups*. San Francisco: Jossey-Bass, 1972, pp. 1–12.

Halpin, A. W., and B J. Winer. *The Leadership Behavior of the Airplane Commander*. Columbus: Ohio State University Research Foundation, 1952.

Hollander, E. P. "Conformity, Status and Idiosyncrasy Credit," *Psychological Review*, 65 (1958), 117–127.

———. "Competence and Conformity in the Acceptance of Influence," *Journal of Abnormal and Social Psychology*, 61 (1960), 365–369.

———, and J. W. Julian. "Contemporary Trends in the Analysis of Leadership Processes," *Psychological Bulletin*, 71 (1969), 387–397.

Jaffe, S. L., and D. J. Scherl. "Acute Psychosis Precipitated by T-Group Experiences," *Archives of General Psychiatry*, 21 (1969), 443–448.

Kissel, S. "Stress Reducing Properties of Social Stimuli," *Journal of Personality and Social Psychology*, 2 (1965), 378–384.

Lefebre, L. B. "Existentialism and Psychotherapy," *Review of Existential Psychology and Psychiatry*, 3 (1963), 271–285.

Lieberman, M., I. Yalom, and M. Miles. "The Impact of Encounter Groups on Participants: Some Preliminary Findings," *Journal of Applied Behavioral Science*, 8 (1972), 29–50.

Lott, A. J., and B. E. Lott. "Group Cohesiveness as Interpersonal Attraction: A Review of Relationships with Antecedent and Consequent Variables," *Psychological Bulletin*, 64 (1965), 259–302.

Luke, R. "The Internal Normative Structure of Sensitivity Training Groups," *Journal of Applied Behavioral Science*, 8 (1972), 421–437.

Mann, R. D. "A Review of the Relationships Between Personality and Performance in Small Groups," *Psychological Bulletin*, 56 (1959), 241–270.

Marquis, D. G., H. Guetzkow, and R. W. Heyns. "A Social Psychological Study of the Decision-Making Conference," in H. Guetzkow (ed.), *Groups, Leadership and Men.* Pittsburgh, Penn.: Carnegie Press, 1951, pp. 55–57.

Moreno, J. L. *Who Shall Survive?* Washington, D. C.: Nervous and Mental Disease Pub., 1934.

Myers, A. "Team Competition, Success and the Adjustment of Group Members," *Journal of Abnormal and Social Psychology,* 65 (1962), 25–32.

Newcomb, T. M. *Personality and Social Change.* New York: Holt, Rinehart and Winston, 1943.

Rogers, C. R. "Process of the Basic Encounter Group," in J. F. Bugental (ed.), *Challenges of Humanistic Psychology.* New York: McGraw-Hill, 1967.

Schachter, S. "Deviation, Rejection and Communication," *Journal of Abnormal and Social Psychology,* 46 (1951), 190–207.
———. *The Psychology of Affiliation.* Stanford, Calif.: Stanford University Press, 1959.
———, and H. Burdick. "A Field Experiment on Rumor Transmission and Distortion," *Journal of Abnormal and Social Psychology,* 50 (1955), 363–371.
———, J. Nuttin, C. De Monchaux, P. H. Maucorps, D. Osmer, H. Duijker, R. Rommetveit, and J. Israel. "Cross-Cultural Experiments on Threat and Rejection," *Human Relations,* 7 (1954), 403–439.

Seashore, S. *Group Cohesiveness in the Industrial Work Group.* Ann Arbor, Mich.: Institute for Social Research, 1954.

Shaw, M. E. *Group Dynamics: The Psychology of Small Group Behavior.* New York: McGraw-Hill, 1971.

Sherif, M., O. J. Harvey, B. J. White, W. R. Hood, and C. W. Sherif. *Intergroup Conflict and Cooperation: The Robbers' Cave Experiment.* Norman: University of Oklahoma, Institute of Group Relations, 1961.

Singer, J. E., and V. L. Shockley. "Ability and Affiliation," *Journal of Personality and Social Psychology,* 1 (1965), 95–100.

Thibaut, J. W., and H. H. Kelley. *The Social Psychology of Groups.* New York: Wiley, 1959.

Tuckman, B. W. "Developmental Sequence in Small Group," *Psychological Bulletin,* 63 (1965), 384–399.

Wiggins, J. A., F. Dill, and R. D. Schwartz. "On 'Status-Liability'," *Sociometry,* 28 (1965), 197–209.

15

Allport, F. H. "The Influence of the Group Upon Association and Thoughts," *Journal of Experimental Psychology,* 3 (1920), 159–182.
———. *Social Psychology.* Boston: Houghton Mifflin, 1924.

Asch, S. E. "Effects of Group Pressure Upon the Modification and Distortion of Judgments," in H. Guetzkow (ed.), *Groups, Leadership and Men.* Pittsburgh, Penn.: Carnegie Press, 1951, pp. 177–190.

Bavelas, A. "Communication Patterns in Task-Oriented Groups," *Journal of the Acoustical Society of America,* 22 (1950), 725–730.

Bergum, B. O., and D. J. Lehr. "Effects of Authoritarianism on Vigilance Performance," *Journal of Applied Psychology,* 47 (1963), 75–77.

Bronfenbrenner, U. "The Mirror Image in Soviet-American Relations: A Social Psychologist's Report," *Journal of Social Issues,* 17 (1961), 45–56.

Brown, R. *Social Psychology.* New York: Free Press, 1965.

Cartwright, D. "Risk Taking by Individuals and Groups: An Assessment of Research Employing Choice Dilemmas," *Journal of Personality and Social Psychology,* 20 (1971), 361–378.
———, and A. Zander. *Group Dynamics,* 3rd ed. New York: Harper & Row, 1968.

Castore, C. H. "Diversity of Group Member Preferences and Commitment to Group Decisions," *Annals of the New York Academy of Sciences* (in press).

Coleman, J. S. *Community Conflict.* New York: Free Press, 1957.

Collins, B. E., and H. Guetzkow. *A Social Psychology of Group Processes for Decision Making.* New York: Wiley, 1964.

Dashiell, J. F. "An Experimental Analysis of Some Group Effects," *Journal of Abnormal and Social Psychology,* 25 (1930), 190–199.
———. "Experimental Studies of the Influence of Social Situations on the Behavior of Individual Human Adults," in C. Murchison (ed.), *Handbook of Social Psychology.* Worcester, Mass.: Clark University Press, 1935, pp. 1097–1158.

Davis, J. H., and F. Restle. "The Analysis of Problems and Prediction of Group Problem Solving," *Journal of Abnormal and Social Psychology,* 66 (1963), 103–116.

Deutsch, M. A. "A Psychological Approach to International Conflict," in G. Sperazzo (ed.), *Psychology and International Relations.* Washington, D. C.: Georgetown University Press, 1965, pp. 1–19.

Driver, M. J. "A Structural Analysis of Aggression, Stress and Personality in an Inter-Nation Simulation," Institute Paper 97. Purdue University: Institute for Research in the Behavioral Economic and Management Sciences, 1965.

Etzioni, A. *Winning Without War.* Garden City, N. Y.: Doubleday, 1964.

Exline, R. V., and R. C. Ziller. "Status Congruency and Interpersonal Conflict in Decision Making Groups," *Human Relations,* 12 (1959), 147–162.

Fiedler, F. E. "A Contingency Model of Leadership Effectiveness," in L. Berkowitz (ed.), *Advances in Experimental Social Psychology.* New York: Academic Press, 1964, pp. 149–190.
———. "Personality and Situational Determinants of Leadership Effectiveness," in D. Cartwright and A. Zander (eds.), *Group Dynamics,* 3rd ed. New York: Harper & Row, 1968, pp. 362–380.

Gergen, K., and M. Gergen. "International Assistance in Psychological Perspective," *Yearbook of World Affairs,* 25 (1971), 87–103.
———, and ———. "Understanding Foreign Assistance Through Public Opinion," *Yearbook of World Affairs,* 27 (1973).
———, ———, and K. Meter. "Individual Orientation to Pro-Social Behavior," *Journal of Social Issues,* 28 (1972), 105–130.
———, and S. Morse. "Material Aid and Social Attraction," *Journal of Applied Social Psychology,* 1 (1971), 150–162.

Gibb, C. A. "Leadership," in G. Lindzey and E. Aronson (eds.), *The Handbook of Social Psychology,* Vol. 4, 2nd ed. Reading, Mass.: Addison-Wesley, 1969, pp. 205–282.

Gilchrist, J. C., M. E. Shaw, and L. C. Walker. "Some Effects of Unequal Distribution of Information in a Wheel Group Structure," *Journal of Abnormal and Social Psychology,* 49 (1954), 554–556.

Guetzkow, H. "A Use of Simulation in the Study of Inter-National Relations," *Behavioral Science,* 4 (1959), 183–191.
———. "Some Correspondences Between Simulations and 'Realities' in International Relations," in M. Kaplan (ed.), *New Approaches to International Relations.* New York: St. Martin's Press, 1968, pp. 202–269.

Hall, E. J., J. S. Mouton, and R. R. Blake. "Group Problem Solving Effectiveness Under Conditions of Pooling Versus Interaction," *Journal of Social Psychology,* 59 (1963), 147–157.

Hare, A. P. "A Study of Interaction and Consensus in Different Sized Groups," *American Sociological Review,* 17 (1952), 261–267.

Higbee, K. L. "Expression of 'Walter Mitty-ness' in Actual Behavior," *Journal of Personality and Social Psychology,* 20 (1971), 416–422.

Hoffman, L. R., E. Harburg, and N. R. Maier. "Differences and Disagreement as Factors in Creative Group Problem Solving," *Journal of Abnormal and Social Psychology,* 64 (1962), 206–214.

Homans, G. C. *The Human Group.* New York: Harcourt, Brace & World, 1950.

Husband, R. W. "Analysis of Methods in Human Maze Learning," *Journal of Genetic Psychology,* 39 (1931), 258–277.

Kelley, H. H., and J. W. Thibaut. "Experimental Studies of Group Problem Solving and Process," in G. Lindzey (ed.), *Handbook of Social Psychology,* Vol. 2, 1st ed. Reading, Mass.: Addison-Wesley, 1954, pp. 735–785.

———, and ———. "Group Problem Solving," in G. Lindzey and E. Aronson (eds.), *The Handbook of Social Psychology,* Vol. 4, 2nd ed. Reading, Mass.: Addison-Wesley, 1969, pp. 1–101.

Krech, D., R. S. Crutchfield, and E. L. Ballachey. *Individual in Society,* 2nd ed. New York: McGraw-Hill, 1962.

Leavitt, H. J. "Some Effects of Certain Communication Patterns on Group Performance," *Journal of Abnormal and Social Psychology,* 46 (1951), 38–50.

Le Bon, G. *The Crowd.* New York: Viking, 1960.

Lipset, S. M. "American Student Activism in Comparative Perspective," *American Psychologist,* 25 (1970), 675–693.

Mills, T. M. "Power Relations in Three Person Groups," *American Sociological Review,* 18 (1953), 351–357.

Mintz, A. "Non-Adaptive Group Behavior," *Journal of Abnormal and Social Psychology,* 46 (1951), 150–159.

Morse, S. "Help, Likeability and Social Influence," *Journal of Applied Social Psychology,* 2 (1972), 34–46.

Newcomb, T. M. *Social Psychology.* New York: Dryden, 1950.

North, R. C., R. A. Brody, and O. R. Holsti. "Some Empirical Data on the Conflict Spiral," *Peace Research Society (International) Papers,* 1 (1964), 1–14.

Osgood, C. E. *Perspectives in Foreign Policy,* 2nd ed. Palo Alto, Calif.: Pacific Books, 1966.

Pessin, J. "The Comparative Effects of Social and Mechanical Stimulation on Memorizing," *American Journal of Psychology,* 45 (1933), 263–270.

Porter, J. W., and E. E. Lawler. "Properties of Organization Structure in Relation to Job Attitudes and Job Behavior," *Psychological Bulletin,* 64 (1965), 23–51.

Pruitt, D. G. "'Walter Mitty' Effect in Individual and Group Risk Taking," *Proceedings of the 77th Annual Convention of the American Psychological Association,* 4 (1969), 425–426.

———. "Choice Shifts in Group Discussion: An Introductory Review," *Journal of Personality and Social Psychology,* 3 (1971), 339–360.

———, and J. P. Gahagan. "Campus Crisis: The Search for Power" (paper presented at the Society for Experimental Social Psychology meeting, Columbus, Ohio, 1971).

Rapoport, A. "Lewis F. Richardson's Mathematical Theory of War," *Journal of Conflict Resolution,* 1 (1957), 249–299.

———. "Formal Games as Probing Tools for Investigating Behavior Motivated By Trust and Suspicion," *Journal of Conflict Resolution,* 7 (1963), 570–579.

———. *Strategy and Conscience.* New York: Harper & Row, 1964.

Restle, F., and J. H. Davis. "Success and Speed of Problem Solving by Individuals and Groups," *Psychological Review,* 69 (1962), 520–536.

Riecken, H. W. "The Effect of Talkativeness on Ability to Influence Group Solutions of Problems," *Sociometry,* 21 (1958), 309–321.

Schelling, T. C. *The Strategy of Conflict.* Cambridge, Mass.: Harvard University Press, 1960.

———. "Signals and Feedback in the Arms Dialogue," *Bulletin of Atomic Scientists,* 21 (1965), 5–10.

Shaw, M. E. "A Note Concerning Homogeneity of Membership and Group Problem Solving," *Journal of Abnormal and Social Psychology,* 60 (1960), 448–450.

———. "Some Factors Influencing the Use of Information in Small Groups," *Psychological Reports,* 8 (1961), 187–198.

———. "Communication Networks," in L. Berkowitz (ed.), *Advances in Experimental Psychology.* New York: Academic Press, 1964, pp. 111–147.

Spence, K. W. *Behavior Theory and Conditioning.* New Haven, Conn.: Yale University Press, 1959.

Stager, P. "Conceptual Level as a Composition Variable in Small Group Decision Making," *Journal of Personality and Social Psychology,* 5 (1967), 152–161.

Stoner, J. A. F. "A Comparison of Individual and Group Decisions Involving Risk" (unpublished master's thesis, Massachusetts Institute of Technology, 1961).

Streufert, S. "Complexity and Complex Decision Making: Convergences Between Differentiation and Integration Approaches to the Prediction of Task Performance," *Journal of Experimental Social Psychology,* 6 (1970), 494–509.

———, and H. L. Fromkin. "Truel Conflict and Complex Decision Making: The Effect of the Three Party Duel on Military and Economic Behavior of Decision Making Groups in Complex Environments," No. 25. Purdue University: Office of Naval Research Technical Report, 1969.

———, and S. Sandler. "A Laboratory Test of the Mirror Image Hypothesis," *Journal of Applied Social Psychology,* 1 (1971), 378–397.

———, and ———. "Perceived Success in Competence of the Opponent, on the Laboratory Dien Bien Phu," *Journal of Applied Social Psychology,* 3 (1973), 84–93.

Thibaut, J. W., and H. H. Kelley. *The Social Psychology of Groups.* New York: Wiley, 1959.

Thomas, E. J., and C. F. Fink. "Models of Group Problem Solving," *Journal of Abnormal and Social Psychology,* 63 (1961), 53–63.

Triandis, H. C., E. R. Hall, and R. B. Ewen. "Member Heterogeneity and Dyadic Creativity," *Human Relations,* 18 (1965), 33–55.

Wallach, M. A., N. Kogan, and D. J. Bem. "Group Influence on Individual Risk Taking," *Journal of Abnormal and Social Psychology,* 65 (1962), 75–86.

———, ———, and ———. "Diffusion of Responsibility and Level of Risk Taking in Groups," *Journal of Abnormal and Social Psychology,* 68 (1964), 263–274.

Wheeler, L., and A. R. Caggiula. "The Contagion of Aggression," *Journal of Experimental Social Psychology,* 2 (1966), 1–10.

White, R. K. "Images in the Context of International Conflict," in H. C. Kelman (ed.), *International Behavior.* New York: Holt, Rinehart and Winston, 1966, pp. 236–276.

———. *Nobody Wanted War: Misperception in Vietnam and Other Wars.* Garden City, N. Y.: Doubleday-Anchor, 1970.

Zajonc, R. B. "Social Facilitation," *Science,* 149 (1965), 269–274.

———. *Social Psychology: An Experimental Approach.* Belmont, Calif.: Brooks-Cole, 1966.

Ziller, R. C. "Scales of Judgment: A Determinant of the Accuracy of Group Decisions," *Human Relations,* 8 (1955), 153–164.

16

Argyris, C. *The Applicability of Organizational Sociology.* Cambridge, England: Cambridge University Press, 1972.

Baritz, L. *The Servants of Power.* Middleton, Conn.: Wesleyan University Press, 1960.

Barnes, L. B., L. E. Greiner, R. R. Blake, and J. S. Mouton. "Breakthrough in Organization Development," *Harvard Business Review*, 6 (1964), 133–155.

Blake, R. R., and J. S. Mouton. *Building a Dynamic Corporation Through Grid Organizational Development*. Reading, Mass.: Addison-Wesley, 1969.

Blau, P. M. *Dynamics of Bureaucracy; A Study of Interpersonal Relations in Two Government Agencies*. Chicago: University of Chicago Press, 1955.

———. *Bureaucracy in Modern Society*. New York: Random House, 1956.

———, and W. R. Scott. *Formal Organizations*. San Francisco: Chandler, 1962.

Copley, F. B. *Frederick W. Taylor: Father of Scientific Management*. New York: Harper & Row, 1923.

Cressey, D. R. "Contradictory Directives in Complex Organizations: The Case of the Prison," *Administrative Science Quarterly*, 4 (1959), 1–9.

Dalton, G. W., and P. R. Lawrence (eds.). *Motivation and Control in Organizations*. Homewood, Ill.: Irwin, 1971.

Fiedler, F. E. "Personality and Situational Determinants of Leadership Effectiveness," in D. Cartwright and A. Zander (eds.), *Group Dynamics*, 3rd ed. New York: Harper & Row, 1968, pp. 362–380.

Friere, P. *The Pedagogy of the Oppressed*. New York: Herder and Herder, 1970.

Gerth, H. H., and C. W. Mills (eds.). *From Max Weber: Essays in Sociology*. New York: Oxford University Press, 1946.

Haire, M., E. E. Ghiselli, and L. W. Porter. "Culture Patterns and the Role of the Manager," *Industrial Relations*, 2 (1963), 95–117.

———, ———, and ———. *Managerial Thinking: An International Study*. New York: Wiley, 1966.

Herzberg, F. I., B. Mausnes, R. O. Peterson, and D. F. Capwell. *Job Attitudes: Review of Research and Opinion*. Pittsburgh, Penn.: Psychological Service of Pittsburgh, 1957.

Hull, R. L., and A. Kolstad. "Morale on the Job," in G. Watson (ed.), *Civilian Morale*. Boston: Houghton Mifflin, 1942, pp. 349–364.

Illich, I. *Deschooling Society*. New York: Harper & Row, 1971.

Kahn, R. L., D. M. Wolfe, R. P. Quinn, J. D. Snoek, J. Diedrich, and R. A. Rosenthal. *Organizational Stress*. New York: Wiley, 1964.

Katz, D., and R. L. Kahn. *The Social Psychology of Organizations*. New York, Wiley, 1966.

Lawrence, P. R., and J. W. Lorsch. *Organization and Environment: Managing Differentiation and Integration*. Boston: Division of Research, Harvard Graduate School of Business Administration, 1967.

Lepper, M. R., D. Greene, and R. E. Nisbett. "Undermining Children's Intrinsic Interest with Extrinsic Reward: A Test of the 'Overjustification' Hypothesis," *Journal of Personality and Social Psychology*, (in press).

Lewin, K., R. Lippitt, and R. K. White. "Patterns of Aggressive Behavior in Experimentally Created 'Social Climates'," *Journal of Social Psychology*, 10 (1939), 271–299.

Likert, R. *The Human Organization*. New York: McGraw-Hill, 1967.

Lippitt, R. "An Experimental Study of the Effect of Democratic and Authoritarian Group Atmospheres," *University of Iowa Studies in Child Welfare*, 16 (1940), 43–195.

———, and R. K. White. "The 'Social Climate' of Children's Groups," in R. G. Barker, J. Kounin, and H. Wright (eds.), *Child Behavior and Development*. New York: McGraw-Hill, 1943, pp. 485–508.

Litwin, G. H. "Climate and Motivation: An Experimental Study," in R. Tagiuri and G. H. Litwin (eds.), *Organizational Climate*. Boston: Division of Research, Harvard Business School, 1968, pp. 167–190.

———, and R. A. Stringer. *Motivation and Organizational Climate*. Boston: Division of Research, Harvard Graduate School of Business Administration, 1968.

Marlowe, L. *Social Psychology: An Interdisciplinary Approach to Human Behavior*. Boston: Holbrook Press, 1971.

Maslow, A. H. *Motivation and Personality*. New York: Harper & Row, 1954.

Mayo, E. *The Human Problems of an Industrial Civilization*. New York: Macmillan, 1933.

Mechanic, D. "The Power to Resist Change Among Low-Ranking Personnel," *Personnel Administration*, 26 (1963), 5–11.

Merton, R. K. *Social Theory and Social Structure*, rev. ed. New York: Free Press, 1968.

Meyer, H. H. "Achievement Motivation and Industrial Climates," in R. Tagiuri and G. H. Litwin (eds.), *Organizational Climate*. Boston: Division of Research, Harvard Business School, 1968, pp. 149–166.

Morse, N. *Satisfactions in the White Collar Job*. Ann Arbor, Mich.: Survey Research Center, 1953.

Packard, V. *Nation of Strangers*. New York: McKay, 1972.

Parsons, T. "Introduction," in M. Weber, *The Theory of Social and Economic Organization*. New York: Free Press, 1947.

Roethlisberger, F. J., and W. J. Dickson. *Management and the Worker*. Cambridge, Mass.: Harvard University Press, 1939.

Scheff, T. J. *Being Mentally Ill: A Sociological Theory*. Chicago: Aldine, 1966.

Schein, E. H. *Organizational Psychology*, 2nd ed. Englewood Cliffs, N.J.: Prentice-Hall, 1970.

Schwartz, M. M., E. Jenusaitis, and H. Stark. "Motivational Factors Among Supervisors in the Utility Industry," *Personnel Psychology*, 16 (1963), 45–53.

Seashore, S. E. *Group Cohesiveness in the Industrial Work Group*. Ann Arbor, Mich.: Institute for Social Research, 1954.

Survey Research Center, University of Michigan. *Survey of Working Conditions, Final Report on Univariate and Bivariate Tables* (for US Employment Standards Administration). Washington, D. C.: US Government Printing Office, 1970.

Tannenbaum, A. S. *Control in Organizations*. New York: McGraw-Hill, 1968.

Taylor, F. W. *The Principles of Scientific Management*. New York: Harper & Row, 1911.

Trist, E. C., G. W. Higgin, H. Murray, and A. B. Pollack. *Organizational Choice*. London: Tavistock Publications, 1963.

Vroom, V. H. *Work and Motivation*. New York: Wiley, 1964.

Walker, C. R., and R. H. Guest. *The Man on the Assembly Line*. Cambridge, Mass.: Harvard University Press, 1952.

Weber, M. *The Theory of Social and Economic Organization*. New York: Free Press, 1947.

Williams, L. K., W. F. Whyte, and C. S. Green. "Do Cultural Differences Affect Worker Attitudes?" *Industrial Relations*, 5 (1966), 105–117.

17

Adorno, T. W., E. Frenkel-Brunswik, D. J. Levinson, and R. N. Sanford. *The Authoritarian Personality*. New York: Harper, 1950.

Allport, F. R. *Social Psychology*. Boston: Houghton Mifflin, 1924.

Allport, G. W., and L. Postman. *The Psychology of Rumor*. New York: Holt, 1947.

Almond, G. A., and S. Verba. *The Civic Culture*. Princeton, N. J.: Princeton University Press, 1963.

Altbach, E. H. "Vanguard of Revolt: Students and Politics in Central Europe, 1815–1848," in S. M. Lipset and P. G. Altbach (eds.), *Students in Revolt*. Boston: Houghton Mifflin, 1969, pp. 451–474.

Bandura, A., and R. Walters. *Social Learning and Personality Development*. New York: Holt, Rinehart and Winston, 1963.

Bayer, A., and A. Astin. "Violence and Disruption on the US Campus," *Educational Record,* 50 (1969), 337–350.

Block, J. H., N. Raan, and M. B. Smith. "Activism and Apathy in Contemporary Adolescents," in J. F. Adams (ed.), *Understanding Adolescence.* Boston: Allyn and Bacon, 1968, pp. 198–231.

Blumer, H. "Collective Behavior," in J. Gould and W. L. Kolb (eds.), *Dictionary of the Social Sciences.* New York: Free Press, 1964, pp. 100–101.

Brown, R. W. "Mass Phenomena," in G. Lindzey (ed.), *The Handbook of Social Psychology,* Vol. 2, 1st ed. Reading, Mass.: Addison-Wesley, 1954, pp. 833–876.

———. *Social Psychology.* New York: Free Press, 1965.

Calhoun, J. B. "Population Density and Social Psychology," *Scientific American,* 206 (1962), 139–148.

Caplan, N. S., and J. M. Paige. "A Study of Ghetto Rioters," *Scientific American,* 219 (1968), 15–21.

Davies, J. C. "Toward a Theory of Revolution," *American Sociological Review,* 27 (1962), 5–19.

DeFleur, M. "Mass Communication and the Study of Rumor," *Sociological Inquiry,* 32 (1962), 51–70.

Fanon, F. *Black Skin, White Masks.* New York: Grove Press, 1967.

Festinger, L., A. Pepitone, and T. Newcomb. "Some Consequences of De-Individuation in a Group," *Journal of Abnormal and Social Psychology,* 47 (1952), 382–389.

Flacks, R. "The Liberated Generation: An Exploration of the Roots of Student Protest," *Journal of Social Issues,* 23 (1967), 52–75.

Freedman, J. L. "The Effects of Crowding on Human Performance" (unpublished manuscript, Columbia University, 1970).

Freud, S. *Group Psychology and the Analysis of the Ego.* London: Hogarth Press, 1922.

Fromm, E. *Escape from Freedom.* New York: Farrar and Rinehart, 1941.

Gore, P. M., and J. B. Rotter. "A Personality Correlate of Social Action," *Journal of Personality,* 31 (1963), 58–64.

Gurin, P., G. Gurin, R. C. Lao, and M. Beattie. "Internal-External Control in the Motivational Dynamics of Negro Youth," *Journal of Social Issues,* 25 (1969), 29–54.

Hall, E. T. *The Hidden Dimension.* Garden City, N. Y.: Doubleday, 1969.

Hoffer, E. *The True Believer.* New York: Harper, 1951.

Hovland, C., I. Janis, and H. H. Kelley. *Communication and Persuasion.* New Haven, Conn.: Yale University Press, 1953.

Hyman, H. H., and P. B. Sheatsley. "'The Authoritarian Personality'—A Methodological Critique," in R. Christie and M. Jahoda (eds.), *Studies in the Scope and Method of 'The Authoritarian Personality.'* New York: Free Press, 1954, pp. 50–122.

Kardiner, A., and L. Ovesey. *The Mark of Oppression.* New York: Norton, 1951.

Keniston, K. *Young Radicals: Notes on Committed Youth.* New York: Harcourt, Brace & World, 1968.

Kerckhoff, A., and K. Back. *The June Bug: A Study of Hysterical Contagion.* New York: Appleton-Century-Crofts, 1968.

Kerpelman, L. *Student Activism and Ideology in Higher Education Institutions.* Office of Education, Washington, D. C.: US Department of Health, Education, and Welfare, 1970.

Lang, K., and G. E. Lang. *Collective Dynamics.* New York: Crowell, 1961.

Latané, B., and J. M. Darley. *The Unresponsive Bystander: Why Doesn't He Help?* New York: Appleton-Century-Crofts, 1970.

Le Bon, G. *The Crowd.* New York: Viking Press, 1960. (French original published 1895.)

Lenski, G. *The Religious Factor.* Garden City, N. Y.: Anchor Books, 1961.

Lipset, S. M. (ed.). *Student Politics.* New York: Basic Books, 1967.

———, and P. G. Altbach (eds.). *Students in Revolt.* Boston: Houghton Mifflin, 1969.

Marx, K., and F. Engels. *Communist Manifesto.* New York: Penguin Books, 1968.

Milgram, S., and H. Toch. "Collective Behavior: Crowds and Social Movements," in G. Lindzey and E. Aronson (eds.), *The Handbook of Social Psychology,* Vol. 4, 2nd ed. Reading, Mass.: Addison-Wesley, 1969, pp. 507–610.

Morse, S. J., and S. Peele. "A Study of Participants in an Anti-Vietnam War Demonstration," *Journal of Social Issues,* 27 (1971), 113–136.

Parsons, T. *The Social System.* New York: Free Press, 1951.

Peterson, R. "Organized Student Protest in 1964–65," *National Association of Women Deans and Counselors Journal,* 30 (1967), 50–56.

———. *The Scope of Organized Student Protest in 1967–68.* Princeton, N. J.: Educational Testing Service, 1968.

Peterson, W., and N. Gist. "Rumor and Public Opinion," *American Journal of Sociology,* 57 (1951), 159–167.

Pettigrew, T. F. "Social Evaluation Theory: Convergencies and Applications," in D. Levine (ed.), *Nebraska Symposium on Motivation.* Lincoln: University of Nebraska Press, 1967, pp. 241–311.

Platt, A. M. *The Politics of Riot Commissions.* New York: Collier, 1971.

Rokeach, M. *The Open and Closed Mind.* New York: Basic Books, 1960.

Rosenhan, D. "The Natural Socialization of Altruistic Autonomy," in L. Berkowitz and J. McCauley (eds.), *Altruism and Helping Behavior.* New York: Academic Press, 1970, pp. 251–268.

Rotter, J. B. "Generalized Expectancies for Internal Versus External Control of Reinforcement," *Psychological Monographs,* 80 (1966), 1–28.

Sampson, E. E. (ed.). "Stirrings Out of Apathy: Student Activism and the Decade of Protest," *Journal of Social Issues,* 23 (1967), 1–34.

Smelser, N. J. *Theory of Collective Behavior.* New York: Free Press, 1963.

Sommer, R. *Personal Space: The Behavioral Basis of Design.* Englewood Cliffs, N. J.: Prentice-Hall, 1969.

Thibaut, J. W., and H. H. Kelley. *The Social Psychology of Groups.* New York: Wiley, 1959.

Trow, M. "Small Businessmen, Political Tolerance, and Support for McCarthy," *American Journal of Sociology,* 64 (1958), 270–281.

Turner, R. H. "Collective Behavior," in R. E. L. Faris (ed.), *Handbook of Modern Sociology.* Chicago: Rand McNally, 1964, pp. 382–425.

———, and L. M. Killian. *Collective Behavior.* Englewood Cliffs, N. J.: Prentice-Hall, 1957.

Watts, W., and D. Whittaker. "Free Speech Advocates at Berkeley," *Journal of Applied Behavioral Science,* 2 (1966), 41–62.

Wheeler, L. *Interpersonal Influence.* Boston: Allyn and Bacon, 1970.

Windsborough, H. H. "The Social Consequence of High Population Density," *Law and Contemporary Problems,* 30 (1965), 120–126.

Zajonc, R. B. "Attitudinal Effects of Mere Exposure," *Journal of Personality and Social Psychology Monograph Supplement,* 9 (1968), 1–27.

Zimbardo, P. G. "The Human Choice: Individuation, Reason, and Order Versus De-Individuation, Impulse, and Chaos," in W. J. Arnold and D. Levine (eds.), *Nebraska Symposium on Motivation.* Lincoln: University of Nebraska Press, 1969, pp. 237–307.

———. "Symposium on Social and Developmental Issues in Moral Research" (paper presented at the meeting of the Western Psychological Association, Los Angeles, April 1970).

GLOSSARY

A

A-B-X model. A cognitive-consistency model often used to explain why similarity facilitates attraction. The model relates the attitudes of two persons to a single object and suggests that two people who agree on issues that are important to a relationship will be attracted because they satisfy one another's needs for consistency.

achievement, need for. A felt requirement to meet standards of excellence in one's performance.

affiliation, need for. A felt requirement to establish and maintain positive ties with others.

aggregate. A group of people not interacting with one another and not organized in any particular way.

aggression. Real or planned acts of physical or verbal abuse directed by one human being against another.

aggressor-defender model. A model of conflict suggesting that one party is the originator of the conflict and is actively responsible for its continuation. See also *conflict-spiral model; structural-change model.*

altercasting. The process whereby, in a social relationship, one influences the role another will adopt by choosing a specific self-definition or role oneself and thereby reducing the other's choices to roles that complement one's own.

altruism. See *prosocial behavior.*

anaclitic identification. The tendency for children to identify with parents who are warm and nurturant. See also *defensive identification.*

arousal jag. A period of indulgence in which people repeatedly seek arousal above their optimum thresholds so that they can have the pleasure of reducing it.

attitude. The disposition to behave in particular ways toward specific objects.

attitude, measure of. See *behavioral measure of attitude; behavioroid measure of attitude; Likert scale; semantic differential; Thurstone scale.*

attraction. A relationship between two parties, characterized by either mutual or one-way interest in, and admiration for, the other party.

authoritarian personality. A personality type characterized by Adorno, Frenkel-Brunswick, Levinson, and Sanford as fascistic, ethnocentric, anti-Semitic, and politically and economically conservative.

autokinetic phenomenon. The apparent motion of a fixed point of light in a darkened room.

averaging model. A model used by social psychologists to explain the process by which people combine their impressions. It suggests that the overall evaluation is formed by averaging the individual evaluations. See also *summation model.*

B

balance. According to Heider, the satisfactory state of psychological affairs that exists when attitudes do not conflict in a given situation. See also *imbalance.*

basic needs. In Maslow's theory of personality, those needs whose satisfaction is vital to the normal functioning of the individual.

behavioral indicators. Specific actions taken to represent certain traits.

behavioral measure of attitude. A means of measuring an overt behavior that reflects a given attitude.

behavior-exchange model. A social-interaction model suggesting that people are rational beings engaged in social bargaining. Behaviors are exchanged in an effort to achieve a mutually satisfying state of affairs for both parties to an exchange. The model is used to explore the successes and failures of relationships.

behavioroid measure of attitude. A means of measuring an intention of or commitment to a behavior, rather than the behavior itself, that reflects a given attitude.

Blake-Mouton Managerial Grid. A popular organizational-development program based on the human-relations philosophy that serves to help managers understand the workings of their organization by mapping its "concern for production" against its "concern for people."

body language. The meanings expressed by the way in which people move, rather than by the words they speak. See also *extralinguistic; paralanguage.*

Bogardus social-distance scale. A scale developed by Bogardus that measures the social distance people desire to maintain between themselves and members of other races or ethnic groups.

C

case study. Study and analysis of a naturally occurring social event or phenomenon.

categorization. Classification or grouping on the basis of perceived similarities.

catharsis hypothesis. Suggests that the release of tensions or aggression through the expression of unconscious impulses or emotions, either through fantasy or action, can render these impulses harmless.

causality, attribution of. The tendency to attach cause-effect relationships to paired phenomena, even when little or no evidence exists for such relationships.

central organizing traits. The specific traits of an individual that have the strongest effects on one's overall evaluation of that individual.

central tendency, measure of. A single number summarizing a set of scores that reveals the trend of the scores. See also *mean; median; mode.*

channel. The means, or modality, by which a message is communicated.

choice shift. The tendency for certain decisions made by groups to shift in degrees of riskiness or caution from those made individually by the members of the group. See also *risky shift.*

circular reaction. The interactive process that occurs when one person's behavior serves as a model for another's and, in turn, the model, observing the other's imitation, becomes stimulated to higher levels of activity.

classical conditioning. A form of learning in which a stimulus that ordinarily evokes a given response is presented with a stimulus that does not usually evoke that response, with the result that the latter stimulus will eventually evoke a similar response when presented alone.

coalition formation. The formation of a subgroup within a larger group in order to influence the decisions or outcomes of one or more other individuals.

coercive power. One of French and Raven's five bases of social power. A person with this type of power is perceived by others as having the ability to administer or mediate punishments, such as reprimands, threats, or reduction of privileges or status. See also *expert power; legitimate power; referent power; reward power.*

cognition. The process or processes by which a person acquires knowledge or becomes aware; anything a person knows or perceives.

cognitive-consistency theory. A broad category of theories based on the principle that people strive for consistency in their feelings, attitudes, and behavior.

cognitive development. The development of a logical method of looking at the world, utilizing one's perceptual and conceptual powers.

cognitive-dissonance theory. Festinger's theory that when people experience discrepancies between two or more cognitions about themselves an uncomfortable psychological state—dissonance—is produced. Dissonance motivates people to act to eliminate or reduce the discrepancy either through reinterpreting their actions, reinterpreting conditions in the environment, or adding new cognitive elements.

collective behavior. Nonnormative, diffusely organized behavior of a large number of interacting people.

complementarity. The general theory that human relationships are most successful when each person is able to satisfy the complementary needs of the other.

complementary projection. The tendency to project onto others characteristics that justify one's own behavior toward those others. See also *similarity projection.*

computer simulation. An all-machine simulation technique in which a computer analyzes hypothetical social interactions.

concept formation. See *conceptualization.*

conceptualization. Grouping perceptions into categories and classifications on the basis of specific similarities. It helps persons to inject order into their lives, but may also introduce distortions in their impressions and understanding.

conditioned response (CR). The learned response to a conditioned stimulus.

conditioned stimulus (CS). A once-neutral stimulus that has come to evoke a given response (CR) after a period in which that stimulus was paired with an unconditioned stimulus that automatically elicited the response.

conditioning. The learning process by which a stimulus becomes linked with some behavior in such a way that the stimulus will cause the behavior to occur. See also *classical conditioning; instrumental conditioning.*

conflict, models of. See *aggressor-defender model; conflict-spiral model; structural-change model.*

conflict-spiral model. A model of conflict focusing on the interaction between conflicting parties and asserting that action by one results in more severe retaliatory action, which in turn causes even more severe action, and so on. See also *aggressor-defender model; structural-change model.*

conformity. The condition of acting in accordance with, or becoming similar to, others.

consistency theory. The general designation for attitude-organization theories.

contagion. The process by which feelings and responses spread from one crowd participant to others.

contingency management. The principle, developed by Lawrence and Lorsch, that optimum management depends on leadership that is flexible enough to embrace the different styles appropriate to a variety of conditions.

continuous reinforcement. A schedule of reinforcement in which every correct response is reinforced.

control mechanism. In organizations, a device that is used to evaluate individual members' performances and to reward or punish them accordingly.

control system. In an organization, a mechanism that serves to keep the organization as a whole on course and that creates and maintains compatible expectations among individual members.

conventional level of moral development. The second level of moral development in Kohlberg's analysis, in which individuals strive to maintain the expectations of their family, group, or nation and perceive this as valuable in its own right.

convivial institution. An institution that exists to help people do the things they naturally want to do. See also *manipulative institution.*

correlation. The relationship between two variables as measured by the correlation coefficient.

correlation coefficient. A number that indicates the extent to which two variables vary together. Correlation coefficients range from +1 (perfect positive correlation) to −1 (perfect negative correlation).

cultural transmission. The passing on of dispositions from one generation to the next or from one cultural context to another.

D

defensive identification. The tendency for children to identify with parents who are punishing and threatening. See also *anaclitic identification.*

deindividuation. In groups, the feeling of anonymity among members and the lack of awareness of individual differences, often resulting in the weakening of social and personal restraints and feelings of personal responsibility. See also *individuation.*

dependent variable. An experimental variable that changes in response to changes in the independent variable.

design-features approach. An approach to language study that focuses on structures of the communication system and compares them in different species.

determinate task. A task that has one or more correct and determinable solutions; for example, algebra problems or crossword puzzles. See also *indeterminate task.*

deviance. Departure from what is considered normal, correct, or standard.

differentiation. According to Lawrence and Lorsch's organizational-development approach, the degree to which the different parts of an organization vary both in the certainty or uncertainty characteristic of their particular environments as well as in the managerial orientations and formal structures that characterize those different parts.

diffusion of responsibility. The principle that the presence of others tends to lessen the responsibility individuals feel for their actions or failure to act.

discounting. A method of resolving apparent inconsistencies in one's impressions of another individual. It involves ignoring, or reducing in importance, part of the inconsistent information. See also *linear combining; relational method.*

discrimination. The ability to detect differences in similar stimuli and to respond accordingly.

displacement. The redirection of hostility from its proper object to a safe and convenient target.

dissonance. According to cognitive-dissonance theory, the uncomfortable psychological state produced by discrepancies in cognition and/or action.

dyadic relationship. A two-member social relationship.

E

ego. According to Freud, the part of the personality that handles transactions with the external environment according to the reality principle. The ego mediates between the demands of the id and the superego.

emergent-norm theory. The contention that crowds often evolve norms that create a certain amount of uniformity in the behavior of participants.

encounter group. An intensive group that emphasizes development and improvement in interpersonal communication.

equal-interval scale. A scale using the differences between two points as a unit of measure and having an arbitrary zero point. The scale is used to determine how many units are contained in a given magnitude.

ethnic group. A group consisting of people who conceive of themselves and are regarded by others as belonging together by virtue of a common ancestry, real or fictitious, and a common cultural background.

ethology. The comparative study of animal behavior.

expectancy-value theory. The general designation for those theories of human motivation that explain human behavior in terms of one's expectations about attaining a goal in a situation in which one's motives might be aroused and in terms of the incentive value of the goal.

experimental artifacts. Phenomena that produce erroneous experimental results because of some problem inherent in the research methodology.

experimental-simulation technique. A man-machine simulation technique in which a participant is pitted against a computer that responds to each action with a predetermined countermove.

experimenter-demand characteristics. The introduction of bias into experiments by the experimenters' subtle communications of their expectations to their subjects.

expert power. One of French and Raven's five bases of social power. A person with this type of power has special resources of knowledge or skill that others need. See also *coercive power; legitimate power; referent power; reward power.*

extinction. The gradual disappearance of a conditioned response, either because of the repeated presentations of the conditioned stimulus without the unconditioned stimulus or because of the withholding of reinforcement for the occurrence of the conditioned response.

extralinguistic. Pertaining to communication by nonlinguistic means, such as hand gestures, facial expressions, and body movements. See also *body language; paralanguage.*

extrinsic payoff. Reward for pursuing a certain course of action that is derived not from the activity itself but on a basis aside from the activity, such as another's response to the activity. See also *intrinsic payoff.*

F

face-work. Goffman's term for the actions taken by people to repair their images by avoiding or correcting situations that threaten the images they want to present.

facilitator. The authorized leader of an intensive psychological group whose role is to keep the group on the right path.

feral. Referring to a child who has been raised in complete social isolation from other human beings.

field experiment. An experiment carried out in a "real-life" social situation.

foot-in-the-door technique. A means of getting people to comply with major requests by first getting them to comply with smaller, minor requests.

forced-compliance paradigm. Used by cognitive-dissonance researchers to demonstrate dissonance reduction. The basic idea is that forced public behavior in a manner contradictory to one's beliefs will create little dissonance and therefore will not cause attitude change, but if individuals can be induced to participate in such a way that they feel the choice is theirs, dissonance will be aroused and attitudes will change to be consistent with behavior.

formal group. A highly structured group that usually has explicit rules and regulations governing the behavior of group members.

frame of reference. A system of concepts, standards, values, or goals developed through experience that affects the evaluations or perceptions of an individual, group, or situation.

free simulation. An all-human simulation technique, used by Guetzkow, in which subjects play the roles of national leaders and interact with one another in economic, military, and political spheres.

frustration. According to Dollard, an interference with goal-directed responses. The term also refers to the emotional state associated with such interference.

frustration-aggression hypothesis. The theory that frustration produces a tendency toward aggression and that aggression is often traceable to frustration.

functional approach to attitudes. Katz's theory of attitude formation and change. It takes into account the functions that attitudes can serve in terms of individual needs and motives.

functional approach to language study. An approach to language study that focuses on the types of messages that are communicated in a particular communication system and on the ways in which they are related to behavior outside that system.

functional autonomy. The theory that behavior that was originally a means to some end may continue after the original motive no longer exists; that is, it becomes an end in itself.

G

gain-loss theory of attraction. Aronson's theory that increments or decrements in esteem given by a person are more important in determining one's attraction to that person than are invariant levels of esteem. Therefore, an enemy turned friend should be more attractive than a person who has always been a friend.

generalization. A phenomenon in which a response learned in reaction to one stimulus is elicited by a separate but similar stimulus.

group. Two or more individuals who are interdependent on one or more dimensions and who perceive the existence of the group and their membership in it. See also *encounter group; ethnic group; formal group; heterogeneous group; homogeneous group; informal group; intensive group; membership group; reference group.*

group cohesiveness. The forces that encourage members to remain in a group and that prevent them from leaving it. Factors that contribute to cohesiveness include attraction among members, satisfaction with the group, and identification with the group.

group norms. Explicit or implicit agreements that dictate acceptable and expected behaviors and attitudes of group members. Group norms also serve as standards by which a group judges the behavior of its members.

group structure. The stabilized patterns of relationships in a group that establish expected and accepted social relations, roles, and status.

guilt. The emotional response, often characterized by regret and lowered self-esteem, that accompanies the realization that one has violated social, legal, or ethical norms.

H

halo effect. The process of basing an entire impression of a person on an emotional evaluation of a few traits.

Hawthorne effect. A general term popularly referring to any instance of improvement in performance that is a by-product of attention.

hedonics. The view that all behavior is directed toward either approaching stimuli associated with pleasure or avoiding stimuli associated with pain.

heterogeneous group. A group in which the members differ with respect to one or more given characteristics, such as a personality trait, gender, and so on.

homogeneous group. A group in which all members possess specified characteristics to a similar degree.

human relations. A school of industrial psychology that attempts to increase productivity by increasing the worker's satisfaction.

I

id. According to Freud, the unconscious and most primitive part of the personality, comprising drives, needs, and instinctual impulses. The id operates according to the pleasure principle and is in constant conflict with the superego.

ideal norm. An ideal standard of social behavior that is neither a true expectation of behavior nor a particularly morally compelling force. See also *norm*.

identification. The act or process of accepting the values, attitudes, and/or behavior of another as one's own.

ideographic approach. An approach to scientific investigation concerned with individual differences rather than aggregates.

imbalance. According to Heider, the uncomfortable state of psychological affairs that exists when attitudes conflict. See also *balance*.

implicational molecule. According to Abelson's theory of psychological implications, the basic unit of cognitive organization. It is a self-contained set of statements that, taken as a whole, are psychologically consistent. It tends toward completion, is resistant to change when complete, and produces pressure to relieve inconsistencies when nonfitting elements are present.

implicit personality theories. Privately held theories about how personality traits fit together. People use these theories to integrate their impressions of others into unified wholes.

impression. An immediate, unanalyzed evaluation of a set of sensations or perceptions. An impression is not based on thorough investigation.

impression formation. The association and integration of various perceptions into a single impression. See also *averaging model; summation model*.

independent variable. A variable that is manipulated by the experimenter. Changes in the independent variable affect the dependent variable if there is a relationship between the two.

indeterminate task. A decision-making task that may have many potential logical solutions, none of which is specifically correct. See also *determinate task*.

individuation. Consciousness of one's individual identity and feelings of personal responsibility. See also *deindividuation*.

informal group. A group that is not highly organized and whose rules and expectations about members' behavior are generally not explicit.

ingratiation. Behavior adopted by persons for the purpose of increasing their attractiveness to others in order to gain something from those others.

inoculation against persuasion. Challenging peoples' beliefs so that their psychological defenses render them less vulnerable to persuasion than if the beliefs had not been challenged.

instinct. Unlearned, biologically based behavior, characteristic of a given species.

institutional aggression. Aggression practiced, controlled, or condoned by an institution or society, either collectively or by individual members. The aggression is usually controlled by the norms, rules, or customs of the institution or society.

instrumental conditioning. A form of learning in which certain of an organism's spontaneous activities are reinforced and consequently learned. Also known as operant conditioning.

intensive psychological group. Types of groups designed to promote personal growth of the participants. Intensive groups include encounter groups, T-groups, sensitivity-training groups, and marathons.

interaction matrix. A matrix illustrating a range of possible exchanges between two or more persons, and the value of each exchange to each person.

interactive approach. An approach to scientific investigation concerned with the way personality and environment combine to influence interactions among individuals and among groups.

internal-external control scale. A scale developed by Rotter for the purpose of measuring the extent to which people believe that they have control over actions and events in their lives. See also *locus of control*.

interpersonal bargaining game. An experimental situation used to study bargaining strategies and cooperative and exploitative behavior.

intrinsic payoff. Reward for pursuing a certain course of action that is derived from the action itself. See also *extrinsic payoff*.

J

job enlargement. The technique of increasing workers' satisfaction by expanding the range of their operations.

just-world hypothesis. According to Lerner and Simmons, the tendency of people to believe that the fortunes or misfortunes that befall another are not random, but are deserved.

L

law of effect. Thorndike's law stating that an act followed by satisfaction is likely to recur, whereas one producing discomfort is less likely to recur.

learning theory. The idea that all behavior is the result of learned responses.

legitimate power. One of French and Raven's five bases of social power. A person with this type of power is perceived by others as having the right to influence their behavior. See also *coercive power; expert power; referent power; reward power*.

Likert scale. A scale developed by Likert for the measurement of attitudes. Subjects indicate agreement or disagreement with statements by means of a five-point scale. Individual attitude scores are derived from the sum of the scores on individual items. This method is also called the summated rating method. See also *Thurstone scale.*

liking relationship. In Heider's balance theory, the positive or negative evaluation of a relationship between any two attitude objects. The relationship is represented by a plus or minus sign.

linear combining. A method of resolving apparent inconsistencies in one's impressions of another individual. It involves adding or subtracting pieces of information in order to arrive at a consistent impression. See also *discounting; relational method.*

linguistic relativity. The notion that different languages have different effects on thought.

linguistics. The science of the origin, structure, and effects of language.

linguistic universals. Structural similarities existing in different languages, pointing to the possible existence of innate language tendencies.

locus of control. A trait dimension hypothesized by Rotter that reflects the degree to which people attribute events to their own actions or to circumstances beyond their control.

M

Machiavellianism. A highly manipulative approach to social interaction.

maintaining face. Goffman's term for the state people are in when they present internally consistent images that are accepted and supported by others.

manipulative institution. An institution that yields products and services for which it must first create an artificial need. See also *convivial institution.*

matching hypothesis. The hypothesis stating that individuals choose partners of approximately the same degree of attractiveness as themselves, rather than partners who are much more or less attractive.

mean. The measure of central tendency computed by dividing the sum of a set of scores by the number of scores in the set. Also referred to as "the average."

mechanical model. An organizational model in which the structure, systems of control, and roles of members are precisely defined.

median. In a set of scores ranked from low to high, the score that has half the scores above it and half below. The median is a measure of central tendency.

membership group. Any group to which a person belongs physically.

metaneeds. In Maslow's theory of personality, needs that are growth needs rather than deficiency or basic needs. Satisfaction for metaneeds is sought once deficiency needs are met. Satisfaction of metaneeds allows self-actualization, but if these needs are ignored, psychological sickness such as alienation and apathy may occur.

minimax strategy. In bargaining situations, the strategy for participants to seek to minimize loss and maximize gain.

mode. In a set of scores, the score that occurs most frequently. The mode is a measure of central tendency.

modeling. Learning based on observation of the behavior of others.

model of equity. Adams' formulation that people need to feel that the resources they expend for others are equal to the resources those other persons expend for them.

moral autonomy, stage of. According to Piaget, the final stage in children's moral development during which they recognize the applicability of abstract principles to moral behavior.

motivation. Goal-directed behavior. This term is used interchangeably with "trait" in this text.

motive. See *trait.*

multiple-stage problem. A problem in which a series of steps must be taken to reach a solution.

mutual accommodation. In interpersonal relationships, the adjustment of both parties to each other's needs, desires, and capabilities.

mutuality. The third level of a relationship, postulated by Levinger and Snoek, characterized by mutual interdependence and interpersonal depth. See also *surface contact; unilateral awareness.*

N

naturalistic study. Observation of naturally occurring events and situations. The observer in the naturalistic study tries to remain inconspicuous.

need hierarchy. Maslow's term for the compulsion to first satisfy basic needs, such as hunger and thirst, before seeking to satisfy metaneeds, which are less urgent.

negative reinforcer. A stimulus whose removal increases the frequency of the response that preceded it.

nominal scale. A scale in which a number or name is arbitrarily assigned to an item or an entity for the purpose of identification.

nomothetic approach. An approach to scientific investigation concerned with aggregates and general principles and laws rather than with specific objects of study.

nonparametric statistics. Statistical techniques designed for use with nominal and ordinal data.

nonsense syllable. A meaningless combination of letters, usually three, that can be pronounced.

norm. A standard of action that specifies what behavior is "normal" or expected and what behavior is abnormal. See also *group norm; ideal norm.*

O

objective morality, stage of. According to Piaget, the first stage in children's moral development in which their moral concepts are simply based on what their parents permit and forbid.

operant conditioning. See *instrumental conditioning.*

ordinal scale. A number system in which numbers are assigned to items according to their rank ordering on some dimension.

organic model. An organizational model in which the structure of the organization and the roles of its members are not predetermined and precisely defined but develop informally during the course of the organization's functioning.

organization. A formal collection of people who have defined relationships, such as authority hierarchies and task differentiations, and who share the purpose of achieving a common goal.

organizational-development programs. Programs serving to resolve dysfunction resulting from outdated policies and to set the organization on a planned course of development that is based on a full assessment of its present situation and up-to-date principles of management. Such programs are usually based on a human-relations philosophy.

organizational psychology. The branch of psychology that studies the ways in which individuals relate to and are affected by organizations and the ways they relate to one another within organizations.

P

paralanguage. The meanings expressed by the way in which a person speaks, rather than by the words used. See also *body language; extralinguistic.*

parametric statistics. Statistical techniques designed for use with equal-interval and ratio data.

peer. A co-member of a given social category, such as age group or social class.

perceived distance. A form of psychological distance expressed in terms of intervening persons rather than actual physical distance.

personal space. The space immediately surrounding a person. Invasion of this space is seen to constitute an invasion of that person's privacy, although the actual dimensions vary from situation to situation and from culture to culture.

persuasibility. The general tendency of an individual to be persuaded toward one viewpoint or another, independent of specific issues.

phenomenology. The study of individual phenomena as people experience them.

piecework-incentive system. A scientific-management technique in which the more workers produce, the more they are paid.

political event. An instance of collective behavior involving participants who are attempting to bring about political change that would alter the way in which power is distributed or exercised within a social system.

political movement. Collective behavior that occurs during a series of coordinated political events and that usually extends over a considerable period of time.

population. The total membership of a group, class of objects, or class of events.

postconventional level of moral development. The third and last level of moral development in Kohlberg's analysis in which the individual defines moral values and principles in relation to their validity and application rather than in relation to the dictates of society or of any particular group. It is characterized by self-chosen ethical principles that are comprehensive, universal, and consistent.

power factor. According to Heider, the ability of a person to carry out a given activity.

power, need for. A felt requirement for control over others.

preconventional level of moral development. The first level of moral development in Kohlberg's analysis in which the child responds to cultural rules and labels of good and bad only in terms of the physical or hedonistic consequences of obeying or disobeying the rules.

prejudice. Preconceived feelings, opinions, or attitudes about and predispositions to act in a certain way toward a diverse group of individuals who have been included in a single category by the perceiver. These prejudgments are formed without sufficient evidence and are not easily changed by opposing facts or circumstances.

primacy effect. The tendency for the earliest impression learned about a person or object to be weighted most heavily in the total impression of that person or object. See also *recency effect.*

primary reinforcer. A stimulus that strengthens a response without the need of prior experience.

process approach to leadership. An approach that views leadership as an ongoing process in which the person who is leader plays a formative part. This approach focuses on an interaction among leader, followers, and situation.

process organization. An organization in which members specialize in separate functions within a larger process and never see a project through all its stages of production.

product organization. An organization in which an individual member is responsible for the entire cycle of a product, from start to finish.

project organization. An organization that combines features of process and product organizations, allowing each member a sense of participation in the overall project but without losing the competence fostered by specialization. Each person's primary organizational identity lies with a process subgroup, but the person is assigned to a succession of temporary project groups, performing more or less the same function in each one.

propaganda. Information that is deliberately spread by an individual, a group, or an institution for the purpose of influencing the attitudes or behavior of others.

prosocial behavior. Voluntary behavior, intended to benefit another person or group of persons, and performed as an end in itself.

psychological implication, theory of. A consistency theory of attitude organization developed by Abelson that focuses on the way that consistency needs either set in motion a search for new information or close off a person from additional facts. The basic unit of cognitive organization is the implicational molecule.

psychological reactance. According to Brehm, a motivational state aroused in response to a feeling that one's freedom is threatened. Reactance directs the person to act to prevent any further loss of freedom and to reestablish the freedom already lost. See *reactance, theory of.*

psychological reference scale. According to Sherif and Hovland, a scale representing the statements or objects that a person accepts or rejects.

Pygmalion effect. See *self-fulfilling prophecy.*

Q

Q-sort. A technique for measuring self-esteem by requiring people to describe themselves as they are and as they would like to be.

R

ratio scale. A scale based on a unit of measurement that is a fraction of a standard difference between two points, in which units are therefore equal, and that has an absolute zero point.

reactance, theory of. According to Brehm, the theory that if one's freedom of choice is threatened, one will attempt to regain that lost freedom.

recency effect. The tendency for the most recent information learned about a person or object to be weighted most heavily in forming the impression of that person or object. See also *primacy effect.*

reciprocity norm. The norm suggesting that persons are expected to return good for good and evil for evil.

reference group. A group with which people identify and whose norms they accept as their own.

referent power. One of French and Raven's five bases of social power. A person with this type of power is liked, respected, or identified with by others and is therefore allowed by others to influence them. See also *coercive power; expert power; legitimate power; reward power.*

refutational defenses. Challenging a person's beliefs but subsequently reinstating those beliefs with counterarguments that refute the challenge.

reinforcement. Any circumstance that increases the probability that a given response will recur in a similar situation. In instrumental conditioning, it is the procedure of immediately following a response with a reinforcer in order to strengthen the response. See also *continuous reinforcement.*

reinforcer. A stimulus that increases the frequency of the response that preceded it.

relational method. A method of resolving apparent inconsistencies in one's impressions of another individual. It involves either changing the meaning of the inconsistent information or adding new traits to relate the inconsistencies in a coherent way. See also *discounting; linear combining.*

relative deprivation. The idea that persons become discontented not because of the absolute severity of their situation but because they compare their actual condition with what it could or should be.

reliability. The dependability and consistency of a measure.

repression. A defense mechanism that guards against anxiety and guilt by the unconscious exclusion of painful and unacceptable ideas or impulses from consciousness.

response set. The tendency to respond to items on questionnaires in a particular way, regardless of the content of the items.

reward power. One of French and Raven's five bases of social power. A person with this type of power is perceived by others as having the ability to give them rewards, such as favors, approval, or increased status. See also *coercive power; expert power; legitimate power; referent power.*

risky shift. The tendency for certain decisions made by groups to be riskier than those made individually by the persons comprising the group. See also *choice shift.*

role. A set of behaviors that characterizes and is expected of a person who occupies a particular position or status.

role differentiation. The process by which roles become different from one another in function.

role playing. The performance of a role.

S

sample. A selected portion of a population, serving to represent the population as a whole.

sanctions. Expressions of social approval or disapproval for appropriate or inappropriate behavior.

scapegoat. An innocent person or group who is blamed by others for the misfortunes of those others.

scientific management. The use of scientific methods to maximize efficiency, discipline, and standardization of jobs. An early school of thought that proved inadequate because it neglected workers' social needs.

secondary reinforcer. A stimulus that increases the frequency of a given response because the stimulus has become associated with a primary reinforcer of that response.

self-actualization. The process of fulfilling one's potentials or the state resulting therefrom. According to Maslow, self-actualization results from the satisfaction of metaneeds.

self-esteem. A person's evaluation or opinion of himself or herself.

self-fulfilling prophecy. A belief, prediction, or expectation that serves to bring about its own fulfillment.

self-perception theory. Bem's theory of attitude change. It states that individuals infer their own attitudes from their behavior.

self-presentation. The conveying of special images of oneself to others.

semantic differential. A method devised by Osgood, Tannenbaum, and Suci to measure the meaning of interpersonal experience. Individuals rate concepts on a series of scales anchored by bipolar adjectives such as good and bad.

sentence-completion test. A projective technique for personality assessment in which the subject is asked to complete sentences without being given any clearly formulated guidelines.

shaping. An aspect of instrumental conditioning in which all acts similar to the desired response are reinforced at first, and then only acts that are progressively more like the desired response are reinforced until the desired response is obtained. This is also called "the method of successive approximations."

similarity projection. The tendency to project onto others one's own undesirable impulses. See also *complementary projection.*

simulation. A representation of reality in simplified form, attempting to maintain the essential components of the reality it represents. Social scientists make use of man-machine simulations, all-man simulations, and computer simulations.

sleeper effect. The tendency for the positive or negative influence of a communicator on the effectiveness of a message to decline with time.

social-comparison theory. Festinger's theory that everyone has a drive to evaluate their opinions and abilities and that, in the absence of objective standards, each person will pick out similar others as standards of comparison.

social distance. According to Bogardus, the degrees and grades of understanding and feeling that persons experience regarding each other.

social facilitation. The positive effect of the presence of others on the performance of an individual group member.

social influence. Influence that an individual or group exerts on the perceptions, attitudes, or behavior of another individual.

socialization. The process through which persons learn the culture and social roles of their society and come to perform the roles expected of them.

social movement. A series of coordinated events that attempt to bring about social change.

social psychology. The scientific study of interpersonal behavior.

socioemotional specialist. Bales' term for the type of leader concerned with interpersonal relationships and morale within the group. See also *task specialist.*

sociogram. The graphic representation of relationships within a group.

standard deviation. In frequency distribution, a number indicating the extent to which measurements within a set differ from one another, expressed as the square root of the squared differences of each measurement from the mean, divided by the number of measurements.

standard experiment. In psychological studies, the experimental situation in which subjects are exposed to a stimulus (the independent variable) and their responses (the dependent variable) are measured.

state of interpersonal accommodation. According to Kelley, a mutually fulfilling social relationship.

statistical significance. The mathematical probability that a given research result was not produced by chance.

statistics. The branch of mathematics involved with making meaningful inferences from collections of data.

stereotypes. Preconceived notions, often having no rational basis, about particular people or groups.

structural approach to leadership. An approach that views leadership as one of many positions in a group that any member can fill.

structural-change model. A model of conflict holding that any conflict modifies the views, actions, and goals of the conflicting parties and consequently may modify the composition of the parties. This modification in turn affects future conflict in various ways. See also *aggressor-defender model; conflict-spiral model.*

subjective morality, stage of. According to Piaget, the stage in children's moral development in which they begin not to take the dictates of their parents literally and begin to realize that the spirit rather than the letter of a rule is more important.

sublimation. In psychoanalytic theory, the unconscious process of redirecting or modifying an instinct or impulse so as to meet the conventional standards of society. Through this modification, one is provided with a substitute activity that allows some means of satisfying the original need.

summated ratings. See *Likert scale.*

summation model. A model used by social psychologists to explain the process by which people combine their impressions. It suggests that people form overall evaluations that are the simple sums of individual evaluations. See also *averaging model.*

superego. According to Freud, the part of the personality that incorporates parental and social standards of morality. The superego inhibits those impulses of the id that are most condemned by society or parents and is thus in constant conflict with the id.

surface contact. The second level of a relationship, postulated by Levinger and Snoek, in which the two parties will begin to interact in a restricted and relatively noninterdependent manner. The interactions will be constrained by the roles each party plays in relation to the other. See also *mutuality; unilateral awareness.*

survey. A technique for obtaining the expressed opinions, beliefs, attitudes, and intentions of selected representative members of a population.

T

task specialist. Bales' term for the type of leader concerned with the completion of tasks and with the movement toward the group's goals. See also *socioemotional specialist.*

taxonomy. The systematic categorization of concepts and entities relevant to a particular field.

territoriality. The tendency in certain animals to stake out particular areas and defend them against encroachment by others.

Thematic Apperception Test (TAT). A projective test in which relatively vague pictures are presented to a subject who is asked to make up stories about them. The subject's responses are taken to reflect underlying needs, motives, and concerns.

Thurstone scale. A scale developed by Thurstone, designed for the measurement of attitudes. It functions when a large number of raters assign values to a group of statements about a particular subject according to the value the raters place on the subject. The statements are then ordered into a scale representing the entire range of opinion on the subject, and respondents indicate either agreement or disagreement. Individual attitude scores are derived from the average scale value of all statements agreed with. See also *Likert scale.*

time-and-motion studies. A scientific-management technique in which the quickest, smoothest series of physical movements by which a given task can be performed is determined.

traits. Stable, or fairly stable, personality tendencies.

tryadic relationship. A three-member social relationship.

U

unconditioned response (UCR). In classical conditioning, an organism's natural reaction to a particular stimulus.

unconditioned stimulus (UCS). In classical conditioning, a stimulus that evokes a given response without previous training.

unilateral awareness. The first level of a relationship, postulated by Levinger and Snoek, in which one party is aware of the other only casually, through observation. See also *mutuality; surface contact.*

unit relationship (U). In Heider's balance theory, the relationship that exists when two or more objects or attitudes form a unit.

V

validity. The extent to which a test adequately measures that which it is intended to measure.

variance. In statistics, the square of a standard deviation. It indicates the variability, or homogeneity, of scores in a distribution.

W

Whorfian hypothesis. The theory developed by Whorf that language tends to determine, in varying degrees, the quality, direction, and content of a person's perceptions and thoughts.

INDEX

unit relationships, 278, 283
University Game, 21
University of Michigan Survey
Research Center, 529

V

validity, 31, 39
Valins, S., 173
values, and collective behavior, 573, 596
Van der Schyff, L., 229
variance, statistical, 32
Veitch, R., 184
Verba, S., 577
Verplanck, W., 412, 413–414
Vertreace, W., 487
Videbeck, R., 130
Vogt, E., 270–271
Von Neumann, J., 424
Vondracek, F., 369
Vroom, V., 532
Vygotsky, L., 113

W

Wagner, C., 385
Walbek, N., 384, 385
Walden Two (Skinner), 52–53
Walder, L., 503
Walker, C. R., 535
Wallach, M., 507
Wallington, S. A., 397, 398
Walster, E., 132, 143, 149, 187, 198, 208–209, 213, 219, 403, 415
Walster, G. W., 187

Walter Mitty effect, 508
Walters, G., 225, 234, 235, 236
Walters, R., 81, 365, 366, 375, 581
Ward, L., 164
Ward, S. H., 49, 249
Waring, P., 6
Warr, P. B., 175
Watson, J. B., 47–48, 49
Watson, P., 240–241
Watts, W., 579
Weakland, J., 92
Webb, E., 260
Weber, M., 547, 548
Weber, S. J., 246
Weiby, M., 169
Weick, C., 563
Weinfeld, F. D., 124
Weinstein, A., 439
Weinstein, E., 399, 400
Weisberg, R., 98
Weiss, W., 287
Weitmen, M., 413
Westie, F., 261, 262
Wheeler, L., 171, 345, 372, 385, 509, 591, 592
White, B. J., 477
White, R., 281, 517, 519, 521, 522, 540–541
Whiting, J. W., 55
Whittaker, D., 579
Whorf, B. L., 101, 103, 104, 106, 113
Whyte, W., 464, 543
Wiens, A., 413
Wiggin, J., 461
Wilke, H., 400
Wilkins, E., 372
Wilkins, P. C., 192
Williams, J., 234, 235, 249
Williams, C. K., 543
Wilson, K. V., 428, 429

Winch, R., 194
Windsborough, H. H., 590
Winer, B. J., 468
Winter, D., 134–135
Wishner, J., 158
Wishnov, B., 441
Wittig, B. A., 62
Wolfe, D. M., 557
Wong, T. S., 232
worker motivation, 530–531, 532–537
Wright, B. A., 392
Wyckoff, B., 418

Y

Yale Communication Research
Program, 285, 296
Yalom, I., 485
Yellin, A., 91
York, R. L., 124
Young Radicals (Keniston), 584

Z

Zajonc, R., 181–182, 269, 494, 495, 581
Zander, A., 466, 472, 473, 493
Zanna, M., 273, 274, 306–307, 315
Zigler, E., 60, 81
Ziller, R., 200, 511–512, 513
Zillman, D., 355, 370
Zimbardo, P., 5, 11, 19, 317, 345, 362, 364, 593
Zimmerman, B. J., 240
Zimmerman, R. R., 60–61
Zweigenhaft, R., 6

PICTURE CREDITS & ACKNOWLEDGMENTS

UNIT I. INTRODUCTION
x—Corita Kent.

Chapter 1. A Science of Social Behavior
2—John Oldenkamp/IBOL;
4—(left) UPI Compix, (right) Ken Heyman; 5—(left) Henri Cartier-Bresson/Magnum Photos, (right) Ian Berry/Magnum Photos; 10—Dick Cortén; 13 and 16—UPI Compix; 17—from C. Y. Glock and R. Stark, *Christian Beliefs and Anti-Semitism*, Harper & Row, 1966; 18 and 19— courtesy of Dr. Philip G. Zimbardo; 20—Mervyn Lew; 23—(left) Bob Towers/Black Star, (right) Fred Keib, Photographic Services, Cornell University; 30—John Oldenkamp/IBOL; 32 and 34—Howard Saunders; 37—Medieval Concept of the Sky, courtesy of the Deutsches Museum, Munich.

UNIT II. SOCIALIZATION: BEING HUMAN
40—Corita Kent.

Chapter 2. Socialization: The Humanizing Processes
42—John Oldenkamp/IBOL;
44 and 45—© 1973 by Jules Feiffer, reprinted by permission of Publishers-Hall Syndicate; 46—Howard Saunders; 47—The Granger Collection; 48—Bonnie Weber adapted from A. W. Staats and C. K. Staats, "Attitudes Established by Classical Conditioning," *Journal of Abnormal and Social Psychology*, 57 (1958), p. 38; 50—Fred Bauman; 54—Bonnie Weber adapted from J. Aronfreed and A. Reber, "Internalization and Timing of Punishment," *Journal of Personality and Social Psychology*, 1 (1965), p. 9; 60— (left) courtesy of Harry Harlow, (right) Arthur Sirdofsky; 61—Mona El-Khadem from H. F. Harlow and R. R. Zimmerman, "Affectional Responses in the Infant Monkey," *Science*, 130 (1959), p. 422; 62—Bonnie Weber from H. L. Rheingold and C. O. Eckerman, "The Infant Separates Himself From His Mother," *Science*, 168 (1970), p. 79; 63—(left) Henri Cartier-Bresson/Magnum Photos, (right) Charles Harbutt/Magnum Photos; 66—The Escher Foundation, Haags Gemeentemuseum, The Hague; 71 and 73—Bonnie Weber from A. Bandura and F. J. McDonald, "Influence of Social Reinforcement and the Behavior of Models in Shaping Children's Moral Judgments," *Journal of Abnormal and Social Psychology*, 67 (1963), p. 278; 74—Mona El-Khadem adapted from J. J. Hill and R. M. Leibert, "Effects of Consistent or Deviant Modeling Cues on the Adoption of a Self-Imposed Standard," *Psychonomic Science*, 13 (1968), p. 243; 76—from Gahan Wilson, *I Paint What I See*, Simon & Schuster, 1971, reprinted by permission of Gahan Wilson; 77—Nacio Jan Brown/BBM Associates.

Chapter 3. Language & Communication
82—John Oldenkamp/IBOL;
85—(top) courtesy of R. A. and B. T. Gardner, (bottom) from John C. Lilly, *The Mind of the Dolphin*, © 1967 by John Cunningham Lilly, used with permission of Doubleday and Co.; 86— Howard Saunders adapted from C. F. Hockett, "The Origin of Speech," © 1960 by Scientific American, Inc., all rights reserved; 87—George Hall; 90—Terry Lamb; 96—Mona El-Khadem from G. A. Miller and J. A. Selfridge, "Verbal Context and the Recall of Meaningful Material," *American Journal of Psychology*, 63 (1950), p. 181; 97—from "Miles and Metaphors, Smiles and Surprises," *Life*, December 17, 1971, pp. 50-51, © 1971 by Time, Inc.; 99—Howard Saunders adapted from R. M. Krauss and S. Gluckman, "The Development of Communication: Competence As a Function of Age," *Child Development*, 40 (1969), p. 258; 104—(left) Gordon Menzie, (top center) Gordon Menzie/Photophile, (top right) Scala, New York/Florence, (bottom right) courtesy of the Henry E. Huntington Library, San Marino, California; 105—(left) John Oldenkamp/IBOL for *Psychology Today*, (center) photo by Gordon Menzie, (right top and bottom) UPI Compix; 106—from the Bentley Collection, 1907, courtesy of *Vermont Life*; 110—Bruce Davidson/Magnum Photos; 111—courtesy of Jet Propulsion Lab/NASA.

Chapter 4. Personalities: Pegs, Round & Square
114—John Oldenkamp/IBOL;
117—Culver Pictures; 118—Terry Lamb; 120—Karl Nicholason; 124—Ian Berry/Magnum Photos; 125—from *Aesop's Life and Fables*, 1476; 128— Harry Coughanour/Pittsburgh Post-Gazette; 129—UPI Compix; 137—Mona El-Khadem from N. Miller, A. N. Doob, D. C. Butler, and D. Marlowe, "The Tendency to Agree: Situational Determinants and Social Desirability," *Journal of Experimental Research in Personality*, 1 (1965), p. 82; 140—(left and center) UPI Compix, (top right) Gary Krueger, (bottom right) René Burri/Magnum Photos.

UNIT III. ENCOUNTERING OTHERS: PERCEPTIONS, FEELINGS & THOUGHTS
144—Corita Kent.

Chapter 5. Perceiving Others
146—John Oldenkamp/IBOL;
148—© 1957 by United Feature Syndicate; 150—The Bettmann Archive, Inc.; 154—UPI Compix; 162—(top left) Brown Brothers, (top center) from Jean Belot, *Oeuvres Diverses*, Lyons, 1649, (bottom left) courtesy of David Werner, (right) courtesy of Clarence V. Elliott; 165—from Gahan Wilson, *I Paint What I See*, Simon & Schuster, 1971, reprinted by permission of Gahan Wilson; 166— (left) UPI Compix, (right) The New York Times; 168—Mona El-Khadem from S. Streufert and S. Streufert, "Structure and Success Effects on Perception and Attitudes," *Journal of Personality and Social Psychology*,
11 (1969), pp. 138-147; 170— *Hand With Reflecting Globe* by M. C. Escher, Escher Foundation, Haags Gemeentemuseum, The Hague; 171 and 172—© 1967 by Jules Feiffer, reprinted by permission of Publishers-Hall Syndicate.

Chapter 6. Interpersonal Attraction
176—John Oldenkamp/IBOL;
180—from L. Festinger, *et.al., Social Pressures in Informal Groups*, Stanford University Press, 1963; 181—Arthur Schatz for *Life*, © 1972 by Time, Inc.; 183—Jane Bown; 186—(left) *Venus and Adonis* by Rubens, courtesy of the Metropolitan Museum of Art, gift of Harry Payne Bingham, 1937, (right) Burt Glinn/Magnum Photos; 189— Mona El-Khadem from D. Byrne, *The Attraction Paradigm*, Academic Press, 1971, p. 58; 191—© 1969 by International Compatibility, Inc.; 195—from *The Only True Mother Goose*, Munroe and Francis, 1833; 198—Werner Bischof/Magnum Photos; 200 and 201—© 1967 by Jules Feiffer, reprinted by permission of Publishers-Hall Syndicate; 202—Bonnie Weber, adapted from E. Aronson and D. Linder, "Gain and Loss of Esteem as Determinants of Interpersonal Attractiveness," *Journal of Experimental Social Psychology*, 1 (1965), pp. 156-172; 204—from *May Time*, Metro-Goldwyn-Mayer; 206 and 207—Mona El-Khadem, adapted from G. Levinger and J. D. Snoek, *Attraction in Relationship; A New Look at Interpersonal Attraction*, General Learning Press, 1972; 209—from *The Crystal Palace Exhibition*, Dover Publications, Inc., 1970.

Chapter 7. Prejudice
214—John Oldenkamp/IBOL;
216—Elliott Erwitt/Magnum Photos; 217—Black Star; 218—Mona El-Khadem adapted from G. W. Allport, *The Nature of Prejudice*, Addison-Wesley, 1958, p. 207; 220 and 221—© 1970 by Jules Feiffer, reprinted with permission of Publishers-Hall Syndicate; 223—Danny Lyon/Magnum Photos; 224—Brown Brothers; 226—Dorothea Lange, courtesy of the National Archives; 228—from T. W. Adorno, E. Frenkel-Brunswick, D. J. Levinson, and R. N. Sanford (eds.), *The Authoritarian Personality*, Harper & Bros., 1950, pp. 225, 110-111, 68-69, and 158; 231—Norris McNamara/Nancy Palmer Photo Agency; 233—(left) Sepp Seitz/Magnum Photos, (right) courtesy of Home Savings and Loan Association, Los Angeles; 238—UPI Compix; 248—Columbia Broadcasting Company.

Chapter 8. Social Attitudes
252—John Oldenkamp/IBOL;
254—Donald Emmerick/Black Star; 255—(left) Harry Crosby, (right) Charles Gatewood; 258—from J. M. Jones, "Psychological Contours of Black Athletic Performance and Expression," a paper prepared for Physical Education Symposium on

Race and Sport, Slippery Rock State College, Slippery Rock, Pennsylvania, June 19-23, 1972; **260**—adapted from J. J. Jenkins, W. A. Russell, and G. J. Suci, "An Atlas of Semantic Profiles for 360 Words," *American Journal of Psychology*, 71 (1958), p. 690; **261**—(left) George Gardner, (right) UPI Compix; **265**— Roger Adams; **266**—courtesy of Antelope Valley Press, Lancaster, California; **269**— Robert Van Doren; **274**—Lynn McLaren/Rapho-Guillumette; **275**—Donna Gibbs after James Jones, 1974; **278** and **280**—Howard Saunders; **281**— Dennis Stock/Magnum Photos.

Chapter 9. Attitude Change
284—John Oldenkamp/IBOL;
286—Howard Saunders; **287**—Bonnie Weber from C. I. Hovland and W. Weiss, "The Influence of Source Credibility on Communication Effectiveness," *Public Opinion Quarterly*, 15 (1951), pp. 635-650; **289**—central panel of *The Last Judgment* by Hieronymus Bosch, courtesy of Akademie der Bildenden Kunste, Vienna, photography by Edeltraut Mandl; **291**—© Press Publishing Co. (New York World) 1929, used by permission of Mrs. H. T. Webster; **293**—(left) Marc Riboud/Magnum Photos, (right) Werner Wolff/Black Star; **295**— Bonnie Weber from L. Mann and I. Janis, "A Follow-Up on the Long-Term Effects of Emotional Role-Playing," *Journal of Personality and Social Psychology*, 8 (1968), pp. 339-342; **297**— from *Gold Rush*, United Artists, 1925; **299**— Charles Gatewood; **302**—drawings by Blechman, from Leon Festinger, "Further Consequences of Making a Difficult Decision," © 1962 by Scientific American, Inc., all rights reserved; **305**—(left) Burk Uzzle/Magnum Photos, (right) Roger Mallock/Magnum Photos; **311**—from *Aesop's Life and Fables*, 1476; **314**— (left) National Museum Vincent Van Gogh, (center) courtesy of the Fogg Art Museum, Harvard University, Bequest-Collection of Maurice Wertheim, (right) courtesy of The Louvre, Paris.

UNIT IV. INTERACTING WITH OTHERS: LIFE & DEATH TOGETHER
318—Corita Kent.

Chapter 10. Social Influence: Advice & Consent
320—John Oldenkamp/IBOL;
322—*Reptiles* by M. C. Escher, Escher Foundation, Haags Gemeentemuseum, The Hague; **329**—courtesy of Stanley Milgram from the film *Obedience*, distributed by New York University Film Library; **330**—from *Dr. Strangelove*, Columbia Pictures, 1964; **331**—(left) UPI Compix, (right) Hank Walker for *Life*, © by Time, Inc.; **334**—from *Twelve Angry Men*, United Artists, 1957; **335**—(top left) Victor Friedman, (bottom left) from *Catch 22*, produced by 20th Century Fox, (right) The Bettmann Archive, Inc.; **336**—from Gahan Wilson, *I Paint What I See*, Simon and Schuster, 1971, reprinted by permission of Gahan Wilson; **337**—from *Tom Sawyer*, Paramount Pictures, 1930; **341**—Karl Nicholason.

Chapter 11. Aggression
346—John Oldenkamp/IBOL;
349—data taken from *Mass Media and Violence: A Staff Report to the National Commission on the Causes and Prevention of Violence*, Robert K. Baker and Sandra Ball Rokeach, U. S. Government Printing Office, 1969; **350**—(top left) R. Van Nostrand/National Audubon Society, (top right) from "The Fighting Behavior of Animals," by Irenaus Eibl-Eibesfeldt, © 1961 by Scientific American, Inc., all rights reserved, (bottom left and right) Leonard L. Rue III/National Audubon Society, (bottom center) Irvin DeVore; **352**—UPI Compix; **355**—art by Karl Nicholason; **356** and **357**—© 1965 by Jules Feiffer, reprinted by

permission of Publishers-Hall Syndicate; **358**—UPI Compix; **360**—(left) Wide World Photos, (right) UPI Compix; **362**—Dr. Philip G. Zimbardo; **363**—Barry Shapiro; **364**—The Bettmann Archive, Inc.; **367**—(left) UPI Compix, (right) George Gardner; **370**—Mona El-Khadem from F. B. Steuer, J. M. Applefield, and R. Smith, "Televised Aggression and the Interpersonal Aggression of Preschool Children," *Journal of Experimental Child Psychology*, 11 (1971), pp. 442-447; **373**—UPI Compix.

Chapter 12. Prosocial Behavior
376—John Oldenkamp/IBOL;
379—(left) Brown Brothers, (right) Arthur Sirdofsky; **380**—John Messina/Rapho-Guillumette; **381**—Tally Photography, courtesy of The Muscular Dystrophy Association of America, Inc., San Diego Chapter; **384**—Ken Heyman; **386**—Calvin Woo; **388**—Bonnie Weber from J. Darley and B. Latané, "Bystander Intervention in Emergencies: Diffusion of Responsibility," *Journal of Personality and Social Psychology*, 8 (1968), pp. 377-383; **391**—(left) Ken Heyman, (right) courtesy of the U. S. Department of Agriculture; **393**—The Bettmann Archive, Inc.; **396**—Bonnie Weber adapted from B. Moore, B. Underwood, and D. Rosenhan, "Affect and Altruism," *Developmental Psychology*, 8 (1973), pp. 99-103; **397**—Richard Carter; **399**— Wenceslaus Hollar for *The Fables of Aesop*, 1665; **400**—Mona El-Khadem adapted from D. G. Pruitt, "Reciprocity and Credit Building in a Laboratory Dyad," *Journal of Personality and Social Psychology*, 8 (1968), p. 145; **402**—(left) Charles Gatewood, (right) Jan Lukas/Rapho-Guillumette; **403**—Rita Freed/Nancy Palmer Photo Agency; **405**—The Bettmann Archive, Inc.

Chapter 13. Exchange and Strategy in Social Life
408—John Oldenkamp/IBOL;
410—© 1967 by Jules Feiffer, reprinted by permission of Publishers-Hall Syndicate; **411**—The Bettmann Archive, Inc.; **412**—Ken Heyman; **413**—UPI Compix; **420**—Mona El-Khadem from J. Sidowski, L. B. Wyckoff, and L. Tabory, "Reinforcement and Punishment in a Minimal Social Situation," *Journal of Abnormal and Social Psychology*, 52 (1956), pp. 115-119; **421**—Culver Pictures; **422**—(left) David Hurn/Magnum Photos, (right) Wayne Miller/Magnum Photos; **424**—Larry Edmunds Bookshop; **427**—Gerhard Julius/Photophile; **430**—Howard Saunders adapted from M. Deutsch and R. Krauss, "The Effect of Threat Upon Interpersonal Bargaining," *Journal of Abnormal and Social Psychology*, 61 (1960), p. 183; **432**—from U. G. Foa, "Interpersonal and Economic Resources," *Science*, 171 (1971), p. 347, a fuller treatment of this topic is given in U. G. Foa and E. B. Foa, *Societal Structures of the Mind*, Charles C. Thomas, 1973; **434**—UPI Compix; **435**—Alan Mercer; **439**—Charles Gatewood; **440**—Alan Mercer; **442**—from *My Little Chickadee*, Universal Productions, 1940; **444**—from *Psychology Today*, November 1970; **445**—Culver Pictures.

UNIT V. BEHAVIOR IN GROUPS: PLANNED & UNPLANNED
450—Corita Kent.

Chapter 14. Informal Groups
452—John Oldenkamp/IBOL;
454—courtesy of Cindy Lyle; **456** and **457**—quiz reprinted by permission of *Rough Times* (formerly *Radical Therapist*) from the April 1972 issue; **458**—Albrecht Dürer, *The Revelations of St. John*, 1498; **460**—UPI Compix; **463**—Howard Saunders; **468** and **469**—The Bettmann Archive, Inc.; **472**—René Burri/Magnum Photos; **474**— Charles Rice/Black Star; **477**—from M. Sherif and C. W. Sherif, *Social Psychology*, Harper & Row, 1969; **482**—Honey/Transworld Feature Syndicate, Inc.; **485**—Arthur Schatz.

Chapter 15. Group Decisions & Conflicts
488—John Oldenkamp/IBOL;
490 and **491**—courtesy of the National Aeronautics Space Administration; **492**—from J. Hall, "Decisions, Decisions," *Psychology Today*, 5 (1971), pp. 51-54; **494**—E. Landy/Magnum Photos; **495**—Stephen Goldblat/Transworld Feature Syndicate, Inc.; **500**—from F. E. Fiedler, "The Trouble with Leadership Training Is That It Doesn't Train Leaders," *Psychology Today*, 6 (1973), p. 26; **502**—Howard Saunders; **506**— Ralph Crane for *Life*, © 1949 by Time, Inc.; **512**— *Lysistrata Haranguing the Athenian Women* by Aubrey Beardsley; **514** and **515**—from *Big Business*, produced by Metro-Goldwyn-Mayer; **516** and **517**—Terry Lamb; **522** and **523**—UPI Compix.

Chapter 16. The Psychology of Organizations
526—John Oldenkamp/IBOL;
529—Pat DeVore; **530**—(left) The Bettmann Archive, Inc., (center) clock courtesy of Olden Tymes Antiques, Solvang, California, photo by Stephen Wells for *Psychology Today*, (top right) courtesy of General Cable Corporation, New York, (bottom right) Erich Hartmann/Magnum Photos; **533**—(left) from the film *Metropolis*, (right) from Paolo Soleri, *Archology: The City in the Image of Man*, © 1969 by M.I.T. Press, used with permission of the publisher; **536**—(left) Brown Brothers, (center) Ted Spiegel/Black Star, (right) Diane Koos Gentry/Black Star; **537**—(left) courtesy of Saab Scania of America, Inc., (right) Michael Mauney for *Life*, © 1972 by Time, Inc.; **541**—Howard Saunders; **543**—from *Oliver*, a Columbia Pictures Presentation, 1968; **548**—United Press International; **549**—Wide World Photos; **550**—Howard Saunders; **553**— Mona El-Khadem from R. R. Blake and J. S. Mouton, *The Managerial Grid*, Gulf Publishing Co., 1964, p. 10; **558**—courtesy of the University of California; **560**—Howard Saunders.

Chapter 17. Collective Behavior
564—John Oldenkamp/IBOL;
567—from Stanley Morse, 1974; **569**—UPI Compix; **571**—(top left and bottom) Ian Berry/Magnum Photos, (top right) UPI Compix; **572**—(left) Ian Berry/Magnum Photos, (top and bottom right) UPI Compix; **573**—from Stanley Morse, 1974; **579**—Gerhard E. Gscheidle/Magnum Photos; **580**—Marc Riboud/Magnum Photos; **581** and **586**—UPI Compix; **588**—Lorenzo Gunn; **594**—UPI Compix.

598 to **601**—drawings by Cliff McReynolds.

COVER—Corita Kent.

A special thanks to Ed Yotka, Vincent DiPrima, and their staff at United Press International, New York and Los Angeles; thank you to the Academy of Motion Picture Arts and Sciences, Larry Edmunds Book Shop, and the Museum of Modern Art for providing film stills.

And for their valuable assistance with the graphics program:
Roland Wilhelmy (preliminary suggestions); Scot Morris (consultation and graphics suggestions); Donna Gibbs and Bonnie Weber (production artists); those actors and actresses of San Francisco who appear in the chapter openers.

A special thanks for the contributions of:
Lee Massey (contributing editor); Martha Straley, Sandylee Williams (proofreaders); David Estrada (indexer); Leslie Bolinger, Melvyn Freilicher, Gary Sawade, Martha Straley, Neil Straussman, Ann Wolff (library researchers); Rolande Angles, Beverly Cefaratti, Rose MacDonald, Allison Pangle, Timothy Sugg (typists and editorial services).

Book Team

Harvey A. Tilker, Ph.D., *Publisher*
Sherred Lane, *Publishing Coordinator*
Cindy Lyle, *Editor*
Rebecca Smith, *Assistant Editor*
Martha Rosler, Cindi Farden, Susan Orlofsky, *Contributing Editors*
Nat Antler, *Designer*
Cynthia Bassett, *Associate Designer*
Nancy Hutchison Sjöberg, *Photo Researcher*
Lyn Smith, *Permissions Assistant*
Sandie Marcus, *Production Assistant*
Howard Smith, *Social Science Marketing Manager*

CRM Books

Richard Holme, *President and Publisher*
Russ Calkins, *Marketing Manager*
Roger G. Emblen, *Publishing Director*
Arlyne Lazerson, *Editorial Director*
William G. Mastous, *Director of Finance and Administration*
Trygve E. Myhren, *Vice-President, Marketing*
John Ochse, *Sales Manager*
Henry Ratz, *Director of Production*
Tom Suzuki, *Director of Design*